Wall Street

and the

Security Markets

This is a volume in the Arno Press collection

Wall Street and the Security Markets

Advisory Editor
Vincent P. Carosso

Associate Editor
Robert Sobel

See last pages of this volume for a complete list of titles

INVESTMENT BANKING

H[enry] Parker Willis
and
Jules I. Bogen

ARNO PRESS
A New York Times Company
New York - 1975

Reprint Edition 1975 by Arno Press Inc.

WALL STREET AND THE SECURITY MARKETS
ISBN for complete set: 0-405-06944-8
See last pages of this volume for titles.

Manufactured in the United States of America

Library of Congress Cataloging in Publication Data

Willis, Henry Parker, 1874-1937.
Investment banking.

(Wall Street and the security markets)
Reprint of the rev. ed. published by Harper, New York.
Includes bibliographical references.
1. Investment banking--United States. 2. Securities--United States. I. Bogen, Jules Irwin, 1903- joint author. II. Title. III. Series.
HG4930.W54 1975 332.6'6'0973 75-14056
ISBN 0-405-07247-3

INVESTMENT BANKING

REVISED EDITION

BY

H. PARKER WILLIS
Professor of Banking, Columbia University

AND

JULES I. BOGEN
Professor of Finance, New York University

HARPER & BROTHERS PUBLISHERS
NEW YORK AND LONDON
MCMXXXVI

CONTENTS

APPENDIX

FIGURES

PREFACE

This book has been written to set forth the principles and practice of investment banking. No systematic exposition of this subject has heretofore been made in book form. Both among bankers and banking teachers the need for a general treatise has long been felt. It is hoped that the volume will supply to the investment banking community for use in its own instructional work, as well as to the college teacher of banking, a comprehensive and usable statement of the economic basis, the policies and the methods characteristic of this fast-developing branch of banking.

During the past few years, the teaching of banking has undergone a complete transformation. Not only has the number of courses offered in academic institutions, as well as the degree of their specialization, been largely increased, but there has been a decided alteration of content as well as a considerable change of method.

The older instruction in banking (so-called), in which predominant emphasis was placed upon the legislative and public aspects of the subject, and in which major attention was given to doctrinal points, has been largely superseded. This has not implied any reduction in the importance assigned to the earlier view of the subject, but has been the result of the great extension of the borders of the study. As in most branches of scientific inquiry, advance in knowledge has produced a lessening of assurance or positiveness in dogmatic instruction, and has tended to defer the presentation of theory until the later stages of the student's work. Discussion of policies applicable to the legislative treatment of banking, and analysis of prices and price movements are logically recognized as best presented to those who have already become acquainted with banking technique and procedure, at least in outline.

Such a change, wherein first attention is given to fact-study and to an understanding of procedure, would naturally broaden the general scope of the material presented to the student. "Banking" unavoidably becomes much more than the analysis or description of the actual procedure of the commercial bank. It is seen as closely connected with other fields of economic thought, a basic analysis of "financial civilization," and hence as a study which must orient itself in the general scheme of economic science. The result has been to broaden the field of what is called "banking" so as to include all phases of the process generically thus designated; while at the same time the increasing attention of the commercial world to long-term financing and the security markets has helped considerably to supply a more adequate and inclusive body of data. Current business tendencies and changes have called for larger recognition of certain types of banking procedure, at the same time that scientific reconsideration of material already available has pointed to new syntheses of banking data.

Among the specific fields indicated by these parallel factors of thought and experience as calling for separate description is investment banking. The field covered by, or included in, this subject comprises some topics formerly sporadically dealt with under such heads as Stock Exchange Speculation, Corporation Finance, Investment Analysis, and the like. It does not in any sense duplicate these older fields, or even include a principal part of the areas covered by them. Like the subject of banking in its commercial aspect, which naturally presupposes some knowledge of accounting, business law, and general economic principle, investment banking makes use of previous studies in the field of speculation and stock market organization, of commercial law, of corporation finance and of banking itself. It is a synthetic treatment of material which, although always available, has not until lately been afforded combined presentation.

The authors firmly believe, furthermore, that more intensive study of investment banking will necessarily occur in courses now devoted to the general field of investment, as well as in the banking curriculum. In the teaching of banking, it has become common to stress the description of banking institutions far more than the instruments of banking, such as notes, checks, etc. In the teaching of investment, on the contrary, almost exclusive attention has been devoted to the instruments—various types of stocks and bonds—and altogether too little to the institutions by which they are evolved and sold. This volume aims to fill this gap, which is a real one since a growing number of students plan to enter the field of investment banking in one or another of its manifold phases. Their needs are not met by a cursory review of the more obvious characteristics of different classes of securities from the viewpoint of the investor.

Teachers of investment banking, like the early teachers of banking in the older sense of the word, have had to encounter serious obstacles growing out of the fact that their material was scattered, fugitive, and hard to present in compact form. There are many valuable books dealing with investment, accounting analysis, corporation finance, and with the specialized investment banking institutions such as trust companies, investment trusts and insurance companies. There are few in which the effort is definitely made to outline the general processes of investment banking which underlie all these institutions, and which condition their activity. In presenting the subject to classes, especially where such classes are too large to permit much detailed work in the library-laboratory, and especially in presenting it to students in the smaller institutions of the country where available current financial sources of information are fewer, the teacher has had to overcome increased difficulty.

This volume is the outgrowth of experience at two universities in which the subject is followed by classes often of considerable size. In presenting investment banking to such classes during past years, it has been found needful to accumulate extensive notes for distribution to students, and to proceed largely by the assignment of library readings, in the absence of a general text covering the entire ground. Within the past two or three years, the question of consolidating portions of this material and giving it a more formal and available shape has been under advisement, and the book as now published is the result. It is intended as a handbook for the use of students of investment banking.

In dealing with the subject, the authors have thought best to make the volume primarily descriptive and to reduce the discussion of theory to the smallest limits possible, while eliminating matter that was in any definite way controversial. Discussion of most of the fundamental problems of theory is thus left for the instructor and his students, the handbook providing merely a convenient basis for the descriptive outlining of the field, with a few essential theoretic discussions. The data presented are chiefly well known, though it is thought that in some chapters it has been possible to furnish more nearly current accounts of methods and technique than are easily available elsewhere. In preparing the chapters which relate to current practice, special care has been taken to "check over" the pages on these topics with practical investment bankers, and to compare them with recent or current discussions. Valuable criticisms were received from Dr. Marcus Nadler of New York University, who read the entire manuscript. Dr. William Howard Steiner contributed interesting material to one of the chapters. While there has been an equal division of work between the authors, they have collaborated at all points, and are jointly responsible for statements made and views expressed.

With the purposes thus set forth, and the circumstances outlined, the volume is presented to the public.

New York, H. PARKER WILLIS
October, 1929 JULES I. BOGEN

PREFACE TO THE REVISED EDITION

In issuing a revised edition of *Investment Banking*, little needs be added to the explanatory statement of aims and methods already furnished in the first edition. The purpose of the revised edition is to bring the discussion of the various topics down to date by taking account of the great changes in governmental supervision and legislative oversight introduced since the first publication of the volume. Some changes in practice, partly consequent upon the legislation already referred to, and partly the result of clearer recognition by the community of some of the necessities, as well as some of the obvious limitations, of investment banking, have likewise altered the background of the subject as far as the United States is concerned, with corresponding modification in the point of view in important particulars.

It so happened that the financial panic of the year 1929 came soon after the publication of *Investment Banking*. During the ensuing period of depression and reconstruction, not a few widely accepted formulations of technique have been severely tested in practice; while the adoption of the Federal Securities Act in 1933 and the Securities Exchange Act in the following year, 1934, with the administrative regulations putting into effect the provisions of these laws, has brought into existence codes of conduct and practice dealing with fundamental investment banking technique that had previously been unknown.

There is no reason to believe that the reorganization of investment banking thus begun has been brought to a close or perhaps has even reached its climax. However, the prevailing situation calls clearly for a restatement of investment banking methods and principles.

In preparing the second edition, the authors have had the use of several competent studies of investment banking, including some unpublished material, prepared by the Securities and Exchange Commission. For this valuable aid we are under obligations to the Commission and to its chairman, the Honorable James M. Landis. We wish also to make acknowledgment here for the numerous courtesies we have received from that body in connection with our request for specific items of information. Valuable criticisms on portions of the manuscript were made by Dr. Raymond W. Goldschmidt, of Washington, D. C. Individual investment bankers and officials of the New York Stock Exchange have also helped greatly with information on pertinent points.

New York, H. PARKER WILLIS
October, 1936 JULES I. BOGEN

Part One

Investment Banking Institutions

Chapter I

INVESTMENT BANKING—CONCEPT AND INSTITUTIONS

Scope of Investment Banking

The term investment banking has come into general use only within recent years. It is now employed to designate a distinct phase or department of banking, which is characterized primarily by the fact that it is concerned with long-term credits.

The old generic term of "banking," on the one hand, has been broadened considerably to permit this inclusion, and, on the other hand, the concept has been more sharply limited and defined through division into the two departments of commercial and investment banking, the one devoted to short-term financing, and the other to the financing of long-term or capital requirements.

The development of this distinction has assumed greater importance during the past few years, and has brought with it sharp differences of opinion as to the proper limitations of each, and the suitable relationship between commercial and investment banking. In nearly all economically advanced countries, and in the United States particularly, the problem has arisen whether it is or is not desirable to have commercial and investment banking carried on through the same institutions. The panic of 1929 and the generally unfortunate experiences of banks from 1929 onward have led in various countries to the confirmation of an older or "classical" view that the two types of banking should be kept as independent and distinct, one from another, as circumstances would permit, and that whatever might abstractly be thought on the subject, there were, in practice, serious dangers from any close combination or union of the two types of financial activity. In the United States this view of the matter was one of the underlying principles embodied in the Banking Act of 1933, and received extensive discussion during the entire period that this act was under consideration, covering the years 1931-1933. By the terms of the Banking Act of 1933, a partial divorce of commercial from investment banking was required. However, subsequent events, as we shall see below, brought about a closer connection between the two types of banking than ever before, as bond investments came to dominate bank portfolios. For some time to come, it may be expected that a separation between commercial and investment banking will continue to be, in theory at least, an accepted canon of American banking management. The fact that this problem has been the subject of fundamental legislation on the subject renders more than ever desirable a clear cut reclassification of American banking functions and institutions.

In its most primitive form, the bank merely receives and safeguards the funds of the individual. In earlier days, this type of banking was well illustrated by the operations of the goldsmith bankers of England, who in the seventeenth century were the chief custodians of the public's money in that country. In our own time, this type of banking is still carried on by safe-deposit companies which are formed by banks to rent space in safe-keeping vaults to individuals and corporations.

A step forward in the evolution of banking occurred when the bankers lent out at interest the funds which they received from the public. This added a vital feature to the banking process—the study and analysis of credit for the purpose of assuring the safety of the loan. The Lombard bankers in Italy and the German bankers in the Rhine cities carried on lending operations, with both their own money and that of depositors, even in the Middle Ages. The bank thus became an intermediary between the owners of capital who could not themselves use it productively and those who wished to utilize this capital in one form or another.

A third step in the evolution of commercial banking was the issue by the bank of its own obligations in the form of notes or deposit credits, while the bank retained from its own funds and those of depositors merely enough actual cash to assure its ability to meet such obligations on demand. Instead of merely handling the existing media of exchange, the bank thus came to create such media. Instead of acting as an intermediary between those who are in possession of cash and those who wish to borrow it, the bank agreed to permit those who are in possession of any form of property or wealth to gain possession of buying power in the form of bank credit. With this property as the basis, the bank made loans which gave current purchasing power to the borrower.

As banking has developed, furthermore, it was inevitable that there should be marked differences in the rate of turnover of bank funds. Some deposits have a low rate of turnover—they are idle or almost idle awaiting the decision of their owner as to the way in which they shall be used. Other funds are active—constantly drawn against, and constantly rebuilt through new deposits. Where these two classes of funds and others representing varying rates of turnover are held and carried by the same institution, there is likely to be a strong tendency toward their intermixture in use.

The bank which feels the pressure of strong demands from borrowers who want funds for long-term uses to create capital goods is inclined to make such loans out of any resources it may have, regardless of whether they are constantly liable to withdrawal by their owners. On the other hand, the bank which finds itself compelled to hold an undue amount of funds with slow turnover may allow itself to make advances for commercial uses that are not as well protected by the actual operations of business as they might be. Accordingly, commercial banks have developed different departments such as those dealing with savings, trust funds, thrift accounts, and the like, and certain of these are more concerned with investment than with commercial banking; the division, however, is based upon the obvious requirements of bookkeeping and administration, rather than the essential nature of the use of the funds received by these departments. The bank carefully classifies its liabilities, but its portfolio of assets is not correspondingly classified.

In the course of this evolution of technique there has been evolved a separate type of banking activity which only in recent years has developed into a distinct division of the credit system with a recognized individuality. Efforts to determine which type of banking first appeared in history would be fruitless, for some of the most primitive banking operations recorded even in ancient times smack of both. Suffice it to say that investment banking has followed a line of development somewhat parallel to commercial banking. In its more primitive form, investment banking involved a loan of the capital of the investment banker, or that of a few clients, on a long-term basis to some sovereign. Such loans were common in Europe in the later Middle Ages and after, and were often represented by long-term securities. Now, however, the investment banker buys issues of securities from governments and corporations which desire capital, after he has made some analysis of the credit risk corresponding to the study of credit made by the commercial banker, and then he resells these obligations to others. In special fields of investment banking, an intermediate step may be taken, where the investment institution sells its own obligations to investors, advancing the proceeds to those who can utilize the capital. The mortgage bank and the investment trust are examples of these.

Functional Distinction between Commercial and Investment Banking

General usage would hardly sanction any single clear-cut and definite distinction between commercial and investment banking. The factor which is most frequently used in making rough practical distinctions between the two is that of time—commercial banking involving short-term advances to borrowers, while investment banking involves long-term advances which generally are represented by negotiable securities. But, as will be seen below, other factors, such as the purpose of the loan, the character of the institution making it, etc., are also frequently to be considered in making a full distinction between these two concepts as they are customarily employed in current usage.

Although there is no intrinsic reason why this must necessarily be the case, commercial banking institutions operate in the main through the system of deposit and discount, while investment banking is carried on through the purchase of security issues and their subsequent sale, at a profit, to investors.

Exceptions may be noted. Commercial paper may be bought and sold like securities; and commercial banks, after making short-term loans, may rediscount such paper with a Federal Reserve Bank. On the other hand, the savings bank, an investment banking institution, receives deposits in much the same way as do commercial banks, but uses the proceeds to buy securities in the capital market and make mortgage loans. Furthermore, investment houses have been known to keep short-term securities purchased from issuing governments and corporations until their maturity, instead of selling them to others. Hence, from the point of view of method of operation, only rough and approximate distinctions can be made.

This distinction, however inadequate and approximate, must not be regarded on that account as any the less real and fundamental. The fact that the community is not always willing to classify its banking practices does not of itself reduce the need for keeping these distinctions clearly in mind in the management of banks. The distinctions indicated above grow out of the essential nature of the banking business. Successful banking over long periods will invariably be dependent upon recognition of the necessity of adapting asset holdings to the nature of the liabilities incurred.

In any case, it must be remembered that the two divisions of banking are closely related, and in practice one cannot be adequately understood without a knowledge of the other. Thus, one connection between the two is found in the fact that the commercial banker is the custodian of the liquid funds of the community, so that when an individual wishes to put his money into investment securities to be purchased from or through an investment banker, he draws the amount he needs out of the commercial bank. Thus, inflation or deflation of commercial bank deposits profoundly affects the volume of funds available in the security markets. It is also true that the commercial banker often finds it desirable, in order to keep his own resources at work, to purchase securities which are issued by an investment banker. A fuller discussion of the rôle of the commercial banks in the field of investment banking is given in Chapters V and VI.

Institutional Distinction

In what has been said thus far, reference has been made to investment and commercial banking as distinct types of financial operations. But it is not possible to pick out or designate certain commercial banks as carrying on the one kind of banking, and certain investment banks as carrying on the other. This clean-cut functional distinction is permissible for the purpose of clarifying underlying ideas, but it does not correspond to what is found in practice. It is, therefore, necessary to consider commercial and investment banking also from the institutional viewpoint, and see how actual banking institutions carry on one, or the other, or both types of operations.

For many years banking or financial institutions have existed which have carried on both kinds of banking concurrently; the practice prevails now perhaps more than ever. The evolution of pure investment banking institutions on a large scale began with the stabilization of government credit in western Europe and the consequent growth of popular investment in government securities. This resulted in the formation of houses of issue, such as those of the early generations of the Rothschilds. The vast development of corporate financing in recent decades has enormously expanded the field of operation of such firms in buying, selling and dealing in securities. At the same time, many institutions have exercised both commercial banking functions and some, or in a few cases all, of the investment banking functions. Such institutions engage in what is sometimes called "department store banking," a separate department in the organization frequently being created to exercise each separate function.

In order to bring out more clearly this institutional overlapping within these two fundamental banking functions we may survey briefly the principal financial institutions found in this country. These include:

1. National Banks.—The national banking system was originally organized as a commercial banking system primarily, but it gradually took on investment banking functions, particularly in the farming regions where a large part of country bank loans came to consist of long-term accommodations secured in one way or another by land, though such loans were nominally not permitted by law. Bond investments by the banks and the receipt of savings deposits also became general without specific legal sanction after 1900. The Federal Reserve Act granted a limited permission to invest in land mortgages, and the McFadden Act of February 26, 1927, greatly broadened the investment functions of the national banks by permitting investment of a large fraction of their time deposits in mortgages on real estate, and also by allowing them to enter the business of security issue and distribution. The McFadden Act furthered the combination of long-term and short-term banking. By encouraging banks to acquire long-term assets, it increased the danger that they would get into a frozen condition. This danger, already apparent before the panic of 1929, became so evident as a result of the collapse that, at the end of 1930, Congress undertook the consideration of a new measure designed in part to rectify the error committed by the McFadden Act. In the Banking Act of 1933, adopted on June 16 of the latter year, the investment banking provisions of the McFadden Act were modified. Member banks of the Federal Reserve System were forbidden to engage in the underwriting and issue of corporate securities, although they were still allowed to continue the purchase and sale of such securities for the account of their customers and themselves. However, as we shall see subsequently, the entry of the commercial banks deeper into investment banking was not really checked by this measure, as the bank portfolios later expanded to record proportions.

2. *State Banks.*—The state banking systems were originally organized along lines paralleling those of the National Bank Act. They also have tended during recent years to develop an investment banking business. In fact, it was because they had led the way that national banks sought the modification of the National Bank Act in 1927. The provisions of the Banking Act of 1933 affecting investment security operations were made applicable not only to national banks, but also to state banks which were or might become members of the Reserve System. Some state legislation, as in New York, has been directed toward a closer examination of all institutions engaged in the business of taking and holding deposits, and this too has tended

to bring about a separation between commercial and investment banking under state charters.

3. Trust Companies.—Trust companies organized under state laws were from the beginning chiefly designed to carry on an investment banking business by managing the investment funds of others. At first, they devoted themselves primarily to the management of the property of clients establishing trusts, but many of them in the course of time, developed commercial banking departments so large as to dominate the rest of the business, while national and state banks have been authorized to conduct trust business on a broad scale. The framers of the Banking Act of 1933 considered the question of separating the trust departments and the performance of fiduciary functions from commercial banking, but the change thus involved was deemed too extreme.

4. Savings Banks.—Savings banks, either mutual or stock, are recognized as investment banking institutions that receive deposits from the community on a time basis and use them to make loans on real estate, as well as to buy other securities allowed by law. Legal limitations prevent them from going into commercial banking. From 1927 onward, there was a strong tendency in many states to broaden the classes of securities which might thus be purchased by the savings banks. This has now been succeeded by an opposite tendency looking in the direction of closer classification of savings bank assets and a restriction of the kinds of securities that may properly be purchased by such banks.

5. Mortgage Banks.—Mortgage banks, best represented in the United States by the Federal Farm Land Banks, devote themselves to the financing of agricultural and real estate development. They sell securities to raise funds to be used in this way, and thus constitute a highly developed, albeit narrowly specialized, type of investment banking institution. The building and loan association is a special, but very important, variant of the mortgage bank. The business of such building and loan associations has grown rapidly of recent years, but the failure to understand the necessity for proper separation between long- and short-term obligations has, in a good many cases, resulted in the taking on of liabilities that could not be satisfied. Accordingly, in many states where building and loan associations have sought to broaden their operating methods, they have found it necessary to work back into their traditional field—a process of devolution which in some cases has been extremely painful.

6. Investment Houses.—The investment house, sometimes called the bond house, devotes itself exclusively to investment banking operations in most instances. The following chapter is devoted to a full discussion of this class of institution, which supplies investment securities for purchase by other financial institutions or individual investors. The Banking Act of 1933 prevents such organizations from maintaining a private deposit banking business, which several of them had conducted previously.

7. Brokerage Houses and the Stock Exchanges.—These organizations buy and sell already issued securities, thus making a market for them. They facilitate the distribution of securities, and constitute a highly important cog in the investment banking machinery.

8. Investment Trusts.—Investment trusts are organizations which issue their own securities for the purpose of raising capital with which to buy other securities. They thus act as securities substitution companies and, as such, facilitate the investment banking process.

9. Other Institutions.—A variety of other types of institutions may be properly classified in the investment banking field, although not always thought of in that connection. Thus, insurance companies are properly grouped as operating on the demand or buying side of investment banking, since they are large buyers and holders of investment securities which they purchase in order to keep the funds of their policyholders profitably employed. Large business corporations and eleemosynary institutions are also frequently large-scale security buyers, thus constituting important factors in the investment banking business.

From the brief descriptive accounts just afforded, it is possible to reclassify American financial institutions on the basis of the functional banking activities they perform, as follows:

1. Institutions engaged primarily in commercial, and secondarily in investment, banking: national banks, state banks and most trust companies. The sharp rise in bank bond hold-

ings in the last few years would, if permanent, modify this condition to some extent.

2. Institutions engaged primarily in investment banking, but with commercial banking as an important auxiliary: some trust companies.

3. Institutions engaged in investment banking pure and simple: investment houses, savings banks, mortgage banks, investment trusts and brokerage houses.

This reclassification is necessarily imperfect, owing to the varying degree in which different institutions engage in the investment banking business. From time to time individual institutions change the scope of their operations and take on new functions or slough off others. On the whole, however, the investment banking structure of the United States is tending to assume a definitely organized form, notwithstanding the fact that the tendency has been in the direction of uniting commercial and investment banking functions under the same institutional control. While the same institution may do both kinds of banking, the underlying functional difference is understood and allowed for by departmental organization or otherwise, so that it may be fairly said that there is today a much more distinct functional separation of the two types of banking than in the past. As has already been seen in preceding paragraphs, this functional separation is today to a degree a basic element in banking law here and abroad.

The Capital Market

The buyers and sellers of securities taken together constitute what is often loosely defined as the capital market. All of the institutions connected with investment banking, as described above, therefore constitute factors in the capital market. The capital market is often distinguished from the money market. The latter includes buyers and sellers of short-term credits, including loans, commercial paper, acceptances and government obligations of short date.

The term investment banking, which at times is used in a narrow sense to signify only the purchase of securities from their original issuers and their sale to all types of investors, institutional and individual, is to an increasing extent being expanded to include the operation of the entire capital market.[1] This is quite proper, as the mechanism which has been evolved to take care of and direct the flow of long-term capital is complicated, and so closely interlocked in its various elements that it can best be studied as a whole.

As a preliminary to a study of the investment banking institutions which together constitute the main factors in the capital market, we may consider in a general way the character of the demand for capital which comes on the market.

Commercial *vs.* Investment Borrowers

The major factor which determines whether a business enterprise shall enter the money market or the capital market to meet its needs for funds is usually the length of time for which an advance is required, although numerous exceptions to this generalization can be cited. However, there are certain purposes for which resort is almost invariably made to the capital market where this is feasible. Among these are the purchase of expensive items of fixed capital, such as plant and equipment, or the raising of a minimum amount of permanent working capital to relieve the business from chronic reliance upon the banks. Repayment of maturing long-term indebtedness is another purpose for which corporations frequently enter the capital market.

The commercial borrower generally seeks funds for temporary purposes, such as seasonal expansion of his inventories to carry him through a busy period in his business, or the anticipation of trade liabilities for the purpose of gaining cash discounts. The special or seasonal nature of commercial banking operation is emphasized by the fact that the customer of the commercial bank is expected to pay off or "clean up" his obligations to it at stated intervals, when such demands are supposed to have passed over. It often happens, however, that such a customer gradually falls into the habit of being more or less permanently indebted to the bank, paying off one note by the issue

[1] The term "investment banker," on the other hand, is generally confined in current parlance to one whose business it is to buy security issues for resale. Brokers would thus be excluded from this appellation in its narrow sense, as would also savings bankers, mortgage bankers, trust company officers, etc.

of another. His borrowing then ceases to be seasonal and becomes permanent or semi-permanent. He has thus become a prospective customer for investment banking accommodation, owing to the change which has taken place in the character of his credit requirements.

Too often the commercial bank fails to recognize this gradual change in the character of its customers. It allows them to become dependent upon a continuous loan, which is regranted each time it matures. A bank which permits its loans to get out of hand in this way may find itself in a frozen condition, unable to meet demands for deposit withdrawals. This is one reason why many commercial banks organized their own investment banking departments or established affiliates for the purpose during the first three decades of this century. Through these, the customer of the type under consideration became an applicant for investment credit and received his accommodation from the capital market. He was thus able to pay off his indebtedness to the bank from which he originally borrowed, retaining only a deposit account with it for the sake of banking service, and borrowing at most only such part of his requirements as were of a purely seasonal and hence commercial credit variety.

The new banking legislation of 1933 has prevented such a direct invasion of investment banking by the commercial banks. However, if commercial banks continue to make frozen loans and buy long-term securities, the change effected by this statute will be more nominal than real.

A still different type of customer is the borrower who wishes to obtain funds for an intermediate period of from six months to three years. Such a borrower might, in certain circumstances, obtain accommodation from the commercial bank on the basis of his statement, and the bank might carry his loan along, either through renewals promised under lines of credit or, where legal restrictions permit, with actual loans running for the full period of the borrowing. Alternative accommodation is afforded by a resort to the investment market with short-term or serial notes.

In the past, American banks have too often encouraged this kind of borrowing in the confident belief that, whenever necessary, such borrowers could be shifted into the investment market and their credits thereby liquidated. It has frequently been found, however, that confidence in the ability to make this shift, although well enough warranted at first, has proved unwarranted when a critical moment arrived. Outside influences affecting credit and money market conditions may so alter the attitude of investors that it will be out of the question to get them to take up such obligations when offered to them, even when the terms are very favorable. Thus, the bank not infrequently has found itself obliged to protect the customer whom it had tolerated in the expectation that when necessary it could eliminate him. This situation is not always the result of a lack of definite lending policy on the part of the bank. Sometimes it grows out of the fact that the borrower himself is not clear in his own mind as to the nature of his own financial needs.

Often the borrower may be uncertain as to which type of bank he should use for his financing. In such borderline cases, the question of comparative cost may become the guiding factor. At times of rising security prices, such as prevailed during most of the third decade of the century, corporations prefer to sell bonds and stocks, and thus gain independence of the banks even for seasonal and special working capital needs. On the other hand, in times of low security prices and high yields, such as the war period, the banks may be called upon to do a good deal of financing, much of it designed to raise funds, directly or indirectly, for fixed capital purposes. It was the large amount of bank borrowing for such non-liquid purposes which accounted in part for the 1920-1921 deflation period.

A similar situation developed in the period before and after 1929, although many of the frozen bank loans at that time were incurred on what was originally meant to be a temporary basis, in anticipation of capital flotations that were never consummated because the markets turned downward. Apparently, the experience of a short decade before had not impressed upon the minds of the financial community the lessons which should then have been learned. Partly, this reflected a belief that fundamental economic conditions had altered, and that a "new era" had set in which had changed the underlying canons of finance and banking. The collapse of the financial markets in the period following the 1929 panic, and the effort to liquidate commitments which followed it, showed that a very large percentage of bank assets had actually assumed a fixed capital form. This did not mean that the commitments so made were necessarily bad, but merely that they could not be realized upon on any large scale when and as desired. Of the numerous bank failures which followed the panic of 1929, it is probably safe to say that a majority were the result not of bad judgment in the use of funds, if long-period standards be applied, much less of dishonesty—but that they were the result of misplaced confidence in the ability to sell to others, and thus to liquidate, securities and enterprises which were thus made the basis of long-term or capital credits.

Limitations of the Capital Market

There are certain definite limitations on the efficacy of the capital market as a channel for financing business enterprises. Perhaps the greatest one is the fact that it is not available for small enterprises in the large majority of cases. The commercial bank, since it means to keep in its own portfolio the paper which it takes from its borrowing customers, must merely be convinced itself of its goodness. The investment house, on the other hand, must also convince its clients that such is the case, for it wants to resell to investors the securities it purchases. This reselling function involves considerable effort and expense, and hence it will not be undertaken unless the issue is large enough to absorb this expense and yield a profit nevertheless. A loan of $50,000, for example, is a fair-sized piece of business for a small bank; but an investment banker can hardly afford to undertake to advertise and sell a stock or bond issue of this size. Only where such smaller loans can be reduced to a uniform basis and handled on a large scale by special institutions, as in the mortgage banking business, does the small borrower enjoy anything like the position of the large one.

Another factor which operates against the small business in the investment banking field is the fact that the large company is already well known to investors through other contacts, and information concerning it is available in financial manuals and other easily accessible places. Thus, the initial sales of securities of the Dodge Brothers' automobile manufacturing enterprise to the public in 1924 was not a particularly difficult matter, since the company already had a nation-wide reputation among buyers of cars. A company like the Great Atlantic & Pacific Tea Company similarly can introduce its securities to the general public on a favorable basis and with little difficulty. But the investor generally hesitates for a long time before purchasing securities of small local enterprises about which he has never heard.

The Demand for Securities

We have thus far considered the relation of the borrowing government or business enterprise to the capital market, and the conditions under which access to it is sought. There are several channels through which the funds of investors are directed into the capital market, where they constitute a demand for securities.

In the simplest case, the investor merely purchases securities from an investment house which has originated them and is selling them for a profit. Such direct investment has always assumed relatively large proportions, but it would be difficult to estimate the share it represents in the placement of new security issues. It has, at times of active popular interest in securities, been estimated that about half of all issues are absorbed in that way; but in a year like 1935 or 1936, when individual investors generally were quite cautious, the proportion of new offerings placed directly with them was relatively small. Institutional investors then constituted the chief market for most new flotations. Enterprises which sell new stock to their own shareholders of course depend primarily on individual investors. This direct investment may also consist in the purchase of already outstanding securities from their former holders, thus placing in the hands of the latter buying power with which to purchase new issues in their turn if they see fit.

But many investors do not care to undertake the difficult function of choosing securities for investment, nor do they want to incur the further task of caring for them and watching conditions affecting their value in the future. The simplest course for the investor is to deposit his savings in a savings bank which promises to pay back such sums on due notice and then proceeds to invest them conservatively and pay a moderate rate of interest. The savings bank thus constitutes an intervening element between the issuer of securities and the investor, performing a number of services for the latter in keeping and profitably using his funds. Also, a special measure of safety for the principal of the investor is thus assured.

Where the investor seeks a higher rate of return without assuming more responsibility for the management of his funds, the investment trust device may be used.[2] This type of institution sells its own securities and utilizes the proceeds for investment. As it does not make any promise of repayment on demand, or after short notice, of funds left in its custody, the investment trust is free to adopt more speculative policies in the management of its funds. Mortgage banks constitute similar institutions operating under special laws in the field of agricultural and real estate finance.

Finally, individuals place their money with institutions that are formed primarily for other purposes, but which nevertheless gather large sums which they must invest. The insurance company and eleemosynary institutions are in this class.

Types of Investment Banking Institutions

There are a number of different types of institutions performing their own particular functions in the capital market, as has already been indicated. The first part of this book is devoted to a detailed description of their organization and operation.

The investment house will first be considered, for, as the security middleman, it is the core of the investment banking system. Taken together, these organizations originate new security issues through purchasing them from governments and corporations that seek to raise funds in the capital market. After the

[2] Freedom from management responsibility should not, however, be confused with the safety factor. Investment trusts may do well or poorly, and the investor must often give such commitments close attention.

investment house, we shall consider the brokers and the stock exchanges, which furnish a market for these securities after they have been issued.

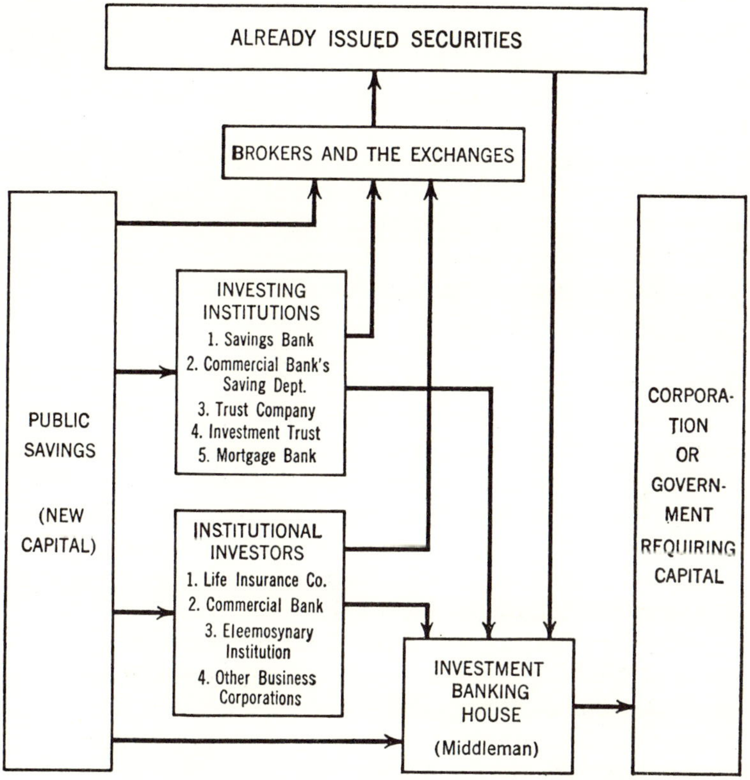

FIG. 1. CHART OF THE INVESTMENT BANKING SYSTEM

This chart shows in schematic form the movement of capital from investors to corporations and governments which sell their securities. Funds flow from investors through investment houses to the user of capital. Part of these funds comes to the investment banking house through investing institutions and institutional investors. Another part goes into already issued securities; but the proceeds of the sale of such securities will, to a large extent, go into new security issues.

After these two broad classes of investment banking institutions, consideration will be given to two other major groups of organizations which devote themselves to purchasing investment securities for others. First, there are the specialized investing institutions, such as the savings bank, investment trust, trust company, and mortgage bank. Secondly, there are institutions which are formed primarily for some other purpose, but which incidentally carry on large-scale security-buying operations because of the vast funds they accumulate in the course of their other activities. The insurance companies, commercial banks, eleemosynary institutions and large business corporations all fall within this class.

This institutional framework of the capital market is outlined in Fig. 1, which seeks to summarize briefly the position of the various types of institutions which have been developed to facilitate the investment of the savings of the public in the securities of governments and corporations that turn to the capital market for funds.

Institutional Transition

It is worthy of renewed emphasis that the classification of investment banking establishments cannot be sharply made according to any logical line of division drawn between institutions performing distinctly separate functions. Functions, as we have noted, are exercised today in combination with one another, and the degree of this combination varies a great deal even over very short periods of time.

This is another way of saying that the form and types of investment banking constantly pass through transitional phases. New functions and duties are being assumed from time to time by existing institutions. For example, national banks are taking up fiduciary duties. Other institutions are sloughing off functions which they have exercised in the past, but which have been found incongruous, unprofitable, or in conflict with the law. The result is to bring about a far-reaching and constant modification of financial relationships.

The years since the close of the World War have witnessed striking transformations among both the banks and the other financial institutions of the country. During the post-war decade, there was a marked tendency to assume new functions and to branch out into unaccustomed fields that led to a great mixture of banking duties, with corresponding danger. Subsequently, efforts have been made to disentangle financial relationships and to simplify the nation's banking structure. Further segregation of functions is now under active debate, as we shall see. There is always a tendency, except in boom times, to modify our institutional structure along lines which have been indicated as safe and constructive by experience. Meanwhile, there is a very large field within which difference of opinion may be successfully sustained by argument as to the shape our financial system should assume, and in which final conclusions will be arrived at only upon an empirical basis.

In addition to these fundamental changes that are taking place in the entire structure of investment banking, still another striking development is to be seen in the organization of new types of institutions whose place is still to be definitely determined. One such has been afforded by investment trusts since the close of the World War. Although the latter institutions had previously been but little known in the United States, they assumed an important place soon after the war, while at the same time they developed along lines that generally were quite unexpected. Instead of being, like their British prototypes, relatively conservative investors in securities purchased for the "long pull," they became quite speculative for the most part, shifting their portfolios constantly, oftentimes in accordance with some untenable theory of the business cycle, or merely haphazardly. Before 1929 they figured largely also in the call loan market, their offerings of funds being an additional disturbing factor in the efforts to control credit. Since the panic of 1929 they have again entered a new phase, having been largely reduced in number and now being more conservatively operated. It seems certain that this process of growth and change will continue for some time not only among investment trusts but among financial institutions generally.

The theoretical bearings of this transitory character of the present situation need to be noted. Some have taken it for granted that because the investment banking structure was by no means complete or final, it was not possible to develop a satisfactory theory of investment banking, much less a definite description of its practice. There would seem to be little basis for any such attitude. The technique of many phases of investment banking has actually attained a practically stereotyped form, at least in its fundamentals. In the same way, the basic principles of investment as a process are, both from the individual and the institutional points of view, becoming increasingly well recognized. They are not likely to change essentially, even though there should be further important modifications of the capitalistic system which has brought them into existence. The capitalistic system is characterized by a particular process for the saving, transfer and use of capital; and whatever changes may be brought about in its motive or purpose, there has as yet been no practical suggestion of a change in the basic technique of carrying on this most fundamental of economic functions. It is, therefore, entirely reasonable to express definite opinions regarding the theory and practice of investment, and to do so with substantial assurance that the underlying factors upon which such views rest will not be materially altered in the near future. The point at which nothing final can be said and no conclusive opinions expressed is in neither of these matters, but is found mainly in the institutional organization of the investment banking system. That can be outlined only as a contemporary matter.

A discussion of the theory of investment banking, therefore, must be developed largely independent of the particular types of institutions by which it is carried on, and with a view chiefly to indicating the processes and methods underlying institutional organization. The latter is important from the immediate standpoint of practical observation. Because, however, it is subject to constant change, the more important analyses of investment banking relate to principles and methods, though they necessarily are represented as being carried out by institutions whose character and form pass through continuous alteration. These fundamental principles and practices are treated in Parts II and III of this volume.

A body of principles relating to investment banking is steadily developing and has already assumed in many respects a definitive form. Some portion of the body of doctrine on the subject is still undoubtedly in the form of mere generalizations of practice which have yet to undergo the test of analysis and criticism before they can be accepted as in any sense ultimate statements of fundamental theory. Still other statements which are frequently put forward as representing the theory or principles of investment banking must be regarded as essentially transitory, growing in some cases out of current legal requirements, and in others being the product of the immediate institutional organization of investment banking. In still other cases, the so-called principles of investment banking will necessarily call for restatement or for adaptation, as institutional organization enters upon new phases.

While these limitations must be constantly borne in mind in dealing with the subject, investment banking has, nevertheless, reached the point at which it deserves recognition as a definite branch of banking, with a set of underlying ideas and a technique which are peculiarly its own. We shall now seek to state these ideas and to relate them so far as practicable to the conduct of investment banking institutions.

References

KNIFFEN, WILLIAM H., *Commercial Banking,* New York, 1923, vol. i, chap. ii.

LAVINGTON, F., *The English Capital Market,* London, 1921, part i.

MOULTON, H. G., *Financial Organization of Society,* Chicago, 1930, chap. x.

RODKEY, ROBERT G., *The Banking Process,* New York, 1928, chap. ii.

SCOTT, WILLIAM A., "Investment *vs.* Commercial Banking," *Investment Bankers Association of America, Proceedings,* 1913, vol. i, pp. 76–80.

SIMMONS, E. H. H., *Modern Capitalism,* New York, 1927, pp. 133–153.

STURGIS, HENRY S., *Investment, A New Profession,* New York, 1924, chaps. i and ii.

WILLIS, H. P., and CHAPMAN, J. M., *The Banking Situation,* New York, 1934, chap. x.

Chapter II

INVESTMENT MIDDLEMEN—THE INVESTMENT HOUSE

The Securities Business

The present-day organization of society is often termed capitalistic, because its most typical feature is the aggregations of capital goods—machines, railroads, power plants, etc.—owned by large business organizations. In the United States we now have more than a score of individual enterprises which report that they have in excess of a billion dollars of fixed assets. But moderate-sized as well as these large companies must raise capital publicly. Not being equipped to reach the widely scattered investment market, they must appeal to middlemen who have developed an organization that is ready and able to gather the funds of thousands of investors.

These middlemen are often defined as "investment bankers" in a more narrow sense. They constitute the nucleus or central factor in the capital market. On the one hand, they gather the funds of the community, either directly from investors or through intermediate institutions presently to be described, by selling them securities. On the other hand, they establish contact with those in need of this capital, and direct the stream of new capital to the most promising channels.

In view of the fact that commitment of capital for investment purposes is to cover a long period of time, it is necessary to evidence it in transferable form, so that the investor may realize upon his investment, should he need the cash for some other purpose.[1] Under legal safeguards, therefore, governments

[1] While the issuance of securities was not unknown in ancient Greece and Rome, and negotiable bonds were issued by the Venetian State in the twelfth century, large public security markets came into existence only with the growth of corporate enterprise after the middle of the eighteenth century. The corporation became the favored form of organization for large enterprises because of the limitation of liability to the shareholder which it accorded; and thus it

and corporations issue negotiable securities. These take the form either of bonds—evidences of debt—or shares of stock—which evidence fractional ownership in the assets of a corporation.

The relatively large issues of securities put out by many corporations lend themselves readily to modern merchandising methods by middlemen. An issue of bonds of the Consolidated Edison Co., for example, can be sold like any other trade-marked article of commerce; it is known and demanded by thousands of prospective buyers. The better and more favorably known the issuer, the less "sales resistance" will be encountered in disposing of its securities. This is because the credit of the company has become established and "seasoned" through extended favorable experience by investors with its securities. The investment banker's problem of distribution differs in various important respects, but not essentially, from that of other merchants.

Security middlemen, buying entire issues on the one hand and distributing them to numerous investors, large and small, institutional and individual, on the other, normally handle the bulk of new security issues other than those of the federal government. However, their services are often dispensed with in the sale of new stock by large corporations which make direct offering of the shares to old stockholders on a *pro rata* basis. The reason for this is partly of a legal nature. Each share of the capital stock of a corporation represents a fractional interest in the equity existing over and above the debts of the enterprise, in the earnings and the voting power. The corporation laws of a number of states require that new issues of capital stock must first be offered to the old stockholders, and only if they refuse or contract themselves out of the privilege of subscribing can the stock be offered on the same terms to outsiders. Investment houses, if used at all in such cases, merely guarantee or *underwrite* the sale, by buying shares not taken up by the corporation's shareholders. In addition to this legal "preemptive right," expediency may suggest the sale of a new issue of shares to existing stockholders of the corporation.

---

came about that the bulk of security issues, other than those of governments, have been those of corporations.

Hence, in the case of a common stock offering, the rôle of the investment banker is frequently limited to the guarantee or underwriting of its purchase by existing shareholders, whereas bonds are almost invariably sold through investment banking houses which offer them to the public.[2] Because most of them handle chiefly bonds, these investment banking houses are often called bond houses, although practically all of them now handle preferred stocks, and not infrequently issues of common stock as well.

The bulk of the funds raised in the American capital market by corporations is obtained, in the first instance, from these middlemen, the investment houses. Every year these organizations put out billions of dollars of new securities. They are in the investment banking field what the ordinary commercial bank is in the field of short-term financing—they gather the capital of the nation and make it available to those able to put it to work profitably. In their method of operation, however, they are fundamentally different, in that they deal in negotiable securities that are generally known and can be bought and sold with ease; whereas, as we have seen in the previous chapter, the commercial bank normally holds the paper which represents its individual commercial loans to maturity. The short term of these advances and the specialized knowledge of each borrower's affairs required make the development of a public demand for individual commercial obligations impracticable.

Kinds of Investment Houses

As in all branches of marketing, there has been a considerable degree of specialization among security-selling houses. The broadest classification on the basis of function is into the three groups of wholesalers, combined wholesalers and retailers, and "dealers," or smaller retailers. Within each of these groups, individual firms exercise a varying degree of specialization, some dealing in all kinds of securities, and others specializing

[2] In several states, the sale of convertible bonds or bonds with warrants attached to buy common stocks at fixed prices must be made first to shareholders because of an extension of the legal doctrine of the preemptive right to such securities.

narrowly in one or more industries, such as railroads, utilities and real estate bonds.

There are but a few exclusively wholesale general investment houses, the most prominent including Morgan Stanley & Company, and Kuhn, Loeb & Company. Other important wholesalers have found it necessary or profitable to supplement their buying or originating activities with retail selling and other activities. The wholesaler relies primarily upon large retailers and the smaller dealers for distributing securities, several of them having a list of retailers usually associated with them in selling their new offerings—a so-called "syndicate list"—numbering up to 1,000 at times.

Most of the larger investment houses of the present day are combination wholesalers and retailers. They both buy, alone or with others in a purchase group, entire issues of securities, and sell them to the ultimate "consumers," either individual investors or institutions. On many recent bond issues, members of the purchase group have themselves accounted for over half of the retail distribution.

Wholesale investment dealers may perform this function either as *originators*, in which case they make contact with the issuing corporation or government and head the purchase group organized to underwrite the issue, or as members or *participants* in the purchase group. The volume of security issues that leading wholesalers handled in a year of relatively moderate investment banking activity, 1935, is shown in the table on page 28.

Retailers may obtain securities to sell from new issues either by joining a *selling group*, which does the actual work of distribution, or by obtaining a dealer's allowance that is usually provided for in the sale of new issues. This allowance will vary from a slight fraction of one per cent to a much larger discount from the public offering price of the new issue, depending upon the quality of the issue, the state of the capital market, etc.

The retailers consummate their sales chiefly through individual salesmen, who make contact with individual and institutional investors and are compensated directly or indirectly in proportion to the volume of their sales. In order to obtain

TABLE I.—BANKING HOUSE PARTICIPATIONS IN REGISTERED ISSUES, 1935[a]

	Stocks and Bonds (000 omitted)		
	Participation as Purchase Group Member	Participation as Manager or Co-manager of Purchase Group	Total Participations
1. First Boston Corporation (New York City)	$ 113,473	$ 99,997	$ 213,470
2. Kuhn, Loeb & Co. (New York City)	38,750	113,153	151,903
3. Brown, Harriman & Co. Inc. (New York City)	137,582	7,760	145,342
4. Edward B. Smith & Co. (New York City)	76,939	49,460	126,399
5. Blyth & Co. (New York City)	79,141	26,684	105,825
6. Salomon Bros. & Hutzler (New York City)[b]	......	93,000	93,000
7. Field, Glore & Co. (Chicago)	52,911	10,918	63,829
8. Lazard Freres (New York City)	41,628	20,400	62,028
9. Dillon, Read & Co. (New York City)	15,920	41,118	57,038
10. Morgan Stanley & Co. (New York City)[c]	4,975	50,792	55,767
11. Kidder, Peabody & Co. (New York City)	53,497	2,061	55,558
12. Bonbright & Co. Inc. (New York City)	28,923	24,208	53,131
13. Halsey, Stuart & Co. Inc. (Chicago)	23,494	23,104	46,598
14. Lehman Bros. (New York City)	25,268	20,696	45,964
15. Lee Higginson Corp. (New York City)	36,004	......	36,004
16. E. H. Rollins & Sons, Inc. (New York City)	35,150	817	35,967
17. Hayden Stone & Co. (New York City)	21,430	13,127	34,557
18. Dean Witter & Co. (San Francisco)	32,330	1,450	33,780
19. Stone & Webster & Blodgett, Inc. (New York City)	22,924	10,352	33,276
20. White, Weld & Co. (New York City)	30,158	312	30,470
21. H. M. Byllesby & Co. (Chicago)	28,040	......	28,040
22. W. C. Langley & Co. (New York City)	18,565	8,800	27,365
23. Coffin & Burr, Inc. (Boston)	15,041	8,658	23,699
24. Spencer Trask & Co. (New York City)	19,076	......	19,076
25. W. E. Hutton & Co. (Cincinnati)	10,273	8,650	18,923
26. Goldman, Sachs & Co. (New York City)	13,553	4,900	18,453
27. Paine, Webber & Co. (Boston)	10,721	7,200	17,921
28. Hornblower & Weeks (Boston)	6,049	11,250	17,299
29. Mellon Securities Co. (Pittsburgh)	15,140	......	15,140
30. F. S. Mosely & Co. (Boston)	13,042	1,000	14,042
31. W. R. Staats Co. (Los Angeles)	10,865	......	10,865
32. Cassatt & Co. (Philadelphia)	8,848	......	8,848
33. Hemphill Noyes & Co. (New York City)	2,215	2,063	4,278
34. Wertheim & Co. (New York City)	3,800	......	3,800
Total	$1,045,725	$661,930	$1,707,655

[a] Includes all houses which had total participations of more than $10,000,000 in distribution of bonds or more than $2,000,000 in distribution of stocks.

[b] The total participations of this house comprise two issues which it distributed as selling agents.

[c] This company was not formed until September 16, 1935.

wider coverage, branch offices are maintained by a number of investment dealers.

Legal Restrictions

Until 1933, almost any type of financial or business organization could participate in the security-selling business. The chief exception, indeed, was the life insurance companies. As a result of the New York State investigation of 1907, such institutions were barred from underwriting.

Nevertheless, up to the World War period, the investment banking business was conducted chiefly by specialized firms, several of which combined their wholesaling and retailing security business with private deposit banking, the acceptance and commercial paper business or some related activity. In the decade of the 'twenties, however, the security business was invaded by *security affiliates* of commercial banks, which for a time seemed destined to dominate it.

Not being authorized specifically by federal banking law to engage in the security business until 1927, and for the most part not having the authority to buy stocks or to underwrite whole issues of securities in any event, commercial banks resorted to indirect means to participate in the larger profits held out by the wholesale and retail security business in the war and post-war period. They organized separate corporations under state law.

These corporations enjoyed virtually unlimited powers. They raised their capital as a rule by an operation under which the stockholders of the parent banks automatically bought shares in the security affiliates *pro rata*. These shares were usually deposited with a trust company for the benefit of the stockholders of the bank, so that identity of ownership and management was assured. Additional funds needed by the affiliate would then be obtained through borrowing from the bank. In a few cases, the same result was attained through printing single certificates that represented shares of stock of both the bank and the security affiliate.

These security affiliates possessed several advantages over independent investment banking houses. They could utilize the same quarters, and had an excellent list of prospective customers in the clientele of the bank. Also, large corporate clients of the bank could furnish new security issues for sale.

In practice, however, the principle of combining the commercial banking business and the business of selling corporate securities within what was virtually one institution was found to involve several serious disadvantages. The business of wholesaling securities can be productive of great loss, and then heavy loans to affiliates may weaken the parent bank. Rumors of these losses can hurt the parent bank even more, through causing deposit withdrawals.

A temptation also exists to shift frozen bank loans to the public from the parent institution through the issue of securities by the affiliate. Affiliates have also been used as a dumping ground for undesirable assets of the bank, or even as an agency for manipulating the market for the bank's own stock. Perhaps the most telling argument against the affiliate system was its abuse by the Bank of United States, a New York institution that failed in 1931 with almost $200,000,000 of deposits. This bank had a security affiliate which, through upwards of 50 subsidiaries of its own, did a variety of things the bank itself could not do, and concealed the true position of the institution. The larger part of the capital of the bank had been borrowed by the affiliate to finance its own operations, particularly the pegging of the bank's own stock.

The Banking Act of 1933 ended the affiliate system by requiring separation of ownership and management of banks and security companies. The shares of a member bank may not now, directly or indirectly, represent the stock of any other corporation except another member bank or a corporation owning the bank's premises. Also, no officer, director or employee of any security underwriting or distributing organization may serve in such capacity with a bank, except "in limited classes of cases in which the Board of Governors of the Federal Reserve System may allow such service by general regulations when in the judgment of the said board it would not unduly influence the investment policies of such member bank or the advice it gives its customers regarding investments."

The Banking Act of 1933 also forbids banks to underwrite new security issues. Commercial banks that choose to do so, however, remain free to act either as wholesalers or as retailers of federal government, state, county or municipal bonds, which are exempted from the restrictions in the law. They are also free to act as retailers of corporate securities, in that they can resell securities which they purchase for their own account. The restrictions affecting such purchases are discussed in Chapter V below.

The Banking Act of 1933 further forbids private bankers to engage in the security wholesaling and retailing business. It was as a result of this provision of the law that organizations like J. P. Morgan & Co. withdrew from the security business, although the same interests were responsible for the organization of Morgan Stanley & Co., which has conducted a large part of the business that the older Morgan firm regularly transacted. Kuhn, Loeb & Co., another private banker who has long conducted an extensive security-wholesaling business, elected to retain the latter and abandoned its deposit banking business.

In the financing of the public utility industry, a number of holding companies built up their own security wholesaling and retailing organizations. The liabilities imposed by the Federal Securities Act, the financial disaster that overtook several of these holding company organizations after 1930, and the provisions of the Public Utility Holding Company Act of 1935 have combined to eliminate these organizations almost entirely from the nation's investment banking mechanism.

In the post-depression period, in fact, the wholesaling and retailing of securities has become almost as highly specialized a function as it was before the war. Only the investment trusts, among other types of financial institutions, have shown a tendency to enter the underwriting field on a material scale. At the same time, through the Federal Securities Act of 1933 and the Securities Exchange Act of 1934, such activities were made subject to extensive federal regulation for the first time.

Specialization in Securities Handled

Specialization among bond houses in particular classes of securities has long been common. This tendency may be encouraged by the special knowledge needed to handle certain types of securities, particularly municipal bonds. In other cases, specialization results from the fact that the house appeals to a definite group of clients with limited interests. An example of this is a house specializing in securities permitted by law as investments for savings banks and insurance companies, termed "legals" in the parlance of Wall Street. Lastly, specialization may result from the financial connections of the investment house. Thus, Bonbright & Co., with close personal connections in the public utility field, has long specialized in the securities of public service companies.

Over a period of time, experience shows, specialization tends to break down in the case of the average investment house. Changing conditions, and the desire to utilize their distribution facilities more intensively, make bond houses extend their interests, despite an original specialized organization. Especially after a corps of salesmen have been gathered and trained, the temptation becomes great to give them a more diversified list of issues to offer clients.

The specialized house possesses several advantages. It can concentrate its organization upon one group of securities, and thus be able to give a better statistical and market service. It acquires a reputation for expert knowledge of this group of securities, and so becomes the focus for inquiries concerning them from both investors and issuers.

On the other hand, a specialized security dealer is at a handicap in serving investors, since he cannot give a well-rounded service to his clients. Also, because of the lack of diversification in his business, he will be at a loss to know how to operate profitably if circumstances contract the volume of business available in his particular field.

Other Investment House Activities

While the basic function of the investment house is to act as middleman in the distribution of new security issues, these organizations have usually branched out into other financial activities to increase their revenues. Since the volume of new financing fluctuates sharply from time to time, such related activities are often found necessary to assure a regular income that will cover overhead expenses at all times.

The most important related activity is the brokerage business in the broad sense, by which is meant the execution of orders for already issued securities. A number of investment houses are members of stock exchanges, and others do a very extensive business in unlisted securities, acting as over-the-counter dealers.

A growing number of investment houses also act as managers of portfolios for individuals or institutions. This involves the creation of an organization similar to that of a specialized investment management concern, such as is described in Chapter V below. Some investment houses have organized and manage investment trusts which they control.

Certain investment houses also conduct foreign exchange, bankers' acceptance, commercial paper and other departments devoted to specialized types of commercial or investment banking.

On the other hand, a large number of stock brokerage houses have opened bond departments, and thus swelled the ranks of investment houses. Here also the desire has been to develop further the connection made with clients in other ways. The efforts of stock brokerage houses to establish profitable bond departments have not been attended with success in every case. The reason for this is that the two activities do not in many instances fit into each other. Where the stock exchange house is one of high repute, with many wealthy customers, the bond department may become nearly as important to it as stock trading activities, and membership in the stock exchange will facilitate such dealings in bonds. But many stock exchange houses which have a more speculative outlook find this does not help them in efforts to sell conservative bonds and preferred stocks on a low-yield basis. In not a few stock exchange houses, in fact, the management seems satisfied if the bond department "breaks even" financially, regarding it as a source of prestige for the firm.

Form of Investment House Organization

The form of organization of investment banking houses shows wide variation at the present time. Originally, practically all the firms were partnerships, in which the several members often possessed equal power. Several of the older firms retain this form of legal organization, and a few of them have a dozen or more partners in the business. Where membership is desired in security exchanges, which generally admit only unincorporated firms, the partnership form of organization is, in fact, compulsory.

The corporate form of organization is now becoming increasingly common among investment houses. Perhaps the greatest advantage thus gained is limited liability for the principals of the concern who own its stock. A second advantage is more centralized organization. In a partnership it is difficult in practice to curtail the powers of individual partners,[3] but in a corporation there is a fixed hierarchy of officers, from the chairman of the board or the president down. The corporate form also permits the sale of stock to outsiders, for the sake of raising additional capital or interesting influential persons in the firm, without passing on at the same time any share in the management of the business. This latter objective has also been attained in many partnerships through securing limited partners who have no voice in the business. However, it is necessary to conform to the legal requirements concerning limited partnerships in each state in which business is transacted, if such limitation of liability is to be assured in practice.

The elimination of the private bankers from the field has tended to increase the number of incorporated security dealers, as a private banker could not incorporate without becoming subject to the banking laws. Thus, when J. P. Morgan & Co., a partnership, withdrew from the security business because of the Banking Act of 1933, a large part of its issue business was taken over by Morgan Stanley & Company, Inc., a corporation in which the partners of J. P. Morgan & Co. held most of the $7,000,000 of non-voting preferred stock, while the officers of Morgan Stanley & Company, Inc., subscribed to its $500,000 of voting common stock.

Most investment banking organizations are themselves privately financed, but a few have raised funds publicly through

[3] One large house has secured centralization of control by requiring each partner, on entering the firm, to give the leading partner an undated letter of resignation, which becomes effective on the latter's acceptance at any time.

security issues. The First Boston Corporation and the Bancamerica Blair Corporation are prominent among the latter.

Internal Organization

Because of the great diversity in types among bond houses, their internal organization shows wide variance. The accompanying chart depicts the actual organization of a typical firm doing a wholesale and retail business. Whatever the division in responsibility among departments and individuals, practically every bond house is organized for the functions of:

1. Purchase of securities
2. Sale of securities
3. Trading in issued securities
4. Statistical analysis of securities
5. Mechanical handling of and accounting for the transactions of the concern

In most investment houses, the departmental organization conforms fairly closely to these basic functions. The management of an investment house is also organized as a rule along these departmental lines. Where the corporate form of organization is adopted, the department heads are frequently vice-presidents and directors. In this respect, investment house organization differs from that of most commercial banks where the board of directors generally consists chiefly of outside persons, and the operating officials are simply employees. In a partnership the different departments are headed largely by partners; and vital decisions, such as the purchase of new security issues or the adoption of general policies, which in a corporation the board of directors would make, are made in conferences of the partners. The general factors governing the operation of each such department will now be discussed.

Purchase of Securities

The purchase of securities from the issuing company, either as member of an originating group or as dealer from other houses, is a difficult matter, especially at times of intensive competition for desirable new issues. In originating a new security issue, the investment banker exercises the important social function of helping to direct the flow of capital into various governmental and corporate channels. He must, for his own protection, determine the ability of the applicant for capital to use investment credit safely and profitably, just as the commercial banker analyzes his customer's statement to fix a safe "line of credit." However, having to resell the securities he buys within a short period, he is more sensitive to the preferences and whims of investors at the moment.

The work incidental to the origination of security issues is concentrated in the buying department. Here proposals for new offerings are received from many sources and put in definite form. Close contact is maintained with the statistical department in the study of these proposals. In a number of houses, the statistical department is included in the buying department, or made auxiliary to it. The legal and other details of security buying are also handled in this department.

The syndicate department, separately organized in many of the larger houses, handles the work involved in the organization of groups of investment houses to cooperate in the sale of securities originated in the buying department.

Usually the ultimate decision as to the purchase of new securities rests with an investment committee, consisting of several or all the partners of the bond house. This investment committee is the counterpart of the loan committee of the board of directors of a bank. It sifts out the desirable proposals from among the many applications for loans and stock sales coming to it. In a well-managed investment house, the decisions of the investment committee are based on a mass of data received from the issuing company, checked and supplemented by the statisticians of the firm and associated engineers and accountants working under the direction of the partner in charge of the buying department.[4]

The question of the relationship between the investment banker and the corporation on whose behalf it has issued securities is a peculiar one. In the case of the commercial bank the borrower, as is well known, submits a statement which is analyzed by the credit department of the lending institution,

[4] For a fuller discussion of the technique of security-issue buying, see chap. xvii.

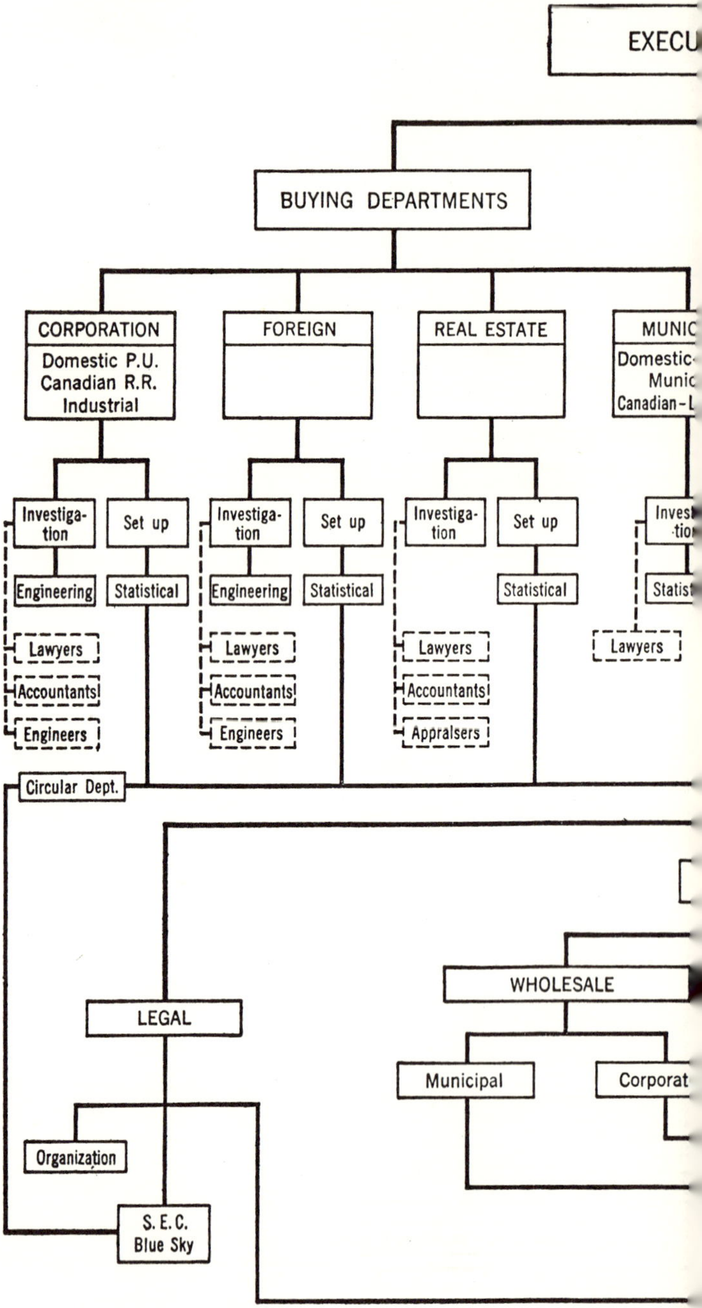

EXECU
BUYING DEPARTMENTS
CORPORATION
Domestic P.U.
Canadian R.R.
Industrial
FOREIGN
REAL ESTATE
MUNIC
Domestic
Munic
Canadian - L
Investiga-tion
Set up
Engineering
Statistical
Lawyers
Accountants
Engineers
Investiga-tion
Set up
Engineering
Statistical
Lawyers
Accountants
Engineers
Investiga-tion
Set up
Statistical
Lawyers
Accountants
Appraisers
Statis
Lawyers
Circular Dept.
LEGAL
Organization
S. E. C.
Blue Sky
WHOLESALE
Municipal
Corporat

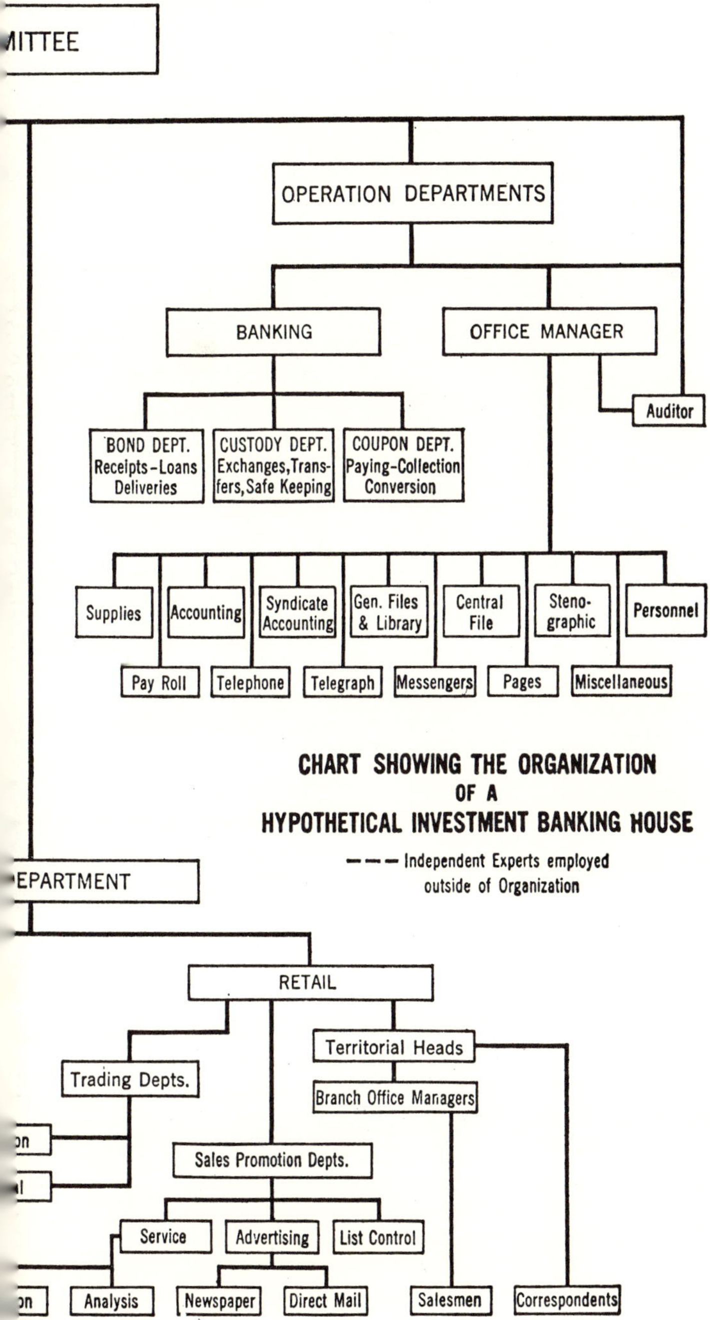

CHART SHOWING THE ORGANIZATION OF A HYPOTHETICAL INVESTMENT BANKING HOUSE

– – – Independent Experts employed outside of Organization

and then, if the statement is approved, funds are placed to the credit of the borrower. The bank is the holder of the paper of the enterprise, although it may and frequently does transfer this paper to some other institution, either through sale in the open market or rediscount. Sometimes, where the amount of money involved is large, some participation of the banker in the affairs of the borrower may be provided. Because he is largely concerned with the liquidity of the borrower, as well as with his solvency, and because he frequently has a title to portions of the property of the borrower, the banker is sometimes even provided with a seat on the board of directors so that he may be able to keep track of what his customer is doing.

In investment banking this closer relationship has hitherto been general. The investment banker, intimately concerned as he is over a long or indefinite period of time with the affairs of the corporation for which he has sold securities to his clients, and with whom his name has been linked publicly by the offering, often takes such a voice in control as a matter of course. He is not as eager as formerly to take a seat on the board of directors of the concern, because of the added liability thus incurred under the Securities Act of 1933. But he may acquire and hold a substantial stock interest in the company.

Where this management function is well performed, it of course gives the buyer of bonds an assurance that the banker has knowledge of what is being done by the borrowing concern, and also of more competent financial policies. This factor may be an important consideration in inducing the bond buyer to part with his money, and explains why some investors place much stress, in purchasing securities, on the character and reputation of the house of issue. However, no banker can afford to assume any obligation to make good on an issue that subsequently proves bad, in view of the small profit margin that usually obtains.

The investment banker now exercises a voice in the management of a number of business enterprises. The "entrepreneur" of the economists, who in traditional economic theory is supposed to bring together and manage the "factors of production," including capital, is a figure fading from the horizon as far as larger business enterprises are concerned. In the railroad industry, with its aggregate investment of more than twenty billions of dollars, the executive is usually closely answerable to the banker who has lent his name as issuer to the hundreds of millions of securities the company has sold to the public. In numerous industrial concerns, the banker element is dominant on the board of directors. Even in the public utility industry, where the technically trained engineer for a long time retained control, the present period of widespread consolidation has resulted in bringing the banker into a more prominent place.

In a competitive society, rivalry among individual enterprises should result in a kind of natural selection and the survival of the fittest—financially. Hence, financial difficulties generally mean that control of an enterprise is to shift from its promoters and executives to the bankers who are asked to help supply new capital. The early history of the General Motors Corporation, involving two separate battles for control between W. C. Durant, its executive head at that time, and a powerful banking group, ended, as most such struggles end, with the victory of the bankers. Similarly, the great packing house of Armour & Company fell under banking control when post-war financial difficulties hurt the fortunes of the controlling family.

The investment banker gains in power not only through the misfortunes of business enterprises, but also through the death or retirement of their founders and chief executives. There are many cases, such as that of the Vanderbilts and the New York Central Railroad, where family management gradually changes to banker management. The descendants of the founders of great family fortunes seldom care to lead the strenuous life of their forbears, and they then welcome the opportunity to shift the responsibility for the continued successful operation of inherited enterprises to some outstanding banking firm, with which they thereafter become affiliated in the control of the property.

Investment Banking a Personal Business

The investment banking business revolves far more around the individuals who make up the chief houses in the field than is the case in commercial banking. This was amply proved when the break-up of the bank security affiliates in 1933 and 1934 brought about a drastic reorganization of the field. Officials of bank security affiliates joined other organizations, and usually carried with them a large part of the business they conducted when with the affiliate.

When a corporation has conducted its investment banking business with a particular investment banker for some years, the latter is held to acquire a claim to it, even if he should change his connection. Investment houses among themselves respect this custom. The story is told of one wholesale security house that negotiated a refunding issue with a public utility. When informed that this utility had formerly carried on its dealings with a bank security affiliate whose head had become the president of another wholesale house, the negotiations were terminated, and it was suggested to the utility that it establish relations with the house headed by the individual who had regularly done its financing in the past.

Thus, a large part of the security origination business is controlled not only by a limited number of large wholesalers, but more particularly by a number of individuals who direct these houses.

Because of its personal character, furthermore, the wholesome investment business is conducted largely within the scope of certain accepted professional ethics. Cutthroat competition for new business, apart from state and municipal issues that have to be sold by competitive bidding, is not considered proper. Houses are, in general, expected to recognize each other's established connections, and where conflicts arise they are usually settled by negotiation, or through sharing the contested business, rather than by outside arbitration or litigation.

Sale of Securities

The sales department is of the greatest importance in all but the large wholesale houses. An efficient selling organization, through assuring distribution power for new security issues, gives the investment house a reputation which makes it a popular member of purchase groups, and thus facilitates the work of the buying department.

The sales department of an investment house consists of a corps of individual salesmen under the supervision of a sales manager. One large New York house reported in 1928 that it had more than 500 salesmen; smaller ones have only a few. In recent years, however, the tendency has been to have far smaller but better-trained sales departments than in the past, as the market for securities has become more largely institutional in character.

These salesmen gather, through the years, customer lists which they are constantly trying to enlarge. The average client of the house deals through one of its salesmen, thus introducing a large personal element which is an outstanding characteristic of retail, as well as wholesale, investment banking. The strength of many an investment house is an adequate, trained and loyal sales force.

The bond salesman depends for his compensation in most cases primarily upon a commission on each bond sold, if the bond is one of a new issue of securities. He gets as a rule no return from obtaining orders for securities already outstanding which must be acquired in the market. This system results in a steady pressure to sell new issues, and may tempt the salesmen to switch his customers too frequently out of securities they already hold and into new offerings. Many houses pay no fixed salaries in addition to these commissions, but allow older men a drawing account against future commissions. Others, recognizing the general good will brought to the institution by a salesman, give a substantial fixed salary which is paid regardless of the commissions earned, and allow commissions on sales in excess of a minimum amount.[5]

The sales department is aided in many houses by an advertising department, which seeks to extend the list of clients constantly by mail, periodical and newspaper advertising.

The Trading Department

In larger bond houses, the trading department assumes substantial proportions even where these houses do not actively seek business as brokers. This is so because of the need for pegging prices of new issues in the market, and for disposing of bonds which are brought into the house by the salesmen as a by-

[5] Security selling and salesmen's compensation are discussed at greater length and in more detail in chaps. xviii and xix.

product of new-issue selling, involving as it does frequent switching of investors from old issues to new.

A new offering of securities is not necessarily the best available securities for merchandising by the sales department. In fact, already outstanding seasoned bonds can often be handled more safely and with far less overhead, and therefore with larger profit. A good trading department can pick up, either in the market or from large private or institutional investors, several hundred bonds of an issue which is recognized as selling too low. These can then be resold at a sufficient advance in price to make the operation profitable, where conditions are favorable.

The trading department is also kept busy disposing of bonds which clients have turned in, receiving in exchange bonds of a new issue which the firm is eager to sell. Frequently, a salesman out to sell a new issue will be met with the cold reply that the investor has no funds available for investment at the moment. But, if experienced, he will not be dismayed, for he can ask the investor to turn in some security he has, perhaps at a price somewhat above the market, and take in exchange the new issue on which a profitable commission is being paid. The trading department then faces the task of passing the bonds received in this way back into the market; and, if ably managed and if market conditions are not adverse, this can frequently be done by gathering substantial blocks of bonds in this way and selling them to some institution or other dealer at a small additional profit to the house.

Another function sometimes performed by the trading department is the making of secondary markets in issues originally offered by the investment house. Finally, the trading department, or the trader attached to the buying or selling department, almost invariably handles the execution of commission orders for customers in securities which must be purchased in the open market.

As a result of the activities of the buying, selling and trading departments, the investment house has a constantly changing volume of inventory. Many houses have sought to give unified thought and control to this problem by establishing an inventory committee composed of the heads of each of these departments. This committee can then determine the wisdom of entering into new originations, the necessity for pressure on the sales department to clear the shelves of unsold issues, and the policy to be followed by the trading department in adding to or reducing the stock of securities on hand through the market.

The Statistical Department

The statistical department, when separately organized, provides the others with facts and figures required to reach intelligent judgments as to values. When a new financing proposal first appears, this department analyzes the company, the industry and the market for similar securities. It helps prepare registration statements and prospectuses, and aids the salesmen in answering questions of prospective clients. It continually analyzes securities to guide the trading department; and, finally, it prepares special studies and circulars. Where the house does an investment management business, the statistical department may bear the brunt of this work. In such cases, it is often conducted autonomously, to assure an independent point of view.

The statistical department helps bring business because it acts as a service agency for the benefit of investors. A bond house of standing receives many general and specific inquiries which must be answered. These are turned over to the statistical department. In this way, contacts are established with investors. One device quite common in the past was to invite investors, both clients of the house and others, to send in their holdings "for analysis." The list was then studied by the statistical department in the light of certain general investment principles, and exchanges were suggested, usually into issues sponsored by the house making the analysis and which it was seeking to distribute to investors. Furthermore, the list was retained and a permanent record of the customer's holdings was thus secured. This was used in selling him securities subsequently by suggesting shifts from time to time from issues on the list into new offerings of the investment house. This was generally done by a salesman assigned to that particular account.

The civil liabilities imposed by the Federal Securities Act and the Securities Exchange Act have made some houses more cautious about such use of the statistical department, although there is wide difference of opinion as to the real practical import of these liabilities.

In any event, the relative importance of the statistical department has become greater as the market for new security issues has become more largely concentrated in a limited number of financial institutions and wealthy investors. For competitive reasons, it has been found necessary by most houses to offer more free statistical service to clients than in the past.

The statistical department also keeps a record of bond redemptions and similar details affecting individual issues. This permits it to advise clients in timely fashion, thus giving them a large measure of personal service and at the same time putting the house in a position to suggest specific exchanges and purchases of securities. Competition among houses raises the standard of this service and investors are coming to expect it.

The Accounting Department

The accounting department of the investment house keeps the records of both security and money transactions. Cost accounting, auditing, budgeting and statistical analysis of records have not been carried far in this field, a study of typical bond houses reveals. However, cooperative studies have been made for the purpose of improving practice in this respect. Many houses restrict their bookkeeping activities to the "cage routine" involved in keeping records of cash and securities, the bookkeeping on customers' accounts, and the income and balance sheet. Few have an auditor permanently attached to the organization, and budgeting of expenses is as yet not at all common. Sales data analysis to determine the average cost of selling bonds has been worked up in a few instances, as has also departmental expense analysis to check on the profitability of the important operating departments. Much remains to be done to bring investment house accounting up to date.[6]

Finally, the investment house must build up an organization for the mechanical handling of securities. This involves a department for the receipt and safe-keeping of securities, a mail-

[6] See Report of the Sub-Committee on Cost Accounting of the Business Problems Committee, *Proceedings* of the Investment Bankers' Association of America, 1928.

ing department, and one for the handling of coupons and redemptions. Where turnover is large, a department for effecting the clearance of transactions must be maintained. This type of service, like the statistical service, is coming to be expected by customers in many places, as a result of keen competition in service among the houses.

Branch Organization

Investment banking is characterized by a greater development of branch organization and activity than is found in commercial banking in this country. The high degree of regulation and government control to which commercial banking has been subjected has hampered normal expansion through branches.

In the investment banking field, which has been regulated to a far lesser extent, the same causes have not existed to localize the operations of the individual investment house. As a result, a number of the leading firms have branches in the principal cities from coast to coast, connected by telephone and leased wire connections so that they may be operated together to a large extent. Correspondent relationships are also well developed with the aid of leased wires.

In a year of great investment activity like 1929, in fact, the Investment Bankers' Association of America reported that its members, numbering a little more than 600, maintained in the aggregate almost 1200 separate branches. In 1935, the association had almost 650 members, and a somewhat smaller number of branches.

Larger branches usually have a complete organization of their own along the lines described in the above discussion. This applies especially to the many houses which began business in some large outside city, like Boston or Chicago, and have since established offices in New York, which has gradually become their most important center. Smaller branches retain a skeleton organization only, usually including a branch manager or assistant sales manager, a corps of salesmen, and a small accounting and cashier department, as the main office may be too distant to permit the handling of customers' accounts there. Where branches are maintained within the same city, as is done, for example, by some New York houses, all bookkeeping and cash transactions may be concentrated in the main office.

While the smaller branches thus largely restrict their activities to the sale of securities, it has usually been found good practice to give each branch as much autonomy as possible, because of the varying tastes of investors in different regions. When the house is putting out a new issue, it is customary to invite branch managers to take on as much of it as they think can be sold within their territory, always having it understood that each branch will cooperate as far as possible. Where efforts have been made to assign arbitrarily a certain quota to a branch, results have frequently proved disappointing.

Not only do the investment houses expand their field of operation through branches, but they also send out sales representatives from the main or branch offices to cover smaller towns and even rich rural districts. These out-of-town salesmen give investors residing within a radius of, say, 200 miles of the city in which the office is located, a direct personal service and the opportunity to do business with a leading house. As the larger houses thus expand their activities geographically, they constitute strong competitors of the local houses and banks which seek to sell securities in their own territory. However, this competition doubtless has raised the standards of the business in the smaller towns, and as such has generally been a desirable development from the point of view of the individual investor. Efforts to impede such outside competition in some states through discriminatory blue-sky laws are discussed in Chapter XXII.

Financing the Investment House

In studying the financial problems facing the investment banker, we may take as a typical house a relatively small firm doing both an issuing and a selling business. The largest houses have such powerful banking connections and financial resources that the same considerations do not always apply to them. The smallest houses, because they seldom purchase securities outright for resale, have few and simple financial needs.

The capital of the investment banker is usually a definitely contributed sum, which should be in some substantial proportion to his average outstanding liabilities, actual and potential. It is quite true that a good many investment bankers regard themselves as being virtually in the brokerage business, and so are disposed to think that they can "get along" with practically no capital at all, provided they have good opportunities for borrowing at banks. This is not as hazardous as it is in the case of the commercial banker, who, a hundred years ago, often undertook to set up a business in this same way. The lower degree of hazard, however, is due merely to the fact that the same insistence on immediate cash payment of liabilities, such as deposits and note issues, does not exist. The internal risk involved for the enterprise itself is not less in one case than it is in the other. An investment house should be reasonably capitalized in relation to the risks assumed, and its capital should be paid in, before beginning business.

The capital of the investment banking house is of course invested in some degree in equipping headquarters, either through purchase or rental. Whatever this outlay may be, it is generally a small percentage of the total capital, and should be regularly reduced by writing off until it has been cut to a nominal amount. After providing for working capital to be used in current running expenses, overhead outlays, developmental work and the like, the remainder of the capital originally contributed constitutes the fund which the concern has in hand for the purpose of buying securities for sale and guaranteeing the fulfillment of obligations it undertakes. The fund so engaged is not only an evidence of good faith—the basis of the concern's business, a necessary supplement to its borrowing—but it represents a guarantee to customers and others that the concern is responsible, and that even though it may incur some losses in the natural conduct of its business, it will be able to write them off.

The methods by which an investment banker finances his business may be observed by taking the case of a house which has embarked upon the business of floating a loan on behalf of a corporation. Let us assume that the capital of the investment banker is $1,000,000, and that he has been asked to float an issue of $1,000,000 in bonds on behalf of some industrial enterprise. It is evident that he is able, making no allowance for his current necessities for running expenses and so forth, to take up this issue and hold it in his portfolio, resorting afterward to the sale of the bonds to others with such profit to himself as he may see fit. If now he finds it possible to dispose of only $750,000 of the bonds, he will be in the position of carrying $250,000 himself out of his own capital. As a matter of fact, however, investment bankers do not like to do this, since they want to embark upon many other operations at the same time, and they regard as distinctly unsuccessful any operation which has left them with a substantial residuum of unsold securities. As he is bringing out successively or simultaneously a number of issues, the investment banker's capital may be almost entirely engaged in carrying the temporarily unsold portions of each issue, with the help of bank credit.

Use of Bank Credit

As a matter of fact, investment bankers normally seek to handle issues which in the aggregate equal several times their own capitalization. The work and detailed investigation involved do not warrant them in undertaking transactions on which the turnover is no larger than their own contributed capital. Accordingly, they must seek the assistance of commercial banks for the purpose of obtaining advances which will practically carry for them the unsold portions of issues in which they have participated, and other securities they hold in their trading and other departments. They thus become perennial or semi-permanent customers at banks, and they look to the latter to furnish the means necessary to the conduct of a large volume of business. In such an event, the capital, originally paid up and deposited in cash with bankers, constitutes a fund which merely supplements the much larger volume of credit which is secured by loans—primarily collateral loans on securities purchased—from the banks.

Before the enactment of the Securities Exchange Act of 1934, security dealers could borrow up to any amount that a bank cared to lend them. At times, they would borrow almost the full market value of a new security issue, and in a few cases this led to severe losses to the banks when the market turned abruptly downward because of some untoward development.

The Securities Exchange Act of 1934 gives to the Board of Governors of the Federal Reserve System the authority to establish minimum margin requirements on security loans. However, very liberal provision has been made to facilitate the financing of investment houses. Bank loans to dealers to aid in financing the distribution of securities to customers, not through the medium of a national securities exchange, are exempt from the minimum margin requirements contained in Regulation U of the Federal Reserve System. Credit extensions by exchange members to distributors, syndicates and similar borrowers are subject to special provisions under Section 3 (c) of Regulation T of the Board of Governors of the Federal Reserve System. Effective April 1, 1936, the board provided that loans extended to such borrowers on registered securities may be up to 80 per cent of the market value. Loans on government and municipal securities are fully exempt from all these limitations.

At the present time, therefore, security dealers do not encounter any legal bars to free borrowing from the banks. However, the banks tend to be more cautious than they were in the pre-depression period. They must also consider the fact that examiners will criticize slow or badly secured loans on securities awaiting distribution.

The use of bank credit by the investment banker enlarges the scope of his operations beyond the limit allowed by his own capital resources. It thus supplements the equally important expedient of forming purchase and selling groups, which reduce the liability of each investment house on any one transaction and vastly speed up the process of distribution to the public, for each must then sell only a relatively small portion of the issue to his clientele. Such cooperation among individual houses on individual loans, which exists in commercial banking in only a rudimentary degree, is discussed fully in Chapters XVII and XVIII.

The investment banking house runs the constant risk of having its liquid capital tied up because of the failure of the public to take new issues of securities after they have been acquired and paid for by the investment house. The retailer avoids this by joining only selling groups, which do no underwriting. The large houses generally have excellent banking connections, and rely upon collateral loans to carry them through difficult periods. Where the investment house retains stock interests in the companies which it finances, where it carries out a number of private "deals" which do not involve public financing in the first instance, such as reorganizations and mergers, and where it maintains big positions in its trading activities, the house must frequently have command over several millions of its own capital free at all times.

While investment houses generally do not make their statements public, neither balance sheet nor income account, the largest organizations are known to utilize from $10,000,000 to sums in excess of $100,000,000 of their own capital, in addition to what is borrowed from the banks.[7] The First Boston Corporation, a leading wholesaler which is also a large trading organization in government and other bonds, published the following statements at the end of 1935:

THE FIRST BOSTON CORPORATION
BALANCE SHEET — DECEMBER 31, 1935

ASSETS:	
Cash	$ 6,738,154.14
Deposits on Securities Borrowed	2,720,480.00
Bankers' Acceptances	140,000.00
United States Government Securities	34,887,072.26
Other Securities, Bonds, and Stocks	10,729,665.16
Securities Carried in Joint Trading Accounts	2,172,893.61
Securities Sold Not Yet Delivered — At Selling Price	37,751,193.96
Good Faith Deposits	210,140.00
Miscellaneous Accounts Receivable and Accrued Interest	332,773.04
Furniture and Fixtures (less depreciation)	105,156.96
Tax Stamps	7,320.31
Deferred Charges	20,367.38
Total	$95,815,216.82
LIABILITIES:	
Collateral Loans Payable	$55,630,077.18
Deposits on Securities Loaned	6,060.00
Securities Sold Not Yet Purchased	1,633,243.75
Securities Purchased Not Yet Received — At Purchase Price	25,154,208.14
Accrued Federal Income and Excess Profits and Other Taxes	588,321.49
Due Customers	272,379.34

[7] In California, the Investment Dealers Audit Association has been formed by investment houses, and once each year a complete detailed financial statement is submitted to a firm of accountants by members. This report is held confidential, however. Blue-sky laws also generally require the submission of financial statements by dealers seeking to be licensed, as shown in chap. xxii.

Miscellaneous Accounts Payable and Accrued Expenses	136,760.03
Reserve for Taxes, Unearned Discount, etc.	55,859.51
Reserve for Contingencies	125,000.00
Capital Stock (authorized and issued, 500,000 shares of $10.00 each)	5,000,000.00
Paid-in Surplus	4,000,000.00
Earned Surplus	3,213,307.38
Total	$95,815,216.82

Notes: The valuation of the securities owned, based on market bid quotations at December 31, 1935, and of the securities sold not yet purchased, based on market offered quotations at that date, is $6,988.10 in excess of the aggregate book values thereof as shown in the above statement.

Securities having a valuation based on market quotations of $59,786,339.62 are pledged as collateral to loans payable.

At December 31, 1935, the Corporation had contingent accounts as follows:

Securities purchased on a "When Issued" basis	$ 601,937.50
Securities sold on a "When Issued" basis	7,991,759.62
Commitment as a member of syndicate formed to purchase securities	7,670,000.00

Summary of Income and Earned Surplus
For the year ended December 31, 1935

Income:		
Profits from trading in securities on own account, in joint accounts, and as participant in syndicate accounts	$7,008,049.82	
Interest, discount, and dividends earned on securities held	1,177,502.78	
Commissions, service charges, and miscellaneous income	111,657.71	
Total		$8,297,210.31
Expenses:		
General expenses	$3,829,843.22	
Interest on bank loans	269,267.63	
Taxes (other than Federal income and excess profits taxes)	302,298.27	
Depreciation of furniture and fixtures	28,037.18	
Miscellaneous	11,712.37	
Total		4,441,158.67
Net Income Before Provision for Federal Income and Excess Profits Taxes		$3,856,051.64
Provision for Federal Income and Excess Profits Taxes		505,086.79
Net Income for the Year		$3,350,964.85
Surplus Credits		52,821.15

Gross Surplus for the Year	$3,403,786.00
Surplus Charge — Provision for Contingencies	95,000.00
Surplus for the Year Before Charging Dividends	$3,308,786.00
Earned Surplus, January 1, 1935	754,521.38
Earned Surplus Before Charging Dividends	$4,063,307.38
Less Dividends Paid	850,000.00
Earned Surplus, December 31, 1935	$3,213,307.38

By contrast with the above, it may be pointed out that numerous small local dealers exist whose capital does not exceed $5,000 to $10,000. It is unfortunate that no publicity is given statements of most investment banking houses, for the public cannot gauge their financial strength, as can be done for banks from statements required by governmental regulating authorities. The Securities and Exchange Commission is taking steps that may lead in time to the regular reporting of financial statements by investment houses to this federal agency.

A way of cutting down the amount of liquid capital which an investment house must possess has been the formation of an investment trust. Several investment houses formed such organizations in the past to aid them in distributing securities, as their assured subscription to new offerings reduced to that extent the possibility of the investment house having to tie up its own liquid capital in any one undertaking. A fuller discussion of the investment trust in relation to the investment house will be found in Chapter V.

The operations and sources of income of a major investment house may be noted from the above financial statements.

Summary

The origination and distribution of security issues, the basic functions of investment banking, are carried on chiefly by specialized institutions called investment houses. These concerns specialize among themselves to a large extent, some stressing wholesaling and others retailing in their activities, while many restrict their activities to specific classes of securities. The ranks of the investment houses have been thinned by the abolition of security affiliates of commercial banks, but many brokerage houses maintain "bond departments" devoted to security origination and distribution.

The departmental organization of the investment house conforms as a rule to its chief functional activities. Houses which engage in originating new security offerings have a buying department which receives and studies proposals for new financing, and prepares them for sale. The work of distribution rests with a sales department, the nucleus of which is a corps of salesmen working largely on a commission basis. Advertising is assuming a growing rôle in supplementing the activities of the salesmen. A trading department is generally maintained to handle purchases and sales for the house and its clients in the open market. The accounting, security-handling and other operating departments are organized separately.

Looked at from a broader point of view, this type of institution appears well suited for expanding the number of investors and building up a wider capital market in a rapidly growing country in which investment is a relatively new popular activity. The stress upon sales effort in the past made the investment house primarily a merchandising institution. Certain aspects of this system have proved not altogether desirable. For one thing, the individual salesman seeking his commissions is not always an impartial advisor to his client. Secondly, aggressive selling and advertising efforts by numerous investment houses involve duplication of effort and may lead to much useless switching from old to new issues. One result has been to encourage the organization of independent investment management concerns, as well as trust companies. To correct this situation, many investment houses now place greater relative stress upon statistical work, and have built up autonomous management departments of their own.

While the investment house is the central factor in the flow of long-term capital from investors to corporations and governments, it is concerned primarily with new issues of securities. But new security offerings appear at any one time only in small amount compared to the total volume of old securities already outstanding. Those who own already outstanding securities, the total amount of which is estimated to be well in excess of one hundred and fifty billion dollars, often wish to sell them, while others may wish to purchase them, for either investment or speculation. Accordingly, brokerage houses and dealers which perform this function of buying or selling already issued securities have assumed an important rôle in the investment banking business; and in the following chapter the characteristics of their business are discussed.

References

Biddle, C. P., and Bates, G. E., *Investment Banking: A Case Book,* New York, 1931, part ii.

Chamberlain, Lawrence, *Work of the Bond House,* New York, 1912.

Dewing, A. S., *Financial Policy of Corporations,* New York, 1934, book v, chap. viii.

Investment Bankers' Association of America, *An Analysis of Investment Banking for Vocational Guidance* (pamphlet).

Jordan, D. F., *Investments,* New York, 1929, chap. xx.

Lincoln, E. E., *Applied Business Finance,* Chicago, 1923, chap. x.

McIntosh, J. W., "The Investment Department of a Country Bank," *American Bankers Association, Proceedings,* 1928.

Townsend, William W., *Bond Salesmanship,* New York, 1924, chaps. i–iv.

Chapter III

FACILITATING INSTITUTIONS—BROKERS, DEALERS, AND THE STOCK EXCHANGES

The Need for a Securities Market

Because investment involves a long-term commitment of funds, one of the greatest problems it gives rise to is the creation of a market where the individual investor, who buys from the investment house described in the preceding chapter, may dispose of his securities at will. A buyer of bonds with, let us say, a maturity of fifty years is almost certain to wish to dispose of his holdings long before this period has elapsed. He may need the money for other purposes, or he may wish to sell them and invest the proceeds in something else. He may die, and the executors of his estate will want to liquidate his investments in order to carry out the provisions of his will.

The quality of being readily salable at a price which is not materially lower than that at which the same security can be purchased at the same time is termed marketability. Every investment that has any apparent value normally has this quality to some degree, as may be seen from the daily reports of the security auction houses, where securities wholly unknown even to most bankers are bought and sold for a consideration. But there is a wide difference between marketability in the highly uncertain market of the auction room and marketability on an organized exchange, where the execution of the orders of numerous buyers and sellers from all over the world results in the maintenance of close markets in which billions of dollars of stocks and bonds may be turned over without necessarily causing any major changes in market prices.

It is the existence of this organized securities market in the background which has made possible the growth of the investment houses described in the preceding chapter, houses which in active years may purchase ten billions of new securities annually and find a ready market for them among all classes of investors. These investors buy so freely only because the bulk of the securities offered are marketable to a greater or lesser degree, so that they can liquidate the investment when the need or desire arises. Furthermore, this market has facilitated enormously the direct sale by corporations of their own stock to shareholders for the same reason. Marketability in the field of investment banking is the counterpart of liquidity in commercial banking.

From the social point of view, the benefits derived from an efficient securities market, including brokers and the stock exchanges, are enormous. To small and little-known enterprises, the cost of securing longer-term capital is often very high, and at times so exorbitant as effectively to prevent expansion, where it is obtainable at all. But large scale corporate organizations able to tap the capital can raise funds freely there at low cost. Doubtless the ideal form of business organization, for the purpose of financing at lowest cost, is the amalgamation within every line of activity of all enterprises into a few powerful companies whose bonds and stocks are listed on stock exchanges. One student of the subject has found that the 200 largest corporations in this country, most of which have securities listed on exchanges, control 25 per cent of the business wealth and 50 per cent of the corporate wealth of the country. This financial ideal is undoubtedly being approached in many countries. Professor Pigou estimated in 1918 that 60 per cent of English wealth was represented by securities. In the United States, the proportion is probably smaller, despite the trend evidenced in recent decades toward consolidation and the capitalization and public issuance of companies even of relatively small size and in highly specialized industries. There are not far from $175,000,000,000 of securities outstanding in this country—approximately half of them listed on the New York Stock Exchange—while the aggregate national wealth is perhaps $325,000,000,000.[1] Thus, rather more than 50 per cent of the national wealth of the United States is represented by securities, according to these very rough estimates. The chief reason why the

[1] The National Industrial Conference Board, New York, estimated the national wealth in 1934 at $287,000,000,000.

percentage is not higher is the vastness of the sums invested in agriculture and real estate.

The organization of a market for already issued securities predates the birth of our investment banking houses. The reason for this market is that it was customary for governments and large enterprises to sell their securities directly to investors before the practice of underwriting their sale by bankers led to the formation of investment houses as middlemen. The sale of Revolutionary War bonds and the formation of banks during the last two decades of the eighteenth century first created an investing class in this country, and it was to serve this group of persons that individuals here and there set up in business as the pioneer brokers.

The typical stock and bond broker differs from the investment house or securities middleman in that he has no dealings with the original issuer of securities. He stands between investor and investment. In some cases, he does not acquire title to the security, but acts merely as agent for the buyer or seller and gets a commission for his services. In others, he may actually buy a security outright from the seller, and then sell it in his own right to the buyer. When he thus acts as a principal and acquires title to the securities in which he deals, he is said to "take a position," and should properly be called a dealer rather than a broker.

Security exchanges are merely aggregations of brokers and dealers who build up machinery which permits them to trade readily one with another at a single place. The security exchange, like the security broker, grew up as the counterpart of the exchanges and brokers already developed for the trade in corn, slaves and other staples of early commerce. These slave and commodity exchanges have existed in commercial centers since ancient times.

Brokers and Dealers

A broker executes an order as agent for a principal. A dealer buys and sells securities for his own account. In the former case, the broker does not take legal title to the securities; in the latter, the dealer assumes and disposes of title to the securities he buys and sells.

Where a securities market has been fully developed, the broker tends to predominate. Where trading is still carried on in relatively informal fashion, and the number of buyers and sellers is not large, those who create a secondary market act mainly in the capacity of dealers. Unless they are willing to do so, in fact, it may prove difficult, if not impossible, to find bids for and offers of less active securities at any one time. The lack of adequate trading machinery for bringing buyers and sellers together and the desire for a larger profit on the transaction than a mere commission would afford, because of the small volume of turnover, further explain this tendency.

There is a fundamental difference in the legal status of brokers and dealers. Under the statute of frauds, in effect in New York and other states, a contract involving $50 or more must be in writing. Hence, a security dealer must have written confirmation of all his transactions, if he wishes to hold those with whom he deals to their contracts. On the other hand, a broker can enforce oral contracts that he makes with his customers, because as an agent he can hold his principal for damages caused by his efforts to carry out the orders of the latter.

It has long been recognized that, when an individual acts as both a broker for another and a dealer for his own account, his functioning in this dual capacity may lead to abuse. The New York Stock Exchange years ago sought to establish rules and regulations to prevent this union of function. Section 11 of the Securities Exchange Act of 1934 is devoted to the subject of "segregation and limitation of functions of members, brokers and dealers." When the act was under debate in Congress, there was considerable sentiment in favor of a complete segregation of function as between brokers and dealers. However, it was pointed out that on many occasions there is a public advantage in combining the two functions, and many individuals could not continue in business if they were restricted in this way. Hence, the law lays down only certain general rules governing the conduct of brokers and dealers on both listed and over-the-counter markets, and in addition it provides that the Securities and Exchange Commission make a comprehensive study of the "feasibility and advisability of the complete segregation of the functions of dealer and broker."

The Commission's report on the subject to Congress, received in June, 1936, reiterated the basic desirability of separating the two functions, particularly on security exchanges, but recognized the practical difficulty involved. It advised that the segregation be worked out gradually and with the full co-operation of stock exchange authorities.

The two general conclusions reached by the Commission were:

1. That the combination of the broker and dealer functions in the same individual or firm involves a conflict of interest which is provocative of abuse of the fiduciary relationship inherent in the brokerage function;
2. That the survey made by the Commission manifests the prevalence upon the exchanges of a type of dealer activity which exerts an undue influence on prices, incites public speculation, leads to disorderly markets and interferes with the effective fulfillment of the brokerage function. These conclusions furnish the basis for fashioning a program for the future.

Exchange Members and Over-the-counter Dealers

Upwards of 5,000 security brokers and dealers registered without delay with the Securities and Exchange Commission when the latter requested this step in 1936. The majority of these were interested in making a secondary market for securities of one kind or another. Most of them conducted their transactions directly with other dealers over the telephone, constituting what is known as the "over the counter" market. Only a fraction of these specialized in the highly complex type of brokerage business conducted upon stock exchanges.

However, brokers who are members of the New York Stock Exchange, and in many cases of other exchanges as well, are by far the most important cogs in the machinery for creating a secondary market for securities beyond the new-issue stage. These brokers stand ready to buy or sell securities on these exchanges in accordance with their rules, receiving uniform commission rates fixed by the exchange authorities. Many of them do business on commodity exchanges also.

An important feature of the service of the brokerage house belonging to the large exchanges is the arrangement of margin transactions, where the buyer of securities merely pays a portion of the purchase price. The broker lends the rest, borrowing such funds as a rule from a bank and giving the securities so purchased as collateral. He thus acts as an agent for the buyer in arranging a bank loan. Another special function of exchange members is to arrange short sales. In such

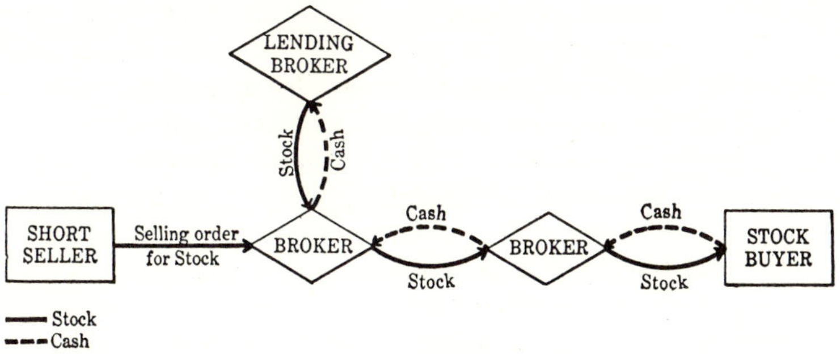

FIG. 3. DIAGRAM ILLUSTRATING A SHORT SALE

The short seller orders his broker to sell stock he does not own, expecting a decline in price and an opportunity to buy back at a lower figure. The sale is made on the floor of the exchange to another broker representing the security buyer. The seller's broker then borrows stock from another lending broker, and delivers it to the buyer's broker. The lending broker happens to be carrying this stock for a customer. The lending broker makes a loan of the stock against the deposit of cash which the short seller's broker has received from the buyer's broker.

cases, the broker sells securities for a client who does not possess them, but who expects they will decline after a time, when he will be able to buy back at a lower price the securities he has sold. The broker arranges to borrow the securities sold short, from a third party, in order to deliver them to the purchaser. The diagram in Fig. 3 explains a short sale.

There are 1,375 members of the New York Stock Exchange, of whom about 800 are partners of some 500 brokerage and investment banking firms having offices in the financial district in New York City. Not all of these members actually spend their time on the floor in the execution of orders. The remainder are members of out-of-town houses and individual traders.

However, the business is largely concentrated. A dozen leading brokerage houses may originate a very large proportion of the public orders which are executed on the floor of the stock exchange.

While the bulk of stock trading takes place on the exchanges, the same cannot be said of dealings in bonds. There are many dealers in the bond market whose chief function is to buy and sell large blocks of issued bonds, both listed and unlisted. It has been estimated that the transactions in bonds on the New York Stock Exchange, the one important organized bond market of the country, represent perhaps 10 per cent of the total sales even of those bond issues which are listed on the exchange. The bulk of the sales are made by large financial institutions directly through brokerage and investment houses acting as bond dealers. An insurance company wishing to dispose of a block of 1,000 bonds of $1,000 denomination would probably find the stock exchange a poor market for so large an offering, since here there are no speculators ready to pick up large blocks of securities at small concessions in price, as is often the case with listed stocks. But a bond dealer who knows of many savings banks and insurance companies ready to take these bonds in large blocks at a uniform price can make a good profit by buying them for his own account at, say, 97½ and selling them at 97¾. This profit of $2,500 can frequently be earned by a well-placed bond dealer in a few minutes of telephoning. However, special efforts have been made recently to encourage and require execution of orders in listed bonds on the floor of the exchange.[2]

The great majority of individual security issues, including nearly all smaller issues, are traded in the unlisted or over-the-counter market, because business is transacted within the office and "over the counter" of the individual dealer, rather than at a central organized trading place known as an exchange. A more correct name under present conditions would be the

[2] Orders for less than 15 bonds are now required to be executed on the floor of the exchange by member firms, under the "fourteen-bond rule," unless a member is able to secure a better bid for his customer off the floor. Also, it has been suggested that over-the-counter bond dealers, not members of the exchange, be permitted to become associate members on some inexpensive basis, to encourage them to put their orders through on the floor.

TABLE 2.—DOLLAR VALUE OF STOCK AND BOND SALES ON REGISTERED SECURITIES EXCHANGES IN 1935

By Exchanges

Names of Exchanges	Market Value of Stock Sales[a]	Market Value of Bond Sales[b]	Total Market Value of All Sales[c]
New York Stock	$13,337,791,388	$2,796,814,845	$16,134,606,233
New York Curb	1,205,287,316	932,550,772	2,137,838,088
Boston Stock	206,204,247 [e]	699,480	206,903,727 [e]
Chicago Stock	182,964,202	216,366	183,180,568
San Francisco Stock	118,414,685	861,440	119,276,125
Philadelphia Stock	92,474,937	458,391	92,933,328
Los Angeles Stock	71,219,114	33,923	71,253,037
Detroit Stock	62,197,033	[h]	62,197,033
Pittsburgh Stock	30,106,882	83,961	30,190,843
San Francisco Curb	24,138,744	323,815	24,462,559
Cleveland Stock	13,956,241	2,075	14,295,153 [g]
Baltimore Stock	10,749,050 [d]	559,767 [d]	11,308,817 [d]
Cincinnati Stock	5,915,316	151,795	6,067,111
St. Louis Stock	3,470,441	51,408	3,521,849
New Orleans Stock	1,108,550	1,995,646	3,104,196
Salt Lake Stock	2,660,159	[h]	2,660,159
Chicago Board of Trade	2,542,235	44,630	2,586,865
Washington Stock	999,651	1,079,867	2,079,518
Buffalo Stock	1,288,577	22,340	1,310,917
Denver Stock	1,071,677	[h]	1,071,677
New York Produce	880,692	14,730	895,422
Chicago Curb[f]	263,698 [f]	56,376 [f]	320,074 [f]
Standard Stock Exchange, Spokane[i]	301,566 [i]	[h]	301,566 [i]
New York Real Estate	1,084	61,570	62,654
Totals	$15,376,007,485	$3,736,083,197	$19,112,427,519

[a] "Stock Sales" include sales of Voting Trust Certificates, American Depositary Receipts, Certificates of Deposit, Warrants and Rights.

[b] "Bond Sales" include sales of Mortgage Certificates and Certificates of Deposit.

[c] Market Value of Stock Sales plus Market Value of Bond Sales. Pass books traded on Cleveland Stock Exchange amounting to $336,837 for the year are also included in the total (although omitted from stock and bond sales).

[d] Excludes transactions made "without record" during the months of January and February, 1935.

[e] Clearing house money values reported for stock sales during the months of January, February, March and April, 1935.

[f] Chicago Curb Exchange became a Registered Securities Exchange on November 1, 1935. Figures include only transactions for November and December, 1935.

[g] Includes market value of pass books traded on the Cleveland Stock Exchange during 1935, amounting to $336,837.

[h] No Bonds listed or traded.

[i] Standard Stock Exchange of Spokane became a Registered Securities Exchange on October 1, 1935. Figures include only transactions for October, November and December, 1935.

"over-the-telephone" market, for the great bulk of the orders are consummated by phone calls from house to house. In over-the-counter trading dealers predominate, for the market is often too narrow to make it practicable for a buyer and a seller to be brought together through the intermediary of the broker. However, there is nothing to prevent an over-the-counter house from acting as broker.

Security Exchanges

The primary purpose of a security exchange is to facilitate the execution of buying and selling orders by furnishing a central floor upon which orders may be executed by the members, who are thus brought into direct contact with one another. There are at the present time 32 registered and exempt stock exchanges in active operation in the United States. Since the enactment of the Securities Exchange Act of 1934, all exchanges whose business is predominantly interstate must be registered with the Securities and Exchange Commission. The relative importance of each of the security exchanges of the country may be gauged from the following table issued by the Securities and Exchange Commission, which follows the volume of turnover for the year 1935. Not all of these exchanges are now in actual operation.

In addition, the following exchanges were in operation, although they were exempt from registration under the Securities Exchange Act of 1934 because of the predominantly local or intrastate character of their business.

The Securities and Exchange Commission now possesses broad regulatory powers over registered stock exchanges. It requires that only securities registered in accordance with its regulations may be listed on these exchanges, although other securities may be admitted to *unlisted* trading privileges with the approval of the Commission. Also, the practices of members of the exchange and its administrative policies are subject to regulation by the Commission.

As will be seen from the above tables, the bulk of the transactions on security exchanges are consummated upon the New York Stock Exchange. For 1935, for example, 87 per cent of the turnover, as measured by value in stocks and 75 per cent

TABLE 3 —DOLLAR VALUE OF STOCK AND BOND SALES ON EXEMPT[a] SECURITIES EXCHANGES IN 1935

By Exchanges

Names of Exchanges	Market Value of Stock Sales[b]	Market Value of Bond Sales[c]	Total Market Value of All Sales
Minneapolis-St. Paul Stock Exchange	$ 3,429,747	$ 32,133	$ 3,461,880
Richmond Stock Exchange	1,887,331	245,464	2,132,795
Standard Stock Exchange of Spokane[g]	2,125,718	[e]	2,125,718
Colo. Springs Stock Exchange	1,443,871	162,290	1,606,161
San Francisco Mining Exchange	856,149	[e]	856,149
Chicago Curb Exchange Ass'n[d]	763,615	2,875	766,490
Wheeling Stock Exchange	729,177	[e]	729,177
Milwaukee Grain & Stock Exchange	346,855	[e]	346,855
Seattle Mining Exchange[f]	205,114	[e]	205,114
Seattle Stock Exchange	140,215	23,280	163,495
Totals	$11,927,792	$466,042	$12,393,834

[a] Exclusive of Honolulu Stock Exchange.
[b] Stock Sales include scrip.
[c] Bond Sales include notes.
[d] Registered October 1, 1935. Figures include transactions to that date.
[e] No bonds listed or traded.
[f] Merged with Seattle Stock Exchange October 1, 1935. Figures include transactions to that date.
[g] Registered November 1, 1935. Figures include transactions to that date.

of the turnover in bonds on all exchanges occurred on the New York Stock Exchange. The New York Curb Market, the second largest market in the country, accounted for 8 per cent of the turnover in stocks and 2 per cent of the turnover in bonds.

Hence, the New York Stock Exchange may be regarded as the prototype of the other security exchanges, and an understanding of its functions and operations will serve to clarify nearly all of the problems encountered by the other security exchanges.

The New York Stock Exchange

The New York Stock Exchange is a voluntary association of 1375 individual members. Only these individual members are allowed on the floor of the exchange to engage in actual trading, except for certain privileges given partners of those members of the exchange who act as its officials. The members of the stock exchange may conduct their business on its floor in their individual capacity, or they may join in partnerships with non-member partners to facilitate such business. These partnerships then become registered firms of the New York Stock Exchange. The partnerships may be either general or limited in character, but in no event may members of the exchange conduct their business through use of the corporate form of organization.

The members of the New York Stock Exchange may be classified into seven main groups. The *commission brokers* are engaged in the business of executing orders for the account of outside customers. They are the members of the exchange with whom the general public comes into constant contact, and they serve as the chief channel through which orders to buy and sell listed securities from all over the world are brought to the floor of the New York Stock Exchange.

On October 1, 1935, 391 members of the exchange, partners in commission houses, were engaged personally in the execution of orders for their firms on the floor of the exchange. In many cases, the exchange member of the commission house does other things, the orders received by the house being turned over to one of the other types of members listed below for execution.

The second type of member of the exchange is a *floor broker*, often termed a "two dollar" broker, who is concerned primarily with executing orders for other members of the exchange, mostly for commission brokers. On October 1, 1935, when a survey was made, it was found that 158 individual members of the exchange were acting primarily as floor brokers. On the New York Curb Exchange, which has 550 regular and an indeterminate number of associate members, 135 individual members were acting as floor brokers at an earlier date.

The "two dollar" brokers obtain their appellation from the fact that they formerly received $2.00 for the execution of each buying or selling order for 100 shares for another stock exchange member. Their compensation has since been increased, and is now a percentage of the regular commission that is paid by the customer through the commission broker with whom he has an account. Commission houses with a large volume of business, and others that do not maintain a member on the floor, make use of these floor brokers freely. In active markets, when a house receives orders for execution at various places on the floor of the exchange, it would be physically impossible to get along without the floor broker.

A third type of member is a *floor trader,* who effects transactions in securities on the exchange for his own account. The New York Stock Exchange on October 1, 1935, had 35 individual members who acted primarily as floor traders. On the New York Curb Exchange, 14 individual members and 6 member-partners of firms acted in this capacity. A floor trader operates in much the same way as an individual customer of a brokerage house, in that he buys and sells for his own account and risk, rather than for others. He possesses several advantages, however, as against the outside trader. In the first place, being directly on the floor of the exchange he can observe the technical situation in the market more intimately than is possible for a non-member of the exchange. Secondly, the floor trader does not have to pay commissions for the execution of his orders, and to that extent he can afford to trade for small profits more easily than an outside trader. Before the imposition of a transfer tax, in fact, the floor trader had a theoretically equal chance of profiting or losing on each transaction and by his superior knowledge of the technical state of the market he could presumably operate to considerable advantage. Now, however, the risk of loss is increased and the possibility of profit decreased because of the transfer taxes he must pay in the execution of his transactions.

The Specialist and Odd-lot Dealer

A fourth and very important group of members of the various stock exchanges are the *specialists,* who largely confine their transactions to one or a group of securities in which they specialize. The specialists at the present time both execute orders for other members in the securities in which they specialize, thus acting as floor brokers, and also trade substantially for their own account in these same issues. Thus, the specialist combines to a high degree the functions of broker and dealer, and proposals to segregate these functions affect him profoundly.

The reader may obtain an idea of the appearance of the

TABLE 4[3]

Bids (No. of Shares)	Price	Offers (No. of Shares)
...	12	100
...	10	100
...	9	400
...	8⅞	300
...	8¼	100
...	8	1,200
...	7	400
...	6⅞	100
...	6¾	100
...	6½	1,000
...	6¼	300
...	6⅛	100
...	6	2,700
...	5⅞	200
...	5¾	1,000
...	5⅝	200
...	5½	3,200
...	5⅜	200
...	5¼	1,800
...	5⅛	300
...	5	20,600 (77 lots)
...	4⅞	3,400
...	4¾	4,300
...	4⅝	1,800
...	4½	13,800 (80 lots)
...	4⅜	3,600
...	4¼	7,700 (50 lots)
...	4⅛	2,200
...	4	16,000 (90 lots)
...	3⅞	2,600
...	3¾	7,000 (40 lots)
...	3⅝	2,500
...	3½	18,400 (116 lots)
...	3⅜	2,800
...	3¼	6,000 (49 lots)
...	3⅛	3,500
...	3	3,300
...	2⅞	100
...	...	...
2,500	2¾	...
1,500	2⅝	...
6,900 (47 lots)	2½	...
1,400	2⅜	...
3,300	2¼	...
2,500	2⅛	...
21,600 (147 lots)	2	100 stop
2,500	1⅞	100 stop
4,900 (37 lots)	1¾	...

[3] Reprinted from The Twentieth Century Fund, Inc., *The Security Markets*, pp. 430-431.

TABLE 4 (*Concluded*)

Bids (No. of Shares)		Price	Offers (No. of Shares)
700		1 5/8	...
9,200	(50 lots)	1 1/2	...
100		1 3/8	...
800		1 1/4	...
300		1 1/8	...
3,300	(25 lots)	1	...
1,100		7/8	...
800		3/4	...
500		1/2	...
100		1/8	...

Stock "A" common:
Day's volume traded........................ 6400 shares
Day's price range......................... High 2 7/8; Low 2 5/8

specialist's book, in which he lists buying and selling orders that he has received from other brokers, by the two samples listed. Table 4 is a transcript of the book of a specialist in an active low-priced common stock at 11:00 A.M. on November 15, 1935. Table 5 shows a specialist's book in a relatively inactive preferred stock, where it will be seen that the amount of stock offered and bid for on both sides of the market is very small. In general, the specialist's books have become considerably

TABLE 5[4]

Bids (No. of Shares)	Price	Offers (No. of Shares)
...	99 7/8	100
...	96 1/2	200
...	96	100
...	95 1/8	100
...	82	100
...	80	100
...	79 7/8	100
...	77 1/2	100
...	75	100
...	74 3/4	100
...	...	...
100	70 1/8	...
100	67 1/2	...
100	66 7/8	...
100	60	...

Day's volume traded............................ No Sales

[4] *Ibid.*, pp. 430-431.

thinner in the volume of orders they list above and below the market as a result of recent restrictions upon their operations.

On October 1, 1935, there were 384 individual members of the New York Stock Exchange who were acting primarily as specialists. On the New York Curb Exchange, 197 members and 65 member-partners of firms were acting for the most part in this capacity at a somewhat earlier date.

The specialist, by bringing together orders to buy and sell particular securities on his book, performs a major function in facilitating the maintenance of close markets on the stock exchanges. It is common for other brokers to turn over to the specialist all orders destined for execution at a price away from the market, as well as orders destined for execution at some future date. In addition, the specialist can himself enter the market on the buying and selling side and thus facilitate the execution of orders; but owing to the possibilities of abuse that arise from this combination of broker and dealer functions, the New York Stock Exchange has itself prohibited a specialist from acting as both broker and dealer in the same transaction, or from preferring his own orders to those received from customers. The Securities and Exchange Commission, after an extended investigation of the subject, has itself recognized the vital rôle played by the specialist in maintaining close and active markets for securities and has restricted itself to suggesting changes in his methods of operation rather than to curb him severely.

The Securities and Exchange Commission, after its thoroughgoing discussion of the advantages and disadvantages that arise from the specialist system, reached the general conclusion that he performs a constructive function in the conduct of the stock exchange business. However, additional regulation was proposed. The Commission's findings were as follows:

1. The specialist enjoys competitive advantages over the general public similar to those of other members on the floor. In addition, by virtue of the great volume of trading in which he participates and by virtue of his exclusive access to the information contained in his "book," he enjoys the advantage of special knowledge of the market for the securities which he handles.

2. The specialist has exceptional opportunities to engage in manipulative activity, by reason of his exclusive information concerning

the existence of bids below and offerings above the market. Since the enactment of the Securities Exchange Act of 1934, however, the Commission has found little evidence of such manipulative activity by specialists.

3. Specialists, during the period under review, traded against the daily trend more often than with it, and thus, on the whole, did not tend to accentuate price trends but contributed to the continuity and orderliness of the market. However, it should be observed that, in so far as they traded with their books, rather than with others, they tended to augment the spread between bid and asked prices and thus to diminish the continuity of the market.

4. During the period studied, specialists traded in moderately active and inactive stocks in relatively greater proportion than in active stocks.

5. In the capacity of broker, the specialist renders a useful service in the execution of limited and stop-loss orders.

6. Although it is argued that the brokerage activity of the specialist renders him peculiarly liable to loss through errors, for which he must find compensation in trading, the evidence is too inconclusive to justify giving any weight to this contention.

7. The specialist has an important incentive to maintain a stable and orderly market.

Its conclusions were expressed as follows:

The Specialist.—Recognition must be given to the fact that the specialist in acting both as broker and dealer has an inherent conflict of interest. From the present evidence it is not possible to conclude whether that conflict can be eliminated in such a way as to enable him to function more adequately in the public interest. Further exploration of such a possibility, together with an appraisal of the exact incidence of this conflict, should be continued.

His trading for his own account, taken as a whole, has not been shown to accentuate trends but has been shown to possess the contrary tendency. Moreover, it does not on the average increase proportionately in activity as other activity increases. Immediate concern for the reduction of this activity is thus not demanded.

In the meantime, pending the acquisition of further knowledge, emphasis should be placed on:

1. Insistence upon the observance of rules against unjustified trading by the specialist for his own account. Trading for his own account should meet an affirmative proof of justification and is

not to be condoned simply because its undesirability cannot be established in each case.

2. The development of appropriate restrictions governing the conditions under which the specialist may trade with his book.

A fifth important group of members of the New York Stock Exchange are the *odd-lot dealers* and *brokers*, who specialize in consummating the large business in lots of less than 100 shares now transacted on the exchange. The odd-lot dealer will buy and sell odd lots at any time within a given fraction of a point, usually 1/8, of the last actual transaction in that security on the floor. Odd-lot dealers receive their orders only through other members, mainly commission brokers. Unlike other members of the exchange, they may offset the buying and selling orders which they secure against each other, evening up their purchases constantly by executing full-lot buying or selling orders on the floor of the exchange. Thus, if an odd-lot dealer receives an aggregation of orders to buy 1,230 shares of United States Steel Corporation common at a given price, and orders to sell 930 shares, he will set the buying and selling orders against each other and execute an order immediately to buy 300 shares on the floor of the exchange. The odd-lot dealer seeks, as a rule, to avoid speculative profits and losses, depending mainly on his differential for his profit, although at times he may maintain a long or short position voluntarily or because of the predominance of odd-lot orders on one side of the market. Because of the need for maintaining a number of members on the floor of the exchange to facilitate the evening up of his position, and expensive office equipment, there are relatively few odd-lot houses. On the New York Stock Exchange, six firms, three exclusively and three partially, conduct an odd-lot business. A total of 25 members of the exchange belong to these odd-lot houses and act as dealers. In addition, 115 members are odd-lot brokers, acting exclusively for odd-lot houses on the floor of the exchange. On the New York Curb Exchange, specialists assume the functions of odd-lot dealers in the securities in which they specialize.

A sixth class of stock exchange members are the *bond brokers* and *dealers*, who specialize in executing orders in bonds for the account of customers or for their own account. On October 1, 1935, 76 members of the exchange were active as brokers and dealers in bonds. The specialized character of the execution of orders in what is known as the "bond crowd" on the floor of the New York Stock Exchange tends to segregate this business from the ordinary stock exchange business. The basic problem of the "bond crowd" is to compete effectively with the over-the-counter market in listed bonds, because, as has been seen above, dealers are often able to make a closer market for a given large lot of bonds than can brokers acting through the New York Stock Exchange. It is in order to safeguard the business of bond brokers that the stock exchange has adopted the "nine bond rule," under which orders up to nine bonds would be executed on the floor of the exchange, when a better market could not definitely be found elsewhere.

A final category of members of the New York Stock Exchange are the inactive members, who are either retired from active participation in business or have purchased their seats chiefly to reduce commissions on their own operations rather than to do business on the floor of the exchange for themselves or others. Sometimes an exchange seat will be bought in the hope of a speculative increase in its value, or investment houses may acquire exchange seats for one or more of their partners in order to be able to execute security transactions on the floor as registered firms. In October, 1935, there were 227 inactive members of the New York Stock Exchange in good standing.

Each member of the exchange is at liberty to act in one or the other of the capacities noted above. He may act as a floor trader or a broker, and in the hope of increasing his earnings he may register with the Committee of Arrangements of the exchange as a specialist in a given stock or group of stocks. He will then, by giving good service, attempt to get as much business as possible in the execution of orders of that particular stock from other brokers. Should he fail to make a living in that way, he may decide to join the "bond crowd" as a bond broker, or he may become associated with some brokerage house as its floor member.

In each case, he must conform to the regulations of the New York Stock Exchange, as well as to the provisions of the Securities Exchange Act of 1934 and the regulations of the Securities and Exchange Commission.

Facilities of the New York Stock Exchange

The stock exchange at the present time consists of a large floor, upon which are seventeen trading posts, each devoted to dealings in a group of stocks. At these posts the members carry on their trading. Around the room are the telephone stalls, each connected with a broker's office. Large annunciator boards call the members by number to their telephone stalls when necessary to take orders. A separate section is devoted to the bond market.

This physical equipment has proved remarkably expansible. Since the World War, the daily volume of trading in stocks has varied from much less than 1,000,000 shares to over 16,000,000; and while individual members have suffered the pinch of inadequate business at times and at other periods have been literally swamped with work, the machinery of the exchange itself has for the most part adjusted itself readily to both conditions. Only during the 1929 panic were trading hours shortened for a while because of the huge volume of trading. The reason for this is that great flexibility is imparted by the specialist, the two-dollar broker and the odd-lot dealer, and the burden of trading can be spread among them as conditions indicate. In 1929, the membership of the exchange was increased from 1,100 to 1,375 because of the great expansion in trading volume which had taken place previously, but subsequently this increase in membership appeared less wise.

In the expansion of the New York Stock Exchange, however, the ticker device for reporting transactions has continually acted as a limiting factor. This device, which in principle is a printing telegraph instrument, was adopted in 1867 for reporting, from the floor of the exchange, the volume and price of each full-lot transaction. Technical improvements have constantly increased its speed, but every improvement merely raises to a limited extent the aggregate number of letters and numbers that can be printed per minute. Inevitably the point has been reached where the ticker falls behind the market. There is some difference of opinion, however, about the value of giving a literally instantaneous record of transactions completed on the floor of the exchange for transmission to every part of the country. It is of importance chiefly to the in-and-out trader, rather than the investor, critics have contended.

The actual buying and selling of securities involves, as a necessary counterpart, the delivery of these securities from seller to buyer. This is a second huge physical task, one which is taken care of by an organization affiliated with the exchange and known as the Stock Clearing Corporation. The Stock Clearing Corporation makes possible an enormous saving in the number of deliveries of securities and cash that must be made by exchange members as a result of each day's trading, by having each firm deliver to or receive from it only those shares and sums due to or from the firm on balance. A firm which has sold for clients 10,000 shares of General Motors and bought 6,000 shares need only deliver 4,000 to the Stock Clearing Corporation, with the net cash balance due on all the transactions. The Stock Clearing Corporation will then settle with each of the other firms involved in these transactions.

Besides the trading floor and the Stock Clearing Corporation, the machinery of the New York Stock Exchange includes facilities where members can borrow on stocks in connection with margin transactions. In one corner of the exchange floor there is a "money desk," at which offers of call loans from the banks are received, and where members resort when they wish such loans. The supply of and demand for this type of loan thus converge at the money desk. As both the bank and the broker in each case prefer to diversify their loans to avoid heavy calls for repayment, such loans are made in units of $100,000 to $500,000. Brokers go to the money desk and apply for loans as offered, while the banks are represented free of charge by brokers who come to the money desk and turn in offers of call loans as received by telephone from the banks. On the basis of these applications and offers, the banks arrange the individual loans. For the machinery behind the work of the money desk and the manner in which call loans are renewed from day to day, the reader is referred to Chapter XI below.

A fourth activity carried on through the agency of the exchange is the loaning of stocks to those who have sold short.

The buyer of the security in such a transaction expects his stock to be delivered in the ordinary way before the close of business the second full business day following. Accordingly, the broker who acts for the short seller must borrow the stock. Either during the day or in the "stock loan crowd" which gathers after the close in one part of the exchange floor, those who wish to borrow arrange to get their stock from other brokers who are carrying the same shares in long accounts. The lending broker receives the market value of the securities he loans, in cash, as collateral for the stock loan. The usual procedure is here reversed, money being deposited as security for a loan of stock. Interest is usually paid on this money, at slightly below the "call money" rate, except where the stock is difficult to borrow.[5] Then the stock is said to loan "flat," and the lender of the stock may have the free use of the money deposited as security, and in extreme cases may also receive a further premium expressed as so many dollars per 100 shares per day.

The stock exchange is primarily an arrangement for economizing effort. Like the clearing house in the field of commercial banking, it seeks to settle a multiplicity of transactions in a central place, with a small force, and with a minimum of derangement to the rest of the banking machinery of the country. The huge volume of stock transactions is settled with the use of a comparatively small amount of deposit currency. One study shows that, for the year 1926, a total of approximately $50,000,000,000 of securities was turned over with the daily use of only a little more than $30,000,000 of bank credit.[6] However, the exchange accomplishes far more than does the bank clearing house, for it provides a central market place where securities can actually be bought and sold, as well as an institution for economically settling such transactions.

Organization and Government of the Exchange

The New York Stock Exchange is managed by a governing committee, consisting of the president, the treasurer, 40 governors elected from the membership of the exchange, and 8

[5] When call money rates are at 1% or below, stock loans are usually made without interest, or "flat."

[6] Rogers, J. H., *Stock Speculation and the Money Market.*

governing members elected from the office partners of member firms. The president is the presiding officer of both the exchange and the board of governors. There is also an advisory group to the governing committee consisting at the present time of eight selected non-members.

Until 1935, only the members of the exchange could be elected to the Board of Governors. Hence, the administration of the exchange tended to represent chiefly floor brokers, specialists and odd-lot dealers, who together constituted a numerical majority of the members, rather than the commission brokers whose contacts with the investing and trading public were closer. In many commission houses, minor partners hold the exchange membership. As a result, it has been charged, past administrations of the exchange were induced to encourage a maximum volume of turnover, rather than relative stability of markets. In accordance with the recommendations of a report on the government of securities exchanges, published by the Securities and Exchange Commission in January, 1935, office partners of exchange members have been made eligible for election to the governing committee of the exchange, and other changes were made to strengthen the influence of commission brokers, as against the floor broker and specialist elements. A move was also made at the same time by some commission house partners to reduce the proportion of commissions that went to floor brokers and specialists, but this failed to make much headway.

The Board of Governors maintains close supervision over members. Its authority is backed by disciplinary powers granted by the constitution of the exchange, which contains the general rules under which it is operated. These disciplinary powers include expulsion, suspension or fine, as the case may be, for any "willful violation of the Constitution of the Exchange or of any resolution of the Governing Committee regulating the conduct or business of members, or of any conduct or proceeding inconsistent with just and equitable principles of trade." In less serious cases, suspension up to a period of one year is provided for members adjudged guilty of any act "detrimental to the interest or welfare of the Exchange."

A number of separate activities are carried on by the several standing committees of the exchange, which consist of from three to fifteen members. There are committees on arbitration, to settle differences between members on contracts executed on the exchange; business conduct, having jurisdiction over customers' accounts; admissions, scrutinizing new members; and securities, regulating the delivery of securities in connection with exchange transactions. Other committees have to do with quotations and commissions, bonds, constitution, public relations, odd lots, foreign business, and customers' men.

One final standing committee is of great importance in the conduct of the exchange—the Committee on Stock List. This committee of nine governors makes recommendations on applications for listing to the governing committee. It also has final power to act on the listing of securities of corporations which have other securities of the same or greater value already listed upon the exchange.

The exchange does not formally take the initiative in listing new securities, but acts only after the companies issuing securities have made formal application. It requires reasonably full information concerning the affairs of the company. It demands that an annual report be published with income account and balance sheet, and endeavors where possible to obtain an agreement to publish periodic reports on a quarterly or semi-annual basis. The exchange also requests information on the distribution of the securities, insisting that the holdings be sufficiently widespread to permit a free and open market. Finally, the Committee on Stock List has been guided by a number of special considerations, such as the total amount of the corporation's securities outstanding, and the stability of the enterprise itself. When the supply of the security is small, the danger of a corner may bring about adverse action on a listing application. Thus, the exchange has avoided the listing of many radio manufacturing stocks and other similar enterprises in their developmental stage in order to avoid securities for which the outlook is unusually uncertain. For such issues a period of seasoning on the over-the-counter or curb markets is often preferred by the exchange authorities.

However, the recent trend has been toward listing smaller issues on the New York Stock Exchange. With the reduction in the volume of speculative trading incident to margin regulation, a larger number of listed issues will tend to make up for the resulting decline in trading volume.

Public Functions of the Exchanges

The securities listed on the New York Stock Exchange had a market value of $90,000,000,000 on July 1, 1936, of which more than $50,000,000,000 represented the value of listed stocks. The value of securities listed solely on other exchanges was in excess of $10,000,000,000, and perhaps $70,000,000,000 more are not listed at all.

A securities exchange is designed to give what might be called a "public market," because the price at which transactions are made is openly stated, while competition exists in the making of purchases and sales. Where no exchange exists, the individual investor must often "shop around" from dealer to dealer in order to learn fully the condition of the market and thus get the best price available. This he is seldom in a position to do. Hence the exchange, when it actually brings all bids for and offers of securities to one central market place, can give a distinctly greater degree of marketability, because it relieves him from reliance on one or a few traders in finding the best bid for his securities.

The chief social functions performed by the exchanges may be summarized as follows:

1. A central market place for numerous buyers and sellers is established for the security, so that its value tends to reflect the judgment of many individuals buying or selling it in competition with other securities and with each other.

2. The quality of increased marketability is imparted to the security, so that it will be less apt to suffer wide and erratic fluctuations merely because of inability to find buyers or sellers for it at a given moment.

3. The security is made available by such marketability for use as collateral for a loan, thus helping the investor and more especially the speculator to hold it without relying wholly on his own resources.

4. Supervision and publicity for securities are assured. Although exchanges generally seek to interfere as little as possi-

ble with the companies whose securities are traded in thereon, they do seek vigorously to prevent out-and-out frauds. The New York Stock Exchange has long set a comparatively high standard in the amount of publicity required from governments and companies whose securities are listed thereon. The Securities Exchange Act of 1934 has further extended these requirements and made them generally applicable.

5. The exchange acts as a shock absorber in times of panic and impaired confidence. At such a period, when the general tendency is to convert claims into cash, the great need is for a place in which property of any kind may be liquidated quickly. Securities are particularly suitable for this purpose, and for this reason economic crises almost invariably witness exaggerated declines in security prices; but nevertheless this ability to liquidate them may help to alleviate the effects of the calamity elsewhere in the business structure.

Other Stock Exchanges

Among the thirty-one other security exchanges in this country, the New York Curb Market stands as the leader in size.

The curb had a very informal beginning as an outdoor market, on which stocks not traded in on the New York Stock Exchange were bought and sold. In its day, it amounted to little more than an "over-the-counter" market, except that it was brought together in one place. In the course of time, especially during the war, its transactions expanded largely, and many stock exchange houses acquired membership. Finally, the curb moved indoors into a building of its own in 1920, and now constitutes an important auxiliary exchange. It furnishes a market for a number of issues that do not seek listing on the New York Stock Exchange because of inadequate size, highly speculative character, unwillingness to pay high listing fees or, in the past, unwillingness of the company to disclose the information about its affairs which is demanded by the Committee on Stock List of the large exchange before the listing privilege is accorded. Also, securities for which initial distribution is desired often have a preliminary listing on the curb.

On the New York Curb Market, as on most exchanges outside of the New York Stock Exchange, a large proportion of the issues traded in are not fully and formally listed, but are admitted to "unlisted trading privileges." In such cases, listing is not arranged by the company, but a member of the curb exchange by paying a small fee applies for and obtains the privilege to trade in these issues. In the past, a majority of the issues traded in on the curb were in this category.

When the Securities Exchange Act of 1934 was enacted, the privilege to trade in unlisted issues on exchanges was extended for a short period, and in 1936 legislation was enacted that permits an indefinite extension of this privilege. It became of particular importance because a security admitted to unlisted trading privileges on an exchange is regarded as a registered issue, and as such is eligible for extensions of credit by banks and brokers.

Under the new legislation of 1936, issues that had been admitted to unlisted trading privileges on March 1, 1934, could continue to enjoy this privilege, with the approval of the Securities Exchange Commission. Additional securities of the following classes could be admitted to unlisted trading privileges on exchanges:

1. Any security duly listed and registered on any other national securities exchange.
2. Any security for which there is available a registration statement and current reports under either the federal Securities Act of 1933 or the Securities Exchange Act of 1934.

It will be noted that under this amendment to the Securities Exchange Act issues which either are listed on other exchanges or have available about themselves information equivalent to that required to qualify for listing on the New York Stock Exchange may be given unlisted trading privileges, and thus become eligible as collateral and margin accounts. However, the option remains with the authorities of each exchange to grant such privileges. The New York Stock Exchange, in accordance with a practice of long standing, does not admit securities to unlisted trading privileges, insisting that each issue in which trading is conducted on its floor be fully listed.

References

CRAGG, ALLISON, *Understanding the Stock Market,* New York, 1929, *passim.*

DICE, CHARLES AMOS, *The Stock Market,* Chicago, 1929.

HUEBNER, S. S., *The Stock Market,* New York, 1922.

MEEKER, J. EDWARD, *The Work of the Stock Exchange,* New York, 1930.

MEYER, CHARLES H., *The Securities Exchange Act of 1934,* New York, 1934.

MOULTON, H. G., *Financial Organization of Society,* Chicago, 1925, chap. xv.

PRATT, S. S., *The Work of Wall Street,* New York, 1921, chaps. x–xv.

SCHABACKER, R. W., *Stock Market Theory and Practice,* New York, 1930.

SECURITIES AND EXCHANGE COMMISSION, *Report on Segregation of the Functions of Dealer and Broker,* Washington, 1936.

SECURITIES AND EXCHANGE COMMISSION, *Report on Trading in Unlisted Securities upon Exchanges,* Washington, 1936.

SHULTZ, B. E., *Stock Exchange Procedure,* New York, 1936.

SMITLEY, ROBERT L., *Course of Study for Brokerage, Stock Exchange and Investment Banking,* New York, 1923, pp. 77–138.

Stock Exchange Practices. Hearings before the Senate Committee on Banking and Currency, 73rd Congress, Washington, 1934.

TODMAN, F. S., *Wall Street Accounting,* New York, 1921, chap. i.

TWENTIETH CENTURY FUND, *The Security Markets,* New York, 1935.

Appendix

RULES FOR THE REGULATION OF TRADING ON EXCHANGES

RECOMMENDED BY THE SECURITIES AND EXCHANGE COMMISSION FOR ADOPTION BY NATIONAL SECURITIES EXCHANGES

First Rule. *Excessive Trading by Members.* No member, and no firm of which he is a partner and no partner of such firm shall effect on the exchange purchases or sales for any account in which such member, firm, or partner is directly or indirectly interested, which purchases or sales are excessive in view of the financial resources of such member, firm or partner or in view of the market for such security.

Second Rule. *Trading for Joint Account.* (a) No member, while on the floor, shall, without the prior approval of the exchange, initiate the purchase or sale on the exchange of any security classified for trading as a stock by the exchange for any account in which he, or the firm of which he is a partner or any partner of such firm, is directly or indirectly interested with any person other than such firm or partner.

(b) The provisions of this rule shall not apply to any purchase or sale (1) by any member for any joint account maintained solely for effecting *bona fide* domestic or foreign arbitrage transactions, or (2) by an odd-lot dealer or a specialist for any joint account in which he is expressly permitted to have an interest or participation by the Eleventh or Fourteenth Rules, respectively.

Third Rule. *Report of Joint Accounts.* (a) No member, and no firm of which he is a partner and no partner of such firm, shall, directly or indirectly, hold any interest or participation in any joint account for buying or selling any security on the exchange, unless such joint account is reported to and not disapproved by the exchange.

(b) Such report shall be filed with the exchange by any member, firm or partner participating in such joint account before any transactions are effected on the exchange for such joint account and shall include in substance the following:

(1) Names of persons participating in such account and their respective interests therein.
(2) Purpose of such account.
(3) Amount of commitments in such account.
(4) A copy of any written agreement or instrument in writing relative to such account.

(c) Every member, the firm of which he is a partner and every partner of such firm, shall file with the exchange not later than Saturday of each week with respect to every joint account existing at the close of business on the preceding Wednesday in which such member, firm or partner is directly or indirectly interested, a report containing in substance the following information, unless such information is reported to the exchange by some other member, firm or partner:

(1) Name and amount of each security purchased or sold during the week ending on such Wednesday.
(2) Amount of commitments in such account at the close of business on such Wednesday.
(3) Any change which renders no longer accurate any portion of the original statement filed.

(d) Every member, the firm of which he is a partner and every partner of such firm, shall file with the exchange not later than Saturday of each week with respect to every joint account existing at the close of business on the preceding Wednesday of which such member, firm or partner has knowledge by reason of transactions executed by or through such member, firm or partner for such account, a report containing in substance the following information, unless such information has previously been reported to the exchange:

(1) Names of persons participating in such account and their respective interests therein.
(2) Purpose of such account.
(3) Name and amount of each security purchased or sold during the week ending on such Wednesday.
(4) Amount of commitments in such account at the close of business on such Wednesday.

Fourth Rule. *Discretionary Transactions.* (a) No member, while on the floor, shall execute or cause to be executed on the exchange any transaction for the purchase or sale of any security classified for trading as a stock by the exchange with respect to which transaction such member is vested with discretion as to (1) the choice of security to be bought or sold, (2) the total amount of any security to be bought or sold, or (3) whether any such transaction shall be one of purchase or sale.

(b) The provisions of paragraph (a) of this rule shall not apply (1) to any discretionary transaction executed by such member for any *bona fide* cash investment account or for the account of any person, who due to illness, absence or similar circumstances, is actually unable to effect transactions for his own account; provided that such member shall keep available for inspection a detailed record of any such transaction and the grounds for exercising such discretion and shall file with the exchange on August 1, 1935, and quarter annually thereafter a report covering the preceding quarterly period showing the name of each account for which any such transaction was executed, the amount of such discretionary purchases or sales and the grounds for exercising such discretion with respect to each account, or (2) to any transaction permitted under the second rule for any account in which the member executing such transaction is directly or indirectly interested.

(c) No member, and no firm of which he is a partner and no partner of such firm shall execute or cause to be executed on the exchange purchases or sales of any security classified for trading as a stock by the exchange for any account with respect to which such member, firm or partner is vested with any discretionary power, which purchases or sales are excessive in size or frequency in view of the financial resources in such account.

Fifth Rule. *Trading by Member while Acting as Broker.* (a) No member shall (1) personally buy or initiate the purchase of any security on the exchange for his own account or for any account in which he, or the firm of which he is a partner or any partner of such firm, is directly or indirectly interested, while such member personally holds or has knowledge that his firm or any partner thereof holds an unexecuted market order to buy such security in the unit of trading for a customer, or (2) personally sell or initiate the sale of any security on the exchange for any such account, while he personally holds or has knowledge that his firm or any partner thereof holds an unexecuted market order to sell such security in the unit of trading for a customer.

(b) No member shall (1) personally buy or initiate the purchase of any security on the exchange for any such account, at or below the price at which he personally holds or has knowledge that his firm or any partner thereof holds an unexecuted limited price order to buy such security in the unit of trading for a customer, or (2) personally sell or initiate the sale of any security on the exchange for any such account at or above the price at which he personally holds or has knowledge that his firm or any partner thereof holds an unexecuted limited price order to sell such security in the unit of trading for a customer.

(c) The provisions of this rule shall not apply (1) to any purchase or sale of any security in an amount of less than the unit of trading made by an odd-lot dealer to offset odd-lot orders of customers, or (2) to any purchase or sale of any security, delivery of which is to be upon a day other than the day of delivery provided in such unexecuted market or limited price order.

Sixth Rule. *Successive Transactions by Members.* No member, and no firm of which he is a partner and no partner of such firm shall execute or cause to be executed on the exchange the purchase of any security at successively higher prices or the sale of any security at successively lower prices for the purpose of creating or inducing a false, misleading or artificial appearance of activity in such security, or for the purpose of unduly or improperly influencing the market price of such security, or for the purpose of making a price which does not reflect the true state of the market in such security.

Seventh Rule. *Trading by Members Holding Options.* No member, while on the floor, shall initiate the purchase or sale on the exchange for his own account or for any account in which he, or the firm of which he is a partner or any partner of such firm, is directly or indirectly interested, of any security classified for trading as a stock by the exchange, in which he holds or has granted any put, call, straddle, or option, or in which he has knowledge that the firm of which he is a partner or any partner of such firm holds or has granted any put, call, straddle, or option.

Eighth Rule. *Record of Orders.* (a) Every member or the firm of which he is a partner or any partner of such firm shall preserve for at least twelve months a record of every order transmitted by such member, firm or partner to the floor of the exchange, which record shall include the name, amount and price of the security and the time when such order was so transmitted.

(b) Every member shall preserve for at least twelve months a record of every order originating on the floor of the exchange given to such member for execution, and of every order originating off the floor, transmitted by any person other than a member, firm or partner, to such member on the floor, which record shall include the name, amount and price of the security and the time when such order was so given or transmitted.

Ninth Rule. *Registration of Specialists.* No member shall act as a specialist in any security unless such member is registered as a specialist in such security by the exchange.

Tenth Rule. *Trading by Specialists.* No specialist shall effect on the exchange purchases or sales of any security in which such specialist is registered, for any account in which he, or the firm of which he is a partner, or any partner of such firm, is directly or indirectly interested, unless such dealings are reasonably necessary to permit such specialist to maintain a fair and orderly market, or to act as an odd-lot dealer in such security.

Eleventh Rule. *Joint Accounts of Specialists.* No specialists, and no firm of which he is a partner, and no partner of such firm, shall, directly or indirectly, acquire or hold any interest or participation in any joint account for buying or selling on the exchange any security classified for trading by the exchange as a stock in which such specialist is registered, except a joint account with a partner of such specialist, a member of the exchange, or a firm of which a member is a partner.

Twelfth Rule. *Records of Specialists.* Every specialist shall keep a legible record of all orders placed with him in the securities in which he is registered as a specialist and of all executions, modifications and cancellations of such orders, and shall preserve such record and all memoranda relating thereto for a period of at least twelve months.

Thirteenth Rule. *Registration of Odd-Lot Dealers.* No member of the exchange shall act as an odd-lot dealer in a security unless such member is registered as an odd-lot dealer in such security by the exchange.

Fourteenth Rule. *Joint Accounts of Odd-Lot Dealers.* No odd-lot dealer, and no firm of which he is a partner, and no partner of such firm, shall, directly or indirectly, acquire or hold any interest or participation in any joint account for buying or selling on the exchange any security in which such odd-lot dealer is registered, except a joint account with a partner of such odd-lot dealer, a member of the exchange, or a firm of which a member is a partner.

Fifteenth Rule. *Options of Specialists and Odd-Lot Dealers.* No specialist or odd-lot dealer, and no firm of which such specialist or odd-lot dealer is a partner and no partner of such firm, shall acquire, hold, or grant, directly or indirectly, any interest in any put, call, straddle, or option in any security classified for trading as a stock by the exchange in which such specialist or odd-lot dealer is registered.

Sixteenth Rule. *Short Selling.* (a) No member shall use any facility of the exchange to effect on the exchange a short sale of any security in the unit of trading at a price below the last sale price of such security on the exchange.

(b) The provisions of this rule shall not apply to any short sale (1) by an odd-lot dealer to offset odd-lot orders of customers, (2) by an odd-lot dealer to liquidate a long position which is less than the unit of trading, provided the net change in the position of such odd-lot dealer after any such short sale is not more than the unit of trading in such security, or (3) by any member, with the approval of the exchange, for the purpose of equalizing the price of a security on the exchange with the price of the same security on another national securities exchange which is the principal market for such security.

Chapter IV

THE BROKERAGE BUSINESS

Commission House Organization

Every firm registered as a member of the New York Stock Exchange must adopt the partnership form of organization in order to insure unlimited liability for the protection of customers.[1] The partnership consists of a group of individuals who contribute varying sums to constitute the initial capital of the business. An important part of the capital goes to buy one or more seats on the New York Stock Exchange, and as many other exchanges as the firm decides to do business upon. The rest of the money goes into furniture and fixtures for the brokers' quarters, and into bank accounts, usually in several leading institutions, to facilitate its ordinary business. Owing to the high cost of exchange seats, brokerage houses require substantial capital, unless arrangements are made to bring in upon a special basis some individual exchange member who already owns his seat.

The organization of a typical stock exchange commission house is shown in Fig. 4. The same essential principle of organization is used generally, although individual firms show wide variations in accordance with the peculiar features of their business. It will be seen that brokerage house organization follows functional lines. The several departments may be grouped, according to function, into six divisions:

1. Relations with customers
2. Handling of orders
3. Handling of securities
4. Handling of cash and collateral loans

[1] The liability of inactive partners may be limited by forming a limited partnership. To gain such limited liability for the special partnership, it must be registered as such. See Gerstenberg, C. W., *Financial Organization and Management,* pp. 54-55.

5. Records
6. Statistical

1. *Relations with Customers.*—This function of the firm is usually under the direction of one or more of the partners. These latter may have special connections with financial institutions or substantial investors who provide the firm with a great part of its business. As the cost of executing an order for several thousand shares is not much greater than that of executing one for ten shares, several big accounts may provide the house with the major portion of its profit.

ORGANIZATION OF A BROKERAGE HOUSE

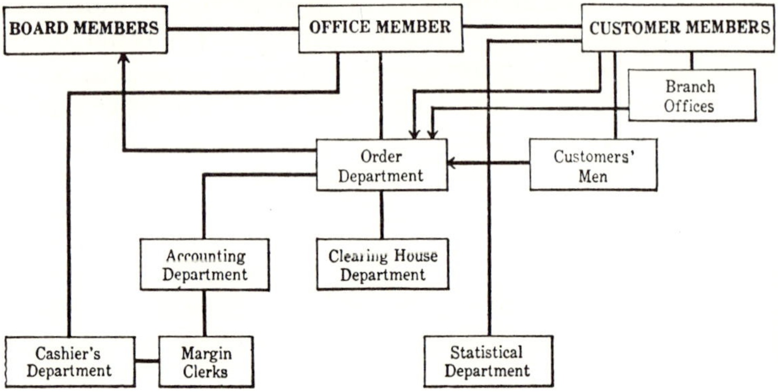

FIG. 4

In addition to one or more partners who establish relations with the customers of the firm, the larger brokerage houses will have a number of customers' men, the counterpart of the salesmen in the investment banking house. The customers' man receives orders to buy and sell securities, by personal call, telephone, telegraph or mail. The New York Stock Exchange forbids the payment of a commission to customers' men based on the volume of business transacted, in an effort to make the latter a disinterested adviser. But, in fact, records of the business brought in by each customers' man are carefully compiled by most houses, and those that fail to obtain sufficient orders either are dropped or have their salaries reduced, while those with a successful record enjoy corresponding increases in remuneration. Salaries may not be changed more often than every three months. The Stock Exchange also requires six months' previous experience as a junior customers' man, or its equivalent, and a clean record, before it will permit an individual to serve in this capacity with a member firm. Since 1936, all new customers' men have been required to pass a compre hensive examination prepared by an exchange committee.

The customers' man is an important cog in the stock-trading machinery. Through his hands pass the bulk of the orders from individual investors and traders to buy and sell stocks listed on the big exchanges. Usually only the larger clients deal directly through partners of the firm. If the customers' man's advice is inept, serious loss may ensue. The customers' man has, however, increasingly become a mere agent for receiving buying and selling orders, the advice-giving function being left to the trained men of the statistical department.

The bulk of the orders in many commission houses come from margin account customers, although the volume of orders to be executed on a full-payment or cash basis has become proportionately far larger in recent years. A margin account is one in which the customer buys securities with a partial cash payment, the balance being borrowed from his broker, who, in turn, may finance the transaction through a bank loan. Thus, a customer who buys 100 shares of Union Pacific at 200 owes the broker $20,030 for this transaction, including the commission. He may be expected to deposit only 60 per cent of this amount, or $12,018, the broker lending him the balance, the loan being secured by the deposit of the stock certificate as collateral.

2. *Handling of Orders.*—Orders received by the customers' men take several forms. They are:

1. Market orders: These are executed immediately at the best price obtainable at the time the order reaches the floor of the exchange.

2. Limit orders: Most orders set a price limit which the customer is willing to pay, or to receive. Such orders are

subdivided into various types, according to the length of time they remain in force, unless executed.

(a) Day orders: Such orders are automatically canceled if not executed during the day in which they are placed. All orders are day orders unless otherwise specified.

(b) Good until countermanded (G.T.C.): Orders of this kind remain valid until either executed or canceled by express order of the customer.

(c) Good this week (G.T.W.): Such orders are automatically canceled if not executed by the close of business on Saturday of the week in which the order is placed.

(d) Good this month (G.T.M.): These orders are automatically canceled if not executed by the close of business on the last business day of the month in which the order is placed.

3. A "stop-loss" order is one which becomes an order to buy or sell, as the case may be, at the market, as soon as a certain named price has been reached by the stock.

The order department is responsible for keeping files of these various orders up to date, as an error may be costly and prove a source of both monetary loss to the firm and serious friction with the customer.

The orders are executed by the floor members, who receive them from the order department. The orders are turned in by the customers' men and through other channels to the order clerks, who transmit them by telephone to the floor of the exchange. There the orders are executed and reports of them are immediately telephoned back to the office. A record of each transaction is then sent to the clearing house department, which arranges the actual delivery or receipt of the stock certificates; to the report department, which sends a confirmation to the customer through the mails; and to the accounting department, which makes the necessary entries on the books of the firm. The accounting department, in turn, quickly notifies the margin clerk, whose sole function is to see that the individual accounts of clients are adequately protected by deposit of sufficient cash and securities.

3. *The Physical Handling of Securities.*—This is the work of the clearing house department, so called because the bulk of the work attached to this task has been enormously simplified through the organization of the Stock Clearing Corporation and a central delivery system by the stock exchange. The exchange clearing mechanism will be described presently. Attached to this department is a fleet of runners, who carry securities and checks hither and thither in the financial district as the business of the firm requires.

4. *The Handling of Cash.*—The cashier's department is responsible for the handling of cash. By handling receipts and disbursements, the cashier knows at about 2:15 P.M. of each day the approximate money position of the firm, and therefore the amount of new loans needed. Accordingly he, or a subordinate loan clerk, arranges to borrow money, generally using customers' securities as collateral, or to call loans which he is able to pay off, thus reducing the interest charges which the firm must pay. Old loans are either renewed or called in the forenoon. The cashier's department also has jurisdiction over the securities in the possession of the firm, keeping a record of each certificate received and delivered, thus supplementing the work of the clearing house department in the physical handling of securities. The margin clerk is often attached to the cashier's department, and his approval is required before a client can withdraw cash or securities from his account.

5. *The Handling of the Records.*—This is the work of the accounting or bookkeeping department, although in many firms this work is placed within the jurisdiction of the cashier's department. Not only are the accounts of customers and the firm itself kept here, but also the records of payment of interest and dividends on customers' securities, and the accounts of branch offices.

6. *The Statistical Department.*—The statistical department of a large brokerage house does more than the name implies. It not only serves the present customers of the house, but it also seeks to gain new ones through giving service to prospective clients and through advertising.

The direct service given by the statistical department takes many forms. The most characteristic is the market letter, a daily sheet discussing market trends and individual securities. In their efforts to avoid committing themselves as to the actual trend of events, many market letter writers have gained a reputation for proverbial tergiversation. In addition, individual securities in which the brokerage house may or may not have a special interest are described in circulars, booklets and, during trading hours, "flashes." A "flash" is a short statement on an individual stock or group of stocks advising immediate action, and it goes out over the wires to all the offices and correspondents of the house, and at times to its chief clients. Of course, the provisions of the Securities Exchange Act of 1934 should be kept in mind constantly in the operation of the statistical department, to avoid conflict with the law.

The work of the statistical department is made the basis of the firm's bids for business from new clients. The literature described is sent by mail to selected lists of prospective customers, and to the newspapers for possible quotation. Also, the advertising of most brokerage houses is built around the statistical department, the typical advertisement of many such houses consisting of invitations to inquire for circulars or letters which have been prepared on specific topics or securities of general interest.

The statistical or service department also handles inquiries from clients and others on individual securities. The direct personal service thus given often proves an important builder of new business.

Financing the Brokerage Business

In active years, the value of securities traded in on the New York Stock Exchange may be in excess of $50,000,000,000. The brokerage business is one which involves the handling of large sums of money.

A brokerage must possess a substantial amount of capital to gain the confidence of the banks and thus secure the credit needed for effecting this turnover, and it must also finance the expenses of its own organization.

The average stock exchange house includes three types of partners: floor members, business getters, and moneyed men—the latter to supply the capital. This capital may be in the form of cash or securities. Often only the *use* of securities is contributed, equitable title to the securities remaining with the contributor, who also receives interest and dividends as paid. Whether cash, securities or merely the use of securities is contributed, the result is the same; the firm has working capital with which to facilitate purchases and sales of securities, cover part of the balance due over and above customers' margin in the unusual cases when this is necessary, take positions in stocks, and, in many cases, engage in the flotation of new issues from time to time as an investment house.

However wealthy the firm, the capital contributed by the partners is usually only a small fraction of the working capital used in the business. The bulk of the capital comes from loans. New loans are frequently secured in the first instance as a "day loan" accommodation or "clearing loan" from the bank. Checks against this loan are paid out through the day as needed in the firm's business. These advances, sometimes termed "over-certifications," are repayable the same day they are made. No interest was charged by the banks on such advances until recently, but now one per cent is charged. A brokerage house usually leaves its unsecured note with the bank to cover such advances from day to day as they are made. Such loans are granted by a bank as an accommodation to a brokerage house customer, and in return the brokerage house leaves a fair-sized balance with the bank. For a firm that gets day loan accommodation up to $1,000,000, it is customary to leave an average balance of $70,000. Very large houses will keep such accounts in several banks. Brokers belonging to the Stock Clearing Corporation obtain temporary accommodation for the day from the latter, which greatly reduces their need for day loans from banks.

Brokers' day loans are never carried overnight, and are expected to be paid up by 3 o'clock of the day on which they are contracted. By that time, the loan clerk of the firm knows what receipts have come in, and therefore how large his overnight requirements are going to be. He can then adjust his collateral loans accordingly. Carrying such loans until 4 o'clock may entail a penalty charge by the bank, such as one day's interest at the full call money rate.

The loan clerk arranges in the afternoon to borrow as much money as is needed to repay the accommodation loan and make any other payments due. Under normal conditions, most of his borrowings will be call loans, and the balance time loans. This will vary, however, according to the prevailing interest rates on the two types of loans. The rate on time loans usually is lower than on call loans, and furthermore it is immune, during the period of the loan, from the sharp flurries which sometimes characterize the call loan market. On the other hand, a sudden influx may depress the call rate well below the time rate.[2] A fuller description of the collateral loan market will be found below in Chapter XI.

The brokerage firm, like the investment house, is free from the necessity of periodically making public its statement of condition and subjecting itself to rigid government regulation, as is the case with commercial banks. Therefore, the public is necessarily in the dark as to the condition of any specific firm, although periodic statements are required of brokers by security commissioners in many states, and by the New York Stock Exchange of its members carrying margin accounts.

One brokerage house in 1929 broke precedent and sent a statement of its condition to its customers. This statement indicates the large volume of business a broker can do with a relatively small capital of his own. The statement follows:

ASSETS

Cash in banks	$ 488,072
Cash on hand	2,253
Deposit with Stock Clearing Corp.	75,000
Memberships	633,500
Customers' debit balances	30,586,603
Securities borrowed	353,900
Securities to deliver	382,108
Unlisted department	270,205
Bank loans receivable	200,000
Dividends receivable	9,587
Commission receivable	25,247
Revenue tax stamps	2,733
Furniture, fixtures and good will	1
Total	$33,029,209

[2] In times of high interest rates, such as 1928-1929, time loans become of negligible importance because they are not exempt from the usury law.

LIABILITIES

Capital	$ 2,610,980
Undivided surplus	576,543
Bank loans payable	23,642,000
Customers' credit balances	1,160,572
Customers' short commitments	558,296
Securities loaned	3,044,700
Securities to receive	710,670
Accounts with other brokers	557,586
Commission payable	8,629
Interest	70,778
Reserve	88,455
Total	$33,029,209

It will be noted that in this case the bank loans of the house, together with credit balances due customers and securities loaned to short sellers who turn over cash as collateral, aggregate about eight times the capital and surplus of the broker. It must be borne in mind, however, in connection with statements of this kind, that they do not reflect the real position of the firm. The basic protection against difficulties lies in the value of the securities held for customers, against which they owe the firm $30,586,603. If this value remains largely in excess of the debit balances of the customers, the position of the house is not endangered even if its own capital is negligible. The size of this margin of excess value depends on the state of the market and the rigidity of the firm's margin requirements.

The minimum amount of capital required by a brokerage house has been set by the Securities Exchange Act of 1934. In the first place, this statute provides that the total indebtedness of a broker, including customers' credit balances, shall not exceed twenty times the net capital of the firm, exclusive of fixed assets and the value of its exchange membership. A similar requirement has long been imposed on its members by the New York Stock Exchange.[3] The Securities and Exchange Commis-

[3] The registration statement of the New York Stock Exchange contains the following on this point:

"LIMITATIONS ON MEMBERS' MAXIMUM INDEBTEDNESS, OR RATIO OF INDEBTEDNESS TO CAPITAL: The Exchange does not prescribe specific rules or regulations in regard to maximum indebtedness or ratio of indebtedness to capital. The Committee on Business Conduct requires that the 'working capital' of any member or registered firm carrying margin accounts for customers shall be equal at least to the greater of (1) $25,000 or (2) the equivalent of 5% of the total debit sion may by regulation further curtail the proportion of indebtedness to capital of a brokerage house.

Furthermore, under Regulation U, as it stood in the autumn of 1936, of the Board of Governors of the Federal Reserve System, member banks are not permitted to lend more than 60 per cent of the value of registered securities to exchange members on securities carried by the broker for his customers. Since, under Regulation T of the Federal Reserve Board, stock exchange firms may in turn lend to their customers no more than 45 per cent of the value of registered securities, it would appear that the broker would need no capital of his own in order to finance his customers' accounts. However, as will be explained later, these minimum requirements apply only to initial extensions of credit by banks or brokerage houses. If the collateral of the customer should subsequently decline in value, then the broker, who must constantly renew his loans at the banks because of shifts in customers' collateral, may find that he can borrow less than the amount which he lends to his customers. Under the rules of the New York Stock Exchange, a broker may lend to his customers up to approximately 77 per cent of the value of his collateral. Hence, a broker may, if he so wishes, carry securities for his customers in margin accounts after they have declined severely, but it is likely that he will have to utilize his own capital in large measure in doing so.

Sources of Income of the Broker

The brokerage business, like any other business enterprise in a capitalistic order of society, is operated to earn a profit.

---

balances carried for customers having secured accounts, plus 30% of the market value of securities (other than government obligations) carried in firm and partners' accounts and in customers' accounts which are in deficit. In determining what constitutes the 'working capital' of a firm, assets which, in the opinion of the Committee on Business Conduct, are not readily marketable or readily acceptable as loan collateral are excluded, and all unsecured customers' debit balances are deducted and also the aggregate amount necessary to make any insufficiently margined customers' accounts meet the requirements of ten points on short commitments and 30% of the debit balance on long commitments. Open commitments in securities, commodities, foreign exchange and other similar transactions are marked to the market and any deficits in such commitments are likewise deducted before the 'working capital' is determined."

The foregoing represents the usual minimum requirements of the committee on business conduct. Additional or special requirements are made in cases involving unusual situations.

Brokerage house expenses are large. First, there are the expensive quarters which most of the larger houses maintain in the financial districts of New York and other important cities. Large clerical forces are required to handle the routine; and the partners, outside of a return on their investment, naturally expect to receive substantial compensation for the time spent in the strenuous task of running a securities trading business. Finally, the profit must be sufficient to give an ample rate of return on the capital invested in exchange memberships and the working capital put into the business by the partners.

The income of the broker on the ordinary margin account consists of two elements: commissions, and a differential interest charge. Minimum commissions on the leading exchanges are fixed at uniform rates for all members; the cutting of commissions is rare, and is generally considered cause for expulsion or fine. On the New York Stock Exchange, the following rates were established in 1923, and, with minor changes, have been maintained since:

For Shares Selling at:	Commission Rate per Share:
under 50c.	any rate agreed upon
50c.–99c.	3c.
\$ 1–\$ 9.99	7½c.
10– 24.99	12½c.
25– 49.99	15c.
50– 74.99	17½c.
75– 99.99	20c.
100– 199.99	25c.
200 and above	30c. plus 5c. for each \$50 or fraction thereof above \$250 per share

A minimum commission varying from \$1 to \$5 is charged by most brokerage houses for any one transaction.

The rates above are reduced to \$2.50 per hundred shares (on stocks selling at 10 to 124.99 a share) when transacted for other members and not "cleared." A slightly higher rate must be charged if the delivery and payment for the transaction are contemplated through the member executing the order.

The second source of income for the brokerage house is the interest charged by the broker on the debit balance due from the customer, over and above the amount paid by the broker to the bank. This charge is generally regarded as constituting a service charge by the broker for arranging the loan. Thus, when the average rate for money through the month is 1 per cent, most brokerage houses will charge their customers on their debit balances from 3 to 5½ per cent, depending on the size of the account. The broker's "spread" is often more than appears from the prevailing call money rate, for he usually borrows a part of his requirements on a time basis at less than the average call rate. Furthermore, he pays those customers who have a credit balance a relatively low rate of interest, often one or two per cent below the average call rate; but such credit balances cut the amount of bank loans he makes. Finally, lending stocks to short sellers may give the broker substantial sums at low interest rates.

Demand collateral loans are exempt from the usury laws in New York and most other states. This exemption does not apply to time loans, however, or to demand loans of less than $5,000. Therefore time loans become unpopular with lenders after the rate rises above 6 per cent, for the interest cannot be collected at law. Also, a few brokers will not charge more than 6 per cent on debit balances of less than $5,000, despite legal decisions holding such higher charges permissible because the broker borrows in large amounts without regard to specific requirements of individual small accounts.

The New York Stock Exchange favors the same uniformity in interest charges as in commissions, although some differential for the size of the account is allowed in practice. The by-laws of the New York Stock Exchange state that allowing a client a preferential rate of interest for the purpose of getting business is an act against the interest and welfare of the exchange.

The broker's revenue from short sales is usually larger than on "long accounts." When stocks are sold short, the proceeds received from the sale are turned over to the broker from whom stock is borrowed, the borrowed stock then being turned over to the purchaser in fulfillment of the sale. Now the lender of the stock usually pays a specified rate of interest on the money he receives as security for the stock loaned. The interest thus paid is retained by the broker who made the short sale, and constitutes clear profit for him, in addition to the commissions received. Furthermore, the broker lending the stock, which be longs as a rule to clients holding it on margin, generally pays less than the market rate of interest for the use of the money, thus cutting the average cost of his funds.

Besides the income from commissions and interest charges, most brokerage houses eke out their profits in a number of ways. Some establish commodity trading departments; others, trading departments for over-the-counter securities, acting as dealers and brokers in this important market. A few do a foreign exchange, arbitrage or commercial paper and acceptance business. The majority at one time or another take positions in securities on their own account, or open investment departments where they act as investment bankers in floating new enterprises or bringing out new issues of securities. Another source of profit that has been tapped lately by some brokers is the establishment of investment trusts or investment management departments, usually in cooperation with other interests. These investment trusts then become important clients of the brokerage house, and thus greatly increase its commission business. Besides, the brokers may make large profits from the ownership of the junior securities of the investment trust.

Relation between the Broker and his Client

Owing to the comparatively complex dealings which take place between the broker and his customers, a number of fine legal points have been determined only after a long course of litigation. The law of the brokerage business has now been largely clarified, so that the relation of the broker to his client can be stated in definite terms.

The broker occupies more than one legal position in his dealings. In fact, four distinct relationships are involved in the handling of the usual brokerage account. These are:

1. The broker as agent, the customer as principal. This is the basic relationship, typical of the brokerage business generally. In executing orders the broker is subject to the usual liabilities of agents, and in practice, owing to the superior financial responsibility of the broker, he is looked to in case contracts are broken by the customer.

2. The broker as creditor, the customer as debtor. This relationship applies to the unpaid balance of the customer owed

on the stocks he may purchase. It will also apply in case of any loss suffered by the customer in his account, as where short sales prove unprofitable.

3. The broker as pledgee, the customer as pledgor. This relationship applies to the stock which, purchased for the customer on margin, is then pledged by him to secure the unpaid balance. The unpaid balance due to the broker from the owner of a margin account actually constitutes a secured debt, with the purchased securities themselves hypothecated as security. In lieu of cash margin, a customer will frequently deposit other securities that he owns, which are also then considered pledged.

4. The broker as trustee, the customer as beneficiary. This relationship applies to stocks and bonds owned by the customer and deposited with the broker when no debt is due to the latter. Frequently customers will have credit balances in their account, or the debit balance due is far less than the value of the deposited securities. It has been held that the broker cannot freely use the customers' securities as collateral for bank loans in such a case, but must consider himself as a fiduciary holding them for the client as beneficiary. Sections 956-957 of the New York Penal Code define penalties to which the broker is subject for illegal pledging of such securities; but a waiver of this provision on a so-called "hypothecation card" is usually required by brokerage houses, to permit them to hypothecate all securities in a margin account, regardless of the size of the *debit balance*, as the amount owed to the broker by the customer is called.[4]

While the brokerage relationship has these four different aspects, the major one is that of agent and principal. The broker in practice undertakes and agrees to do the following:[5]

1. To buy or sell the stocks indicated by the customer at once.

2. To advance all the money required for such purchases beyond the *usual and customary* margin required of the customer.

3. To carry or to hold such stocks for the customers' benefit

[4] A rule of the New York Stock Exchange provides, however, that more of the customers' securities may not be pledged than is "fair and reasonable" in view of the indebtedness of the customer, regardless of such agreement.

[5] See Markham *vs.* Jaudon, 41 N. Y. 235, decided in 1869. This is an old but leading case on this subject.

so long as that usual and customary margin is kept good, or until notice is given by either party that the account be closed.

4. To have within his control and ready for delivery to the customer at all times the shares purchased, or an equal amount of other shares of the same issue within the broker's right of reclamation or possession.

5. To deliver such shares to the customer when required, upon payment of the balance due.

6. To sell such securities upon the order of the customer, and to account to the customer for the proceeds of such sale.

The relationship between the broker and his client is usually put to a test when the latter's account is impaired through an adverse movement in the price of the securities held. When a fall in stock prices impairs the margin of a customer, the broker, to protect himself, calls for an additional deposit of funds. When these are not forthcoming, the broker may, and in fairness to his other clients and the solvency of his house should, place stop-loss orders without specific notice after the customer fails to respond to the margin call. The broker's right to place a stop-loss order is based on the legal principle that an agent with an interest in the subject matter of a contract reserves his right to protect his interest in that contract. It has been held judicially that reasonable notice must be given the customer of the broker's intention to close out his account when the margin deficiency is not made good, for the brokerage relationship constitutes an agency terminable at will.[6]

In the case of a short sale, the broker may buy in the stock sold short immediately when it can no longer be borrowed, for the implied agency contract is then abrogated by impossibility of performance.

Since the broker is primarily an agent, it is best as a rule to restrict his activity accordingly. Discretionary accounts or orders, where the broker is given the right to buy or sell for a client without consulting him, usually lead to dissatisfaction, and most houses and customers' men discourage this practice.

[6] This notice usually states the securities to be sold, and the time and the place of sale. It is sent by registered mail, with a return receipt required. This sale amounts to a foreclosure on hypothecated property, and the customer is liable for any remaining deficit in his account.

Wire System

In the brokerage business, because of the nation-wide dependence upon the market furnished by the New York Stock Exchange, branch and correspondent relationships have long been highly developed. In 1936, there were more than 1,000 branch offices of stock exchange houses, and more than 3,000 non-member correspondents, several houses having a dozen and more out-of-town offices, as well as numerous correspondents for whom they execute orders. A small group of the larger houses have as many as fifty branch offices each, including correspondents.

The leased wire system is a remarkable example of mechanical efficiency, and has been developed to a point where the different parts of the country are closely tied in with the major market places, especially New York. The maintenance of this service at a very low cost is made possible through the use of so-called "carrier current," by which a single pair of telephone wires may be used simultaneously for 24 telegraph conversations. This is accomplished through carrying on the telegraph conversations by currents of different frequencies going over the same wires, and separated at each end by a "selecting circuit" device.

Fig. 5 shows the private wire system of a large stock exchange house with connections from coast to coast, from Boston to New Orleans, from Los Angeles to Seattle.

Margin Regulation

The brokerage business has been vitally affected by regulation of margins provided in the Securities Exchange Act of 1934. That statute gave to the Board of Governors of the Federal Reserve System the power to determine and to vary the maximum amount of credit that could be extended, either by brokerage houses or by banks, on registered securities. This authority has been utilized to discourage widespread margin trading or purchasing of securities with bank credit, such as developed during the period before 1929. (See Appendix III.)

When an account becomes undermargined under the provisions of Regulation T of the Federal Reserve Board, the broker is under no obligation to insist on additional margin or, in the

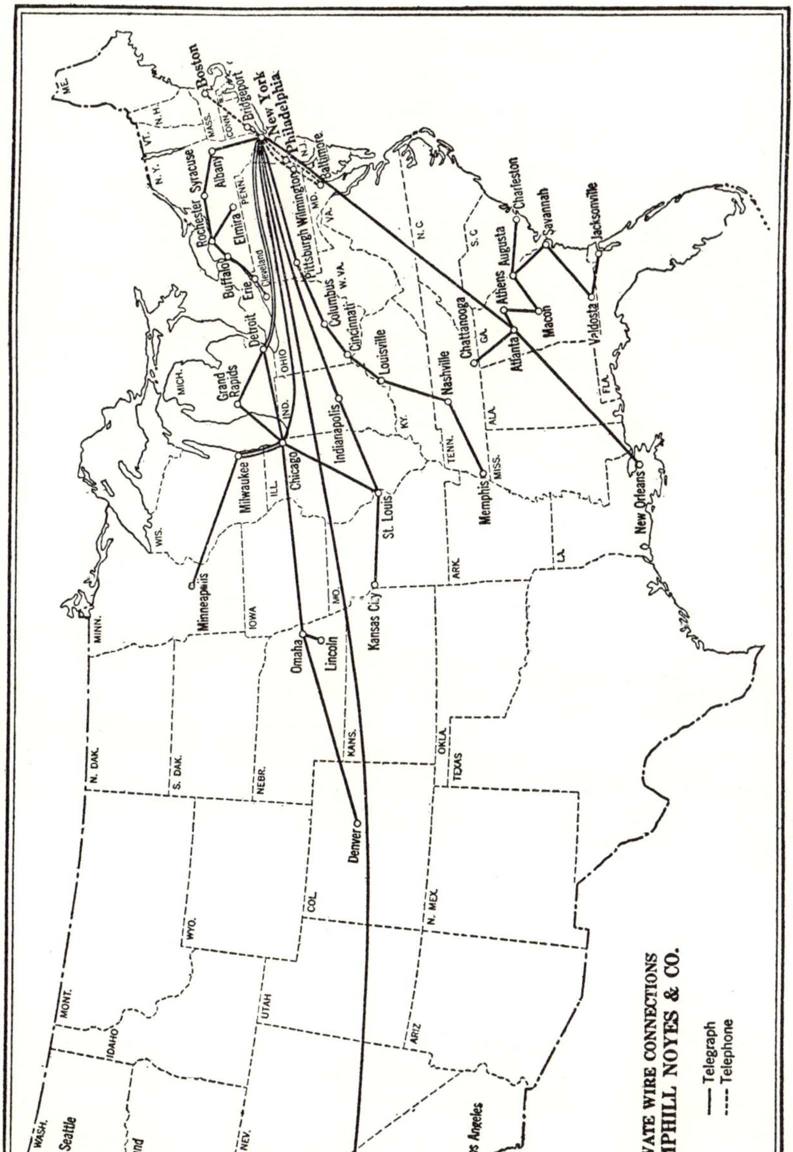

Fig. 5. Wire System of a Large Brokerage House

alternative, sell out the account. It merely falls into the category of a restricted account, in which no transaction may be effected that will have the result of increasing the customer's debit balance. The broker can then establish his own rules to govern calls for additional margin or forced selling, subject to the New York Stock Exchange requirement that a minimum margin of 30 per cent of the debit balance, equivalent to slightly over 23 per cent of the market price, be maintained.

Hence, the technical position of the market has been strengthened as compared to the situation prevailing before 1935, when reactions usually brought heavy selling from thinly margined accounts that had become impaired. Now, on a reaction, numerous accounts become restricted, so that their buying power is exhausted, but forced selling is avoided until the individual broker's or the exchange's margin requirements are no longer met. Also, by putting up sufficient additional cash or collateral to margin new commitments, a customer may be permitted to add to his holdings in a restricted account, without first making good the deficiency in his margin, under Regulation T.

With the establishment early in 1936 of a flat 55 per cent margin requirement, or 45 per cent maximum loan value, for both brokerage houses and banks, the volume of margin trading was materially reduced. As a result, brokerage houses must depend more largely upon investment rather than speculative business. Furthermore, even during periods of major price changes, the total volume of turnover on the exchange is likely to be smaller because of this curtailment of margin speculation.

The reduced volume of margin trading has also tended to increase the emphasis upon investment service and investment advice on the part of brokerage houses. Several houses have, in fact, entered the field of investment management, both because of the fees they can thus obtain and because of the increased volume of commission business which comes to them through accepting advisory and discretionary accounts.

Margin regulation by the Federal Reserve Board also makes it necessary for those who are responsible for the conduct of a commission house to keep abreast of credit developments, and to foresee, as far as possible, likely changes in margin regulations from time to time.

The brokerage business has thus been transformed into one which caters more largely than formerly to an investment clientele. For that reason, standards of service, statistical and otherwise, have been raised higher than ever before, and there is less dependence upon the in-and-out speculative traders who formerly often accounted for the bulk of the business on the exchange. The provisions barring manipulation of security prices and restrictions on trading for their own accounts by officials, directors and large stockholders of corporations have emphasized this tendency.

The Over-the-counter Markets

Outside the organized exchanges, a vast amount of security trading is conducted on the over-the-counter market. In the aggregate, as we have seen, a vastly larger number of security issues enjoy whatever marketability they possess on this over-the-counter market, particularly in the case of stock and bond issues of small enterprises, the obligations of municipalities, and the securities of special group corporations such as banks, insurance companies and investment trusts.

Section 15 of the Securities Exchange Act of 1934 for the first time subjects the over-the-counter market to federal regulation. However, the constitutional basis of federal regulation of unlisted trading is far less clear than in the case of securities exchanges on which orders from all over the country are executed. As a result, the Securities and Exchange Commission has been hesitant about applying to the over-the-counter markets the same type of control that it has upon the registered securities exchanges.

The Commission has been influenced by two main considerations in the evolution of its regulatory policies applicable to over-the-counter markets. On the one hand, it has sought to avoid discouraging corporations and governments from listing their securities, for in that event the whole purpose of security market regulation would be defeated. On the other hand, the Commission has recognized the fact that to stamp out the over-the-counter markets would be to injure the public interests severely by greatly limiting or eliminating the quality of marketability which that market confers upon a large number of individual securities that find there their sole market.

Registration of Dealers

In its regulation of the security exchanges, the Securities and Exchange Commission requires the registration of individual security issues as well as of the exchanges themselves. In the over-the-counter markets, no attempt has yet been made to register the securities there traded in, because of the lack of certainty that issuing corporations would care to do so. Rather, regulation has been sought through requiring dealers to register with the Commission.

In 1936, the Securities Exchange Act was amended to require over-the-counter brokers and dealers to register. Such registration is effected by filing with the Commission an application in which certain information about the applicant and his business is presented. Thirty days after the application has been received by the Commission, the registration is effective unless denied for cause. When denied in this way, or when revoked after its effective date, the Commission must furnish appropriate notice and an opportunity for a hearing. Among the causes for such denial of registration specifically stated in the statute are:

1. Willful misrepresentation in the application for registration.
2. Conviction for a felony or misdemeanor involving the purchase or sale of any security within ten years preceding the filing of the application.
3. The existence of a temporary or permanent injunction against the applicant which bars him from engaging in the purchase or sale of any security.
4. A willful violation of the Securities Act of 1933 or of the Securities Exchange Act.

Regulation of Over-the-counter Practices

In the spring of 1936 the Securities and Exchange Commission promulgated a number of regulations affecting the over-the-counter markets. Registered brokers and dealers must conform to these regulations; if they do not, their registration may be revoked, and they would thus be barred by the statute from the use of the mails or of any other means or instrumentality of interstate commerce to effect their transactions.

One fundamental rule, MA10, provides that:

(a) No registered broker shall act as agent of both buyer and seller in any security transaction on an over-the-counter market unless (1) he procures the written or telegraphic consent of both such buyer and seller at or before the completion of the transaction; or (2) he makes written disclosure to both such buyer and seller before the completion of the transaction that he is so acting.

(b) The terms "buyer" and "seller" as used in this rule shall not include a broker or dealer as defined in the Securities Exchange Act of 1934.

Accordingly, if circumstances should arise where an over-the-counter broker wishes to act in this capacity for both buyer and seller, he must arrange a specific agreement with both parties to this effect to avoid running the risk of a revocation of his registration with the Securities and Exchange Commission.

Another fundamental rule, known as MA11, provides that:

(a) No registered broker or dealer shall effect any transaction in a security for or with a customer on an over-the-counter market, unless such broker or dealer at or before the completion of such transaction clearly discloses to such customer in writing (1) whether he is acting as a dealer for his own account, as a broker for such customer, or as a broker for some other person; (2) if he acts as broker for such customer, either the name of the person from whom such security was purchased or to whom it was sold for such customer and the day and time when such transaction took place, or the fact that such information will be furnished upon request of such customer; (3) if he acts as broker for such customer, the amount of the commission or service fee charged by him to such customer, and the amount of commission paid by him to any other broker employed by him in such transaction; and (4) that he is controlled by, or controls, or is under common control with the issuer of such security if such be the fact.

(b) The term "customer" as used in this rule shall not include a broker or dealer as defined in the Securities Exchange Act of 1934.

It is apparent, therefore, that an over-the-counter dealer acting for his own account may not also act as a broker for his customer, charging him a commission, or as a broker for a third party selling to his customer. In order to conform to this section of the law, it is necessary for the security broker or dealer to utilize suitable forms in communicating with his customers. The Investment Bankers' Association of America has prepared a set of specimen forms which it advises its members to use or adapt to their particular business.[7]

A third fundamental rule, MA12, restricts the conduct of discretionary accounts or investment counsel activities by registered over-the-counter brokers. It states:

(a) No registered broker or dealer who receives or has promise of receiving a fee for advising a customer with respect to any security or is vested by a customer with discretion as to the choice or the total amount of a security to be bought or sold or as to whether the transaction shall be one of purchase or sale, shall on an over-the-counter market

(1) effect any transaction for or with such customer in any security in which in the course of his business as a broker or dealer he has a long or short position, or in the distribution or accumulation of which he has any direct or indirect financial interest, or in which he holds or has granted or has knowledge that any principal for whom he is acting holds or has granted any option, unless he clearly discloses to such customer the fact of such opinion, interest, or option and obtains the written or telegraphic consent of such customer to each such transaction;

(2) buy from or sell to such customer any security for any account in which he or any principal for whom he is acting is interested, unless he obtains the written or telegraphic consent of such customer to each such purchase or sale.

(b) The term "customer" as used in this rule, shall not include a broker or dealer as defined in the Securities Exchange Act of 1934.

Over-the-Counter Quotations

Trading on over-the-counter markets differs in several important respects from that on security exchanges. Perhaps the

[7] Printed in *Investment Banking*, vol. vi, no. 6, pp. 193-197.

most fundamental is the fact that whereas on security exchanges the volume of turnover and the price at which a transaction actually takes place are made public, on the over-the-counter markets publicity is given at most only to the bid and asked prices at a particular time.

In New York through the New York Security Dealers Association, which includes most of the large over-the-counter dealers in that city, and elsewhere by action of individual dealers, newspapers receive lists of quotations of bid and asked prices of particular groups of securities on the over-the-counter market. An example of such quotations for New York City bank stocks is presented herewith:

NEW YORK BANKS

	Bid	Asked	Monday Bid
Bank of the Manhattan Co. (1½)	31	33	31
Bank Yorktown (2)	58	68	58
Chase (1.40)	46½	48½	46½
City (1)	41½	43½	41½
Commercial (8)	193	*199	194
Fifth Av. (†34)	995	1025	995
First National (100)	2135	2175	2145
Merchants (4)	90	105	90
National Bronx	25	30	25
Nat. Safety (25c)	14½	16½	14½
Penn. Exch. (20c)	10	11½	10
Public (1½)	49½	51½	49½
Sterling	34½	36	34½
Trade	32	40	32

† Includes extras.
* Ex dividend.

NEW YORK TRUST COMPANIES

	Bid	Asked	Monday Bid
Bankers (2)	69½	71½	70
Banca Comm. Ital.	105	115	105
Bank of New York (14)	505	510	508
Bank of Sicily	10	12	10
Bronx	9	10	9
Cent. Hanover (4)	132	135	132
Chemical (1.80)	66½	68½	66½
Clinton (†3)	80	84	80
Colonial	14	16	14
Continental (80c)	18¼	19¾	18¼
Corn Exch. (3)	66	67	66
Empire (1)	26¾	27¾	27

Fulton (10)	250	265	250
Guaranty (12)	357	362	356
Irving (60c)	15¾	16¾	16
Lawyers (2.40)	53½	56½	53½
Manufacturers (2)	50	52	50½
Do cum pf. (2)	51½	53½	51½
New York (5)	141	144	141
Title Guarantee	10¼	11¼	10¼
Underwriters	80	90	80
Un States (†70)	2030	2080	2040

† Includes extras.

Very often, an investor or trader can sell the issue above the bid price here shown, and he can buy it below the asked price. In order to protect themselves, dealers may maintain a wider difference between the bid and asked prices that they make public than they actually maintain in practice. Of course, the relative activity of a given issue, the size of orders transacted in it, and the degree of competition among dealers will determine the size of the spread between the bid and the asked quotations.

In addition to the limited number of over-the-counter quotations published in the newspapers, a far greater number of prices are maintained by larger dealers, as well as by financial services that compile and publish such quotations.

References

Dice, Charles Amos, *The Stock Market,* Chicago, 1929.

Meeker, J. Edward, *The Work of the Stock Exchange,* New York, 1930.

Pratt, S. S., *The Work of Wall Street,* New York, 1921, chaps. x–xv.

Schabacker, R. W., *Stock Market Theory and Practice,* New York, 1930.

Securities and Exchange Commission, *Report on Segregation of the Functions of Dealer and Broker,* Washington, 1936.

Senate Committee on Banking and Currency, *Hearings,* Stock Exchange Practices, 73rd Congress, Washington, 1934.

Shultz, B. E., *Stock Exchange Procedure,* New York, 1936.

Smitley, Robert L., *Course of Study for Brokerage, Stock Exchange and Investment Banking,* New York, 1923, pp. 77–138.

Todman, F. S., *Wall Street Accounting,* New York, 1921, chap. i.

Twentieth Century Fund, *The Security Markets, New York,* 1935.

Chapter V

INVESTING INSTITUTIONS

Direct *vs.* Indirect Investment

In the simple investment banking transaction, the investor buys securities directly from a bond house or through a broker from another investor. The burden of choice and the risk of loss rest on him alone.

As the volume of outstanding investment securities has expanded to huge proportions, and the types of issues offered have multiplied many times over, the choice of investments has become increasingly difficult. The investing process at any one moment is, to a large extent, a matter of comparing values. No matter what the state of business in general or the condition of the securities markets, there are always securities which are "out of line," because their quotations, compared with those for other securities, are too high or too low. To appraise individual securities and thus find issues undervalued in the market, and to foresee broad changes in the general level of security prices so as properly to time individual purchases, are the major functions of investment analysis.

Under these conditions, the investor whose primary personal interest is elsewhere has a strong incentive to use an intermediate institution, placed between himself and the seller of securities, which can adequately perform the tasks of investment analysis. These intermediate institutions, formed for the specific purpose of investing other people's money, have grown to such large proportions that they are now a very important part of the investment banking machinery. Although exact inclusive figures are not available, the capital which they now hold and invest is certainly upward of fifty billions of dollars.

There are three basically different types of investing institutions which have been fully developed in this country. The first of these, typified by the savings bank, operates as an institution of deposit, investing these deposits in securities. A second group of investing institutions issues its own securities and invests the proceeds of their sale. This group, which may be called securities substitution companies, comprises investment trusts, mortgage banks, building and loan associations and other organizations sometimes loosely described as finance companies. The third and, as measured by the volume of funds managed, the most important type of investing institution, typified by the trust company, manages the funds of each investor individually, giving a special and personal service not possible with the other kinds of investing institutions. Investment counsel firms offer investment advice alone, and fall within this third category.

In this chapter, the organization of these investing institutions and the legal and economic aspects of their work are studied. Some appraisal of their activities is also made from the point of view of the investor. A fuller discussion of the broad problem of investment management policy is contained in Chapter XXI.

The Mutual Savings Bank

The mutual savings bank is the prototype of the intermediate investing institution. It had its root in charitable and benevolent organizations formed to promote thrift among the wage-earning classes. The profit-making motive has been, at least nominally, left out of mutual savings bank operation.

Instances of mutual savings bank organizations were found in Germany in the latter half of the eighteenth century. In Scotland, now characteristically enough regarded as the original home of savings banking, such a bank was first established in 1810. The idea spread rapidly, and in 1816 such institutions were proposed in Boston and New York. During the next few years, savings banks were chartered in most of the important towns in New England and the Atlantic states.

The mutual savings bank, as an intermediate investing institution, possesses a number of important features which give it a distinct character. This character has largely been preserved through the years, because of rigid legal regulation and the extreme conservatism of legislators in changing savings bank laws.

As the custodian of the surplus funds of the poorer classes, ultra-conservative management and iron-bound safeguards have been held necessary. The peculiar features of the mutual savings bank are the following:

1. It is a mutual institution.
2. It is dominantly non-commercial in character.
3. Its investments are rigidly restricted by law.

Each of these characteristics will be considered in its turn.

1. The mutual savings bank is a non-stock institution, so that its assets are in effect the property of depositors. The sole exceptions are moderate initial guaranty and expense funds, which are returned to the trustees who advance them after the bank has been fully established. Earnings of the bank on its investments are similarly the property of depositors, after expenses have been deducted. The bulk of the income is paid out, *after it is earned,* as a stated rate of interest. The rest goes into a reserve fund, or surplus, against which losses may be written off, and which in time provides income to cover the operating expenses of the institution.

2. The savings bank, as a benevolent institution, is non-profit-making. In a leading savings bank case, a New York court stated:

> Savings banks are not organized as business enterprises. They have no stockholders, and are not to engage in speculation, or money-making in a business sense. They are simply to take the deposits, usually small, which are offered, aggregate them and keep and invest them safely, paying such interest to the depositors as is thus made, after deducting expenses, and paying the principal on demand.[1]

The non-commercial aspect applies both to the mutual savings bank itself and to its managing body. The trustees in some states are permitted no fee whatsoever for their services. Elsewhere they are allowed only "what is just and reasonable" for actual services performed. Also, no loans may be made to directors, and provisions exist for restricting, although not always

[1] Hun *vs.* Carey, 82 N. Y. 65, decided in 1880.

with success, indirect gain that may come to officers and trustees from connection with the bank.

3. In the operation of the savings bank, safety of the principal of depositors is made the first consideration. Accordingly, the individual states where mutual savings banks operate have passed laws governing their investments, usually within very narrow limits. Many of these laws were enacted a long time ago, and have been very reluctantly changed since, so that they often appear out-of-date in the light of present-day conditions and knowledge of investment matters. When investment conditions change, as has been the case especially during the past ten years, such laws may be found to hamper seriously, rather than to advance, sound investment policies.

The mutual savings bank, as described above, is the original and typical form of savings bank. In the South and West, however, it has made practically no headway, and in the East it has met in later years with increasing competition from other less restricted types of intermediate investing institutions which are described later in this chapter. The stock savings bank, run on a commercial basis, is still found in California, Iowa and several other states, but is not an important type of investing institution in this country.

Organization and Operation of the Mutual Savings Bank

Mutual savings banks are found in seventeen states at the present time. More than 90 per cent of these banks, however, are located in New England, New York, New Jersey and Pennsylvania. Thus, the mutual savings bank as an investment banking institution is of sectional importance only.

Under the laws of these states, mutual savings banks may be organized by individuals willing to assume the burden of becoming trustees. The trustees are a self-perpetuating body in whom rests the management of the institution. The office of trustee is presumably sought only for the honor thereof, and as a result the liability of the trustee is limited to gross neglect of duty or violations of the law. In practice, however, other motives besides those of honor and prestige do admittedly operate, and generally without adverse effects upon the value of the institution. Those who can, directly or indirectly, benefit from starting a mutual savings bank are:

1. Investment bankers, who can thus influence investment policy. Investment bankers have not played an important rôle in savings banking, by and large.

2. Lawyers, who may receive considerable business, directly or indirectly, in connection with mortgage loans, etc. The Attorney-General of New York State has held that trustees may search real estate titles, in connection with mortgage loans made by their institutions, provided the fee is paid by the borrower and not by the savings bank itself.

3. Commercial bankers, who welcome savings bank deposit accounts. Savings banks may keep 5 per cent or more of their funds on deposit with commercial banks to meet current demands for cash and to await satisfactory investment opportunities.

4. Persons who wish to become salaried officials.

Savings banks receive only time deposits, on which they may demand advance notice of 30 or 60 days, varying according to state law, before depositors may withdraw their funds. The theory is that the funds will be placed in permanent investments, so that day-to-day liquidity need not be maintained. The size of individual deposits is limited, $7,500 being the maximum in New York, to prevent large individual depositors from jeopardizing the investment program of the bank through sudden withdrawals of substantial sums. As a result of these safeguards against large and sudden withdrawals, no legal reserve requirements exist for mutual savings institutions.

The deposit is evidenced by a pass book, which possesses more than the ordinary bank-book significance, since withdrawals are made as a rule only on presentation of this pass book. The pass book may be used as security for loans.

The savings bank is peculiar among investing institutions in that the depositor is not dependent upon the market-ability factor. He is entitled at all times, subject to the notice just mentioned, to withdraw his principal and accumulated interest. His investment is always worth its par value. His savings, as long as the bank is solvent—and mutual savings bank history has witnessed very few failures—are thus completely under his control.

The investments of a mutual savings bank are rigidly regulated by state law. In general, these laws limit investment to real estate first mortgages, government and municipal bonds, and a limited group of the better railroad and utility bonds meeting specific tests. Stocks are not permitted as investments in any important savings bank state.

These investment restrictions involve three adverse factors. In the first place, the bank cannot achieve full diversification in its investment portfolio, for it is limited to fixed-income-bearing securities.[2] Secondly, by limiting these banks to a relatively small number of investments, the market prices of the securities which pass the test and thus become "legal investments" are raised relative to other equally good but non-legal securities. The fact that trustees may be subject to the same restrictions intensifies this effect. As a result, depositors may have to be satisfied with a lower return than would otherwise be the case. In the third place, the fact that a limited number of financial institutions own these "legal" issues in large blocks, makes liquidation by them extremely difficult, if not impossible, on declining markets. On the other hand, the limitation of investment to a restricted group of "legal" securities may bring greater market stability for them in more prosperous times since, regardless of investment conditions as a whole, there is always a substantial demand for these "legals." In the fourth place, these restrictions encourage large investments in groups of securities favored in the past, such as railroad bonds, which may become less desirable as a group because of technological and economic changes.

The periodical payment made by the savings bank out of its net earnings is erroneously termed interest. It is strictly a dividend, which is contingent upon earnings; and in many states, such as New York, no fixed rate can even be promised in advance. Interest on invested deposits and on the invested sur-

[2] The depositor in the mutual savings bank has one advantage over the direct investor in gilt-edge securities, in that his principal, expressed in dollars, is not impaired by a rise in interest rates and a consequent general drop in bond prices. The savings bank's surplus protects the depositor against adverse effects from this contingency, but it is itself subject to this risk.

plus of the bank is the source of these earnings, but the accumulated surplus itself is seldom used to meet current dividend payments.

Annual expenses and write-offs may amount to about 1 per cent on the deposits of an institution. Hence, when an average of 4 per cent is earned on the portfolio, 3 per cent may be paid as interest. Where a large surplus exists, earnings on it may be sufficient for expenses, so that all earnings on the invested deposits may be paid out. In order to discourage undesirable competition, maximum interest rates are now set by administrative bodies in New York State, and for all members of the Federal Deposit Insurance Corporation by the latter.

The Investment Problem

The objective of savings bank legal investment restrictions is to compel these institutions to purchase only the highest grades of bonds and real estate first mortgages. For example, the New York State law has provided that railroad bonds could not be purchased by mutual savings bank unless the issuing railroad earned its fixed charges at least one and one-half times during at least five out of six years before investment, including the year before. Beginning with 1931, however, it proved necessary for the legislature to pass a moratorium on this provision each year, in order to keep the bulk of railroad bonds on the legal list to prevent impairment of their marketability. Only where a bond actually suffered default was it taken off the list during this period.

As a result of this experience, there is growing belief in more flexible institutional investment restrictions that will not favor unduly particular groups of securities like railroad bonds, as does the present savings bank statute.

Artificial government measures tending to depress mortgage rates and competition of other lending institutions also make more difficult the obtaining of a reasonable rate of return from mortgage investments. The investment policies of mutual savings banks during recent years may be observed from the following comparison of their investments in 1930 and 1935 (statistics as of June 30, in thousands of dollars, taken from reports of the Comptroller of the Currency):

	1930	1935
Mortgage loans	$ 5,895,095	$5,240,255
Other loans	245,461	102,222
U. S. government bonds	530,666	1,379,429
Government-guaranteed bonds	....	191,343
Federal Land Bank bonds, etc.	....	15,377
State and municipal bonds	1,102,416	885,439
Railroad and public utility bonds, etc.	2,347,953	1,868,840
Stocks	142,558	108,508
Foreign securities	70,979	62,468
	$10,335,128	$9,853,881

It will be noted from the above table that savings banks have increased their holdings of United States government bonds to an important extent in recent years. This has tended to improve the liquidity of their portfolio. It has also reflected the lack of an adequate supply of satisfactory investments in other categories during this period.

Liquidity and Safety.—Until the depression, the mutual savings banks received time deposits, repayable on short notice, and invested the great bulk of their resources in real estate mortgages and long-term bonds. As long as depositors did not withdraw their funds on a large scale, this arrangement proved quite satisfactory. However, when in 1932 and early in 1933 withdrawals grew heavier, it became apparent that special provisions to take care of such situations, however unusual they might be, were desirable.

The mutual savings banks have taken the following measures to improve their ability to meet concerted depositor withdrawals, should the need ever arise again:

1. United States government bonds have been bought in large amount. In the future, it is likely that from 10 to 20 per cent of mutual savings bank deposits will be kept in thi form.

2. Special funds or institutions have been set up to rediscount mortgages or make loans to mutual savings banks desir ing to raise cash. In New York State, the Savings Banks Trus Co. and the Institutional Securities Corporation were set up fo the purpose. Massachusetts, Connecticut, New Hampshire an Maine also established such funds. Also, mutual savings bank were made eligible for membership in the Federal Reserve Sy

tem by the Banking Act of 1933, and a limited number of such banks have joined it.

3. Deposit insurance has been established for most mutual savings banks. Such institutions are eligible to join the Federal Deposit Insurance Corporation, but many savings banks have felt the rate of premium excessive for them. Hence, only a minority of savings banks joined. In New York State, the Savings Banks Trust Co. has established a separate Mutual Savings Banks Fund which makes small assessments when needed; and Massachusetts saving banks similarly have a fund of their own. The New York and Massachusetts plans emphasize prevention of financial weakness, rather than deposit guarantee, in their operation.

Development and Future of Savings Banks

The growth of mutual savings banks in recent years is shown in the following table:

Year	Number of Banks	Deposits[a]	Number of Depositors	Average Deposit
1914	634	$ 3,915,555	8,277,359	$473.04
1920	620	5,186,952	9,445,327	549.16
1924	613	6,693,246	10,409,776	642.98
1928	616	8,672,823	11,732,080	739.24
1932	594	10,021,852	12,521,750	800.36
1935	571	9,902,107	13,213,211	749.41

[a] 000 omitted.

In view of the enormous expansion of investment activity in this country in recent years, especially in the territory in which the mutual savings bank is most prominent, it is evident that this institution has not kept pace. The reason is that with the increase in average individual wealth and the steady spread of knowledge concerning investments, the purely benevolent type of institution has become less necessary; although efficient and reliable investing organizations, run on business lines and unhampered by obsolete legal restrictions, are needed more than ever before. Accordingly, the savings bank has encountered difficulty in maintaining its relative position.

Mutual savings banks have displayed some tendency to broaden their services to depositors and to seek deposits more aggressively, to hold their own against competitive institutions operated for profit. Years ago, a court in New York held that "it is not legitimate for the trustees of such a bank to seek depositors at the expense of present depositors. It is their business to take deposits when offered." Now, savings banks in many cases do not hesitate to use a very small proportion of their income for publicity and advertising purposes to increase their size by securing new deposits. At the same time they have developed school savings accounts, Christmas savings clubs, investment service departments, etc.

The stock savings bank has lost ground rapidly, as shown below:

Year	Number of Institutions	Deposits[a]	Number of Depositors	Average Deposit
1914	1,466	$1,018,330	2,832,140	$473.04
1920	1,087	1,351,242	1,982,229	681.68
1924	990	1,746,609	3,562,017	490.34
1928	791	1,561,561	3,273,162	477.08
1932	502	832,536	1,617,737	514.63
1935	341	714,900	1,359,414	525.89

[a] 000 omitted.

Because of their location in agricultural areas for the most part, the larger portion of their resources is invested in farm mortgages.

The United States government was long importuned tc establish a government savings bank along the lines of the Euro pean government savings institutions. The postal savings sys tem was finally established by Act of Congress in 1910, but it efficacy as a competitor of private savings institutions has beer curtailed by the establishment of a 2 per cent interest rate. Offices of the postal savings system are established in man post offices throughout the country, and on June 30, 1935, de posits amounted to $1,204,843,784. They were greatly increase by the bank failure epidemic of the early 'thirties. Through th direct sales of ten-year "Baby Bonds" at a discount, with a maxi mum yield of 2.9 per cent per annum, the government has caused some shift of funds from the postal savings system to direct investment in its obligations.

The most important expansion of savings banking in recent years, however, has occurred in commercial banks.

Savings Departments of Commercial Banks

Commercial banks have long sought time deposits.[3] In fact, in parts of the country where lending opportunities have been few, commercial banks and trust companies have long acted chiefly as savings banks for their communities. Many large banks did not actively solicit savings deposits as such until recent years, and some do not do so even now.

The way was opened for the general entry of the large banks into the savings business when the Comptroller of the Currency, in 1903, ruled that "there does not appear to be anything in the National Bank Act which authorizes or prohibits the operation of a savings department by a national bank." The development of savings banking by commercial banks on a permanent basis required permission to purchase securities as well, and this was granted similarly in a ruling of the Comptroller of the Currency under Section 5136 of the Revised Statutes of the United States, which permits a national bank to discount and negotiate promissory notes, drafts, bills of exchange, *and other evidences of debt.*

The Federal Reserve Act recognized the special character of the savings deposit, and required a reserve of only 5, afterwards changed to 3, per cent against all time deposits. The McFadden Act of 1927 further provided for them by authorizing national banks to invest in bonds, stating that "the business of buying and selling investment securities shall hereafter be limited to buying and selling without recourse marketable obligations evidencing indebtedness . . . in the form of bonds, notes or debentures commonly known as 'investment securities' as may by regulation be prescribed by the Comptroller of

[3] Formerly such deposits were handled in a special manner, being evidenced by certificates of deposit. Now commercial banks in their savings departments more nearly approximate the practices of the mutual savings banks, with pass books to record deposits made.

the Currency." The Banking Act of 1935 further modified the statutory authority for member banks to buy bonds.

Member banks of the Federal Reserve System, under the Banking Act of 1935, may buy federal, state and municipal government obligations, and those guaranteed by the federal government. They may also invest in other bonds conforming to regulations issued by the Comptroller of the Currency, but only up to 10 per cent of the capital and surplus of each institution may be placed in the obligations of one obligor.

The Comptroller of the Currency has issued two regulations under this section of the law. The first of these, defining marketability, provides:

Under ordinary circumstances the term "marketable" means that the security in question has such a market as to render sales at intrinsic values readily available.

In determining whether a given security is marketable, it must meet the following minimum requirements:

(a) That the issue be of a sufficiently large total to make marketability possible;

(b) (1) That a public distribution of the securities must have been provided for or made in a manner to protect or insure the marketability of the issue, or, in the alternative (2) other existing securities of the issuer have such a public distribution as to protect or insure the marketability of the issue under consideration, and such issue must be registered under the provisions of the "securities Act of 1933" as amended, unless it is exempt from registration under Section 3 thereof.

(c) That where the security is issued under a trust agreement, the agreement must provide for a trustee independent of the obligor, and such trustee must be a bank or trust company.

The second, concerned with the quality of the security purchased, provides:

The purchase of "investment securities" in which the investment characteristics are distinctly or predominantly speculative, or "investment securities" of a lower designated standard than those which are distinctly or predominantly speculative, is prohibited.[4] The purchase of securities which are in default, either as to principal or interest, is also prohibited.

Purchase of an "investment security" at a price exceeding par is prohibited, unless the bank shall—

(a) Provide for the regular amortization of the premium paid, so that the premium shall be entirely extinguished at or before the maturity of the security and the security (including premium) shall at no intervening date be carried at an amount in excess of that at which the obligor may legally redeem such security; or

(b) Set up a reserve account in order to amortize the premium, said account to be credited periodically with an amount not less than the amount required for amortization under (a) above.

Purchase of securities convertible into stock at the option of the issuer is prohibited.

While the text of the regulation, through a footnote as shown below, provides for dependence upon rating manuals, this is not absolutely necessary. A number of banks insist upon depending on their own analysis to determine whether or not speculative characteristics predominate in any issue on which interest is being paid.

The Banking Acts of 1933 and 1935 provide for the setting of maximum interest rates on time and savings deposits by the Federal Reserve Board and the Federal Deposit Insurance Corporation. The former has issued regulations defining such deposits. A savings deposit under this rule is defined as any deposit for the account of an individual or eleemosynary corporation which is subject to thirty days' advance notice before withdrawal. In January, 1936, the maximum rate of interest was made 2½ per cent under this provision of the law.

The rise in the total of time deposits in commercial banks and trust companies in the pre-depression period and the subsequent decline, is summarized in the following table (in millions of dollars):

[4] "The terms employed herein may be found in recognized rating manuals, and where there is doubt as to the eligibility of a security for purchase, such eligibility must be supported by not less than two rating manuals."

Year	Time Deposits	Percentage of Total Deposits
1922	$ 6,129	20
1926	14,826	34
1928	18,197	42
1932	11,809	31
1935	11,182	28

The time deposits listed above include corporate deposits placed on this basis by the depositors to obtain interest, which is not payable on demand deposits.[5]

Segregation of assets of savings departments of commercial banks, on the ground that otherwise the investment of such funds will be inadequately regulated, has been advocated. Commercial banks may now solicit savings deposits on the same basis as a savings bank, and it may invest such funds in any way in which it would invest its ordinary demand deposits. However, such a segregation of assets would be a doubtful source of safety, since poor quality or frozen assets meeting certain tests could be used for the purpose.

The Investment Trust

The essential feature of savings banking is the assurance it gives the investor that his principal will be kept intact. However, because it is restricted in its operation and may receive only limited deposits, other intermediate investing institutions have arisen, designed to invest other people's money without the narrow restrictions typical of the savings bank. These other investing institutions for the most part stress their ability to give a larger income or appreciation of principal, rather than merely absolute security of principal with a limited rate of return.

Where such investing enterprises combine management with investment functions, they are more properly referred to as holding companies. Such concerns have played an important rôle in the consolidation and conduct of American industrial and public utility enterprises. Our primary concern here is

[5] See a discussion of "Bank Expansion versus Savings," by Benjamin M. Anderson, Jr., in *The Chase Economic Bulletin*, vol. viii, no. 2, June 25, 1928.

with the purely investment intermediaries, generally termed investment trusts.

An investment trust may be defined as an agency which combines the funds of numerous investors through sale of its own securities, and invests them primarily to obtain maximum return and appreciation. Although several types of investment trusts have lately been evolved in this country, the prototype of the investment trust was developed in Great Britain in the latter part of the nineteenth century, at a time when popular investment in securities became general in that country.

The British investment trust at first operated along speculative lines, but the debacle attending the Baring failure of 1890 brought about a drastic change in policy accompanied by an almost universal scaling down of captalization. As a result of the experience of that period, the British investment trust movement adopted more conservative practices, including in most cases the placing of profits realized on investments sold in reserve accounts, to offset actual or possible losses on other security holdings. Further, the British trusts have tended to restrict dividend payments on their shares to actual interest and dividend receipts on the securities held in the portfolio. Most of these trusts have learned also to diversify their holdings carefully, seeking a balance between stocks and bonds, the distribution of their funds among various industries, and geographical distribution of their investments. They have sought a larger return and increased their income chiefly by purchasing higher-yielding foreign securities. More speculative operations, including extensive trading and purchase of control of concerns, are left mainly for a distinct category of enterprises known as "finance companies," which more nearly approach our financial holding companies in character.

Several other features characterize current British investment trust operation. Most trusts aim to hold down operating expenses through obtaining an expert board of directors and through the maintenance of a single statistical organization by a number of trusts, resulting in the formation of several group organizations. They follow a policy of liberal publicity, a majority of them periodically making public a list of their holdings. Finally, they trade on the equity, issuing bonds and two or more classes of stock, thus concentrating speculative risks in the ordinary shares, while placing the senior securities in a strong, protected position, giving their bonds the status of trustee investments.

The investment trust was practically unknown in the United States until after 1920, although a few such investment organizations did arise here and there. Two factors then appeared to make the investment trust a common institution. In the first place, an enormous rise in security values got under way about 1922, and for years thereafter went forward at an accelerating pace. This gave the general public confidence in security investment, and also created numerous speculative opportunities which investment trusts were in a position to take advantage of. The large returns many of them were thus able to secure soon captivated the public imagination, and a veritable swarm of such organizations of various kinds and varying quality resulted. In the second place, the prostration of most capital markets abroad after the Great War created similar opportunities there, and some investment trusts based their appeal to investors on their ability to ferret out and acquire bargains in foreign securities.

The investment trust offers the investor two chief advantages: diversification of his holdings and expert management. For these advantages, the investment trust mechanism exacts a twofold tribute from investors: the original selling cost or "loading" and other benefits to the organizers, which must be deducted from the funds supplied by the investor, and the expenses of administering the trust, including the share in the income which, in one form or another, goes to the management. The investor is supposed to receive something for which he pays. The investment trust, unlike the mutual savings bank, admittedly is run on a straight business basis.

The rapid evolution of the investment trust in this country after 1920 resulted in many departures from the British model, and the development of varied forms of investment trust organizations. The four more important types developed were the general management, the specialized management, the fixed trust and the financial holding company. The relative importance of each type in January, 1929, is indicated by the following compilation:[6]

	Number	Paid-in Capital
General management	119	$ 781,000,000
Specialized management	32	136,000,000
Fixed	21	58,000,000
Financial holding companies	26	550,000,000
Total	198	$1,525,000,000

The General Management, Discretionary or "British-type" Trust or Fund

This type comes nearest to the original English prototype, and American trusts, especially the earlier ones, were often frankly meant to imitate what had been done abroad.

The general management investment trust is usually organized as a corporation, although in a few cases the legal form is that of a business trust. In practice, however, this generally proves a formalistic rather than an essential difference. Many of these organizations have traded on the equity, issuing bonds, preferred stock and common stock. When profits are large, the balance of income left after deducting interest and preferred stock dividends may give a really phenomenal rate of return on the junior shares; the rise in security prices after the war permitted investment trusts to make a remarkably successful record in the early years of their history. The bonds and preferred stocks are meant to appeal to more conservative investors, but such issues often acquire speculative characteristics through being made convertible into common stock, or having attached to them warrants to buy common stock at fixed prices. In January, 1929, the following analysis of capitalization was issued, covering 146 investment trusts of this general type, in terms of paid-in capital:[7]

	Amount	Percentage
Bonds and debentures	$200,000,000	20.5
Preferred stock	439,000,000	45.0
Common stock	337,000,000	34.5
Total	$976,000,000	100.0

[6] Made by Leland Rex Robinson. The financial holding company group excludes pure holding companies. During 1929, about $2,000,000,000 more was absorbed, chiefly by general management and financial holding companies.

[7] From data compiled by Leland Rex Robinson, published in the New York *Journal of Commerce.*

The securities of a general management investment trust have generally been distributed on different bases to the general public and to the management group. The general public, in the usual instance, subscribes for all or the bulk of the senior securities, while the management seeks to hold the junior shares, thus retaining control. Instances abound where the management acquired control with little investment.

The management of the trust is usually allowed to purchase and sell securities for investment at will, subject only to such general restrictions as the limitation of the percentage of resources that may be placed in one security or type of issue, or in one foreign country. It can thus operate for profits on turnover as well as interest and dividend income on investments, seeking security bargains and disposing of these issues when quotations rise to a point where better opportunities may be found elsewhere. By maintaining a statistical organization, at times of an elaborate nature, the management can be on the *qui vive* for opportunities in every industry and in every part of the globe. It can liquidate when security prices rise too high because of general speculative enthusiasm, and buy heavily when prices seem unduly depressed. It not only can help the small investor to avoid putting all his eggs in one basket, but it can see that the investor has most of his eggs in the right baskets.

The accounting practices of American investment trusts have differed radically from those of their British prototypes. When security prices rise, income from turnover may become a very important part—often the major portion—of investment trust earnings here. The usual British practice is to include in the trust's income for the year only interest and dividends received on securities in the portfolio, while trading profits go into a reserve account which protects the trust against future depreciation in the value of its investments. Only when profits have accumulated to a large sum over a period of years is any benefit passed on to shareholders in the form of a stock dividend. The American practice in the boom period after 1929 was diametrically opposite. The trusts reported income from both sources as current earnings, available for dividend payments, thus making a splendid showing. But when the markets subsequently declined sharply, the earning power reported in the year of many profits proved wholly illusory. When heavy losses were incurred, however, it was common here to charge them directly to surplus account.

The British trusts learned to put profits directly into reserves and thus make them unavailable for current dividends as a result of their sad experiences of the 'nineties of the last century. The wisdom of this policy was confirmed during the war, when security prices were sharply depressed generally. Presumably, this lesson has not yet been fully learned here.

The general management investment trusts fall into two broad groups as regards management, one of which includes trusts which are affiliated with investment houses, and the other, trusts which may lay claim to an independent status. Trusts affiliated with investment banking houses are in a position to enjoy certain advantages from being allowed to participate with the latter in their underwriting transactions, getting the full benefit of the underwriting syndicate's profit. The cost of distribution of their securities is reduced in many instances. They also enjoy the benefit of the statistical and other information possessed by the investment banking house, which may permit hem to avoid the burden of overhead expense entailed in the naintenance of a separate statistical organization. To offset hese gains, however, there is the presumptive suspicion that he judgment exercised in making the investments may be varped by the interests of the banking house. In certain cases, he publication of the list of security holdings of such a trust hows that in it were placed securities which the investment ouse found it difficult to dispose of elsewhere.

As practice becomes standardized, a number of these general nanagement investment trusts are raising their standards of peration, including the extent to which they make their affairs ublic. Most British investment trusts make their holdings ublic periodically. In the beginning, hardly any American usts did so; but when a "whispering campaign" was directed gainst several of them, especially those connected with investent banking houses whose underwriting record was not good, they were compelled to drop the veil of secrecy. The New York Stock Exchange thereafter insisted upon such publication, and since the depression this practice has become general.

The Investment Fund

A modification of the general management type of investment trust which has achieved major importance lately in the investment fund. One difficulty with the general management trust has been that their stocks have sold at substantial discounts below liquidating value, thus penalizing investors who have sought to liquidate their holdings through the market. Investors may withdraw from a fund whenever they wish on giving specified notice, at which time they will receive their principal and undistributed earnings, less certain small deductions. This withdrawal feature gives to the investor in the fund independence of the marketability feature. However, unlike the depositor in the mutual savings bank, what he gets on withdrawal is not always the original principal of his investment, for if the fund has suffered losses, he must stand his *pro rata* share of them. In the case of an accumulative fund, holders of certificates in the fund receive no current income, all earnings being reinvested to increase the principal.

The investment fund provides the dual advantages of expert management and diversification, without trading on the equity. Also, it gives the investor automatic liquidity by permitting him to withdraw at will. The management fee is usually a stated percentage of the capital, such as one-half of one per cent per annum. It has proved possible to operate such funds at lower cost than that of most of the other types of investment trusts.

The investment fund has been given a preferred status under the Revenue Act of 1936, which imposed a surtax on undistributed earnings of corporations. Under this law, organizations which qualify as *mutual investment trusts* may deduct dividends paid before computing their normal income tax. They are also exempt from the surtax on undistributed earnings.

Under the law, a mutual investment company is any corporation other than a personal holding company possessing the following characteristics:

1. It is organized for the purpose of and engaged almost exclusively in holding, investing, and reinvesting in stocks or securities.
2. At least 95 per cent of gross income is derived from dividends, interest or gains from sale of stocks or securities.
3. Less than 30 per cent of gross income comes from sale of stocks or securities held for less than six months.
4. At least 90 per cent of net income is distributed to shareholders as taxable dividends during the taxable year.
5. Its shareholders are on reasonable notice entitled to redemption of their stock for their proportionate interests less a discount not in excess of 3 per cent.

Despite the foregoing provisions, a corporation will not be considered as a "mutual investment company" if at any time during the taxable year:

1. It had outstanding any bonds or indebtedness in excess of 10 per cent of its gross assets, taken at cost, or
2. More than 5 per cent of the gross assets, taken at cost, was invested in any corporation, government, or political subdivision—except of the United States government, or
3. It owned more than 10 per cent of the outstanding stock or securities, or both, of any corporation.

Other less important restrictions are included in the statutory definition.

Through the income tax law, therefore, the federal government first sought to regulate the investment trust. This statutory provision has been criticized, however, because it encourages investment trusts to pay out turnover profits, a cardinal weakness of the device in the pre-1929 period, and also because it fails to provide for high standards of operation in other respects.

An independent attempt to regulate them by federal authority was provided for in the Public Utility Holding Company Act of 1935, which required the Securities and Exchange

Commission to investigate the trusts and report on them. This may lead to federal regulation of such institutions by this Commission. About 921 investment trusts and companies were found to come within the scope of this investigation, but not all of them were active when the study was undertaken in 1936.

Specialized Management Trusts

The specialized management investment trusts restrict their operations to a specifically delimited field. Most of them, in fact, operate in the banking, insurance, mining and aviation industries. The thought behind their organization is that certain fields of financial and business activity offer superior investment possibilities for investors who are willing to intrust their funds to the management of a group of men expert in such fields. These experts can then pick out the most desirable securities available there, and trade in and out of them as circumstances may dictate. Furthermore, in the fields of banking and insurance, prices of individual shares may be so high that diversification becomes unusually difficult without an intermediate investment organization which pools the funds of many individuals.

This type of investment trust may assume an important rôle in the future in the financing of new industries in this country. Within such new industries changes are often very rapid, and companies which at one stage of development appear to be very promising may be out of existence a few years later. The average financial analyst may be unable to appraise such securities intelligently, at least without the aid of technical experts who have a thorough knowledge of the industry. A specialized management trust run by technical men and bankers has here an especially broad opportunity. However, the tendency is to add certain control features which transform these organizations into holding companies.

The Fixed Trust

In the pure type of fixed trust, the investors' funds are place in a named list of securities, chosen once and for all at th inception of the trust. Against this list of securities, collatera shares are issued representing fractional ownership, usually i low denomination. The investor thus gains diversification, but the act of management takes place only at the start.

The theory behind the pure fixed trust is that a picked group of leading companies, taken together, should show a steady increase in the value of their equities, regardless of economic, industrial and financial changes. Hence, shares in a fixed trust are offered at all times, regardless of the state of the security markets or the condition of business. Whereas the general management investment trust sells many of its holdings and keeps its funds liquid when general declines in quotations are anticipated, the fixed trust remains undisturbed. It ignores the wide cyclical fluctuations in security prices, and invites the investor to look only on the long, upward secular movement of prices of shares in the leading corporations.

Such fixed trusts may operate either in the general run of securities, or in certain specified groups, such as oil stocks or bank stocks. In either case, the trust shares are issued as a small fractional interest in collateral deposited with a trust company; and those who so wish may, by securing a sufficient number of shares, turn them in to the trust company and get the deposited collateral. Thus, if a trust is formed in 30 named stocks, which together cost $10,000, 1,000 certificates may be sold against them, and the trust company will agree to turn over this collateral at any time against the offer of that number of certificates.

The shares in a fixed trust are generally sold by a sales company formed for the purpose of distribution. The price of the fixed trust shares to the public includes a varying loading charge covering selling, trustee and other expense. This surcharge has averaged about 10 per cent, and has been higher in individual instances. In the case cited, where 1,000 certificates are issued against stocks having a value of $10,000, each certificate would be sold to the public for $11 when a surcharge of 10 per cent is desired.

There are few pure fixed trusts in operation, most such organizations allowing the management some discretion. Thus, several of them permit a shift of the funds of the trust out of any security held which appears to the management to become a poor commitment in the course of time, into call loans, government bonds or securities on a named reserve list. Others operating within special industries, like bank stock trusts, permit the substitution of any other bank stock for one on the list which appears to have been over-priced, or for some other reason becomes undesirable. In such cases, the fixed trust approaches the specialized management trust in character.

Fixed trusts were most popular in 1930 and 1931, but the subsequent regulation in the security markets caused the public to lose interest in them. It became evident that cyclical risks could not be ignored by investors.

Financial Holding Companies

A number of investing organizations have at various times sought to combine with the pure investment function a degree of control and management. This places them midway between the investment trust and the more common holding company. While far from standardized, they are sometimes described as financial holding companies. The financial holding company is a most ubiquitous type of investment trust, being organized under such names as "holding," "omnium" or trust in England, France, Belgium, Germany, Switzerland and Austria.

The combination of investment with control of enterprises in which investments are made is a particularly difficult type of business, as the past records of such organizations as Credit Mobilier, Kreuger & Toll, Goldman Sachs Trading Corporation and others, amply demonstrate. These enterprises buy control, build up a corporation by expansion, merger, reorganization, or otherwise, and then seek to sell out to others, freeing their funds for other similar ventures. It is usually much more difficult to sell out than to buy, however, and when markets decline these enterprises are often found overextended.

The Trust Company

The trust company differs from other investing institutions in that it offers individual and personal service, both during the life and after the death of the investor. For the most part, the trust company necessarily appeals to the individual of relatively large means, although as the volume of business has grown it has become profitable in smaller trust companies to handle accounts even as small as a few thousand dollars.

The trust company has enjoyed its greatest growth in this country, where it has had more than a century of development. The first trust company of which record has been preserved is the Massachusetts Hospital Life Insurance Company, chartered in 1818. Funds placed on deposit with the company as a trust fund were aggregated and managed by it for a fee of one-half of one per cent of the capital. In fact, this company resembled most closely the investment trust fund of the type recently developed and described above. It is still in operation.

The first company which received legislative powers to act in a fiduciary capacity was the Farmers' Fire Insurance and Loan Company, organized in New York in 1822, and later known as the Farmers' Loan and Trust Company. With the subsequent growth in the number of large individual fortunes, trust business grew rapidly, so that by the time of the Civil War about a score of such organizations were in existence. After the war, the large growth of the corporate form of organization created a great deal of so-called corporate trust business in connection with the issuance of securities, while the enormous increase in the number and size of large fortunes at the same time led to a vast increase in the so-called personal trust business. One after another, these companies also entered the banking business, at first without supervision, but gradually under restrictions similar to, but often more liberal than, those governing the operation of commercial banks with state charters.

In accord with the general tendency of banking toward the combination of many functions within one institution, trust departments have been opened by many national and state banks. The Federal Reserve Act of 1913 gave national banks the privilege of exercising trust powers, and this was further facilitated by the McFadden Act of 1927, giving these institutions perpetual charters for the first time. By 1935, national banks held over $9,000,000,000 in personal trust accounts, each trust account amounting to an average of $71,322.

No inclusive data on the total volume of trust funds have ever been compiled, although a survey in the State of Pennsylvania showed that trust companies and trust departments of other banks in that state held in excess of $4,000,000,000 in trust in 1929. For the country as a whole, the total may reach $30,000,000,000, including all types of personal trust business.

Types of Trust Business

The trust company plays several rôles in American investment banking. First, the banking department often possesses a large proportion of time deposits, and thus acts in the same capacity as a stock savings bank. Secondly, the corporate trust business, wherein these companies act as trustees under corporate mortgages and as transfer agents and registrars for stock issues, facilitates the security transactions of other investment banking agencies. In the third place, trust companies, like many commercial banks, may maintain security departments, which operate within the limits laid down by the Banking Act of 1933. Finally, they act as out-and-out investment institutions in the handling of personal trusts. We turn to a discussion of this most important part of their investment banking business.

Under a personal trust, the trust company supervises and manages the investments of individuals under stated conditions. Personal trusts fall into two broad classes, testamentary and living. A testamentary trust, the more important type, involves the rôles of executor and administrator under wills, and appointment as guardian and conservator of the property of infants. Originally, practically all trust business involved the care of property after the death of the creator of the trust. Lately, however, the trust company has to a growing extent been looked upon as a convenient agency for specialized management of an individual's affairs before his death as well.

The trust company is in a position to prove of inestimable value in testamentary trusts because it can give a special and personal service for which no other investing institution is qualified. A trust company not only can act as executor and administrator and supervise the investment of an estate, but it can also manage the expenditure of the income or principal after the death of the owner where this is desired. It claims several advantages over the individual executor or administrator for this function—it has perpetual life, specialized technical ability, and it can better avoid the family and other prejudices and squabbles in which individual trustees are often involved.

A special form of service that may be rendered is the life insurance trust. This trust consists of life insurance policies which will be paid into the trust and invested and disbursed according to the wishes of the testator upon the latter's death. In 1929, life insurance policies at the rate of about $1,000,000,000 yearly were being placed with trust companies, several of which formed special departments for this business. Another special development in this connection was a combination of savings accounts with life insurance which several trust companies developed in their banking departments.

The trust company has one peculiar feature as an investing institution—its fees are limited by law in most states. In New York State, for example, the fee consists of a percentage of the principal, combined with a percentage of the annual income. The fee on the principal, payable one-half when the trust becomes effective and the other half when it is terminated, amounts to 5 per cent on the first $2,000, 2½ per cent on the next $20,000, 1½ per cent on the next $28,000, and 2 per cent on all amounts over $50,000. The income fee, payable annually, consists of 5 per cent on the first $2,000 of income, 2½ per cent on the next $20,000 of income, 1½ per cent on the next $28,000 of income, and 2 per cent on all income over $50,000. Special agreements between the testator and the trustee may supersede these legal fees.

Living trusts are made by an individual for the benefit of himself or others during his lifetime. They come into effect immediately, thus differing from the testamentary trusts, which become effective only after the death of the testator. The living trust is generally revocable.

In addition to full-fledged trusts, the trust companies offer agency services of various kinds. Since they do not then assume full legal responsibility, the fees are substantially smaller. One type of such agency service has been termed by trust men "guardian custodianship." This service includes investment advice, securities analysis, and the development of a definite investment program. The trust companies recognize a trend in investment away from high-grade low-yielding bonds and toward diversified common stock commitments, and they seek to adapt their supervision to such conditions. In discussing this service, a trust officer has said:[8]

> The eight main advantages of guardian custodianship are: authoritative and continuous information, a scientific and carefully balanced program, automatic follow-up, due warning on unfavorable investments, relief from solicitation by unscrupulous security salesmen, automatic attention to subscription rights, conversion privileges, etc., composite judgment of a group of seasoned specialists and financiers, and control with relief from all administrative detail.

The trust company may restrict its activity merely to the physical care and handling of the securities, leaving the owner full control over his investment policy. In this case, the trust company becomes merely the nominee, the securities being vested in its name to facilitate transfer, tax reports, etc. In cases where only safekeeping and collection of current income are desired, the fee is reduced accordingly.

A cardinal principle of trust company operation in general is the segregation of assets, by which the trust funds are kept distinct from the funds of the trustee. In most states, and under the regulations of the Federal Reserve Board governing trust departments of national banks, corporate fiduciaries are specifically forbidden to mingle trust funds either with their own funds or with those of other trusts. However, trust companies hope to work out commingled funds which they can manage for numerous smaller investors along investment fund lines.

Investing Activities

With regard to investment policy, individual trusts may be discretionary as to the manner in which the property of the trust is to be invested. Where the grantor of the trust specifically designates the securities or property that are to stay in the

[8] A. F. Young, Vice-president of the Guardian Trust Company of Cleveland, before the Tenth Mid-winter Trust Conference of the American Bankers Association of America, New York, 1928.

trust, the trustee of course has no voice at all in the matter. This type is sometimes called a designated trust. If no statement as to the manner of investment is made, the trustee is restricted to the purchase of investments which are designated as legal trustee investments by the law of the state. Where the trustee does not adhere to the specific instructions of the trust instrument, or the legal trust investments where none are specified in the trust instrument, he is liable for all losses so incurred, and for each loss so incurred without regard to offsetting profits on other unauthorized investments.

Investments legal for trustees are generally specifically designated in the state laws, although in some states the surrogate's court rules on this matter.[9] The list of legal investments in the eastern states usually coincides roughly with the group of investments which are legal for savings bank funds. In New York State, trustees are allowed to invest in the same securities as savings banks, except that they are subject to less stringent limitations in purchasing real estate mortgages.

The trust company is a very elastic and adaptable type of investing institution. By restricting investment to "legals," which can be done either specifically or simply by making no mention of investments in the trust agreement, the same ultra-conservative canons that govern savings bank investment may be secured for trust funds. On the other hand, the trust agreement may confine the trust to common stocks alone, and this has been done to an increasing degree in recent years.

The law endeavors to assure, as far as feasible, the independence of the trustee. With this in view, a trust department of a banking institution which also has a bond department may not purchase securities directly from the latter, although it may purchase from others securities in which the bond department is interested.

A basic problem in trust company operation is its liability in case of loss on the investments it handles. The trustee is under the control of the courts of equity, and a number of decisions

[9] In Massachusetts, the trustee is given a wide range of discretion in his investing activities when no instructions are given in the trust deed, but his responsibility for loss in case he does not exercise the caution of a "prudent man" is correspondingly greater.

have been handed down in these courts to create general standards governing such liability. The trustee is expected to exercise due diligence in the performance of his trust, and is held liable for losses caused by carelessness or lack of prudence in the management of the trust investments, except where no discretion is allowed him by the terms of the contract. The prime consideration should be safety of principal, although the trustee has also been held bound to secure the best return on the trust investments compatible with safety. The trustee, in other words, is expected to follow the same course of action as a prudent private investor.[10]

An interesting example of the delicacy of this problem of trustee responsibility is the way in which the trust companies reacted to the discussion over the status of German investments which arose in 1927. Many trust companies held German bonds in clients' accounts. Owing to the so-called transfer clause in the Dawes Plan and the terms of the Treaty of Versailles, which made reparations payments a first charge on Germany, the ability of the obligors on these bonds to make interest payments abroad was subject to some question. At least one trust company, in the desire to avoid liability later, as well as to protect clients' interests, felt called upon to dispose of such bonds when held in estates, and to give notice that such issues should be disposed of where there were individual co-trustees sharing investment responsibility.

The experience of the depression has caused trust companies generally to expand their statistical and research departments. Numerous suits to recover damages from trust companies on account of alleged gross neglect of duty and lack of due diligence were brought by beneficiaries. It was found that the ability to show that extensive statistical work was being done in connection with investments made it less likely that the trust company would be surcharged in such suits.

Increased tax and other legal work, as well as this enlarged analytical service, has raised the cost of trust company operation considerably. Hence, profit margins have become much more narrow; and it is likely that if these trends persist, the

[10] A fuller discussion of the practical aspects of these investment responsibilities is given in Chapter XXI below.

average level of fees may in time have to be raised considerably. This will be true particularly if large trusts continue to become less common because of heavy taxation on wealth. In fact, some trust men believe that the chief administrative problem for this type of financial institution in the future will be the evolution of a technique for handling numerous small trusts at fees sufficient to yield a moderate profit.

Investment Counsel

The investing institutions thus far considered take over the management of the funds of the investor and keep custody of the securities purchased. In the case of the savings bank and investment trust, these funds are merged with those of numerous other investors. The trust company keeps the securities of each individual separately. More recently, there has been a marked growth of a group of organizations that restrict themselves entirely to the management of portfolios. These investment counsel organizations merely advise investors and supervise their holdings. They do not take custody of securities, and the client is at liberty to decide whether or not he will follow this professional advice.

The investment counsel thus gives part of the service which the trust company performs, but it specializes solely in this work. Its fees are smaller, averaging less than one-half of one per cent per annum for large accounts. For the large investor who wants expert advice, without giving up control over the investment of his funds to secure it, the investment counsel has often proved adequate. Financial statistical agencies and, as we have already seen, investment and brokerage houses have developed investment counsel as a by-product of their other functions.

It will be noted that in this advisory capacity the investment counsel may do virtually the same work as the sales and service departments of the investment house. However, the investment counsel has the advantage of being impartial in his service, if he is true to the best interests of his client, since he has nothing to sell.

The investment counsel organization is created along well-defined lines. It has a statistical and research department in which trained security analysts study broad economic trends, the status of individual industries and particular companies. These data are then made available to the supervisors, who translate the work of the statistical and research department into specific suggestions for individual accounts that are watched directly by account executives.

Some investment counsel organizations now manage upwards of $100,000,000 of funds. However, the cost of acquiring accounts and of renewing them early constitutes a serious item of expense, running as high as 30 per cent of the fees received. In this respect, trust companies are in a much more favorable position, since they are not concerned about the annual renewal of contracts with clients. Their total cost of acquiring and keeping business on the books is estimated at about 5 per cent of the fees received.

Summary

Three important types of investing institutions have been organized in this country to invest the money of numerous individual investors. The savings bank, collecting the funds of investors in the form of deposits, invests them under rigid legal restrictions designed for great safety at the expense of the size of the return. It assures the investor conservation of, and the right to withdraw, his principal at all times. The investment trust, in its numerous forms, sells its securities to collect the funds of investors, and invests these funds subject only to any self-imposed regulations the management chooses to adopt. Safety of principal is subordinated for the most part to securing a larger return. Thirdly, the trust company and investment counsel stand ready to give an individualized type of service, caring for the property and funds of each individual separately, both in life and after death.

As the function of investment calls for more and more specialized skill, and as the volume of invested wealth increases, these investing institutions grow in size and importance, and profoundly affect the whole field of investment banking. The investment house, which originates and distributes securities, finds that its selling is done increasingly to these investing institutions, rather than directly to private investors. Conversely, the individual investor finds that his investment requirements can be handled more effectively by one or another of these investing institutions, as they increase in number and in the extent of the services they perform.

From the point of view of the investment houses, these investing institutions constitute a wholesale market of great size for their issues, but of a special nature. In the first place, the investing is subject to certain regulations, which have been summarized in this chapter. Secondly, in the case of the investment trust especially, the investment houses have gained a measure of control over these institutions to assure their power of distribution.

From the individual investor's standpoint, these investing institutions must be appraised by the same tests that he applies to securities—safety of principal, stability and size of income, possibilities of appreciation, convenience and freedom from care, etc. In addition, the investor must determine how much he pays for the service and other benefits which the investing institution performs. If, for example, in a well-managed investment trust too large a part of the income is absorbed by the management, he may pay too dearly for this expert supervision of his investments.

One illuminating study of comparative costs to the investor for having his funds managed by various investing institutions shows that, for each $1,000 of property managed, the annual cost is about $5 in a savings bank or investment trust; $10 to $20 in a testamentary trust where the trust company acts as executor and $2.50 where it acts as trustee, and $5 to $10 where the property is managed by an investment counsel.[11]

References

Fowler, J. E., Jr., *American Investment Trusts,* New York, 1928.

Grayson, T. J., *Investment Trusts, Their Origin, Development and Operation,* New York, 1928.

Kniffen, William H., *The Savings Bank and Its Practical Work,* New York, 1928.

Moulton, H. G., *Financial Organization of Society,* Chicago, 1925, chaps. xiv, xvi, xvii.

[11] von Tresckow, Walter, *Can Trust Profits be Improved?* Young & Ottley, Inc., 1935.

RIDDLE, N. G., *Investment Policy of Trust Institutions,* Chicago, 1934.

ROBINSON, L. R., *Investment Trust Organization and Management,* New York, 1926.

SMITH, J. G., *The Development of Trust Companies in the U. S.,* New York, 1928, chaps. iv and xvii.

STEINER, W. H., *Investment Trusts—American Experience,* New York, 1929.

STEPHENSON, G. T., *Living Trusts,* New York, 1926, chaps. ii and iii.

TRESCKOW, WALTER VON, *Can Trust Profits be Improved?* Young & Ottley, Inc., 1935.

TWENTIETH CENTURY FUND, *The Security Markets,* New York, 1935, chaps. vi and xvi.

Chapter VI

INSTITUTIONAL INVESTORS

Types of Institutional Investors

The preceding chapters have been devoted to a description of those institutions which are concerned with investment banking as their primary purpose. The security middleman—the investment house—forms the link between the capital market in general and the borrower or issuer of capital stock. A secondary market for these securities, which imparts marketability to them, has been developed with the aid of brokers, dealers and the stock exchanges. Specializing in the function of investing other people's money, and thereby forming a link between the investor and the capital market, is the investing institution—be it the savings bank, the investment trust or the trust company.

In addition, a number of institutions formed primarily to carry on other functions play an important rôle in the capital market as huge buyers of securities. Their other activities lead to the accumulation of funds which they must invest. When these funds take on very large proportions, the investment function, originally incidental, assumes great importance in the operation of these organizations.

The most important of these institutions for which investing is an incidental rather than a primary function is the insurance company. Formed for the purpose of spreading risks over the community, the insurance companies in the course of their operation accumulate reserves which make them at the present time the most important single class of buyers of investment bonds. Life insurance companies have investments aggregating well over twenty billions of dollars today.

The commercial bank, long defined as an institution of discount, deposit and issue or exchange, has been profoundly modified by recent economic and financial developments. Its investment functions have been largely expanded, even outside of the field of the savings department. Thus, in addition to being an investing institution, the commercial bank is becoming, even in connection with its commercial banking functions, an institutional investor as well, placing in bonds the funds held as demand, as well as time, deposits.

The general run of business corporations are also becoming increasingly important as institutional investors. Many individual corporations act incidentally as investment trusts, holding hundreds of millions of dollars of securities of other companies, both within and without their own individual field of activity. Naturally, they cannot be ignored as factors in the capital market.

Universities, hospitals, churches, charitable organizations and foundations are all important buyers of securities. Their holdings in the aggregate amount to billions of dollars. Furthermore, the wealth in the hands of these institutions tends to increase from year to year, as the men who made great fortunes in the recent rapid expansion of the country's business structure pass on and follow the usual custom of leaving some part of their wealth to these eleemosynary institutions.

Insurance Companies

The business of insurance, one of the oldest in our economic order, steadily grows in importance with the increasing complexity and scope of economic activity. Insurance seeks to protect the individual by spreading the economic risks to which he is subject over large numbers of people. It is based on the fundamental rule that death and accidents happen to only a small number of people at one time, and therefore the individual may be protected from their adverse financial effects by means of small regular payments to a common fund. This is effected by collecting small sums from numerous people and using the fund thus gathered to pay losses to the individuals subject to the hazard against which it is sought to guard them.

The fund gathered to pay losses naturally assumes very large proportions as the insurance enterprise grows in size. It must be kept as a reserve from which losses are paid, thus making the insurance companies large holders of capital collected from the whole community, and kept for it. While the individuals taking out insurance protection do not always consider saving their major objective, the insurance company incidentally becomes the largest single type of saving and investing machine in the country.

There are two important types of insurance, differentiated by the nature of the hazard. Life insurance and such related types as old age and pension insurance seek to insure against a hazard certain to occur. The purpose of such insurance is to give economic protection to those who will be affected by the death of the individual insured, and the protective fund must be kept intact until this occurs. Hence, the reserves of life insurance companies become particularly large, for they must keep the funds of the insured over a long series of years until death closes the contract and makes payable the amount of the insurance. By including large numbers of people, the individual insurance company can avoid suffering very heavy losses at one time, and can keep payments from the reserve fund to a fairly regular rate. In fact, owing to the general growth of wealth, the improvement of medical science and the steady spread of the practice of taking out life insurance, the assets of these companies have increased by leaps and bounds during the past decade, and the reserve funds have grown rapidly despite the steady drain caused by payments on policies which have matured, either because of their limited term or because of the death of the insured.

Another group of insurance companies insures against a hazard which is by no means certain. The oldest form of insurance is marine insurance, which protects shipowners from casualties of the sea. Fire insurance is of a similar nature, as are accident, surety and other forms of insurance against events which may or may not happen. Casualty insurance of all kinds is generally written to cover one particular event, such as the voyage of a ship, or a short period of time, such as one- to five-year policies for fire insurance. The reserves of these companies naturally are much smaller as a result, and there is no steady accumulation of premiums over long periods of time against an eventual certain risk such as death. At the end of the period of insurance, all liability of the company ends, and any sums left over after all losses and expenses have been paid constitute its underwriting profit.

From the point of view of investment banking, the insurance companies are of special interest in two respects. In the first place, as large investors, the nature of their investment needs and the conditions under which they may and do purchase securities are of vital import. Secondly, from the point of view of the individual, their efficiency and desirability as investment institutions must be compared with other investing institutions and institutional investors.

Life Insurance Operation

To furnish a background for understanding the problems facing life insurance companies as investors, a brief review of their operating methods is necessary.

All life insurance involves the payment of premiums, as individual contributions to an insurance fund are called, out of which benefits are paid to the beneficiaries named by those insured persons who die during the period for which they are insured. It is evident that insurance companies must determine these probable death losses in advance. This is done on the basis of an American experience table of mortality, which gives the probable number of deaths which would occur at each age in a group of 1,000 persons. The American experience table was prepared from empirical data many years ago, and is now considerably out of date, as the average expectation of life has risen materially in the meanwhile. Its continued use therefore, means that premium rates are more conservative than need be.

From the point of view of the insurance company, premiums received are its chief source of income, and death benefits paid constitute the mortality cost. Income is further increased by earnings on the investment of premium funds, pending the time when they are distributed to beneficiaries as death losses. This investment income may be regarded as certain if the investments of the company are conservatively made. For this reason, life insurance premiums are reduced to allow for these expected earnings on the reserves. As a matter of fact, American companies, in computing their premiums, generally allow for earnings of 3 per cent on their reserves, and reduce the amount due from policyholders accordingly. On the other hand, premiums are increased because of the expenses of operation of the insurance companies, resulting in a "loading," or additional charge.

The net earnings of the insurance company arise from three important sources. In the first place, because of the use of the obsolete American experience table and because of the rising standard of health in this country which accompanies the rising standard of living, death losses, or mortality expenses as they are called, are smaller than anticipated. In the second place, earnings on invested reserves generally have amounted to considerably more than the 3 per cent expected. Thirdly, most companies, especially in view of the rapid growing volume of insurance written, keep their expenses below the "loading" which is added to the premium. These net earnings in the case of mutual companies, which are owned by policyholders in much the same way as mutual savings banks are owned by depositors, are distributed to policyholders in the form of "dividends." They are obviously not true "dividends," however, but really represent an overcharge made to policyholders in their premiums, which is returned in this way. Where these "dividends" are paid, policies are said to be participating. Where the company is privately organized and these net earnings belong to the stockholders, the policies are called non-participating.

A final important feature of insurance company operation is the so-called level premium plan which is in general use. If an individual takes out an ordinary life insurance policy calling for the payment of a fixed sum to his beneficiary at the time of his death, he will be required to make yearly payments as long as he lives. Actually, these payments should be on an ascending scale, for as he grows older there is greater likelihood of death, and therefore larger payments are required from all persons insured in that particular age group. But a scheme of rising annual premiums, while mathematically necessary, is in point of fact impractical, since the individual's ability to pay premiums tends to decline with age, after a peak of earning power is reached somewhere in middle life. Furthermore, the average individual's living expenses rise with age up to a certain point. Hence, the universal practice has been adopted by life insurance companies of fixing a uniform annual premium, involving overpayments in the earlier period of the life of the policy so as to build up a reserve which reduces the amount of insurance provided. It is these overpayments which are largely responsible for the great size of insurance company reserves. They constitute a form of savings, rather than insurance proper.

Were it not for this level premium plan, insurance companies would tend to pay out yearly almost as much as they receive in premiums. Under this plan, however, a gradually declining portion goes into the reserve out of which part of the death benefit can be paid. The size of this reserve is increased when the policy calls for payments for only a limited number of years, or when premium payments are further enlarged in endowment policies. The reserve accumulated against any policy constitutes its "cash surrender value," which the company will return to the insured if he wishes to cancel the policy. If also constitutes the "loan value" of the policy, or the amount which it is willing to lend to the policyholder with the policy as collateral.

Insurance Company Investments

Insurance companies, because of their close contact with the mass of the population, are subject to regulation by state law Although state laws are far from uniform, nevertheless the requirements of the stricter states are generally complied with by life insurance companies. The reason for this is that the insurance company, while incorporated in one state, generally does business in many others as well. In order to be permitted to do business in, or be "admitted" to, others than their home state, insurance companies must conform to the laws of the strictest state in which they operate.

The insurance company usually has three funds from which its investments are made. First, there is the capital provided by the stockholders, except in the case of a mutual company which is run on the same principle as the mutual savings bank and is owned by the policyholders. In the second place, there is the surplus retained by the company from its past earnings

Last and by far the most important, and constituting the great bulk of the investment fund, there is the premium reserve paid in by policyholders, and held against future mortality losses.

The laws governing the investments of life insurance companies are less strict than those applicable to mutual savings banks; and the tendency has lately been to liberalize them further, in order to permit these companies to obtain moderately high yields on their investments as the volume of their assets has continued to grow from year to year. The annual increase in reserves has recently been in the neighborhood of a billion dollars annually, a very large sum to be newly invested each year. The laws are not always designed to give maximum return consistent with safety, which should be the case in justice to policyholders. Frequently, extraneous considerations, such as the desire to induce companies to invest in favored localities or industries, govern. Thus, in Iowa and Nebraska, life insurance companies are restricted in the main to local securities, which means that the larger part of their funds actually go into farm mortgages in these agricultural states. The serious dangers of thus artificially delimiting the field of investment are readily apparent.

Laws governing life insurance company investments in the everal states usually provide three separate sets of rules. The apital and surplus, usually up to the minimum required by aw, are subject to specially stringent regulations. For foreign ompanies doing business within a state, the laws usually proide for special deposits of securities, subject to similar stringent equirements, that must be left with the superintendent of inurance. The remaining funds of the company, including the eserves and any part of the capital and surplus not covered by he above laws, are generally regulated by a third and less ringent series of regulations. These latter regulations determine, of course, the investment of the great bulk of insurance unds.

Under the laws of New York State, which govern the investment of more than half of all life insurance company funds in his country, the companies are allowed to purchase:

1. United States government and municipal bonds.
2. First mortgages on improved real estate up to 66 2/3 per cent of the value of the property.
3. Bonds of corporations which have earned at least 4 per cent on their capital stock for at least five years.
4. Secured bonds of solvent corporations, of which not more than one-third of the security is capital stock.
5. Preferred stocks of corporations which have earned at least 4 per cent on their capital stock for at least five years.

There was in this country in 1929 over $23,000,000,000 of life insurance company funds invested according to the legal requirements. This fund represented payments made by 63,000,000 individual policyholders, covering some $100,000,000,000 of life insurance policies. The distribution of this investment fund has been determined by the Association of Life Insurance Presidents, which makes an annual study of changes therein. A chart showing these changes over a period of years is shown in Fig. 6. Data made available by the association, covering more than 90 per cent of the assets of all life insurance companies held by 52 reporting companies, show the following distribution of assets on December 31, 1935:[1]

Security	Amount	Percentage of Total Assets
Farm mortgages	$ 927,000,000	4.4
Other mortgages	3,914,000,000	18.3
United States government bonds	2,502,000,000	11.7
Other government bonds	1,659,000,000	7.8
Railroad bonds and stocks	2,930,000,000	13.7
Public utility bonds and stocks	2,212,000,000	10.4
Other bonds and stocks	793,000,000	3.7
Policy loans	3,221,000,000	15.1
Real estate	1,905,000,000	8.9
Cash	750,000,000	3.5
Other admitted assets	537,000,000	2.5
	$21,350,000,000	100.0

The above figures show that 22.7 per cent of the assets of these companies were in the form of mortgages, about half the

[1] *Proceedings* of the Association of Life Insurance Presidents, New York, 1935 pp. 12-13.

RELATIVE GROWTH OF LIFE INSURANCE ASSETS, 1906-1935

(Of Companies Holding from 91.6% to 98.4% of the Assets of all U.S. Legal Reserve Companies, See Table I)

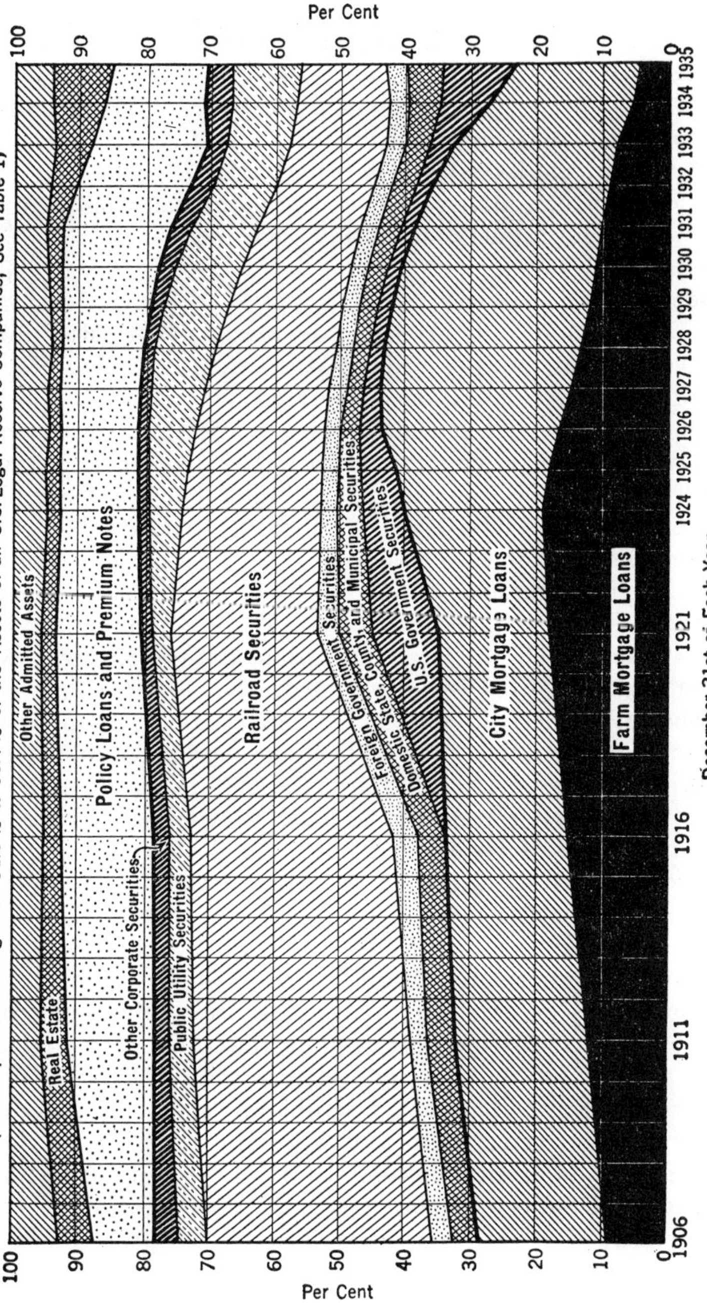

December 31st of Each Year

Fig. 6

rates of a decade ago, while 47.3 per cent were in bonds and stocks, almost entirely the former. They also show a preponderance of security investment in the railroad field, although there has lately been a strong tendency in favor of United States government and public utility issues, so that the percentage invested in the latter field is rising at the expense of railroad issues as the new money received by the companies as premiums flows into government and utility securities.

Depression Experience

The widespread deflation and depression of the early 'thirties served to bring out the elements of strength, as well as of weakness, in the various types of investing institutions and institutional investors. Those which possessed assets that corresponded in a general way with the character of their liabilities were able to meet the test with good results. On the other hand, where frozen or slow assets were held to cover current obligations, disaster often intervened.

The life insurance companies, in general, met the test of the depression in impressive fashion. While a number of smaller companies failed, the large institutions did not require any direct assistance from the government, their cash income being sufficient to meet the outgo. The basic reason for this was, of course, the fact that their obligations mostly become payable only in the event of death. Only the policy loan privilege and the right to permit policies to lapse caused a serious drain on cash, and after the banking moratorium of 1933 these privileges were restricted for a time. As long as policyholders may borrow the bulk of their reserves from the company, the insurance company must stand ready to perform a banking service and should be sufficiently liquid to meet such demands, even though they become large only under quite abnormal conditions. The sharp increase in the proportion of government bonds held by life insurance companies during the past few years represents, therefore, a significant additional precaution against heavy demands for policy loans.

However, life insurance companies did sustain severe losses through defaults on mortgages and subsequent foreclosures, and through interest defaults and decline in price of some of the bonds held, particularly railroad bonds. Here, again, it is possible for the companies to adjust their operations to unfavorable conditions through a reduction in dividends paid to policyholders, and moderate reductions have been made. Furthermore, since the mortality experience table in use is more conservative than need be, the reserves on hand are actually larger than will be required.

The period of extremely low money rates inaugurated in 1934 created new problems for the companies. Current premium rates allow for earnings of 3 per cent on the reserves, and if this rate cannot be obtained then savings on mortality costs and expenses will have to be used to make up the difference. This would tend to force further reductions in dividends to policyholders in the future. However, this problem would arise only if the decline in interest rates should continue, and if they should remain at a low level for a period of years.

Life Insurance as an Investment

We have thus far considered the life insurance company as an investor. In reaching a definite appraisal of the full value of this type of institution as currently operated, it is also necessary to consider it from the point of view of the individual investor.

The purest type of life insurance is called term insurance, which runs for a limited period of years. In the case of a one-year term policy, no reserve need be set up out of the premium at the end of the year, so that the premium need be large enough to cover only the death losses paid on such policies during the year, plus expenses of operation. There is no investment element involved. But in actual practice, the bulk of insurance policies are not of the term variety. There are three important types of life insurance policies, in addition to the term policies. These are:

1. *Straight or ordinary life insurance,* which gives protection for life and requires annual premiums to be paid as long as the policyholder lives. The excess premiums paid at a declining rate in a straight life insurance policy actually constitute an investment for the insured, on which he is allowed 3 per cent and any excess earnings which the company may distribute

in the form of "dividends." The investment character of these excess payments is indicated by the fact that the policyholder may withdraw them by canceling his insurance, getting back the "cash surrender value," or excess payments. In the event of death, the payment to the beneficiary consists of this reserve, plus insurance sufficient to make up the face value of the policy.

2. *Limited payment life insurance* gives protection for life, but limits the number of payments due to a specified number of years. Here the savings or investment feature is further developed. The annual payments are larger than the premiums due in straight life insurance, the overpayments with interest thereon constituting a sum sufficient to pay the premiums for the balance of the expected life span of the individual. This form of insurance is in essence a combination of straight life insurance with an additional savings plan whereby an individual in his years of larger earnings accumulates a reserve out of which to pay premiums in the later years of reduced earning power.

3. *Endowment insurance* emphasizes equally the insurance and savings and investment aims of the individual. The annual payments here are much larger, equaling, with 3 per cent compound interest, at the end of a stated period of time the full face value named in the policy. The insurance equals this amount throughout the life of the policy, but if the insured survives to the end of the policy term he receives the accumulated sum intact. This type of contract is the equivalent of insurance protection for the period during which payments are made, plus a savings feature whereby the individual accumulates for his own benefit a sum of money paid to him in full at the end of the policy period, for which he makes additional payments to the insurance company.

It will be noted that these four forms of insurance policies differ primarily in the extent to which the investment element is added to the pure insurance factor. Considered purely in an investment aspect, life insurance naturally results in the accumulation of a considerably smaller sum than is possible through the placing of funds in savings banks or in conservative investment securities. The reason for this is that a part of the premium, or annual payment, goes to pay mortality losses of the company. The table below compares the accumulation which results from purchase of different types of insurance policies with that possible from investment of an equivalent sum at 4½ per cent compound interest, assuming an investor could obtain this rate with safety from investing institutions or securities. Of course, it must be remembered that the investor does not then get the insurance protection which creates a substantial estate for his beneficiaries before he has had the opportunity to accumulate a large fund for them out of savings.

Type of Policy	Annual Premium[a]	Accumulated Reserve, Equal to "Cash Surrender Value"			Sum Accumulated by 4½ Per Cent Compound Interest in 20 Years
		End of 5 years	End of 10 years	End of 20 years	
Straight life.....	20.38	$ 45.76	$ 98.94	$ 230.50	$ 653.31
20-payment life..	30.56	95.49	208.95	504.59	949.80
20-payment endowment......	48.27	185.39	407.79	1,000.00	1,500.23

[a] Average, 8 large companies.

The majority of persons taking out life insurance do so because they want immediate protection against the hazard of death, and are not in a position to wait for the long and slow process of accumulating a large principal sum through investment. From their point of view, the problem is not one of whether or not insurance is desirable in itself, for the answer to that question is necessarily in the affirmative. The real question is which of the several types of insurance is most desirable.

There are three factors to consider in answering this question. In the first place, the insurance policy has an advantage over most other forms of investment, in that it constitutes an automatic system for regular savings so that the investor has little opportunity for succumbing to the temptation of failing to make his payments. From the point of view of the rate of return received, on the other hand, the insurance company does not always measure up as favorably. Investors could obtain more flexible management for their funds by taking out the cheaper kinds of insurance—preferably term or straight life policies—and investing through a trust company, investment counsel or directly any additional sums they have available.[2] To offset this larger return, however, there is the greater risk element usually connected with individual investment, except when carried on through a savings bank.

The weakest point in the investment position of insurance policies is that, as investments, they constitute a gamble on the chance of life, while as insurance they constitute protection against the chance of death. If an individual dies during the period of payment on a limited payment life insurance policy or on an endowment policy, his estate gets no more than if he had had a term or straight life policy. He has gambled on the chance of life and lost, in so far as he made the larger payments. Only if he lives does he get any benefit at all from these additional payments in the form of larger premiums. If his estate is small, this gamble on the chance of life is unfair to his dependents, whose share in the estate is thus reduced.

A recent study analyzed the rate of investment return received from the purchase of insurance with investment features by comparing cash surrender values of limited payment and endowment policies with straight life insurance policies, ignoring the small element of investment found in the latter. It was found that, at age 25, the limited payment and endowment policies gave an average return, as measured by the cash surrender value, of 2½ per cent on the extra payments over and above the straight life insurance premiums if the insured lived 5 years; 4 per cent if he lived 10 years, and 5 per cent if he lived 20 years. These are average figures based on data of 12 large companies. If insured at the age of 50, however, a return of 3¼ per cent was earned if he lived 5 years, and fully 8 per cent if he lived 20 years. The accumulation was, of course, entirely lost if the policyholder died before collecting from the company. Then his estate received merely the face amount of the policy, which would have been payable in any case. Thus, at the age of 50, the chance of the policyholder's getting his

[2] Disadvantages arising from investing regulations compelling these companies to buy fixed income securities are discussed below in chap. xiii.

accumulation, with income at the compound rate of 8 per cent, at the end of 20 years is found to be only 55¾ out of 100, based on his chances of living at least until the age of 70, as shown by the experience table.

As a conclusion of this study, the author says:[3] "A careful analysis of the situation indicates that in most instances it is desirable to keep life-insurance contracts separate and distinct from investment contracts—to buy life-insurance services from a life-insurance carrier and investment services from an investment institution."

This conclusion would be challenged by a number of life insurance authorities, however. In particular, advice to shift from high-premium to low-premium types of policies, referred to as "twisting," is condemned by them as usually unwarranted.[4]

The combination of insurance and investment activities through a bank and trust company has been tried in recent years, in order to avoid the disadvantages mentioned above attaching to the insurance company as an investing medium. Several banks have worked out schemes for acquiring insurance for savings depositors, paying premiums out of the interest earned on savings accounts. The Harris Trust & Savings Bank of Chicago installed such a combined savings-insurance system in 1921.

Another combination of life insurance and investment activity is present in the insurance trust, especially where the individual who creates the trust places securities as well as life insurance policies in it. The earnings from the securities can then be used to pay premiums on the insurance policies; or some other arrangement can be perfected to assure that the investment side of the transaction, both before and after death, shall be handled by the trust company, while the insurance company merely furnishes the term or straight life insurance contract.

[3] Nerlove, S. H., "The Investment Element in Life Insurance Contracts," *Journal of Business of the University of Chicago*, vol. i, pp. 273-293, July, 1928.

[4] For an extreme statement of this point of view, see Speicher, Paul, *The Truth About Life Insurance*, Indianapolis, 1936; especially chap. v, "The Truth About the Twister."

Social Security Funds

A new investment problem of gigantic scope is being created by the inauguration of government social insurance. The federal Social Security Act as enacted in 1935 sets up two funds from which payments would be made to beneficiaries. The first of these, the Unemployment Insurance Fund, would be managed by the Secretary of the Treasury for the various states that enact unemployment insurance legislation. It has been estimated that this fund would probably not rise much above $2,000,000,000, as payments out of it to idle persons would constantly tend to reduce the amount held.

In the second place, the Social Security Act creates on Old Age Reserve Account, from which benefit payments would be made to contributors. As originally set up, it has been estimated by actuaries that this fund would in time surpass the vast reserves of the life insurance companies themselves, and that by 1960 it would exceed $26,000,000,000, and by 1970 it might go above $32,000,000,000.

These two social insurance funds differ greatly, however, from those of the life insurance companies. They may be invested only in United States government bonds. The Secretary of the Treasury has the choice of buying bonds in the open market or of issuing new bonds if necessary to provide investments for this fund. Furthermore, the statute requires that 3 per cent shall be paid by the Treasury annually as interest on the bonds held by these funds, even though the coupon rate on the bond may fall to a materially lower yield.

It is apparent, therefore, that these funds would operate much like a sinking fund for the national debt. The point has been made, however, that there is little purpose in having a large reserve accumulated against the insurance liabilities of the federal government, since through taxation it would always be in a position to meet its obligations as necessary. For that reason, a sounder program would be a reduction in the social security taxes and contributions, so as to place the whole scheme as far as possible upon a self-supporting basis, but without the accumulation of reserves to a larger extent than necessary.

Needless to say, the existence of a large social security reserve fund would further reduce the supply of gilt-edged securities by creating a demand for virtually all of the government bonds that are now outstanding. To the extent that these bonds would be repurchased from commercial banks, the result would be a deflation of credit.

Fire and Casualty Insurance Companies

The other types of insurance companies are far less important as institutional investors. This is the case chiefly because of their method of operation, since they write insurance for short periods and do not build up large reserves. Furthermore, these companies, since they do not affect the general public so largely, are subject to far less stringent regulation than is the case with the life insurance companies, so that many of them buy heavily of common stocks and seek large speculative profits on their security holdings.

As a matter of fact, most fire and casualty companies do not charge enough in premiums to cover their loss payments. The difference, as well as their profits, is made up from earnings obtained by investing these premium payments as rapidly as received, and before losses are paid out. In fact, taken together, fire insurance companies show underwriting losses almost yearly, but investment and speculative profits have made many of these companies highly prosperous.

A study of 63 leading American fire insurance companies showed that they had investments aggregating nearly $1,250,000 in 1927, of which nearly one-half was in stocks. Several companies had the larger portion of their funds invested in industrial and utility common stocks, while others, more conservatively inclined, continued to rely chiefly upon bonds as investment media. The depression undermined a number of the companies that invested heavily in stocks, and as a result investment policies have tended to become more conservative. A total of 25 leading casualty companies in 1927 had more than $550,000,000 of investments, and displayed at the time a tendency to invest more heavily in stocks, in which they had about one-fourth of their funds.

The Revolution in Commercial Banking

The increase in size and financial strength of the average American business corporation after the war, making it less dependent upon bank loans than ever before, has had a profound effect upon the activities of the commercial banks. Many a corporation which formerly turned to the commercial bank for credit facilities built up a surplus of liquid capital which

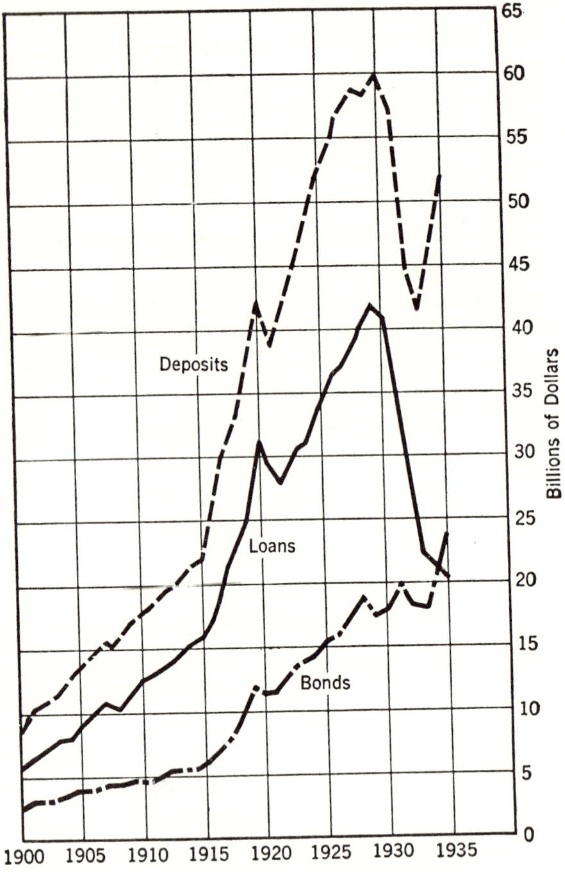

FIG. 7. DEPOSITS, LOANS AND BONDS OF ALL BANKS IN THE UNITED STATES, 1900 TO 1935[5]

has transformed it into its own banker. Even in the case of co[r]porations which need additional capital, the great expansion [o]f popular investment in securities has permitted the raising [o]f money through the sale of stocks or bonds.

The commercial bank, finding it less and less possible [to] utilize its resources in wonted channels, has branched out in[to]

[5] Source: *Annual Reports* of the United States Comptroller of Currency. Us[ed] by permission of Young & Ottley, Inc.

other fields, notably security loans and bond investment. Since the deflation of security advances after 1930, they have become increasingly investors in bonds. Fig. 7 illustrates what has happened since 1900.

Loans and investments of the commercial banks of the country on June 30, 1935, aggregated $33,512,000,000. This total was distributed in the following manner:

United States government bonds (including fully guaranteed issues)	$12,239,000,000
Other stocks and bonds	6,692,000,000
Loans on securities	4,550,000,000
Loans on real estate security	3,121,000,000
Loans to other customers	6,901,000,000
Total loans and investments	$33,503,000,000

The true nature of the revolution that has taken place in the position of the commercial bank may be understood only by differentiating investments and investment loans made with time deposits from those made with demand deposits. In so far as the commercial bank receives time deposits and invests them as does the savings bank, it may contend that it is acting merely as an investing institution, in the manner described in the preceding chapter. It is only when it invests its resources over and above its savings deposits in securities that the commercial bank also acts as an institutional investor. The change that has occurred in the nature of the distribution of commercial bank assets is shown in the following table:

TABLE 6.—CHANGES IN DISTRIBUTION OF ASSETS NATIONAL AND STATE BANKS AND TRUST COMPANIES

(Percentage Distribution)

Type of Asset	June 30, 1921[a]	June 30, 1930[a]	June 30, 1934[b]
"All other loans" (chiefly commercial)	37	28	15
Security loans	18	19	10
Real estate loans	5	7	8
Federal, state and municipal bonds	9	8	29
Other investments	11	14	10
Cash and miscellaneous assets	20	24	28
Total	100	100	100

[a] *Annual Report*, Comptroller of the Currency.
[b] Call Report of Insured Banks, Federal Deposit Insurance Corporation.

The investments of commercial banks and banking departments of trust companies were distributed as follows in June, 1935, according to the report of the Comptroller of the Currency (in millions):

Type of Bond	National Banks	State Banks	Trust Companies
United States government	$ 7,173	$1,393	$3,673
State and Municipal	1,399	601	527
Railroad	593		
Public utility	536	507	791
Industrial, etc.	403		
Foreign government	104	197	526
Other domestic and foreign securities	508		
Total investments	$10,716	$2,698	$5,517

The Corporation as Investor

There is one peculiarity of American corporate accounting practice which has had a remarkable effect upon the investment process in this country. As a result of the kaleidoscopic changes through which most of our industries have passed, and especially on account of the great scope for expansion they have enjoyed, the corporate surplus account became ubiquitous in American finance. Whereas in Great Britain and on the Continent the rule was for the corporation to pay out to its stockholders the great bulk or all of its reported earnings, after putting aside certain relatively small statutory and other reserves, the practice here has been to pay out to stockholders in dividends only a fraction of the annual corporate income. The balance is plowed back into the property.

The corporate surplus was a natural outgrowth of the special conditions under which American industry grew up. This is revealed by a study of our early corporations. The first railroads, for instance, originally followed the policy of paying out in dividends all their earnings. The annual income, in fact, was considered a "dividend reserve," and anything not paid out was immediately labeled in this way, to be paid out as soon as practicable. Any other course, it was thought, was an imposition on the stockholders.

The rapid progress of industrial change soon showed that such accounting practice was not suitable to American conditions. This was early discovered by the large railroads. Intensive new railroad building brought competition, and competition and rate-cutting brought about the failure of the companies which did not have extra resources to carry them through lean years. Also, with the rapid change in technique, facilities often became obsolete long before the termination of their estimated lease of life. Corporations without a corporate surplus were then compelled to reorganize, in order to raise the needed capital to modernize their properties. The philosophy of a corporate surplus was one of the chief factors that made the early Morgan railroad reorganizations successful. Finally, with the growth of the country, many profitable opportunities for expansion arose, and boards of directors frequently preferred to use current earnings to take advantage of these opportunities, instead of turning their income over to stockholders and issuing additional securities to finance new ventures of doubtful immediate profitability.

As time went on, the accumulation of a corporate surplus of large size, and continued payments of only a fraction of earnings as dividends, became one of the habitual practices of American business life. The practice followed in the railroad field is shown in the following table, giving the percentage of earnngs paid out in dividends by such companies over a period of years:

Year	Net Income	All Dividends Paid	Percentage Net Income Paid as Dividends
890	$106,270,095	$ 87,071,613	81.9
900	252,760,482	139,597,972	55.2
910	583,191,124	405,771,416	69.6
920	481,950,969	331,102,938	68.9
925	771,053,077	409,645,051	53.1

The surplus accumulated by many industrial corporations as exceeded their outstanding capital. However, it was necessary in many cases to make heavy charge-offs against surplus accounts during the depression, owing to the retirement of obsolete and unneeded facilities and the decline in plant replacement and accordingly in values.

The Revenue Act of 1936 for the first time penalized the accumulation of a corporate surplus. A graduated surtax was levied on undistributed earnings of corporations.

The habit of building up large surpluses has given corporations funds to invest both in their own and in other enterprises, thus tending to transform them into investment organizations. A spectacular example, one of many which might be cited, is the du Pont Corporation. Founded in 1799 as a munitions manufacturing plant, this company in the latter years of the nineteenth century built up a large business as a manufacturer of powder and explosives, used for the most part in mining and building operations. The company's activities then were extended into the chemical field. During the World War, it took a foremost place in the manufacture of both munitions and chemicals, the main source of supply of the latter having been cut off through the closing down of trade with Germany.

The huge profits obtained during the war period were not paid out to stockholders in the main. Although the vast liquid capital which the company accumulated certainly could not be used in the munitions business, and the chemical business was expanding at a rate which held out prospects for profitable employment of only a fraction of it, the balance was not distributed. Instead, the company turned to an entirely different industry, automobile manufacturing, where the difficulties of one leading promoter permitted it to acquire a controlling stock interest in the General Motors Corporation. Thus the company became a leading powder and explosive manufacturer, a manufacturer of chemicals with stock interests in numerous other concerns in the same field, and finally the holding company for the largest automobile manufacturing concern in the world. The relationship between the market valuation of the General Motors investment of the company and its own total valuation, as measured by security prices on April 1, 1929, was as follows:

Market value of du Pont capitalization	$1,751,284,150
Market value of shares of General Motors held as investment	823,450,650
Market valuation of balance of du Pont assets	927,833,500

Corporations, through their surplus accounts, have, in fact, become a major savings agency. The device of the corporate surplus, designed at first to strengthen a corporation's position in its own industry, has led to the accumulation of large amounts of capital which have been kept in liquid form, awaiting use in one channel or another, or to take care of contingencies.

This brings us to the second phase of development of the corporate surplus, where it assumes merely the form of excess liquid capital awaiting use in the indefinite future. A number of corporations, following a business practice quite suitable to conditions of an earlier day, have accumulated huge amounts of cash for which they find no foreseeable use. Pending the finding of favorable use for these funds, corporations generally seek some profitable investment for them. They can place their money in short-term securities, in the corporation's own shares, or they may act virtually as investment trusts, buying and selling securities for profit as well as current income. Such investing activities have not always had happy results, and it is difficult to defend them from the stockholders' point of view.

The growth of surplus cash reserves of corporations is merely one instance of the fundamental change in the position of this country from a debtor to a creditor nation. This is reflected in the individual corporation by the fact that, instead of having to borrow additional capital to expand its activities, it has a surplus for which no definite use is in sight. The same process is repeated here as occurs in the country as a whole, where a surplus of liquid capital is available now for investment abroad, whereas formerly resort had to be had to foreign capital markets in order to raise the funds needed for the development of home industry by American corporations.

Eleemosynary Institutions as Investors

A large and growing group of eleemosynary institutions constitutes an important factor in the capital market. A recent study estimates their property investment and endowment at more than $9,000,000,000. A large part of the endowment is invested in securities. The volume of resources possessed by each major group of institutions was found to be as follows:

Institutions	*Endowment and Property*
Religious	$3,839,500,000
Higher education	2,815,000,000
Hospitals	1,400,000,000
Foundations	1,000,000,000
Organized charity	239,000,000
	$9,293,500,000

Among eleemosynary institutional investors, colleges and universities have by far the largest endowment funds, as a group. Most American institutions of higher learning, outside of the state and municipal institutions, do not receive enough in fees or subsidies to cover the cost of the educational work offered. The balance is made up from income earned on endowments presented to the institutions by benevolent individuals. These endowments sometimes take the form of land or securities which the institution is expected to retain. To a growing extent, however, they are free endowments which the institution is at liberty to invest or reinvest at the discretion of its board of trustees.

A study of 30 institutions which possessed $536,000,000 of endowment funds in 1931, or 74 per cent of the investments of all institutions of higher learning in this country at the time, showed 50 per cent of the funds invested in bonds, 8 per cent preferred stocks, 10 per cent common stocks, 13 per cent real estate mortgages, 13 per cent realty, and 6 per cent other assets.[6]

Harvard University reported on June 30, 1928, endowment funds totaling $86,702,876. However, this amount was substantially below the market value of the securities held, as many common stock holdings of the university were valued at nominal or very low quotations.

It has been found that only a limited number of institutions of higher learning have adopted well-defined and consistent investment policies. They are hampered in this by the fact that

[6] Wood Struthers & Co., *Trusteeship of American Endowments*, 1932.

much of the endowment is received in the form of securities or real property.

Benevolent foundations, such as the Rockefeller and Carnegie, possess about a billion dollars, all invested in securities. By their very nature, however, they tend to keep the securities originally donated, although in the course of time they may also accumulate large general investment funds which may be managed in the usual way.

The investing activities of these religious, educational and benevolent institutions are not subject to legal regulation. They are limited in some cases by the wishes of the donors of the property, where these are specified in the deed of gift. In other instances, conservative and rigid regulations have been self-imposed by the board of trustees of the institution to govern their activities. While many of these institutions keep within the limits of securities legal for savings bank investment in the interest of safety, others show a greater disposition to sacrifice unnecessary marketability and to seek appreciation in or protection from a rise in commodity prices by the purchase of common stocks. In the operation of their investment accounts, many of these institutions rely on the advice of investment or commercial bankers who are on their board of trustees. In other cases, financial statisticians may be employed to search out investment opportunities. To a growing extent, however, it has been found desirable to place supervision of the portfolio in professionally qualified hands.

The Institutional Investment Problem

In this and the foregoing chapters, we have surveyed the investment policies and restrictions applicable to a variety of investing institutions and institutional investors. We have seen that for the most part these agencies are seeking to invest billions of capital each year in high-grade bonds, and that to a large extent they are prevented from buying other types of securities by legal contractual restrictions. On the other hand, there has been a tendency in corporate financing for various types of enterprises to rely less upon bond financing, and instead to raise needed capital through the sale of stock. This situation is leading to a famine in the high-grade bond market as a result of diverse tendencies in the policies of institutional investments on the one hand and corporate issues of securities on the other.

This raises a fundamental problem with regard to the future operation of these institutions and the need for modifying their investment policies. The tendency for yields to fall to unprecedentedly low levels after 1934 brought considerable pressure for institutional investors to compromise with their standards in order to obtain higher rates of return. In the long run, it may prove necessary to modify investment restrictions and policies generally to conform with new financing methods.

Summary

There is a large and important group of institutions, not formed for the primary purpose of investing funds of individuals, which nevertheless gather in the course of their business large sums which must be kept profitably employed. These institutions play an important rôle in the capital market.

The leader among these institutional investors is the insurance company. In the case of life insurance companies, the business of insurance is complicated by a very large investment element, because of the adoption of the level premium plan of payments and the addition of endowment features to policies. These methods of operation have caused the life companies to accumulate huge reserves, the investment of which is regulated by state law. From the investor's standpoint, on the other hand, the combination of insurance and investment activities which results raises a number of problems.

Other insurance companies and commercial banks also accumulate substantial funds which are kept invested in securities, under regulations imposed by state laws. Numerous business corporations have large sums available for general investment, to a great extent a result of the common practice of American corporations over a period of years of paying out only a portion of their earnings as dividends, regardless of the immediate expansion needs of the enterprise.

Finally, eleemosynary institutions are gaining control of increasing amounts of money which are being largely invested by them in securities. Colleges and universities are most important in this respect; but churches, hospitals and other religious, benevolent and educational foundations are also becoming important institutional buyers of securities, and their investing activities play a conspicuous part in the capital market.

REFERENCES

ACKERMAN, SAUL B., *Insurance,* New York, 1928, chaps. iii and xxviii.

BORDEN, ALBERT G., *The Investment Trust Service of Life Insurance,* New York, 1928.

HUEBNER, S. S., *Life Insurance,* New York, 1935.

NERLOVE, S. H., "The Investment Element in Life Insurance Contracts," *Journal of Business of the University of Chicago,* vol. i, pp. 273–293.

RICHTER, E. E., and STANDISH, A., "Bank and Insurance Company Investments," *Harvard Business Review,* vol. iii, pp. 414–423.

RIEGEL, R., and LOMAN, H. J., *Insurance,* New York, 1923, chaps. v. and viii.

SPEICHER, P., *The Truth about Life Insurance,* Indianapolis, 1936.

TOWNSEND, W. W., *Bond Salesmanship,* New York, 1924, chap. x.

TWENTIETH CENTURY FUND, *The Security Markets,* New York, 1935.

VON TRESCKOW, W., *Merchants of Debt,* New York, 1936.

WOOD, STRUTHERS & CO., *Trusteeship of American Endowments,* New York, 1932.

Chapter VII

MORTGAGE BANKING

Purpose and Types

The institutional development of investment banking has produced a special type of organization in the financing of rural and urban real property development known as the mortgage bank.[1] It is based upon the concept of substitution of joint for individual credit, and in some cases is equivalent to a joint guarantee of individual credit. The special peculiarity of mortgage banking is, in fact, its attempt to strengthen credit, and make it broadly acceptable, by averaging or combining risks.

The term "mortgage banking" also includes the converse service of distributing risks through reducing the risk carried by any one owner by giving him only a share or fraction of a large mortgage.

As the name implies, mortgage banking is a form of investment banking whose purpose is to finance the purchase and development of real properties through the sale of mortgages. Under it are included two major divisions: one usually called rural credit or farm finance, and the other, real estate financing or city mortgage banking. Both have a common purpose, but their methods are widely different. Of the two branches of mortgage banking, the rural phase is by far the older, and has been more perfectly worked out than has city mortgage banking. Rural mortgage banking also has the advantage of resting upon definite legislation in most countries.[2] Many nations have

[1] Mortgage banking is not a term that applies narrowly to the making of mortgages. In the first stage of mortgage banking, the basic instrument was a first mortgage secured on land. As the system is working out today, mortgage banking is considerably broader, including the origination of collateral trust bonds of which the basic security consists of instruments which are secured by a lien on land or buildings.

[2] Mortgage banking of any kind is successful not merely when it helps the lender, but when it helps the borrower as well. So we may say that the social object of mortgage banking from the standpoint of the borrower (the farmer) is

adopted rural credit legislation which aims at the financing of farm purchases and the development of land with the aid of mortgage loans.

There are only a few countries in which the development of mortgage banking in cities has been subjected to legislative control, or has been given any legislative recognition or aid. This discrimination is due to the fact that in most countries the so-called agricultural problem—that of keeping the farmer on the land and of providing him with reasonably cheap working capital—has been regarded as of primary importance from several standpoints, so that much more attention has been given to it than to the parallel problem of city real estate financing.

In the United States this non-participation of the state was the rule until after the depression of 1930-33; then this policy was reversed. As subsequent investigation showed, the inflationary policies of the post-war decade lead to the creation of an enormous burden of urban real estate mortgage debts. The Twentieth Century Fund estimated the amount as well over $27,000,000,000 for the United States as a whole. This was close to three times the amount that was owed upon farms, the latter being somewhat less than $9,500,000,000. The city mortgages which were thus floated in many cases represented loans based upon fictitious property values. Accordingly, the depression, with its shrinkage of incomes and of employment, necessarily resulted in cutting away the economic basis of the values upon which these mortgages had been issued. When holders of property ceased to meet the interest on their mortgages and, of course, became unable to pay them at maturity, a general revaluation with widespread changes of ownership seemed to impend. The result was action by the United States government in adopting legislation designed to assist those who were un-

to give him better access to the capital market. In most countries he has only poor access, and thus mortgage banking is a system specially designed to meet his needs. In this country he could formerly get his funds from the local bank or from the individual mortgage lenders who were engaged in the business and getting high commissions and high rates of interest. These conditions have been improved by developing a special system framed from the borrower's standpoint, as illustrated in our farm loan system—that of giving the borrower access to capital steadily, consistently and at a lower rate of interest. Rates have been reduced sharply during the past twenty years, in relation to other interest rates, as a result.

able to obtain refinancing for their mortgages. The Federal Home Loan Banks (created in 1932), and, later, the Home Owners Loan Corporation (created in 1934) came into existence for the purpose of relieving distressed borrowers; by the year 1935 an extensive system of government mortgage banking operating upon city real estate had been developed.

The Nature of Mortgage Banking

Real estate, in the broad sense, constitutes the nation's greatest business. The financing of urban and farm real estate development, therefore, has become one of the major divisions of the field of finance, and is performed by a large number of institutions, some specialized and others more general in character.

The financing of urban and farm realty is characterized, in the first place, by the predominance of the small unit. While there are a number of very large buildings in our cities and several large-scale farming enterprises, individual homes and smaller farms still account for the great bulk of the real estate of the country. Secondly, while income is important in supporting real estate, like all business, credit, nevertheless special stress has traditionally been laid on the protection given by the pledged real property itself, which can be sold to satisfy the loan in the event of a default. Thirdly, the legal procedure for the protection of mortgages is relatively well defined, so that it is usually easier for the holder of a real estate mortgage to protect himself in case of default than is the case with other types of creditors.

The business of mortgage banking is especially important in the United States because of the great expanse of the country and the very important rôle that urban real estate and agriculture have played in our economic development. Furthermore, the speed with which this development has taken place has tended to make the burden of indebtedness resting on American real property relatively larger than is the case elsewhere in the world. As a result, mortgage banking in the past has not always been conducted upon a sound basis, and failures of financial institutions caused by the inability of mortgagors to meet their obligations have been frequent.

History of Mortgage Banking in the United States

During the colonial period, and also in the decades shortly following the adoption of the Constitution, specialized mortgage banks were promoted to lend money on the security of farms. In many cases, the loans were made on an excessively liberal basis because they were incurred during boom periods in which farm values soared to high levels justified only by speculative considerations. When values subsequently dropped and deflation of agricultural prices cut farm incomes simultaneously, the net burden proved excessive, and defaults became widespread. Since early mortgage banks usually had but meager capital resources, their record was far from good.

During this earlier period also many commercial banks made real estate and farm loans, with or without mortgage security. Hence, each recurring crisis brought in its wake numerous bank failures caused primarily by defaults on mortgage loans. The panic of 1837, for example, witnessed an epidemic of bank failures that in some respects compared with that of 1930-1933. The primary cause was the failure of numerous "wild-cat" banks whose chief activity was lending money directly or indirectly on farm and town realty.

The Civil War period witnessed the establishment of a national banking system from which mortgage lending was excluded. As a result, the business of real estate financing was largely shifted to state banks and trust companies. As the pace of economic development of the country gathered momentum following the conflict, a number of other financial institutions entered the mortgage lending field also. Foremost among these were the life insurance companies, the building and loan associations and, later, real estate mortgage bond houses.

The severe depression and deflation of the years 1930-1933, following upon twenty years of rapid increase in both farm and urban mortgage debt, effected another revolution in this, as in other, phases of our financial machinery. A number of new institutions, some emergency and some designed to be permanent, were quickly brought into being to meet the crisis and to supersede institutions that suspended or curtailed their operations during the deflation era.

Farm Mortgage Banking

We shall consider first farm mortgage banking, both because its development preceded the evolution of urban mortgage banking and because, being simpler, its fundamental principles may be more easily understood.

At the present time, the total mortgage debt resting upon American farms is probably less than $8,000,000,000. The Bureau of Agricultural Economics reports that the outstanding total of farm mortgages rose from $3,330,000,000 in 1910 to $7,857,700,000 in 1920 and $9,468,526,000 in 1928. Thereafter, there was a considerable deflation of farm mortgage indebtedness. Nevertheless, the majority of American farms, either because of their small size or because of the policy of their owners, are not mortgaged. In fact, only about 40 per cent of all American farms are mortgaged.

Furthermore, it is likely that the total of farm indebtedness will decline further. An increasing proportion of farm mortgages are of the installment type, and so will be gradually repaid over a period of years. In the past, too many mortgages, both farm and urban, did not contain regular amortization provisions. As a result, the tendency was for the total farm mortgage debt burden to rise steadily, making periodic wholesale defaults virtually inevitable. The use of the installment mortgage on which the mortgagor makes regular payments, a logical and sensible scheme for the gradual liquidation of mortgage debts resting on real property, has been established as standard practice. Hence, the record of farm mortgages, other things being equal, may well be better in the future than in the past.

The Federal Land Bank System

The federal government has for many years, in line with the practice followed in other countries, sought to facilitate borrowing on attractive terms by farmers. Although the Federal Reserve Act, passed in 1913, contained special provisions to facilitate agricultural financing, such as the authority given the Federal Reserve Banks to rediscount agricultural paper with a six months' maturity while ordinary commercial paper had to have a maturity of ninety days or less to be eligible, it naturally did not concern itself with long-term lending to farmers.

There was criticism of this in western states, where it was argued that industry was being aided more than agriculture. Accordingly, Congress in 1917 passed the Federal Farm Loan Act, which set up a Federal Land Bank System. Subsequent legislation has enhanced its rôle, so that the Land Banks have become the most important lenders on farm mortgages. In time, a large part, if not the larger part, of outstanding farm mortgages in the United States will probably be held by these banks.

The Federal Land Banks, twelve in number, serve as many districts embracing the entire United States. These banks operate under the supervision of the Governor of the Farm Credit Administration, who is located in Washington and is responsible to the Secretary of the Treasury.

The business of the Federal Land Banks is to lend on mort-ages having a value of not more than 50 per cent of the value f the farm land and 20 per cent of the value of permanent im-rovements pledged as security for the advance. These loans ear a rate of interest that is normally not more than 1 per cent igher than the interest rate on the last issue of bonds sold by ie Federal Land Banks, and in no event higher than 6 per ent. Under emergency legislation, however, the banks were uthorized to make loans at 3½ per cent in 1933, the Federal reasury making this possible by subscribing to additional ock of the Land Banks. Amortization is effected through regu-r repayments over from 5 to 40 years. Farm relief legislation iacted in 1933 reduced the interest rate and alleviated the iking fund provisions on mortgage loans previously arranged.

The Federal Land Banks obtain money from two sources. rst and by far the more important, they sell their own issues bonds secured by farm mortgages. These bonds are the joint d several obligations of the twelve Land Banks. Their in-stment status is enhanced by the general understanding that e United States government will come to the aid of the deral Land Banks whenever they get into difficulty, although is not under legal obligation to do so. The purchase of large iounts of additional stock in the Land Banks by the federal vernment in 1933, when defaults on mortgages held had be-me numerous, has tended to confirm this impression. Be-ise they are an "instrumentality of the Government of the

United States," interest on Federal Land Bank bonds are ex empt from income taxes. Secondly, the Federal Land Bank raise capital by selling stock to borrowers and the Treasury

Most Federal Land Bank loans are made not directly, bu through National Farm Loan Associations. These association are cooperative groups of ten or more farmers who wish t borrow $20,000 or more from the Federal Land Bank of th district. The farmer members turn over their mortgages, whic meet the requirements laid down by the Farm Credit Admin istration and the law, to the National Farm Loan Association from which they receive 95 per cent of the face value in cas and 5 per cent in stock of the Association. The Associatio in turn turns over these mortgages to the Federal Lan Bank and receives 95 per cent of their face value in cash and per cent in stock of the Land Bank.

As long as defaults on mortgage loans made by one Nation Farm Loan Association do not exceed 5 per cent of the aggr gate, there is no loss to the Federal Land Bank, since the stoc of the latter held by the National Farm Loan Association canceled up to such an amount. Similarly, the individu farmers who have borrowed through a National Farm Loa Association may have to absorb losses up to 5 per cent of th amount of their own borrowing if fellow members of the particular Association default. Thus, the initial burden of d faults rests upon the stock in the Association. In this way, loc groups of farmers in effect guarantee each other's loans from th Federal Land Bank System up to 5 per cent of the amount each advance.

The emergency legislation of 1933 and subsequent legis tion also authorized direct loans by the Federal Land Ban themselves, at a rate of interest one-half of one per cent high than on loans made through the Farm Loan Associations.

The operations of the Federal Land Bank System and t present status of these institutions are reflected in the balan sheet of the twelve Federal Land Banks combined, which is p sented herewith:

The original Federal Farm Loan Act also provided for t creation of a privately owned system of Joint-stock Land Ban to supplement the Federal Land Banks and assure more aggr

FEDERAL LAND BANKS

Consolidated Statement (twelve banks combined), September 30, 1935

Assets

Mortgage loans, less matured principal unpaid	$2,045,591,438.45
Extensions, less reserves	33,655,432.34
Delinquent installments, less partial payments, delinquent installments and reserves	12,311,151.08
Accounts receivable (tax advances, insurance advances, etc.)	8,137,091.78
Purchase money mortgages and contracts	49,966,565.56
Cash	23,194,209.32
Deposits for matured or called obligations	17,819,504.16
Due from Secretary of the Treasury (interest reductions and paid-in surplus)	10,867,703.10
United States government obligations, direct and fully guaranteed	43,914,688.60
Other bonds and securities	76,993.90
Accrued interest receivable (not yet due)	34,669,832.25
Real estate owned, less reserves	72,875,742.19
Sheriffs' certificates, judgments, etc., less reserves	19,529,655.67
Banking house, furniture, fixtures, equipment, etc., less reserves	6,052,672.80
Prepaid and deferred expenses	5,135,048.14
Other assets	808,023.74
Total	$2,384,605,753.08

Liabilities

arm loan bonds outstanding, less bonds held by banks	$1,903,374,340.00
latured obligations (farm loan bonds including interest)	17,815,504.46
otes payable	56,079,720.27
ccrued interest payable (not yet due)	23,159,572.63
eferred proceeds of loans	6,422,680.93
ccounts payable	787,438.90
ividends declared but unpaid	356,195.21
rust accounts	6,752,009.47
dvance installment payments	2,247,716.52
rtial payments on extensions, purchase money mortgages, contracts, etc.	1,417,247.94
her liabilities	1,609,219.93
ferred income	5,819,160.68
pital stock	234,525,717.00
id-in surplus	87,897,892.74
gal reserves	25,656,426.59
serves for contingencies	9,732,156.02
divided profits	952,753.79
Total	$2,384,605,753.08

sive competition in the lending of money to farmers. How-ever, these institutions were not well managed in several cases and a number of them went into receivership. Under legislatio passed in 1933, lending by the Joint-stock Land Banks wa stopped and they are now in process of liquidation. Thus, th Federal Land Banks, non-profit institutions, were left alon in the field among active farm mortgage banks.

The Federal Farm Mortgage Corporation

The Federal Land Banks, which constitute virtually a gov ernmental agency, are the most important single lenders o farm mortgages. In addition, the federal government set up i 1933 the Federal Farm Mortgage Corporation to facilitate r funding of outstanding farm mortgages into obligations with lower rate of interest. This Corporation no longer makes loan being engaged in liquidating the mortgages it took over in 193 and 1934. It was authorized to exchange its own bonds, o which the payment of interest and principal is guaranteed b the federal government, for outstanding farm mortgages hel by financial institutions and individuals. These mortgages ha to be scaled down, where excessive in amount, to 50 per ce of the value of the land and 20 per cent of the value of improv ments pledged as security. The interest rate on such converte mortgages was reduced to that prevailing on Federal Land Ba Loans. The present status of the Federal Farm Mortgage Co poration may be gauged from its balance sheet as of Septemb 30, 1935, which is presented herewith:

FEDERAL FARM MORTGAGE CORPORATION

Statement of Condition, September 30, 1935

ASSETS

Mortgage loans	$ 765,319,311.
Accounts receivable	115,517.
Purchase money mortgages and contracts	8,145.
Cash with Treasurer of the United States	79,992,170.
Consolidated Federal Farm loan bonds (par value)	729,179,840.
Accrued interest receivable (not yet due)	19,904,535.
Furniture, fixtures and equipment	1.
Deferred expense (unamortized discount on bonds sold)	1,407,312.
Total	$1,595,926,833.

LIABILITIES

Federal Farm Mortgage Corporation bonds	$1,367,566,800.00
Accrued interest on Federal Farm Mortgage Corporation (not yet due)	11,588,066.97
Deferred proceeds of loans	3,564,400.28
Vouchers payable	2,719,800.19
Trust accounts	1,238,393.59
Other liabilities	77,871.73
Deferred income (unamortized premium on bonds sold)	1,444,992.26
Reserve for losses on mortgage loans	7,726,508.77
Capital stock	200,000,000.00
Total	$1,595,926,833.79

The federal government, through the Federal Land Banks and the Federal Farm Mortgage Corporation, holds indirectly upwards of 40 per cent of the total amount of farm mortgages outstanding. The large-scale participation of the federal government in the farm mortgage lending business has been defended by many, including some who regard the government's entry into banking generally as of doubtful wisdom, as an emergency measure to ameliorate the effects upon helpless farmers of a major era of deflation.

However, serious question has been raised as to whether the government will be able to liquidate the Federal Farm Mortgage Corporation without loss. Foreclosures on individual farms by the federal government might have serious political repercussions, and would doubtless lead to strong pressure upon Congress and the Administration to give extensions of time to the mortgagors. While it is easy enough for the government to make a great number of farm loans, and thus to become a mortgage banker on a large scale, it may prove difficult indeed to get out through insisting upon repayment.

The experience of the government as a mortgagee will depend largely on future economic conditions. If agriculture remains relatively prosperous, farmers will not encounter as much hardship in making interest and principal payments, particularly in view of the reduction in the amount and the interest rate on such indebtedness that has been effected. Experience of both the Federal Land Banks and the Federal Farm Mortgage Corporation will throw a good deal of light upon what government conduct of banking may mean in other fields.

Other Farm Lending Institutions

Among private lending institutions, the most important in the farm mortgage field are the life insurance companies. At the end of 1935, they reported holding upwards of $900,000,000 of farm mortgage loans. This represented a sharp reduction, however, from the total of more than $2,000,000,000 of mortgages on farm properties held in 1920. The deflation of farm prices and resulting numerous mortgage defaults, competition from government agencies and moratorium legislation combined to make farm mortgages less attractive as investments. Government competition has depressed rates, and made farm mortgages less attractive as investments for all private holders. These lower rates are the more discouraging because many states have passed moratorium statutes, under which mortgagors have been able to stop payment of interest and principal for a period without incurring the risk of foreclosure. Several such statutes have been upheld by the United States Supreme Court. Congress passed a modified national moratorium statute on farm mortgages, the Frazier-Lemke Act of 1934, but this was subsequently held unconstitutional by the Supreme Court.

Next to the life insurance companies, the most important lenders on farm mortgages are national and state banks, which held $568,553,000 of such loans at the end of 1935. The balance of farm mortgage indebtedness is owned chiefly by individual investors.

A number of government and private agencies specialize in making intermediate and short-term loans to farmers and livestock raisers. Because of the relatively longer period required to finance farmers' working capital requirements and the special risks involved because of weather, commercial banks have met these needs only in part. The Federal Intermediate Credit Banks, twelve in number, make loans that usually run from three months to a year to cooperative marketing and purchasing associations and local institutions that lend to farmers for intermediate terms up to three years. The Central Bank for Cooperatives and twelve District Banks for Cooperatives also help to finance cooperative marketing associations. Short-term loans are made by Production Credit Associations, financed through twelve Production Credit Corporations. Emergency crop and feed loans are made directly by the Farm Credit Administration.

Urban Mortgage Lending

Urban real estate financing has in recent decades exceeded by far the total of farm mortgage financing. The Twentieth Century Fund has estimated that the volume of outstanding urban realty mortgages rose from $13,000,000,000 at the beginning of the century to $35,000,000,000 in 1928. From that high level the volume of urban mortgage indebtedness outstanding has declined by about $7,000,000,000 to $28,000,000,000, as a result of defaults and foreclosures, repayments and a subnormal volume of new building from 1931 to 1936. Of this total, it has been estimated that about $18,000,000,000 are loans on small homes, and the balance loans on larger residential, commercial or eleemosynary structures.

In a number of cities there has developed a system of mortgage banking parallel to and in some respects like the rural credit system which has just been reviewed.

Mortgage Middlemen

In the first place, there are mortgage middlemen, which correspond in the real estate field to the investment houses discussed in Chapter II. These have often been more than mere middlemen, however. Thus, a number of mortgage companies in the past assumed the task of insuring titles to property, and from this they passed to insurance of the principal and interest of mortgages. Such insurance was possible by reason of the fact that the companies had made careful investigations of titles, security, and the like, and were the holders of large masses of records, besides being equipped with substantial capital. The number of mortgages which they normally had to redeem, as a result of some flaw which rendered the debt uncollectible, was small where the business had been carefully done, and thus their losses were often nominal. At all events, the losses were never so great but that a moderate insurance charge, spread out over the general body of mortgages and deducted from the interest paid to the lender, would cover them. Thus a kind of mortgage banking could be practiced, even without the use of the principle of trusteeing the mortgages and issuing bonds against them. This latter principle, however, had been found very useful and profitable in furnishing rural credit, and its application to city real estate financing was only a question of adaptation to the different conditions that presented themselves in city land finance.

By pooling the mortgages which had been taken by the guaranteed mortgage companies, placing them in the hands of a trust company or other trustee for safeguarding, and issuing bonds or certificates against them, city mortgage bankers finally took the step which has usually been regarded as characteristic of mortgage banking in the full sense—the establishment of a fund or pool of mortgages against which securities are issued. In this way, they were able to proceed with mortgage lending operations up to the time when a substantial part of their capital was engaged in it, and could then get back their capital by placing the mortgages already taken in trust and selling certificates against them.

The mortgage companies profited to the extent of the difference between the interest on the mortgages and the interest on the bonds or certificates which they sold against them, and they of course earned an income from fees for title examination, brokerage, and other services. On the other hand, the buyer of the bonds or certificates was better off than the buyer of individual mortgages so far as security was concerned, because he was now in possession of a direct claim upon the issuing company which at the same time was protected by a great number of mortgages, and so was free of any except that general risk which might be regarded as inhering in all such investments.

Of course, he was not able to expect as high a rate of interest as he would have received on the individual mortgage. Because of the greater safety furnished by guaranteed mortgages and by the pooling of risks, he was freed of worry about the flaws that might exist in any particular loan and could base his confidence entirely upon general conditions as they might exist in any given community. Thus the bonds and certificates of the kind created in this way gradually came to be regarded as an exceptionally safe type of real estate investment with a correspondingly moderate interest rate.

Weaknesses of the Guaranteed Mortgage System

But this system had some real, inherent weaknesses. Before the panic of 1929 many were unwilling to admit their existence, and the advertising of companies engaged in urban land financing often made extravagant claims of freedom from loss and ultimate safety, even under the most adverse conditions. These claims were put to a severe test during the panic and the depression which followed it. The depression experience showed that urban mortgages as such were not necessarily more safe than those that had been written on agricultural lands—in some places not as much so, particularly where resort had been had to mortgage banking for the purpose of financing reckless real estate operations. Two kinds of difficulty exhibited themselves: (1) the shrinkage of land values caused by over-promotion and over-pricing in the first place, and subsequent falling off of demand for space on account of shrinkage of incomes of occupants and tenants in the second place; and (2) the fact that mortgage and title companies, in guaranteeing the mortgages and the bonds which rested upon them, had in a large proportion of cases undertaken an excessive volume of obligations. Thus in New York some companies which had been engaged in the mortgage guarantee business reported total guaranties up to forty times their capital and surplus. Evidently, then, a shrinkage of one-fortieth or 2½ per cent of the values would wipe out the insurance fund (capital and surplus of the guaranteeing corporation). Accordingly, most of the companies engaged in the mortgage business found it necessary to go into bankruptcy or receivership, while partial or total moratoria were established in their favor by the government. The investors who had bought the mortgage certificates found themselves obliged to depend entirely upon the underlying mortgages as a result. Like the persons who had bought the guaranteed mortgages themselves, they were in the position of having to undertake the administration of the mortgages—the collection of interest, the foreclosure of defaulted loans, and the like. There was, of course, an immediate suspension of interest in many cases, and in others the eventual liquidation was slow and the investor was subjected to serious ultimate losses. Guaranteed mortgage obligations were quoted at 20 or 30 per cent of par value over long periods, and in cases of need when sales had to be made quickly sometimes hardly anything was realized.

Financing Office Buildings and Apartment Houses

Mortgage financing as applied to city real estate has in recent decades been given a new turn in connection with the financing of office and apartment buildings and large structures in general. Modern American city development has come to demand the erection of very large and costly structures which, in ordinary circumstances, could not be built by the efforts of any one individual, or even by a small group of individuals. Accordingly, it has been necessary to find a means by which the ownership in such buildings could be subdivided and capital for their construction obtained from a large body of investors.

In order to carry out this plan, it has become customary to place a mortgage upon a given building, either before, during or immediately after construction, and with its proceeds pay off the expenses involved in building. The mortgage is made out in favor of a trustee, usually a trust company, which acts as a fiduciary on behalf of the bondholder. An equal amount of bonds is issued and offered to investors. Thus, when the bonds have been sold, the investors become part owners, in proportion to the number of bonds taken, of the underlying mortgage itself. The trust company or trustee thus assumes the duty of paying the coupons on the bonds out of interest which it has collected from the owners of the building. It retires the bonds as they fall due under an amortization scheme, which has usually been put into effect to protect them; and, should the building owners default, it will foreclose the mortgage and take possession of the building on behalf of the bondholders by bidding it in at special sale on their behalf. The assumption in the whole undertaking, of course, is that this latter step will not be necessary, that the investment is a sound one, and that the issue of bonds has merely enabled participation in a security that would otherwise have been outside the reach of the ordinary investor.

The nature of large-scale urban real estate financing of the pre-depression period is indicated by the following classification of such issues publicly made in 1927, when such financing was at its peak:

Apartments	$ 403,752,400
Office buildings	271,725,750
Hotels	102,897,000
Theaters	100,201,300
Semi-commercial, industrial, etc.	57,410,000
Clubs, churches, hospitals, etc.	80,303,150
Total	$1,016,289,600

Since 1929, the volume of such financing has dwindled to very small proportions.

Considerable differences existed in the types of financing carried on by various houses which specialized in this field. Some sold bonds representing a fractional interest in a large commercial building or apartment house mortgage, but they emphasized their own responsibility for the bond rather than the ascertained worth of the underlying security. In other cases urban real estate financing firms undertook the selling of preferred and common stocks instead of bonds. The largest attempt of this kind was made in New York City by the Fred F. French companies, which placed a 50 per cent first mortgage on a large building which they themselves were to construct and operate, and sold preferred stock to cover the balance of the cost. The financing company then kept half the common stock equity, giving the other half to the preferred stockholders. In effect, this resulted in giving investors a preferred stock in place of a mortgage, and the decreased security is offset by the common stock equity.

A number of concerns operated similarly in the second mortgage field. Rates on second mortgages naturally ran much higher; and therefore this business, involving a much greater risk than first mortgage financing, gave a considerably higher margin of profit to the mortgage company which handled the deals.

This type of financing, like the guaranteed mortgage business, fell deeply into discredit during the depression. It is well to remember, however, that certain real estate mortgage bond issues received interest and amortization payments throughout the depression.

The lesson of the depression is not adverse to this method of land financing as such, but it does emphasize the necessity of using the same basic precautions in real estate financing as in any other kind. It is complete folly to assume that the natural growth of an American city or the increasing density in population will furnish an increment to value which can be relied upon to make sound a loan based on excessive appraisals of value or income.

Future of Direct Mortgage Financing

The serious breakdown which has occurred since the panic of 1929 in the field of guaranteed mortgages necessitated some reorganization of the system of urban real estate lending. In New York State, it was thought best to create a Mortgage Commission upon which fell the duty of taking over for adjustment about $800,000,000 of mortgages represented by certificates outstanding which had been guaranteed by title and mortgage companies, the latter finding themselves unable to collect the sums due them from debtors and hence unable to meet their obligations to investors in the mortgage certificates. The importance of this situation from the standpoint of the small saver and investor is obvious. Mr. George S. Van Schaick, Superintendent of Insurance of the State of New York, in an address delivered to the Bar Association of the City of New York in 1935, in considering the future of the business, expressed the following opinions:

> A consideration of the probable future course of urban mortgage financing is pertinent. For purposes of discussion urban mortgages can be grouped into two classes. The first class consists of small mortgages on private homes. The second class consists of large mortgages on exceptional homes, apartment houses and commercial properties of all descriptions.
>
> *Future Financing of Small Mortgages on Homes*
>
> The outlook for the first class of securities is relatively clear. The federal government has planned a comprehensive program for

the financing of small-home mortgages composing this class. As a temporary expedient there has been the Home Owners' Loan Corporation. On the permanent side a federal system involving both mutual and stock corporation institutions has been developed about the central principle of a long-term 80 per cent amortized mortgage. Federal savings and loan associations with an insurance feature and a central discount system promise to afford a steady flow of investment funds. Insured mortgages under Title II of the Federal Housing Act probably will be used widely by state savings banks, insurance companies and other financial institutions. Additional stability to investments of this class apparently will be provided by national mortgage associations under Title III of the Federal Housing Act, which are stock corporation institutions under the supervision of the federal government designed to afford market facilities for insured mortgages.

The indications are that this federal program if amended to obviate weaknesses as disclosed will play an important part in the future. It is quite likely that the amortized mortgage will dominate the mortgage market in the future so far as small mortgages on private homes are concerned.

If the amortized mortgage is economically and socially sounder than the standing mortgage, and this is coming generally to be accepted as true, it is doubtful whether the guaranteed mortgage business should be revived for small mortgages on private homes. These mortgages are so small that there is no necessity for certificating them. On the other hand, the sale of such mortgages as whole guaranteed mortgages might be handicapped by the amortization features. Individual investors are apt to shun a form of investment where small amounts of principal are periodically returned to them. Institutional investors are less likely to be attracted by a guaranty. Perhaps there will always be some demand for small standing mortgages. If the amortized mortgage is a sounder form from a social standpoint, standing mortgages should be restricted to a relatively low percentage of the appraisal value (50 per cent or less). In this event, payment of a premium for the guaranty would in many cases appeal to investors as unnecessary.

Future Financing of Large Mortgages

. In General

The outlook for the second class of urban mortgages, which includes most of the mortgages securing guaranteed mortgage certificates, is still uncertain. The federal government has developed no program up to the present time for large mortgages on exceptional homes, apartment houses and commercial properties. There is an exception. The Reconstruction Finance Corporation recently offered to aid state trust companies, and to a lesser extent state mortgage companies, specializing in this class of mortgages, by the purchase of preferred stock or capital notes and by the establishment of substantial discount privileges. The primary obligation, therefore, of reestablishing a sound system for the revival of this class of mortgage investments rests with the state government.

2. New System of Guaranteed Mortgages

An obvious course is to provide for a new system of guaranteed mortgage companies. This is suggested by the Moreland Commissioner who has investigated various phases of this subject. His suggestion is accompanied by a carefully worked-out set of specifications designed to insure the safety of investments made in the securities of such companies. The Insurance Department concurs heartily with his proposed safeguards. The proposals to regulate appraisals are particularly important. Appraisals are fundamental in mortgage finance. In one important respect perhaps he could go further.

Should not the principle of amortization be extended to this class of mortgages? The report of the Moreland Commissioner seems to be silent upon this point. Perhaps it might be inferred from the fact that he limits the guaranty and service charges to one-half of one per cent that he contemplates the continuance of a short-term mortgage with renewal fees. Otherwise, with guaranties limited to ten times capital, it would be difficult for the companies to make sufficient profit to justify their existence. The Department prefers to see the elimination both of short-term mortgages and the renewal fee. If this results in making it impossible to retain both the limitation of ten to one on guaranties with a maximum of one-half of one per cent service and guaranty charge, then the latter charge should be raised. It is better to run the risk of curtailing somewhat the sale of such securities than to weaken the safety factor of a sound ratio.

If the guaranty companies could be revived to handle this class of mortgages, both past experience and reason indicate that the mortgages would for the most part have to be certificated. Individual investors as a rule cannot handle large mortgages and it is wiser perhaps for institutional investors to diversify their holdings. This circumstance points to an interesting possibility which deserves careful consideration.

3. System of Mortgage Banking

Students of mortgage finance tell us that the most satisfactory method of financing large real estate loans is through mortgage banking. Experience in Europe indicates that over a long period of time real estate securities by this method are stabilized almost on a level with government bonds. Occasionally it has been found possible to secure even more favorable interest terms for the issues of the mortgage banks than for government issues of the country in which the bank was located.

There is no vital difference between mortgage banking and a guaranteed mortgage certificate system. In the latter case the investor has a specific collateral interest in one or more mortgages and gains the benefit of diversification through the guaranty obligation of the company backed up by all company assets. In the case of the mortgage bank, diversification is gained directly because the bonds of the bank are secured by all of its mortgages and other assets upon an undifferentiated basis.

At first glance, the guaranteed mortgage certificate system might seem to offer a more attractive security to investors. This is largely illusory. Purchasers of guaranteed mortgage certificates, unlike purchasers of whole mortgages, are notably inexperienced in real estate matters. For the most part they purchase their securities not upon the basis of judgment of value of the real estate securing their certificates but upon confidence in the general responsibility of the issuing institution.

On the other hand, mortgage banking has definite superiorities over the guaranteed mortgage certificate system. The self-interest of the bank is identified completely with its investors in so far as concerns quality of its security. The conflict of interest which is fundamentally responsible for the condition of the group series of the companies in rehabilitation is lacking. In the event of delinquency of the issuing institution the position of the debenture holder of a mortgage bank is superior to that of a guaranteed mortgage certificate holder. A unitary reorganization generally is to be preferred over piece-meal handling. A mortgage bank could be reorganized with one proceeding in the nature of a "Schackno" reorganization of which thousands of separate proceedings are necessary in the case of the present companies. In point of marketability the mortgage bank debenture is to be preferred over guaranteed mortgage certificates. This is so because the issues are much larger and therefore become better known and can be listed on exchanges. Furthermore, mortgage banking is conducive to the development of a central banking system. A central bank increases marketability to a marked degree which in turn serves to reduce interest rates, thereby stimulating construction and the use of real estate. A central bank also might afford, if it is desired, a sound medium for the control of cut-throat competitive building which has been one of the outstanding evils of the past.

We now turn our attention to the investing institutions organized for the purpose of financing real estate.

Building and Loan Associations

Chief among investing institutions exclusively devoted to lending on urban mortgages are the building and loan associations which function throughout the country. At the end of 1935, these associations were responsible for more than $4,500,000,000 of such loans, which compared with a peak level of almost $8,000,000,000 before the depression.

Building and loan associations are organized on the cooperative principle, and are not normally operated for profit. They lend on the security of first mortgages on homes, usually up to 70 or 80 per cent of the appraised value. Funds for this purpose are obtained through selling shares to be paid for on the installment plan. The shares as a rule have a par value of $200, and are paid for by subscribers in regular weekly or monthly payments. The period of payment is shortened by application, to the principal, of dividends declared on the shares.

When a building and loan association encounters adverse conditions because of defaults on interest and principal payments and declines in the value of pledged property, it can meet the situation simply by ceasing to pay dividends on its shares. Hence, if operated strictly in accordance with the basic principles just outlined, it would be quite unusual for a building and loan association to fail. Unfortunately, many such institutions, in order to hasten their growth, have accepted deposits subject to withdrawal and given shareholders the privilege of withdrawing their payments, under certain conditions, before the shares have been fully paid up. When they do this, their operation tends to resemble more that of a savings bank, and they become more easily subject to failure. Hundreds of building and loan associations did fail during the deflation period following 1929.

Individual accounts in eligible building and loan associations up to $5,000 may now be insured against loss through the Federal Savings and Loan Insurance Corporation. The insured associations then pay annual premiums of 1/8 of one per cent of the insured accounts, until a reserve fund has been set up equal to 5 per cent of the total insured accounts by the Federal Insurance Corporation.

Until 1933, building and loan associations were chartered only under state law. The Home Owners' Loan Act of 1933 provided for Federal Savings and Loan Associations, which were to be under the supervision of the Federal Home Loan Board, would be entitled to federal aid, and would automatically enjoy insurance of individual accounts up to $5,000. More than a thousand such associations had taken out federal charters by the end of 1935.

The future of the building and loan association as an active, expanding mortgage banking agency seems assured, and these institutions may in time dominate the home loan field. Federal insurance of individual accounts, described above, should enhance their importance.

Mutual Savings Banks and Insurance Companies

Mutual savings banks are responsible for the largest volume of real estate mortgage loans among investing institutions. At the end of 1935, they had outstanding almost $5,500,000,000 of such advances.

The states in which mutual savings banks operate maintain their own restrictions on mortgage loans made by them. In general, the criteria set up approximate those of New York, where these institutions may lend up to 60 per cent of the value of improved and 40 per cent of the value of unimproved property.

A third important group of institutions lending on urban mortgages are the life insurance companies. In the aggregate, the life insurance companies held more than $3,900,000,000 in real estate mortgages at the end of 1935, a figure which represented a substantial decline, resulting from foreclosures and repayments, from the peak of well over $5,000,000,000. State moratorium statutes and government measures tending to reduce interest rates on real estate loans have made life insurance companies more cautious. Therefore, these institutions may not play as important a rôle in the urban lending field in the future as they have in the past.

Commercial banks also have been responsible for a large volume of urban mortgage loans, the total held in 1935 being $2,640,000,000. The Banking Act of 1935, as has been already seen, both liberalized the mortgage lending powers of national banks and permitted them to lend up to the amount of their capital and surplus, or up to 60 per cent of the amount of their time deposits, whichever is larger, in this way. However, the same factors that have made insurance companies slow to expand their mortgage loans apply to the banks also.

A very important source of demand for real estate mortgages is the trust companies, which purchase large amounts of such liens for trust accounts. In making such loans, they are subject to the restrictions on trustee investments contained in state laws. In New York State, unless a trustee is specifically released by the deed of trust, it may lend from trust funds no more than 66 2/3 per cent of the value of real property. Exact figures are not available, but trust company holdings of real estate mortgages in trust accounts aggregate several billions of dollars.

The Home Owners' Loan Corporation and Mortgage Insurance

To facilitate the refunding of home mortgages into lower-interest liens during the depression emergency, the Home Owners' Loan Corporation was established in 1933. This agency, like the Federal Farm Mortgage Corporation, no longer makes loans, but it continues active as a liquidating organization. It loaned upwards of $3,000,000,000 to more than 1,000,000 home owners.

The Corporation's chief function was to exchange government guaranteed bonds, mostly bearing 2¾ per cent interest, for outstanding home mortgages. Such bonds were issued only up to 80 per cent of the value of pledged property. Mortgages taken over by the Home Owners' Loan Corporation were to be amortized by regular payments within 15 years. Thus, the

Corporation has helped to establish the principle of gradual repayment of mortgage debt, which had been even less common in urban than in agricultural mortgage lending.

Apart from the Home Owners' Loan Corporation, which was an emergency agency, there had been set up as early as 1932 the Federal Home Loan Banks. These institutions constitute a permanent group of lending institutions to building and loan associations, savings banks and insurance companies. They apply the principle of rediscounting to urban mortgages. However, their lending power is limited to a maximum of 12 per cent of all the home mortgages owned by a member agency, and hence they are restricted in the extent to which they may aid their members. At the end of 1935, more than 3,500 home lending institutions had joined this secondary mortgage lending system.

The federal government has also set up a system of insurance of individual mortgages when held by banks and trust companies, building and loan associations and other approved lending institutions, as a further means of facilitating the borrowing of money for home building at low cost. This insurance, effected by the Federal Housing Administration, is available on first mortgages on one to four family dwellings up to 80 per cent of the appraised value of the pledged property, with a maximum of $16,000 on any one home. Insured mortgages must be of the installment type, and may have a maturity up to 20 years. A premium of ½ or 1 per cent per annum, depending on the type of transaction, is charged, but if it proves too large the excess will go to extinguish part of the debt.

By requiring that insured mortgages be the sole lien on pledged property, and by requiring that they shall be amortized by monthly payments during a period up to a maximum of twenty years, federal mortgage insurance has contributed materially to the improvement of real estate lending standards in this country. More than 12,000 lending institutions have been approved for the making of such insured loans. Also, attempts have been made to market bonds secured by mortgages guaranteed by the Federal Housing Administration, thus creating a standardized type of mortgage bond that would replace the old-fashioned real estate mortgage bonds and guaranteed mortgage certificates, which caused heavy losses to investors during the deflation era of the early 'thirties.

Basic Principles of Mortgage Banking

On the basis of the experience of both mortgage middlemen and investing institutions in the past, it might be said that mortgage banking is conducted soundly when it conforms to the following basic principles:

1. Individual loans should bear a reasonable proportion to the conservatively appraised value of the property, such valuation to reflect earning power as well as market prices of similar property.
2. Mortgage loans should not be made on special purpose property which is not likely to enjoy a fair market during normal times.
3. Mortgage loans should be based in part upon the income of the mortgagor or that which is obtained regularly from the pledged property.
4. Provision should be made for the gradual repayment of these loans, so that a definite plan for the retirement of indebtedness against the property is assured.
5. The rate of the amortization should be sufficient to assure that the loan will decline at least as rapidly as depreciation and obsolescence reduce the value of the pledged property and the income derived from it.

It is a function of an efficient mortgage banking system to provide a regular flow of funds at reasonably low but remunerative rates of interest to owners of farm and urban realty, within the scope of these principles. While it cannot be said that the American mortgage banking system fully measures up to these requirements, progress has been made in that direction. If the government will refrain from efforts to depress interest rates on such loans to unremunerative levels, considering the expenses to the lender and the risks involved, and if moratorium statutes and other such artificial weakening of the quality of real estate liens are ended, considerable further advance toward the development of a sound and efficient mortgage banking system in the United States should be witnessed. Such a system would contribute materially to the stability of real estate values and building activity throughout the country.

The principles of sound city real estate financing are not materially different from those which apply to rural mortgage lending, except for the underlying economic differences. In rural lending, as in city financing, it is essentially necessary to have a sound appraisal of the value of the mortgaged property. In the country, the appraisal has a definite economic basis furnished by the use to which the land can be put and the gross earnings that can be made through such use. A piece of land, for example, may be satisfactory for the cultivation of both corn and wheat. One of the two crops is usually the more profitable, and he amount which can be harvested from it over a series of years urnishes, on the average, the test of its income-producing power and, therefore, the ultimate test of the amount which may safely be lent upon it. A different test is necessary in the ity.

This test is furnished by the rental capacity of the city building, and this rental capacity is a complex matter which involves uestions of the management of the structure, changing curents of trade and of population in urban centers, and many ther elements. It is necessary also to remember that, whereas ie value of land is determined by broad general economic facrs which underlie the question of demand for farm products nd the prices of such products, the value of a city structure dependent upon conditions affecting building costs, and is tered by fashions in building, new methods of meeting the onvenience of occupants of offices, and a variety of other elements. All this may be summed up by saying that the problem city real estate financing is not, as in the country, largely a atter of appraisal based upon ability to produce articles havg a wide market, but appraisal based upon capacity to sell a ghly localized and special service—the provision of space.

Behind any mortgage structure is, as a conditioning factor, e question: How sound is the general financial condition of e community? If the community is in a position which renrs probable some severe shock or violent transformation because of currency disorganization or financial failures on a nation-wide scale, those who borrow upon mortgage will probably be unable to meet the liabilities which they have thus incurred. After all, appraisals depend for their validity upon the income of the community, which must be maintained if there is to be a stable balance between the effective demand and the supply of space for living uses or for business. A general disturbance of the habits of the community in regard to the payment of wages and the receipt of incomes may result in rendering great blocks of mortgages unsafe. This, however, is equivalent to a general statement that all credit tends to be a unit and is controlled by the same general conditions. Disturbances of this kind are likely to be transitory and to be followed by the re-establishment of mortgage banking practice substantially along the same more basic lines. The financing methods represented by mortgage banking have established themselves too firmly in the practice of the community to warrant their being displaced. Some have foreshadowed a condition in which the government might succeed private mortgage banking institutions, so that future mortgage loans would be granted as a kind of subsidy to encourage this or that type of building or of "relieving" this or that class or group in the community, by placing at their disposal inexpensive housing accommodation or low-rent apartments where these were believed to be necessary as a means of maintaining the efficiency and morale of the population. Once mortgage banking assumes a charitable character, however, it will undoubtedly lead to economic maladjustments, as is always the case where subsidized industry competes with free enterprise. The future of this method of financing—as, indeed, of all banking in the United States—will necessarily be profoundly affected by the maintenance of private ownership and the so-called capitalistic system upon lines somewhat similar to those heretofore employed. This is not the place to discuss the probability of such continuance or of the rehabilitation or restoration of older methods of capital formation and distribution. It is only necessary to indicate here that the success of mortgage banking depends upon its being an integral part of the existing type of organization of society.

Marketing Real Estate Securities

The mere fact that a rural or urban mortgage banking institution is ready to issue a series of bonds does not place these bonds in the hands of investors. It is necessary to find a means of distributing them—a process which might be carried on by direct sale to investors in small lots or by advertising the availability of the bonds and leaving it to the investors to come in voluntarily and take them up. As a matter of fact, land banks and building and loan associations have found it necessary to develop distributing facilities to reach the sources of investment funds.

The situation which has thus been described may be compared to advantage with a method formerly widely employed in Germany, where agricultural credit has long had a very elaborate and systematic development. In accordance with this plan, it was the practice in Germany to form groups of farmers who jointly undertook to guarantee one another's credit. Applications from members of the group, when made to the office jointly representing the entire body of farmers, would be considered with care; and, if granted, the applicant would be allowed to present a mortgage upon his land, receiving in return the joint bond of the organization for an equivalent amount, less expenses. These bonds usually bore a rate of interest believed to correspond roughly with the rate prevailing in the market for similar sound securities, and they would then be handed to the farmer-borrower to dispose of as he thought fit. This placed upon him the necessity of marketing the bonds; and the result of the borrowing transaction was merely to give him, instead of his own obligation, another obligation representing the credit of the group to which he belonged. It was as if all members of the group had united to endorse the paper of any one of them who might be accepted as a borrower. This obviously gave to the farmer a much stronger and more widely acceptable credit instrument than his own individual obligation could ever be. He could at times sell it to some neighboring organization, such as a savings bank, while at other times he was obliged to have it sold in a distant market. But the task of selling rested upon him.

Eventually, German farmers developed a plan of creating

mortgage banks whose duty it was to deal in these bonds, and thus a system very similar to our plan of marketing was evolved. In most countries, the task of marketing is regarded as too technical for the local borrower to undertake. Obviously, he cannot market such paper with success, unless there is a substantial demand for it in his immediate neighborhood. Such a plan works well, therefore, only where the savings of a community are about equal to the new capital which that community wants to use in development. Mortgage banking then becomes a means of cooperatively guaranteeing the paper of borrowers, which is carried by those who possess the requisite liquid funds. Where, as in the United States, saving sections and capital-using sections are not identical—the West, for example, being a habitual consumer of capital, while the eastern states are habitual exporters of it—mortgage banking involves both the element of cooperative guarantee and the element of disposal or distribution of securities in a distant market. It thus performs the function of bringing together two widely separated geographic areas.

General Service of Mortgage Banking

From this sketch of the mortgage banking situation, it i easy to recognize the essential place it occupies in the invest ment field. It performs the function of bringing together cap ital and opportunity in one particular branch of industry— that of improving the soil or of adding to it capital improve ments in the form of buildings. It finds groups of investors wh prefer this particular kind of security, and who are willin therefore to furnish the means for larger exploitation of natura resources through this means. Again, the service of investmer banking in this field is seen in the fact that it has been possibl to place capital obligations in large amounts, made availabl for buyers in a shape that is much more acceptable than th actual mortgages themselves would be.

The relation of mortgage banking to other investment insti tutions is changing. Hitherto the great buyers of mortgag have been savings banks, commercial banks, insurance compa nies, title and mortgage companies and others which had sp cial facilities for testing and judging of the qualities of the mortgages offered to them. It sometimes happened that such institutions have constituted so nearly exclusive a market for loans of that type as to enable them to fix rates of interest within very well-defined limits, so that the borrower, with some degree of justice, sometimes felt that he was in the grasp of a "trust." The trend now is for building and loan associations and similar specialized mortgage banks to do a larger share of the business. This should distribute mortgage investments more and more widely.

There may thus be a tendency to eliminate a considerable portion of mortgage loans from the portfolios of the institutions which have thus far carried them, and they in turn will find it necessary to look elsewhere for their investments or to substitute for direct mortgages the mortgage bonds which are gradually taking their place as a general or popular form of investment. The result should be a decided strengthening of the portfolios of investment institutions, and at the same time a smoothing out of the inequalities of interest rates. This change should prove beneficial to the institutions themselves by giving them a better and more widely diversified portfolio, while it should also give to the borrower on mortgage a rate of interest much more closely in accordance with the general market rate prevailing at the time he obtains his loan.

It so happens that in most communities land and the structures built upon it have come to be regarded as a fundamental object of taxation. Some economists, indeed, have been inclined to urge that they should be the chief, if not the only, basis and measure of taxation. Few would go so far today; but as a matter of practice as well as of theory, land and its improvements do constitute a well-nigh universal tax basis. On the other hand, many governments have given to real estate bonds a preferred taxable status, as in fact our federal government has determined to do in the case of Federal Land Bank bonds. In consequence, rates of interest upon bonds which are thus preferred naturally tend to go lower in the degree to which they enjoy tax exemption, and they thus become more suitable as investments for persons who profit most from such tax exemption.

References

Bingham, R. F., and Andrews, E. L., *Financing Real Estate,* Cleveland, 1924.

Clark, H. F., and Chase, F. A., *Elements of the Modern Building and Loan Association,* New York, 1925, chaps. i–iii.

Lyon, H., *Investment,* New York, 1926, chaps. xiii–xv.

National Industrial Conference Board, *Private Long-Term Debt and Interest in the United States,* New York, 1936.

North, N. L., Van Buren, D. V., and Smith, C. E., *Real Estate Financing,* New York, 1928.

Riegel, R., and Doubman, J. R., *The Building and Loan Association,* New York, 1927, chaps. i and xii.

Steiner, W. H., *Money and Banking,* New York, 1933, chaps. xx and xxi.

Twentieth Century Fund, *The Internal Debts of the United States,* New York, 1934.

Wiprud, A. C., *The Federal Farm Loan System,* New York, 1921.

Wright, Ivan, *Farm Mortgage Financing,* New York, 1923.

Van Schaick, George S., *Future of the Title and Mortgage Guaranty Business,* New York, 1935.

Chapter VIII

HISTORY OF AMERICAN INVESTMENT BANKING

The Lesson of History

Students of commercial banking generally devote much study to an examination of the development of the present banking system of the United States. Such an examination, it is usually felt, is of value in understanding many features of our system that otherwise seem obscure. Furthermore, banking history has been of special value in connection with proposals for changes in our banking laws or practices, since many a suggestion advanced as new, has been tested in one form or another in the past.

The same is true of the history of investment banking. The issue and sale of securities have been carried on in this country since colonial days, and many changes have occurred in the methods which have been followed and in the institutions devised to accomplish these transactions. The process of evolution of an investment banking mechanism, fully articulated and adequate to satisfy the capital needs of this country and other nations able to borrow here, is now going forward at a more rapid pace than ever before. By revealing their causes and historical setting, such study may also help to disclose many unnecessary and outworn features of our present organization and laws, and thus help lead to their elimination.

The reason why currency and commercial banking history have been stressed in the past, to the neglect of investment banking, is partly the great political interest attaching to these questions, and partly their dominating importance in the early financial life of the country. Investment banking problems are of later growth, and not until recent years have they affected more than a small percentage of the population. Hence, this is a relatively virgin field, in which much study will be necessary before the full significance of the many changes which have taken place can be clearly realized.

The Beginnings

The first investment banking activities known in this country were the abortive efforts to establish mortgage banks in several of the thirteen colonies before the Revolution. The basic distinction between commercial and investment banking operations was to be learned in our banking history at so great a cost that the lesson was learned perhaps too well, with the result that our laws at times have distinguished between the two kinds of activity to an exaggerated extent. But this was not so in the early days; and the colonists, eager for cheap money in quantity, sought to develop mortgage banks which would issue currency to them in return for mortgages on their farms. As one recent student of early banking theory says, "The earliest sentiment seems to have been that banks should serve all classes alike with their loans, regardless of whether or not liquid assets result."[1] The early state banks, even after the Revolution, were expected to advance long-term loans to farmers. The charter of a bank in Massachusetts established in 1792, for example, required that one-fifth of the loans be reserved for the benefit of "the agricultural interest."[2] This was in conservative New England. The southern and western states went much further in a similar direction.

No investment banking mechanism existed for those few colonists who did not employ their wealth directly. Local real estate or a share in a ship were the chief forms of private investment, and these were generally purchased directly, without the aid of any intermediary.

The first major financial operations to take place in this country had to do with the financing of the Revolutionary War. The original thirteen colonies were primarily agricultural communities, industry having been restricted by the British laws so that whatever activities of this kind flourished were on a small scale, involving very little fixed capital. Several fortunes were built up on the basis of the shipping trade, with or without

[1] Miller, H. E., *Banking Theories in the United States before 1860*, p. 171.
[2] *Massachusetts Acts and Resolves, 1792-1793*, p. 18.

the aid of smuggling, but they were not numerous before the Revolution. Manufacturing activity was all but non-existent.

The revolutionary government was in great need of money, and it incurred a bonded debt of several millions, in addition to issuing a mass of currency which later became practically worthless. It borrowed money at home chiefly through Robert Morris, a wealthy Philadelphia shipping magnate who became banker and commissary for the armies in the field. It sent Dr. Benjamin Franklin abroad, and he borrowed substantial sums in Paris and Holland, giving bonds of the government in exchange for much-needed supplies. In this way a debt of $11,710,000 was gradually accumulated abroad, and one of over $40,000,000 at home, including accrued and unpaid interest.[3] The domestic debt was partly incurred originally by the states. These debts were all recognized by the constitutional government, and were exchanged for 6 and 3 per cent bonds on a fixed basis in Hamilton's funding scheme. Although calling for some concessions from the bondholders, Hamilton's proposals were so much better than had been expected that they served to establish the credit of the United States, and resulted in the first extensive security speculation known in this country, consisting of a rapid rise in the old bonds to discount the unexpectedly favorable treatment they received at the hands of the new government.

From the close of the Revolution it was realized that a central bank was needed to regulate the currency and aid in the government finance of the republic. Hamilton's original thought on the subject was that a land mortgage bank was needed; but by 1790, when his celebrated report was handed to Congress, he had apparently grasped the distinction between investment and commercial banking. He advocated the restriction of the new bank to the latter field, except for government financing; and Clause X of the bank's charter restricted its dealings to bills of exchange and gold or silver bullion.

That the accumulation of capital within the country was already going on at a fairly rapid pace, partly from profits earned through supplying the army during the war and the removal of trade restrictions following its close, is clearly evi-

[3] Channing, Edward, *History of the United States,* vol. iv, p. 95.

dent. The $8,000,000 capital of the first Bank of the United States was offered publicly, and over-subscribed within two hours. However, part of this stock quickly found its way to England, which was now rapidly forging ahead to the forefront among the capital markets of the world. The Industrial Revolution was then shifting the dominance in international finance from Holland to London, and it is noteworthy that the United States Revolutionary bonds which were sold originally in France and Holland were partly absorbed by London after 1790.[4] After the reestablishment of British confidence in this country which followed the organization of the constitutional government and the adoption of Hamilton's funding scheme, the London banking world took a growing interest in the infant republic.

The wave of security speculation which accompanied Hamilton's funding scheme and the formation of the First Bank of the United States resulted in the formation of small groups of brokers in Philadelphia and New York who specialized in executing purchases and sales for others. In New York these brokers would foregather in Wall Street; and by 1792 we find twenty-four of them signing an agreement to maintain a uniform commission of one-quarter of one per cent of the selling price of the shares, and to give preference to each other in their dealings. This agreement was meant to prevent the competition of commodity auction houses in the security business, and marked the beginnings of organized brokerage activities.

Early Period of Capital Accumulation (1790-1817)

The Napoleonic Wars in Europe led to a boom in the foreign trade of the United States which resulted in a fairly rapid accumulation of wealth in the seaboard cities of Philadelphia, New York, Boston and Baltimore. In each of these towns, a class of wealthy traders and shipowners arose who had a surplus of capital and so were in a position to purchase securities for the purpose of financing larger enterprises.

The capital market which thus came into being was not,

[4] In 1791, Bird, Savage & Company, London stockbrokers, bought several million dollars' worth of these bonds in Holland and disposed of them to customers in London.

however, adequate at first to permit the sale of any large issue of securities. The supply of funds available for the purchase of securities down to the last years of the Napoleonic Wars was not more than several million dollars annually. When any important need for large sums of money arose, foreign sources still had to be tapped. The $15,000,000 needed to finance the Louisiana Purchase in 1803 was raised chiefly in Holland. As late as 1805, the house of Baring in London, as agent there for the United States government, paid the coupons on United States government bonds of a par value of $28,500,000. When the federal government wished to dispose of its remaining holdings in the First Bank of the United States in 1802, it sold them to the Barings in one block of 2,220 shares.[5]

The situation changed when the European wars reached a more advanced stage. The more rapid accumulation of capital within this country that followed, and the simultaneous rise in money rates abroad caused by the great conflict, resulted in the gradual repatriation of both government bonds and shares in the Bank of the United States. This process was hastened by the steady redemption of the government debt, and the liquidation of the First Bank of the United States in 1812.

The accumulation of capital and the growth of trade resulted in the formation of a number of banks and insurance companies. By 1801 there had been formed twenty-three banks, with a combined capital of $35,550,000. The primitive condition of the country, the preponderant importance of trade, and the requirements of state laws caused these banks to restrict their activities almost entirely to purely commercial banking transactions. Thus, the Bank of New York, founded in 1784, was specifically forbidden to trade in stocks of the federal or state governments, or to lend on the security of real estate.

The banks in the commercial communities of the East tended to conform to Adam Smith's dictum, that a bank was to advance only that part of the capital of a merchant "which he would otherwise be obliged to keep by him, unemployed, and in ready money, for answering occasional demands." The Brit-

[5] Jenks, L. H., *The Migration of British Capital to 1875*, p. 66. This work may be regarded as the definitive account of Anglo-American finance before the Civil War.

ish idea of strictly commercial banking was not followed in the agricultural areas to the West and South, where strictly commercial loans were much scarcer. But with the increase in wealth and the development of a spirit of speculation, the line of demarcation between commercial and investment banking was still further broken down in the period which followed. In 1816, the first mutual savings bank was established in New

Prices of Stocks

6 per Cent. Funded Debt	98⅜ per cent.
3 per Cent. do do	56½ a 57
8 per Cent. Loan	112½
6 per Cent. Navy Loan	par

Bank Stock

United States Bank	143 a 143½ p. ct.
New York (dividend off)	131½
Manhattan	132

Insurance Shares

New York Insurance Co.	128 per cent.
Columbian ditto	137 a 138
United ditto	118 a 119

Bills of Exchange at 60 days sight

On London	100 a 101 per cent.
On Hamburgh	36 a 38 cts. p. mk. b.
On Amsterdam	40 cents per guilder

E. Benjamin, Stock and Exchange Broker,
No. 50 Wall Street.

November 14.

Fig. 8. Advertisement of Stock Quotations Appearing in the *Evening Post*, New York, November 16, 1801.

York State as a purely investment institution, and this type of institution, which fostered small savings, showed a slow but steady growth thereafter.

In addition to bank and some insurance company flotations, there were canal and turnpike promotions. Davis reports 328 individual incorporations in all were formed before 1800, the great majority of them for small local improvement projects.[6] A great number, however, remained paper projects.

[6] Davis, Joseph S., *Essays in the Earlier History of American Corporations*, pp. 24 ff.

The methods of raising capital were primitive because no investment banking mechanism existed. The shares in these enterprises were as a rule offered directly to the public at some tavern or other public meeting place. There the investor would appear in person, and his name and the number of shares desired would be inscribed in great "books," which still lead a figurative existence in the terminology of Wall Street today. After the original flotation of the shares in this way, those of the larger companies attracted the interest of brokers, who often gave their quotations for publication to the newspapers and periodicals of the time. In order to acquire securities for sale, these brokers would at times subscribe for new issues in their own names. A typical list of quotations, taken from the New York *Evening Post* of 1801, is shown in Fig. 8.

The first formal stock exchange to be opened in this country was organized in Philadelphia in 1800. Philadelphia was the commercial and financial metropolis at the close of the Revolution, and it retained its financial primacy practically down to the War of 1812, although it lost its trade leadership a decade earlier. In New York, after the speculation in governments in he early 'nineties came to a close, the security market became very restricted, and many of the brokers turned their attention o other affairs. In fact, it was not until 1817 that the New York Stock Exchange was formally organized and a written onstitution adopted.[7]

The War of 1812 had to be financed entirely at home. The overnment's efforts to raise money were attended by the greatst difficulties, to a large extent because of the sharp division f opinion as to the wisdom of the conflict and the failure to echarter the First Bank of the United States. However, the ar did show that capital accumulation had proceeded to a oint where large sums could be raised in the domestic market. When in 1813, with bankruptcy staring it in the face, the Treasury asked for $16,000,000, the public bought only about 5,000,000 of its bonds. Secretary Gallatin then called in the ree leading capitalists of the day, Stephen Girard, John Jacob stor and David Parish, and they took the remaining 6 per cent

[7] Stedman, E. C., *The New York Stock Exchange*, pp. 62 ff.

bonds at approximately 88 per cent of par.[8] Similarly, the sale of the $35,000,000 of capital stock of the Second Bank of the United States, also through direct public offering, was successfully accomplished with the aid of the large fortunes of the day in 1816. A balance of more than $3,000,000 of the stock of the institution not taken by the public was subscribed for in one block by Stephen Girard.

Internal Improvements and the Import of Capital (1817-1840)

Following the close of the War of 1812, three important factors combined to change investment banking conditions in this country radically. In the first place, a mania for internal improvements arose which created a need for large amounts of capital far in excess of visible supplies, whereas previously the accumulation of capital here seemed to equal domestic requirements. In the second place, the close of the war in Europe resulted in a surplus of capital in England which eagerly sought the higher rates of return available abroad. In the third place, nascent industrial development in New England and other seaboard areas, and the opening up of new areas across the Appalachians, sharply reduced the supply of free capital within the country available to finance the internal improvement program.

The period of internal improvements was ushered in by the phenomenal success of the Erie Canal. Financed through the sale of state bonds, at first sold to Albany banks, this enterprise paid for itself from the start. The great increase in commerce and wealth it brought the City and State of New York resulted in a host of projects by other states to imitate it. The other states, like New York, were ready to back these projects with their own credit.

Conditions were peculiarly favorable at the time for the attracting of British capital to this country. In the first place, the rapid repayment of the national debt of the United States after the close of the War of 1812 tended to create confidence. Secondly, Hamilton had taken over the state debts after the Revolution, and there was a strong tendency to ascribe to the states on this account approximately the same credit standing as that possessed by the federal government. Thirdly, the lead

[8] "National Finances," *Bankers' Magazine,* vol. i, p. 257.

ing banking house in London was closely affiliated with American finance, and helped to confirm the already favorable attitude of the English investors toward their Anglo-Saxon cousins across the seas.

The house of Baring Brothers & Company was to play the chief rôle in the drama which followed. Originally wool manufacturers from Bremen, this family turned their interests to trade to an increasing extent during the eighteenth century. Alexander Baring late in the century allied himself by marriage with the wealthy Bingham family of Philadelphia, which both added largely to his wealth and centered his attention upon the United States. When the Napoleonic Wars came to a close, not even the Rothschilds had the prestige and wealth possessed by the Barings in England, and the firm was foremost in the financing of American trade and, later, the American states.

About 1817, British purchases of American securities began to take on sizable proportions. Two years later, an observer writes that this practice already was "of many years' standing, and therefore escapes observation."[9] New York State issued $7,000,000 of its bonds between 1817 and 1825 to finance the construction of the Erie Canal, and these bonds rapidly found their way to London. New York 6's appeared there in quantity in 1817, and were officially quoted on the London Stock Exchange in that year. A great stimulus was given to British investments here by the collapse of South American securities on the London market in 1825. This brought into vogue "reproductive investments," and within this classification American state and municipal bonds issued for internal improvements had a foremost place.

By 1836, there had been invested $90,000,000 in canals and railways in the northern states. More than half of this sum was raised through the pledging of state credit and the sale of bonds in England. In addition, the southern states borrowed for both internal improvements and, more especially, land mortgage banks, since the plantation system in the South created capital needs for the purchase of slaves, etc. The British also held about that time $14,000,000 in federal government

[9] *Niles Register*, vol. xlv, p. 178.

bonds and $8,000,000 in United States Bank stock, as well as substantial tracts of land for speculative appreciation.

It is highly significant that the British favored public securities, and shares of institutions like the Bank of the United States, in which foreign shareholders had no right to vote. Had they insisted and developed a suitable organization for the purpose, the British might have secured control of the railroads and other large enterprises then initiated in much the same way as they have subsequently in South America and other parts of the world. In Argentina, the great bulk of the railroads and public utilities, and many of the large agricultural and business enterprises, are directed from London. But despite large imports of capital made by the United States at various times in its history, actual ownership and operation of its leading enterprises have, with very few and minor exceptions, been retained by American citizens. The British in this early period did buy the bonds of a few railroads in the East and the stock of a few New York and New Orleans banks and some mining shares. But the aggregate of these was small and the only substantial institution which they controlled wa the Bank of the Manhattan Company, which the Marquis o Carmarthen was said to own "body and breeches," except fo directors' qualifying shares, for its board had to be composed o citizens of New York. This provision in the charter probabl hastened the later repatriation of the ownership of this financial institution.

The Machinery for the Import of Capital

The investment banking mechanism which was created t finance the internal improvement program at home and abroa was relatively simple. There were practically no public offerings through underwriters. The state and municipal bonds wer generally sold here through commissioners, appointed by stat governments, who acted as agents and solicited bids, or by contract to merchants or bankers. Thus they were originally Amer can issues, although they often contained provisions for th payment of the coupons in London at a fixed rate of exchang at the option of the holder. Large blocks of bonds were pu chased in this way in New York at various times by Astor

Sons, by the leading brokerage house of Prime, Ward & King,[10] and by such banks as the Morris Canal & Banking Company and the Bank of the Manhattan Company.

These bonds were then sent abroad in large amounts to build up balances upon which these American bankers could draw to help pay for our imports. The financing of American trade was gradually concentrated in the hands of a small number of large merchants and banking houses. The Yankee dry-goods houses were especially prominent in this connection, and many of them gradually developed a substantial banking business as an offshoot of their trading operations. In order to build up balances in London against which they could draw in order to make payments for their purchases both in Europe and the Far East, where the United States had a heavy import excess, these houses remitted large blocks of these state securities. They were sent to the leading London banking houses, who in turn distributed them to favored country banks for distribution to favored clients.[11]

A marked change took place in the method by which Ameri-an securities were distributed to English investors after 1836. In that year, the charter of the Second Bank of the United States expired and was not renewed. This institution, with a apital of $35,000,000, was then transformed into a Pennsyl-ania corporation, and its business was modified to include a umber of investment banking transactions found necessary o secure full employment for the large capital. An agency vas opened in London, and Nicholas Biddle, the president, egan to bid for entire issues of American securities, which he ent to his London agency for disposal there. In fact, the vowed purpose of the opening of this agency was to "popu-arize American securities," which were in turn to be sold broad in order to maintain the speculative structure at home. This had been badly shaken by the panic of 1837 and Jack-on's insistence on specie payments for sales of public lands, en taking place on a large scale for speculative purposes. The

[10] Nathaniel Prime was regarded as the first real private banker in the city. e "Banking in New York, 1822-1922," issued by the Farmers' Loan & Trust ompany.

[11] Jenks, L. H., *The Migration of British Capital to 1875*, p. 78.

agency became the chief channel for the raising of investment capital abroad for the United States.

By thus providing the means for meeting indebtedness incurred by this country abroad on account of imports of merchandise and interest payments due, Biddle succeeded in keeping the bubble of internal improvements and speculation, accompanied by the wholesale issue of new indebtedness, inflated for several years more. In the end, the Bank of the United States was hopelessly bankrupt, and simultaneously, in 1841 and 1842, nine states stopped payment of interest on their indebtedness.

As an example of the way in which capital was raised for American use in this period, the case of the $5,000,000 Mississippi bond issue may be cited. In 1838, the State of Mississipp decided to establish a mortgage bank to aid planters, and i subscribed for the stock of the institution, paying with $5,000,000 of its bonds. Three commissioners were then designate by the directors of the bank to sell these bonds in order to rais liquid capital for the bank. They negotiated with Nichola Biddle for the sale of the entire amount. The bonds wer made payable at the agency of the Bank of the United Stat in London, thus facilitating their sales to British investors. M Biddle promised to pay for the issue in five annual installment The Bank of the United States in the meanwhile used the bonds in Europe as collateral for loans which it obtained fro such leading bankers as Hope & Company of Amsterdam. Th bonds were gradually sold in England, although Biddle nev succeeded in selling the entire issue.

Within less than two years, it is interesting to note, th Mississippi bank was hopelessly insolvent because of the ra manner in which it made its loans. The state shortly thereaft repudiated the bonds, charging that a number of technicaliti in the enabling act had not been complied with.[12]

The example of the Bank of the United States in establishi direct ties between the American borrowers and the Lond capital market was followed by others. George Peabody, Yankee dry-goods merchant, went to London and founded t house which later became Morgan, Grenfell & Company

[12] "The Origin of Repudiation," *Bankers' Magazine*, vol. i, p. 337.

1837, to specialize in Maryland securities. The Rothschilds sent August Belmont to make his headquarters in New York as their personal representative. The French house of Hottinguer, also interested in American securities, sent a representative to this country who cooperated closely with Biddle. Finally, many Americans went overseas to negotiate loans di-rectly for a commission.

The Domestic Capital Market

In the meanwhile, the accumulation of capital within this ountry went on, and the home money market began to assume izable proportions. Foreign capital did not play any signifiant part in the financing of American manufacturing indusries, such as the textile mills of New England and the iron nanufactories of Pennsylvania. In the first place, the British vere not accustomed to joint-stock industrial companies, having ractically none of these in their own market at that time. Secndly, the British merchant bankers, who were also engaged to large extent in exporting manufactured products to the Jnited States, did not relish fostering competition here. As a esult, American industry remained independent of foreign apital, a fact which was fraught with great significance for the ture. Another factor was that British houses which would ave been likely to take over control of industries here, such as ie Rothschilds, did not play an important rôle in financing ie United States. Until 1835, the Rothschilds, the "bankers legitimacy" as they were called, refused to have anything to with the new republic, which they regarded askance as a volutionary affair.

In the 'thirties, the American capital market consisted of a umber of moneyed families in the seaboard cities, a group of surance companies in the leading cities, the banks which were ringing up everywhere and, finally, a growing class of merants and manufacturers who invested in relatively small nounts and appeared at the time to favor stocks in railroads d financial institutions. The latter class constituted the chief ents of the brokers who were then building up exchanges in e leading centers.

A compilation made in 1831 showed that in New York City

alone there were sixteen banks with a combined capital of $18,130,000, eight marine insurance companies with a capital of $3,050,000, and twenty-five fire insurance companies with a capital of $7,800,000. Boston, which had forged ahead to second place in financial importance, had eighteen banks with a capital of $13,900,000, and Philadelphia had thirteen banks with a capital of $10,792,000. In arriving at these figures, each office of the Bank of the United States was allowed a capital of $1,500,000.[13]

The commercial banks exercised investment banking functions in two ways. First, they bought the new state and municipal securities in large blocks for their own account wherever their charters made this possible. Secondly, they made large loans to promoters and others on the security of stocks and bonds. The Bank of the United States did both on a large scale. It turned over entire issues of bonds which it sold or pawned in Europe, and it also loaned over $20,000,000 on the security of turnpike, canal, railroad and land companies, often directly to these companies themselves to help them to complete their projects. Numerous smaller banks—347 were chartered between 1830 and 1837—also sprang up, "willing to finance almost any conceivable proposal."[14] "Wildcat banking," in which the distinction between commercial and investment operations disappeared, was flourishing at this time.

The three years following the panic of 1837 closed a period of rapid internal development and widespread speculation throughout the country. During this period, a substantial capital market was developed for the first time, a number of canals and railways were built, and the frontier was pushed farther westward to the Mississippi.

The three least fortunate developments were the mania for speculative land purchases, the defaults on the debts of many of the states held abroad, and the spread of unsound banking methods. Many of the new banks, especially in the West and South, although designed as commercial banks, actually turned out to be land banks run on very unsound principles. In the "wildcat" days, banks were organized which sold their stock i

[13] Goddard, Thomas H., *A General History of Banking.*

[14] McGrane, R. C., *The Panic of 1837*, p. 17.

return for real estate mortgages, and then utilized to the full their right under state law to issue currency up to two and one-half times the amount of their capital. In the seaboard states, however, a sounder view of the relation of the banks to the real estate market generally obtained, even during the speculative period. The general banking law of Massachusetts, first passed in 1829, provided that banks should not invest more than 12 per cent of their capital in real estate, including the banking premises.

The panic of 1837 and subsequent large losses suffered by banks through dealing in securities caused many states once again to seek a more rigid separation of commercial and investment banking. The spectacular failure of the Bank if the United States in 1841, in which it was found that the depreciation of its security holdings had wiped out its capital of $35,-000,000, accentuated this tendency. Charters of banks organized in New York under the safety fund scheme provided invariably that the bank "shall not directly or indirectly deal or trade in . . . buying or selling any stock created under any act of the United States or any particular State, unless in selling the same when truly pledged by way of security for debts due." In commenting on this legal provision, the *Bankers' Magazine* said, "The object of the statute was doubtless to prevent banks from hazarding their capital, especially in stock jobbing, to which they are often strongly tempted, and from which disastrous consequences often follow."[15]

In the eastern cities, notably New York, call loan markets were already established, thus making the liquid funds of the banks the means of financing the holding of investment securities representing long-term commitments of capital. During the panic of 1837, when the drastic decline in securities made it impossible to realize on many such loans, they were severely criticized in the public press, although the practice was recognized as long-established, and therefore perhaps a necessary evil.

Moreover, in this period there is already visible the beginning of a tendency to separate real estate financing from commercial banking, and to leave the latter to specialized institu-

[15] *Bankers' Magazine,* vol. ii, p. 741.

tions. Thus in 1835, an Illinois lawyer, Francis B. Peabody by name, found his eastern clients so eager for sound mortgages on Illinois property that he opened a mortgage banking house, one of the first in the country, and certainly the first in the West.[16]

Recuperation and Growth (1840-1860)

With the cutting off of the supplies of foreign capital after the collapse of the second Bank of the United States in 1839 and the numerous defaults of the states in the same period, the growth of the country continued for a time at a slower pace, but also without the symptoms of exaggerated speculation which had marked the preceding era. The experience of the wildcat banks resulted in a general disposition to curtail banking activity, and especially to differentiate commercial from investment banking.

In the southern states, for example, where some of the worst examples of unsound banking had occurred, amendments were generally passed severely restricting investments by banks in real estate and securities. There was a general disposition to recognize the essential differences between banking with liquid and with illiquid assets, and doubtless the experience of the panic period played an important rôle in making relatively complete the segregation of commercial and investment banking institutions in this country, which thereafter became a marked feature of American financial organization.

Railroad building attracted increasing interest during this era, but this time the banks did not play an important part in their development. Instead, a number of brokerage houses became specially interested in their securities, and these houses in several cases advanced money to the railroads and secured representation on the boards of directors as a result. Thus we find the firm of Drew, Robinson & Company active in this connection in the 'forties, the Drew being none other than Daniel Drew, who was to become the prototype of a new type of predatory financier twenty years later. Drew helped finance the Erie Railroad when it was being built across southern Ne

[16] *Financing an Empire—History of Banking in Illinois,* pp. 536 ff. This fir has continued down to the present day in the house of Peabody, Smith Company.

York State, lending money on the collateral of its stock and convertible bonds, which he later took over in payment for the loan. In this way he secured a place on the board of directors of the company. Jacob Little shares with Drew the rôle of founding a line of more predatory speculators. Another figure who was later to play an important rôle, Jay Gould, also appeared in Wall Street in the late 'fifties as head of a brokerage house interested in railroad securities.

The growing speculation in railroad and miscellaneous securities caused a rapid expansion of the exchanges. The following table traces the growth of the New York Stock Exchange, as shown by fragmentary data available:

Year	Number of Brokers	Approximate Average Daily Turnover
1817	20	Several shares
1820	39	" "
1827	..	100
1828	..	600
1830	..	1,000
1848	112	5,000

So great had speculative interest become, that a New Board of Brokers was founded as a separate exchange, which competed for a time with the original Old Board. The former, however, gradually died out.

While the financial supremacy of New York was unquestioned after the early 'thirties, the other seaboard cities were often close competitors. Thus, in Philadelphia the house of E. W. Clark & Company financed the Mexican war, and the Philadelphia investment market rivaled that of New York in wealth and influence. This firm, as did that of Corcoran & Riggs in Washington, had great influence with rich investors and a substantial distribution power, and they played an important part in promoting new railroads and reorganizing bankrupt canal and railway companies.

In the late 'forties, European interest in American finance began to revive, but henceforth the foreign investor favored railroad securities issued by private corporations. August Schoenberg had come from Vienna in 1837 to establish an agency here for the Rothschilds, which developed into the international banking house of August Belmont & Company, and played a leading rôle in directing a new flow of foreign capital into American enterprise. An official compilation made in 1854 clearly illustrates the relative importance of foreign holdings in each group of securities outstanding.[17]

Security	Total Outstanding	Foreign Owned	Percentage Foreign Owned
United States government...	$ 58,205,000	$ 27,000,000	46
States....................	190,718,000	110,972,000	58
Counties and cities..........	93,280,000	21,462,000	23
Railroad bonds.............	170,112,000	43,889,000	26
Railroad stocks.............	309,894,000	8,026,000	3
Banks and insurance.......	279,555,000	7,067,000	3
Canals and navigation......	58,019,000	2,522,000	4
Miscellaneous..............	18,814,000	1,068,000	6
Total.................	$1,178,597,000	$222,006,000	18

In the years preceding the panic of 1857 speculation again became active, especially in stocks. The call money market developed enormously to keep pace with the demand for securities. The attitude of the time toward this feature of the market for securities, which facilitated the carrying of stocks for speculative purposes and made of such loans the most liquid investments available for the banks, is expressed in the following statement from the Report of the Massachusetts Banking Commissioners made public in 1855: "Extension upon the basis of business paper is a very different thing from distention created by speculation upon mere capital—that is, loans upon stocks, instead of discounts of promises representing something that has an intrinsic value."

The free use of the call loan, which has been common since the period of internal improvements and bank incorporations that began with the War of 1812, has been a factor little appreciated in keeping the control of American industry within this country during the period when large imports of capital made

[17] Secretary of the Treasury, *Report on Foreign Holdings of American Securities,* made to Congress in 1854.

it possible for foreign control to gain a strong foothold in the management of our industry. During this era, the foreign investor sought to minimize his risks at the very time that the American, fired with pioneer optimistic zeal, was ready to take more than an ordinary chance for a large profit. The free use of the call loan opened up to the speculator the means of easily financing his operations by making available to him on a low-cost basis the funds of the commercial banks, usually an ample source of liquid capital in the growing commercial and industrial communities of the seaboard cities.

A sequel to the rapid development of the call loan market was the evolution of the peculiar American system of daily settlements on the exchange. In the early days of the exchange, most transactions involved delivery of stock after an interval, usually up to 60 days. The average period of settlement tended to become shorter, and by 1857 daily settlements were formally adopted.

The Civil War and the Rise of the American Bond House

By the opening of the Civil War, the financing of the railroads and states and cities had created an investment banking machinery of substantial proportions. However, American investment banking practice was not then differentiated, as it was later to be, from methods pursued in other countries. Owing to the small clientele available for investment issues, they were sold through consultation by the investment banker with his client in the latter's office. The salesman, and other "high pressure" agents for achieving security distribution which characterized the further development of the business, were not yet in evidence. A radical change in the character of the investment banking business was to be brought about during the Civil War, just as another revolution in methods and size was to be accomplished by another war more than half a century later.

The development of investment middlemen here, as elsewhere, was a direct outgrowth of the practice of underwriting, or insuring, an issue of securities. Originally, as has been seen, new security issues were often offered directly by the company to the public. To avoid the uncertainty of the public response —especially in cases where the proceeds had been spent in advance on the property—the company turned to a banking or brokerage house and, for a fee, induced it to guarantee the sale of the issue, the unsold portion being taken up by the underwriters. There is but one step from this procedure to the outright purchase of the entire issue by the investment banker; in fact, the purchase of an issue of securities for subsequent resale is still called an underwriting operation, but the term is an anachronism in the modern method of bond issue. In England, new security issues are in fact frequently offered to the public by the issuing company, and the bankers merely appear as the underwriters who will take over only the unsold portion of the offering.

The sale of government bonds during the Civil War witnessed the first outburst of active bond selling in this country, although rudimentary cases existed during the preceding era of railroad promotion. The credit of the government was poor, and the European market, to which borrowers here had been in the custom of resorting for large bond issues, was unfriendly to the union cause. Accordingly, the Treasury was faced with the immediate necessity of creating a great market for government bonds. Jay Cooke, a Philadelphia banker trained in the old house of E. W. Clarke & Company, accomplished this task, and helped revolutionize the American investment banking business more than any other single individual. In 1861, he formed his own firm and joined with the older house of Drexel & Company in selling a $3,000,000 Pennsylvania State Loan at par, above the market price, through an appeal to patriotic principles. He then took an interest in the federal government bonds at that time appearing on the market in increasing quantities to finance the war. Already the market for them was showing signs of exhaustion, and grave fears were expressed concerning the ability of the government to continue to raise money. Jay Cooke achieved remarkable success in selling bonds locally through salesmen and with the aid of widespread advertising, and Secretary Chase finally appointed him Government Loan Sales Agent, in which capacity he directed the sale of federal bonds during the period of the conflict. He was the original bond salesman, the prototype of the thousands of men and women who now earn a living by selling securities. At one time, he alone employed 5,000 such salesmen.

Jay Cooke first developed many of the most prominent characteristics of American investment banking—developed them through the application to bond selling of the pioneer psychology which was evident in many other economic activities in this country. His methods have been graphically described by one biographer as follows:[18]

"Mr. Cooke's agents—he employed some five thousand during the second 'seven-thirty drive'—went everywhere. They overran the countryside visiting very hamlet and farm, appealing to every living person they could find. They distributed posters and circulars—broadsides, some of them, with eagles and mothers on one side and popular songs on the back—in railroad stations, courthouses and hotels, in factories, in stores, in trains; they gave them to toll gate keepers, to postmasters, to the teamsters on the roads; they pasted them on walls, they put them up on trees, they tacked them on telegraph poles; and they interviewed newspaper editors."

Cooke was the first American financier to realize to the full the power of the press in finance, and to use it. From that day to this, the lesson he taught has been well learned and applied by a host of imitators. He won the favor of editors and writers by flattery, by threats, by dangling advertising contracts before them and by doing favors. In return, the news and editorial columns resounded with his name and with his message—the maximum purchase of government bonds by every individual in the country. And the result was that the Treasury was able to sell $2,000,000,000 of bonds during the war period. He was also the pioneer financial advertiser.

It may be asked why the number of security holders dwindled after Cooke's efforts ended; why the United States did not become right then and there a "nation of bondholders," a phrase much used sixty years later. The answer is that individual business opportunities were so great that capital was withdrawn from securities and put back into individual business enterprises—agricultural, industrial, and commercial—as soon as the war came to an end and pressure to purchase and hold bonds

[18] Minnigerode, Meade, *Certain Rich Men*, pp. 65-66.

was removed. However, the dimensions of the permanent market for investment securities were greatly enlarged by Cooke's efforts, despite the contraction which followed the panic of 1873.

Next to Jay Cooke's management of the sale of government bonds, the most significant event of the Civil War from the investment banking viewpoint was the passage of the National Bank Act of 1862. Designed to furnish a sound and stable currency in the form of bond-secured bank notes, these national banks became, shortly after the war, the chief group of financial institutions in the country. Outside of their purchase of government bonds as note-issue security, they were expected to restrict their activities to commercial banking. The law permitted them to negotiate "promissory notes, drafts, bills of exchange and other evidences of debt." It was only later that the Comptroller of the Currency ruled that "other evidences of debt" might include bonds.

The development of the investment banking business in this country after the Civil War may be divided into three great historic eras:

1. The period of railroad promotion
2. The period of industrial consolidation
3. The period of the export of capital and widespread popular security distribution (the post-war boom).

Railroad Building and Industrial Development—The Rise of the International Bankers (1865-1893)

The period from the end of the Civil War to the panic of 1893 was dominated by the rapid growth of our transportation network and the evolution of the great railroad systems. More than 30,000 miles of new track were laid between the close of the Civil War and the panic of 1873. These railroads were the cause for the rise of the United States to the first rank among agricultural exporting nations. This period also witnessed the coming of age of the American capital market, although at the same time some $2,000,000,000 of European capital is estimated to have been invested in this country, almost entirely in railroad securities.

Industrial development in this era was rapid, but it assumed largely the form of relatively small individual enterprises and local corporations, so that the industrials did not as yet play an important part in American finance. But this period of the growth of numerous small enterprises made possible its spectacular sequel, the combination and trust era. However, even in the 'eighties a few industrial combinations aiming at substantial monopoly power already appeared on the horizon—the oil, sugar and whiskey trusts. Also, the investment bankers were not important as yet in the industrial field. The more important combinations were then being evolved by the industrialists themselves—people like the Rockefellers in oil and the Havemeyers in sugar.

One outstanding exception to the rule was the exploitation of the copper resources of Michigan with Boston capital. The Boston exchange became the chief market for copper securities in the world in the 'seventies and 'eighties, and a number of banking houses were formed there to specialize in them. Several of these houses have survived as leading financial institutions down to the present day. For a time, it seemed that the financial capital of conservative New England was to become the most speculative market in the country, but enthusiasm gradually simmered down as the industry gained stability.

In the investment banking field, this period witnessed a curious evolution in the decline, after 1873, of the distributing houses built up during and directly after the Civil War, and the rise to dominance of the so-called international bankers, whose chief source of power was their foreign connections—their ability to sell American securities which they sponsored to bankers in England, Holland and Germany. Directly after the Civil War, Jay Cooke and a number of bond houses turned their energies to the financing of railroads. The financial press of that period is full of railroad offerings of such companies as the Northern Pacific, Chesapeake & Ohio, and what later became the New York, Ontario & Western. These issues were sponsored by houses with extensive sales forces, who often based their selling appeal on the superior yields in these securities over those offered by the government bonds they had originally sold to their clients. Municipal securities also were recommended by these houses, especially high-yielding issues of the southern and western states.

The panic of 1873, chiefly marked by the failure of Jay Cooke and his associated banks, was brought on by the collapse of several of the railroads which were being financed by the distributing houses. Jay Cooke, who sold Northern Pacific bonds "almost exclusively to persons who rely upon our recommendations rather than upon their own judgment," finally discovered that "there is a limit to this class and their money." Having tied up his own funds in an endeavor to finance the company pending the sale of its bonds, he was forced into bankruptcy when the road lost its credit. A number of the big distributing houses disappeared during the panic and subsequent depression, and in many cases the properties they originally financed came to look to the international bankers, with their access to wider capital markets, for funds.

The government loans of 1878 and 1879, issued in connection with the resumption of specie payments, were handled by a group of international bankers, of which August Belmont was the head. These transactions definitely established the preeminence of the international bankers. The rise of the international banking houses was accompanied by largely increased flotations abroad of American securities. This is illustrated in the following table (in millions of dollars) of offerings in the London market:[19]

Year	U. S. Securities	State and Municipal	Railwa
1860–1865.........	None	2	27.
1866–1870.........	None	17	51.5
1871–1875.........	800	40	275.

In addition, several relatively small utility and industria issues were made in London after 1870.

Another characteristic of the period ending with the panic c 1873 was the appearance on the speculative markets, whic had grown apace, especially under the stimulus of the eas money of the greenback régime, of a number of unscrupulou operators who acquired control of several American corpor tions through purchase of their shares on the open marke Daniel Drew, Jim Fisk and Jay Gould were the more conspic

[19] Jenks, L. H., *The Migration of British Capital to 1875*, p. 426.

ous figures, and the last-named continued on his course of successful speculative control of giant corporations, generally at the expense of the smaller stockholders and speculators, down to the end of the period. In individual instances, battles for control of railroads between these speculators and the international bankers were already occurring. The defeat of the speculator, however, was not finally accomplished until the panic of 1893.

A different type of promoter-operator was typified by Commodore Vanderbilt, who invested a fortune of $10,000,000, earned in the shipping business, in railroads in the 'sixties, and within twenty years had increased his wealth tenfold through the purchase and consolidation of railroad properties. Vanderbilt ran his properties with at least one eye glued to the stock market, but he did not neglect to put these properties under efficient management and to make them highly useful, even if at times grasping and monopolistic, public servants. In his constructive efforts, he often came into bitter conflict with the speculators of the Gould type, who in the memorable battle over control of the Erie Railroad in 1868 outdid him in shrewdness and lack of scruple.[20]

The multiplication of stock and bond issues of railroad companies on the American stock exchanges gave these institutions a decidedly speculative character probably unequaled in any other important financial center. The essentially speculative nature of much of the railroad building and financing, resulting from the fact that railroads were being built ahead of the need for them to an unprecedented extent in this country, furnished the necessary background for the operations of such men as Gould and Drew. And the temper of the security-buying public in this market was such as to welcome the opportunity to assume the risks involved in the stock and junior bond issues, while European markets took mainly the senior bonds and the junior issues of only the better properties. European investors became holders of the more speculative American securities at this time principally only as a result of the recurrent waves

[20] See Adams, Charles Francis, and Henry, A., *Chapter of Erie and Other Essays*, for an interesting account of this episode.

of receiverships and reorganizations among the transportation companies.

The extent to which the speculative machinery expanded after 1875 may be traced in the following statistics of the volume of trading on the New York Stock Exchange:

Year	Average Volume of Shares Sold Annually
1875–1879	51,244,048
1880–1884	104,388,480
1885–1889	83,096,264
1890–1893	76,791,376

While the old large security-distributing houses of the East, such as Jay Cooke & Company, Fisk & Hatch, etc., were eclipsed by the panic of 1873, a new group, also of a purely domestic character, made its appearance at this time. The price of capital in the West was naturally much higher than in the East, and there were many types of high-yielding western securities which, for one reason or another, could not be sold in Europe. Hence, a market for them had to be built up in our eastern cities. In the early 'eighties, several houses arose to sell western municipals and mortgages, and these houses gradually revived the methods of Jay Cooke, first developed in the sale of Civil War bonds. Thus N. W. Harris & Company of Chicago was at first ridiculed for efforts to sell bonds by the method of "ringing door-bells," as the widespread use of salesmen was termed. But it prospered nevertheless, and developed into a large wholesaling and distributing house under the name of Harris, Forbes & Company.

The end of this period witnessed the rise of the international banking houses to a position of complete domination in the financial organization. Numerous failures among the railroads brought about foreclosures which wiped out the equities of the original promoters and the later speculative managers, and they were replaced by the bankers who had sold the bond issues to investors here and abroad. These banking houses gained further prestige when the government had to resort to them in 1894 and 1895 for large loans in order to replenish its disappearing gold reserve, scattered by the disastrous experiment in large-scale silver coinage between 1890 and 1893. The prestige and wealth gained by the important banking houses at this time permitted them to play the leading rôle in the next stage of financial evolution, the consolidation of American industry into giant units.[21]

Trust and Consolidation Period (1893-1914)

The recovery of the country from the panic of 1893 was accomplished within a few years; and by 1896 a combination of bountiful harvests and industrial recovery had abruptly changed the financial position of the country, in the words of Noyes, from "the crippled industrial and financial state of 1894, with the country's principal industries declining, its great corporations drifting into bankruptcy and its Government forced to borrow on usurious terms from Europe to maintain the public credit," to that of "a community whose prosperity had become the wonder of the outside world, whose productive industries had developed such strength that the 'American invasion' was discussed abroad as threatening ruin to our European competitors."[22]

The accumulation of capital within the country ran for a time beyond the demand at home. One English estimate placed this annual capital accretion at $450,000,000.[23] Accordingly, a curious period of capital export developed, foreshadowing what was to happen on an immensely larger scale twenty years later. The international banking houses, whose chief function had been to furnish a link between the foreign capital markets and American corporations and governments, now began to participate in English, German, Cuban, Japanese and Mexican financing to acquire securities for distribution in this market. In 1896 and 1897 alone, nearly $200,000,000 of foreign securities were offered in this market because of the plethora of capital seeking investment. At the same time, a large part of the American securities held in Europe flowed back to this market.

[21] Raymond, Wm. L., "History of American Investment Banking," *Barron's Finance Weekly,* May 31 and June 7, 1926.

[22] Noyes, A. D., *Forty Years of American Finance,* p. 257.

[23] Ford, Walter F., "American Investments in England," *Contemporary Review,* Vol. lxxix.

By 1901, it has been estimated, about one-fourth of the Amer ican securities theretofore held in Europe had been repurchased and brought back here.

But this capital export movement was not destined to continue. It was merely a by-product of the rapid accumulation of capital at a time when public confidence in the domestic situation was still only partially reestablished. Before long, huge drafts were being made on the domestic supplies of capital in rehabilitating the railroads. The Union Pacific, Reading, Northern Pacific and a number of others issued large amounts of securities and levied huge assessments on their stockholders in order to finance their rehabilitation. Within a short time, we find the European capital markets again being called upon to purchase issues of American securities because of the resumption of large-scale expansion here. Railroad development soon assumed an unprecedented scale because of numerous consolidations which resulted in the evolution of larger and sounder units in the industry. It was in this period that Hill and Harriman, the New York Central and the Pennsylvania, were engaged in purchasing control of most of the independent systems of the country in order to weld them into great communities of interest. The ability to sell 3½ and 4 per cent bonds at par for the stronger properties stimulated these plans.

New issues of railway securities expanded as follows:

1898	$ 67,000,000
1899	107,000,000
1900	199,000,000
1901	434,000,000
1902	527,000,000

But the reorganization of the American railroad system was a relatively small task compared with the achievement which followed—consolidation of many individual plants in each of the important industries of the country into nation-wide organizations. The protection of the tariff, the rapid growth of the home and foreign markets, the desire to avoid cutthroat competition and the avidity of the capital markets for new securities combined to favor this development; and between 1899 and 1901 there were formed 200 of our most important industrial combinations, such as the United States Steel Corporation, the American Can Company, the American Locomotive Company, the International Harvester Company, etc. Within this two-year period, new corporations with a total capital of $10,000,000,000 were formed, an achievement not again equaled for more than a quarter of a century. Most of this capitalization represented capital stock issued against good will or excess earning power—that is, it constituted "water." The public paid its money for this "water," thus transferring its accumulations of wealth to the previous owners of the different enterprises going into the combinations, and to the promoters and bankers who facilitated this transfer of ownership of large equities in our great industries to the public.

The investment banking mechanism expanded to a great extent to help in the absorption of these vast issues of securities. In order to attract public confidence, the great international banking houses and many of the older brokerage houses were given leading rôles in accomplishing such consolidations. This was a natural development, also, because large amounts of liquid capital were needed to accomplish these transactions; and, as was later revealed in the New York insurance investigation of 1906, funds of the life insurance companies themselves, which they controlled, had been utilized by the bankers in organizing the United States Steel Corporation, the International Mercantile Marine Corporation, etc.

As a natural corollary to the introduction of vast amounts of new industrial securities into the domestic capital market, there was an enormous expansion in the volume of securities turned over on the stock exchanges. Public speculation was rife, and the brokerage houses did a flourishing business. The securities of the new industrial combinations, although greatly watered, were eagerly bid up for a time by the outside public after they were listed on the stock exchanges. A world-wide rise in commodity prices stimulated both business activity and speculation—especially the latter—and the mass of the population was soon involved in the speculative vortex in one way or another, through dealing in securities or real estate.

The extensive capitalization of industrial enterprises and the sale of their securities to the public during these years made new types of securities available for investment and speculation here. Until this period, government and municipal bonds, railroad securities and bank and insurance stocks constituted the great bulk of the issues available. The only other staple investment was the individual real estate mortgage, for the largest portion of the national wealth still took the form of rural and urban real estate. After 1901, however, public utility and industrial securities gradually assumed a preponderant rôle in the securities markets. In 1898, there were only twenty industrial issues listed on the New York Stock Exchange, but by 1915, the number had grown to one hundred and seventy-three. In 1902, industrials and utilities accounted for only 25 per cent of the turnover on the exchange. By 1928, this figure had risen to over 94 per cent.

The industrial and financial expansion of this period naturally led to excesses, all the more so because of the sound basis upon which it originally began. The panic of 1907 and subsequent liquidation brought down values to a more normal level, and squeezed out a large part of the credit advanced by the banks for the purpose of carrying securities for a rise. Speculation for the rise in securities continued intermittently in the following years, largely because of the efforts of the expanded speculative machinery to keep going at a higher rate despite public apathy. The record of capital issues and security trading on the New York Stock Exchange on page 233 indicates the extent to which financial operations quieted down prior to the European war, as compared with the preceding period of reckless expansion and speculation.

The regulation of investment banking came to the fore as a vital problem of the day after the public became directly interested in the security markets, especially as an aftermath of the panic of 1907. Many investors suffered heavy losses on account of both speculation and fraud, which had a sobering effect on the popular mind. Early regulation had concerned itself with incorporated financial institutions only and, as has been seen above, tended for the most part to the limitation of security holding and dealing powers of commercial and savings banks. Insurance companies were subjected to more rigid regulation after the Hughes investigation of 1906 had unearthed unsound practices. But the investment banker and the broker, carrying

Year	Stock Exchange Stock Dealings (in shares)	Stock Exchange Bond Dealings (par value)	New Capital Issues	New Incorporations (000 omitted)
1896	56,663,023	$ 394,329,000		
1899	175,073,855	336,451,120		
1900	138,312,266	578,359,230		
1901	265,577,354	999,404,920	No data available	No data available[24]
1902	188,321,181	891,305,150		
1903	100,748,366	684,200,850		
1904	186,429,384	1,036,810,569		
1905	263,040,993	1,018,090,420		
1906	283,707,955	676,392,500		
1907	195,445,321	527,166,350	$1,393,913	$2,545,053
1908	196,821,875	1,084,454,020	1,423,199	2,059,184
1909	214,425,978	1,314,656,200	1,681,621	2,465,073
1910	163,882,956	634,091,000	1,518,272	2,869,073
1911	126,515,906	889,567,100	1,739,488	2,906,002
1912	131,051,116	674,215,000	2,253,587	3,288,245
1913	83,083,585	501,155,920	1,645,736	2,191,659
1914	47,899,593	461,898,100	1,436,518	1,581,418

on their business for the most part as private individuals or in partnerships, were practically unregulated.

With the growing wealth of the country and the spread of security speculation appeared also a wider field of operations for the sellers of fraudulent securities. This hastened the popular demand for regulation of security selling, and led to the passage of the first blue-sky law in Kansas in 1911. The purpose of this Act was "to provide for the regulation and supervision of investment companies and providing penalties for the violation thereof." The Bank Commissioner was to receive data on all securities offered within the state, and also semi-annual statements of the condition of all investment companies doing business in the state. The operation of the law resulted in the revelation of a surprising condition. During the first year of its operation, out of 1500 applications for permission to sell securities filed, more than 75 per cent were adjudged fraudulent,

[24] A compilation of the authorized capitalization of industrial companies alone of $1,000,000 or more formed in this earlier period appears in an article by Charles A. Conant in the *Journal of the American Statistical Association* for 1901. The figures are:

1896	$ 49,850,000
1897	81,000,000
1898	708,600,000
1899	2,243,995,000
1900	831,415,000

about eleven per cent (162) highly speculative, and only about seven per cent (100) passed muster.

Kansas had a host of imitators. Within three years, twenty other states had passed similar laws; and the number was doubled after the constitutionality of the principle underlying these various acts was established. Efforts to pass a federal blue-sky law have failed but a certain amount of protection is provided in interstate commerce through the anti-fraud section of the United States criminal code referring to attempts to use the mails for purposes of fraud. In New York, New Jersey and Maryland, blue-sky laws failed of passage; but instead, anti-fraud statutes were passed, which gave the state attorney special powers to prosecute after the fraud was committed. The subject of blue-sky laws receives fuller treatment in Chapter XXII below.

The World War Period

The war-time period of American finance was characterized by an unparalleled expansion, first, of the industrial machinery and, secondly, of the financial mechanism of the nation, so that within ten years what had been vaguely predicted in 1897 became an actual fact, and the primacy in world finance definitely passed to this country. With the industrial consolidation movement largely completed before the war began, the basic industries were in a position to expand without difficulty as the need arose; and the financial strength and efficiency of many of the leading corporations permitted them a large degree of flexibility which stood them in good stead when Europe began to call upon this country to help supply war materials and supplies to her armies, as well as food and other materials available in reduced quantities because of the absence of millions of farmers and city workers at the front.

The consequent rise in prices caused a great increase in business profits and spread apparent phenomenal prosperity throughout the land, all the more because immigration was interrupted and labor was thus in a position to secure more than ordinary participation in the larger earnings available. With the large increase in the production of surplus wealth, we were able to absorb within a few years the great bulk of

American securities which had been held abroad. In addition, several foreign loans were floated in this market, the most notable of them being the $500,000,000 Anglo-French 5½ per cent loan of 1915, which the market absorbed fairly well.

With the entry of this country into the war in 1916, the situation was not essentially changed. The great demands from Europe were now met through direct advances by this government, instead of the resale of American securities owned abroad or the flotation of foreign bonds here. This government, in turn, raised by 1919 more than $20,000,000,000 in the domestic market through the sale of its own obligations, for the most part of long term. Although bank credit inflation was liberally applied as a lubricant in raising these vast amounts of capital, the actual disturbance in the money and capital markets was comparatively moderate.

Popular ownership of securities was vastly stimulated by wartime finance. One investment banker estimated that there were 200,000 holders of securities in this country before the war, and 20,000,000 afterward.[25] That the latter figure is not exaggerated is indicated by the fact that the $5,249,908,000 of Victory Loan bonds were sold in 1919 to 11,803,895 individual subscribers. The Liberty Loan campaigns, and customer and employee ownership plans as carried out by individual corporations, paved the way for the expanded efforts of investment banking houses after the war to develop the security-buying habit in the American people.

The Post-war Boom

The post-war organization of investment banking in this country has been partly outlined in the chapters preceding. The following outstanding features made their appearance during this period of credit inflation and industrial expansion:

1. *The Increased Importance of Distribution in the Investment Banking Process.*—Before the war, the investment banker in this country depended, at least to a partial extent, upon the foreign market to absorb new security issues. Furthermore, sales for the most part were made to institutional investors and a limited number of wealthy individuals and estates. Under these

[25] Warburg, Paul M., *Some Problems of the Investment Banker.*

conditions, the banking house which originated a new issue constituted the most important cog in the machinery, since selling was a limited and simple problem.

With the vast increase in the number of investors, the problem of distribution grew apace. At the same time, those houses which had developed extensive distribution power found little reason to depend further upon the big originating houses, so that the tendency was toward the combination of the origination and distribution functions within one investment house. The problem of reducing the cost of distribution because of the smaller average size of individual sales also became urgent.

2. *The Growth of the Investment Trust.*—It is only since 1925 that the investment trust has been more than an exotic experiment in this country. It has gone through various stages of evolution since, as rapidly changing conditions have affected it, in many instances adversely.

3. *Stocks Replaced Bonds as the Favored Popular Investing Medium.*—Three decades ago, one widely discussed question in the field of investments was the relative merit of real estate mortgages and corporation bonds as investments. In recent years, the same question arises between bonds and stocks, with the latter enjoying the greater popularity. When American industry was new and the individual enterprise was in its developmental stage, stock equities tended to be speculative and ill suited for long-term investment. With the relative stabilization of the industrial situation and the development of giant corporations abundantly supplied with fixed equipment and liquid resources, common stocks, constituting equities which share in the growth of earnings, have gained wide favor. This increased popularity of stocks brought about a great expansion of the stock brokerage business.

4. *The United States Became a Leading Creditor Nation.*—During the decade following the close of the World War, some $15,000,000,000 of foreign securities were sold in this market. The greatly increased productive capacity of the country resulted in a surplus available for investment abroad, which was eagerly taken advantage of by foreign lenders during the post-war reconstruction period. Capital flowed abroad not only through the sale of foreign issues here, but also through large

purchases of foreign internal securities by Americans, and through the purchase or development by American corporations of subsidiaries abroad. Under the conditions that prevailed in the post-war world, a large part of these foreign investments proved ill-advised, and caused serious losses to investors.

5. *Changes in Methods of Corporate Financing.*—As the individual enterprise has gained in financial strength, it has tended to rely less upon the commercial bank, and has built up instead large cash reserves through the reinvestment of earnings and the liberal issue of securities in the expanded capital market. As a result, the many major business corporations have become institutional investors.

6. *The Tendency Toward "Department Store" Banking.*—This tendency brought both commercial and investment banking functions within one institution. The commercial banks, encouraged by liberal legislation, opened security departments, organized security affiliates, and bought vast amounts of bonds for their own portfolios. They also went heavily into the trust business. Similarly, many brokerage houses entered the investment banking field, especially as stocks rose to a position of prime importance as investment media. Finally, commercial banks, investment houses and brokerage houses alike went into the business of organizing, operating and managing investing institutions through their investment trust affiliations.

Deflation and Depression

When the decade of credit expansion and business prosperity which followed the World War gave way inevitably to deflation and business depression after the stock market panic of 1929, investment banking in all its phases was profoundly affected. Just because the preceding expansion of credit had so largely been based upon security loans and investments, the subsequent deflation was particularly severe in the stock and bond markets. Industrial stock prices declined by almost 90 per cent from the high point of the late fall of 1929 to the low level reached about the time of the nation-wide banking moratorium early in 1933.

Each major panic and subsequent depression have, as we have seen in the foregoing pages, affected investment banking greatly.

The panic of 1837 and its aftermath largely cut off the flow of capital from abroad, and made this country more dependent upon its own capital accumulations for a time. The panic of 1873, on the other hand, discouraged individual investment in bonds within this country, and made our great railway enterprises turn to the international investment bankers and foreign sources of capital to raise needed funds. The panic of 1893 had less profound effects, although it led to a protracted period of abnormally low demand for capital and easy money that culminated in the industrial consolidation boom about the turn of the century.

The series of financial panics that beset this country from 1929 to 1933 was precipitated by a variety of causes, but the most aggravating factors were the failures of thousands of commercial banks, large and small, and the forced liquidation of billions of dollars of security loans. The resulting hardships to the country were so extreme that a great revulsion of popular sentiment against deflationary policies resulted, which will doubtless have a profound effect upon the attitude of the government toward banking for a long time to come. Just as the Roosevelt Administration took drastic action to check further deflation when it assumed office in 1933, it seems likely that future administrations of whatever party will similarly resort to political remedies whenever wholesale credit contraction again contracts business activity and forces the level of commodity prices sharply downward.

The depression period was marked by a severe contraction in the volume of both new issue and security trading activity, great losses to all types of investing institutions and institutional investors, discouragement of individual investment, a cessation of the export of American capital abroad, and a shaking of confidence in many established institutions and ways of doing business in this country. Congressional investigations into banking practices in particular tended to crystallize sentiment in favor of reform which was often based upon emotional considerations that failed to keep a long-range perspective as regards what had happened and what was needed to remedy the situation.

The New Deal and Its Aftermath

The ambitious reform and recovery program of the Roosevelt Administration, launched after it took office in 1933, affected investment banking in the following respects:

1. Bank failures were checked through government subscriptions to bank stock, federal deposit insurance, and the indirect effect of the other measures taken to check the deflationary tendency in the nation's economic life. This lifted the burden of forced liquidation from the security markets, and so paved the way to the reestablishment of the nation's investment banking business on more normal lines.

2. Commercial banks were required to limit their direct participation in investment banking through the segregation of security affiliates and the imposition of other restrictions on their security activities, under the Banking Act of 1933, drafted before, but not passed until, the change in administration.

3. Flotations of new securities were brought under federal regulation by the federal Securities Act of 1933.

4. The security exchanges, the over-the-counter markets, and lending on securities were brought under full federal control by the Securities Exchange Act of 1934.

5. The Board of Governors of the Federal Reserve System was given greatly increased power over both the commercial and the investment banking systems by the Banking Act of 1935, which has gone far to centralize credit regulation in the United States.

6. Through its deliberate deficit policy, the Roosevelt Administration floated and sold to the banks vast amounts of government securities, thus forcing the commercial banks into the investment banking business through a new channel and basing the outstanding bank deposits of the nation largely on government credit.

7. Through devaluation of the dollar, open market purchases of government bonds by the Federal Reserve Banks, and gold imports, vast excess reserves were created in the Federal Reserve System which brought down the level of interest rates to an unprecedentedly low point, and hence profoundly affected investment banking activity.

8. Mortgage banking was reorganized, with a large measure

of government intervention, in the interests of relief for farm and home owners and speedier recovery in new building.

9. Investment trusts were subjected to federal investigation and regulation through the Public Utility Holding Company Act of 1935 and the Revenue Act of 1936.

The capital markets enjoyed a distinct revival beginning with the spring of 1935, spurred by the inflationary credit policies sponsored by the government at the time. However, the bond market remained largely an institutional affair in comparison with the pre-depression period, individual investors taking largely to common stocks. The recovery in stock prices, once the pressure of deflation was definitely ended, was accelerated by vague popular fears of commodity price inflation following the devaluation of the dollar. This factor helped to overcome fear of investment in stocks that had been engendered by the severity of the declines in the 1930-1933 period.

Another striking development in the American capital market was the great inflow of capital from abroad, especially Great Britain and western Europe, that began in 1934. The Department of Commerce estimated that at the end of 1935 some $5,000,000,000 of American stocks were being held for foreign account. The relative political tranquillity that prevailed in this country, its remaining large undeveloped natural resources, and the disturbed conditions that existed in most other parts of the world accounted for this abnormal flow of both "nervous" and investment capital to a country that was already amply provided with capital resources of its own, and that should logically have exported capital on a large scale. This inflow of foreign funds added to the plethora of capital, helped depress interest rates further, and raised stock prices. It also added to the volume of funds seeking expert guidance or management to escape the evident dangers to the integrity of capital created by such abnormal conditions.

References

DEWEY, D. R., *Financial History of the United States,* New York, 1903.

HOGGSON, N. F., *Epochs in American Banking,* New York, 1929.

JENKS, L. H., *The Migration of British Capital to 1875,* New York, 1927, chaps. iii and iv.

LANIER, H. W., *A Century of Banking in New York, 1822–1922,* New York, 1922.

LAWSON, W. R., *American Finance,* Edinburgh, 1906, chaps. i–v.

MEEKER, J. EDWARD, *The Work of the Stock Exchange,* New York, 1930, chaps. i and ii.

MILLER, H. E., *Banking Theories in the United States Before 1860,* Cambridge, 1927.

MINNIGERODE, MEADE, *Certain Rich Men,* New York, 1927.

MYERS, M. G., *The New York Money Market,* New York, 1931.

NADLER, M. N., and BOGEN, J. I., *The Banking Crisis,* New York, 1933.

NOYES, A. D., *Forty Years of American Finance,* New York, 1909.

NOYES, A. D., *War Period of American Finance,* New York, 1926.

PRATT, SERENO S., *The Work of Wall Street,* New York, 1921, chap. i.

STEDMAN, E. C., *History of the New York Stock Exchange,* New York, 1904.

WILLIS, H. P. and CHAPMAN, JOHN M., *The Banking Problem,* New York, 1934.

Part Two

The Theory of Investment Banking

Chapter IX

THE THEORY OF INVESTMENT

The Basic Concepts

There has been extensive controversy in recent years regarding the relationship between money, savings, goods, and capital, as well as with reference to the bearings of these various concepts, one upon the other. A brief summary of the usage that will be followed in the present discussion is necessary at this point. The conception of wealth from the investment banking standpoint is perhaps the simplest and may therefore be used as a starting point. By wealth is meant, in the present discussion, any economic good or service which satisfies a human need, and has, consequently, the power of commanding other goods or services in exchange.

The "exchange value" resulting from the fact that a given object or service is desired must, however, be measured in erms of some standard or unit, and the rate of exchange beween goods is their price. One such good is money, which makes money a form of wealth devised for the special purpose of acting as a means of promoting exchange and of measuring he value of commodities in exchange. We thus include money under the head of wealth, but, of course, cannot regard wealth in any sense as money, except that it is indirectly a means of ommanding money.

Production is the process of bringing wealth into existence—hat is to say, of changing the character or form of goods and ervices so as to adapt them for use. Consumption, on the other and, is the application of these goods and services to their speific objects, that is, to the satisfaction of human needs or deres. Capital comprises forms of wealth especially adapted for urther production, as, for example, tools and machines, which hemselves do not satisfy any consumption desires.

Ordinarily, savings are defined as that part of the periodic production of wealth which is devoted to the creation of capital, or, in other words, used in preparing for further wealth production.

Investment is the process of applying such savings to the creation of specific forms of capital. There has been a long controversy about the question whether savings are or are not, in fact, practically equivalent to investments. The use made of the term in this volume, however, differentiates the two concepts, and regards saving as the mere decision not to consume produced goods, whereas investment is the actual application of the savings thus made to some specified purpose.

Difficulty is found in the preservation of these distinction when they are stated in terms of money rather than goods and services, as above. If an individual, for example, has received an income of $2000 in the form of a check on a bank and has determined to save $500 of it, while the other $1500 is "drawn" or "checked out" for current expenses, what has happened has been that $1500 of the bank's deposits has been applied t payment for consumption goods—food, clothing, etc.—while i retains a credit on its books, in his favor, of $500. This $50 will be offset by assets held by the banks in order to earn a income. Such investment, moreover, may be made in the obl gations of some industry that is producing consumption good or that is annually incurring a deficit which eventually ma either result in bankruptcy, thereby lessening the value of th banker's claim upon it or the worth of the securities which h may have accepted as collateral protection for the advance. Th "saving" which the customer of the bank has thought he mad thus turns into a loss—in other words, his saving is not equiv lent to the investment of his funds in the positive sense. It m be answered that here the loss does not fall upon such a save but upon the bank itself which has guaranteed his deposit wi it, or, under a régime of bank deposit guaranty, it may ul mately fall upon the associated banks of the country. Th however, is an apparent and not a real difficulty inherent the reasoning. It allows differences of ownership to obscure t true economic situation which is involved. If we regard t depositors of the bank as a unit, it then appears that the acti of the original customer in saving a part of his income is n complete, but depends for its completion upon parallel action originating with the banking mechanism of the country. For our purposes, it is necessary to treat the question of savings and investments explicitly from either the social standpoint or that of the individual—a distinction which should, in all discussion of investment banking, be clearly made.

The Social Point of View

The theory of investment may thus be considered from either he social or the individual standpoint. The social point of view which regards the flow of the annual income into investment, he influence of speculation upon the community, etc., is im-ortant in connection with the control of investment banking, s well as the forecasting of changes in investment conditions. For the individual investment banker and investor, a corre-ponding series of problems arises, involving the shaping of olicies that best conform to these broad social changes.

As the more fundamental set of considerations, those which elate to the social theory of investment should receive first ttention. Viewing investment as a process which goes on in very community, we may ask exactly what this process con-sts of, and what limits or conditions it. By investment in the rger sense of the term is meant what is usually referred to by conomists under the head of "saving," but including the fur-ner thought that money savings are actually applied to the eation of what are called capital goods.

By capital in the economic sense is meant the forms of wealth hose service is found in the production of consumable goods, ther directly or indirectly. They do not themselves yield any tisfactions, but they make it possible to obtain such satisfac-ons through the use of the product which they turn out. If A, r example, having a credit of $100,000 in the bank, devotes mself to the construction of a water-power system, and there-ter sells the power or energy so developed, he has used his 00,000 in the creation of capital, and that capital yields a rvice—in this case, power—which can be sold and so recon-rted into current funds. This process may be described as in-stment. The outcome of investment is the establishment of a flow of income from the capital in question, corresponding to a continuous stream of resulting economic goods or services.

It is thus clear that investment is a process of converting funds into capital, using the capital for the production of goods and services which are sold for funds that can be expended as may be desired. This last process of reconversion is the earning or receipt of income, such income being the flow of values which comes from the application of capital in the way indicated. It is clear that the process has no necessary connection with money, although it is usually described in terms of money, so that we habitually speak of "investing money" or getting money income out of investment.

We may next ask the question: When is a country better off and how is it better off, in an economic sense, as compared with some previous time? Evidently the measure of economic improvement is found in the increase, immediate or ultimate, of ability to command consumption goods, and this may come about as a result of new discovery, improvement in processes, or better organization of labor. It is quite possible that a change such as the better organization of labor might bring about a larger production of wealth from the same equipment and with the same number of persons at work. Ordinarily, however this improved organization is rendered possible only through the use of machines, or the increase of fixed capital employed for the purpose of applying labor in a more efficient and satisfactory way. Better processes are usually dependent upon better and more effective employment of machines.

In short, the conditions which determine whether a country is or is not better off have to do with the volume of fixed capital which is employed in its processes of production, and the extent to which it can accordingly turn out goods without having to depend upon direct human labor. Investment is concerned with the creation of new capital goods and their use in the strengthening and improvement of the processes of production. It is a process for rendering human economic activity more productive and efficient.

The Question of Over-production

It is worth while at this point to consider briefly a problem arising from the investment of capital which is ordinarily r ferred to as "over-production." It was the view of the classical economists that no such thing as "general over-production" could be conceived of as taking place—if for no other reason than simply because there was no limit to the extent of human wants. These economists could not conceive of a situation in which a body of human beings existed whose wants for material comforts had been completely satisfied. Their underlying theory was that competition would in time distribute capital throughout the entire field of investment, while changes in the rate of return would automatically regulate both the total volume and the allocation of savings.

While accepting the general views thus expressed, subject to the extremely arbitrary underlying assumptions upon which they rested, later economists have been inclined to emphasize two factors affecting investment which were probably underestimated by the classical economists. These were: (1) the cumulative increase in productive power brought about by intensive use of machine methods of production, and (2) the difficulty of obtaining a smooth and steady consumption of the products of machine industry, such difficulty being attributable directly to a faulty distribution of wealth with inadequate consumption power in the hands of the rank and file of wage earners. By emphasizing these two factors, contemporary writers have at times developed what seemed like a new philosophy of over-production, committing themselves to the view that the existing organization of economic society necessarily tended toward spasmodic dislocations in production and consumption. A period of full operation of the production machinery was, according to them, followed by a "glut" of consumable goods, in excess of what wage earners could buy with funds placed in their hands as the reward of labor. Various suggestions have been made for the relief of this condition—one a prohibition of the introduction of new labor-saving devices, to the end that there might be more work and hence more wages for expenditure in purchasing. Another supposed remedy has been the raising of rates of wages far above the "subsistence minimum" described by the older economists, in order that wage recipients might have adequate buying power out of which to purchase the commodities they desire, and thus enlarge their consumption, end the glut and enable the capitalistic organization to proceed with its normal productive processes. The so-called "technocratic" doctrine represented one very extreme statement of the over-production theory, while the payment of high wages, as a principle, ascribed to various American industrialists, embodies the second.

Evidently these considerations have an important bearing upon the question of investment. The limit of desirable investment is obviously determined by the amounts which can be appropriately used in producing goods that are wanted, and ir effecting the sale of such goods under conditions that assure a reasonable return to the owner of the capital. Individual diffi culty in accomplishing this end is not due to the fact that ma chinery becomes too powerful for economic society to use, bu that industry often contains the seeds of its own failure by re fusing to the employee the means which will enable him tc make a satisfactory demand for commodities. The situation i simply one in which faulty conditions of investment have per mitted an excessive amount of fixed capital to be supplied i turning out given classes of goods. This dislocation may hav taken place because of unexpected inventions which hav brought about the introduction of new processes in given field of production, and thus rendered a good deal of existing ma chinery partly obsolete, or it may be due to the existence of ten porary excessive additions to capital in given industries whic have led to a massing of investment funds there. The probler is one of distribution, and the reason why it has sometimes a peared as an especially "new" or "modern" issue is the fact th the increasing complexity of modern business organization h occasionally seemed to make a satisfactory distribution of ca ital difficult or impossible. Excessive production in given lin of industry has ensued and surpluses have developed the which could not be disposed of. By the time that this situatic was discovered, it was usually too late to bring about a redi tribution of capital into other fields where more attractive ope ings were offering themselves. Such a shift of capital w impossible because of the specialized forms which it had a sumed, and the difficulty or impossibility of reshaping them such a way as to adapt them to the production of other kinds wealth. The situation thus depicted may be summed up in the statement that modern capitalism results in a very high degree of specialization of production mechanisms and constantly tends to render obsolete even comparatively recent types of productive machinery. The effort of owners to obtain some residual value by still working the older machines has often led to an effort to have labor absorb the cost of obsolescence in some measure, and has at the same time resulted in the production of goods which could not be absorbed at prices that would yield a profit to their producers. But none of these factors warrant the view that there is danger of protracted over-production of goods, beyond the capacity of the public to pay for or consume. There is an increasing danger in the over-specialization of capital and in the necessity of constantly writing off large volumes of investments which have been rendered obsolete by new methods of manufacture or of labor reorganization.

Further perfecting of industrial processes and enlargement of the power to turn out goods cheaply and in great masses is the essential basis of a rising standard of living. It is desirable that there shall be a sufficient diffusion of business statistics to discourage unnecessary duplication of productive capacity; and at times it may be possible through joint action of those engaging in a given industry to regulate or "smooth out" the rate at which new capital is applied there. The safe extent of such possible interference with the automatic processes of saving and investment is still uncertain. The problem, at any rate, is one of distribution of income and investment, and is not a matter which calls for restriction in productive power.

Application of Money Income

Suppose that an individual is in possession of money income or command over wealth of which he has become possessed as a result of his activities in various directions. He evidently has the choice of (1) "using" this money in consumption, (2) allowing it to lie idle, or (3) applying it to a purpose which does not involve immediate use on the part of the owner. This third means of employment of the fund is usually thought of and described as investment.

Investment of money thus involves the application of current funds for a purpose other than to satisfy the immediate consumption needs of the owner. This is spoken of as investing or lending "money." It is an operation which involves, as a rule, the transfer of titles to money or bank credit, they being passed into the hands of others who agree to return them with a payment for their use which is known as "interest" or "profit." These others who obtain the use of such funds cannot pay interest or profit, however, unless they succeed in earning it. They must therefore use what they thus borrow not for consumption but for the purpose of producing more goods or services which are disposed of to others, and which consequently bring back a larger amount of goods or, in current phrase, "money," than what was parted with. If we eliminate these intermediaries, and look simply at the fundamental character of the operation, we shall see that it consists of applying current funds to the production of more wealth.

In a capitalistic society, this usually means the application of such funds to the manufacture or purchase of machinery or improvements of some kind—in other words, to the creation of what are called "capital goods" as distinct from "consumption goods." These goods are purchased or created because their owner will thus be able to pay the interest or profit which is demanded in return for the use of the "money" parted with by the person who had originally acquired or saved it.

The Ubiquitous Risk Element

Every application of wealth necessarily involves risk and the use of business judgment as to the wisdom of incurring it. The individual may succeed in transferring his responsibility to others. He may put his funds into a savings bank or investment trust, but such a transfer of responsibility does not eliminate it. It merely places the duty of making the decision upon the shoulders of others. Eventually someone has to make the decision where every unit of wealth is to be applied—whether in the creation of more machinery for the manufacture of automobiles or in extending the cultivation of wheat or cotton. Judgments thus arrived at may be correct or incorrect, or, what is more troublesome still, they may be partially correct and partially incorrect. There is no sharp dividing line between sound and unsound investment judgment. In proportion as decisions of the kind referred to prove to be well-founded, the investment of capital which takes place by the methods already outlined becomes remunerative or productive. In proportion as the judgments referred to are incorrect, the application of capital which is made turns out to be erroneous, hence, unproductive or unprofitable. The percentage of accuracy in the placement of funds which on the average is attained by the community in making its investments determines the percentage of loss of capital which occurs as a result. It also determines what we may call the "risk element" in investment. This may be understood by assuming that an individual determined to spread his capital out evenly over the entire field of investment, so that (we may suppose) he purchases an equal number of units of ownership in every business enterprise whose shares are available for general sale. He will not receive equal return from all, and from some he will receive nothing or next to nothing, while in others he will soon find that his capital has been completely lost. Therefore, in order to induce the investor to go on applying his funds he must receive rather more than would otherwise be necessary from those enterprises that do actually pay. This risk element in investment eventually has an important influence in determining the rate of interest that must be offered by borrowers.

The typical investor wishes, of course, to find enterprises for the use of his funds in which this element of risk has been kept to a minimum, but he can never find one in which it is eliminated. Risk is, therefore, a regular element in investment, and every theory of investment must recognize the function of risk-bearing as a part of the process by which capital is placed at the service of the community, and is made to yield an income. It is often hastily assumed that there is some kind of "planning" which can direct the movement of capital in such a way as to eliminate risk, but it is evidently possible only to the extent that it is possible to foretell or dictate the volume and character of human consumption. That is ordinarily outside of the scope of planning, except in societies where complete regimentation has been successfully introduced. Even there, serious blunders and errors of judgment are constantly occurring.

The element of risk will continue in the field of industry as long as human judgment is fallible. So long as it thus continues, investment processes will have to carry or absorb a correspondingly large proportion of loss resulting from misjudgment in the placing of funds. Obviously this question of risk is an important factor in determining the availability of new capital. It exerts its influence partly upon the mind of the saver of new capital and partly upon the market conditions which determine the allocation of capital among various uses.

The Flow of Income into Investment

In studying the flow of income into investment, attention may first be given to the factors which direct funds to the purchase of production goods—goods which are not to be immediately used up or consumed. There is a steady flow of new capital which is thus coming into the market from savers, and which represents the economic surpluses of individuals over and above the amount expended or used for their current support. Thus A, the recipient of a salary of $5,000, may use $4,000 in paying his current expenses, so that at the end of the year he has $1,000 remaining as a bank deposit—current funds. He uses this surplus in buying part ownership in a business which he expects to yield him an income, or in developing some natural resource, such as a mine, or in building some piece of machinery which will facilitate the productive work of the business in which he is already engaged. In this way, investment takes place through additions to the existing total of funds which has been rendered available through the processes of labor and saving already described.

These additions, made as the result of saving, are usually "net." The replacement of older capital goods, for capital of all kinds is wearing out from day to day, should be effected through depreciation reserves. That part of capital which has taken the form of machinery, or physical assets, usually has only a comparatively short life. Other capital goods are being lost in any one of a number of ways: through fire, natural disasters, wars, etc. More frequent still are the cases in which losses of capital occur through badly conceived investment. Railroads may be built where there is an insufficient amount of business, and may later be abandoned on that account. Canals or roads may be constructed where natural conditions are unfavorable, so that the incomplete work has eventually to be abandoned. Perhaps the most important of all these factors is the very rapid process of industrial change in the modern world, which is constantly rendering capital goods obsolete. Industrial methods are changing. Given kinds of machines are being abandoned, and others substituted. Processes which were once economical have become less so, on account of changes in cost of material or the discovery of new methods. The result is the abandonment of machinery which may have practically no worth at all, or only a scrap or recovery value. Unless depreciation reserves are adequate, new capital must be found for such needed replacements.

In what has thus been said we have assumed that the direction of the flow of capital is decided by individuals whom we have described as "savers." To a certain extent this method of determining the flow of capital still prevails, but it has been supplemented by the process of corporate savings and investment. Corporate managements find themselves in possession of net earnings at the end of the fiscal period. These they may declare as dividends to stockholders or decide to "plow back" into the business.

Corporate Control of Saving

From this it may be inferred that under the corporate system of business organization the control over investment is not in the hands of the individual. Such, in fact, is the case. A large part of current savings is made by corporate organizations which are already in possession of the investment funds of the community. A, for example, is the owner of stock in X Corporation, which, at the end of the fiscal year, finds that it has earned 25 per cent on the original capital used by A in becoming the owner of the stock. The corporation might evidently declare a "dividend" of 25 per cent—that is to say, might return to A the total amount of net earnings obtained by the operation of the business with the use of A's capital. Or it might declare a dividend of 10 per cent in favor of A and hope to extend the plant of the business by using the additional 15 per cent which has been earned. Here the board of directors would assume the right to decide that A's 15 per cent should be invested in the extension of the same business. A evidently has no decisive voice whatever in the matter. It may be answered that, as the affairs of the corporation are more or less public, the value of A's stock in the market will be immediately enhanced by 15 per cent, so that he can possess himself of the funds by selling a portion of his stock if he so wishes. This may or may not be the fact; but even if the entire enhancement of value is reflected in the worth of the stock so that A has no difficulty in actually converting it into money, the fact remains that the community as a whole has accepted the decision of the board of directors of the X Corporation and has assented to the investment of the earnings for the year in question in the extension of the particular business which has reported them. The management has, in any case, alone determined the amount and the application of this particular section of the year's profits.

This automatic savings function of the corporation has grown more and more important of recent years and has been the object of some criticism by both economists and public men.

"Undistributed" Income

President Roosevelt, in his proposal of March 3, 1936, to revise the corporate income tax, urged that the retention of corporate earnings in business without passing them through the hands of the stockholders had the effect of preventing a total which he estimated as $4,500,000,000 of corporate income from being distributed to stockholders. These funds were savings effected by these corporations. The estimate thus given may or may not be accurate, but it illustrates the great rôle played by the modern corporation in the determination of the volume of savings and their direction.

It has been contended that this power of determination of the volume of reinvestment may have undesirable effects. One of those which is chiefly emphasized is the possibility that the corporations, unduly influenced by large profits in favorable years, may "over-invest"—that is to say, establish too large a plant as compared with present or probable needs of consumers. The effect of such faulty decisions may be to bring about the production of commodities that are not wanted at the time or which cannot be sold at a price that will yield profits. Hence, plant facilities may have to be shut down, with resulting unemployment and aggravation of the "business cycle." Some weight must, of course, be given to this suggestion. The recommendation that, in order to cure the evils thus complained of, corporations be compelled to distribute most or all of their earnings to stockholders, overlooks the fact that a surplus may merely offset inadequate depreciation deductions from income, and assumes that the individual investor is able to exercise better and sounder judgment regarding the industrial future than is the corporate board of directors. Facts do not always warrant such assumptions; on the contrary, they show that the individual who has made a substantial profit in a given industry through the ownership of securities therein is prone to go back into the industry with fully as little forethought as would be shown by the board of directors. A striking illustration of this situation was afforded during the five years before 1929 by the readiness with which corporations were able to obtain new capital for practically nothing in the way of promised current return. Exorbitant prices were paid for new stock offered shareholders through subscription rights.

New Investment and a Managed Economy

Another point of view has been developed in connection with he proposal that a so-called "managed economy" would be ble to direct the flow of investment into channels where it was conomically needed and would probably result in continuous roduction and continuous employment. By this means of versight through "social" or governmental action, it is asrted that far wiser and better use could be made of the annual avings of the community than is actually made under the soalled "capitalistic" system. Here is an assumption that "socity" or "the government" can use the savings of the community etter and with greater foresight than can the individual at the resent time or the corporate organization acting for him. To nis is sometimes added the thought that the central bank of a ven country (usually under government control) can direct nese investments and serve as a medium for determining when nd how they shall be made.

This contention has been advanced, particularly in countries with a socialistic bias. Evidence is lacking to substantiate the basic assumption of planning advocates. There is no satisfactory experience in any of the industrial countries to show that greater success is likely to be had by vesting in the hands of public officers or official boards of bank directors the power to make decisions regarding the placement of new funds. Most students of the subject are fully disposed to admit that mistakes are constantly being made in investment matters, and that greater wisdom and foresight and the avoidance of experiments with inflationary credit policies will necessarily bring about important improvements in this regard, with corresponding reduction of the danger of alternating periods of unwarranted prosperity and severe depression. They doubt, however, that the judgment of government officials is better than the automatic adjustments effected by a free economy. The proneness of government personnel to the shifts and changes incident to political life prevents continuity of policy, while they afford opportunity for the acceptance and application of erroneous theories of price-fixing and price-raising and of economic stimulation that result often in serious disturbance.

Institutional Influences

This doctrine of "management" in its positive form is less attractive than the argument advanced by some, that existing conditions and the institutional organization of society sometimes tend to lead to "over-saving," with consequent bad effects and that these will be avoided by endeavoring to liberate the individual from the influence of this institutional organization, leaving his action regarding investment to be determined by his own instincts. British economists, particularly, have urged the abandonment of constant effort to stimulate saving—the constant presentation of the thought that the individual should "lay up something for a rainy day." They point out that it is frequently true that the individual cannot make a better investment than by using his funds in self-development or education, or in broadening or liberalizing his consumption.

This argument is frequently well-taken in individual cases

The undiscriminating demand for larger saving is often injurious rather than helpful. There is certainly substantial basis for the view that the institutional organization of society sometimes results in the continued application of savings to production, without careful or discriminating thought as to whether the production is really likely to find a market for the goods which result. Here too, however, the question is not merely that of pointing out faults or errors in the investment process, but that of developing alternative or substitute means of determining whether investment should be carried further, or not.

Measurement of Investment

In what has just been said it may seem to be assumed that "investment" is always more or less successful. "Investment," however, must be regarded as either positive or negative. It may result in rendering existing capital forms obsolete and thus (from the bookkeeping standpoint) result in loss, though the effect of it may be the turning out of a much greater supply of goods than was previously available. On the other hand, it may simply result in marginal gains or profits, or, in rare cases, it may produce practically no effect whatever from the standpoint of earnings.

A balance sheet representing these items of gain or loss can theoretically be drawn up from period to period, not merely for the individual in terms of money, but also for the community in terms of capital goods. Such a balance sheet may be difficult to put into concrete form, but the data underlying it are present. Countries or communities are advancing or declining in their control over wealth. In order to ascertain their position at any given moment, some process of investment measurement is needed.

It is often asked how the process of investment, viewed from the social standpoint, can actually be gauged. Various measures suggest themselves, the obvious one being simply to ascertain the difference between the annual production and the annual consumption of goods in a community. If the annual production is taken as may be expressed by x number of dollars, and the annual consumption by a specified number y, the margin of saving or investment is the difference between the two, or

x minus y. It is quite true that saving is not necessarily investment, but the money income available for saving may be thought of as offering the limit for such investment, if we leave out the factor of bank credit inflation we shall consider subsequently. All saved wealth may be invested; and if it is, then the difference between consumption and production measures both the savings margin and the investment volume. It is customary to measure the savings or investment margin in terms of dollars, a process which assumes that it is possible to ascertain the price of each unit of capital entering into the aggregate savings fund, and, further, that each such unit may theoretically be expected to command its price if sold. With these broad assumptions, estimates of saving power or investment are, as stated, currently made in terms of dollars and have at least a comparative interest as relating to different periods of times. One such estimate by Professor Willford I. King indicates the percentage saved between 1909 and 1917 as running from 12 to 27 per cent of the total national income.

The determination of the size of the investment surplus in terms of goods is not practicable. An indirect measure is furnished by productivity statistics. Thus the National Industrial Conference Board has prepared the figure shown on page 261, which measures the extent of the increase in physical product of all industries since 1899 that is traceable to improved equipment and organization.

Factors of Supply and Demand

In the analysis of the investment process from the money point of view, it is desirable to consider the factors entering into demand for, and supply of, investment funds. This furnishes a means by which to gauge the tendencies at work at any given time to change the character or extent of the flow of funds into the investment market.

Looking at the subject of the demand for investment fund analytically, we are able to recognize four or five distinct factor which determine its intensity. Important among them is the rate of economic development in the country, including such questions as the state of its industrial arts, the degree of fluidity or permanence which has been attained by its economic organization, the relations between capital and labor, and a variety of other factors. Of importance also are the character of its financial market, the degree of initiative that is shown by its promoters and investment bankers in their search for new opportunities, and, generally, the degree of success attained in bringing about a prompt response on the part of active business men to the opening up of new opportunities through in-

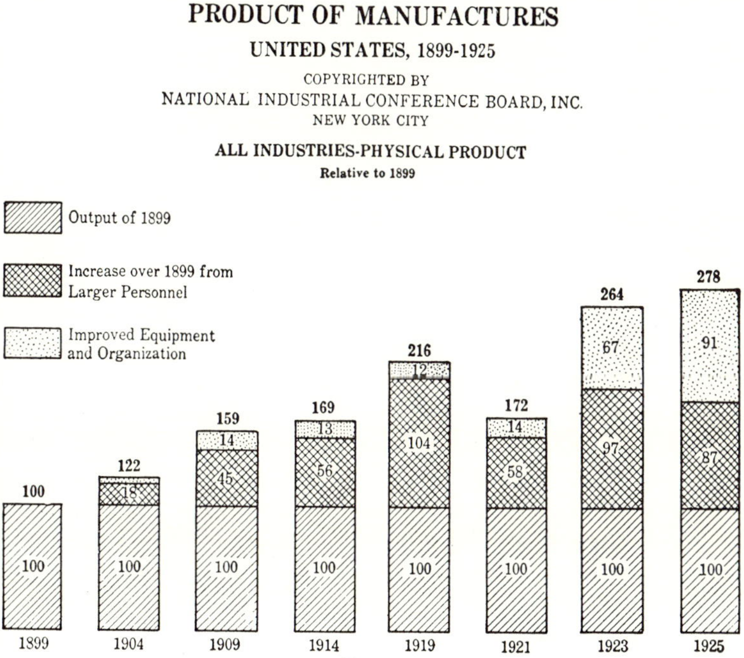

Fig. 9

vention, through change in international relationships, or otherwise. Finally, a place of some importance must be assigned to the position in the business cycle that has been reached at any given moment by the economic organization of the country. The activity of demand for investment resources, other things being equal, will be greater or less as the business cycle passes through one or the other of its various phases, as set forth in Chapter XV. The demand for capital in the United States is discussed in the following chapter.

On the other hand, analysis of the supply of capital may be made in the same way. Such analysis emphasizes the stage of economic development as a determining factor just as does demand, since in some of the various stages of national economic growth there is a much larger fund of savings forthcoming than at other times. National habits in connection with the use of wealth and savings—the extent to which profits and earnings are employed as a basis for luxurious outlay or are used for further production—have an important bearing. The extent of the distribution of wealth among various classes, and the influence thereby exerted upon the volume of savings, as well as the character of the opportunities afforded to savings by the investment banking organization of the country, also have an important share in determining the amount of the supply of funds going into investment.

The factors of supply of and demand for capital thus referred to raise a variety of important theoretical questions. We may ask in any given case, in what circumstances do investments increase most rapidly? Is investment assisted by industrialization? Does a given kind of distribution of wealth facilitate its growth? Is it aided or retarded by specified forms of economic organization, such, for instance, as cooperation? All these questions must be answered before final conclusions with respect to the growth of social capital can be drawn. They open a large field of discussion and can only be raised here, without any effort to furnish a solution even of the major issues involved.

Capital and Economic Development

A somewhat closer view of the major factors already suggested as influencing supply and demand will be worth while. Attention may first be given to the stage reached by a country in its economic development. As is generally known, the study of economic history shows various well-marked phases through which practically every country passes in the process of combining labor with its natural resources. In the United States, for example, we first passed through a period in which the main problem was that of establishing communication and transportation and bringing the whole country under general control. This was succeeded by a more intensive period of capital application and development, during which natural resources were being exploited, and industrial centers located at strategic points. This, in turn, has been followed by a period of corporate consolidation and reorganization, in which effort has been made to intensify the division of labor and to establish more effective working relationships among the different elements of industry.

The supply of actual funds growing out of the economic activities of the country, and particularly that portion of the supply which may be regarded as a "surplus," in the sense that it is available for transfer into this, that or the other field, varies widely, and tends to become more abundant as a country reaches the full measure of its control of natural resources combined with effective machinery for developing and marketing its products. Each enterprise then tends in time to accumulate a large surplus of its own, to pay substantial dividends to stockholders and to have little need for new capital, as the openings for new investment become more limited.

The demand for capital, at least for domestic investment, reaches a peak when industrial growth attains its full measure of development, and it tends to decline thereafter. Many of the European countries, such as England or Holland, have reached this latter stage. They are making fairly full use of their natural resources, as far as present-day technique allows, and they cannot expect to open up many new enterprises within their home territory which may be capitalized and represented by security issues. In the United States, on the other hand, industry is still in a dynamic condition, and there is great opportunity for the application of additional funds in the opening up of new branches of business, and hence a large field for exploitation through securities issued. The demand for capital here is still extensive, though not fully equal to some former periods.

In a country which is practically fully exploited and in which industry is amply equipped, the need for new investment funds is likely to be small; and even if savings are large, it is difficult to find an outlet for them at home. It is for this reason that many countries are habitual exporters of capital, and that in a good many cases they have found it necessary to seek outlets in so-called "colonies." In such countries, the volume of saving is greater than the opportunity for investment, with the result that funds must be placed elsewhere. In the converse case, in which a country has reached a phase of active economic exploitation, and has large opportunities opened to it wherein new capital can be employed to advantage in increasing production, every effort will be made to attract savings; and when their supply is insufficient at home, the attempt will be made to draw them from abroad by the offer of high rates of return, freedom from taxation, or superior advantages of one sort or another.

Risk and the Supply of Capital

The supply of investment resources is always largely affected by the amount of risk which is involved in their use. In looking at this factor in the supply of capital, just as in studying the influence of different stages of development, we may obtain a valuable illustration from the experience of different countries. In some, where rich natural opportunities have presented themselves, exploitation appears to be accompanied by small hazard of loss. Almost anyone with funds can find a safe opportunity for their employment, with a reasonable probability of at least moderate returns. Into such countries, capital naturally flows freely from outside sources, while the rate of saving on the part of inhabitants tends to reach a high point.

Most sections of the United States furnish satisfactory examples of the development of capital flow through limitation of risk. On the other hand, in new countries, such as some of the South American states, where political uncertainties often arise, where natural resources, although abundant, are hard to reach, or where distance makes marketing expensive, the risk of investment is fairly high. In the Philippines, for example, it is usually stated that, while profitable openings can be found for those with large capital who can afford to take risks and lose money for a time, it is difficult for the small man to find a safe opportunity for the use of limited quantities of funds. Accordingly, rates of interest necessarily have to be high, and it is customary there to say that the risk element is large and that otherwise the cost necessary to induce capitalists to furnish funds for investment would be lower. Where risk is limited, the return on investments is lower, and the result is a steady, reliable flow of funds into investment channels at reasonable cost.

National Habits and Wealth Distribution

How national habits affect the supply of capital may be understood from a comparison of such a country as Russia, as organized under the old form of government, with such a country as Holland or England. In Russia, the ownership of wealth was largely in the hands of a small group who preferred to spend much of their time abroad, and who drew heavily upon the revenues of their estates in order to meet their extensive expenditures incurred through luxurious living. As a result, capital was always scarce in Russia, and the country was underdeveloped, possessing before the war little machinery and only a poorly organized system for the exploitation of its very valuable and extensive natural resources.

Holland, on the other hand, much smaller in area, and with a much less satisfactory supply of natural resources, was occupied by a thrifty population. The inhabitants were disposed to make the most of the opportunities open to them, and did so; with the result that the margin of savings, always substantial, was employed to the best advantage, thereby greatly enlarging the available supply of capital and rendering it possible for business to equip itself with practically any facilities it might require for the more effective prosecution of its efforts.

Similar though less well-marked distinctions between the practices and ideas of different communities may be found within various countries, and may be noted, for example, in the United States. Some sections of the country, like New England, are given to thrifty use of incomes, with constant reinvestment and an abundant supply of capital; whereas other regions are far less well equipped, less disposed to save, and consequently find it necessary to draw their capital from other sections of the country by borrowing. In the former regions, the rate of interest tends to be comparatively low, while in the latter a high level of charges is the rule.

The influence of the distribution of wealth upon the investment situation should be given a foremost place in any study of the social theory of investment. Which condition of affairs best promotes the growth of capital: a situation in which wealth is widely divided among the different members of the population, or one in which wealth is highly centralized? As we have seen, it is the total savings margin, or difference between production and consumption, which determines from year to year how much can be saved, and accordingly how much will be. But within this margin, the determination of the actual amount going to savings is a matter which must depend fundamentally upon the determination of members of the community who have this margin within their control. It is they and they only who can furnish the ultimate decision as to whether income will be saved or not, and also (in individual investment) what form will be given to the saving through its distribution among investment demands.

The question which is thus raised with reference to the effect of the distribution of wealth upon investment can be generally answered without much difficulty; the effect of distribution depends upon the relative inclination of the various classes in the community with regard to the use of their funds. In a society in which living standards are simple and mere extravagance is not admired for its own sake, it is undoubtedly true that a high concentration of wealth favors a high rate of saving. Conversely, a situation in which wealth is widely divided among a frugal population greatly devoted to saving also tends to maximize the amount of investment from the social standpoint.

Investment Banking Mechanism

Along with these broader factors which tend to control the supply of capital available, it is desirable to consider also the character of the investment mechanism that can be used by the community. Thus, for instance, the existence of satisfactory arrangements for banking and security distribution invariably tends to stimulate the growth of savings. Much has been said about the question of farm credit in the United States within recent years, and the discussion has brought out the fact that mortgage banking has stimulated the flow of funds into rural investment. Postal savings systems have been found in many of the older countries to be great stimulators of savings, and the same thing is true of the so-called popular banks, or people's banks, which are numerous in some European countries. In the United States, mutual savings banks and building and loan associations collected over $16,000,000,000, much of which might probably never have been accumulated if these organizations had not existed. The presence of stock exchanges tends to create an interest in securities, and a more receptive attitude on the part of the community at large with respect to the investment of funds in enterprises which involve some risk. The satisfactory organization of banking largely influences the ability of business men to obtain the funds needed for the development of their operations. Thus it may be fairly said that both the supply and the use of capital are greatly affected by the character of the machinery which is available for saving, distributing and using it, and that two countries of equal resources and natural strength will vary widely in the volume and cost of their capital, according to whether they make use of better or less satisfactorily adapted investment machinery.

In fact, as we have already seen, modern industrial society has made a beginning in the development of an automatic saving mechanism. The modern corporation has it in its power to limit the distribution of its earnings among stockholders. It must determine what proportion of its earnings is to be paid to the owner, and what proportion is to go back into the business. Most large corporations reinvest a substantial part of their earnings, which are devoted to the extension of the capital plant of the undertaking. This, it would seem, is a function which, taken in the aggregate, has a large effect in determining the immediate use of the current earnings of business enterprises, and may operate to enlarge, and sometimes to overspecialize, the plant equipment of the country. At times the greater part of our annual savings is made in this way. The punitive tax on undistributed corporate earnings enacted in 1936 may reduce, but hardly can check, such automatic savings.

Somewhat the same may be said of the influence of institutional investment, such as that carried on by the insurance companies. Such investors have been intrusted by the community with a part of its current income for a specific purpose. It is within the power of such an institutional investor to decide how its funds shall be used. Thus, in studying the investment margin of any country, attention is properly given to the relative degree of development that has been attained by corporate and individual investors of the types above mentioned.

The demand for capital is greatest in countries where active corporate promotion is going on. At times, the optimistic business man and financiers who have held rather too hopeful a view of the possibilities may be too encouraging in their representations to prospective investors. Ordinarily, the investor is not particularly well qualified to judge of the true worth of securities. He has to depend more or less upon advisers in the financial field who enjoy his confidence; and when these have quite generally fallen under the influence of a speculative fever, their opinions are not to be trusted. During such a boom period, active promotional work usually results in floating considerable quantities of securities which either are ahead of their time, representing investments that may become valuable at a later date, or are perhaps largely or wholly bad, representing misjudgment or even dishonesty. Sometimes a situation of this kind has results which are serious and long lasting. For example, the commercial disturbance or panic of 1873 has often been ascribed to excessive absorption of capital and savings in the construction of the transcontinental and other railroads which had been built just after the close of the Civil War for the purpose of linking the different parts of the United States more closely. There was undoubtedly good reason for this investment, but there was not enough business, either present or immediately prospective, to warrant investors making so large an outlay, if they expected to get any adequate return in the way of income. The late 'twenties of the present century witnessed a similar period of excessive activity by the nation's investment mechanism and corporate managements. But while American corporate promotion has been quite venturesome, often leading to substantial losses, it has also been remarkably successful in the long run, and has greatly helped in placing this country in the forefront among industrial nations.

Relation to the Business Cycle

The stage which has been reached in the business cycle in any country materially influences the volume of income and savings which are available for investment, as well as the demand for investment funds that makes itself felt. When business (and perhaps prices) are advancing, and when the whole economic mechanism is active, the natural tendency is to see profit possibilities in many directions which have formerly been viewed with some degree of pessimism. Promoters are anxious to develop given branches of business and to sell securities for that purpose. Investment bankers see the opportunity to place offerings which they believe will appeal to the popular fancy of the moment, or which are the outgrowth of new *bona fide* industrial undertakings which are just appearing. The result is that during the upward movement of the business cycle, there is invariably a strong tendency for the demand for capital to increase, which may at times result in the offering of higher rates of interest or more attractive participation in earnings to investors.

The downward movement of a depression is accompanied by a falling off of new offerings, and by an indisposition on the part of the public to buy them. This is partly the result of changes in the attitude of mind or psychology of the community as regards the whole subject, but it may also be due to actual changes in the need for funds. It frequently happens that during the upswing of business many industries are overprovided with capital. During the downward movement, they of course are not in the market for new capital. The relation of the business cycle to the field of investment is discussed more fully in Chapter XV.

Cost or Price of Capital

This analysis of the factors of demand for and supply of capital naturally raises the question of how an adjustment is brought about between them. As in most economic relationships, this adjustment is effected through changes in the current remuneration which is paid for the use of investment funds, which takes the form of interest yields on banks and dividend yields on stocks.

Income on investment is a payment to the owner of the funds for their use. It must be sufficient in amount to induce him to prefer the application of these resources to investment rather than to immediate purchase of commodities. If an absolutely safe investment could be conceived, the interest on that investment would be merely the minimum amount necessary to induce owners of funds to save and part with them. No such investments, however, can be found; and accordingly, income on investments must be regarded as consisting of at least two elements—interest on capital, and payment for risk or hazard in connection with the repayment of the funds at their full face value. In addition to these two elements, a third is usually to be recognized—a payment for management to cover the time and expense involved in dealing with the funds, transferring them, rendering them available, keeping them idle for the average time between investment changes, and the like. Other additional payments may be included in the rate of income required to induce an individual owner of funds to make a given investment, but these are undoubtedly the chief. Expectations of special future benefits, such as special disbursements, will cause current yields on stocks in many cases to fall far below this figure.

Like other economic payments which are made to harmonize demand and supply, interest rates move higher when demand is strong and supply small, and lower when supply is large and demand inadequate to absorb it. The factors of demand and supply have been analyzed in the foregoing paragraphs, and no recapitulation is necessary at this point. It is enough to say that in the capital market demand and supply are quite closely and delicately balanced, so that the rate of interest commonly affords a very reliable barometer of changes in the capital situation. It must of course be remembered, as is explained in Chapter XI on the money market, that the capital market is divisible into several sections corresponding to different purposes, so that there is seldom or never perfect competition between lenders and borrowers in all parts of it.

Over- and Under-saving

In the process of investment there is always an open question as to the capacity of a given market to "absorb" the investment surplus of the community. It does not follow, merely because an individual or a group are of saving habits and can put aside a proportion of their income from year to year, that there is always a satisfactory way in which to apply these savings so as to bring the owner thereof a regular income. The older economists were of the opinion that in almost all countries gradual expansion of population, and what they called the pressure of population upon subsistence, would eventually bring a community to a "marginal point" at which it was doubtful whether the further investment of savings would produce a large enough additional income to be worth while. Examples of this kind have been furnished by some of the older European countries, in which practically all natural resources have been brought close to the point of marginal productivity. In other countries, however, which are very far from having reached any such point, as in the United States, there is always a question as to whether a given field of business may not have been developed about as far as there is any occasion for it. For example, it may well be questioned at any given moment whether any further investment of funds in factories devoted to the manufacture of farm machinery will bring a return on the amount so spent. If capital is put into fields which are thus close to the margin of productiveness, it may be expected that the returns will be small and that the investor will be correspondingly disappointed.

The converse of this situation also holds good. Industries may easily pay too high a price for the funds they seek. If they offer securities on the market under certain conditions, they may find that there is no demand. Either the savings fund of the community has already been absorbed, or all that part of it which can be expected to be available at the rate of interest on the new securities has been exhausted. There is probably seldom a time when higher rates of interest will not call forth new savings funds in some quantity; but the question is whether or not the users can afford to pay more in order to bring about the offer of such funds. It is the function of the capital market to bring about an adjustment between demand and supply, at a price which will equalize the two sides of the dealings, without regard to such questions.

It is thus a frequent occurrence that the investment market machinery already described fails to function perfectly. Because of a variety of causes, it may easily happen that there will be an excess of investment securities brought into the market and offered for sale, with the result that the volume of current saving is not able to absorb them. In the same way, it may be that large savings occur, with the consequent placing upon the market of an undue volume of such savings offered as purchasing power for securities. When either of these conditions takes place, there is a lack of adjustment or balance between supply and demand, with a consequent tendency to raise the values of securities above reasonable quotations or to depress them below such a level, according as the supply of securities, as compared with savings funds, is scanty or over-abundant. These variations result in corresponding variations in the yield to be derived from the securities which are thus purchased by investors. Advances in such income or a tendency to decline below the normal level tend in turn to stimulate or retard the rate at which savings are made, and thus again a condition of balance may finally be brought about.

It will be noted that frequent reference has been made to the so-called normal adjustment. As in all economic writing, it is desirable not to use this word without assigning to it a definite meaning; and that meaning is for our purposes the level at which demand and supply are in balance, producing a rate of interest just sufficient to bring forward continuous additional supplies of savings adequate to meet the demand originating with those who are willing to pay a reasonable rate of return. When savings are available in excess amount or when money is unduly easy, the result is to enable some users of capital to get it more cheaply than they should. This condition of things tends to bring about an excess production of the goods that are being turned out by the industries which are thus enabled to obtain funds for capital use at unduly low rates. In a similar way, whenever some industry or industries are able to obtain the use of funds for working capital purposes only by paying rates that are unduly high, the effect is to restrict the total amount of output which should come from such enterprises. Unduly cheap or over-costly capital has the effect of throwing out of gear the industrial mechanism which is linked up with the investment market.

Over-saving or under-saving, over-borrowing or under-consumption of capital, all react upon the industrial output, affect prices in one way or another, thus influence the net earnings of the enterprises which are responsible for the change in production and distribution, and thus eventually work back into the investment field by affecting the quoted value of the securities of the enterprises which have been dependent upon unduly costly or unusually cheap supplies of capital. Thus the circle of saving-investment-industrial development-earnings-securities value is completed. The aid given in the performance of this function by the stock exchanges and by other securities markets is perhaps the most fundamental justification of their existence —the best illustration of the service which they render to the economic organization of society. The question of investment credit control is discussed more fully in Chapter XII.

It often happens, of course, that the processes which are iere described are proceeding at a different rate in different narkets. Accordingly different levels of prices for similar seurities exist in the two markets. Consider, for example, the ase of govenment securities in a country which is unquestionbly sound and stable but relatively short of capital, and the ame class of securities in another country similarly stable in s position but with much better assurance of the capital it eeds. In the second country, investors will be willing to pay iore and to accept a lower rate on the public issues than they ill in the first. A similar parallelism with lack of exact identity ay be traced in almost any class of securities as between two ven markets at the same time. The "lag" in one as compared ith another is the result of many causes of friction or retardaon which differ in differing instances. When the existence of ch a situation is perceived, investors in one country are likely try to transfer their funds to another by purchasing securities the country whose markets afford the best returns, provided litical, monetary or similar risks do not restrain them.

Bank Credit as Capital

The size of the fund available for capital investment at any one time may be expanded or contracted by the policy being pursued by the commercial banks of the community. Bank deposits represent the liquid funds of the community which can be directed to any one of several different channels. Any unit of it may be employed for consumption or devoted to investment, according to the decision of its owner.

The rate charged for bank funds, or the rate of interest for short-term loans, is ordinarily more sensitive and readily changed than is the rate on long-term investments, such as bonds. Both, of course, go back to the same general determining factors of supply and demand. The same elements which tend to make the charge for money high will in the long run exert the same effect upon capital funds, and *vice versa.* However, there frequently are periods of divergent fluctuation, in which the two groups of rates move separately from each other, perhaps, in fact, in opposite directions. Possibly the most influential factor tending to bring about this kind of divergence between the two classes of rates is speculation. Speculation ordinarily requires as a basis substantial advances of current funds, and these will normally be obtained from the banks. It is thus an added element of demand for the current resources of the community, and its influence is to raise or accentuate rates of interest for money. This may occur at the time when rates of return upon long-term capital are actually falling or are nearly stable. Good illustrations of these tendencies are found in the movements of long- and short-term funds at various periods during the years 1926-1929, especially in the New York market.

On the other hand, the policies of the central bank authorities may depress artificially rates of interest on long-term capital advances, through creating a plethora of short-term funds available for investment. This occurred in the period following 1933, as is more fully discussed below.

Control Over Capital Flow

From what has been said, it will be apparent that capital movements, like other economic shifts and changes, are likely to go at times too far in one direction before an opposing movement sets in and furnishes the corrective to a change that is possibly being overdone. It is never desirable for a community to pass from one extreme to another, as it is likely to do where competition is unrestricted. Accordingly, the effort of the financial community has always been that of bringing about some kind of control or regulation of capital movements which may operate more or less effectively to prevent unwise extremes from occurring. Several such types of efforts at control may be recognized. One is that of direct regulation, such as legislation; another is indirect regulation through the banking structure and the money market, as considered in Chapter XI.

A second possible method of control is through the application of the insurance principle by creation of special agencies or devices to spread risks. From the purely theoretical standpoint, the function of insurance is not merely that of protecting the individual against loss, but also of equalizing the losses resulting from unwise investments and spreading them out over the entire field of capital use. As different lines of business reveal through experience greater or smaller hazards, application of the insurance principle to them may become feasible.

Careful analysis of the credit risk of individual enterprises similarly results in regulating the investing process. The setting up of standards of safe investment for financial institutions, by law or otherwise, operates to restrain those who might otherwise be induced to apply capital funds in unpromising directions, and who might thus divert resources which are needed by essential industries to lines of business in which the outlook is not promising or is merely specious. This process of analysis is necessarily an expert one, hence the necessity of intrusting it more and more to those who are technically familiar with sound procedure.

References

Badger, R. E., *Investment Principles and Practices*, New York, 1928, chap. ii.

Durbin, E. F., *The Problem of Credit Policy*, New York, 1935.

Hawtrey, R. G., *The Economic Problem*, London, 1926, chaps. vi and vii.

Keynes, J. M., *The General Theory of Employment, Interest and Money*, New York, 1936.

KIRSHMAN, J. E., *Principles of Investment,* Chicago, 1924, chap. ii.
LAVINGTON, F., *The English Capital Market,* London, 1921, chap. ii.
MARSHALL, ALFRED, *Principles of Economics,* London, 1922, book ii, chap. iv; book iv, chap. vii; book v, chap. iv.
MOULTON, H. G., *The Formation of Capital,* Washington, 1934.
WILLIS, H. P., *The Theory and Practice of Central Banking,* New York, 1936, chaps. xvi and xviii.
WILLIS, H. P., and CHAPMAN, J. M., *The Economics of Inflation,* New York, 1935, part i, xi, and part ii, essays 5-7.

Chapter X

THE DEMAND FOR CAPITAL

The Flow of Capital

The investment surplus described in the preceding chapter does not flow as one steady and unchanging stream through the various channels of saving into the several classes of investment. It may rather be likened to a mountain torrent, which is constantly shifting its course to new channels in response to changing conditions.

Sometimes these shifts occur in response to rational causes, such as the promise of higher rates of return in new industries. In other instances, they occur in purely random fashion. Legal restrictions constantly affect the channels into which savings go. Furthermore, the total volume of new financing varies sharply with changes in conditions in the money and capital markets.

The net annual addition to the capital of the country may be defined as the increase in income-producing assets, tangible and intangible, which takes place during each year. This addition to the capital of the community is not necessarily the same as the surplus income, or savings, of individuals and corporations. There is a gap between money savings and the capital gross which constitutes productive business capital.

The savings of individuals are invested in part directly in buildings, real estate mortgages bought direct from the borrower, and other forms of wealth not requiring the intervention of the investment banking mechanism. Therefore, only a portion of current income is free for investment in securities, and thus constitutes a demand for new security issues. When the individual investor has a surplus of funds available for investment, it does not matter, from the point of view of the market as a whole, whether he buys a new security or one already outstanding. Should he purchase an outstanding bond or stock through his broker on the stock exchange, he turns over his free capital to the seller of that security, who will then be in a position to buy a newly issued security. Capital is thus made available for the purchase of new securities, regardless of whether the investor buys new or already outstanding securities with his savings.

The surplus earnings of a corporation, in so far as they are not distributed to shareholders as dividends, thus constituting individual income, are retained by it for use in its own business. This direct reinvestment of surplus income is an automatic savings process beyond the pale of investment banking, and a very large proportion of the annual savings of the community is made in this way. It tends to be reflected in time in a steady rise in the quoted market value of the shares issued by these corporations.

The stream of free investment capital which thus originates in the main as surplus earnings of individuals divides itself into many substreams and rivulets. One major division is the separation of a large fraction of the total for export abroad. The remainder, invested at home, goes into the various types of domestic enterprises, being diverted from one field to another from time to time according to the returns offered and the prevailing sentiment of the investing public. Finally, there may be a shift in the form of financing between stocks and bonds in response to various stimuli.

Interpretation of New Security Issue Statistics

The statistics of new security issues, as presented and analyzed in this chapter, must not be accepted as measuring the extent to which money savings are being invested in securities through the capital market at any one time. The data are useful only after their limitations are understood.

In the first place, a large part of the new security offering represents refunding of new issues put out to replace other previously outstanding. Such refunding operations may be fo the purpose of paying off a maturing obligation, or reducin the rate of interest on outstanding bonds by selling a new issu with a lower rate of interest. The proportion of new financin consisting of refunding is greatest in periods of rising bon prices, when many corporations rush to refund their high-coupon bonds with issues of low yields. It is also large in the earlier periods of a boom in stock prices, when corporations often call in bonds and replace them with stock issues. The percentage of new financing representing refunding in 1925, 1930, and 1935 was as follows:[1]

Year	Refunding Issues	Percentages of Total New Financing
1925	$ 905,854,350	13
1930	637,692,758	8
1935	3,271,095,399	69

In addition to refunding, a large proportion of new financing represents the sale of securities of established but privately owned businesses to the public. In this case, no new capital goes into the enterprise whose securities are offered by the investment banker, but the securities formerly closely held are issued for public subscription. Thus, in 1924 Dodge Brothers, Inc., after having been closely held by the Dodge family since its inception, was sold to bankers for $146,000,000 in cash, and the bankers then sold securities largely in excess of this amount to the public. Did the issues of Dodge securities represent new capital?

The answer is that no new capital went into the Dodge enterprise itself. The financing merely represented a transfer of ownership, the funds of investors being turned over to the Dodge owners for the purchase price, and the balance going to the bankers as profit. If the recipients of the investors' money invested it directly in some other productive enterprise, the Dodge issue would represent the raising of new capital going into industry. More usually, however, capital raised through the sale of a closely held corporation to the public is put into already outstanding securities, so that the free capital is transferred to other holders in the market. If this capital, after passing from hand to hand through the purchase and sale of already outstanding securities, is finally invested in a productive enterprise by some individual who sells his securities to invest the proceeds in his own business, then the capital origi-

[1] "Summary of New Financing," from *The Commercial and Financial Chronicle.*

nally invested in Dodge securities represents an addition to the total accumulation of capital in the community. On the other hand, should the money be invested eventually in a new security issue, then the same amount of capital has been counted twice in the new total of new security offerings—once when it was placed in the securities of an established business being sold to the public, and a second time when the proceeds, having passed from hand to hand in the securities markets, are finally invested in some other new security issue. There is duplication resulting from issues of securities previously privately held, therefore, in addition to the element of refunding, that must be borne in mind in interpreting statistics of new security flotations. Flotations of investment trusts and other organizations formed for the purpose of buying already outstanding securities similarly may not reflect in themselves a net accretion to the aggregate net savings of the community.

Finally, it must be remembered that a substantial portion of new security issues is not distributed to investors immediately, but is carried on credit. In the case of new stock issues, a large part may be carried indefinitely in margin accounts by brokers, so that the amount of the issue does not represent savings received from investors, but only partly that and partly credit provided by the banking system. The relation of the money and capital markets is discussed in the following chapter.

These various factors make statistics of new financing only partially representative of the process of money investment as it is constantly going on in an economically advanced country. In so far as refunding issues, sales of closely held stocks to the public, and investment trust and many holding company issues are concerned, statistics of new capital flotations overstate the volume of savings. Since direct investments made without public offering, the reinvestment of corporate savings, and investments in individual realty mortgages, etc., are generally omitted, the volume of savings is understated by such statistics. However, they are the best figures available for measuring the current volume of savings, and if used as approximations they throw considerable light on variations in the direction of the flow of investment resources into various channels and on indicated changes in the aggregate investment fund from year to year.

Classes of Domestic Issues

Until the beginning of this century, the railroads absorbed the largest portion of the new capital which flowed through the investment market. During the period of industrial consolidation which followed, basic manufacturing industries, like steel, forged to the front as the largest issuers of new securities. In recent years, with the enormous advance in electrical technology, the public utilities have taken a leading place.

The following table classifies new domestic financing in 1924 and 1928, illustrating the pre-depression situation:

Year	Total Financing[a]	Percentages of Total					
		Railroad	Public Utility	Industrial	Real Estate	Farm Loan	Municipal
1924.....	$5,416,630,222	17.4	28.2	19.1	6.2	3.3	25.8
1928.....	9,232,402,520	7.9	28.6	38.8	8.7	0.7	15.3

[a] Except foreign government issues.

The shifts that occurred during the depression period are shown by the following summary of new financing during the five years 1931 to 1935, inclusive. These statistics show how the capital market was dried up to a large extent while the recession process was going on, but a sharp recovery, largely due

Year	Total Financing	State and Municipal	Farm Loan, etc.	Railroads	Public Utilities	Industrial, etc.	Canadian Government, etc.
1931.....	$4,023,000,010	31	3	12	38	15	1
1932.....	1,864,000,000	46	9	3	29	9	4
1933.....	1,134,000,000	46	8	9	8	24	5
1934.....	2,262,000,000	41	32	11	7	6	3
1935.....	4,747,000,000	26	24	4	27	17	2

to a wave of refunding attracted by low money rates, followed. This recovery occurred despite the application of an extensive system of federal control to investment banking during this period.

The statistics above also reflect the fundamental changes that have taken place in the relative position of different industries in the investment markets. The railroads, under conditions of rigid government regulation and suffering largely from the competition of other forms of transportation, are loath to borrow money which they are not certain they can use profitably. The carriers have found that there is strong resistance to any substantial increase to their earning power; hence to add to their capital liabilities through the sale of additional bonds and stocks is seldom attempted except where there is virtual certainty that earnings will be large enough to cover the capital requirements in the new securities by an adequate margin.

There is no reason to believe that railroad financing in this country will ever recover a dominant position. The railroad net of the country as at present laid down gives adequate facilities to most of the well-populated areas. For local traffic, the automobile and motor truck are in many instances replacing existing branch lines of railroad, and there is certainly no basis for much future building of short lines. Hence, financing for new construction will be small. With business men and farmers agitating steadily for lower rates also, improvements to existing lines must be made in moderation if capitalization is not to outrun earning power.

Railroad financing has been strongly influenced by the fact that their seasoned character long gave to railroad bonds a preferred position in the laws governing legality for institutional investment of savings banks, insurance companies and trustees —a position which their present status would hardly justify. Well over one-third of all outstanding railroad bonds are held directly by financial institutions, and a large part of the balance is in trust accounts.

The public utilities, enjoying a steady increase in business and liberal regulation at the hand of state commissions under the protection of Supreme Court valuation decisions, absorbed during the 'twenties great and increasing amounts of capital which investors, impressed by their record, were more than willing to provide. Among the public utilities, the electric light and power industry, with its $10,000,000,000 investment, has been the largest factor. The persistent expansion in its output, along with steady improvement in methods, has permitted the industry to do just what the railroads could not do—cut rates generally without impairing income permanently.

After the depression of the early 'thirties, the legal status of the public utilities was changed through the enactment of legislation to impose strict federal regulation upon holding companies. The federal government also embarked upon direct competition with private companies to further its "yardstick program," and also made loans and grants to municipalities to permit them to embark upon the production and distribution of electricity. However, these legal changes did not impair the basic economic strength of this growing industry, although it tended to slow up new investment by many utility companies. Since 1928, a selected group of utility bonds was made legal for the first time for savings bank investment in New York State.

The communications industries represent an investment of some $6,000,000,000, of which the bulk is in telephones. This industry and the gas industry, whose investment is above $2,000,000,000, are enjoying steady growth, although at a rather slower rate than in the case of the electric utilities. The water and street railway utilities absorb little new capital.

In summary, therefore, it would appear that public utilities should retain the foremost place among American industries in absorbing new capital through the securities market.

Industrial Financing

The volume of industrial financing tends to be reduced by the practice of financing a large portion of new capital requirements through plowing back surplus earnings rather than by issuing new securities for cash. In the course of time, earnings thus retained by stockholders are frequently represented by securities issued as stock dividends, but these are not properly included in the totals of new financing. It is not clear how far the surtax on undistributed earnings imposed in 1936 will change this practice over a period of years, but in the aggregate such direct corporate savings will doubtless remain large. The attempt to keep down, by legislative or judicial action, the rate of earnings on railroad and public utility investment to a fair return has limited surplus earnings in these industries. The aim of regulation has been to allow these companies to earn merely enough to attract the necessary new capital for expansion and improvements.

Among the various industries included in the general classification of industrial financing, however, there has been a substantial shifting of new capital requirements from older industries to the new. The following analysis of industrial financing during the five-year period, 1924-1928, gives an indication of the changes that took place in that period:

Year	Iron, Steel, Coal, Copper, etc.	Equipment Manufacturing	Motors and Accessories	Oil
1924.........	$229,319,160	$19,016,100	$ 56,521,760	$187,525,968
1925.........	153,928,996	13,766,000	190,063,110	282,538,338
1926.........	280,382,200	30,787,500	131,573,624	499,716,415
1927.........	187,054,250	23,815,000	94,788,790	425,337,500
1928.........	320,575,859	9,135,000	107,653,468	263,110,305

Year	Rubber	Shipping	Other Industrial, etc.	Total Industrial Financing
1924.........	$ 2,000,000	$13,800,000	$524,949,923	$1,033,132,911
1925.........	65,550,000	34,420,120	1,005,443,343	1,745,709,907
1926.........	43,214,537	26,500,000	1,154,180,118	2,166,354,394
1927.........	72,701,675	34,210,000	1,845,489,796	2,683,397,011
1928.........	64,424,795	21,150,855	2,796,360,384	3,582,412,666

The Securities and Exchange Commission issues regular annual, quarterly and monthly statistics on the nature of new capital issues registered with it. Its group classification of issuers covering registration statements that became effective in 1935, with comparable percentages for 1934, was as follows:

TABLE 7.—GROUP CLASSIFICATION OF ISSUERS OF NEW SECURITIES FULLY EFFECTIVE FROM JANUARY 1 TO DECEMBER 31, 1935

Group	Number of Issues	Gross Amount (in Dollars)	Per Cent of Total	
			1935	1934
Agriculture	1	$ 125,000	0.0	0.0
Extractive industries				
Coal Mines	1	13,770,315	0.5	0.1
Gold and silver mines	54	27,435,275	1.0	3.3
Other metal mines	2	17,412,518	0.7	
Oil and gas wells	28	14,857,169	0.5	0.5
Quarries and non-metal mines	1	4,646,000	0.2	0.0
Total extractive industries	86	78,121,277	2.9	3.9
Manufacturing industries				
Food and related products	24	166,529,270	6.2	0.4
Tobacco products	2	199,625	0.1	....
Beverages (incl. breweries and distilleries)	15	47,324,716	1.8	8.1
Textile and textile products	3	137,960	0.0	0.1
Lumber and lumber products	2	1,240,000	0.1	1.1
Paper and paper products	3	13,106,425	0.5	0.2
Printing and publishing	2	2,990,000	0.1	0.1
Chemicals and allied products	12	8,920,917	0.3	0.5
Mineral oil refining	10	129,921,250	4.8	0.1
Tire and other rubber products	..	....	....	0.1
Leather and manufactures	1	4,000,000	0.2	0.0
Building and related products	5	27,325,287	1.0	....
Iron and steel	18	253,224,698	9.4	0.3
Non-ferrous metals	5	64,409,000	2.4	0.3
Machinery and tools	23	43,863,629	1.6	0.3
Transportation equipment	16	15,569,881	0.6	2.2
Miscellaneous products	7	18,789,000	0.7	0.2
Total manufacturing industries	148	797,551,658	29.8	14.0
Financial and investment companies				
Investment and trading companies				
General and limited mortgage companies	61	235,137,369	8.8	42.1
Fixed trusts	17	73,969,869	2.7	10.3
Total investment and trading companies	78	309,107,238	11.5	52.4
Holding companies	3	52,241,910	1.9	2.9

TABLE 7—(*Continued*)

Group	Number of Issues	Gross Amount (in dollars)	Per Cent of Total 1935	Per Cent of Total 1934
Commercial credit, finance and mortgage companies	25	100,782,662	3.8	1.4
Industrial and personal loan companies	8	3,978,290	0.2	0.5
Insurance companies	3	2,075,000	0.1	0.3
Other financial and investment companies	11	11,512,718	0.4	2.4
Total financial and investment companies	128	479,697,818	17.9	59.9
Merchandising	12	16,734,375	0.6	0.7
Real estate	4	587,820	0.0	1.0
Construction	..	....	....	0.1
Transportation and communication	14	128,984,767	4.8	....
Service industries	14	11,649,997	0.5	0.5
Electric light, power, heat, water and gas companies				
Diversified companies	30	506,517,861	18.9	18.2
Electric light and power companies	19	488,091,892	18.2	
Gas and/or steam heat companies	7	25,080,250	0.9	
Water companies	10	28,110,205	1.1	
Total electric light, power, heat, water and gas companies	66	1,047,800,208	39.1	18.2
Miscellaneous domestic companies	4	2,250,000	0.1	0.2
Foreign governments and municipalities	2	114,190,000	4.3	1.5
Total	479	2,677,692,920	100.0	100.0

Financing New Industries

That much of the venturesome quality of American business enterprise in general is shown by free capital in this country is attested to by the volume of new financing for new and untried industries, particularly in more prosperous periods.

Every so often, some new industry becomes a financing "fad" of the moment. During the period in which the industry retains its popularity, practically any issue of the group can be sold. But when the bubble bursts, the industry suffers a penalty, for then it may lose all power to raise money on reasonable terms.

The radio industry originated such a bubble in 1924, when almost any radio stock was readily salable. Where this "fad" stage is followed by solid growth, however, no interruption need be experienced in the ability of the industry to obtain constant new supplies of capital. The trend of chain store financing, for example, has reflected the expansion of this type of merchandising into various lines. Thus, of the 69 offerings noted in 1928, an active financing year for this industry, the following lines were represented:

Type of Chain	Number of Offerings	Amount
Drug	12	$ 67,791,000
Department store	11	66,947,000
Five and ten cent	8	34,044,000
Grocery	10	29,174,000
Shoe	7	10,473,000
Restaurant	2	9,622,000
Women's apparel	7	8,464,000
Other	12	11,398,000
Total	69	$237,913,000

The financing of individual industries generally follows a fairly uniform course of evolution. In the early stage of an industry's life, capital is difficult to secure, and financing takes the form of speculative stock issues, not always sponsored by established banking houses, for the latter may be unwilling to risk their reputation and prestige with a new and untried security. Then, as individual enterprises become firmly established and earning power is more definitely developed, a great deal of financing takes place, the success of some companies inducing the public to invest in others. Finally, the industry tends to reach a saturation point, where it has expanded sufficiently to meet the normal demand for its product or services. Furthermore, at this stage surplus earnings are sufficient to furnish a large share of the capital needed for expansion purposes. As a result, the volume of new financing in the industry tends to fall off sharply.

During a subsequent period of decadence, capital investments are scrapped or abandoned. As invention advances, it becomes possible to take the place of labor by the introduction of mechanical devices. Whether or not it will be wise to do so depends a good deal upon the amount which must be paid for capital. When capital can be cheaply borrowed, the tendency is to displace labor as far as possible and to substitute mechanization. This mechanization may thus give rise to what is called "technological unemployment." One result of it is to cause a great deal of "excess capital" in plants, many of which close the sections which operate with older and more expensive machinery, keeping them idle except in seasons of very high demand or periods in which prices have been artificially advanced, so that a profit can still be made by calling into employment the older equipment which is not so advantageous as the newly mechanized devices which have been brought in as the result of invention. As we have seen, it is usual in this stage to employ the surplus earnings of the enterprise to finance its own expansion, but a state of affairs in which new capital may be had at an exceedingly favorable rate may prove equally influential in bringing about a change of the capital equipment. Such a condition presented itself in the middle 'thirties in various industries, when interest rates were very low.

The railroads passed through this cycle during the first century of their existence. The utilities are still far from the saturation point; and as long as they extend their facilities they will require large amounts of new capital which must be obtained through security issues because of the limitation in earnings already referred to. The steel, automobile, and other better-established industries have been obtaining most or all of the capital they need from earnings. On the other hand, the airplane, chain store, and some branches of the chemical and amusement industries are among those which have only in recent years established a recognized basis for investment credit.

Real Estate and Municipal Financing

An important component element of new security offerings before the depression was issues of bonds secured by real estate mortgages. While the separate real estate mortgage is perhaps the oldest popular investment medium in this country, only in more recent years have bond issues secured exclusively by liens on land and buildings become a major factor in the investment market.

Such real estate financing in the pre-depression period varied as follows:

Year	New City Construction[a]	Real Estate Bond Issues	Percentage of Bond Issues to Building Volume
1923	$3,449,465,740	$240,613,000	7.0
1924	3,614,662,440	324,573,000	9.0
1925	4,302,696,723	722,325,800	16.8
1926	4,008,309,244	657,066,000	13.9
1927	3,541,388,042	613,609,000	17.3
1928	3,413,091,835	723,633,650	21.2

[a] Figures from 310 cities, compiled by *The Commercial and Financial Chronicle.*

Adverse experience with such liens during the depression, involving the collapse of a number of real estate bond houses, constituted a severe setback for this type of financing.

Municipal financing is stimulated by an artificial factor—tax exemption. Because of their freedom from federal and certain state imposts on income, these bonds are especially attractive to persons of large means who purchase them to avoid heavy income tax payments. High income tax rates keep municipal financing relatively large.

There is little reason for expecting a sharp drop in municipal financing. Attempts to take away the tax exemption feature of these bonds, which would tend to discourage their issuance, have been defeated in Congress thus far.

United States Government Financing

After its huge Liberty Loan issues floated during the war, and a Victory Loan sold subsequent to the conflict, the United States government ceased to be a borrower of new capital. Instead, it steadily reduced its debt through sinking fund payments, so that only refunding issues were necessary.

The severe depression of the early 'thirties again made the government a heavy borrower, and the tendency to increase the national debt was accentuated after 1933 by the New Deal program, which involved large investments by the national government in various federal agencies designed to extend the activities of the government in the economic field. Also, several billion dollars of mortgage bank bonds were guaranteed by the United States government, so that the federal credit was loaned to facilitate the program of relieving the burden of indebtedness resting upon farmers and home owners.

When the federal government issues bonds and invests the proceeds in productive enterprise, the process is similar to that which occurs under private auspices. When the government raises money for non-productive purposes, on the other hand, it effects merely a change in the distribution of national income for the future. A part of the population will pay taxes in order to permit the payment of interest and principal to a future generation of holders of government bonds. Similarly, when the government increases its debt, it takes over the determination of the spending of a portion of the nation's current income—that portion which is subscribed to new bond issues. When the government sells its bonds chiefly to banks, rather than to individual investors, then the additional spending power thus acquired by the federal Treasury is not deducted from the total national income, as expressed in terms of money but that total is inflated by the amount of additional bank credit written up on the books of the banks through such purchases of federal bonds.

As far as the investment banking mechanism is concerned government financing is of less moment than private. Th government uses the Federal Reserve Banks as its investmen banker, paying them only a nominal fee for this service; bu large banks and government bond dealers help in the distribu tion of new issues as a rule by taking large positions whic they reduce over a period of time as the government debt absorbed by the rank and file of institutional and individu investors. By pricing new issues somewhat below the lev justified by prevailing market quotations, the dealers obtai what corresponds to the gross spread in the flotation of oth securities, except that it is not recognized as such. Of cours government financing is exempt from all the statutory restri tions and safeguards that have been established for other typ of securities.

The Yield Factor

Relative yields on different classes of securities have changed constantly in response to changing preferences of institutional and individual investors, legal investment restrictions and the demand for new funds. United States government bonds being backed by the unlimited taxing power of the federal government, being rediscountable when owned by member banks at the Federal Reserve Banks at par, and, finally, being backed by the ability of the government to print paper money if necessary to pay interest, are virtually devoid of the credit risk, although it is true that the currency in which interest and principal are payable may depreciate sharply in purchasing power. However, this latter consideration is true of all bonds.

Municipals, particularly because of their tax exemption, generally come next as a class, followed by railroad and public utility issues. In recent years, the former price position of railroad obligations among corporate obligations has been largely lost.

The relative levels of short-term and long-term interest rates will vary with the main trend of the rate of interest. When it is feared that long-term interest rates will decline, short-term rates may drop to nominal levels, as was the case in the early 'thirties. Also, lack of confidence in the stability of the currency will cause investors to prefer short-term to long-term commitments, although this is not always logical, particularly where short-terms are replaced as fast as they come due by other short-dated obligations.

The volume of new bond financing tends to follow closely interest rates, rising when interest rates advance and falling when they drop. In other words, bond financing will conform rather closely to the trend of bond prices. This close relationship beween new financing volume and price is similarly marked in he case of stocks. The accompanying charts illustrate this reationship.

A factor of great importance since 1933 has been the unprecedented decline of the rate of interest for capital. The esult has been to alter the conditions of demand for and supply f various types of securities. Taken in conjunction with the alling off in the volume of new issues, the credit inflation of

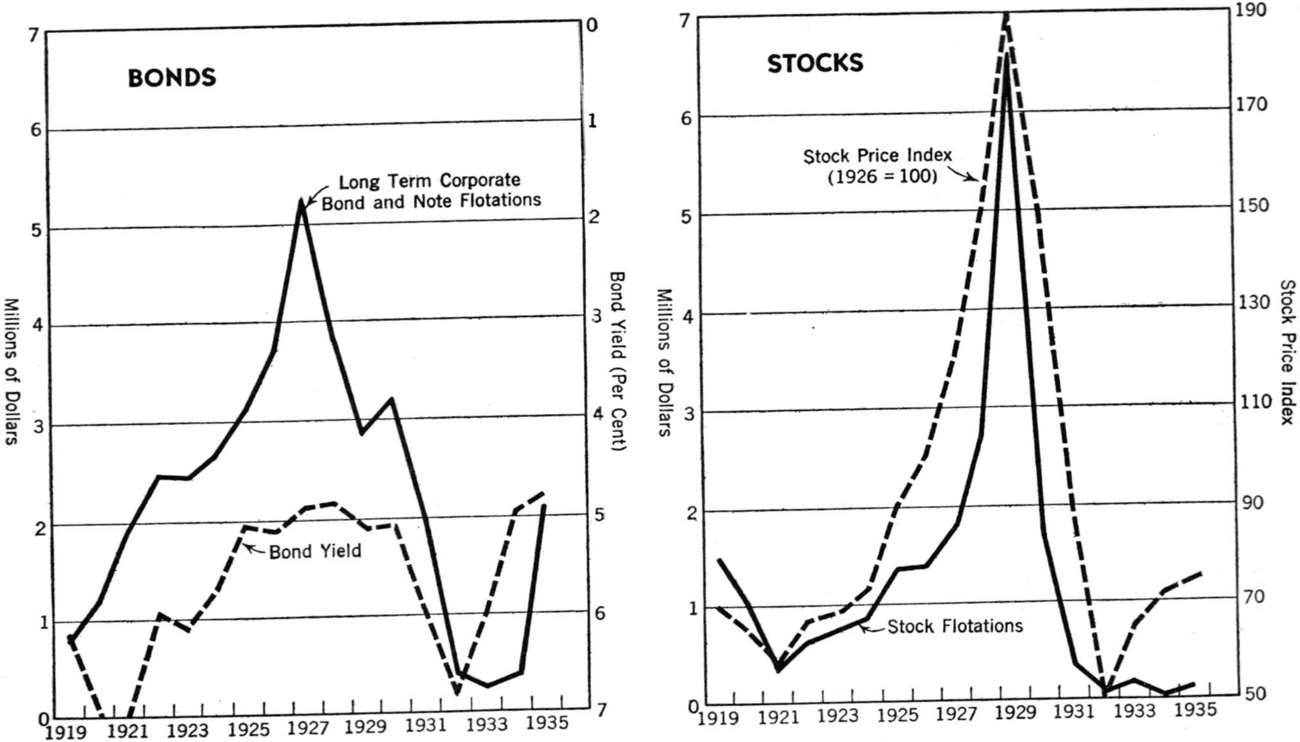

FIG. 10. RELATION OF TYPE OF FINANCING TO MARKET CONDITIONS

that period generated a virtual famine of the best-secured types of investment. This has resulted in the advance in price of such issues to heights relatively unknown in times past; and the tendency to go into bonds rather than stocks finally extended itself to the second-grade speculative securities, with the effect of putting them up to levels formerly typical of gilt-edge securities only. The history of the five years 1930-1935 emphatically demonstrates the inpermanence of any general classification of securities as "good," "bad," or "indifferent," and lays emphasis upon the necessity of subjecting securities of all kinds to constant and repeated analysis for the purpose of testing them in every possible way from the standpoint of their soundness and suitability for the purposes for which they are intended.

Stocks and Bonds

Statistics of new financing during the third and fourth decades of the twentieth century show a dominance of bond issues to 1928 while bond prices rose, and an excess of stock issues while bond prices reacted in 1928 and 1929. Thereafter, bond financing again predominated. The proportion of stock issues to total security flotations is shown in the following table, covering the years 1926-1935 (in millions of dollars):

TABLE 8.—BOND AND STOCK FINANCING

Year	Corporate New Capital Issues			Corporate Refunding Issues		
	Total	Bonds and Notes	Stocks	Total	Bonds and Notes	Stocks
1926	3,754	2,667	1,087	820	687	133
1927	4,658	3,184	1,474	1,850	1,586	264
1928	5,346	2,385	2,961	1,584	1,054	530
1929	8,002	2,078	5,924	1,374	542	833
1930	4,483	2,980	1,503	474	451	23
1931	1,551	1,239	311	821	789	32
1932	325	305	20	319	315	4
1933	161	40	120	219	187	32
1934	178	144	35	312	312	0
1935	404	334	69	1,864	1,782	81

Other things being equal, corporate managements have several reasons for absorbing new capital through stock rather than bond issues. They thus avoid fixed charges and the risk of default and foreclosure during periods of small earnings. However, as shown by the above table, only during periods of prosperity do stock issues attain large proportions. In addition, through the sale of convertible bonds, stock financing may be accomplished indirectly, since later conversion of the bonds frees the company from fixed income obligations.

The great prosperity of American industry during the years following the war resulted in a general rise in stock prices which attracted an unprecedented amount of popular speculation and which also gave to common stocks a place of paramount importance as an investment instrument. This change in the relative position of stocks seemed temporary during the depression, but again asserted itself during the subsequent period of credit inflation. While it is impossible to speak of a normal situation in these matters, it is fair to say that usually a larger yield should be obtained on stocks than on bonds, because of the fact that the bond presumably represents a claim upon actually existing assets, while the stock is, in some proportion at least, dependent upon good will or earning power for its value. A good deal of absurdity attaches to some theories about common stocks as long-term investments, and erroneous notions have been advanced with respect to an alleged certainty that in the "long run" or "on the average" such investments not only would be secure but would participate in the "natural" growth of values, as against preferred stocks or bonds which, by the terms of their agreement, are limited in their participation of profits.

The relative merits of the two chief types of securities are discussed at greater length in Chapter XIII below.

Foreign Financing

When the accumulation of capital within a country proceeds at a rapid pace, it is natural that a portion of the stream of savings shall be deflected from domestic investments into foreign securities as more profitable opportunities arise abroad. This was the case in the United States after 1920, although, as was seen in Chapter VIII, we enjoyed a short period of capital export before the era of industrial consolidation began in 1899. During the decade following the end of the Great War, approximately $15,000,000,000 of foreign securities were floated in this market. The amount of foreign financing, and the proportion of total new capital issues which represented foreign issues, are shown in the following table:[2]

Year	Foreign Financing	Percentage of Total Financing
1920	$ 538,725,887	13.4
1921	604,662,000	14.4
1922	802,799,034	15.3
1923	368,402,279	7.5
1924	1,253,625,765	19.7
1925	1,316,022,500	18.5
1926	1,360,215,540	18.4
1927	1,737,618,425	17.5
1928	1,582,982,400	15.9

The stream of capital destined for foreign investment turned in the first post-war years to the old countries of Europe, but gradually spread over practically the whole world as the confidence of the investor increased and the lure of higher yields attracted him farther afield, largely regardless, as later experience was to show, of safety or soundness. Thus the Department of Commerce reports the following geographic distribution of American foreign financing between January 1, 1914, and January 1, 1928:

Territory	Amount	Percentage of Total
Europe	$ 5,653,262,025	48.5
Canada and Newfoundland	2,711,242,015	23.3
Latin America	2,426,848,849	20.8
Far East	694,771,800	5.9
Territories and possessions	173,258,840	1.5
Total	$11,659,383,529	100.0

[2] Compiled by *The Commercial and Financial Chronicle.*

This flow of American capital abroad benefited both governments and corporations of other countries and might have been far more helpful had more competent management prevailed. The proportion of corporate financing grew steadily, following the reconstruction of government finances in many countries after the war, and made additional loans abroad unnecessary for them for a while. The character of the industries which were thus financed by foreign corporate security flotations in this country is shown by the compilation below.

Industry	Foreign Financing, 1914–1927 (inclusive)
Public utilities	$ 722,925,000
Railways	720,114,750
Banks	492,729,075
Sugar companies	347,673,990
Paper	346,769,450
Mining	239,425,500
Oil	175,524,745
Iron and steel	135,930,000
Miscellaneous	532,215,399
Total	$3,713,307,909

This heavy export of capital in the post-war period was not accompanied by any lowering of our tariff barriers to facilitate imports that would permit foreign borrowers to pay interest and principal on their debts to this country. The situation was further aggravated by simultaneous attempts by this country to collect the war debts from its erstwhile allies, and by the latter to collect vast amounts of reparations payments from Germany.

The result was a severe international financial crisis which began in the spring of 1931 and within a short time brought about the abandonment of the gold standard by Great Britain and other countries, the imposition of strict foreign exchange control in other nations like Germany and Italy, and numerous defaults on foreign bonds. In these circumstances, investors in this country developed a keen distaste for nearly all foreign securities that will probably persist for a long time. Instead, a heavy influx of capital seeking safety came into this country from abroad. The consequent disappearance of foreign financing during the early 'thirties is shown by the following table giving figures for such financing from 1929 to 1935 (000,000 omitted):

Year	Foreign Financing	Percentage of Total Financing
1929	$671	6.7
1930	905	13.1
1931	229	7.6
1932	29	0.24
1933	12	1.7
1934	0	0.0

The period since 1929 has been punctuated here and there also by legislation and actual efforts in foreign countries to prevent the growth of American control of enterprises in which large financial interests have been acquired. In many cases these attacks upon American rights have been successful, usually employing as vehicles various elaborations in corporate law or in the voting power of various classes of stockholders. Americans who bought participations in German banks have been disappointed by the outcome of their investments—a situation well illustrated in the changes introduced into the bargain which the Reichsbank itself had made with them. In other cases, even in England, obstacles have been thrown in the way of the transfer back to the United States of money representing the purchase price of enterprises which American owners had succeeded in selling to foreigners. In those countries in which strict exchange control has been instituted, wholly owned subsidiaries of American manufacturing enterprises have been compelled to continue their process of production without being permitted to transfer profits when earned to their parent offices in the United States, and in some cases under the necessity, as well, of turning over to the central bank any foreign exchange that they might obtain as a result of sales of their goods in other countries. The effect of all these aggressions has undoubtedly been that of checking and limiting in a material degree the expansion of American enterprise and its normal development in countries where there was real need of outside capital and where a legitimate field for expansion might have been found, had it not been for nationalistic feeling which forbade any assurance of safety or continued enjoyment of the funds so placed abroad.

Other Forms of Capital Export

In tracing the volume of foreign investment, the total of new capital flotations for the account of foreign government and corporations is not an inclusive figure. In addition to these foreign securities floated abroad, large purchases of securities originally issued internally in those countries have been made at times by Americans. Purchases of such internal issues cannot be traced, but the number of investment houses and brokers interested in trading in such securities was at one time so large as to indicate that the aggregate was then quite substantial. Furthermore, some investment trusts have at times in the past put a sizable proportion of their funds into such foreign internal issues.

In addition to public security flotations here and the purchase of internally issued securities, the export of capital may take the form of the shifting of liquid cash balances from one market to the other. This, however, is more a banking than an investment matter, at least nominally, although when a large volume of foreign funds is shifted to New York, they may influence domestic speculative and investment conditions substantially.

A final and important channel for foreign investment is the direct investment by corporations in the property or securities of concerns doing the same line of business abroad. Thus, the Electric Bond & Share Company, a leading holding company in this country, has invested hundreds of millions in its subsidiary, the American & Foreign Power Company, which operates solely abroad. The International Telephone & Telegraph Company similarly is an American corporation, although it operates almost entirely abroad. Numerous leading American industrial companies, such as the Ford Motor Company, the General Motors Corporation, the International Harvester Company, F. W. Woolworth & Company, the Westinghouse Air Brake Company and the General Electric Company, have extensive interests in foreign countries, and through these interests send abroad a large amount of American capital which, for the most part, is not recorded in statistics on the subject. The tendency to build and operate American-owned concerns in foreign countries gave rise to the creation of some 1,200 such plants before 1929, but was then checked. Exchange control and high tariffs, however, have given it some renewed stimulus.

The Future of New Financing

This analysis of new financing indicates that a number of fundamental changes have taken place in recent years. Capital flotations on the American market have tended increasingly to represent new or rapidly growing industries. Railroads, traction companies, iron and steel companies and other industries which have seen their period of greatest growth in the past no longer absorb as large a share of the annual increment of new free capital as was formerly the case. The federal government may absorb new capital through bond issues for some time to come.

From what has been seen, the chief demand for new capital in this country will probably come from new industries. The one outstanding exception is the electric power and light industry, which has assumed the leadership in new financing and will probably retain it. Lastly, foreign financing, direct or indirect, may again, when normal economic conditions are restored, absorb some portion of the annual accretion of capital in the United States.

When established channels for the investment of new capital again absorb the savings of the country at the rate established in the pre-depression years, and when artificial easy-money policies are abandoned by central banking authorities, it would appear that there is no real plethora of free capital in sight. Experience shows that extremely low interest rates in one country are affected when rates are high in other economically developed parts of the globe. But a long time may be required for this tendency to assert itself.

There have been periods in the past when excess free capital sought employment at very low rates. The most remarkable period was noted at the turn of the century, when governments could finance at a cost of less than 3 per cent, and first-class corporation bonds yielded less than 4 per cent. This era witnessed extremely low interest rates in France, England, Germany and Holland, as well as in this country. The era of great industrial consolidations and public utility development had not started then on the scale which drove interest rates steadily higher in the period which followed. Also, investment funds were largely concentrated at that period in a relatively limited number of government and railroad bonds.

Up to the time of the depression, it was thought by many that there would be a steady expansion in popular interest in foreign securities in this country, while the domestic demand for capital from industry would contribute to maintain returns to owners of such capital. The over-financing and over-stimulation of the pre-panic years brought a reaction, however, during which the economic machinery of the country was disrupted. This period was marked by the inability of capital to earn a reasonable rate of remuneration in high-grade investments. One factor that had much to do with this situation was the lack of confidence which characterized large sections of the public with regard to the future of business, and the nation's currency and banking systems.

References

Hawtrey, R. G., *The Economic Problem,* New York, 1926, chap. xxiv.

Hobson, C. K., *The Export of Capital,* London, 1914.

Kirshman, J. E., *Principles of Investment,* Chicago, 1924, chap. iii.

Madden, John T., and Nadler, Marcus, *Foreign Securities,* New York, 1929, chap. iii.

National Industrial Conference Board, *The International Financial Position of the United States,* New York, 1929, chaps. i and x.

Stone & Webster and Blodget, Inc., *One Thousand Dollars a Second—America as a World Investment Market.*

Chapter XI

THE MONEY MARKET AND INVESTMENT BANKING

The Sources of Funds

In the preceding chapter, we have been concerned with the chief sources of demand for capital.

On the supply side, a complicating factor is introduced by the fact that investment funds flow into the capital market from several sources. The current stream of money savings of individuals and investing institutions is one such source. In addition, however, the supply of funds available for long-term investment is affected by the short-term funds or money market. The volume of funds available for investment may be reduced by diversion into short-term commitments, by application of current income to the repayment of maturing short-term debts, or by the creation of new investment funds through short-term credits available for the purpose.

The supply of capital, therefore, may be expanded or contracted through the operation of the money market.

The close relation that exists between the money and capital markets is in large part an outcome of the fact that the commercial banks of the country do both types of business—making short-term loans and also making advances on securities and buying bonds directly for their portfolios on a large scale. As commercial banks have turned increasingly to investments, the closeness of the relationship between the money and capital markets has become greater than ever.

Scope of the Money Market

The term money market is usually assigned to the aggregate of buyers and sellers who are concerned with short-term credits. Included under this head are commercial and financial loans made on both a call and a short-term basis. While in current parlance the term is often used in a restricted sense to denote the market for call loans secured by stock and bond collateral, the latter is really only one section of the larger money market. Sometimes, also, the money markets denote the long-term, or capital, market, as well as the market for short-term credits.

It is hardly necessary to call attention to the fact that the terms "short" and "long" are of purely relative significance in any such discussion as this. However, this distinction between short- and long-term loans and securities is made, and it is possible to draw a rough line of demarcation between these two branches of the investment field. Securities of even short term, when issued by investment bankers, are seldom included within the operations of the money market, although short-term government obligations often are. Furthermore, the money market trades only in loans and obligations, equities being naturally excluded.

A general characteristic of the money market is the fact that loans and obligations are transferred within it in terms of a stated rate of interest, rather than in quotations which represent certain percentages of par value, as is the case in the bond market, or so many dollars for each share, as is the case in the stock market. It is true that such long-term securities as railroad equipment trust certificates and municipal bonds are also generally traded in on a yield basis, but they constitute the exceptions in the security markets. The near maturity of money market obligations and the fact that they are payable at their par value when they fall due account for this general practice of making quotations in terms of the interest or discount rate.

The price for the use of the short-term loans which are secured in the money market is, therefore, stated as a certain rate of interest. Before examining the money market in greater detail, we shall consider the general rôle played in it by the interest rate.

Definition of Interest

The definition of interest has formed the subject of extended discussion among economists and students of finance for many years, but there has been no definite agreement as to any one basis for the payment of interest. There is agreement that in ordinary competitive societies, with private ownership of wealth, a payment made by the active user of wealth to the owner of it is necessary in order to insure the maintenance both of the amount and of the availability of wealth adequate for the current needs of industry.

The interest rate, or the price paid for the use of money or free purchasing power, thus reflects supply and demand forces just as do other prices. It is also agreed that, within broad limits and subject to some limitations which at times become controlling, a change in the amount thus paid tends to determine the capital made available for particular uses. A higher rate of interest payment may result in inducing persons to save more, while a reduction in the rate of interest tends to slow down the amount produced or the amount of the existing fund which is turned over to industrialists. Accordingly, the rate of interest is looked to as a partial means for bringing about the regulation of the amount of actual new capital which is coming forward for investment, and the amount of such capital which is made available through short-term channels, as compared with the amount which is being used in long-term channels.

Evidently, this kind of definition necessitates a conclusion as to what limits the interest rate. Substantial agreement prevails to the effect that a rate cannot be paid in excess of the capacity of the borrowed capital to produce a money income; the limit of the rate that can be paid at any time is thus the amount of money income which can be obtained through the application of the capital. This notion is evidently almost axiomatic when it is stated in this broad way. The difficulty with it is found in the fact that nearly every industry differs from every other with regard to the amount of additional productiveness that could be obtained through the use of more units of capital. Productiveness of funds in industry varies. The money and capital markets iron out these differences and establish a relatively uniform rate which is to be paid by various individual groups of those who want new capital. It reduces the great differences which would exist between rates if they were left to depend upon the ability of those who are using them to produce actual increases in wealth.

The first general rôle of the rate of interest is to regulate the total amount of funds which is offered and sought. As this rate is not uniform but differs for various kinds of loans, it performs a second function in regulating the proportion of loanable funds which are available for any one specific kind of loan in the money market. In fact, the market is competitive, and each user or group of users undertakes to protect itself against others by offering higher or lower rates for the funds needed. As a matter of fact, we never have a single rate of interest in any market; we have a variety of rates which have been adapted to the particular kind of loan for which they are intended, and which represent the notions of the groups of traders with respect to the relative urgency or desirability of that particular use as compared with other uses which are to be contrasted with it.

These varying rates of interest fluctuate greatly, not only absolutely but in relation to one another among themselves. The study of the rates, or "rate structure" as it may be called, in any given community furnishes the clue to the actual distribution of funds at any given time, as well as to the underlying conditions which determine the willingness of borrowers to pay more or less for what they want. Just as a thermometer measures the temperature in a room, and may lead by mechanical contrivance to alteration of the inflow of air before those in the room have had time to feel very uncomfortable, so the rate of interest is an indicator to determine the time and conditions in which alterations of the supply of, and demand for, capital take place, and corrective steps may be taken if interest rate changes indicate that abnormal conditions may develop in the business structure.

While each type of interest rate is determined by the relation between the supply and demand factors affecting it, local conditions of demand and supply constantly vary, causing fluctuating rates in each money market. Thus, for example, we may give first attention to the rate which is charged by banks for loans to their customers.

Normally, the minimum rates of interest are fixed by the costs of lending institutions. The banker has a definite overhead cost in making a loan which he must always cover; but above that there is a large field of fluctuation or uncertainty within which variation is caused by the changing conditions referred to. In the United States, rates for ordinary individual bank loans on unquestionable security seldom go below 4 or 4½ per cent; but in some parts of the country, where the demand is large enough, they may be as high as 8 or 10 per cent, even when the security is paper of an irreproachable character.

Types of Loans

With these general considerations concerning interest rates in mind, we shall now turn to a survey of the different sections of the money market, each of which has its own particular set of rates. Seven important sections in the money market can be distinguished. They are:

1. The call money market, for loans secured almost exclusively by stocks and bonds
2. The time money market, which is also a security collateral loan market
3. The market for short-term government securities
4. The market for bankers' acceptances
5. The market for negotiable commercial paper
6. "Over-the-counter" loans by banks to their regular borrowing customers
7. The market for credit at the central bank—in this country, credit at a reserve bank which member banks may secure through the process of rediscounting, as provided by law.

The money market is largely concerned with kinds and classes of credit with which commercial banks have to deal, as disinguished from those with which purely investment banking nstitutions are more directly concerned. The bank, particularly he American bank, has its own "market" which consists of its own group of customers, while the money market in the broad ense comprises what is also termed the "open market," which ncludes all those who are engaged in dealing in obligations which are suitable for bank holdings. The investment bankers nd the brokers have contact with the commercial banker in he open market, since they borrow from him there; the comnercial banker on the other hand buys investment securities in he capital market.

Call Loans

Call loans are repayable at the option of lender or borrower within twenty-four hours. When not called, these loans may continue in force indefinitely. A special significance, however, has been given to the term "call funds," so that it is now applied to funds lent on demand notes backed by stock and bond collateral. The term call loans is practically identical with brokers' loans. However, a bank could also make considerable amounts of call loans directly to individuals who want to use them in carrying securities.

Up to this point any "market for call funds" we have considered has been a purely theoretical one, since it has involved only two parties, the banker and the borrower, whether the latter be a broker or a speculator. The "market" arises only when the broker or other borrower endeavors to find out where he can get his funds most cheaply and "shops about" for the purpose of making the most satisfactory and profitable connection with an actual lender of money. This kind of market development may be brought about through the efforts of money brokers who mediate between lenders and borrowers. In the New York market, however, it has been provided for through the establishment of a "money desk" on the floor of the New York Stock Exchange, at which offers of and bids for money are received, and lenders and borrowers brought into contact with one another to the end that demand and supply may be equalized and that rates may be adjusted one to another. Evidently this kind of adjustment, aiming as it does at an equalization of demand and supply over very short periods, results in establishing a highly sensitive rate responsive to changes in the relationship between demand and supply.

As a matter of fact, the great bulk of the call loans made on the New York money market, the dominant money market in the country, are made at the rate fixed at the money desk of the New York Stock Exchange. Each morning at 11 A.M a "renewal rate" for call loans is determined by the Stock Clearing Corporation, based on expectations of what the supply of and demand for funds will be during the day. Any borrower or lender not satisfied with this rate can call his loan and make a new loan in the market. During the day, brokers file applications for new loans at the money desk, while banks, through friendly brokers, turn in offers of money at various rates. When the supply of funds at one rate is exhausted, the rate rises. Conversely, if the demand for funds can be satisfied out of offers made at a lower rate, the official rate declines. Many loans may be arranged also on the "outside market," that is, directly from banks or through money brokers off the floor of the exchange.

Time Loans

The market for time funds, consisting of collateral loans running from 30 to 180 days, does not differ in any important respect from the call loan market.

The trading takes place at the hands of the same group of dealers and operators, and the factors of demand and supply are much the same in both cases. Differences in rates for the two types of loans are primarily due to the fact that borrowers themselves at times shift their demand from call to time funds and back again, according as the situation in the speculative field seems to indicate the probability of early changes in the call money rate. Trading in time funds is resorted to as practically an insurance of a steady money supply at a given rate for a specified period; or, in other words, it may be viewed as a forward order for call money. It need not, therefore, be given any very extended treatment, so far as its technique goes, by students of the investment banking situation.

There is one phase of the time money situation, however, which is worthy of special study. This is the function it performs in bridging the gap between call money and the shorter-term forms of investment paper. As a rule, the time money rate is higher than that for call money, and is intermediate between the call rate and the rate on short-term investment paper. This intermediation is not of course permanent, for at times both the call and the time rate may temporarily be pushed considerably higher than the investment paper figure, as happened in 1928 and 1929. But in normal times the lowest rate in the open market is usually that for call money; time funds are slightly above it, and short-term investment paper occupies a still higher stage in the general scale of rates prevailing at any time in the market.

Time loans become relatively unimportant when the rate moves up above 6 per cent for any period of time, because such loans are not exempt from the usury law, which in New York State provides for a maximum rate of 6 per cent on loans to individuals and partnerships, except in the case of call loans of more than $5,000 secured by collateral. In the case of a time loan, when more than 6 per cent is charged, the interest is not collectible at law. Hence, the volume of time loans declines sharply in periods of high interest rates, being made chiefly to first-class firms who would not, it is supposed, contest the payment of interest under any circumstances.

Security Loan Statistics

An increasing interest came to be centered upon security loans in the middle 'twenties because of their rapid expansion and their importance for business and speculation. Regular statistics began to be published. At the present time, the Federal Reserve Bank of New York furnishes weekly the total of loans made by the New York and Chicago reporting member banks for their own account and for out-of-town banks. These figures are issued Thursday afternoon for publication in the newspapers Friday morning. The New York Stock Exchange makes its own compilation of loans made to its members in New York City from all sources, and this appears shortly after the beginning of each month. Neither of the two statements is comprehensive. The weekly report of loans made by and through New York member banks does not include advances from other sources or those made to out-of-town brokers or dealers. The monthly statement of the New York Stock Exchange fails to include loans from whatever source made to others than members of the exchange. The quarterly statement of all member banks shows loans made by them to brokers and dealers in and outside New York City.

In addition, weekly member bank reports furnish regular statistics of security loans to other borrowers.

Collateral Loan Restrictions

During the security market boom of the late 'twenties, American banking entered upon a peculiar phase that has already had a profound effect upon banking legislation and national credit policy. (See Appendices III and IV.)

Attracted by the desire to profit from the spectacular rise in prices then going on, hundreds of thousands of persons all over the country began to borrow money with which to buy securities on margin in one way or another. As a result, the money market was tapped to an unprecedented degree to finance a security market boom. The resulting expansion of security loans by the banks entailed a corresponding expansion in bank deposits, since the latter rise *pari passu* with an increase in loans or investments for the banks of the country as a whole. Thus, a mass of bank deposits was created on the basis of security loans, both to brokers and to other borrowers.

The nature of this vast expansion in security loans may be noted by the changes that occurred in the volume of this type of credit outstanding during the last year of the boom. The distribution of all security loans in October, 1928, and October, 1929, was as follows:

	October, 1928	October, 1929
Bank loans to brokers and dealers.......	$ 2,749,000,000	$ 2,824,000,000
Bank security loans to other customers...	6,375,000,000	7,875,000,000
Loans to brokers and dealers by others..	3,701,000,000	6,416,000,000
Total of security loans.............	$12,825,000,000	$17,115,000,000

The unsound nature of a banking system in which deposits are created through security loans became apparent during the subsequent deflation period. It was then found that the decline in quotations created a "vicious spiral" of deflation, each material fall in security prices forcing liquidation of impaired bank loans and margin accounts, which depressed prices further and impaired additional collateral loans. The inflation and deflation of security loans during this period were more drastic by far than in the case of other types of loans, as shown by the chart on page 310.

The outcome was a series of measures to prevent for the future such a drastic expansion in security loans as occurred during the late 'twenties. These measures are likely to prove one of the most effective and constructive of the banking changes of recent years. They include:

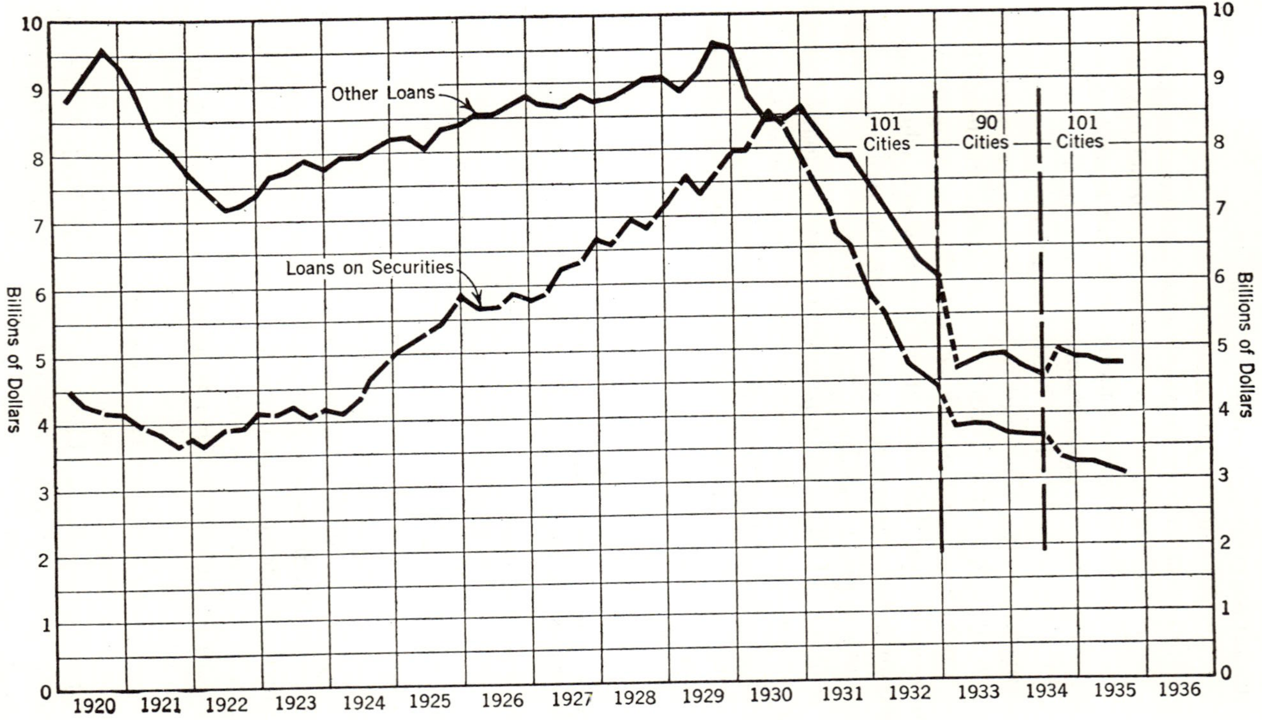

FIG. 11. SECURITY AND OTHER LOANS OF REPORTING BANKS, 1920-1935
(Used by permission of Young & Ottley, Inc.)

1. Brokers' loans by other than banking lenders, which are beyond the control of the Federal Reserve System and were largely responsible for setting at naught the restrictive credit control policies of the 1928-1929 period, have been practically abolished by the Banking Act of 1933 and the Securities Exchange Act of 1934.

2. The Federal Reserve authorities can move to limit direct security loans by banks, under the Banking Act of 1933, by limiting the percentage of a bank's capital and surplus that may be loaned on securities, and by limiting rediscount privileges for banks that expand security loans after being asked not to do so.

3. Most powerful of all, maximum loan values on registered securities may be fixed by the Board of Governors of the Federal Reserve System. By fixing such loan values at a relatively low point, such as the 45 per cent limit set in 1936, a powerful obstacle to the expansion of security loans can be interposed.

If properly used, there is reason to believe that these measures, taken together, can be used effectively to check any undue expansion in security loans by the banking system in the future.

Other Sections of the Money Market

Special attention has been given to the collateral loan sections of the money market, because of their intimate bearing on the investment banking business.

The rate on short-term government securities reflects the price of the highest grade of credit in the market. However, treasury bills are so largely dealt in by the Federal Reserve Banks that the rate is usually highly artificial.

The bankers' acceptance, used in foreign trade financing, also represents a very safe and sometimes liquid instrument when properly used. The rate on bankers' acceptances, too, does not accurately reflect the state of the money market because of sporadic Federal Reserve buying. Today the volume of acceptances, like the volume of other commercial paper, has fallen off greatly from the level of almost $2,000,000,000 outstanding early in the decade. However, a large part of the acceptances which the Federal Reserve Banks bought in the 'twenties were virtually investment paper issued on a renewal basis at a time when it was easier to get accommodations from the banks than from the investment market. The fact that a good deal of such paper has disappeared today merely means that this roundabout way of obtaining investment funds is no longer thought necessary.

Commercial paper, as broadly used, signifies obligations of commercial borrowers who obtain funds in one way or another from the banking community on short term. Thus, straight customers' notes held by a bank are frequently referred to rather loosely as commercial paper. In a narrower and more professional sense, it implies paper which is sold in blocks to dealers for the purpose of providing working capital for enterprises which do not care to borrow from their local banks, or who prefer to get at least a part of their requirements without recourse to them. The volume of open-market commercial paper outstanding fell sharply after the early 'twenties, as other methods of short-term financing by business came to be preferred.

Federal Reserve Bank credit constitutes the basis for the other types of credit just reviewed. Bank loans and investments of whatever type bring about a corresponding expansion in deposits for the banks of the country. These deposits involve certain legal reserve requirements which, for member banks, consist of deposits of their own with the Federal Reserve Banks. At this writing, member banks in central reserve cities must keep 19½ per cent, in reserve cities 15 per cent, and in other localities 10½ per cent, of their demand deposits in the form of a deposit with the Federal Reserve, while on time deposits a flat 4½ per cent is required. These percentages are 50 per cent higher than those prevailing before August 15, 1936.

A fuller discussion of Reserve Bank credit is presented in the following chapter on investment credit control.

Some International Aspects

The international aspects of money markets deserve comment at this point. There was a strong tendency to internationalize money and capital markets in the post-war decade so that the chief centers which had been separated one from another now tended to become in a real sense sections of one international market. Several factors tended to bring about this development. One was the growing number of banks which possessed foreign branches, or which had created agencies or named foreign correspondents who worked in direct harmony with them abroad. Foreign banks, moreover, increased the number of their branches in the United States, that number, including both branches and agencies, being estimated in 1929 at 150. The international cooperation of central banks also tended in a like direction. Summed up, the situation just before the panic of 1929 was one marked by the increasing internationalization of banking. This tended to adjust differences in rates of discount and interest, so that the inflow and outflow of foreign funds was one of the chief factors in the New York money market.

These tendencies were greatly altered after 1929. Within the past six years, the steady growth of foreign exchange restrictions and the effort to centralize the control of exchange in the hands of central banks has tended to prevent normal international movements of funds. Currency uncertainties also tended to nationalize money markets more than ever, except for considerable accumulations of "nervous money" and investment funds in New York, the favored market for the purpose, and London. This flow of capital from poor to rich countries was obviously abnormal, and could only cause trouble to both in the long run, since funds flowed from where they were needed to places already possessing a surfeit of liquid funds available for investment.

References

Anderson, B. M., "Brokers' Loans and Bank Credit," *The Chase Economic Bulletin,* vol. viii, no. 4, October 31, 1928.

Blaisdell, William M., *Financing Security Trading,* Philadelphia, 1936.

Burgess, W. R., *The Reserve Banks and the Money Market,* New York, 1936, chaps. ix-xii.

Hickernell, W. F., *Financial and Business Forecasting,* New York, 1928, chap. v.

Koch, Karin, *A Study of Interest Rates,* London, 1929, chaps. ii and iv.

Madden, John T., and Nadler, Marcus, *International Money Markets,* New York, 1936.

SIMMONS, E. H. H., *Modern Capitalism,* New York, 1927, pp. 173–190.

SUBCOMMITTEE OF THE COMMITTEE ON BANKING AND CURRENCY, United States Senate, 71st Congress, Third Session, *Operation of the National and Federal Reserve Banking System,* Appendix, Part VII.

WILLIS, H. P., and CHAPMAN, J. M., *The Banking Situation,* New York, 1934.

Chapter XII

INVESTMENT CREDIT CONTROL

Need for Investment Credit Control

In the preceding chapters, the flow of funds into the capital market has been considered. The relation of the money to the capital market and the effect of the phenomenon of speculation upon both have also been taken up. The process has been regarded as largely automatic and determined by the institutional environment. However, efforts have been made to control the capital market through organized intervention, and it is to those efforts that the present chapter is devoted.

From early days, the need for some agency for controlling banking activity has been felt. This need has grown steadily with the increasing size and complexity of the banking systems of the leading countries of the world. Since, as has been seen, the money and capital markets are closely related in a number of ways, and to an increasing degree in recent years, control of commercial banking necessarily implies investment banking control as well.

Control has been found necessary to assure the ultimate soundness and stability of the credit structure, and, by the same token, of economic conditions generally. It may be exercised in a variety of ways. The usual method is the establishment of a central bank under government auspices, which operates not for its own profit primarily, but for the purpose of keeping the credit structure of the country on a sound basis. In modern central banking practice, this has been done through operations in the money market which the central bank, with its great resources, is able to carry out on a scale sufficiently large to affect the entire banking and business structure.

The chief concern of the central banks, like the Bank of England, the Bank of France and the Federal Reserve Banks, was formerly the money market, the organization of which has been described in Chapter XI. They were interested primarily in the market for short-term loans and paper, for they were formed for the purpose of acting as bankers' banks, controlling the volume of credit made available to business and agriculture. Investment banking, or the supplying of long-term capital, does not, in the first instance, fall within the province of central banking activity, except in so far as the supply of capital to the government is concerned. Invariably, central banks become fiscal agencies of the government, despite many past and present attempts to separate the two.

While, in theory at least, most central banks are expected to concern themselves primarily with the money market, they inevitably affect the capital market as well, for, as was shown in Chapter XI, one of the prime functions exercised by the money market is the regulation of the supply of capital which flows into the securities market and into speculation. Changes in the money market always affect the flow of funds into investment and speculation, and hence the activity of the agency which controls the one will affect the other. Conversely, no agency controlling the money market can afford to close its eyes to the condition of the capital markets. Again and again in the past, excessive activity in the capital market, through either unwarrantedly large new capital issues or widespread speculation in stocks, has tightened the money market, and, by creating an unbalanced expansion of bank credit, has compelled corrective measures on the part of the banking authorities.

In recent years, central banks have come to depend increasingly upon open market operations in the exercise of their control policies. These affect the capital market more directly by influencing prices of high-grade bonds.

Besides the control, generally indirect, exercised by the central bank on the capital market, a certain amount is also exercised by the investment banking houses themselves. As yet, no agency resembling a central investment bank has been evolved, but several of the largest investment banking houses have, in the leading investment banking centers, developed sufficient contact among themselves and control over other banking institutions to work together to a considerable extent.

Finally, the government exercises some control over investment credit in unusual circumstances, especially in time of war or during depression and readjustment periods by means of institutions like the Reconstruction Finance Corporation.

Supervision of Investment Credit

There has been for many years a wide divergence of opinion among both economists and public men with regard to the desirability of investment control and the lines along which it is to be exerted. About the only direct outcome of this agitation until after the war was the adoption of so-called "blue-sky" laws in various states (see Chapter XXII). The objects of these laws was usually nothing more than the securing of publicity concerning the facts relating to new investment offerings, and the assurance that promotion and selling operations were being carried on honestly and by enterprises whose directors or managers were known to be reliable men of good reputation. The abuses which developed during the decade 1920-1930 however, culminating as they did in a panic of the first order of severity, led to a widespread demand for the installation of means of controlling more directly the use of investment credit and the application of such credit to industry, as well as for the control of stock exchange trading in securities of all classes.

A comprehensive system of federal security legislation was the outcome. Also, the Federal Reserve authorities largely extended their interest in security market conditions in connection with the formulation of credit policies.

Types of Control

Control over credit may be essentially either quantitative or qualitative. It may seek to regulate the total volume of credit sought, or determine the type of borrower who shall get the credit available. In central banking practice, both types of control are exercised. Through manipulation of the rediscount rate, through purchases and sales of bankers' acceptances and through similar operations in government securities, the central bank exercises a profound effect on the total volume of liquid funds in the market. At the same time, by favoring agricultural and business paper to some degree, and by seeking to discriminate against paper arising out of speculative transactions, the central banks in some countries, and notably in the United States, have been expected to endeavor to install a régime of qualitative credit control as well. If this régime worked successfully, rates for speculative credit might soar at the same time that the cost of money for purely business and agricultural uses remained unchanged. This policy of qualitative credit control is practicable only if the reserve banks can actually direct the disposition of the credit they grant; and their lack of ability to do so was proved when such a "straddle" policy was pursued in 1928 and 1929.[1]

As investment credit control is largely indirect, arising through control of the money market, qualitative control of it is particularly difficult. Hence, when it becomes necessary owing to special circumstances, the government usually intervenes, as it did during the war when the Capital Issues Committee was established to give financing of war needs priority over other capital flotations, by requiring preliminary approval of all new flotations by this body.

Control of the capital market on a qualitative basis through discrimination between investment and speculative activity has been attempted in the past. Federal Reserve authorities have sought to withhold the use of short-term funds for the purpose of carrying stocks for a rise in price, especially in the form of brokers' loans. At the same time, they have expressed themselves as unwilling to interfere with the flow of credit into industry through the issuance and sale of investment securities.

A qualitative distinction between investment and speculative security loans is extremely difficult to make because of the impossibility of distinguishing between these two types of transactions from the point of view of the capital market as a whole, as will be seen in a subsequent chapter. It is there concluded that the major distinction from the market point of view is the extent to which bank credit is absorbed to carry securities, re-

[1] This is the expressed aim of the original Federal Reserve Act. Some writers deny that this policy can be enforced. Thus Burgess says, "The Reserve System cannot prescribe the uses to which credit shall be put. That decision rests with the individual member bank." See Burgess, W. R., *The Reserve Banks and the Money Market,* p. 179. The views of the Federal Reserve Board on this topic were stated before the Senate subcommittee on Banking in 1932 (Hearings, Part I).

gardless of the amount of risk involved in the securities purchased and whether new or old issues are involved. In fact, loans made to speculative security buyers to permit them to purchase stocks on margin permit them to pay for securities bought from those who desire to place the proceeds in new security offerings, directly in privately-owned business enterprises or for the purchase of consumption goods.

However, as was seen in Part I of this book, investment and speculative activities in the securities markets are carried on to a large extent by different institutions. Efforts to control each, therefore, involve different problems. Accordingly, while the close interconnection of investment and speculative activity in the capital market is recognized, each will be separately treated here.

Control of Investment Credit

The market for investment securities is subject to constantly changing conditions. If the supply of funds seeking permanent investment is large, and the demand for capital, as reflected by the volume of new security offerings, is small, bond prices tend to rise. This rise in prices encourages investors to hasten their purchases, and a certain amount of speculative buying for the rise enters the market to expand further its power to absorb new securities. On the other hand, declining bond prices, from whatever cause, discourage buyers and thus tend to slow up the flow of investment capital, and at times to halt it practically entirely.

Any tightening of the money market will affect the capital market only in so far as it increases the supply of investment securities in the market and thus adversely affects the price level. Let us assume, for example, that, as a result of rapidly expanding business activity and a resulting expansion of commercial credit, money rates rise, and the central bank seeks to prevent further expansion by raising its rediscount rate and selling in the open market some of its holdings of government securities. The immediate effect is to increase the supply of bonds in the market from several sources. Commercial banks are large holders of bonds. On June 30, 1928, all banks were reported officially to hold, in round numbers, $6,000,000,000 of government bonds and $12,000,000,000 of other securities, mainly corporate bonds. These holdings were materially reduced through liquidation during the subsequent months when interest rates rose sharply. The commercial banks hold these securities in their portfolios only so long as they give a larger return than can be secured from other sources, reserve position, liquidity and marketability being considered. When higher rates are available elsewhere, and especially when they need funds because of a tightening of the money market by the action of the reserve banks, the commercial banks sell securities if they can do so without too great price depreciation. This increases the supply of bonds in the market, and has an adverse effect on their prices. Bank buying and selling have become far more important than ever before in the past few years, when bank resources have been far more heavily invested in bonds.

When commercial banks invest in bonds, the effect is different from that which follows individual investment in securities in one essential respect, in that additional deposit credit is thereby created on the books of the banks.

This point is of the first importance in understanding the operation of the credit system. It can be clearly understood only if we distinguish the operation of a single bank from that of the banking system as a whole. An individual bank makes loans or investments out of its reserves, which are increased through the receipt of additional deposits. For the banking system as a whole, however, the making of new loans or investments by individual institutions brings about a corresponding rise in deposits unless the proceeds of such loans or investments should be withdrawn in the form of currency, which is the unusual contingency. As the proceeds of new loans or investments are withdrawn from one bank, they are generally deposited in others, thus increasing the deposit total of the banking system correspondingly. The limiting factor of such expansion is, as we have seen, the maintenance, by the member banks as a whole, of adequate legal reserves on deposit in the form of balances with their Federal Reserve Banks.

When commercial banks buy bonds, they cause a corresponding increase in deposits in individual and corporate accounts. These deposits in turn are available for investment in securities by their owners, so that the inflation thus made possible is twofold in character. The great inflation of bank holdings of government bonds in connection with the Treasury deficits of the years following 1932 thus was accompanied by a corresponding expansion of bank deposits, which provided huge purchasing power for individual investment in securities.

A less important way in which the tightening of short-term money rates adversely affects prices for long-term bonds may now be stated. As was seen in Chapter II, investment banking houses carry new issues of securities, pending their distribution to investors, on collateral loan with commercial banks. When money rates are high, it becomes expensive to carry securities in this way, as the interest received on them does not, in many cases, cover the interest paid the banks on the collateral loans. The result is that bond houses become eager to dispose of bonds more quickly, and to hold down their inventories to a minimum.

Formerly higher money rates caused certain investors to shift from the capital to the money markets because of the higher return obtainable in the latter. Thus, in the latter part of 1928, when call money rates above 7 per cent frequently ruled, institutional and individual investors sold bonds giving returns in many instances of 5 per cent or less, and instead put out the proceeds in the call market. Thus, the supply of bonds in the market was increased and prices dropped. This process was greatly extended during the following year, when the call money rate reached 20 per cent. Lending by non-banking lenders on call has since been prohibited.

Conversely, low short-term money rates tend to expand the demand for investment securities from banks and investors, and to encourage investment banking houses to put out new issues which can be carried cheaply at the banks. When money rates are tending downward, furthermore, individual and institutional buying is hastened, because a future rise in prices is then discounted.

As a rule, the volume of new security offerings reflects the state of the bond market more than any other factor. In other words, the effective demand for new capital is largely a function of the condition of its supply. When the market is in good shape, investment bankers hasten to put out issues which they have been working on for some time, and borrowers are tempted in turn to enter the market by declining rates. On the other hand, adverse conditions in the market cause investment bankers to discourage would-be borrowers from entering the market, and to hold up as long as possible issues which they do take on. Therefore, when a rise of substantial proportions in money rates takes place, resulting in depressed conditions in the bond market, there is an immediate tendency for the supply of new issues to decline and for the flow of funds into investment channels to be reduced.

High money rates, therefore, tend to cause a condition of indigestion in the bond market. The market being oversupplied with bonds, investment banking houses tend to accumulate, against their will, inventories of both old and new issues, which they find they cannot sell rapidly enough. The accumulation of unsold securities discourages new issues and interferes with the regular functioning of the investment banking mechanism. The Securities and Exchange Commission has urged the desirability of publishing regular statistics on aggregate inventories of unsold securities of new issues in process of distribution.

The manner in which the rise in money rates affected bond prices and the volume of new security issues during 1928, a year in which short-term money rates rose, is shown in the following table:

Month	Average Call Money Rate (per cent)	Mean of Bond Prices (per cent)	Volume of New Bond Offerings
January	4.26	93.05	$598,198,937
February	4.36	92.66	645,931,500
March	4.47	92.50	569,624,208
April	5.03	93.31	726,881,350
May	5.68	92.67	630,612,825
June	6.17	91.25	582,846,017
July	6.66	90.46	192,932,841
August	6.77	89.72	126,430,040
September	7.25	90.58	309,872,450
October	6.94	90.68	355,279,000
November	6.75	90.96	429,745,000
December	8.74	90.23	302,040,200

Control of the supply of investment capital which central banking authorities can exercise through their jurisdiction over the money market is further limited during periods of large-scale security speculation by the ability of corporations to sell more or less speculative stocks, instead of bonds or preferred stock of investment character. At such times, although money rates may rise to high levels and bond prices be much depressed, the public appetite for securities with possibilities of appreciation may be so keen as to permit the volume of new security issues to remain large. This was illustrated by the experience of 1928 and 1929. The following table shows how a rising call money rate was accompanied by a sharp increase in the relative proportion of stock financing in the market. The tendency was further accentuated by the large number of bonds with speculative conversion and option warrant features which were sold largely on the basis of the latter, rather than on any intrinsic investment merit.

Month	Average Call Money Rate (per cent)	Total New Financing (in millions of dollars)	Percentage in Stock Issues
July, 1928	6.66	625	69
August	6.77	274	54
September	7.25	476	40
October	6.94	783	55
November	6.75	875	50
December	8.74	986	60
January, 1929	7.07	703	51
February	6.98	1,021	59
March	9.52	1,050	50
April	8.75	618	53
May	8.70	634	59
June	7.60	813	65

However, the failure of the federal authorities to show more substantial results from their restrictive efforts in 1928 and 1929 also reflected a lack of consistency in the measures adopted and the failure to check the expansion of brokers' loans for the account of others than banks, which reached a total of several billion dollars before the panic.

Control Over Interest Rates

One interesting phase of central banking policy that has stood out in recent years has been the effort to establish and to maintain indefinitely low interest rates in a country, regardless of gold movements, the state of business, or relative price levels. Whereas formerly the main issue in central banking policy was whether or not it should be conducted with a view to stabilization of the commodity price level, control over interest rates has latterly tended to dominate the stage of discussion in central banking theory.

For example, after the Bank of England abandoned gold conversion in September, 1931, English credit policy ceased to reflect the movement of gold into or out of the country, and also showed little tendency to be influenced by commodity price movements. On the other hand, there was a persistent effort to depress and to keep down the level of interest rates for both short-term and long-term credit; and special measures, often quite unorthodox in character, were undertaken to prevent increases in interest rates whenever circumstances tended to bring them about.

Under such a system, the interest rate ceases to perform its historic rôle of measuring supply and demand forces at work in the capital market. Instead, through resort to credit inflation of one form or another, a permanent excess of supply of funds is created, which prevents interest rates from rising over indefinite periods of time. Hence, the capital market ceases to be automatically self-regulating, and the inflationary forces thus invoked can be checked before they go too far only by drastic restrictive measures of opposite character, applied in good time.

Such a policy was pursued in the United States during the years following 1932. As a result of the purchase of almost $2,500,000,000 of government bonds by the Federal Reserve Banks, an increase in the nation's gold supply of about two thirds through the devaluation of the dollar in 1933-1934, and a further heavy influx of gold from abroad resulting from unbalanced international economic and financial conditions, member banks of the Federal Reserve System were given some $3,000,000,000 of excess reserves, over and above their legal requirements. As a result, short-term interest rates were driven down toward the vanishing point, long-term interest rates dropped to unprecedentedly low levels, and a redistribution of the national income was brought about, in effect, through thus artificially reducing the share that goes to the owner of capital invested in bonds in the form of interest. As the fall in bond yields tends to reduce the average yields of preferred and common stocks as well, the effect was to reduce the share of the national income going to the owners of capital generally.

Control by Investment Houses

A state of indigestion in the bond market can also be brought about through failure of issue houses to keep down the volume of new offerings to a figure which the market can absorb, regardless of what the relative size of the demand may happen to be. No matter whether the demand be small or large, if the stream of new offerings is excessive in relation to that demand, the market will soon be burdened by an excess supply of investment securities, bringing about a general decline in prices.

Such a condition developed, for example, in the summer of 1927, at a time when the money market was abnormally low, as a result of the efforts of the reserve banks to aid European financial rehabilitation by encouraging the flow of funds abroad. The bond market was in good condition, but investment banking houses sought to take excessive advantage of it by putting out too many individual issues, often too highly priced. Before long they found themselves in the position of being unable to distribute them to investors, and they were left "holding the bag." In order to cut down the rapidly accumulating stocks of unsold bonds, they had to offer them below the original price. When they had cut the price of the new issues and sharply reduced the volume of new offerings for about three months, the market quickly corrected itself and large-scale financing was resumed on a sound basis.

At such periods of congestion, brought about by unintelligent multiplication of offerings, the need for some cooperative action by investment banking houses is keenly felt. As a result of experience in such periods, informal efforts to time new offerings so that they will not interfere with one another are frequently made. The 90-day waiting period before registration is effective in facilitating such informal cooperation.

Proposals have been put forward from time to time for a "stagger plan" for new bond offerings, which would permit timing of new offerings in a more orderly fashion, thus giving the investment houses themselves control over the supply of new securities, and therefore, to some extent, over the volume of investment credit currently made available. Central banks in some countries since the depression have sought to exercise this type of control also by consultation with issue houses.

Government Control

Efforts to control the volume of investment credit sought by issuers of securities through governmental agencies took place first during war time. The aim of the government in such times is to mobilize the financial resources of the country for war purposes, and, as far as feasible, available funds in the market must be diverted into government bonds to assure an adequate supply of purchasing power for the government. Hence, except in so far as capital issues are made for the benefit of allies or are to foster war industries, they are distinctly discouraged.[2]

Government control, as described above, may be qualitative as well as quantitative. During the World War, the authorities in Washington sought to keep down the volume of investment credit obtained by industry in general, and also to distinguish between demands for capital on a qualitative basis, favoring some and forbidding others, according to whether the industry produced goods or services needed in the war.

In times of peace, investment credit control may be applied by the government, often to stimulate business recovery after a depression. In the 1933-1935 period, this was attempted by loans at low rates of interest offered by the Reconstruction Finance Corporation, by the creation of subsidized mortgage banking institutions, and by federal public works and grants to

[2] This was the aim of the so-called Capital Issues Committee in Washington during the World War.

municipal and other bodies, by building power plants or bridges and by the construction of similar works. Government control of credit may be employed in time of peace also for the purpose of shifting the control or enjoyment of wealth from one group of persons to another, as in using the available resources of banks in making loans for the carrying of cotton and wheat at exceptionally low rates. This kind of political control may be defended on the ground that it is necessary in order to assist some class in the community that is suffering from unfavorable conditions of economic life, and it may likewise be defended as helping to assist some particular industry or the producers of a given crop, so that they may be relieved of pressure from low prices. This is not the place to discuss the ultimate results of such credit "management." It is enough to say here that control of the type already referred to has, in one form or another, been applied in the United States and elsewhere, especially during the past few years. For a short period at least, such measures may result in an apparent attainment, either complete or partial, of the objects sought—aid to depressed industries or classes in the community.

In normal times, there is in practically every important country an effort to exercise qualitative control over investment credit in one field—that of foreign investment. In the United States, the government assumed such qualitative control with the rise of the New York market as an international financing center of the first importance after the war. At a conference in 1921 between leading investment bankers and several Cabinet members, the former agreed to keep the State Department informed of such issues. In 1922, the government issued a statement in which it said: "The Department of State cannot of course require American bankers to consult it. . . . The Department believes that in view of the possible national interests involved, it should have the opportunity of saying to the underwriters concerned, should it appear advisable to do so, that there is or is not objection to any particular issue."

Under this policy, the administration barred the sale here of securities of nations which had not arranged to pay their debts to this government, and also of those governments which had not been recognized by our own. The Johnson Act passed in

1934 prohibits new loans to countries in default on their debts to the government of the United States. In other individual cases, as in the instances of a São Paulo coffee stabilization loan and a German potash loan, the State Department took the initiative in discouraging foreign loans because they were intended to keep up the price of commodities used by the American consumer. Otherwise, our government has avoided interference in the export of American capital abroad. Other nations, like France and Germany, have endeavored to regulate the export of capital in the interests of the political and economic aggrandizement of the nation as a whole, or, as in the case of Great Britain, to safeguard the stability of the currency. In the case of Germany, the government interfered also in the import of capital by establishing in 1924 a central bureau to approve before issuance all government and municipal loans proposed.

Control of Speculation

The problem of control of investment credit is inseparably connected with the control of speculation in already outstanding securities, especially on the exchanges. Speculation, if carried on moderately, may broaden the market for new bond issues through increasing buying power in the hands of security buyers. When extensive enough, however, it may result in a sharp decline in the demand for bonds and a general rush to buy speculative securities—above all, common stocks. In times of over-extended speculation, investment banking houses seek to meet the desires of the buying public by including a larger proportion of speculative securities in their offerings, and thus may greatly expand the aggregate ability of the capital market to absorb new security offerings of all kinds.

The type of speculative activity in securities which affects the capital market is carried on with the aid of bank credit. Securities bought with bank credit are held on margin with brokers, or are bought outright and then carried with the aid of bank loans. Hence, the connection between the volume of security speculation and the money market is far more direct than is the case with the volume of investment credit.

Before the establishment of the reserve system, there were

recurrent periods of speculation which ended abruptly through a severe stringency in the money markets, the skyrocketing of money rates to such figures as 148 per cent, and simultaneous commercial catastrophe and disorganization resulting from the lack of credit facilities to finance ordinary business needs. The reserve system was planned to obviate these old-fashioned panics by permitting the banks at such times to transfer their best assets to the reserve institutions, thus getting into a position where they could make additional advances of credit without forcing rates up to ruinous levels.

At the same time, through its control of the money market, the reserve system was so placed that it could discourage speculation to some degree. The law was originally designed to serve only the "legitimate" needs of business and agriculture, and it specifically stated that no paper "covering merely investments or issued or drawn for the purpose of carrying or trading in stocks, bonds or other investment securities, except bonds and notes of the government of the United States," shall have the privilege of rediscount. The fact is, however, that if the banks desire additional credit to finance speculation, they can get it by turning over their commercial paper, government securities or acceptances to the reserve banks and using the credit so obtained for speculative purposes, if the Reserve authorities do not object.

These expectations of credit control were long believed well warranted. Indeed, there were many who were of the opinion at the time the Reserve Act was adopted that it would operate to kill stock trading. The best comment upon any such fears is, of course, afforded by the actual development of stock market operations during the twenty years of the history of the Federal Reserve System. The practice of reserve banks in making loans upon collateral consisting of eligible paper or government bonds, and, above all, the fact that new reserve credit however created could be used for a multiple expansion of member bank credit, would, in any case, have defeated the whole purpose of this kind of control. We may, however, well question whether the various devices that have for years past been urged to tighten the control of credit—the regulation of the rates of discount, open market operations, etc.—are likely to exert the desired effect. Generally speaking, it is entirely feasible to defeat almost any kind of artificial regulation of this kind by simply resorting to roundabout methods of credit expansion. The "control" which reserve banks may exert most effectively arises from judicious use of their own credit-granting facilities, as well as supervision over the whole body of outstanding credit-bank and commercial, short-term and long-term.

The Nature of Reserve Bank Credit

It must be clearly kept in mind that credit provided by the reserve banks through these operations is entirely different from credit provided by member banks. Reserve bank credit permits member banks to increase their reserves by equivalent amount. When a member bank rediscounts $1,000,000 of its obligations, secured by government paper, it gets a credit balance on the books of its reserve banks of that amount. This credit is normally utilized as soon as possible by making a loan or investment for an amount roughly equivalent. The proceeds of a loan so made are largely withdrawn by the borrower and paid over to his creditors, who deposit the sums as received in their respective banks. The $1,000,000 of reserve credit is thus transferred in large part to other banks. Each bank receiving these deposits gets part of the reserve credit originated by the $1,000,000 rediscount, and can use it as a basis for more loans and investments, so that eventually the $1,000,000 of new bank reserve permits an expansion of several times that amount in the banking system as a whole.

The practical limit on such expansion is the legal reserve requirement against the new deposits created as a result of these new loans and investments.

This fact is of great significance for the speculative markets. Let us say that the member banks as a whole wish to increase loans by $500,000,000 for the purpose of carrying securities. How can they finance such a huge expansion in brokers' loans? Merely by taking about $60,000,000 of government securities from their portfolios and using this as collateral to rediscount their notes of that amount with the reserve banks. Such a rise in rediscounts is so small as to make little difference in the position of the reserve system. The same effect can be achieved if $60,000,000 of gold is imported into the country and deposited by the member banks with reserve institutions, or if the reserve banks purchase in the open market $60,000,000 of government securities or acceptances. In any case, the final result is a credit for that amount on the books of the reserve banks, making possible a multiple credit expansion.

Excess reserves exist when the member banks have on the books of Federal Reserve Banks, credits in amounts greater than the reserves required by law. In normal times, banks are unwilling to permit such excess reserves to accumulate, for they earn no interest when on deposit at the Federal Reserve Banks. They make new loans and investments until their reserves stand at the legal minimum balance which they are expected to keep. When demand for funds is at a low ebb, or when banks are unwilling to expand loans and investments to the extent permitted by their surplus balances at the Federal Reserve Banks because they fear they may not prove permanent, as in the period after 1933, excess reserves may persist over long periods, and become a lasting phenomenon. However, it must be remembered that the banking system then is much like a ship without a rudder, and credit control can hardly be said to exist as such.

Restrictive Powers

We have seen that through open market operations, the devaluation of the gold content of the dollar, and the adoption of policies that encourage gold imports, it has been possible to stimulate an inflation of bank credit largely through increasing reserves that member banks possess in the Federal Reserve Banks. Furthermore, when such inflationary methods are pursued intensively enough, they may give rise to an expansion of credit of an uncontrolled variety that will give business an unhealthy stimulus and thus make it vulnerable to a subsequent severe reaction. Powerful restrictive measures are in time required in order to check such tendencies.

The conventional method of credit restriction formerly pursued involved the sale by the reserve banks of government securities in the open market, which led to an increase in rediscounts and advances in rediscount rates, with a consequent tightening of the money market, a rise in interest rates, and a fall in bond prices. Such restrictive measures were attempted on a considerable scale in 1928 and 1929, but with indifferent results, as we have already seen. Especially at times when the Treasury has a budget deficit and is eager to facilitate the sale of new government bonds as far as possible, the central bank, normally sensitive to the needs of the government, hesitates to sell Treasury bonds for fear that it will interfere with necessary new government financing.

Hence, new restrictive measures have lately been devised to curtail credit. One of them is to build up deposits of the Treasury at the Federal Reserve Banks, which reduces member bank reserves to a corresponding extent. A second is to segregate part of the gold reserve of the country into a special fund apart from the central bank, such as the Exchange Stabilization Fund that was set up in the United States by the Gold Reserve Act of 1934. Third and most significant of all is the power to change legal reserve requirements given to the Board of Governors of the Federal Reserve System by the Banking Act of 1935. This latter power aims at the heart of the problem of quantitative credit control, in that it permits direct manipulation of the volume of reserves that member banks possess. In addition, the relationship between bank reserves and potential member bank deposit expansion is changed also. Thus, before August 15, 1936, $100,000,000 of excess reserves could normally be counted upon to support more than a tenfold expansion of member bank credit for the banking system as a whole. After that date, when a 50 per cent rise in legal reserve requirements became effective, the same amount of surplus reserves could make possible an expansion of member bank deposits only six to seven times as great.

The Gold Reserve Act of 1935 also resulted in transferring a large part of ultimate responsibility for credit control from the Federal Reserve Banks to the federal Treasury. By taking part of the "gold profit" resulting from the devaluation of the dollar in 1934 and using it to establish an Exchange Stabilization Fund of $2,000,000,000 in the Treasury, the latter was placed in a position to expand the reserves of member banks at will through depositing portions of this Fund with the reserve banks and spending the proceeds. Similarly, the Silver Purchase Act of 1934 gave the Treasury a large silver seigniorage which could be used to expand member bank reserves in the same way. Also, by shifting its own cash balances from member banks to reserve banks and back again, the Treasury could influence member bank reserves within more narrow limits. Finally, when it incurs heavy deficits, the Treasury influences reserve policy indirectly, since central banks are traditionally sensitive to the needs of the government in the formulation of their policies. By financing such deficits through the sale of government bonds to the banks, furthermore, the Treasury can make certain that excess reserve will actually be used as the basis for credit expansion, for bank purchases of its bonds cause a corresponding expansion of deposits.

Also, under Regulations "T" and "U" of the Reserve Board, as we have seen, margin requirements on security loans are today not only those that would be exacted by conservative brokers and dealers, but are designed to prevent any sharp increase in their volume. At the same time, in declining markets, they can be lowered and thus some encouragement can be given to speculative purchasing on the decline.

Recent History of the Federal Reserve Policy

That investment as well as commercial credit has largely influenced Federal Reserve policy, and at times been a dominant factor in shaping it, is readily revealed by a survey of outstanding developments in recent Federal Reserve history. In the summer of 1927, the reserve banks bought several hundred million dollars of government securities in the open market and reduced rediscount rates. This was done in conjunction with European central banks, which resorted to easy-money policies at the time, seeking to prevent an incipient worldwide business depression and deflation of commodity prices, which they correctly felt to be in the offing as a sequel to the maladjusted international economic situation left by the absurd arrangements set up by the treaties of peace that followed the World War and the widespread internal and international credit inflation of the post-war period.

These easy money measures, as some foresaw, led to a wave

of intensive speculation in stocks in the United States. The question of control of speculation by the reserve banks became acute in 1928, when extensive public participation in stock speculation at rapidly rising prices caused an unprecedented increase in brokers' loans. At the same time, exports of gold amounting to approximately half a billion dollars seemed to call for a sharp curtailment in the total volume of outstanding bank credit. Instead, the export of gold and the growing volume of speculative credit were both offset by a sharp rise in rediscounts. The reserve banks were thus called upon to finance a credit expansion at the very time that a contraction was logical.

The reserve banks at first resorted to conventional steps to halt the credit expansion. They sold nearly $500,000,000 of securities, largely for the purpose of further tightening credit conditions and so discouraging expansion. The sale of securities, and the subsequent rise in rediscount rates in most reserve banks from 3½ to 5 per cent, finally appeared to take effect, especially since the reserve banks combined their action with several warnings to the effect that speculative curtailment was necessary. But speculative activity was soon resumed on a more violent scale than before, and simultaneously the reserve banks ceased fighting the expansion of credit for fear of disturbing the fall seasonal expansion in business then due. Instead, they bought liberally of acceptances, not raising the buying rate when the volume of bills held by them rose to unprecedented levels. Only in the spring of 1929 was the policy of restriction resumed with renewed vigor through sales of government security and acceptance holdings. By August, 1929, we find a return to the "traditional policy of free purchase of acceptances."

The policy of 1927-1929 has been the subject of much recrimination. The Hon. A. C. Miller, a member of the Federal Reserve Board, issued in June, 1935, a long defense of the policy of the Board during the pre-panic period and subsequently, in the *American Economic Review* for August, 1935, developed the same argument in a slightly different manner. Previous to these two utterances, Mr. Miller had, when a witness before the Senate Banking and Currency Committee in January, 1931, presented his views at substantial length. Generally

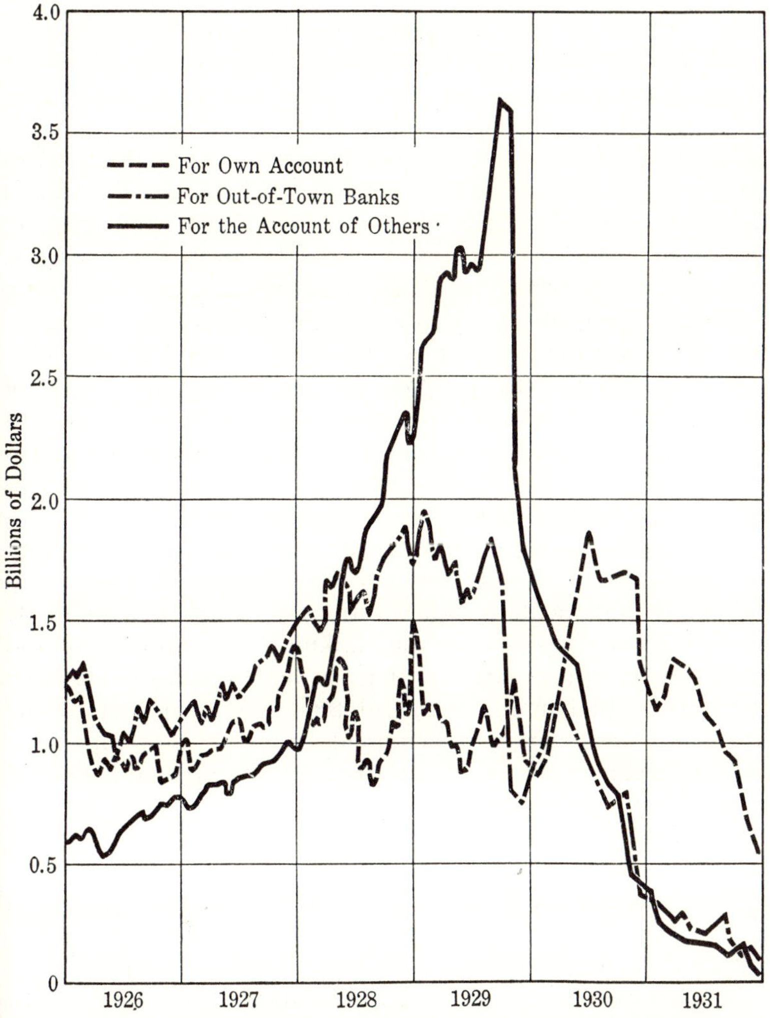

FIG. 12. SOURCES OF BROKERS' LOANS MADE BY AND THROUGH NEW YORK CITY REPORTING MEMBER BANKS, 1926 TO 1931

Statistics published by the Federal Reserve Bank of New York.

speaking, his opinion was that the Federal Reserve System was blameworthy in maintaining an over-liberal open market policy during the years after 1926, and that it failed to raise its rate of discount sharply and decisively as soon as it should have in 1928. This failure to act Mr. Miller attributes to the reluctance of the Federal Reserve Banks and their managements to take decisive action. The latter, however, have contended that the fault lay in the Federal Reserve Board which, at times when they were anxious to raise their rates, held back. The Board and the reserve banks differed as to the dates when changes in discount rates were called for, the banks desiring to raise rates at periods when the Board was opposed, and vice versa. Without attempting to decide this controverted question, we may safely say that the machinery of the Federal Reserve System provided for the purpose of controlling the supply of credit has never worked either promptly or efficiently. Various conflicting interests have constantly sought to employ it for ulterior purposes, no doubt honestly, and there has been as constantly a reluctance to have it employed at all.

The success of the elaborate safeguards lately enacted into law must, after all, depend upon the exercise of a wise and deliberate judgment by some authoritative body. That body never has been supplied by the banking community itself, and the governmental mechanism that has been organized has been less, rather than more, successful than that furnished by the banks. The problem of judicious measurement and apportionment of credit thus remains an unsettled one in American commercial and investment banking.

Loans for the Account of Others

When the reserve banks sought to curtail speculation in the spring of 1928, the New York member banks were induced to reduce their loans to brokers sharply. To make peace with the Reserve System, they cut such loans by about 35 per cent within a few months.

The rate on call money rose perpendicularly in response to these withdrawals. But the expected result of reducing the total was not accomplished. Instead, large amounts of credit were soon made available to the stock market from non-banking sources. The great New York banks, for a small charge, placed in the collateral loan market sums of $100,000 or multiples thereof. These loans were listed in their statement to the reserve bank as placed "for the account of others." The chart on page 335 shows the variation of loans by New York City reporting member banks for their own account, for that of out-of-town banks, and for the account of others during the period 1926-1931, inclusive.

Experience during and after the panic of 1929 again illustrated the dangers of these loans, and led to the provision in he Banking Act of 1933, that no bank should make such loans or the account of non-bankers. This left open the possibility hat, when demand for such credit again became very active, he business of lending on collateral would be taken up by those who had spare funds in their possession and who were inclined o operate through money-brokers and other non-banking intermediaries. The Securities Exchange Act of 1934 has proibited brokers from borrowing from banks other than members of the Federal Reserve System and those who subject hemselves to the provisions of the Federal Reserve Act appliable to security loans. Brokers' loans to other brokers who re members of registered exchanges are now also limited, so hat it would appear quite unlikely that this troublesome probem in central bank supervision will again arise under our resent banking laws.

he "New Deal" Expansionist Policies

When the inflation movement collapsed of its own weight the fall of 1929, the reserve banks bought government securities in the open market, expanded their portfolio of banks' acceptances, and reduced rediscount rates. During the ink failure epidemic and international financial collapse that llowed, the pressure of deflation was so great that these easyoney measures proved entirely futile, and they were even bandoned for a time in an effort to discourage exports of gold.

Beginning with 1932, reserve policy entered a new phase. xcess reserves were created on a substantial scale for the first me by open market buying operations. These excess reserves ere very largely expanded by the Roosevelt Administration, hich made the artificial reduction of interest rates a cardinal ature of its economic policy, taking measures to lower rates of interest on farm and urban mortgages and other types of long-term investments, as well as those on short-term commitments.

At the same time, steps were taken to expand the rôle of the Treasury in the control of credit, and largely to centralize and expand the powers of the Board of Governors of the Federal Reserve System both to curtail reserve credit quantitatively and to restrict the use of credit qualitatively by granting power to fix minimum margin requirements on security loans to brokers or banks and to limit by regulation the extent to which individual banks could make security advances, when that was held desirable. Margin requirements were increased to 40 per cent by a number of houses during the bull market of 1928-1929, and a long list of speculative leaders, subject to particularly wide fluctuations, was carried only on a margin of 50 per cent, and more. Furthermore, curb stocks and unlisted issues were no longer carried on margin by most houses. Although designed solely as a safety measure, this also resulted in cutting down the possible maximum purchases which individual speculators could make. The legislation of 1933 and 1934, however, made federal control over the volume of security loans practically complete, as has been seen.

References

Beckhart, B. H., *The Discount Policy of the Federal Reserve System,* New York, 1924.

Burgess, W. R., *The Reserve Banks and the Money Market,* New York, 1936, chaps. xii-xviii.

Goldenweiser, E. A., *The Federal Reserve System in Operation,* New York, 1925, chaps. ii–v, and xv.

Lawrence, J. S., *Wall Street and Washington,* Princeton, 1929.

Owens, Richard N., and Hardy, C. O., *Interest Rates and Stoc Speculation,* New York, 1925.

Sprague, O. M. W., and Burgess, W. R., "Money and Credit and Their Effect on Business," in *Recent Economic Changes,* New York, 1929, vol. ii, chap. x.

Willis, H. P., *The Federal Reserve System,* New York, 192 chap. iv.

Willis, H. P., *The Theory and Practice of Central Banking,* New York, 1936.

Chapter XIII

STOCKS *vs.* BONDS

Types of Securities

Modern finance has evolved two radically different types of securities to represent control over capital. The older form is the promise to repay a fixed sum of money, with periodic interest payments, and is typified by the bond. The other, which, with the growth of corporate enterprise, has become of the first importance, is the share of stock, which represents direct ownership of a fractional equity in a business enterprise.

These two great types of securities—bonds or evidences of debt, and stocks or evidences of proprietorship—have undergone numerous variations as the complexity of modern business and the capital market have created new needs and new methods of attracting investors' funds. The great bulk of securities have to be sold at one time or another, creating a merchandising problem which has a great influence on the form of security adopted. Governments, corporations and bankers are all interested in reducing to a minimum "sales resistance" in the distribution of their securities to investors; and as a result, they are usually quite ready to alter the form of the security if this will mean lower selling costs and a smaller promised return to the buyer. Hence the numerous variations which have been played in modern finance on the two major themes of stocks and bonds.

The bond, originally merely an evidence of an obligation to pay a sum of money and interest for its use, has developed a number of special features. First, it has been given a lien on specific property in many cases, in order to enhance its superior claim to the assets of the obligor in event of default as against other claimants. This creates the mortgage bond. Secondly, numerous instances arose where the bond has been made more attractive through the granting of conversion privileges into stock or rights to buy stock at certain specified prices. Here the aim was to give to the bondholder certain of the advantages possessed by the holders of the equity in the property, the stockholders. Other less important features, such as payment of some taxes by the issuer, participating features, etc., have been added to the original simple bond in many instances to make it more attractive.

On the other hand, shares of ownership have been differentiated into preferred and common shares, or into Class A shares and Class B shares, giving a part of the stock capitalization a claim to income superior to that of the rest. The genus preferred stock has been especially subject to mutation, so that it becomes difficult at times to distinguish, except in a formal legal sense, between a specially well-secured preferred stock and a bond.

The legal distinction between the stock and bond—the equity and the debt—has in fact been partially broken down in practice. From the point of view of the investor and the corporation, any security with limited income is similar to a bond, in that it does not benefit directly from an increase in earning power of the corporation beyond the amount required to pay its fixed rate of return. Owing to the peculiar nature of modern economic organization, a distinction of the greatest importance arises between securities of limited income and those representing equities in properties. Holders of bonds and preferred stocks have claims for the payment to them of a fixed sum in money. Hence, any variation in the purchasing power of money will have a profound effect on the value of their securities as compared with the worth of common stocks, representing ownership of property. The relative position of stocks and bonds as investment media involves a number of complex factors creating a difficult theoretical problem, the correct understanding of which is of the utmost importance.

Advantages of Bonds

For many years, bonds were regarded as the investment medium *par excellence*. Large institutional investors, such as banks and insurance companies, have been compelled by law to restrict their investments almost entirely to bonds. Trustees have been similarly restricted in most states, except where the deed of trust provided otherwise. What, then, are the advantages of bonds that gave them such a high place in the field of investment?

The basic advantage of the bond is its superior relative claim to the assets and the earnings of an enterprise. The bond has, first, a prior claim on the income of the obligor, so that, if anyone is to suffer from reduced earning power, the stockholder first foregoes his income. In the second place, the bondholder's claim to a regular return is a compulsory one, except in the case of the income bond. If earning power disappears temporarily, the bondholder is protected nevertheless, for he has the power to put the corporation into receivership. A third advantage of the bondholder is his prior claim to the assets of the corporation in case of receivership, so that he can take over control of the entire property and rule out the interests of stockholders if necessary in order to secure his interest and principal.

In point of fact, a corporation issuing bonds strikes a bargain whereby, in return for a prior claim to earnings and assets, money is raised for long periods on a promise to pay only a limited return. A fixed rate of income is promised the bondholders; and the directors, acting for the stockholders whom they represent, then strive to earn a larger return on the capital thus obtained, the income over and above bond interest going to the stockholders.

A final general advantage of well-secured bonds is that they do not enter actively into speculation as a rule. As a result, exaggerated price movements are avoided, and a fairly stable market usually exists for the investor, should he seek to dispose of his commitment.

The Changing Value of Money

The outcome of this bargain between bondholder and stockholder, whereby bonds are issued with a fixed promise to pay interest periodically and the principal on maturity, is vitally affected by factors not known at the time the bargain is first made. One of the most important of these is a change in the value of money.

The value of money is its purchasing power over goods and services, as reflected in the level of commodity prices. Since 1790, the price level in the United States, as roughly measured by available commodity price indices, has varied as shown in Fig. 13. In a study of the relative position of stocks and bonds published in 1925, Kenneth S. Van Strum points out a remark-

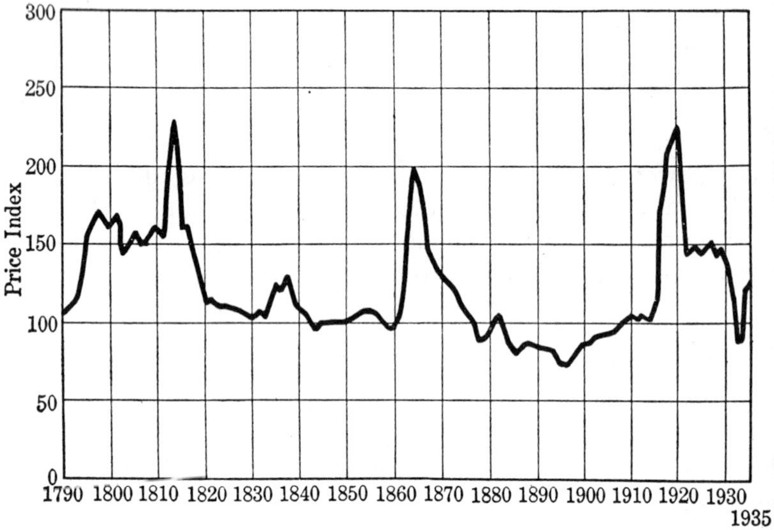

FIG. 13. THE COURSE OF COMMODITY PRICES, 1790-1935

able correspondence between English commodity price movements and changes in the yield on British consols between 1790 and 1923. He concludes from this statistically observed correspondence:[1]

> When commodity prices were low the yield on consols was low and when commodity prices were high the yield on consols was high. In other words, the return which the investor in consols demanded for the use of his money was fixed by the purchasing power of money. If the purchasing power of money was low, the yield on consols was high, and if the purchasing power of money was high, the yield on consols was low.

It is evident to the reader of Chapter X that the above

[1] Van Strum, Kenneth S., *Investing in Purchasing Power*, p. 8.

statement is superficial and, in the form given, erroneous. Investors do not in practice carefully scrutinize commodity price index numbers before buying bonds, and demand lower prices as the index number rises. They generally pay what they must to get the kind of investment they prefer. Bond prices are fixed by a variety of demand and supply forces, most of which are not directly influenced by changes in commodity prices, although the latter may themselves reflect the same underlying factors. If purchasing power declines rapidly they will boycott bond issues, as happened in Germany and France during the period of rapid decline of currency values. But if the movement of prices is slow, as is the case normally, the psychological attitude of the investor will not be influenced by price movements as such to any significant extent.

Rising and falling commodity prices may influence bond prices so that they often move together in the fashion noted by Van Strum in his statistical study. Rising prices mean larger profits, expanding business, and a greater demand for capital. This results in bond prices going lower and yields rising. Furthermore, high prices often correspond with war periods when heavy government financing tends to raise bond prices and depress bond yields. On the other hand, falling commodity prices often bring business depression, a surplus of capital awaiting investment, higher bond prices, and lower yields. Changes in the demand for capital because of variations in business profits, rather than omniscience on the part of capitalists in determining the rate of return they want, cause bond prices often to follow in their movements the level of commodity prices. Moreover, business prosperity influences people to buy stocks because of the larger returns indicated; depression makes them return to bonds for greater security of return and principal.

As a matter of fact, changing commodity prices influence the position of bondholders in two distinct ways. In the first place, they influence bond prices in the manner indicated above, through changing the demand for and supply of capital. Secondly, changes in the price level automatically change the value of dollars which the bondholder receives in payment of the interest and principal of his bond. Let us consider the case of the buyer of Atchison, Topeka & Santa Fe general 4's in April, 1902, a time of abnormally high bond prices. It has been pointed out that the bonds at that time could have been obtained at a price of 103½, giving a yield of 3.87 per cent.[2] In July, 1920, when the commodity price level had considerably more than doubled, these bonds had dropped to 71, a decline of 32½ points. But this decline represented only a minor part of the loss incurred. As a matter of fact, the greater actual loss in real income resulted from the decline in the purchasing power of the dollar to only 37 per cent of what it had been in 1902, so that the buyer of the bond in 1902 had only 25.5? per cent of his original purchasing power left in 1920.

In periods of rising prices, it is doubtless true that the bond holder loses while the stockholder gains. A principal sum in vested entirely in bonds may suffer diminution through a de cline in the market value of the bonds—it will suffer even more through a decline in the purchasing power of the income re ceived thereon.[3] Conversely, when prices fall, the position o

[2] Smith, Edgar Lawrence, *Common Stocks as Long-term Investments,* p. 93.

[3] The following episode related by Van Strum in 1925 graphically illustrate this point:

"About twenty years ago a certain Boston business man, feeling that he ha reached a discreet age for business retirement, sold his business and investe the proceeds in what he considered to be gilt-edge bonds. The yield from the securities was ample for his needs and, he thought, would enable him to li for the rest of his life in the style to which he had been accustomed. H maintained a winter residence on dignified Beacon Street, a summer home the shore and all the accoutrements which accompanied such a standard living.

"Satisfied that he would be able to continue his old mode of living, he co tinued his daily life heedless of the encroachment that the rising cost of livi was having upon his plans, until one day it was brought forcibly to his atte tion. He was planning a trip abroad with his family and was surprised discover that the increased cost of a thousand and one items used in daily li had so eaten into his reserves that it would be necessary for him to draw up his principal in order to make the trip.

"A few years later he found it necessary to do without several of his servan some of his club memberships; and one by one he found that there we pleasures which he must forego. By degrees he was forced to curb his standa of living until today the income from his bonds is downright inadequate assure him the comforts and pleasures he had in the early years of his reti ment. But what has happened to his investments? His bonds are as high-gra today as they were twenty years ago and they command the same income dollars. The answer is to be found in the increased cost of living, and not in t fact that he received any smaller dollar income from his investments."

the bondholder improves at the expense of the stockholder, particularly where default does not occur.

The Effects of Devaluation

The year 1931 introduced a new era of monetary uncertainty all over the world, a sequel to the unsound basis of post-war currency stabilization. Hence, investors were called upon to contend with monetary uncertainty on a scale to which they had not been accustomed for decades especially in the United States, where the gold content of the dollar and the convertibility of the currency unit into yellow metal had been maintained unchanged since 1879.

During the immediate post-war years, currency inflation and devaluation in various countries had been accompanied by sharply rising commodity prices. The extreme case of the kind occurred in Germany, where commodity prices rose to fantastic levels and the old mark was finally stabilized on the basis of 23 trillion per dollar. Hence, when Great Britain abandoned the gold standard in 1931 and the United States followed suit in the spring of 1933, a similar rise in commodity prices and consequent sharp decline in the purchasing power of the dollar were feared here. To investors, this indicated the wisdom of a flight from fixed-income securities into equities.

However, during the post-war years in Europe an artificial shortage of commodities existed which accounted for the manner in which the price level rose at that time. Under more normal conditions, especially in view of the increased productive capacity of industry and agriculture of recent years, currency and credit inflation tend to cause an expansion in the volume of production and trade rather than an increase in the average price level at which they are conducted.

In point of fact, the devaluation of the dollar effected in 1933 and 1934 did not of itself cause a material rise in the general price level. The fact that the United States is so largely self-sufficient tended to make the resulting change in the external value of its currency of much less importance than would be the case with a country that imports a large part of its raw materials and foodstuffs and depends largely upon export markets for its products.

The chief effect of devaluation was the resulting increase in the nation's gold supply, which greatly broadened the basis for credit expansion in the form of reserves of member banks with the Federal Reserve Banks, and so made possible a return of the expansionist conditions that prevailed in this country before 1929. The sequel of devaluation, therefore, was a sharp rise in bond prices and, at a later date as credit inflation exerted its wonted effects, in stock prices as well. The predictions of some economists that devaluation would lead to a corresponding commodity price increase that would seriously injure the purchasing power of bond interest overlooked the fact that gold is not of itself a medium of exchange, but merely the basis of the credit structure.

Stocks and Corporate Financial Policy

The relative position of stockholders in the long run is further benefited by the corporate policy pursued by numerous American enterprises. It has long been customary for corporations in this country to pay out only a portion of their earnings as dividends, retaining the rest in a surplus account from which plant extensions and improvements are financed. The rapid growth of the country has constantly provided opportunities for profitable investment of much of this capital. If such retained earnings are really profitably invested each year, the value of the equity thus tends to increase at the same rate as a sum of money placed at compound interest; hence Edgar Lawrence Smith concluded that "over a period of years, the principal value of a well-diversified holding of the common stocks of representative corporations, in essential industries, tends to increase in accordance with the operation of compound interest."[4] This increase in value is in addition to the dividend income yielded by the stocks held, and it may be reflected in stock dividend "split-ups" or rights to subscribe to new shares at relatively low prices.

These benefits to stockholders have often been increased, and the bondholders' position made worse, by making bonds callable at the option of the management. When yields fall to a low point and bond prices generally rise, the bonds can be

[4] Smith, E. L., *Common Stocks as Long-term Investments*, p. 77.

called in and refunded with others bearing a lower coupon rate. This cuts the fixed charges and raises the net income of the company; but it also deprives the bondholder of his investment at a time when bond prices are high and he is at a relative disadvantage in the market in seeking to replace his called security. Legislation facilitating reorganizations may further weaken the bondholders' position. Irving Fisher has concluded:

> It seems, then, that the market overrates the safety of "safe" securities and pays too much for them, that it underrates the risk of risky securities and pays too little for them, that it pays too much for immediate and too little for remote returns, and, finally, that it mistakes the steadiness of money income from a bond for a steadiness of real income which it does not possess. In steadiness of real income, or purchasing power, a list of diversified common stocks surpasses bonds.

Past Experience and the Future

In this last statement of Professor Fisher's, the experience of the post-war decade is tersely summarized. Statistical studies carried down to the end of the third decade of the twentieth century have shown that stocks were almost consistently undervalued and bonds largely over-valued. The upward movement of commodity prices, the rapid growth of the wealth and enterprise of the country, the attitude of investors—all tended to favor stockholders, and the market seldom appeared to appreciate the fact fully during this period.

But in applying the lessons of the past to the future, it is necessary to exercise caution. This was proved during the period of falling prices from 1930 to 1933, when the average of stock prices fell by more than 80 per cent and bonds also declined sharply, but generally much less and recovered sooner than did stocks. Will commodity prices tend upward for the future? About this question there is great difference of opinion among experts. Some point to the increasing efficiency of credit systems and the popularity of inflationary policies, and believe that the tendency to rise displayed by the price level from 1896 to 1913 will be resumed. Others point to the efficiency of industry, and deduce that prices will tend downward from these causes.

A second question which must be answered is whether the

value of corporate equities in the future, as in the past, will tend to increase at a rate similar to a compound interest curve because of reinvested earnings. This question cannot be answered with the same degree of confidence which would have been possible years ago. Several of our basic industries, such as the railroads and steel manufacturing, show signs of over-developed capacity; and during the depression, few companies have found it possible to reinvest their surplus earnings profitably. In fact, this is merely one by-product of the fact that the country as a whole has changed into a creditor nation. We are producing more free capital annually than we can ourselves consume, and many individual corporations find themselves with a surplus of cash on hand which they cannot profitably employ. The tax on undistributed corporate earnings will also have the effect of discouraging continuous expansion of corporate surpluses.

In Europe, it is customary for large corporations to pay out their entire earnings, after certain specified reserves, as dividends. In this country, where opportunities for profitably investing additional sums of money annually have been widely available, a different corporate policy has been prevalent. But in the future it appears likely that an increasing number of American corporations will have to adopt the practice of paying out practically all of their income as dividends. The result will be a less rapid increase in the value of equities; and the compound interest curve may no longer apply to the movement of an average of stock prices, as it did during the first three decades of the century when many of the great American industrial combinations first made their appearance and enjoyed a period of rapid growth.

A third factor which must be kept in mind regarding the relative position of stocks and bonds in the future is the possible change in the accuracy with which investors value the advantage of each type of security. In the past, investors have often under-valued stocks. But this error in judgment has been brought forcibly to their attention by such writers as Irving Fisher, Edgar Lawrence Smith and Kenneth S. Van Strum as well as numerous practical investment authorities. Investment trusts, trust companies, and investment counsel have em phasized the advantages of stock investment, and the small investor has turned to stocks as an investment medium to an extent never known before. Under the circumstances, it is natural that investors may easily get to over-value stocks from time to time, especially if in the future the trend of commodity prices should be downward.

Finally, a number of criticisms may be leveled against the statistical methods followed in such studies as that of Edgar Lawrence Smith, which analyzed the past price movements of groups of securities chosen at random, to determine the relative merits of stocks and bonds. These studies, in order to achieve universal application, assumed a total absence of judgment on the part of the investor. As a matter of fact, however, it has been the experience of brokers for many years that the average investor or speculator not only shows little judgment, but that he labors under the handicap of a negative quantity of this faculty, which might be termed bad judgment. Not only will he not do what past experience and common sense appear to dictate, but he is likely to do just the opposite.

Furthermore, it is questionable to what extent the tests developed to prove the relative merits of bonds and common stocks really assume a lack of judgment on the part of the investor. In choosing his "diversified list of common stocks," Smith used a number of methods of sampling designed to eliminate the element of judgment. One of these was the choice of the ten most active stocks. In the first place, it is often difficult to tell in advance which are going to be the most active stocks, and hence it is a violent assumption to hold that investors can obtain these shares at their average prices for the period taken, especially during rising markets. In the second place, it is often difficult to secure a diversified list of stocks, which investors usually desire, by taking the most active ones, especially if there is a group movement under way. In the third place, picking the most active stocks in any one week, as Smith did, necessitates trying a number of different weeks through the year as tests of the results from the sample week chosen, which he did not do. Other tests since made have partially overcome these objections, but the fact remains that many investors who have bought common stocks for investment in the past have found this a very costly move.

Hence, while the experience of the past warns that the merits of common stocks as investments may at times be under-valued, in the future the investor should ascertain in self-protection that he is not paying too much for equities purchased.

The Time Hazard in Stock Purchases

Owing to the marked cyclical movements in stock prices, as well as the influence of speculation as described in Chapter XIV, there are times when the general body of stocks is at a level so high that the investor stands to lose a substantial part of his principal by purchasing then. Some students of the subject have tended to minimize this danger through excessive emphasis upon the secular trend of stock prices. In a study of stock prices over the period from 1837 to 1922, Edgar Lawrence Smith, who has already been quoted, found that "in buying a well-diversified group of representative common stocks in essential industries, our chances of coming out even, or of making a profit in principal values, are: Within 1 year, 78 in 100; 2 years, 87 in 100; 4 years, 94 in 100."[5] Generalizations of this kind became absurd in the light of the experience of the depression and deflation period during the early 'thirties.

This kind of study has but little value as a guide for future action. In the first place, average prices are taken, which eliminate the greatest bulges. It is true that if stocks are bought at the average prices of the current year, for example, any decline which may take place will probably be regained at some time over a period of years. It is not as likely that the highest prices of the year will be seen again within the near future, however. In the second place, this study shifts from one group of stocks to another in a way that an investor seldom does. The list is changed three times: in 1880, 1892, and 1901. In the process of industrial change, new concerns come forward and earn large profits, while the old ones decline or move forward at a much slower rate. By shifting from one group to another it is possible to avoid loss, but this requires considerable vision Finally, the fundamental fact remains that basic economic con

[5] *Ibid.*, p. 82.

ditions have changed in this country, and therefore conditions surrounding common stock investment in the future may not be as favorable as they have been in the past. As a result, it may be increasingly difficult for a list of diversified stocks bought at a period of peak prices quickly to regain losses caused by a subsequent decline in the market. The time hazard has become more important. Cyclical movements are more significant, and secular swings less so than in an earlier stage of our economic evolution.

In the past, the growth of this country and its chief corporations was so phenomenal as to make reckless stock speculation very profitable at times. But this is no reason to believe that the same policy can be followed in the future with impunity, any more than that the primitive but, on the whole, successful farming of the pioneer can still be followed by the farmer today, whose produce competes on the world market with that of cheaper lands elsewhere. The railroads today, under stress of motor vehicle competition and rigid federal regulation, cannot afford to support the reckless expansion and speculative manipulation of the old Erie days, when the inevitably rapid growth of traffic could be counted upon to make up in the future for the sins of the present. In the same way, an increasing number of other industries face a slower rate of growth, or an actual decline, making the secular increase in equity values much slower and thus increasing the danger that payment of an unwarranted high price for a given stock, based on the expectation of a large gain in earnings in the future, may result in the impairment of the capital value of the investment over a period of time.

The reasoning of the whole "common stock school" leads to the conclusion that shares, instead of yielding a return equal to a pure rate of interest plus a premium for risk, as some theorists have held, should yield a current cash return equivalent to a pure interest return less a liberal allowance for future benefits expected. However, common stock prices tend to reflect actual and prospective earning power far more than yields based on current and future dividends and other benefits.

Considerations which govern the approximate determination of periods when speculative and cyclical factors place security prices on an exorbitant level are considered in Chapters XII above and XV below.

Growth of Stock Holding

Public interest in common stocks as investments increased enormously after the close of the World War. Several factors combined to bring this result about. Most fundamental was the inflation of bank credit at that time. Others were the increased prosperity of American corporations already referred to, the spread of security ownership in general, owing to the great increase in individual wealth, and the customer and employee stock ownership campaigns of utilities and other large corporations which habituated many people to stock ownership for the first time in their lives.

Estimates of the number of individual shareholders in this country can be made only with the greatest difficulty, because of the many companies for which data are unavailable, and the many cases of duplication in shareholders even among companies which make public the number of individual names on their stock books. Thus, the American Telephone & Telegraph Company had in 1935, some 700,000 individual shareholders, but many of these were large holders of stocks in other companies as well. Some recent estimates which have been made place the total number of stockholders in this country at 15,000,000 and more; others, working from income tax statistics, arrive at a far lower figure.

Concrete evidence that stock holding is taking the place of real estate and bonds as the most prevalent form of investment in this country is given by statistics of estates filed for tax purposes with the federal government. The variation from 1923 to 1927 in the relative proportions of real estate, bonds and stocks in such estates is distinctly a favor of stocks. The changes were as follows:

	1923	1924	1925	1926	1927
Real estate	24.68	23.55	22.01	19.13	18.23
Bonds	14.96	14.79	15.57	16.17	14.77
Stocks	31.29	31.41	32.92	37.40	38.90

It is interesting to note that these figures of estates filed for tax purposes also reveal that real estate becomes of decreasing importance with the size of the estate. In gross estates of less than $50,000 in 1927, real estate constituted 39 per cent. This percentage decreased until it was less than 1 per cent in estates of more than $10,000,000.

Institutional Investments

Life insurance companies, savings banks, national banks, trust companies and other financial institutions which are supposed to be guided by considerations of maximum conservatism in their investment policies are almost universally restricted to bonds by law. In 1928, New York life insurance companies were allowed to invest in preferred stocks as well; but, as has been seen above, a well-protected preferred stock may be essentially different from a bond only from a legal point of view.

Strange to say, proponents of the thesis that common stocks rather than bonds constitute the ideal investment medium have been especially vehement in their insistence that institutions of this kind, especially life insurance companies, should continue to be limited to bonds and mortgages in investing their funds. Thus, it has been stated:

> There is a vast difference between the investment needs and purposes of such institutions from those of the individual investor, or the family estate. Take an insurance company, for example. It is by the nature of its business perfectly safeguarded against any possible loss through the depreciation of the dollar. It deals in nothing but dollars. Its contracts call for the payment of future dollars. It therefore requires to know only that it will receive from its investments more future dollars than it will have to pay out. The purchasing power of these future dollars is of no concern to it. If dollars have shrunk in value, the beneficiary under its policies absorbs the shrinkage, the company does not.[6]

The same reasoning is applied to savings banks, commercial banks and trust companies.

A fallacy underlies this reasoning from the investor's point of view. The writer assumes that these institutions are run for their own sake, and not for the investors who use them as media of investment. But they succeed in their object as investing

[6] *Ibid.*, p. 11.

institutions only in so far as they furnish a safe and reasonably lucrative investment medium. If the bondholder fares as badly as is claimed, then surely the savings bank depositor and the holder of a life insurance policy deserve equal sympathy. It is necessary for some purposes to look beyond the institution to the men for whom the institution operates.

It is true that these institutions must be ready to meet their obligations in dollars whenever called upon to do so. But the experience of the past shows that at any one time only a small portion of their liabilities is likely to become payable, and they can surely realize as quickly upon a list of highly marketable stocks as upon a portfolio of long-term bonds.

Whatever conclusion is applied to the position of the individual investor in the question of the relative merits of stocks and bonds applies, with suitable modifications, to the investing institution and the institutional investor as well. At least a limited portion of the assets of such institutions should be permitted to take the form of high-grade common stocks meeting certain accepted tests of quality, whenever experience shows that these are actually the better form of investment. The basi reason why both institutional and individual investors must b cautious about common stock investment is the severe risk o adverse cyclical fluctuation involved. But to favor commor stocks for the estates of orphans, and to forbid them to th insurance companies formed to protect these same orphans involves an obviously large element of contradiction.

To make such changes as a more enlightened, but not fanati cal, attitude toward common stocks dictates would require number of changes in the laws governing investments by thes institutions, which have been reviewed briefly in Part I c this book in connection with these various institutions. This necessarily a slow and long-drawn-out process. The rapid growt of the investment trust and investment counsel reflects th trend.

Trust companies have been especially active in considerin the wisdom of buying stocks for fiduciary investment, sinc they may secure the full right to invest in them through ma ing suitable provision in the trust agreement. That this polic has had a certain amount of judicial sanction, as revealed i cases where beneficiaries have sought to recover losses from stock investment by trustees, is shown in the following statement of a trust officer:[7]

> The public who are the customers of the banks and trust companies not only request, they demand that trustees under wills and deeds of trust avail themselves of the advantages which the purchase of common stocks affords.
>
> This demand has already been met by some trustees. It is high time that all trust men declare unhesitatingly that it is and will continue to be part of their investment policy to buy common stocks for trust estates when properly authorized to do so.
>
> In every case which I have read in which the trustee has been surcharged for an investment in common stocks, anyone who had the proper conception of the duties of trusteeship, particularly the trust officers of the banks and trust companies of this country, would condemn the original action of the trustee in making the purchase and would give whole-hearted approval to the decisions of the courts.
>
> Where the stocks bought are in any way representative and belong to that indefinite category of "investment" stocks, the cases disclose a tolerant and generous attitude on the part of the courts.
>
> We may confidently expect the support of the courts in an intelligent and reasonable investment program, including some common stocks, under a broad general power. But we must be highly discriminating in the selection of stocks before we buy them; and once bought, we must watch them with a minute and vigorous attentiveness.

Legal decisions handed down during and after the depression have tended to bear out this prediction.

Another aspect of the problem of the relative advantages of bonds and stocks for institutional investment is the prevailing habits of corporate issuers of securities. As a result of depression experiences, many corporations prefer to finance by the sale of stocks, which do not involve fixed-interest charges that must be paid regardless of earnings. The consequent shortage of bonds became all the more marked as financial institutions that were compelled by legal and other restrictions to buy

[7] C. Allison Scully, Vice President of the National Bank of Commerce, before nth Mid-Winter Conference of the trust companies division of the American ankers' Association, 1929.

fixed-interest-bearing obligations mopped up available supplies on the market. As a result, during the great refunding era of 1935-1937, many bonds of quite limited investment merit could be sold at yields of 4 per cent and less, formerly typical of the best grade of obligations, especially when conversion or stock purchase options are not attached. The shortage of bonds suitable for institutional investment constitutes an additional powerful argument for making legal restrictions on investments of financial institutions more flexible, so that, when necessary, higher grades of stocks can be utilized for this purpose to supplement an inadequate bond supply.

Preferred Stocks

The discussion thus far has been concerned with the char acteristic features of common stocks and bonds when these type of securities are found in their original and typical forms. How ever, special intermediate types of securities exist which pa take of the nature of one or both of these forms, while havin certain special characteristics. The earliest form of special se curity is the preferred stock.

As preferred stocks constitute a large group of securitie their position is naturally a matter of importance. Essentiall a preferred stock is like a bond, if its legal features be ignore Unless it has participating, convertible, or other rights to larger return than the stated preferential rate of dividend pa ments, it is a fixed-income security adversely affected by d clines in the purchasing power of money and not benefitin from the piling up of equities through the corporate surplu

The situation is different, of course, where the company not in a strong cash position and where the preferred sto sells down to a relatively low level on account of uncertain over dividend payments. In such circumstances, preferred stoc will move much as common stocks will, especially if dividen are cumulative and thus pile up when not paid. Thus, depen ing on the earning power of a corporation and its capitalizatic preferred stocks vary in character from well-secured senior curities of large companies to non-dividend-paying stocks wi remote possibilities of a return.

A statistical study of the past record of preferred stocks has been made to determine their market price performance, which resulted in the following conclusion:

It appears that preferred stocks are a better investment than common stocks about as often as the opposite is true, when purchase is made for one year only. But it also appears that, when the line of common stocks swings above, it goes considerably farther above the line of preferred stocks than it goes below this line in the years when it swings below. That is to say, when the common stocks are better, their superiority is quite marked. When the preferred stocks are better, their superiority is much less in amount.[8]

Hybrid Securities

The investment banking business, like any other, seeks to please the fancies of the public in order to stimulate its patronage. In the case of securities, this can often be effectively done by attaching to a bond or preferred stock which holds out to the investor safety of principal and regularity of income, indirect participation in the ownership of the company.

Five important ways of doing this have been devised. The oldest and most common, until recently, was the convertible bond, which permits the bondholder to turn in his security and get stock in exchange at a fixed rate of conversion. A second method for accomplishing the same result is the giving of shares of stock as a bonus with the bonds or preferred stock, a method which had its heyday in the period of the early railroad promotions when the bonds covered the cost of the property and the stock was given away free to represent the good will. Strange to say, this scheme was revived in floating a number of investment trusts. A third method is the granting of option warrants to holders of bonds and preferred stock, which permit them to buy stock at specified prices. Fourthly, the practice is not uncommon of selling blocks of bonds or preferred stocks with common shares, at a fixed price for the package. Thus, two shares of preferred stock may be sold with one share of common at a fixed price for the three, and the investor is given no choice

[8] Jackson, James Roy, "Common and Preferred Stocks as Investments," *Journal of Business of the University of Chicago,* vol. i, pp. 294-323.

in the matter—he must take the whole block or leave it. This method of financing also has been used extensively in the investment trust field and the financing of small industrials. Lastly, a senior security may be participating, obtaining a higher rate of return when the common stock does so on an agreed-upon basis.

Fashions in the investment field change frequently. In times of rising stock prices, the attachment of the various indirect participations in the equity is often absolutely necessary to sell many issues. When prices are falling in the stock market, however, and confidence is at low ebb, such features often aid little in selling bonds or preferred stocks, price stability and yield then being the prime consideration.

The convertible bond or the bond with option or common stock attached is from many points of view the ideal security. It seems to protect the investor both ways. If the company is successful and conditions are favorable, the bondholder shares in the prosperity through conversion or purchase of stock below the market prices. On the other hand, should the value of the common stock decline sharply, it is altogether unlikely that the bond or preferred stock, with prior claims to earnings and assets, would suffer nearly as much.

However, the investor must be careful not to pay too much for such participation in the future prosperity of the enterprise. There are many cases on record in which the conversion or warrant feature merely concealed the innate weakness of bond. Where the intrinsic investment security is weak, the investor should not be tempted to purchase an issue merely because a conversion or warrant feature of doubtful value added.

Thus, a bond with warrant attached and a 3½ per cent coupon may be offered at 100, to give the investor a yield 3½ per cent. As a straight investment, let us assume that yield of almost 5 per cent should be expected, based on yields of similar securities in the market, so that the price would be say, 75. The investor actually pays, in this case, 25 points f the warrant privilege, and he should decide whether it is wor the price before making his commitment.

References

Chamberlain, L., and Edwards, G. W., *Principles of Bond Investment,* New York, 1927, chap. v.

Chamberlain, L., and Hay, W. W., *Investment and Speculation,* New York, 1931.

Fisher, Irving, *How to Invest When Prices Are Rising,* Scranton, 1912.

Jackson, J. R., "Common and Preferred Stocks as Investments," *Journal of Business of the University of Chicago,* vol. i, pp. 294–323.

Rose, Dwight C., *Practical Application to Investment Management,* New York, 1934.

Rose, Dwight C., *Investment Management,* New York, 1928, chap. xi.

Rodkey, R. G., *Preferred Stocks as Long-Term Investments,* Ann Arbor, 1932.

Smith, Edgar Lawrence, *Common Stocks as Long-term Investments,* New York, 1924.

Van Strum, Kenneth S., *Investing in Purchasing Power,* New York, 1925.

Chapter XIV

SPECULATION AND MANIPULATION

Investment *vs.* Speculation

Few economic concepts have been subject to so much confused thinking as speculation. Much of this confusion arises from the fact that what constitutes speculation from the point of view of the individual does not necessarily affect the capital market as a whole in a way different from any ordinary investment. In this chapter, an effort is made to distinguish carefully between these two aspects of the term, and to trace in detail the precise effects individual speculation has on security price movements.

From the social standpoint, or that of the capital market as a whole, an investment may be defined as any commitment of funds, whether in one's own business or in securities. This appears to have been the original meaning of the word in financial parlance. In this broad sense, the term investment carries no added implication of safety. In fact, from the standpoint of the capital market as a whole, all commitments of capital are of equal importance and constitute investments, regardless of the risks that arise for the individual investor. It is at least equally important that capital be forthcoming for new and untried enterprises, such as airplane lines and the exploitation of new inventions, as that it be available for old, established public utilities to permit them to make extensions to their service. Both represent an investment of the free capita of the community in what are meant to be productive enterprises.

From the point of view of the individual investor, on the other hand, there is a sharp distinction between investment and speculation. This distinction is one of the degree of risk involved in the commitment made; for the investor, if his securit is fully protected, is not vitally concerned with the use t which his funds are put by the borrower. Where the risk is small, the process is called investment; as the risk increases, the commitment becomes more and more speculative.

An initial difficulty arises, however, in attempting to draw a distinction between these two terms because it is no easy matter to tell in advance how large a degree of risk attaches to any specific security. It is easier to be wise after than before the event. The intention of the buyer of securities to invest rather than to speculate, through the avoidance of risk, may not prove successful. Thus, many an investor in high-grade government bonds has fared badly because of a rise in the level of money rates at the time of sale. Long-term federal obligations have been quoted in the low 'eighties on several occasions since the war. Buyers of Russian government bonds before the war, when these bonds were considered a high-grade investment, have seen their holdings wiped out. But holders of these bonds bought them as investments, and few will deny that these buyers must be included in the category of investors. It is necessary to distinguish, therefore, between the intention of the security buyer in making the original commitment, and the final outcome of the transaction.

Considering merely the intention of the security buyer, we may define investment as the *purchase of securities or other income-producing wealth with the intention of avoiding all substantial risks.* Generally the investor finds that he must be satisfied with only a moderate rate of return on his capital in order to achieve this aim, although a well-informed investor naturally will frequently discover opportunities giving large promise of income and profit, but which nevertheless involve so slight a degree of risk as to constitute the commitment a pure investment.

Speculation, on the other hand, may be defined as the *act of consciously assuming risks to secure a profit which is expected to result from the favorable outcome of the enterprise in which the risk is assumed.* Speculation thus becomes a matter of judging risks and choosing those which offer the promise of largest returns for the degree of uncertainty involved.

Gambling, as the term is commonly used, is an activity of an entirely different sort. It consists in assuming risks for their own sake, without specifically evaluating them. By almost general consent, the man who takes a "flier" in stocks, by which is meant the purchase of shares for quick and very large profits utterly without knowledge of what they represent, is termed a gambler. And this distinction appears only fair to that other type of individual, the speculator, who is engaged in delicately weighing risks in order to pick that which offers the largest measure of profit in return for the degree of uncertainty involved. The gambler *par excellence* is the player, at cards or dice, who artificially creates risks having no relation to business activity, and eliminates as far as is reasonably possible the elements of judgment and foresight. It is also properly used to define all kinds of wagers, such as those on the outcome of horse races and other partly foreseeable events, where the individual does not take an interest in what is intended to be a money-making, or so-called productive, enterprise.

The distinction between investment and speculation, however, cannot be made on the basis of intention alone. It is further conditioned by the *degree of knowledge* which the security buyer possesses. To one without any knowledge of security values, any commitment, unless made in accordance with expert advice, would be a gamble. This would be the case, for example, with the widow sometimes depicted in trust company advertisements, brought into contact with financial matters for the first time in her life through the death of her husband. She may use her funds to buy a government bond, or she may put her money into fraudulent oil stocks; but in either case she proceeds, at least until enlightened by some financial adviser, wholly in the gambling spirit. On the other hand, to the banker, with his special sources of information and his expert judgment, a wild-cat oil security which he has made the subject of special investigation may be a good investment. He has evaluated the risks, having the knowledge to do so, and has perhaps found that they are virtually non-existent.

An investor, then, is one who commits his funds in such a manner as to seek to avoid all major risks. The speculator purposely assumes risks when he feels that the profit possibilities or the higher rate of return justifies them. Exactly what constitutes risk to each individual, however, depends upon hi knowledge of the circumstances surrounding the safety of the commitment. Where such knowledge is wholly lacking, the commitment is a gamble. In investment, where individual knowledge differs so greatly, "one man's meat is another man's poison."

Of course, we have assumed up to this point a purely rational attitude on the part of the security buyer. Needless to say, emotional considerations, habits, and imitation determine acts of investors to a large extent, and cause them to buy securities without intelligent appraisal of risks.

Criteria of Speculation

The definition of speculation advanced above attempts no clear-cut demarcation between it and investment. Many attempts have been made to define arbitrarily the border line between investment and speculation. Thus, one writer asserts that an investor is one who is satisfied with a return equal to a theoretically pure rate of interest, as approximately fixed by the yield of government bonds plus a "premium for risk" that, at most, is no greater than this amount. If government bonds yield three per cent, an investment according to this definition yields up to six per cent, and a speculative security is one which yields more than the latter figure. Such a distinction is entirely useless, for it is based upon a series of *a priori* assumptions without foundation in fact. The yield on a government bond is not a pure rate of interest for there are a number of factors entering into the determination of the quotation of such a bond, such as tax exemption, borrowing privileges at Federal Reserve Banks, availability for institutional or trustee investment, and the fact that it is so well known to all classes of investors that the yield may be depressed far below any tenable "pure rate of interest"; but even more important is the fact that there are many securities on which the yield is not much greater, or is even less than that on government bonds, but which, to those able to appraise the situation fully, are quite speculative.

There is another test which is frequently used as a touchstone to distinguish between investment and speculation. Buying for income, it is said, constitutes investment; buying for appreciation, speculation. This view is not always tenable in the light of actual facts. Some of the most conservative of investors buy securities which give little or no return but which they feel are certain to appreciate in value. Standard Oil stocks and stocks in many banks and insurance companies have been included in this class. In fact, many of our most conservative corporations have preferred, particularly before it was sought to impose corporation income taxes upon undistributed income, to reinvest a large proportion of their earnings in their business and consequently to pay relatively small dividends. This policy has resulted in low yield on their shares, but a steady appreciation in the prices of their common stocks. Conversely, many bonds bought solely for income give a large current yield, but constitute outright speculations. It is true, however, that the great bulk of speculative security purchases are made in the hope of quick capital appreciation, rather than larger current income. Similarly, practically all short sales are speculative. The speculator, in search of large profits from the assumption of risks, naturally prefers to carry the risk for as short a time as possible.

A final test frequently applied to determine this point is whether the commitment is made in whole or in part with borrowed capital. The security buyer, as already indicated, makes an investment if he knowingly avoids all reasonable risks. When he uses borrowed funds to help pay for the securities, he increases the risk in the hope of larger profits. But this fact does not *per se* make the commitment a speculation. Those who borrowed at the banks to buy Liberty Bonds during the war—and millions of investors did so—were not necessarily speculating. It is true that there is an additional element of risk in that the loan might become payable at a time when the bonds show some depreciation in market value, but this risk may be so small as to be negligible. Furthermore, when an individual buys securities on margin with the purpose of paying for them in full during a period of time, he may be said to make an investment on the installment plan.

While these last two criteria are not absolute distinctions between investment and speculation, they do furnish approximate tests of such transactions. The bulk of speculative security transactions are made for rapid appreciation, and they are made on margin.

Ubiquity of Speculation

Speculation has been described above as the conscious assumption of risks for the sake of gain. The term has often been applied exclusively to trading in organized markets for stocks and commodities. While speculative activity is highly developed here, it is a mistake to distinguish speculation on the exchanges from the assumption of risks in any other form of economic activity. The risks of the security markets, in fact, largely reflect those inherent in all business ventures.

The element of speculation, it is conceivable, could be largely eliminated from economic society; but this would involve the development first of an absolutely static state of society, such as that conceived at times by the classical economists. If it were possible to eliminate, first, changes in population, secondly, changes in the volume of production of agricultural and mineral products, and, thirdly, changes in technology and money and credit conditions, such a static state would be largely realized and speculation would die a natural death except for climatic, seasonal, and catastrophic risks. Lacking such a consummation, efforts to curtail speculation have often proved ineffectual and have frequently defeated their purpose by stifling production and trade.

The speculative nature of business in general has been particularly emphasized in the economic discussions of the past two decades, in which the business cycle has played so prominent a part. Business men have sought to avoid the adverse effects of the cycle through a proper speculative policy. In part this consists in avoiding speculative risks by cutting down inventories in times of activity and rising prices; and in part it involves the assumption of risks at the right time through anticipating shortages and higher prices of labor and material.

As economic organization becomes more highly articulated, risk-bearing becomes a more and more specialized function. Institutions are organized to reduce and eliminate certain risks —hence the growth of insurance in its various phases. By means of more effective social control through private and public agencies, risks may be reduced. Cooperative marketing and similar schemes have been advanced as methods of reducing large innate risks of agriculture, and risks arising from money and credit changes are supposed to be reduced through central banking. Again, where risks cannot be avoided by being spread over large sections of the community, they can be shifted from the community in general to a small group who specialize in assuming them for the sake of profit. This is the case on the exchanges. Finally, through the spread of information, risks resulting from ignorance or inability to appraise the uncertainties of a situation are reduced.

The tendency under present conditions, therefore, is for risks to increase because of the growing complexity of economic life, and at the same time to be reduced, as far as the individual is concerned, by the social agencies mentioned above.

Speculation in Securities

Securities represent claims to money or to property of present or potential income-producing capacity. As such, they reflect in each case not only the risks inherent in the enterprise or governmental credit which they represent, but the additional ones incident to the market in which they are traded. To cite one example of thousands which might be mentioned, Argentine railroad stocks lost the greater part of their quoted value on the London market in the early years of the World War because the British holders in many cases had to sell them, and a market existed for these securities nowhere else in the world. On the basic risk of the enterprise were thus superimposed the additional risks peculiar to the marketability factor.

In order to redistribute and allocate the risks in the security markets, financial practice has developed a number of devices. The most significant one from the point of view of risk-bearing is that of "trading on the equity," a term borrowed from legal usage and connoting in its broad sense the raising of funds on a comparatively low-cost basis through the issue of prior claims to income or assets. The junior security holders thus assume greater risks in the hope of securing larger profits through the sale by the enterprise of bonds and preferred stocks. "Trading on the equity" or "leverage" denotes that part of the issued securities of the company are given what is meant to be an investment status, while the junior issues bear more than their share of the speculative risk in return for greater ultimate profit possibilities. It thus becomes possible to segregate much of the risk element, to be borne by those willing to specialize in assuming it for the sake of a larger possible return.

An important factor of uncertainty resulting from this present-day financial practice is the effect of variations in the purchasing power of money. Trading on the equity involves the issue of bonds and preferred stocks with generally a fixed annual income. The common stock is entitled to all the residual income. Any pronounced decline in the value of money thus reacts very unfavorably upon the fixed-income-bearing security in the enterprise, whereas a rise in the purchasing power of the dollar has an opposite effect. This was more fully discussed in Chapter XIII.

A second factor affecting the distribution of risks within the corporation is the financial policy followed by its management. Where a corporation builds up large reserves, puts its plants in excellent shape and pays dividends only after these requirements have been fulfilled, it is placing a cushion of financial strength between itself and its security holders, so that shocks felt by one are passed on to only a partial extent, if at all, to the other. In other cases, the ordinary risks of the enterprise are multiplied many times over by a policy of alternatingly overpaying dividends and sharply retrenching for the purpose of physical rehabilitation.

The distribution of risks through methods of capitalization thus determines the types of securities issued by corporate enterprises. These securities are then bought and sold in the market, and their quotations are placed at the mercy of the multiple forces which determine fluctuations in prices. These forces are numerous, and at different times play more or less important parts in determining market values. The two major market factors, as distinct from changes in business conditions, are the general level of interest rates, already discussed in Chapter I, and the degree of confidence felt at the time by the security-buying public, as reflected in its willingness to buy freely. The following diagram summarizes the distribution of risks in the security markets:

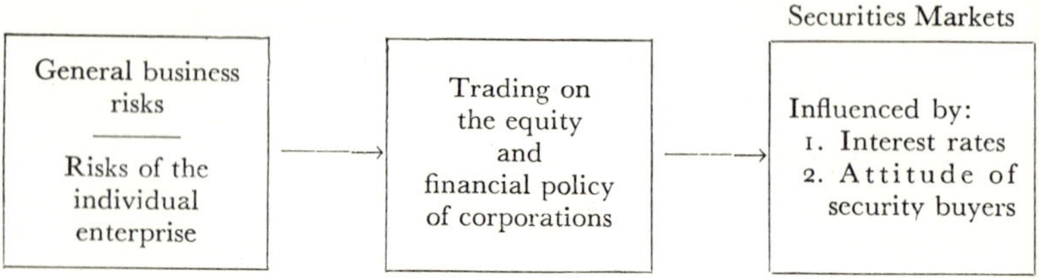

The market for securities is thus seen to be a highly uncertain affair, involving not only the ordinary risks of business, but a number of additional factors arising out of the market itself. These risks are to some extent segregated by the process of issuing prior securities or trading on the equity, and they are reduced or increased, as the case may be, by the financial policies followed by individual corporations.

Speculation and the Security Markets

We have thus far considered speculation as an individual activity, consisting of the assumption of risks for the sake of profit. We now turn to the effects of such speculative activity on security prices, especially in the organized security markets.

The only way in which speculation affects the security market as a whole is in the extent to which it results in purchases and sales of securities over and above what would be the case if speculative activity were non-existent. The purchaser of speculative securities who buys them outright and holds them for profit is an investor from the standpoint of the market—he makes his purchase and pays for it just as he would for a high-grade investment issue. We often read of "investment buying" going on in the stock market. This refers to purchases of all kinds of securities, regardless of the risk involved, by those who mean to pay for them and retain them for some period of time.

Only that kind of speculation affects the market in a special way which creates a demand for securities over and above such "investment buying." Such a demand is created when securities are bought on margin, for in this way an individual uses bank credit to buy more securities than he can afford to contro with his own funds. Such purchases are seldom designed as permanent commitments. Rather it is hoped that the price of the security will rise within the shortest possible period, and that after it has risen the speculator will be able to resell to someone else, either another speculator or an investor, who will pay for and hold it more or less permanently. Secondly, those who buy and sell large amounts of securities with their own funds for the sake of quick profits exercise a distinct effect on the level of prices, especially when such trading is designed to bring about substantial price change, as in pool manipulation. Finally, floor traders on exchanges and other professional buyers and sellers of securities, including short sellers who cover their commitments, contribute to broader markets at times, and thus influence the course of quotations.

The effects of large-scale speculation upon the course of security prices have often been discussed in the past. The optimistic view of such effects, frequently presented at some length by apologists for speculative activity who feel called upon to answer popular criticism of the stock exchanges, holds that the speculator limits price fluctuations and thus benefits the public. Stability of security prices is obviously desirable from the investment and social points of view. The speculator, it is contended, through buying when investment demand is small for one reason or another, keeps prices from falling, or, at any rate, from falling too rapidly. He is willing to utilize bank credit and assume the risk of carrying securities for the sake of a gain he is said to earn abundantly in terms of social service. Similarly, the short seller is found to exercise a beneficent influence in maintaining the relative stability of prices. When prices go up too fast, it is argued, the short sales of the speculator limit the rise. Conversely, when prices decline too rapidly, covering operations by short sellers similarly limit the amplitude of the fluctuations.

This optimistic view is based on an assumption very common to classical economics. One of the best-known expositions of it, in fact, was furnished by John Stuart Mill. It assumes that the speculator is an entirely rational and far-sighted, as well as successful, being. By buying when prices would otherwise be low and selling when they are high, he helps both himself and society. This assumption perhaps is borne out on certain occasions, but there are many instances when the contrary has proved to be the case.

There is a strong psychological attraction in the assumption of risks which few persons escape. Often this tendency is gratified in purely gambling activities of a minor sort, such as card playing and sports. However, what financial writers are pleased to term "the public" is now ever ready to gratify this tendency in the stock market also if prices rise steadily; and the history of stock speculation is replete with such periods of widespread public participation in the stock market, during which reasoned analysis of values becomes a poor guide to price movements, and even the able and shrewd professional speculator may feel he must throw caution to the winds and swim with the tide if he is to escape being swept away. Speculation at such periods doubtless greatly increases the amplitude of price fluctuations, instead of making for price stability.

When we consider not the broad movements of the market, but changes in individual securities, speculation doubtless plays a much larger rôle in increasing the amplitude of fluctuations. Frequently a stock declines in price after a major upswing, on the announcement of the news that the upswing had anticipated. The speculator explains the drop by the fact that "the news is out." What he means is that speculation has more than anticipated the rise. But the tendency of speculation to exaggerate price movements is even greater when popular attention is attracted to one particular security or group of securities by some rumor or report, the exact import of which is not correctly gauged. Fig. 14 shows the movement in the price of American Telephone & Telegraph capital stock, from January 1, 1927, to May 3, 1929, when no significant news was published about the company, but speculation was rampant in the security market generally. While a free market may stabilize prices in general, and over a period of time, it does cause wide discrepancies in the case of individual issues.

There is no need to defend speculation on moral or ethical grounds by alleging that it limits security price fluctuations. The fact is that, without a free market for such speculative securities, it would not be possible freely to secure capital for new and uncertain enterprises. Numerous sound investment securities of the present day passed through a long period in

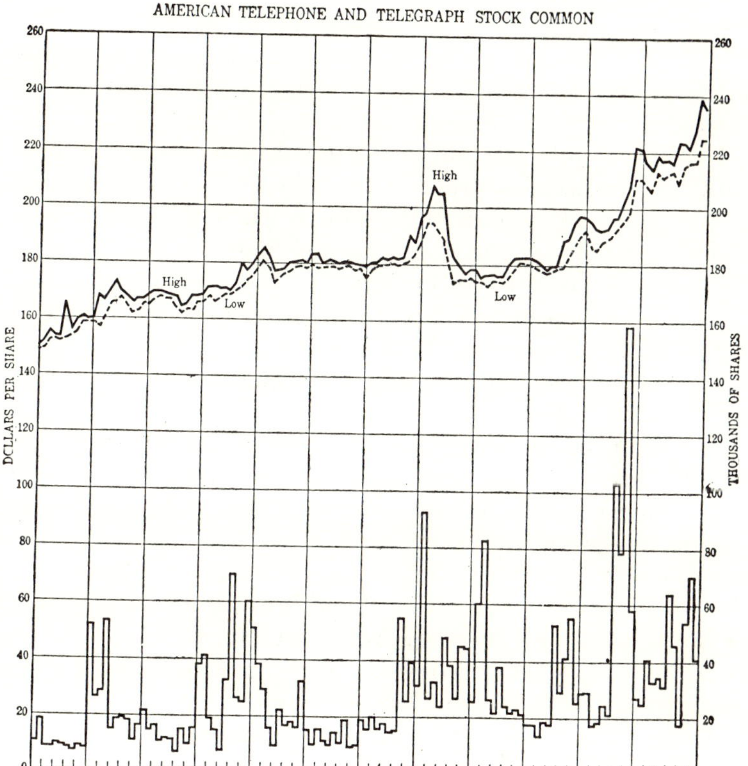

FIG. 14. WEEKLY HIGH AND LOW PRICES FOR AMERICAN TELEPHONE & TELEGRAPH CAPITAL STOCK ON THE NEW YORK STOCK EXCHANGE, WITH VOLUME OF TRADING. JANUARY 1, 1927—MAY 3, 1929.

which they underwent wild and exaggerated fluctuations because of keen speculation in their shares. It was chiefly the appeal of these speculative movements to the stock trader which made it possible to float these shares in the first place. In the light of these developments, security speculation as a force facilitating technical progress may be socially more desirable than investment in seasoned securities long outstanding.

Economic and Social Effects of Security Speculation

The chief general economic effects of security speculation as now carried on are three in number. These are:

1. Capital is made available for almost any new enterprise which promises large returns through the development of a demand for speculative securities.

The automobile, the radio and the airplane industries have, within recent decades, proved that substantial amounts of capital can be raised within this country when the industry for which capital is sought is hardly out of its embryonic stage. This is easier because promoters can point to the success of other new industries in the past—the number of such cases has been legion. An argument by analogy may not always be sound, but it is invariably effective, especially in a new and ever-growing country.

As a result of the many cases of fabulous profits earned from the purchase of speculative securities, a large part of the security-buying public in this country is hungry for speculative possibilities, even at the expense of stability and safety. National psychology differs greatly in this respect. Just as the average French investor carefully tries to avoid risk, although he does not always succeed, American investors, even of the conservative type, will frequently place their money in a speculative issue "with long-pull possibilities." This tendency has been invariably associated with the pioneer spirit.

2. The savings and bank credit resources of the country are opened to the use of enterprises of a speculative nature.

One aspect of security speculation of the characteristic margin-trading type is that it makes a speculative security purchase the basis of a bank loan generally considered of the most liquid and safe kind. The margin trader, specializing in the assumption of such risks, advances only a part of the market price of the security, the rest being secured from a bank on a collateral loan. This loan, usually of the call type, then is considered a liquid part of the bank's portfolio, although it is, at the same time, the means which permit the creation of a market for the speculative security in question. Bank security loans, therefore, represent largely a tapping of the liquid credit resources of the country for the purposes of financing speculative enterprises. The risk element in the transaction is segregated and borne by the speculator, because he is lured by the possibilities of large profits.

3. Speculation acts as a stabilizer, although an imperfect one, in the market for securities.

It has been seen above that frequently, owing to the imperfections of the speculator himself and the alternating ebb and flow of public participation in the market, speculation may exaggerate ordinary fluctuations in security prices. It remains true, however, that speculators may frequently be the only buyers when investors are generally eager to sell out their holdings, while conversely he may be a short seller when a temporary heavy demand bids fair to overvalue securities.

The social effects of speculation are more intangible and difficult to measure. Doubtless there have been numerous occasions—the more picturesque of which have been the tulip craze in Holland and the South Sea bubble in England—when popular participation in speculation became so keen that the ordinary life of the community was disrupted and a part of the populace demoralized by the get-rich-quick idea. On the other hand, speculation has proved for some an avenue to that more highly regarded habit known as thrift. The meager return of the pure investment security may not be able to lure into the fold of investors those of a more speculative temperament; but the combination of investment and speculative features held out by many securities now traded in on the market does have the effect of breaking them into the security-buying habit. A more extreme case of the kind is the lottery bond issue, used in some countries abroad, to attract investment funds by making a gambling appeal.

Speculation and Bank Credit

Security speculation is carried on to a large extent with the use of bank credit, secured either through brokers' loans or through direct loans to speculators from their banks, the securities bought being used as collateral. The volume of bank credit absorbed in such speculative purchases of securities varies widely with the state of the security markets. At the peak in 1929, the banks of this country had roundly $3,000,000,000 of brokers' loans outstanding, and $10,000,000,000 of loans made to other borrowers secured by stocks and bonds. While some part of this latter sum represented loans made for commercial and industrial purposes, the bulk of these security loans doubtless represented the use of bank credit in the carrying of securities for a rise.

When the volume of bank credit absorbed in security speculation expands, as it did rapidly in 1927, 1928 and 1929, a serious question arises in connection with the effect of this speculative expansion upon the general banking structure of the country and the condition of business. Does this speculative credit expansion make much less credit available for business needs as was commonly asserted at the time? What happens to the credit thus advanced to speculators? If bank reserves are adequate, as was the case at that time, security loans should not impair the ability of banks to lend adequately to commercial borrowers also. However, if the desire to curb speculative loans brings a general tightening of money rates through corrective measures by the credit authorities, commercial borrowers would then be penalized.

The superficial view is frequently advanced in answer to the second question, that the security markets absorb credit like a sponge, so that credit outstanding against securities performs no agricultural, commercial and industrial service for "legitimate" business use. Actually, however, it will be found that practically all of the bank credit which originally takes the form of a loan to a broker or a security speculator becomes purchasing power in the hands either of business corporations or of sellers of securities.

To prove this thesis, it is necessary to trace the course of the credit which originates as a loan for the purpose of carrying securities. The buyer of securities, or his broker, uses the bank credit to help pay for the securities. The seller of the securities who thus receives this buying power may do one of several things. If he buys other outstanding securities, he merely transfers the credit to another seller of securities, and the problem remains in its original form. Sooner or later, however, many sellers buy new issues of securities with the purchasing power so obtained, and thus transfer the proceeds of brokers' loans, at one or more removes, to the business corporations and governments that issue securities. In so far, therefore, as security loans go into new capital issues, directly or indirectly, they represent credit created in the first instance for speculative purposes, but transferred to business. These security loans permit the sale of new securities in much larger volume than would otherwise be the case, and constitute the means for financing business through the security markets instead of, as in the old-fashioned way, through the banks.

But not all those selling securities to buyers who pay with the aid of security loans put the proceeds into other securities. Many individuals put such proceeds directly into business enterprises which they own. Here the broker's loan is used to finance business even more directly. Others put such proceeds into real estate where, once again, the broker's loan is used to finance an important productive industry.

Finally, in times of rising security prices, a large part of the profits realized because banks make security loans to brokers and individuals goes directly into consumption goods. Fine automobiles, sumptuous residences and other more or less luxurious forms of spending are made possible through sales of securities at large profits—sales made to others who borrow from the bank to pay for their purchases.

Therefore, we may conclude that bank credit finances business, no matter whether advances are made directly to corporations and farmers or indirectly through security loans, the proceeds of which are either used to buy new security issues or are placed by the sellers directly in their businesses, or are spent for consumption goods and thus transferred to the business enterprises selling the goods. As a matter of fact, this illustrates one general truth of banking—that bank credit normally cannot be destroyed, but is merely transferred from one account to another until repaid. The credit which takes the form of a security loan is thus transferred practically entirely to business firms. Roughly, this might be called a case of the law of the conservation of bank credit, corresponding to the laws of the conservation of energy and the conservation of matter in physics.

From the social point of view, however, there is a vast difference between credit expansion through security loans and credit expansion through business loans. The latter are made by individual bankers, generally after analysis of the credit of the borrower and some scrutiny of the purpose of the advance. The banker's influence is all on the side of conservatism, liquidity and safety. When business raises money via the security markets, however, the amount thus brought into being and the disposition of the credit are largely at the mercy of the security speculator, who picks securities which give immediate indication of appreciation. If the proceeds of the security loans go into consumption, the buyer of luxuries has the control over the flow of credit. Therefore, a large volume of security loans reflects the fact that the speculator instead of the banker has been made arbiter of the flow of credit. Hence, the measures taken to limit the volume of security loans represent a major financial reform in a country where during past years they have assumed so large a rôle.

Manipulation and Security Prices

In the discussion of speculation above, care has been taken to avoid reference to one concomitant of organized speculative activity, which has been especially conspicuous during past years —manipulation. The Stock Exchange has been called a mere den of iniquitous manipulation—obviously a superficial exaggeration. Equally exaggerated is the claim of those who have solemnly asserted that prices of speculative securities have always reflected solely the "free play of the forces of supply and demand." Manipulation formerly played an important part—one that made the term "organized speculation" particularly appropriate in security price movements. How much it has been reduced through present govenmental supervision in the United States is still a debated question. The Securities Exchange Act has doubtless largely reduced the importance of the manipulative factor, but to an extent that only experience over a period of years will reveal.

One apologist of stock exchange speculation has expressed himself as follows:[1]

> The most easily manipulated market is the limited market. The market you cannot manipulate is the big, open, easy, facile market where everybody can trade with the least restriction. . . . There is no man so big he can manipulate the market into which the whole public comes. The idea that a big man can manipulate a market is greatly exaggerated anyway, but the bigger the market the harder it is for the big man to manipulate it. If the market is bigger than the man, he cannot manipulate it. The public determines the price of the stock in the long run, and the more easily you let the public come in, the harder it is for the big man to manipulate.

This sort of ratiocination is based upon a superficial view of the nature of the securities markets. There is actually no one uniform commodity there which the public can come in to buy and sell as the market moves higher and lower. Instead, there are numerous individual securities, in each of which a different technical market situation may arise. In one case where the ownership of the security is widely spread among the public a major fluctuation could hardly occur without public confidence, although a group with the proper financial sponsorship could create such confidence by artificial means, especially before legal restrictions upon the use of such means were imposed by Section 9 of the Securities and Exchange Act of 1934. As a matter of fact, however, many large and well-distributed stock issues have so small a floating supply as not to permit of wide manipulative movements. In other cases where the stock is largely held by a few individuals possessed of plentiful means, there is no reason why a major movement may not occur with only limited public participation.

The inequality of knowledge and financial resources of the several classes of participants in the business of stock speculation largely explains the importance of the various forms of "manipulation," including those that may still be carried on under present statutory provisions. First, there is the "public"

[1] Testimony of H. C. Emery, in Regulation of the Stock Exchange, Hearings before the Committee on Banking and Currency, U. S. Senate, 63d Congress, Second Session, on S 3895, Washington, 1914.

consisting mainly of relatively small traders and investors, often with a very imperfect notion of conditions surrounding security values, and with distinctly limited resources. Public trading often makes for erratic price fluctuations, for it is not directed toward any particular end. When stocks are free of manipulation and the public has the market in its own hands, prices are likely to move uncertainly up and down until there is special and definite news forthcoming about the issue and its prospects. Furthermore, as a rule, the public buys on a large scale only when there is a sharp rise in prices.[2]

A second group of participants in the stock market are the professional traders, who know the ways of the market and make a business of operating on it. These professionals, while armed with much better knowledge and much larger resources than the average outside trader, also follow rather than direct the trend of the market. The average professional speculator is eager to follow the trend once it is established, whether it be for a rise or a fall, relying as a rule on others to initiate and direct the movement. Federal regulation has tended to curb the operations of these professional speculators.

The third factor in the speculative security markets is the operations of the leading financiers and industrialists—people sometimes vaguely termed "insiders." These leaders, with powerful banking connections, and controlling as they do the management of many of the corporations whose shares are traded in on the security markets, are in a position to make market trends to a considerable extent, provided they do not flout fundamental economic conditions for any length of time. Within this select group are found the leading bankers of the country, the great investment bankers, a number of heads of stock exchange houses, and the executives of sundry corporations.

On the other hand, it must be remembered that the backbone of the market is the buying of institutional and individual investors who acquire securities to hold rather than to sell out as soon as possible to someone else at a higher price. This investment buying may not exercise much effect on the trend of

[2] The factors in the speculative market are fully discussed by Bond, Frederic Drew, *Stock Movements and Speculation,* chap. iii.

prices at a time when such buying constitutes a relatively small proportion of the total volume of transactions in active stocks. Investment buying is accomplished once and for all, whereas speculative trading results in a heavy turnover of stock again and again. But over a period of time investment buying cuts down the floating supply of a security, the latter connoting the portion registered in the names of brokers and held for speculative appreciation. The less speculative activity there is at any given time, the more buying and selling by investors dominates price movements.

In the long run, investment buying and selling will determine the selling price of a security. No one cares artificially to maintain the price of a security indefinitely unless the public follows suit and buys it at the higher prices. But a major manipulative operation may be carried on over a period of years, during which the price is kept at an artificial level. Yet if the public does not join in, the price must sooner or later find a level at which those seeking to affect the market can relieve themselves of the holdings bought for this purpose.

Effect on Investment Securities

The ebb and flow of speculative activity thus has a considerable effect on the market for investment security. Common stocks especially are subject to wide price fluctuations in response to such activity reducing their worth as investment media. This is particularly the case in times of widespread public participation in security speculation, when many conservative issues are taken in hand and forced up to unjustified heights. At such a time, many considerations may be forthcoming to rationalize what happens, such as assertions or predictions of the unlimited future growth of the country, its change from a "debtor" to a "creditor" nation, etc., but the inevitable subsequent deflation soon corrects such notions.

It would undoubtedly be desirable to avoid fluctuations in investment securities if this could be done without losing the benefits that accrue from speculation, as already described. Stability is from the long-range point of view a desirable quality in investment and constitutes a source of encouragement to the accumulation of savings. Through publishing a mass of information on operations of the railroads, and through rigid control of their financial policies, the Interstate Commerce Commission sought to stabilize investment values of railroad securities, but adverse economic and regulatory conditions rendered such efforts of no avail. Experience shows that capital can be raised most quickly for any purpose while similar securities are rising sharply. Hence, in a new industry or a new country, highly fluctuating and speculative security markets prove helpful to those seeking to raise capital for productive ventures while the general trend is upward. Then heavy purchases by speculators create an adequate supply of capital where investors would be slow to place their funds. As the country emerges from its pioneer phases, however, the relative value of untrammeled speculation tends to decline.

Reduction of Risk through Financial Organization

Through expert management and proper diversification of risks, speculative reverses may be largely reduced for the individual investor.

The financial institutions discussed in the first part of this volume are devoted in part to the reduction or isolation of the risk element. The savings bank and investment trust, by careful investigation in purchasing and diversification in holding securities, seek to eliminate it. The general management type of investment trust may further segregate risk by the process of trading on the equity on its own account. In this way, while the senior securities are high grade, the junior issues represent those with the risk element isolated, and are frequently of a highly speculative nature.

The investment banking house, which acts as the middleman between the issuing corporation and the buyers of securities, plays a rôle in the stabilization of investment. By its investigation and sponsorship, it often eliminates part of the uncertainty surrounding the security. After the issue has been put out, the market is generally supported, at least during the period in which it is being distributed. Finally, many concerns or their bankers may seek to stabilize markets over a longer period of time. Price fluctuations may be reduced by buying of the issue when the supply appears to be too large, and selling back when the market appears able to absorb offerings readily. Of course, when outside buying and selling orders become heavy enough, such stabilization efforts may be swept aside.

Combining Speculation and Investment

While part of the machinery of investment banking and corporation finance seeks to delimit the field of investment from that of speculation, a tendency exists also to combine the two. Many an investor seeks to combine his investment with some speculative feature which will enable him to profit from any unusual prosperity which may befall the enterprise issuing the security, while at the same time his risk of loss is limited. Hence, the great vogue of convertible securities and those with options attached, especially within recent years.

A security of this kind really consists of two portions—an investment bond or preferred stock, and a call on a more or less speculative common stock. This call is generally a highly speculative item with a small immediate value. Nevertheless, so many of these features have proved profitable in the past, over a period of years, that they have a special fascination for even conservative investors. Especially in times of a general rise in the security markets, convertible securities and those with options attached are in great demand. Then even *bona fide* investors may demand a speculative "kick" to their securities.

This mixture of investment and speculative features often results in complicating the value of the security to a considerable extent, because of the presence of both features. On the other hand, where an enterprise is not strongly enough established to justify the issue of bonds which can be offered as high-grade investments, this feature proves a convenient means of raising money at relatively low cost. In the case of senior security issues of smaller industrials, the Industrial Securities Committee of the Investment Bankers Association has gone so far as to consider that the investor has some right to such a speculative feature, in view of the risk he necessarily assumes.

Effects of Regulation

The New York Stock Exchange officially, and many economists and others who have been concerned with the theory of organized markets, have emphasized the need for maintaining them on a free and open basis. It has been argued that only by permitting both investors and traders from all over the world free access to the market, regardless of whether they come with their own or with borrowed funds, could the market be made broad enough to prevent manipulation of prices, to assure a correspondence between underlying conditions and security quotations, and to provide sufficient buying and selling orders to impart liquidity to listed securities at all times. Hence, government regulation of exchanges was opposed because of the threat therein implied to the maintenance of free and open markets.

However, the adverse consequences of the stock market boom of 1924-1929 were so severe, and the practices revealed by an investigation of financial markets conducted subsequently were found in some cases to be so undesirable, that Congress passed the Securities Exchange Act of 1934 without material opposition, after certain more restrictive proposals originally included in the draft of the bill had been dropped. The chief features of this measure are:

1. Standards are laid down for the publication of information by managements of companies whose securities are listed. This reflects the theory that a free and open market is impossible unless reasonably adequate information is available to the general public, as well as to "insiders." This portion of the law attracted little opposition in affected circles.

2. Manipulation of security markets is prohibited as far as feasible, and pegging of quotations to stabilize markets is subjected to regulations of the Securities and Exchange Commission. The theory here is that as long as persons with large financial resources act to manipulate prices, markets do not really remain free and open. The Stock Exchange authorities did not oppose the theory behind this section of the law, but argued that manipulation was far less prevalent than was popularly supposed, and that efforts to prevent it might do more harm

than good by interfering with the free flow of orders to the floor of the exchange.

3. Operations of the stock exchanges and their members, and of security brokers and dealers generally, are subjected to regulation by the Securities and Exchange Commission. This is designed to give assurance that public buyers and sellers shall be placed on an equal basis, as far as possible, without the creation of inequalities through the functioning of the mechanism of the security markets themselves.

4. Security loans by brokers and banks are made subject to regulation by the Federal Reserve Board. In this way, it is desired to prevent the ebb and flow of speculation from determining in large measure the volume of bank credit that shall be outstanding, and thereby from affecting business conditions. Also, through maintaining relatively high margin requirements, it is hoped to limit the dependence of the market upon buyers using borrowed money, and make it more an investors' affair. This has been opposed by more extreme advocates of the free and open market theory.

5. Corporate "insiders" are placed in a special category. Directors, officers and owners of 10 per cent of any class of equity securities must report changes in ownership of equity issues monthly. They may not sell their securities short, and they may be compelled to return to the corporation profits made on sales of its stock issues within six months after purchase. By thus limiting trading by corporate "insiders" possessing special knowledge, it is sought to make the market more "free and open" as far as the rank and file of public buyers and sellers are concerned.

These regulations have doubtless tended to reduce the volume of speculative trading, and thus to make the market thinner at any given time. However, advocates of this type of regulation maintain that even if minute-to-minute liquidity is thereby sacrificed, these limitations on certain types of speculation will tend to iron out major fluctuations in prices of securities to some extent, especially many price movements of a needless character, while leaving the markets sensitive to broad changes in general economic conditions and the position of particular industries and corporations.

References

BOND, F. D., *Stock Movements and Speculation,* New York, 1928, chaps. viii–xi.

CASSEL, GUSTAV, "Discount Policy and Stock Exchange Speculation," *Skandinaviska Kreditaktiebolaget Quarterly,* October, 1928.

DICE, C. A., *The Stock Market,* Chicago, 1926, chap. xxii.

FLYNN, JOHN T., *Security Speculation,* New York, 1934.

HADLEY, ARTHUR T., *Economics,* New York, 1904, chap. iv.

HARDY, C. O., *Risk and Risk Bearing,* Chicago, 1923, chaps. i–iv and vii–ix.

HUEBNER, S. S., *The Stock Market,* New York, 1928, chap. xx.

KIRSHMAN, J. E., *Principles of Investment,* Chicago, 1924, chaps. i and vi.

LAVINGTON, F., *The Work of the Stock Exchange,* New York, 1922, chap. xv.

MEEKER, J. E., *The Work of the Stock Exchange,* New York, 1931.

SIMMONS, E. H. H., *Modern Capitalism,* New York, 1927, pp. 43–60.

SLOAN, L. H., *Security Speculation,* New York, 1926, chap. ix.

Chapter XV

INVESTMENT BANKING AND THE BUSINESS CYCLE

Business Fluctuations

The rate of business activity is in a constant state of flux. Periods of prosperity alternate with periods of depression. The volume of production rises and falls. There are times when employment is easy to secure and business enterprises are earning large profits, and other periods when unemployment is widespread, losses common, and economic conditions become generally bad.

This constantly changing state of business naturally has a powerful repercussion on the security markets, and therefore upon the business of investment banking. In this chapter, we are primarily concerned with the relation of business changes to securities; but in order to trace it clearly it is necessary briefly to review the nature and causes of the business changes themselves.

Types of Business Fluctuations

Economists have for more than a century given careful hought to business fluctuations. For a long time they were articularly concerned with the periodic spectacular collapse n business prosperity, or panic, which occurred several times luring the nineteenth century—otherwise a time of rapid ecoomic progress in western Europe and the United States—and heories of changes in business were called theories of panics or rises. In later years, they have come to consider changes in usiness as an organic whole, including in their studies the auses of prosperity as well as of panic and depression. This rocess of successive rise and fall is now generally defined as ne "business cycle," a term applied to such changes many years ago by French writers and popularized in this country more recently by Wesley Clair Mitchell and others.

A major forward step in the study of business cycles was taken nearly a century ago by a French engineer and mathematical economist, obscure during his own lifetime but since celebrated as a remarkably original thinker in this field. A. A. Cournot distinguished three important types of changes in business, which are now termed secular, seasonal and cyclical.[1]

If we examine the trend of industrial and trade activity in a country over a long period of time we find a long term or "secular" upswing. Several reasons account for this usual trend under these conditions. The opening up of new lands, the discovery of new natural resources, increasing technical knowledge, the development of new industries, and the growth of international commerce—all of these factors are enabling the more advanced countries of the world, and especially regions possessed of extensive natural resources relative to population, such as the United States, to enjoy an expansion of economic activity and a rise in living standards.

A second form of change now generally segregated is the variation in business activity which occurs from one season of the year to another, reflecting special climatic and other factors. Thus, industrial activity in this country is greatest in the early spring and fall, as a rule. Agriculture is most active in the fall, when the majority of crops in the temperate zone are harvested. These regular seasonal changes in business continue to occur from year to year, despite the effects of secular growth. What secular growth, when it continues, does accomplish is to make each seasonal peak higher than before, while in the regular "slack" seasons business activity does not decline as far as previously.

"Cyclical" Changes

But it has long been observed that secular and seasonal changes in business activity do not alone explain the variations which regularly take place. In the United States, for example

[1] Cournot did not distinguish seasonal fluctuations as such, using a category of "random" variations instead. See Moore, Henry Ludlow, *Generating Economic Cycles*, p. 2.

there has been a secular growth in business activity from colonial times down to the present. Seasonal changes occur fairly regularly from year to year, although interrupted on occasion by special factors. Still, over and above these two types of variations, we have alternating periods of prosperity and depression. For several years, expansion becomes much more rapid than what is regarded as "normal," and the business organization of the country appears to enjoy an unwonted stimulation; then, more or less suddenly, a retrograde movement sets in, and perhaps for several successive years the secular upward movement comes to a halt and industrial activity declines sharply. Secular expansion, therefore, does not proceed at a steady pace, but consists of periodic spurts of unusual activity, and subsequent reactions or recessions of greater or less duration.

It has become quite customary to measure the various stages of the business cycle statistically by indices based on car loadings, production of pig iron, building contracts, and similar data. The secular trend may be measured by fitting, through one or another of the common mathematical methods, a "trend line," while seasonal variations can be determined by a 12-months' moving average, or the link relative method.[2] When the secular and seasonal trends have been eliminated from the index, there is left the cyclical change alone, which shows deviations above or below a normal line.

The application of these mathematical methods results in a quantitative measurement of business changes which is to some extent spuriously precise. An index of general business velocity is a rough average which only partially and approximately represents the true general business situation as it exists at any time. The application of mathematical curve-fitting methods to such statistics, for the purpose of eliminating secular trend, and of other methods for getting rid of seasonal variation, represents further approximations which make the final results subject to a wide margin of error. Hence, it is wise for the student to use these undoubtedly valuable statistical devices for segregating and measuring cyclical business changes with a full realization of their approximate character, in order to avoid

[2] For a description of these techniques cf. Mills, F. C., *Statistical Methods.*

unjustifiable dogmatizing with them as a basis, as some advocates and extreme exponents of the use of these methods are in the habit of doing.

True Nature of the Business Cycle

The usual representation of a business cycle as a periodic change in statistical averages of business activity conceals the fact that different industries often pass through cycles of their own, quite apart from that represented by an average or combination of different industries.

In particular, there is inevitably a marked discrepancy between the average rate of activity of the capital goods or heavy industries and that of the consumers' goods or light industries at different phases of the business cycle. During a severe depression, the heavy industries may come almost to a standstill for a time, as the nation finds its available capital equipment excessive and the incentive for expanding capacity further disappears. On the other hand, the consumers' goods industries, serving as they do the necessary current needs of the population, may suffer only a small recession. The more highly developed a country becomes, and the larger the proportion of its industrial equipment that is devoted to the manufacture of production goods, the wider the possible range of fluctuation of general industrial activity.

On the other hand, certain new industries may enjoy a persistent growth of their own for a time without much regard to cyclical changes elsewhere—the automobile, radio, rayon and airplane industries being in this class.

The fact of the matter is, therefore, that the business cycle is a composite and approximate affair. During a period of prosperity more individual industries are active and profitable while during a period of depression an unusual number of industries reduce their operations, throw people out of employment and report losses from operations.

The business cycle is largely influenced, although to a varying degree in each case, by financial developments. A period of prosperity may be greatly extended by bank credit expansion which increases the buying power available for both capital goods and consumers' goods for a time. Conversely, rapid credit contraction intensifies a depression, since part of the purchasing power of the community is diverted from new purchases to the repayment of old debts. If at the same time the depression is marked by numerous failures of banks and other financial institutions, as was the case in the 1930-1933 period, the contraction of purchasing power, and hence of industrial and trade activity, will be all the more severe. At such times, credit contraction may in fact become by far the most important factor determining the course of the business cycle.

The fact that individual industries enjoy their own cycles, and that the generalized "business cycle" usually referred to represents merely an average of conditions, is a factor of great importance to the security markets. It means that different groups of securities will be subjected to varying conditions during any given period of prosperity or depression. Hence, any effects of the business cycle as a whole on the security markets which are here traced are understood to be general or average effects, subject to numerous exceptions and variations in individual cases.

Duration and Amplitude of Business Cycles

During the earlier period of business cycle studies, efforts were made to find a regular periodicity in such changes and thus to develop a method of controlling or at least of forecasting them. Some writers spoke of twenty-year cycles, others of eight-year cycles, others of eleven-year cycles. They then sought to prove their contention as to the length of the cycle by applying refined curve-fitting methods to statistics of business changes. In this way, they succumbed to the dangers of regarding rough and approximate though mathematically correct methods as exact and accurate representations of the very complex business situation.

More recently, most writers on the subject have adopted a more realistic attitude, and have come to agree that the business cycle is a generalized affair of varying length and amplitude, and that any regularity in its rhythm may be destroyed by such special events as wars, new inventions, new currency or banking changes, etc. Periods of more or less sustained prosperity can be isolated covering five or six years on end, while others may last a year or two. The cyclical movement is in itself a generally admitted fact, but any regularity in its length or degree of variation is widely doubted.

Since the panic of 1929 a good many observers have attempted to use the enormous amounts of statistical data which had been developed from many sources as a result of the 1929 breakdown, for the purpose of throwing further light on the amplitude of business cycles. One phase of the matter which especially attracted attention was the extraordinary length of the depression which opened in 1930 and which appeared to run counter to all of the previously accepted views as to the probable duration of the period from "trough" to "trough" in a depression. Professor H. L. Reed of Cornell University has examined some of these efforts, and particularly the view that the prolongation of the present depression is due to a contraction of the outstanding credit volume in the United States. His opinion is that proof is lacking to show that the long continuance of the depression which began in 1930 was due to the failure to expand the volume of credit sufficiently early, and that many extraneous events contributed to making the depression longer and more severe than it would otherwise have been. Bank failures, international financial troubles, and the excesses of the preceding boom period may be mentioned as some of them. Continuous testing of banking conditions and the application of conservative methods of credit control seem to him proper as a preliminary to successful economic managemen during a crisis or depression. Both Professor Reed and othe careful students are evidently disposed to regard the duratio of the "cycle" as a matter greatly influenced by government an central bank management, and in no way fixed or automati

Causes of the Cycle

Students of business fluctuations have differed over thei causes. Several score of explanations for the cycle have bee advanced at one time or another, and many of them have en joyed considerable vogue and have occasionally become a popu lar fashion in economic discussion.

These explanations fall into two broad groups—single an pluralistic. Among the single causes which have been advance to explain the business cycle are rainfall variation, variation in the volume of building construction, excessive savings, excessive competition, over-capitalization of profits, changes in the volume of bank credit outstanding, etc. Leading students of the subject have to an increasing extent recognized that cyclical business movements are the resultant of a variety of factors. At one time one of these factors, at other times another, plays the dominant rôle.

The record of past theories is chiefly valuable, perhaps, as a caution against future attempts to dogmatize narrowly on the subject. The truth is that what has thus far been done in business cycle theory is purely tentative and preliminary.

Prices and the Business Cycle

Commodity price changes have played a major rôle in business cycle discussion. Here an average of price changes can be obtained through the device known as the index number which generalizes the changes in a group of individual commodity prices.

Changes in prices have been ascribed by some writers chiefly to variations in the volume of gold production and by others to changes in the supply of bank credit. Others have emphasized the importance of the evolution of the more efficient production methods. At any rate, price changes have not been cyclical in character and they cannot be said to parallel cyclical changes in business activity. Hence, while price changes may exercise an important rôle in shaping the course of business cycle change, they can hardly be said to be a major cause, although one authority has actually written that such change in commodity prices—that is, in the value or purchasing power of money—is the business cycle." Such views are today without material support.

The greatly increased technical proficiency of American industry, as well as the large extent to which the country is self-sufficient, has tended to make the price level relatively less sensitive to cyclical changes in business activity. In addition, efforts in various industries to control prices by mergers, agreements and cooperation have also contributed to price stabilization in the face of fluctuating business conditions. Thus, during the decade of credit inflation following the war, commodity prices were remarkably stable because the stimulus thereby given was offset by the increased volume of production, rather than by a rise in price. When this stimulus was withdrawn and credit deflation followed, commodity prices declined sharply. Beginning with 1933, despite the numerous measures then taken to boost prices, only a relatively moderate recovery in the price level followed. This experience tends to support the view that greatly increased technical efficiency causes the main price trend to be downward, so that periods of deflation may be regularly marked in the future by material recessions in commodity prices, while subsequent recoveries may witness far more moderate advances in the price level.

The question thus incidentally raised is in a sense the really fundamental issue for this phase of the subject. Is money and change in its various forms the cause, either sole or primary, of changes in prices, and thus the originator of cyclical movements, or do the latter produce changes in prices? The issue thus brought to the front appears in many phases of contemporary economic discussion. It would be impossible in a general work such as the present to follow through these ramifications of economic controversy. What is chiefly important is to express a general opinion for use in connection with investment discussion as here presented. This is, that while changes in the volume and velocity of money and credit have important effects upon commodity values, they certainly cannot be isolated in such a way as to assign them as the sole or main cause of extensive business changes. What is called "inflation" is frequently spoken of as a primary cause of an upward followed by a sharp downward movement of business, but careful study o the subject has shown that periods of large and expanding busi ness are often periods of downward movement of commodit prices, as in the years from 1926 to 1929; while it has sometime happened that decline of business is accompanied by risin prices because of special factors which have operated to alte the relationship between money and commodities. The olde idea, that an enlargement of the quantity of gold available o a great expansion of bank credit—"easy money," in short—ad vances prices and so forces a return of prosperity, is pretty ger erally abandoned, although it sometimes figures as a political doctrine. Thus, for example, President Roosevelt early in his administration undertook to "restore" the price level of 1926, because by so doing he would alter the relation between debtors and creditors to the advantage of the former. He sought this end by lowering the gold content of the dollar and by introducing a régime of easy money and lax bank credit, urging the discounting of paper based upon real estate. When these methods were unsuccessful, he insisted on the necessity of forcing the desired change of prices, and added, "Do it we will"—apparently in the belief that a favorable turn in the "business cycle" could be compelled through monetary and credit manipulation.

The tendency of recent discussion has undoubtedly been to regard money and credit in the business cycle as merely a medium through which the volume of business activity is influenced by reason of the variations in profits that may grow out of such changes. If, for example, public policy results in cheapening the cost of capital by reducing rates of interest for accommodation, it may be possible for businesses that are operating on a narrow margin of return to continue or expand their activities without running into the "red," as they otherwise might be driven to do. In this case it might be said that more abundant supplies of credit had forced a return of business activity, whereas the truth would be that the acceptance by some government institution of the responsibility for providing loans at less than their current economic value had resulted in enlarging profits in given industries and, hence, in enabling the latter to continue to do business when they would otherwise have curtailed operations because of the absence of profits.

Many economists would at any rate assert that a major change in prices would at any one time constitute a dominating factor in the business cycle; for if prices advance sharply at any one time, the result is a material increase in business profits and a strong temptation to business men to expand their productivity in order to profit further from the rising prices. On the other hand, a sharp drop in general prices will cause most business men to lose money and therefore to curtail their operations. However, in many cases price changes and variations in the level of business activity are both caused by the same factor—such as, at times, credit and banking changes.

Business Cycles and Securities

The above *résumé* of business cycle theory is presented as a background for the purpose of tracing the effects of business fluctuations upon prices and markets.

In the first place, a clear-cut division must be made for this purpose between securities receiving a fixed income, such as straight bonds and preferred stocks, and those receiving an income contingent upon earning power, that is, common stocks or convertible or participating bonds and preferred stocks. Each of these two main groups of securities is affected in a special way by changes in the business cycle, and to a large extent their prices vary in opposite directions.

There is, of course, no automatic or mechanical effect of business changes upon security prices. Whatever effects the business cycle may have are exercised through its influence upon the supply of, or demand for, any particular type of security. If changes in business activity resulted in no change in these two sets of factors, there would be no occasion for any resulting major variation in the level of security prices.

As a rule, however, changes in the state of business do exercise a profound effect upon the factors of supply and demand in the capital markets. More active business and higher profits mean a larger demand for capital, and thus lead to willingness by borrowers to pay a higher rate of interest on the securities they issue. On the other hand, rising business profits attract additional buying, partly of a speculative character based on borrowed funds, in the capital market. The bulk of this additional demand for securities, of course, turns at such times to issues not limited as to return which are in a position to benefit fully from the increase in the earning power of business enterprises, primarily common stocks.

It would be of great significance and value from the standpoint of an investment policy and as a practical guide in the making of investments, if some generalizations, even of the roughest kind, could be laid down with respect to the probable recurrence of the cyclical movements already mentioned. If this could be done, it is evident that intending purchasers could avoid placing their orders while prices were moving downward, and would wait for the most favorable conditions. In attempting to establish a basis for foreshadowing cyclical movements for this practical purpose, two factors appear to be of most interest. The first is the period which may be expected to elapse between "peaks" in security prices or, on the other hand, the low points of such prices. The second and more important is the group of symptoms that are to be taken as indicative of the fact that the curve of business and values has reached or is about to reach the turning point, whether up or down. If actual light on these two problems can be had, the investor, particularly the large investor, is furnished with information of the utmost value to him. He may make serious mistakes in judgment with respect to any particular security, but these will tend to "average out," when judged in connection with the large number of securities.

Phases of the Business Cycle

Do statistical data furnish any actual light on the first of these questions—the probable period of the business cycle? We have already seen that economists believe that data are wanting to establish any given length of cycle. To them the only essential or interesting phase of the whole question is the recognition of the distinguishing marks or phases characteristic of the upward and downward movements of business and values.

Four such successive phases are listed by recent authoritative writers, and the business cycle is identified with the successive recurrence of these phases in regular order. These are revival, prosperity, liquidation and, at times, panic and depression. Evidently, if it be true that a business cycle is merely a succession of these phases in regular order, what is necessary is to recognize the particular phase through which the cycle is at the moment passing. It is then possible, presumably, to foreshadow coming stages.

In order to trace more clearly the effects of the business cycle on the security markets through these supply and demand factors, the status of the two important classes of securities—those that receive fixed income and those entitled to residual earnings, shares of common stock—should be studied in each stage of the cycle. Let us examine therefore the four phases through which values of all kinds are believed to pass in order to fulfill a complete cycle of movement. The first is designated by some writers as a phase of revival from a period of depression, and is characterized by increasing activity.

Security Markets in Periods of Business Revival

During such a period of increasing activity, the confidence of the investing public in the security market is not at first very great. Accordingly, there is a general tendency to seek what appear to be "safer" securities, and bonds are therefore in demand. At the same time, the increasing demand for credit as the revival proceeds may tend to raise interest rates slowly, so that the advancing tendency in bond prices may be halted as the revival enters its later stages. However, easy-money policies of central banks may, as in 1934-1936, intensify the rise in bond prices and postpone any turn in their trend.

Stock prices, on the other hand, will reflect the change in the business situation more slowly but more decisively. As prices begin to rise with the revival of business, deferred liquidation may prevent the advance from assuming larger proportions for some time. On other occasions, when optimism concerning the future business situation is quickly established, a rapid advance may occur forthwith. Stocks of companies in the capital goods industries, especially as the revival proceeds, tend to rise in price more rapidly than the more stable consumers' goods issues.

This may be called the typical period of accumulation in the stock market. It is characterized by an effort on the part of better-informed investors, and especially large financial and industrial interests, to obtain as large quantities as possible of given issues in which they have confidence. Their optimism leads them to stand ready to pay higher prices than those which on the average have seemed to the rank and file of investors to be warranted. As a result, values advance, while the floating supply tends to become more and more closely massed in a relatively small number of hands. This is reflected in a preponderance of odd-lot selling orders and full-lot buying orders in the statistics on trading gathered by the Securities and Exchange Commission.

Phase of Prosperity and Distribution

The prosperity phase of the business cycle is reached when the volume of activity goes above that indicated by the "normal" rate of growth. When the revival has proceeded far enough, the capital goods industries generally find that they have an unusual quantity of orders, and expansion is in order. Thus, heavy building operations lead to large orders for steel, which in turn call for heavy coal production and increased railway traffic. The stimulation thus spreads from industry to industry, and may be hastened by firmer prices occasioned by the keener demand. Any fear of higher prices that prevails may result in large forward orders; and when this occurs on a sufficiently large scale "boom" conditions may be said to prevail.

The expansion characteristic of such periods results in an increasing demand for capital and in rising interest rates. This tends to depress bond prices if central banking authorities do not interfere. If they seek to check the "boom" by tightening interest rates the decline in bond prices may be accentuated. In addition, the rapid growth of earnings reported at such times attracts the public to stocks, so that bonds decline in relative favor among investors. In the stock market, as prosperity unfolds itself, stocks rise sharply, above all as public enthusiasm is engendered by hopes of large speculative profits. The sharp increase in the volume of trading which usually occurs at such times is the best indication of the fact that the public is flocking into the market.

A time comes when, in the opinion of those informed buyers who have been purchasing stocks during the revival period, advantage may be gained by selling them. From their point of view, the general level of values is regarded as "too high." When is a security or group of securities too high? Fundamentally, of course, when prospective earnings are being over-discounted. When such a situation occurs, those who are holding the security are warranted in the belief that a lower level of prices will shortly be established for it. A period of distribution or "unloading" then sets in; and during this period prices may remain unchanged and then move downward, as better-informed holders endeavor to dispose of their securities at prices which they believe are still in advance of the true levels of value dictated by information or new developments which have become known in connection with securities. At such times pool operations to facilitate distribution were formerly common. As during the period of accumulation, there may be and probably are many exceptions furnished by the issues which have power to resist the general trend of things. But liquidation in one section of the market tends to affect others, so that if the selling becomes drastic, few securities may be able to avoid its effects.

As the decline in stocks gets under way at the end of a period of prosperity, bond prices generally continue to drop for a time. The liquidation of bonds is partly a result of efforts by speculators to curtail their operations by selling securities which have declined least. That a change in the trend of interest rates is at hand may be ignored by the market under such circumstances. Liquidation by financial institutions desiring to get into a more liquid position may also be a factor. Efforts of large industrial and financial interests to distribute blocks of stocks may or may not be accompanied by a downward price movement at first. Such sales may be made at a time when rumors of actual evidence indicate improved earnings and higher dividends, so that a buying fever sets in and a large enough demand is called into play to absorb the offerings placed on the market. Distribution, then, often takes place with a well-maintained or even rising price level, because of the fact that the rank and file of small investors and traders are of the opinion that business opportunities warrant strong confidence in the future price level.

It should, moreover, be remembered that the basic factors which influence the prices for stocks and bonds are of a deep-seated economic character, and that as they work more or less powerfully upon given issues of securities, the latter move up or down with reference to one another. Thus it may be that, in a period of depression, a given share or group of shares maintains its stability or reaches a higher level at the same time that others fall. This is particularly likely to be true of issues that represent a new industry that is proof against depression influences. The basic factor of earning power, present and prospective, may thus cause individual securities and groups of securities to move contrary to the general trend. It remains true that such exceptions rather tend to prove the rule since they depend for their validity ordinarily upon the fact that the security in question is new, the industry which it represents not having been subject to the same general factors of development and exploitation that have regulated the investment of capital in other and competing enterprises.

Liquidation or Panic

The pendulum of business prosperity inevitably swings too far, leading to a reaction which often is proportional in its severity and extent to the preceding upswing. In the business field, this reaction reflects the over-production and credit inflation which usually occur during the enthusiasm of the boom, leading to a falling off of orders and, often, decline in commodity prices. On the security markets, speculation based on the discounting of future increases in corporate earnings and dividends collapses, and liquidation follows in which values may soon be drastically adjusted.

The symptoms of this change in the business situation differ in individual cases. In most instances in the past, persistent expansion in the volume of production, rising commodity prices, an apparent shortage of many types of goods, and high interest rates have been common characteristic symptoms of such an approaching turn in the business situation. When the liquidation reaches panic proportions, all security prices may be swept downward without exception. When the reaction is less severe, selling of stocks may be accompanied before long by buying of bonds as investors seek to safeguard their principal by placing their money in protected, fixed-income-bearing securities. Also, as short-term interest rates drop with the decline in the demand for funds, encouragement is given to the buying of bonds. A major rise in bond prices has, in the past, often dated from a period of severe liquidation or panic in the stock market.

The rise in stock prices generally has culminated before the period of severe liquidation or panic arrives. By that time, the leading financial and industrial interests have generally distributed large blocks of stock to the public. Professional speculators may still be active in the market, but it is common for this element to be caught in the toils of the panic because of their desire to continue profitable operations as long as possible. As liquidation develops, the decline in stock prices tends to be extremely rapid because of the impairment of speculative margin accounts. Just as in the rise of stock prices speculators pyramid their commitments, using paper profits on one transaction to support another, so on the decline the wiping out of margins in one commitment compels throwing other holdings overboard.

Credit Management

Within recent years, a new variant of an old theory has been put forward as a phase of what is called "managed currency" or credit management. This is the notion that the moment when prices begin to turn downward—as, say, at the end of 1929—it is possible for the banking mechanism to arrest liquidation and check depression tendencies by simply expanding the volume of credit available to the community through resort by the central bank to open market buying operations particularly of government securities. Thus, for example, it has been suggested that in 1930, "it was not sufficient for the reserve banks to reduce discount rates sharply and rapidly. Open market management through purchases of government securities should have been carried beyond the point at which, generally speaking, the average member bank was relieved of debt," thus leading to the creation of excess reserves.

Politicians have found in this theory a useful issue for application in current contests in several countries. They have won a following because the hardships of "deflation" have always been unpopular.

This contention presupposes (1) that prices should never be allowed to recede, but should be kept stable or rising; or else (2) that if prices do recede the recession should not be allowed to go beyond a certain "normal" level whose nature and location are not indicated. There is here a large field of discussion in which opinion is far from uniform among economists, although most of them have rejected the cruder forms of the "credit control" doctrine. What is admitted is that at a time of panic or sharp recession any effort to hold business within check and limit speculation then under way should be discontinued, leaving the economic mechanism to right itself. The reply made by many advocates of "planned money" is substantially this: Why wait for an automatic righting of a disturbed economy when the work can be so much more promptly and effectually done through planning or combined effort? The answer, of course, would be favorable to the use of the planning method, provided there were any assurance of its success. Thus far, there is little conclusive evidence that the planners who propose to take charge of the process of rectifying conditions are any more reliable or possess better judgment than the business men and bankers whose over-optimism had brought about the difficulty in the first place. However, control is doubtless more effective when used to curb a boom han to check a panic.

Phase of Depression

The final stage in the so-called cycle of investment events may be described as a period of depression. During this period usiness conditions are at low ebb. Stock prices are adjusting hemselves to the new circumstances through further sharp eclines. After a while, the stock market becomes dull and quoations fluctuate irregularly around the low level established y the decline.

As the period of depression and impaired general confidence ontinues, a surplus of funds awaiting investment accumulates. his surplus gradually finds its way into high-grade bonds. iterest rates decline as the demand for capital continues small the face of this increasing supply, so that bond prices may ell enjoy a major upward movement before the depression over. Only as signs of business revival multiply does buying stocks, especially of a speculative character, again attain subantial proportions.

Relation to an Investment Policy

The cyclical movements we have traced naturally have an important relation to our theory of investment. The investor will normally desire to stay out of the stock market and to keep his funds in high-grade bonds as far as possible in periods of prosperity, even when things appear most reassuring. Conversely, he will want to shift his funds and bonds into stocks whenever he believes that a revival of business is at hand. Obviously if all investors were perfectly informed and acted under the same influences, the investment cycle would be largely "ironed out," since all would refrain from buying at the high point and all would enter the market at the low, and high and low points would tend to disappear; but confronted by the actual phenomena of booms and depressions, the rank and file of investors and speculators continue to buy freely in good times and to sell in periods of decline.

Buyers and sellers are not actuated by any common motive or body of information. A great many of them analyze the market quite differently from others, and buy when others are selling. Again, it is also true that there are numerous investors who find it necessary, because of large income, to buy practically steadily regardless of cyclical fluctuations of this sort. There are others who prefer not to sacrifice the regular income which is lost in keeping funds idle, but make long term commitments without regard to capital gains.

Problem of Forecasting

In the effort to adapt himself to changes in the busines cycle the investor naturally encounters the question whethe it is possible to forecast market changes. Various agencies whic purport thus to forecast the course of prices have been formed and they offer "services" which are designed to perform thi function in some way.

Clearly, they all depend for their success upon the existenc of a business cycle. They are able to furnish only approximat indications of broad changes in values; and those who are wise undertake to do no more than to indicate alterations in funda mental factors, such as activity of trade, employment, outpu price movements and the like, leaving the investor to draw h own inferences. Their value is greatest, as a rule, in compiling and presenting data relating to individual securities and the businesses the latter represent.

Experience since the panic of 1929 illustrates this condition. During the five years following this panic, the end of the depression and the return of prosperity were repeatedly predicted without success, and as a result buying policies were prematurely initiated.

Immediately prior to the panic of 1929, there was a small group of investors, as well as some bankers and industrialists, who felt rather vaguely that conditions were dangerous and that an important reversal of trend was near. They converted their holdings of stocks into government bonds, and their action in so doing doubtless helped to modify the trend of events which began with the panic of October, 1929. The end of the year 1929 found a certain number of large investors, and investment trusts, with their funds in securities of the type just indicated, or in cash.

The question then became urgent: What should be the policy of those who had thus placed themselves in a position to buy securities more cheaply than they could have acquired them for a long time preceding? Three lines of policy were indicated. The first was the immediate repurchase of securities, particularly of stocks, in order to gain the advantage of the advance which many asserted would shortly be resumed. Those who followed this advice, and so helped to start the "pseudo-boom market" of the spring of 1930, suffered from the further severe declines of the second phase of the depression which began about the middle of 1930. It was this policy that was publicly advocated by President Hoover.

A second group of observers advocated continuous conversion of stocks into bonds on the ground that an extended depression and a further shrinkage of values were likely and that bonds, although still high, would probably not fall in any such degree as would stocks. A large number of investors followed this plan, the result being to accelerate the decline of stock prices after the summer of 1930, or to cause comparative firmness in bonds for a time. Because of the fact that many issues of bonds then on the market were "bonds" in name only, there were great differences in the course of prices of various groups of bonds; only the best liens succeeded in holding their value in any considerable degree, many others falling off as sharply as preferred or common stocks. Generally speaking, those who followed this policy did so at a loss, except in cases where bond purchases were of the highest grade. The latter, and especially those who confined themselves largely to government bonds, succeeded substantially in maintaining the value of their capital.

The third policy involved the retention of cash or government bonds until stocks had reached a level at which they seemed completely "liquidated"; bonds were then to be sold and stocks taken on. This advice became especially urgent after the announcement of a policy of devaluation by the Roosevelt Administration in 1933. Meantime, however, so many unexpected industrial and political factors had begun to influence our business life that those who undertook to convert their bonds into stocks did not benefit immediately, and certain groups of stocks, like those of many utility holding companies and railroads, barely participated in the recovery.

The entire experience showed that an investment policy designed to benefit from cyclical business and credit changes can usually be applied only within limits, and is no substitute for the exercise of considered judgment based upon the course of events, many of which are the outgrowth of psychological or legislative changes.

Forecasting as to individual securities or groups of securitie in which earnings, assets, management, and the like are care fully estimated and then studied in their relationship to th more general influences operative in the market is a more re stricted but more practical task.

International Aspects

Business cycles have necessarily displayed considerable co respondence in various countries in view of the many com mercial and financial relations that prevail internationall However, relatively stable and self-contained countries lik France and Russia are less subject to such fluctuations than ar nations like Great Britain and the United States.

Movements of security prices may begin in one country and proceed to a considerable extent before being followed anywhere else. Noting this difference in the stages, or degree of progress, of the cyclical movement in the various countries, some investors have felt that they could transfer funds from one country to another in such a way as to anticipate local changes in security prices. This effort has been made, for example, by some investment trusts which believed that they could successfully sell out in a country where securities had been overvalued and thereafter shift their funds to a country where securities were depressed.

The fact is that there often exists a plethora of funds in one market, and at the same time a corresponding shortage in another. But these discrepancies do not automatically adjust themselves, and hence such international diversification may not prove to be a profitable policy. The "high" market may go much higher, while the depressed market remains low. This was the case after 1926 with investment trusts which sought to protect themselves from a decline in the rapidly rising American market by buying in such countries as Germany where money was very scarce and prices remained low. Since 1931, owing to unprecedentedly high trade barriers, interferences with the international flow of capital, foreign exchange restrictions and monetary changes, security prices in one country have had little relation to those elsewhere. In such conditions, it is especially dangerous for investors to follow a policy of international diversification, especially when investment conditions at home are relatively untrammeled, as in the United States. There is good argument in favor of a policy of buying only in hose markets of which investors possess immediate personal knowledge, and where expert advice is available, instead of being guided by the assumption that outsiders may successfully qualize their returns or escape unfavorable conditions in one market by hastily buying in another.

The Business Cycle and Investment Banking

The investment banking business, serving as it does industry and trade in general, is much affected by the business cycle. irst, cyclical changes affect quotations of securities, and therefore the conditions and prices at which new issues can be marketed. Secondly, the business cycle has an important influence upon the business of the various types of financial institutions. The policy of the investment banker necessarily must be to adapt himself to such changes and to avoid any injurious or embarrassing effects which they may produce upon his own operations. Such possible influences may be briefly summarized as follows:

1. Dealers and brokers may build up large organizations that involve operating losses when activity falls off sharply.

2. Excess inventories are more dangerous to a security dealer than to other industries. Such a situation, resulting as it does in serious loss, may be avoided only through careful watching of the market and more or less successful forecasting of tendencies.

The Senate sub-Committee on Banking which investigated the operations of security affiliates of banks in 1931-1932, received reports showing the results of their underwriting operations after a period of prosperity. In one conspicuous case, it appeared that a commitment made by the affiliate on the verge of the 1929 panic had resulted in a loss greater than its entire profits during the preceding ten years. Other illustrations of the same sort, although none of quite so striking a character, were observed. The risk involved in single underwriting operations is very great in relation to the banker's capital, particularly at times of critical change in the securities market; it cannot be eliminated but may be greatly reduced by care and prudence.

3. Financial institutions may suffer declines in quotations and impairment of liquidity of portfolio investments, causing losses and perhaps endangering solvency.

Investment bankers may in some measure protect themselves against adverse effects from the business cycle through the combining of several types of business within one organization; and this factor has been one of the major incentives to the combination of functions which has been common in recent years Thus, a house handling only bonds may have little to do in times of active stock market speculation; but if it has a stock brokerage department also, or an unlisted trading department it is prepared to expand its stock business at such times. Bro kerage houses with commodity trading departments may make money from these when the security markets are relatively inactive. The aim of the Securities and Exchange Commission to segregate brokers' from dealers' functions may hamper such efforts in the future.

References

Adams, A. B., *Economics of Business Cycles,* New York, 1925, chaps. v-ix.

Chamberlain, L., and Edwards, G. W., *Principles of Bond Investment,* New York, 1927, chap. xlii.

Edie, Lionel D., *Money, Bank Credit and Prices,* New York, 1928, chap. xviii.

Kirshman, J. E., *Principles of Investment,* Chicago, 1924, chaps. xxvi–xxvii.

Mitchell, Wesley C., *Business Cycles,* New York, 1927, chaps. i, ii and v.

Moore, Henry L., *Generating Economic Cycles,* New York, 1923.

Reed, Harold L., "Stabilization Doctrine," *Quarterly Journal of Economics,* August, 1935, pp. 600 ff.

Snyder, Carl, *Business Cycles and Business Measurements,* New York, 1927, chaps. i and xii.

Twentieth Century Fund, *The Security Markets,* New York, 1935, chap. vii.

Willis, H. P., and Chapman, J. M., *The Economics of Inflation,* New York, 1935.

Part Three

Investment Banking Practice

Chapter XVI

THE LEGAL FRAMEWORK

Securities Legislation

Until the early years of this century, as we have already seen, the investment banking business was largely free from regulation by specific legislation. While fraud was punishable here as in other relations, the rule of *caveat emptor*—let the buyer beware—prevailed to a large extent. As we shall see presently, purchasers of securities did have some well-defined legal remedies in the event of misrepresentation, but these stemmed from general common law principles.

Special legislation to regulate the sale of securities was first passed by the states, beginning with Kansas in 1911. However, since the jurisdiction of such statutes could not cross state lines, and since the state blue-sky laws varied greatly in their scope and character, such regulation was of limited effectiveness. The widespread losses caused to investors by the violent deflation in the security markets during the early 'thirties, and the evidences of loose practices brought out by the Senate investigations of 1932 and 1933, led to the enactment of a comprehensive scheme of federal regulation designed to prevent certain abuses and undesirable conditions in the financial markets. Two major pieces of legislation, the Federal Securities Act of 1933 and the Securities Exchange Act of 1934, were the outcome.

The Federal Securities Act is concerned with the flotation of new issues of securities. It provides for adequate disclosure by the issuer, underwriters and dealers who are concerned with a new security offering. It also imposes civil and criminal liabilities upon sellers of securities who fail to conform to its provisions, or who make misrepresentations of material fact or omit material facts.

The Securities Exchange Act of 1934 provides for federal regulation of security exchanges and their members, requires certain disclosures of fact from companies whose securities are listed, subjects security loans to the regulation of the Board of Governors of the Federal Reserve System, and brings the over-the-counter markets under a measure of federal regulation. It is so comprehensive in character, however, that it affects the business of originating and distributing securities in several respects, as well as trading in already issued securities.

Despite the enactment of federal legislation, the state blue-sky laws continue in effect, and sellers of securities must conform to them. They are discussed in a later chapter.

It must not be supposed that the federal security legislation to safeguard investors from misrepresentations was altogether a new departure. Before studying this legislation, it will help the reader to gain a proper perspective if he will first consider the traditional common law provisions affecting such transactions.

Common Law Liability

Even before the states or Congress legislated on the subject, the vendor of securities was subject to certain common law liabilities in connection with their sale. The vendor, through his offering circulars and through his salesmen, made certain representations with regard to the security being offered. Under the common law, the buyer is entitled to recover from the seller when the latter makes a false representation of fact which is known to him to be false when made, which is made with the intent of influencing the buyer and which causes damage to him. It is also necessary to prove, however, that the buyer acted on this false representation.

This type of suit is known among lawyers as the action of "deceit." It is evident that the buyer must prove:

1. That a misrepresentation of fact was made to him.
2. That the misrepresentation was made knowingly.
3. That it was made with intent that the buyer act on it.
4. That the buyer does rely on this representation.
5. That he has been caused damage.

In practice, however, it is generally difficult, if not impossible, to prove that the vendor himself made a misrepresentation of fact, and made it knowingly. Mere carelessness is not sufficient to impose liability. Bankers formerly sought to escape liability for statements in their offering circulars by including a "hedge clause" to the effect that the contents of the offering circular "though taken from sources believed to be reliable, are not guaranteed by us." But since liability for false statements cannot generally be escaped by attributing them to other persons, it is doubtful whether such hedge clauses had any practical significance. An added difficulty in bringing an action of deceit is that it must revolve around a representation of fact, and not the assertion of mere opinion.

A second and easier remedy for the buyer of securities who purchased on the strength of misstatement is provided by the common law in the shape of an action known as "rescission." Such actions may be brought only by the original buyer who has bought from the person circulating a false statement about a security. The buyer in this case must merely prove that he relied upon a misrepresentation of fact. Upon discovering such misrepresentation, he must demand cancellation of the sale, tendering the securities in return for his money. It is not necessary to prove that the person who makes or circulates a false fact, or who conceals a material fact, was himself possessed of any intent to misrepresent.

This common law protection which the buyer of securities shares with the purchaser of any other good is not infringed by federal legislation. Such actions may still be brought, but under the statute the liabilities of security sellers have now been made more specific, and have been extended.

The Registration Procedure

The fundamental change in investment banking practice effected by the Federal Securities Act is the requirement that securities must be registered before sale. The purpose of this step is twofold. First, it makes necessary the filing of pertinent facts about each offering in advance with the Securities and Exchange Commission, so that the latter can prevent its sale if found desirable for any reason in the public interest. Secondly, a record of the representations made by the security seller is thus preserved, so that false or misleading statements, or omissions of material facts, can be more readily proved and the buyer protected. As has commonly been stated, it is thus sought to change the basic rule from that of *caveat emptor* to that of *caveat vendor.*

The Act, in an appendix, outlines the contents of a registration statement, but gives the Securities and Exchange Commission the authority to modify the requirements by its regulations. The Commission has promulgated a series of forms that prospective issuers of securities must use in registering their securities in advance of sale. The most common form, known as A-2, is to be utilized in the registration of most corporate issues. Special forms have been devised for the registration of issues of investment trusts, companies undergoing reorganization, certificates of deposit, oil royalty interests, etc. The Commission has also prepared an instruction book to facilitate the registration process.

Unless a security is exempt from the registration requirement of the Act, a registration statement must be filed with the Commission in triplicate, and at least one copy must be signed by the issuing corporation, its principal executive, financial, and accounting officers, and the majority of its board of directors. In the case of a foreign corporation, the statement must be signed by its duly authorized representative in the United States, although in the case of a foreign government flotation the underwriter alone need sign. The effective date of the registration statement is the twentieth day after the filing, except in the case of foreign government issues where it is seven days. The statement may be amended, however, during the waiting period without changing the effective date, with the approval of the Commission. As a matter of fact, the Commission has adopted a very flexible policy in this respect, permitting the corporation to withhold from the registration statement the price of offering, the names of the underwriters, and other important details until shortly before the date when selling may begin.

Whenever the Commission finds that a registration statement is incomplete or inaccurate in any material respects, it may issue an order refusing to permit the statement to become effective until amended in the manner desired. The Commission may also issue a stop order suspending the effectiveness of a registration statement, but in such event it must give the applicant a personal hearing within fifteen days after serving the notice. Where fraud is involved, sale may be stopped by application for an injunction from a federal court.

It is thus apparent that a registration statement becomes effective when the Securities and Exchange Commission does nothing to prevent this from taking place. It does not have to take any affirmative action, therefore, in order to permit the distribution of the securities to begin.

Exemptions

Under the Federal Securities Act, certain groups of securities are specifically exempted from the registration requirements. The exemptions include United States government, state and municipal obligations, securities issued by eleemosynary corporations, building and loan securities, railroad issues which require the approval of the Interstate Commerce Commission, certificates issued by a trustee in bankruptcy, insurance and annuity contracts and other security issues up to $100,000 in size that are exempted under the special regulations of the Securities and Exchange Commission covering such smaller offerings.

Where a security is exchanged by the issuer with its existing security holders exclusively, and where no commission or other remuneration is solicited for committing such exchange, exemption is given. This facilitates corporate readjustments. Also, securities issued under reorganizations approved by a court, and offerings sold to persons residing within a single state or territory, thus constituting a purely intrastate transaction, are also released from the registration requirement.

The registration requirement applies only to securities publicly offered by an issuer and those sold by an issuer through underwriters or dealers. Brokerage transactions executed upon customers' orders are naturally exempted from the provisions of the Federal Securities Act.

The sale of a security requiring registration before the statement becomes effective is made unlawful under the Act, and is subject to both criminal penalties and civil liabilities.

The Prospectus

In addition to registration with the Securities and Exchange Commission, the Federal Securities Act requires that every buyer of an issue not exempt from its provisions be furnished with a prospectus that meets the specifications laid down in the statute. In general, the prospectus must contain the bulk of the information given in the registration statement, although through its regulations a very material shortening of the prospectus has been authorized by the Commission. As a result of rulings which permit mere mention of certain exhibits in the registration statement, the size of the prospectus has been reduced markedly. Furthermore, the Commission has authorized the use of a short form of prospectus in newspaper advertisements, so that the latter have come to resemble increasingly those used before the Federal Securities Act was enacted.

In order to meet the requirements that every buyer of a security be furnished with a prospectus, it has become common to mail a copy of the prospectus along with the securities when they are delivered to the purchaser, unless it is known that the latter has received a copy from some other source. Dealers who are asked to join in the distribution of the issue receive preliminary prospectuses which omit certain items such as price, banking commissions, etc., so that they will have a clearer idea of the nature of the security which they are invited to help sell. This preliminary print is commonly known as the "red herring" prospectus, since its tentative and unofficial character is clearly indicated by a suitable notice in red ink printed across its face.

A prospectus in the broad sense may also take the form of a radio broadcast or any form of literature sent to buyers. However, it is necessary to state in connection with the use of such other selling material that a prospectus as defined in Section 10 of the Federal Securities Act may be obtained; or such other selling devices are preceded by a prospectus, as defined in the Act, which is sent to prospective buyers.

Information for Security Buyers

In the prospectus which each buyer of a security subject to the Act receives, and in the registration statement which he is admittedly to consult in Washington and from which facts are broadcast through the financial services and the press, the public is assured a certain minimum amount of information about a new security offering, not all of which was available formerly. In addition to standardized financial statements, such added data are now made available as the gross spread between the price received by the issuer and that paid by the public, the commissions paid underwriters and the other compensation they receive, the compensation paid directors and officers and other persons receiving more than $25,000 a year, and, more particularly, various unfavorable facts of a material character affecting the issue.

Unfortunately, there is evidence that only a limited number of security buyers are taking advantage of the greatly enlarged facilities now available to them for analyzing new security issues. However, the mere availability of this information and the need for publishing it do make less likely a repetition of some of the worst examples of unsound and undesirable public financing of the past.

It should be kept clearly in mind that the Securities and Exchange Commission is not authorized to stop the distribution of a security offering merely because of its poor quality or because it is held to be over-priced. Its powers do not extend so far. As long as there is no evidence of fraud, and as long as the registration and prospectus requirements are conformed with, the Commission must stand aside and rely upon the intelligence of security buyers to protect themselves. It is for this reason that the designation "Truth in Securities Act" sometimes given this law is a suitable one.

Civil Liabilities

When the Federal Securities Act was originally enacted, new corporate financing came almost to a complete halt because of fears on the part of issuers, underwriters and dealers, of the civil liabilities imposed upon them by the statute. Subsequently, the liability provisions of the law were amended and made less severe, but nevertheless the existence of these liabilities in their modified form constitutes a constant threat to investment houses concerned with new financing.

Section 11 of the law outlines the civil liabilities that may be incurred in connection with untrue statements of material facts or omissions of material facts in a registration statement. The persons who are made liable are those who sign the registration statement, all directors of the issuing corporation, accountants, engineers or other professional experts who help prepare or certify any part of the registration statement, and every underwriter. Individuals other than the issuer may escape this liability if the misstatement or omission occurs in an extract from a public official document, an expert report, or was taken from some other source in the accuracy of which there were reasonable grounds to believe. The statute specifically states that the standard of what constitutes a reasonable ground for belief "shall be that required of a prudent man in the management of his own property."

Any buyer of a security where a misstatement or omission of material fact is found on the registration statement may bring suit to recover from any or all of the persons liable the difference between the amount paid for the security, not exceeding the public offering price, and either the value at the time the suit was brought or the price at which the security had been subsequently disposed of in the market. However, such suit must be brought within one year after the discovery of the untrue statement or omission, or after such discovery should have been made by the exercise of reasonable diligence on the part of the buyer. In no event can such action be brought later than three years after the effective date of the registration statement.

The defendant in such a recovery suit can reduce his liability, if the decision goes against him, if he proves that part or all of the damages for which recovery is sought was not caused by the depreciation in value of the security caused by the misstatement or omission. In any event, each underwriter's liability is limited to a maximum amount of damages not in excess of the total price at which the securities underwritten by him are offered for sale to the public.

The statute also imposes similar civil liabilities for misstatements or omissions in a prospectus, but in such case the dealer is liable only to those who have purchased from him. Any provision in a contract waiving these protections in the law are specifically stated to be void in the statute.

We may summarize the liability provisions in the Federal Securities Act in the following manner:

1. Common law protection that security buyers formerly enjoyed has been expanded by permitting buyers to recover damages they suffer through misstatements and omissions of material fact in connection with the sale of a security, from a variety of persons involved, instead of merely from the particular seller from whom they purchased.

2. Buyers do not have to prove that they relied specifically upon the misstatement or omission of material fact, which was the case under the common law, in actions both of deceit and of rescission.

3. "Good faith" alone is no longer a defense, where the seller of a security is sued because he had relied upon misstatements or omissions of material fact. Only where he has made a "reasonable investigation" or where he relies upon an expert and has no reasonable ground to believe that the statements made on such authority are untrue, does he have a defense. As a result, it has become common to state in the registration statement that suitable investigation has been made as regards statements not made on the authority of an expert, and to refer to certain parts of the registration statement as "made on the authority of an expert."[1]

The Cost of Registration

It is obvious that this procedure developed by the Federal Securities Act for the protection of investors involves a material addition to the expense of originating and distributing securities. A study of the costs imposed by the Federal Securities Act, made some time after its enactment, showed that for issues sold during 1935 issuers alone incurred expenses in connection with the preparation, registration and issuance of the securities averaging .7 of 1 per cent of the gross proceeds.

However, since many of these expenses do not vary materially

[1] The rôle of engineers in connection with the preparation of registration statements is described in a pamphlet entitled, "Recent Practice and Procedure in Securities Act Registration," by Ford, Bacon and Davis, Inc.

with the size of the issue, the burden is far greater for small issues than for large ones. It should be pointed out that certain of these costs, such as revenue stamps and trustee charges, would be incurred in any event, regardless of the law. The fact remains, however, that on issues of less than $1,000,000 the added costs imposed by the Federal Securities Act may make new financing burdensome. On issues of $200,000 and less, the cost has often run considerably above 2 per cent of the gross proceeds.

The Securities and Exchange Commission has shown that it is aware of this problem and that special measures will probably be taken in time to facilitate the registration of smaller offerings at lower cost. It has also been contended that there has been a tendency on the part of some accountants, engineers, lawyers and other professional experts to exaggerate the risks involved in the process of registration so as to increase the fees for their own work.

Because of the liabilities they incur under the Act, furthermore, bankers who act as underwriters now have reason to increase their gross spread. On the other hand, the publicity given their spread through the registration statement and prospectus tends to have a restraining influence. There is no reason to believe, therefore, that the average spread is any higher now than it was formerly, although it continues to vary widely, depending on the type of issue, the state of the market and other pertinent factors. On ninety bond flotations consummated in 1934 and 1935, the average gross spread was 3.09 per cent of the face value and ranged in individual instances from 8.5 per cent to 1.10 per cent of such face value.

The Investment Bankers' Code

Shortly after the Federal Securities Act was enacted, the investment bankers of the country sought to improve standards in their profession by voluntary action of their own. This in part was stimulated by the government, and in part represented a desire on the part of the bankers to establish higher standards of dealing and a restraint on competitive practices that would end undesirable business practices and would strengthen the confidence of the public in the investment banking business

The outcome was the Code of Fair Competition for Investment Bankers, promulgated under the National Industrial Recovery Act.

Following the invalidation of that law by the Supreme Court in May, 1935, the code lapsed. However, many bankers continue to conform in general to its provisions, and in 1936 an Investment Bankers' Conference was launched for the purpose of reestablishing the code by voluntary action. This movement was encouraged by the Securities and Exchange Commission, which hoped that the regulation of over-the-counter dealers could be facilitated through such voluntary contract, since serious doubts were felt about the constitutionality of federal regulation of over-the-counter markets at that time.

In its provision applicable to salesmen, syndicate practices and other aspects of the investment banking business, the code was even more far reaching than the securities legislation and the regulations of the Securities and Exchange Commission. We shall have reason to refer to its major provisions in subsequent chapters. The Securities and Exchange Commission, through its revival, hopes to achieve, among other things, solutions of the following problems:

1. The desirability and practicability of efforts by the Commis-ion or by an appropriate organization of investment bankers and lealers to perfect a mechanism of publicity for purchases and sales n the over-the-counter markets by registered brokers and dealers.

2. Methods of eliminating nominal or fictitious quotations, and ontrol of wide spreads between bid and asked prices of securities raded in over-the-counter.

3. The standardization and simplification of trust indentures in onnection with securities issued by public utility holding com-anies and public utility operating companies; and other rules and egulations relating to public utility companies.

4. Development of reporting system for inventory of unsold se-urities in the hands of security dealers.

5. Advisability of permitting on offering sheets such additional formation as ratings by statistical organizations, etc. Control of arket letters, circulars, and other literature.

6. Control of registered brokers and dealers who carry customers margin.

7. Requirements for the segregation of securities and funds held

in trust and segregation of capital employed in brokerage business from capital employed in dealer and underwriter activities.

The existence of the new securities legislation on the federal statute books makes it necessary for those in the investment banking business to familiarize themselves with its major provisions. As has long been the case with commercial banking, the legal aspect has become of fundamental importance.

However, novel and complicated statutes of this kind take years to interpret. Shortly after their enactment, the tendency was to exaggerate the importance of the liability involved. Subsequently, there was a reaction in the other direction, and the tendency developed among investment and brokerage houses to give little weight to the legal restrictions, beyond obtaining the advice of counsel. However, there can be little question that, with any sharp decline in security prices, the civil liabilities imposed by the Federal Securities Act and the Securities Exchange Act may assume quite substantial proportions.

We shall now proceed with a description and analysis of the practical process of originating and distributing securities as it is now conducted within the framework of the new legislation.

References

Lasser, J. K., and Gerardi, F. A., *Federal Securities Act Procedure*, New York, 1934.

Meyer, C. H., *The Securities Exchange Act of 1934 Explained*, New York, 1934.

Michelet, S., *Handbook of the Securities Act of 1933*, Washington, 1933.

Securities and Exchange Commission, Form A-2 and Instruction Book.

Securities and Exchange Commission, *General Rules and Regulations under the Federal Securities Act of 1933 and the Securities Exchange Act of 1934*.

Chapter XVII

NEGOTIATION AND PURCHASE OF NEW SECURITY ISSUES

Policy in Purchasing

Socially, the origination of new security issues is the most difficult and important of the functions of the investment banking machinery of the country. From a purely selfish point of view also, sound purchasing policies are essential for two vital reasons. In the first place, a security issue well bought is half sold, a rule of merchandising that applies in the securities business as much as, or more than, it does elsewhere. Secondly, he future of the investment house is closely bound up with he character and record of its past offerings. The ability to sell ecurities possessed by these houses is based on public confidence in them, and the confidence of the public can be secured only through a successful record of issues which have been ound and profitable over a period of time.

From the social point of view, the purchase function of the nvestment house is of first importance. As the investment anker chooses, among the numerous financing propositions rought to him, those he will accept, he unconsciously directs he flow of the community's capital into certain channels and way from others. In this way, he acts as arbiter of the future f governments and industries. It is true that this dependence n the investment banker varies with the strength of the organiations with which he deals, for governments like those of the nited States and Great Britain and corporations like the Ford Iotor Company and the Standard Oil Company are so strong to need little, if any, aid from investment bankers in aproaching the capital market. But the rank and file of our rger corporate enterprises largely depend on the investment ouse for effective access to the capital markets at reasonable ost.

In this chapter, current practice in the negotiation and purchase of new security issues is described. Wide variations exist in the methods followed by different houses, so what is presented here is chiefly an exposition of practices used by the larger houses, and may be regarded as representing a fairly standardized mode of procedure. The whole process has been profoundly affected and modified in recent years as a result of the enactment of the federal Securities Act of 1933.

Channels for New Financing Proposals

Most of the larger investment houses receive regularly far more proposals for new financing than they care to, or can, handle. Before considering the methods by which these proposals are analyzed and then rejected or accepted, we shall first take up the various channels by which most of these propositions reach the individual investment house. Six of the most important channels are:

1. Financial and personal relations between the investment banking house and the applicant
2. Branches and traveling representatives, negotiators and "finders"
3. Banks and correspondents
4. Direct application to the investment house
5. Competitive bids
6. Joining with originating houses in syndicates

Each of these channels will be considered in turn.

1. It is a general rule followed in relations between invest ment bankers and their customers, that "one good deal de serves another." Therefore, when the investment house ha once given satisfaction by selling a security issue effectivel there results as a rule a permanent connection between th issuing government or corporation and the banker. Sometime it is merely informal, while in other cases it is cemented by th banker's acquiring a stock interest or a place on the board c directors of the corporation. Among the larger banking house this custom has been so generally adopted that one firm wi frequently refuse to consider financing for corporations whic have been definitely affiliated with another.

In the larger originating houses, financial relations with the applicants assume a major rôle. J. P. Morgan & Company established its prestige first as a railroad reorganization firm. Early success with such reorganizations made investors ready to put money in the rehabilitation of railroad properties when their management was turned over to this firm and its associates through a voting trust. By thus becoming affiliated with the management of these properties, J. P. Morgan & Company, with or without large stock holdings in the property, became recognized as the "banker" for the railroad, and often was represented on its board of directors. Personal contacts of great value resulted, so that it became quite unusual for the railroad company to do its later financing through any other house.

The success of such firms as Morgan, and Kuhn, Loeb & Company in directing and financing railroad reorganizations was followed by similar ventures in the industrial field, this time chiefly in the realm of combination rather than reorganization, but with substantially the same results. A long string of companies thus tied themselves up to one or another of the major houses of issue, and this tendency has persisted down to the present day, although it has been less strong since the depression. A banker who can once successfully float an issue of a company's securities, especially when this is connected with the acquisition of a block of the company's stock or assuming a place on its board of directors, traditionally becomes affiliated with the future issues of that company. To some extent, this practice has invaded the field of government finance as well, with the result that several European and South American countries have their accredited "bankers" in London and New York. Here again houses with a large measure of public prestige are dominant. J. P. Morgan & Company has been in the past the official "banker" in this country of the governments of Great Britain, France and Italy; while Chile, Uruguay and several other South American countries formerly looked to the National City Company as their permanent financial connection here. Whenever foreign financing in this country revives, similar relationships will doubtless be reestablished.

When an investment house has established itself in a definitive relationship with a vigorous and expanding enterprise, the result may be that a steady stream of new financing proposals may come to it from numerous subsidiaries and affiliations of the company it originally finances. This may be assured by a written prior financing contract, under which the banker has the prior option on new issues of the corporation before they may be sold on the same terms to other originators.

2. Independent intermediaries, known as "finders," have often uncovered suitable issues and presented them to banking houses, especially in newer and less well-developed industries. The professional promoter of new enterprises or combinations often works in this way. Compensation takes the form of a fee or percentage of either the gross or the net profit on the issue, usually paid by the banker. At other times in the past, an allotment of junior securities has been the consideration paid the finder.

In the foreign financing field, the special representative and finder have played a particularly important rôle in the past, for the usual banking connections are not as generally developed in this department of financing. Negotiators who have made a constructive contribution have been men with wide banking and business connections abroad, who have evinced a knowledge of finance and business both in the originating country and in the home capital market. Many of them have also had to have a knowledge of the intricate international legal problems involved, especially in the case of foreign corporate issues, for this is needed even to begin negotiations on a practical basis, before it is feasible to call in expensive outside legal advice. In some instances, however, intermediaries of this kind have been concerned with political and personal connections to obtain new issues, with at times unhappy results.

3. A well-established investment banking house often has numerous contacts with other banks that bring it business. An investment house on friendly terms with a commercial bank is in an especially favorable position in this respect, since the latter can recommend a security issue to their clients whenever bank borrowing becomes excessive or large needs for new capital arise. Many a foreign bond issue floated here before 1929 originally went to a European banking house long affiliated

with that particular issuer, the American firm being called in later to assure adequate distribution.

Commercial banks also are influential in bringing to city investment bankers corporations whose activities are chiefly in the interior of the country. As a result, a series of mutual relationships have grown up which bind banks and investment houses together in a manner that resembles the correspondent relations among banks in different localities.

Trading relations tend to cement these connections. The Banking Act sought to assure the independence of each *vis-à-vis* the other, by prohibiting interlocking directors and employes.

4. A certain number of issues are sold through direct application by a company to a banker, without previous acquaintance or other intermediaries, but they comprise a rather small minority of the total new financing. To a large extent, such direct dealing is restricted to highly speculative issues, houses specializing in the latter sometimes advertising in the daily newspapers for new security offerings. As a result, a certain amount of suspicion often rests on direct applications by unknown parties to investment banking houses. And when a financing proposal becomes known as one which has been "shopped around" in numerous quarters, this suspicion becomes acute.

Investment bankers are averse to such practices also because of the expense involved in a preliminary investigation of a new proposition; therefore they want assurance that if the finding is favorable they will have the financing for themselves.

On the other hand, many instances are known where desirable propositions were brought directly to the investment house by the vendors. This is especially true for firms which have established a reputation for successful financing in some specialized and relatively new field, such as chain stores, natural gas or airplane manufacture.

5. While most of the securities offered in the New York market are purchased by investment banking houses as a result of direct negotiation with the vendor, large amounts of bonds are regularly sold through competitive bidding. At the present time, the great bulk of municipal issues and some foreign government bonds are sold in this way, and the Interstate Commerce Commission has been experimenting with this method

of sale for the railroads, restricting it to equipment trust certificates. The Treasury has disposed of weekly bill offerings similarly, and the Reconstruction Finance Corporation has used a like method to dispose of some of its holdings. A few New England states, such as New Hampshire, require operating utilities within their borders to sell new issues by competitive bidding.

The arguments usually advanced in favor of competitive bidding are the following:

1. The vendor gets the highest possible price for the issue.
2. By ending special relations between the vendor and individual bankers, more firms become interested in its issues, leading eventually to a wider distribution of its securities.
3. Banker domination of the issues is eliminated.

Against competitive bidding the following arguments have been frequently advanced:

1. Bankers withdraw the advantage of special support when competitive bidding takes away the motive they have in supporting the credit of a vendor with whom they are specifically identified.
2. The eagerness of competition leads to too high prices for individual issues of securities, causing loss to the bankers and the public, poor distribution, and unsound general conditions in the securities market.
3. In adverse times, no bids may be forthcoming.
4. Establishment of permanent financing channels tends to cut the cost of distribution and eventually to lower the price of securities to the public.
5. The strongest banking houses tend to restrict their activities to business they are certain of getting, leaving securities available by competitive bids open to weak and speculative organizations.
6. Investigation is less complete.

In practice, competitive bidding appears to have established itself permanently in municipal finance, where advantages of tax exemption, standardization and the general financial strength of American municipalities make special banking connections less essential.

It has been found that competitive bidding is usually suitable only where the issue is of a standard variety that can be readily analyzed by a large number of interested houses. Municipal bonds and railroad equipment trust certificates have hitherto proved to be the only important classes of securities, apart from Treasury bills, which meet these requirements. As the conditions surrounding the operation and financing of railroads, public utilities and other basic industries become more stable and uniform, it is possible that the practice will spread.

6. The great majority of bond houses get a share in new security issues by joining with other houses in forming purchase and selling groups. The operations of such syndicates are discussed later in this and the following chapter. Invitations to join are sent out by the original issuing house, usually a few days before the actual offering. Some study, usually of a cursory nature, is made of the new issue, and then the investment committee in the bond house decides whether or not to accept the participation rendered. Participations vary greatly in size according to the position of each house and its relation with the originator. If the latter is one of the more important houses of origination, it may be bad policy to antagonize it on future issues by turning down a proffered participation. A house which has done yeoman's service in distributing previous offerings put out by the syndicate manager may seek and get a larger allotment than is first offered to it when a really desirable issue comes along.

Negotiation of Security Issues

From whatever source the proposal for new financing is received, it is turned over to the buying department of the investment house for investigation and negotiation. Where banking relations have been firmly established, negotiation may be a routine matter and take but little time. However, in order to bring out all of the problems which face the investment banker in the negotiation of new issues, this section will outline the steps taken in the study. and negotiation of an entirely new security offering, it being understood that the process is abbreviated when additional financing is done for the same client.

When a new financing proposal is first received, a rapid preliminary study is normally made. This study includes for a corporation an analysis of the industry in which it operates, and a study of its financial and other available statistics. From this study, made by statisticians and other experts in the buying department of the house of issue, and often supplemented by a quick check with a bank or other outside source of information, the investment house, usually through an "investment committee" of partners, decides whether or not it is interested. If it is, the house generally tries to secure from the prospective vendor of the security issue a memorandum or preliminary contract, giving it an option on the issue for a certain period of time, thus protecting the house against negotiations with competitors while a more extended and expensive investigation is carried on. Without this option, the issue may be sold to someone else before the investigation is completed, thus causing to the house loss of effort and money expended.

In making the full investigation of the proposition which follows, the method varies widely according to the type of issue and vendor, as well as its size. One leading house gives the following outline of the facts it seeks in most cases. This outline serves as a check list, and data are sought on as many items mentioned as is feasible.

A. General and Commercial Investigations

(Conducted by the Buying Department)

1. Ownership and management
2. Credit position
3. Location of property
4. Character of products
5. Market
6. Competition
7. Labor conditions
8. Public relations
9. Office analysis of earnings, balance sheet, etc.

B. Engineering Examination

(Conducted by engineering experts employed by the Buying Department)

1. Description of service or product.
2. Valuation of property, taking into consideration the replacement value less depreciation, and intangible values such as franchises, processes, patents, good will, etc.
3. Physical condition of the property, including its present condition, the improvements necessary to put the property into first-class business condition and operating efficiency, the policy of the company with reference to additions, betterments and maintenance, the rate of depreciation and the expense and percentage of gross earnings necessary to maintain the property in the most efficient operating condition. Is the property economically and strategically located as to efficiency and economy of distribution—availability of transportation, availability to supply of raw materials, etc.?
4. Present and probable future sources of competition, and the extent to which they do or may affect the status of the company.
5. The labor situation, especially the relationship between the management and employees.
6. Comparison of earnings and expenses with other similar companies; do they give adequate return on the value of the property? What has been the effect of rates, prices of materials, wages, etc., on earnings?
7. To what extent will money be required for future improvements?

C. Legal Examination

(Conducted by legal experts employed by the Buying Department, usually a well-known firm of corporation attorneys)

1. Has the company been legally and validly organized, and is it currently in good standing with the authorities under which it was organized?
2. Has it all franchise, charter and other rights necessary to enable it to carry on its business?
3. Has it good title to its various properties sufficient for the use to which they are put? To what extent are they subject to any liens, charges or encumbrances which would interfere with the operations of the company or impair the rights of the bondholders?

4. Are all legal papers affecting proposed bond issue, including any contracts, leases and agreements, indenture, the bonds themselves, in proper form?
5. How difficult will registration be under the federal Securities Act?

D. Audit

(Conducted by accounting experts employed by the Buying Department)

1. Comparative earning statements and balance sheets over a period of years.
2. Comparative statements of charges to maintenance and depreciation.
3. Analysis of the accounting system. Is it adequate and sufficient? Have items been charged to the proper accounts?
4. Audit of accounts in detail.

Before the enactment of the Federal Securities Act of 1933, a single originator normally conducted the negotiations with the issuer and signed the purchase agreement. Now, however, because of the added liability that is incurred under the provisions of this statute between the time that the underwriting contract is signed and the beginning of actual selling, originators prefer to share the risk by having all the members of the purchase group sign the contract. Hence, by the time that the negotiations with the issuer are completed but before the contract is signed, the originator has organized his purchase group, varying in size from a few to twenty-five or more members, to sign the purchase agreement with him.

The Purchase Agreement

When the full examination is completed, the investment committee or the partner in charge of the buying in the investment house reaches a final conclusion. If favorable, the bankers generally send a letter or telegram to the vendor expressing a willingness to purchase the issue on stated terms, often including the price they are willing to pay. This letter thus constitutes an offer to purchase, which may be accepted by the board of directors of the corporation, or an accredited official in the case of a government bond issue. Often final approval must also be secured from the stockholders of a corporation or the legislative body of a government before the purchase can be legally consummated.

When such approval as is required has been secured, it is the usual practice to embody the terms of the transaction in a purchase or underwriting agreement, usually a lengthy and formal document. At other times, a letter from the bankers to the issuer, or vice versa, alone constitutes the purchase agreement.

Before the enactment of the Federal Securities Act, when the actual public offering of the issue usually is effected almost immediately after the signing of the purchase agreement, these contracts were for the most part irrevocable, so that the issuer was assured of obtaining the proceeds unconditionally. With the introduction of a twenty-day waiting period under the Federal Securities Act, however, and the requirement that the details of the purchase agreement be filed in advance of the date of public offering, investment houses have inserted hedge clauses in purchase contracts which would release them from he underwriting obligation in the event of stated unfavorable onditions. The most significant type of hedge clause is known s the "market clause," which usually provides that the origiator, as representative of the purchase group, "may, in its disretion, terminate this agreement without liability on the part f the members thereof, if prior to the time for delivery any ibstantial change in the position of our company, or any subdiary, or in the existing operating, political, economic or *maret* conditions shall have taken place which, in our opinion, nders it impracticable or inadvisable to market the bonds at ie price to the public named."

These market clauses may provide in extreme cases that the ırchase group may withdraw from its commitment because of lverse market conditions not only before the date of public fering, but even after that. An examination of registration itements filed with the Securities and Exchange Commission date will show that most of the purchase agreements involved re cancelable in the event of adverse market conditions, not ly before but sometimes even after actual public offering. few large houses have refrained from the practice of using e market hedge clause in their underwritings.

Another common type of hedge clause provides that the issuer will indemnify purchase group members for losses incurred because of misstatements or omissions in registration statements or prospectuses.

The chief items generally found in a purchase agreement are:[1]

1. A full description of the securities to be issued.
2. The price to the corporation, and the method and time of payment and delivery of the bonds. It has become common to make payment to the corporation before the public pays for the issue.
3. Provision for a carefully drawn registration statemen and prospectus under the federal Securities Act. Th issuer also agrees to pay all costs and expenses in con nection with delivery of the bonds, sometimes includin counsel and other expenses incurred by the underwriters compliance with state blue-sky laws and listing on ex changes. It is usual for the issuer to give specific permis sion to the purchase group and dealers to use the pros pectus, of which an adequate number of copies is to b furnished them.
4. An agreement by the underwriters to make the publi offering, usually as soon as possible after the registratio statement becomes effective.
5. Disposition of proceeds of issue, future financing an reports to the bankers.
6. An agreement to indemnify underwriters against Fe eral Securities Act and common law liabilities incurre in connection with the issue.
7. The whole transaction is made contingent on findi representations of the company correct as stated.

In most cases, the lawyers cannot render a final opinion the validity of the issue until after the purchase agreement h been signed and the securities, perhaps, sold. In such instanc it is carefully provided in the agreement that the purchase contingent wholly upon a satisfactory finding of the lawyers this respect. At times, when the auditors' report is especia

[1] A sample purchase agreement is shown in the appendix to this chapter.

complex, a favorable report from them may also be included as a condition for the completion of the deal.[2]

In arriving at the price to be paid for a new security issue, the investment banker is governed by the state of the market and the known preferences of buyers. Like wholesalers in other lines of business, buyers of entire issues of securities must keep in mind that what they buy is to be sold again. Hence, bankers are quick to sense changes in fashions, turning from bonds to stocks and from one industry to another, as tastes of investors vary.

In the case of new bond issues, the terms are determined approximately by the yields of similar securities as shown by market prices. If a similar issue already traded in gives a yield of, say, a little less than 6 per cent, that fact will fix the other terms. A maturity date which is common for the industry—ten to twenty years for the general run of industrials, twenty to forty for basic industrials, and thirty to fifty for utilities—s chosen. Then a coupon rate will be fixed which will permit he pricing of the issue at a point a little under par. Investors, ike other buyers, seem to prefer such a price. In part, this reflects the same psychology as underlies the popularity of prices ike 98 cents or $1.98 in the general merchandising field—it gives the impression of a bargain price and sounds much more ttractive than prices like $1 or $2.[3] Secondly, investors prefer o buy bonds at a discount because in that way they gain asurance that the principal of their fund will not be impaired. Ience, in the present instance, the bond will in all likelihood e a 5½ per cent issue which will be offered at about 97½.

'he Bankers' Spread

The price that the bankers will pay will be the expected maret price reduced by the gross spread desired. This spread, of ourse, varies with the type of issue and the state of the mar-

[2] The National City Company canceled a contract to purchase an issue of nds of a steel company in 1926 when the auditors' statement disproved figures the company.

[3] This peculiar merchandising practice is said to have been originated many ars ago by R. H. Macy & Company, New York department store, to "check " on sales by clerks by fixing prices which would require getting change at a tral desk where sales records were kept.

ket. In the case of standardized, tax-exempt municipals, easily sold in large blocks, it may reach barely one point, or one per cent of the par value. It may be over ten points in the case of speculative issues. A place on the board of directors, a stock interest and expectations of future profitable financing may cause bankers to reduce their usual spreads.

In order to determine spreads on security issues on a more precise basis, the application of cost accounting principles has been advocated. The pricing of new security issues has hitherto been a rather haphazard affair, immediate expediency and practical judgment being relied upon by the investment banker. While cost accounting has made great progress in the industrial and merchandising field, little has been done in the direction of applying it to investment banking. So large a part of the expenditure of the investment house is of a general or overhead nature, and so little uniformity exists in departmental organization, accounting systems and methods of compensating salesmen—often the main expense item—that the application of cost principles becomes a very complex problem.

A survey made in 1928 revealed that out of twenty typical investment houses in different cities, only one had anything like a complete cost system. Five others had some income and expense analysis by departments, and three made some tentative analysis of income and expense per item sold.[4] Following this survey, the Investment Bankers Association of America set a subcommittee to work out a cost accounting system for the business which would pave the way to the determination of proper price spreads, through pointing out the unprofitable kinds of securities handled which can be dropped unless a larger spread can be secured upon them. The following data are said by this subcommittee to be desirable for such cost control:

1. Actual Gross Profit of each issue of securities offered for sale. This would be analyzed so as to show for each issue:

(a) Buying Profit (for originations)
(b) Buying Expense (for originations)
(c) Underwriting Profit

[4] See *Proceedings* of the Investment Bankers Association of America, 1928, pp. 143-161.

(d) Banking Profit (when this is not merely a quantity discount)
(e) Selling Group Profit
(f) Loss of Selling Group Profit due to repurchases by syndicate managers
(g) Secondary Profit

Not all of these items would occur in every issue. These figures should be analyzed from the point of view of finding out why the issue is or is not successful, so that buying policies may be based on factual experience in addition to pure judgment.

2. Speculative Profit or Loss of each security issue. This is the difference between budget selling profit, consisting of the difference between the cost of the issue, plus expenses, and the formal public offering price, and actual selling profit; and when considered with general external economic conditions gives an idea of the risk factor which may be expected in various circumstances.

3. Distribution Cost of each issue. This is one of the most important records and, when sufficient information is built up, gives an idea of how many points profit should be allowed for selling costs of various types of securities under various marketing conditions and with various prevailing interest rates. Some issues are brought out with, for example, two points selling group profit at such a price that they are sold practically without effort. In that case, from the point of view of the issuing house, they may be priced too cheap, or the selling group commissions may be too great, or both. It scarcely need be pointed out that if it were possible for the issuing house to establish with scientific precision for various external marketing conditions and interest rates the correct price and the correct selling group commission, the advantage in knowing what to allow for distribution costs in making the bid when buying the issue, and in conserving profits when selling the issue, would be enormous. Such a state of precision cannot be hoped for, but many of the factors can be reduced to a definitely known basis so that judgment need not be exercised on so many variables as is now customary.[5]

In the case of stock issues, the price is often fixed at a figure believed most attractive to buyers at the moment. Generally, and especially in the financing of newer promotions, the spread

[5] "Interim Report of the Sub-Committee on Cost Accounting of the Business Problems Committee," *Investment Bankers of America Bulletin*, vol. xvii, pp. 02-110.

is considerably larger than in the case of bonds, and stock bonuses play a more important rôle.

The publicity given spreads under the Federal Securities Act has doubtless tended to reduce their size. The average gross spread on $2,664,000,000 of securities registered with the Securities and Exchange Commission in the first half of 1936 was 3.2 per cent. On several high-grade bond issues, it was as low as 1 per cent.

Practice differs widely in arranging payment for new security issues. In certain instances, the full purchase price may be turned over on the signing of the purchase agreement. In other cases, payment is provided for only after a certain period of time—for example, a month—has elapsed, to permit the bankers to sell the securities before having to pay for them. In still other instances, a part of the purchase price is paid on the signing of the purchase agreement, and the balance is payable at stated intervals. Since 1933, it is common to provide for payment just before the selling group or retail customers pay the members of the purchase group for their bonds. The latter can then finance the transaction by a short-term overdraft at the banks.

The Code and Origination

The Code of Fair Competition for Investment Bankers provided that an originator "make such investigation as may be reasonably necessary to determine the merit of such issue, and to satisfy himself that the business risk of the investors who purchase such securities is reasonable and that there are appropriate provisions to safeguard the interests of such investors." Dealers who distribute securities originated by another house were expected to satisfy themselves that the investigation as outlined has been made by the originator.

The code further provided that originators of issues exceeding $100,000 shall require the issuer of the securities to agree to publish audited financial statements and to conform to accepted accounting standards in handling stock dividends received, surplus credits and charges, etc. Special requirements as to the information published were laid down for municipal issues. It also required that the titles of new issues of securities shall not be misleading as to the lien, terms or priority.

The code, through which voluntary regulation of investment banking practices can be developed to supplement federal regulation, may be utilized over a period of years as a means for further standardizing and improving practices of investment bankers originating new issues.

Organization for Security Purchasing

The investment house is gregarious. It does not like to do business alone; most of its operations are done in conjunction with other houses. There are two important reasons for this. In the first place, there is a desire to share the liability involved in any one transaction, so that, should the position of the specific issue or the general market take an unfavorable turn, or a sudden panic develop, the house need not be tied up in one or a few big commitments which endanger its solvency. In the second place, when the actual task of selling securities must be accomplished, there is a desire to share the selling effort by bringing in an adequate number of houses with distributing power to help assure the complete and successful disposition of the issue within a reasonable length of time.[6]

The simplest form of cooperation in security purchasing is the joint account, in which two firms join to handle a single transaction. Many of the principles underlying the cooperation of three or more houses in what are generally known as syndicate transactions may be seen in simplified form in the working of the joint account. These transactions involve a manager, usually the house which originated the issue, in order to assure centralized control and to prevent more sales being made than are necessary to sell the entire issue. Since the enactment of the federal Securities Act, the desire to share the risk on underwriting commitments has been greater than ever, so that joint accounts have been less common than before, except on small issues.

The essential features of the joint account are brought out

[6] The Investment Bankers Association of America sought to summarize the best practice, and in some degree to advance the cause of greater uniformity in syndicate operation, by sponsoring the volume known as *Security Syndicate Operations,* written under its auspices by Arthur Galston. The student is referred to this work for a more detailed discussion of syndication as it was conducted before the enactment of the federal Securities Act of 1933.

in the following typical letter sent by the house originating the business to the one which is invited to join it:

Confirming our verbal understanding, we have ceded to you an interest of 50 per cent in our purchase, at 90 and accrued interest, of $1,000,000 X Power & Light Company 5-per-cent bonds. To facilitate the handling of this Joint Account, we shall act as Managers and keep the records. The offering price of these bonds to the public will be 92 and accrued interest, from which price there will be allowed to either of us on confirmed sales a selling commission of 1 per cent. All sales, however, will be subject to confirmation by us as Managers, and will be applied against the total obligation of the Joint Account. The Joint Account will continue for a period of two months from the date of this letter, unless sooner terminated, or unless extended by mutual agreement.

Kindly confirm the above as being in accordance with your understanding.

In the above instance, the corporation receives $900,000 for its bonds. The bonds are to be sold to the public for $920,000. If each of the two houses in this joint account sells $400,000 of the bonds, they each make the selling commission of 1 per cent or $4,000 on the bonds sold, and they each take over $100,000 of the bonds left unsold. The profits remaining in the syndicate, consisting of 1 per cent on the $800,000 of bonds sold, or $8,000, less expenses, is then divided between the two houses.

The operation of the joint account may be further clarified by summarizing the accounting entries as they would appear on the books of the manager, who opens up a special book of account to cover the transactions. Under the assumptions as outlined above, the journal entries would be as follows:

Joint Purchase Account

	Debit	Credit
$1,000,000 of bonds, purchased at 90	$900,000	
$400,000 sold by A at 92 less 1 per cent		$364,000
$400,000 sold by B at 92 less 1 per cent		364,000
$100,000 delivered to A at 90		90,000
$100,000 delivered to B at 90		90,000
Expenses	1,800	
Profit to A	3,100	
Profit to B	3,100	
	$908,000	$908,000

In the joint account outlined here, the arrangements for purchasing the issue through cooperation between the two banking houses are made simultaneously with the selling arrangements. As the size of individual issues increases and the number of houses joining the syndicate expands, the arrangements become more complex, and buying activities tend to become divorced from the selling. However, the basic accounting principles are the same.

The Purchase Group

In the usual case, a group of underwriters signs the purchase agreement with the issuer. These underwriting houses agree among themselves to act as a purchase group, and make a formal agreement to that effect. This purchase group, because it assumes the sole underwriting liability as a rule, has the key rôle in origination today.

The originating banker usually acts as manager of a purchase group, unless he prefers to defer to another, better-known or larger house. A portion of the commission retained by the purchase group is usually turned over to the originator in recognition of his leading rôle in the transaction. The other members of the purchase group, however, being "underwriters" as the term is defined by the federal Securities Act and being liable accordingly, conduct some investigation of their own also.

The purchase group now usually consists on an average of about ten members, although in a few instances a much larger number of houses are included. Each member of this group makes a definite underwriting commitment, by which he agrees to purchase a stated amount of the issue on the date set in the purchase contract.

The members usually assume also an obligation in connection with market support operations during the initial period of distribution, a function formerly often fulfilled by the distribution syndicate.

It is common to limit the maximum liability on this support account to 5 per cent of the face amount of the issue. Thus if X & Co. have a $4,000,000 participation in a purchase group for an issue of $40,000,000 of bonds, it makes a definite contract to buy these bonds and also to take an additional 5 per cent or

$200,000 which the purchase group manager has repurchased in the market in connection with his pegging operations.

A typical purchase group contract is reproduced in the appendix to this chapter. It will be noted that it takes the form of a letter to the two originating houses from the other members of the purchase group, that it lists the outright underwriting commitment of each member, and that a special commission of 1/4 of 1 per cent is given the originators for their efforts.

An important factor to be considered by originating houses whose organizations are not nation-wide in the true sense is the need for securing proper distribution in the Middle West, Northwest, South and the Pacific coast, where in recent years large buying power has been developed. This can often be done by including in the purchase group houses well known in these sections of the country, usually leading investment bankers with main offices in the chief city of the area in which its influence is important. These houses then act as "regional" or "key" distributors, and wholesale the issue in their territory up to the amount of their participation. Thus, of a $20,000,000 issue, a Chicago house might be allotted $5,000,000 for the Middle West, the territory being clearly defined. This Chicago house then invites local houses by which it is well known to take a participation in the selling group. The out-of-town distribution thus gained is often especially desirable in respect to permanence, thus enhancing the stability of the market for the issue after the public offering.

Formerly, purchase group participations were either on a divided or an undivided basis. This distinction was highly important, for it fixed the liability of the members. A divided or limited syndicate limited the liability of each member to the amount of his participation, so that his liability at the dissolution of the syndicate was limited to the difference between the amount of the securities sold or taken over and the participation. Thus a house which had a $100,000 participation in a divided syndicate, and which disposed of $95,000 of securities, on dissolution was asked to take up a maximum of only $5,000. The divided syndicate is in universal use now.

In an undivided or unlimited syndicate, on the other hand, securities unsold on the termination of the syndicate agreement were divided among the members in proportion to their participations, regardless of the amount of bonds or stock they sold or otherwise disposed of during the life of the syndicate. In such instances, the final liability of a member of a syndicate could be for a materially larger amount of bonds than his participation called for, because of the failure of other members to dispose of their portion. In the purchase syndicate, however, this liability was usually theoretical, since the securities were to be turned over to another distribution syndicate *in toto*. Only when failure was met in the effort to form a selling syndicate to take over the whole issue was there question of further liability.[7]

Banking Groups and Sub-underwriters

In the case of large issues, a second purchase group was formerly often formed which was larger than the original purchase group. While the desire to share liability was one factor in forming the purchase group, a more frequent factor was the desire to bring large banking houses into a purchase group which would allow such organizations a larger profit than if they joined only the selling syndicate. Hence, organizations with substantial distributing power, and those which could place large blocks of bonds with institutions, were invited to take substantial participations in a second purchase group. Another factor was the desire to obtain the aid of more houses in financing the carrying of the unsold portions of the issue, pending its final distribution. This intermediate group was usually known as a "banking group."

The formation of intermediate groups has been relatively unusual since the federal Securities Act was enacted. The chief reason for this is that the securities may not be sold until the effective date of the registration statement. Hence, once the underwriting is completed, outright sale of the issue to an intermediate group before the effective date of the registration becomes technically impossible. The present-day purchase group, because it both underwrites and manages the distribution of an issue, performs the functions both of the old original

[7] The divided syndicate was sometimes called the "western" type, and the undivided the "eastern," since these forms found favor in the respective regions.

purchase group and of the intermediate groups that were in vogue in the past. However, circumstances could well bring about a recrudescence of banking groups, with a resulting broadening of the membership of underwriting syndicates, once the technical legal obstacles to their use have been overcome.

In several cases, in fact, sub-underwriters who have about the same position as members of the old banking groups have been used. These sub-underwriters agree to purchase from the purchase group members a stated proportion of the unsold balance of the issue up to the date of final determination of the selling group. Thus, in an issue of $10,000,000 a sub-underwriter taking a $1,000,000 commitment would be responsible for taking over 10 per cent of the unsold portion of a new offering.

As a result of the elimination of intermediate groups, the purchase group naturally receives a larger proportion of the gross spread between the price to the issuer and the public offering price than formerly.

In the case of most municipal issues, bids are made directly by purchase groups, several of which may be organized for the purpose. The small margin of profit militates against the multiplication of syndicates in municipal bond operations, although cases have arisen where one syndicate which acted as both the purchase and the selling group, having failed to dispose of the entire issue, has sold the unsold portion to a different syndicate in order to dissolve.

Dissolution of the Purchase Group

Since the purchase group now constitutes the sole underwriting group, it must be maintained as long as any material part of the issue remains unsold and it is desired to support the market price. In the subsequent chapter, we shall be concerned with the considerations that govern the pegging of the market for the issue during this period, and the way in which this is done.

Opinions differ on the most desirable duration of a purchase group. Where the issue is quickly oversubscribed and goes to a premium in the open market, no real problem is presented.

Where subscriptions through the selling group and directly to purchase group members come in slowly, and the bonds are "sticky," in the parlance of investment houses, a delicate question arises. Maintenance of the life of the syndicate is costly, in that it is necessary to buy back bonds through the market. It also ties up the selling organization of the members, who might otherwise be free to turn to pushing other issues. On the other hand, a quick dissolution, with a consequent removal of the price peg and a decline of several points in the issue, may bring dissatisfaction among dealers, customers and the issuer. There may be a feeling that insufficient effort was made to distribute the whole issue before support was removed from the market.

Individual investment houses adopt differing policies as regards the most desirable time of dissolution of purchase groups.

Private Placements and Agency Distribution

Before the American capital market achieved its present scope, it was not uncommon for security issues to be placed by issuers or other investment houses with a few institutional buyers, without public offering. Such private placements became uncommon in the war and post-war period. Since 1933, however, it has again become common, chiefly because a private offering is exempt from the registration requirement of the Federal Securities Act, thus permitting a reduction in the cost of distribution. The increased importance of institutional buyers in the capital market, however, would itself explain some increase in the popularity of the private placement of new security offerings. Sometimes an issue is placed privately without registration, and then is registered in due course to assure full marketability.

The highest grade of bond issue that can be placed readily with a half dozen or so of financial institutions, such as life insurance companies or savings banks, lends itself most readily to such private placement.

Regardless of whether an issue is placed privately or by public distribution, the corporation may itself retain the risk, using investment bankers merely as agents. A large proportion of these private placements were effected with the aid of investment houses who negotiated the transaction. Also, in a very few cases, securities have been offered by the corporation with investment houses acting merely as "selling agent," accepting subscriptions and taking care of the physical handling of the issue, and receiving a reduced fee for the service. The tendency for bankers' spreads to decline in ordinary financing has tended to make agency distributions unattractive.

The Pure Underwriting Syndicate

It is customary for established corporations to sell their stock issues directly to their own stockholders, rather than to the general public through an investment banker. In many individual cases, furthermore, bond issues, especially where they are convertible, are also offered first to shareholders. Sometimes this is necessary because shareholders enjoy a preemptive right to new stock issues. In other cases, it is done in any event as the cheapest and most effective method for raising new capital. Where this practice is followed, the corporation frequently finds it desirable to assure itself that the securities so offered will be taken up by the shareholders through the formation of an underwriting syndicate.

Such an underwriting syndicate consists of a group of bankers which, for a consideration, guarantees the sale of the issue by contracting to purchase, on the same terms as the shareholders, any portion which the latter do not subscribe for Thus, an issue of $1,000,000 of stock may be offered share holders at 100. If they take only $400,000 of the issue, then the underwriters' syndicate will take over the balance of $600,00c at the same price. However, the actual price to the syndicate will be reduced by the commission it receives.

Compensation to the underwriters is arranged in two ways In many instances, a flat commission is paid on the whole amount of the offering. Thus, when the Baltimore & Ohio ir 1927 offered $63,242,500 in new common stock at 107½, the underwriting syndicate received a flat commission of 2¼ pe cent on the entire issue, regardless of how many shares stock holders took up. As a matter of fact, shareholders took up prac tically the whole issue, and the commission of $1,422,956 re ceived by the bankers was largely in the nature of an insuranc premium paid by the company to cover a contingency—failure to sell the new stock to shareholders—which did not occur.

A second way of arranging compensation for the underwriting syndicate is to fix a small rate of commission on the underwriting of the entire issue, and a higher rate on those shares or bonds which the underwriters must take up. It may be provided, for example, that a commission of 1 per cent will be paid on the entire amount of the issue underwritten, but that a commission of 5 per cent will be paid on any portion of the issue taken up by the underwriters. The first payment is in the nature of an insurance premium, which is to be received even if stockholders take the whole offering. The second payment represents the usual differential between the purchase price and the price of sale to the public of a new security issue.

Registration is effected in such cases much as with a public issue. The underwriters each take a participation in the total, but their purchase is conditional on prior subscriptions by shareholders. If any large portion of the issue is left on the hands of the underwriters, a selling group may be formed to effect its distribution.

Inventory Policy

The buying department of an investment house, whether it purchases for wholesale or retail distribution, faces the problem of providing as many securities as can be sold at a profit, without permitting so great an accumulation of unsold issues at any one time as would create a serious problem of inflated inventories.

Sudden changes in business conditions or in the money market may sharply curtail the ability of the market to absorb new issues. The large originating houses at such times are often asked by smaller firms and dealers to take back securities sold to them, in order to relieve the latter, with their limited resources, of the necessity of carrying substantial amounts of temporarily unsalable securities. In the past, it has often proved to the ultimate interest of the large houses to oblige the small firms in this respect, for their cooperation at other times in the distribution of securities is thus secured. As a result, the large investment houses have found it profitable to draw increasingly close to commercial banks, which have facilities for carrying them through periods of large inventories with collateral loans at moderate rates, even when the money market becomes unusually tight.

Proposals have been advanced to put the management of the inventory problem upon a more scientific basis through the application of budgeting methods for sales. On the basis of past performances of salesmen, branch offices and other outlets, the house may work out a monthly sales budget which the buying department must meet in order to satisfy the requirements of the sales department. This requires the closest cooperation between the two sides of the business of the investment banking house, buying and selling.

For a fuller understanding of the buyer operations of the investment house, it is necessary to have a clear view of the complementary function of securities selling, and this is taken up in the following chapter.

References

Badger, R. E., *Valuation of Industrial Securities,* New York, 1925.

Biddle, C. P., and Bates, G. E., *Investment Banking: A Case Book,* New York, 1931.

Code of Fair Competition for Investment Bankers. Published by the Investment Bankers Association of America, Chicago, 1934.

Eaton, William D., *Explanatory Outline of the Functions and Requirements of Bankers, Trustees, Registrars, Transfer Agents and Lawyers in Connection with the Issue of Investment Securities,* Boston, 1928.

Galston, Arthur, *Security Syndicate Operations,* New York, 1928, chaps. i–iii.

Investment Bankers Association of America, *An Analysis of Investment Banking for Vocational Guidance* (pamphlet), Chicago, 1929, chaps. iii–v.

Kraft, K., and Starkweather, L., *Analysis of Industrial Securities,* New York, 1929.

Lincoln, E. E., *Applied Business Finance,* Chicago, 1925, chap. x

Madden, John T., and Nadler, Marcus, *Foreign Securities,* New York, 1929, chaps. iv–v.

Nelson, M. N., *Readings in Corporation Finance,* New York, 1926, pp. 244–271.

Appendix I

PURCHASE CONTRACT (UNDERWRITING AGREEMENT)[1] (1935)

October 14, 1935.

MORGAN STANLEY & CO., INCORPORATED
2 Wall Street,
New York, N. Y.

Dear Sirs:

Illinois Bell Telephone Company (hereinafter called the "Company") proposes to issue $45,000,000 principal amount of its First and Refunding Mortgage 3½% Bonds, Series B (hereinafter designated the "Series B Bonds"), to be dated October 1, 1935, to mature October 1, 1970, and otherwise described in the Amended Registration Statement and Amended Prospectus (Exhibits B and D) attached hereto, as amended by the further amendments attached hereto as Exhibit E, and to be issued pursuant to the provisions of and to be secured by the First and Refunding Mortgage dated June 1, 1923, executed by the Company to First Trust and Savings Bank (Chicago), Trustee, as supplemented by a Supplemental Indenture dated as of October 1, 1935, and executed by the Company to The First National Bank of Chicago, Trustee. Copies of such First and Refunding Mortgage and said Supplemental Indenture are filed as Exhibits B 1 and B 2 to the Registration Statement (Exhibit A) hereto attached.

I

The Company represents and warrants to each Underwriter hereafter mentioned that:

(a) It prepared and on September 26, 1935, filed with the Securities and Exchange Commission in Washington, D. C., a Registration Statement, a copy of which is attached as Exhibit A; it also prepared and on October 11, 1935, filed with said Commission an amended Registration Statement substantially in the form attached hereto as Exhibit B;

(b) In connection with said Registration Statement it filed a

[1] Source: Registration Statement filed under the Securities Act of 1933. Docket 2-1671, Exhibit F.

Prospectus, a copy of which is attached as Exhibit C, and in connection with said Amended Registration Statement it filed an Amended Prospectus substantially in the form attached hereto as Exhibit D;

(c) It is about to file certain further amendments to the Registration Statement and the Prospectus, such further amendments being substantially in the form attached hereto as Exhibit E;

(d) When said Registration Statement becomes effective, the Registration Statement and the Prospectus as amended will fully comply with the provisions of the Securities Act of 1933, as amended, and the Rules and Regulations of said Commission, and neither said Registration Statement nor said Prospectus as amended will contain any untrue statement of a material fact or omit to state any material fact required to be stated therein or necessary to make the statements therein not misleading;

(e) It has approved for use in connection with advertising the Series B Bonds a form of "newspaper prospectus" (which is not an Offering Prospectus) and said "newspaper prospectus" does not contain an untrue statement of a material fact or omit to state a material fact necessary to make the statements therein not misleading.

II

Upon the basis of the foregoing representations and warranties but subject to conditions hereinafter stated, the Company hereby agrees to sell to you and your associates named below (on whose behalf you are acting), severally and not jointly, and you and your associates named below (hereinafter collectively referred to as the "Underwriters") agree to purchase from the Company, severally and not jointly, at 100½% of the principal amount thereof, plus interest accrued thereon from October 1, 1935, to the date of payment and delivery, an aggregate of $43,700,000 principal amount of Series B Bonds (out of the total authorized issue of $45,000,000 principal amount of Series B Bonds) in the several principal amounts below set forth opposite their respective names:

Names	Amounts
Morgan Stanley & Co., Incorporated	$13,600,000
Kuhn, Loeb & Co.	6,800,000
Kidder, Peabody & Co.	5,300,000
Lee Higginson Corporation	2,500,000
The First Boston Corporation	4,500,000
Brown Harriman & Co., Incorporated	4,000,000
Edward B. Smith & Co.	4,000,000
Mellon Securities Company	2,000,000
Bonbright & Company, Incorporated	1,000,000

III

If any Underwriter shall fail or refuse because of financial inability to purchase the principal amount of Series B Bonds which it is required to purchase under this Agreement, the Company will immediately notify you and you agree, within three days of receipt of such notice, to purchase for your own account or to find purchasers for such Series B Bonds on the terms herein set forth. In any such case you will have the right to postpone the date of payment for an additional period of not more than one week in order to effect whatever changes shall be necessary.

IV

The Company expects to sell the remaining $1,300,000 principal amount of Series B Bonds on or before December 1, 1935, to the Trustee of Pension Funds established by the Company and by other ompanies of the Bell System at 100½% of the principal amount hereof, plus interest accrued thereon from October 1, 1935, to the ate of payment.

V

You have advised us that the Underwriters expect to offer their espective portions of the Series B Bonds, as soon after the effective ate of the Registration Statement as in their judgment it is feasible) do so, at 100½% of their principal amount, plus accrued interest) the date of payment, when, as and if issued, and accepted by the nderwriters, and subject to the approval of their counsel. In conection with this offering you, on behalf of the Underwriters severly, expect to form a Selling Group, in which some of the several nderwriters may participate, to which Selling Group all or part f the Series B Bonds which the Underwriters undertake to purase are to be offered at the public offering price less a concession 1% of the principal amount thereof, of which the Underwriters ay retain not in excess of ¼% for the pro rata share of expenses curred in connection with the issue and sale of the Series B Bonds her than the amount of expense for advertising to be reimbursed the Underwriters by the Company as provided in the third paraaph of this Article V. A copy of the proposed Selling Group Agreeent is attached hereto as Exhibit F.

The Company authorizes the Underwriters, and the members of y Selling Group formed by you on behalf of the Underwriters r the purpose of selling the Series B Bonds, and all dealers to hom the Series B Bonds may be sold by the Underwriters or by e members of such Selling Group to use the Prospectus, Exhibit

D, as amended by the amendments to the Prospectus set forth in Exhibit E, in connection with the sale of the Series B Bonds.

The Company authorizes the Underwriters to advertise the Series B Bonds by means of a "newspaper prospectus" approved by the Company (which is not to be used as an Offering Prospectus) containing certain information in regard to the issue as permitted by the Regulations of the Securities and Exchange Commission and the Company agrees to reimburse the Underwriters on account of the additional cost of such "newspaper prospectus" as compared with the so-called short form advertisement in an amount not to exceed $25,000.

Payment for the Series B Bonds which the Underwriters undertake to purchase shall be made to the Company or its order by certified check in New York funds for the respective accounts of the Underwriters, at the office of J. P. Morgan & Co., 23 Wall Street New York, N. Y., at any time, at the option of the Underwriter on or after October 22, 1935, but not later than November 1, 1935 upon delivery of the Series B Bonds in temporary form, in such authorized denominations as the Underwriters may request, exchangeable for definitive Series B Bonds without expense to th holders as soon as possible after the preparation and authenticatio of the definitive Series B Bonds. The date of such payment an delivery is hereinafter referred to as the "closing date."

VI

The several obligations of the Underwriters hereunder are subje to the following conditions:

(a) The Registration Statement and any and all amendmen thereto shall have become effective not later than October 18, 193 and no stop order suspending the effectiveness thereof shall ha been issued prior to the closing date, nor any proceedings for th purpose have been taken or threatened prior to such date;

(b) The form and validity of the Series B Bonds, and of t corporate proceedings and other related matters incident to t issuance of the Series B Bonds, and the form of the Registratic Statement as amended and the Prospectus as amended shall ha been approved by Messrs. Davis, Polk, Wardwell, Gardiner & Ree counsel for the Underwriters;

(c) The receipt by you prior to payment by the Underwrit for the Series B Bonds of an opinion, satisfactory to counsel f the Underwriters, of counsel for the Company, Messrs. Cutti Moore & Sidley, with respect to (1) the validity of the Series Bonds, the First and Refunding Mortgage, and the Supplemen

Indenture, (2) the validity of the lien of the First and Refunding Mortgage, as set forth in the Registration Statement and Prospectus, as amended, (3) the titles of the Company to the property owned by it and subject to the lien of said First and Refunding Mortgage, as set forth in the Registration Statement as amended and Prospectus as amended, and (4) the order or orders of the Illinois Commerce Commission authorizing the issuance and sale of the Series B Bonds and the sufficiency of such order or orders;

(d) The receipt by you prior to payment by the Underwriters for the Series B Bonds of a certificate dated not earlier than the day before the closing date, of the President or a Vice President of the Company, to the effect that there has been no change in the financial condition of the Company from that set forth in the Registration Statement as amended and the Prospectus as amended, other than changes arising from transactions in the ordinary course of business.

VII

In further consideration of the purchase by the Underwriters of Series B Bonds as provided herein, the Company covenants as follows:

(a) As soon as the Company is advised thereof, to advise you, and confirm the advice in writing, (1) when the Registration Statement as amended has become effective and (2) in the event of the issuance by the Securities and Exchange Commission of any stop order suspending the effectiveness of the Registration Statement or of the initiation of any proceedings for that purpose;

(b) To deliver to each of the Underwriters on the effective date of the Registration Statement as amended, so many copies of the Prospectus in final form (Exhibit D as amended by the amendments to the Prospectus set forth in Exhibit E) as you may reasonably request;

(c) To furnish to you without charge a copy of the Registration Statement and financial statements and of all exhibits and amendments thereto, and to furnish to each of the other Underwriters without charge a copy of the Registration Statement and financial statements and of all amendments thereto;

(d) Before filing any amendment to the Registration Statement as amended after the latter has become effective, to furnish you with a copy of such proposed amendment;

(e) For a period of one year after the public offering of the Series B Bonds, if any change shall have occurred as a result of which the Prospectus in final form includes an untrue statement of a material fact or omits to state a material fact necessary in order to make the statements in the light of the circumstances under which they were made not misleading, to forthwith prepare and furnish to each Underwriter and to each dealer in the Selling Group referred to in Article V above an amendment or amendments to said Prospectus which will correct such Prospectus so that as corrected it will not contain any untrue statement of a material fact or omit to state any material fact necessary in order to make the statements in the light of the circumstances in which they were made not misleading. The Underwriters will furnish to the Company promptly after the public offering of the Series B Bonds a list of the names and addresses of the dealers in the Selling Group referred to in Article V above;

(f) To make generally available to the Company's security holders as soon as practicable after November 1, 1936, but not later than December 31, 1936, an earnings statement covering the period for the twelve months ended October 31, 1936;

(g) To indemnify and hold harmless the Underwriters against any and all losses, claims, damages or liabilities, joint or several, which they or any of them may become subject to under the Securities Act of 1933, as amended, and to reimburse the Underwriters for any legal or other expenses incurred by them in connection with defending any actions, in so far as such losses, claims, damages liabilities or actions arise out of or are based upon any untrue statement or alleged untrue statement of a material fact contained in the Registration Statement as amended or Prospectus as amended or "newspaper prospectus" referred to in Article I, or arise out of or are based upon the omission or alleged omission to state therein material fact required to be stated therein or necessary to mak the statements therein not misleading, except in so far as suc losses, claims, damages, liabilities or actions arise out of or ar based upon any such untrue statement or alleged untrue statemer or any such omission or alleged omission, which was made c omitted in such Registration Statement as amended or Prospect as amended or "newspaper prospectus" referred to in Article in reliance upon information furnished in writing to the Compar by any Underwriter. Each Underwriter agrees promptly upon tl commencement of any action against such Underwriter in respe to which indemnity may be sought from the Company on accou of its agreement contained in this paragraph to notify the Cor pany in writing of the commencement thereof, but the omissic of such Underwriter so to notify the Company of any such actic shall not relieve the Company from any liability which it may have to such Underwriter otherwise than on account of the indemnity agreement contained in this paragraph. In case any such action shall be brought against any Underwriter and such Underwriter shall notify the Company of the commencement thereof, the Company will be entitled to participate in (and, to the extent that it shall wish, including the selection of counsel, to direct) the defense thereof at its own expense. Any Underwriter shall have the right to employ its own counsel in any such case, but the fees and expenses of such counsel shall be at the expense of such Underwriter unless the employment of such counsel has been authorized by the Company in connection with defending such action. Each Underwriter agrees to indemnify and hold harmless the Company against any and all losses, claims, damages or liabilities, joint or several, which it may become subject to under the Securities Act of 1933, as amended, and to reimburse the Company for any legal or other expenses incurred by it in connection with defending any actions, in so far as such losses, claims, damages, liabilities or actions arise out of or are based upon any untrue statement or alleged untrue statement of a material fact contained in the Registration Statement as amended or Prospectus as amended or "newspaper prospectus" referred to in Article I, or arise out of or are based upon he omission or alleged omission to state therein a material fact equired to be stated therein or necessary to make the statements herein not misleading, which untrue statement or alleged untrue tatement or omission or alleged omission was made or omitted in uch Registration Statement as amended or Prospectus as amended r "newspaper prospectus" referred to in Article I, in reliance upon nformation furnished in writing to the Company by such Underriter. The Company agrees promptly upon the commencement f any action against the Company in respect of which indemnity ay be sought from an Underwriter on account of its agreement ntained in this paragraph to notify such Underwriter in writing f the commencement thereof, but the omission of the Company to notify such Underwriter of any such action shall not release ch Underwriter from any liability which it may have to the Comny otherwise than on account of the indemnity agreement conined in this paragraph. In case any such action shall be brought ainst the Company and the Company shall notify an Underwriter om paragraph of the commencement thereof, such Underwriter all be entitled to participate in (and, to the extent that it will sh, to direct) the defense thereof at its own expense;

(h) To make application for the listing of the Series B Bonds on the New York Stock Exchange and the Chicago Stock Exchange and their registration under the Securities Exchange Act of 1934.

VIII

(a) This Agreement shall become effective when the Registration Statement referred to above becomes effective and until such time this Agreement may be terminated by the Company, by notifying you at your office in New York, N. Y., or by such number of Underwriters as have in the aggregate agreed to purchase more than 50% of the principal amount of the Series B Bonds, by notifying the Company at its office in Chicago, Illinois. Any such notice may be in writing or by telegraph or by telephone.

(b) If this Agreement shall be terminated by the Underwriters because of any failure or refusal on the part of the Company to comply with the terms of this Agreement or to fulfill any of the conditions of this Agreement, or if for any reason the Company shall be unable to perform its obligations under this Agreement, the Company will reimburse the Underwriters severally for all of their out-of-pocket expenses (including the fees and disbursements of their counsel) reasonably incurred by them or by any Selling Group which they may have formed or caused to be formed in connection with the purchase or sale of the Series B Bonds.

IX

The agreement herein set forth has been and is made solely for the benefit of the Underwriters and the Company and no other person shall acquire or have any right under or by virtue of this Agreement.

Please confirm that the foregoing correctly sets forth the agreement between us.

Very truly yours,
ILLINOIS BELL TELEPHONE COMPANY
By F. O. Hale
President

Confirmed:
MORGAN STANLEY & CO., INCORPORATED
By Harold Stanley
President
Acting on behalf of itself and its associates severally.

Appendix II

PURCHASE GROUP AGREEMENT[1]
(1935)

$20,000,000
WILSON & CO., INC.
First Mortgage Twenty Year Bonds—Series A, 4%
Due July 15, 1935

July 26, 1935

Edward B. Smith & Co.,
31 Nassau Street,
New York, N. Y.

Field, Glore & Co.,
123 South La Salle Street,
Chicago, Illinois.

Dear Sirs:

We wish to confirm as follows the agreement between yourselves and each of the undersigned with respect to the purchase by yourselves and the undersigned severally (yourselves and the undersigned being sometimes hereinafter collectively referred to as the "Purchase Group") and the sale to the public of an aggregate of $20,000,000 principal amount of First Mortgage Twenty Year Bonds —Series A, 4%, due July 15, 1935 (hereinafter sometimes referred to as the "Bonds") of Wilson & Co., Inc.

1. You are hereby authorized to enter into an agreement with Wilson & Co., Inc. (hereinafter sometimes referred to as the "Company") on behalf of each of the undersigned, covering the purchase of the Bonds, in substantially the form of the agreement attached hereto (without the exhibits therein referred to, copies of which have been received by each of the undersigned) as Exhibit A. As specifically stated in said agreement, it is understood that all of the obligations of the various members of the Purchase Group thereunder shall not be joint but shall be several in the following amounts and proportions, except as set forth in paragraph 8 hereof:

[1] Source: Registration Statement under the Securities Act of 1933, Docket No. 2-1538, Exhibit F-2.

Name	Principal Amount	Percentage
Edward B. Smith & Co.	$4,500,000	22.5%
Field, Glore & Co.	4,500,000	22.5%
Speyer & Co.	1,800,000	9.0%
The First Boston Corporation	1,800,000	9.0%
Hallgarten & Co.	1,800,000	9.0%
Goldman, Sachs & Co.	720,000	3.6%
Bancamerica-Blair Corporation	720,000	3.6%
Lazard Freres & Company, Incorporated	720,000	3.6%
Hornblower & Weeks	720,000	3.6%
Lee Higginson Corporation	720,000	3.6%
Kuhn, Loeb & Co.	2,000,000	10.0%

You are further authorized by the undersigned to act as agents of the Purchase Group in managing the public offering and as Managers of the Selling Groups hereinafter referred to, and it is understood that all things pertaining thereto are to be managed by you.

2. The general plan for the public offering of the Bonds is set forth in the agreement, Exhibit A. You may allot such amount of Bonds which you and the undersigned shall severally purchase from the Company pursuant to the aforementioned agreement, in such proportions (which may vary as among the different members of the Purchase Group) as the several members of the Purchase Group, respectively, shall have agreed with you for sale to the Selling Groups of selected dealers referred to in Paragraph 3 of Exhibit A in accordance with the terms and conditions of the Selling Group letters which shall be substantially in the form attached hereto as Exhibit B. The allocation of Bonds as between the two groups referred to therein shall be determined by you, and both groups shall be terminated at the same time.

It is our understanding that we will be advised by you by telegraph or telephone when the issue is released for offer.

Any of the Bonds offered to members of the Selling Groups which are not sold and delivered to members of the Selling Groups may during the life of the Selling Groups, be sold by you at the public offering price for the account of the several members of the Purchase Group in the proportion that the amount of each member's Bonds offered to members of the Selling Groups bears to the total amount of Bonds offered to the Selling Groups, or, either prior to or at the termination of the Selling Groups, be divided among the several members of the Purchase Group in the same proportion.

You are authorized, for the account of the several members of the Purchase Group in proportion to their respective participation in the original purchase of the Bonds from the Company, to purchase any of the Bonds from any of the several members of the Purchase Group or of the Selling Groups, at the public offering price less the Selling Group discount or any part thereof.

Except as above provided and as provided in the Selling Group letters, during the life of the Selling Groups the members of the Purchase Group shall not offer any of the Bonds for resale at a price below the public offering price, nor allow any concession from said public offering price to any one, and during said period the several members of the Purchase Group shall otherwise be governed by the terms and conditions of the Selling Group letters whether or not they are members of such Selling Groups.

3. On the closing date provided in said agreement, Exhibit A (hereinafter sometimes referred to as the "closing date"), each of the undersigned members of the Purchase Group will deliver to you at the office of the Guaranty Trust Company of New York, Corporation Trust Department, 140 Broadway, New York City, its certified check in New York Clearing House funds payable to the order of Wilson & Co., Inc., for the full purchase price for the entire amount of Bonds which such member has agreed to purchase at 97⅜% of the principal amount plus accrued interest against delivery of Bonds in temporary form to such member. Each member of the Purchase Group agrees promptly to deliver to you for its account such of the Bonds purchased by such member as shall have been sold to the Selling Groups for its account or otherwise sold by you for its account pursuant to the provisions of this agreement. Upon receipt by you of payment for Bonds sold to the Selling Groups you will remit to each member, in the proportion that the amount of such member's Bonds offered to the members of the Selling Groups bears to the total amount of Bonds offered to the Selling Groups, out of the payment so received, 97⅜% of the principal amount of the Bonds so paid for, plus accrued interest. Upon receipt by you of payment for Bonds otherwise sold by you for the account of the several members of the Purchase Group you will remit to each member out of the payments so received in the proportion in which such member shall be entitled to receive payment, 97⅜% of the principal amount of the Bonds so paid for, plus accrued interest.

4. As compensation for your services in managing the public offering and the Selling Groups, we agree to pay to you ¼ of 1% of the principal amount of the Bonds purchased by us from the Company. Such payment will be made by us at the time of your final accounting hereinafter referred to.

It is our understanding that all expenses incurred by you, other than those for which Wilson & Co., Inc., reimburses the Purchase Group, in connection with the purchase, carrying and distribution of the Bonds, including without limiting the generality of the foregoing, all transfer taxes, all legal fees and all other expenses arising under the terms of the agreement, Exhibit A, and this agreement, shall be charged 50% against the compensation granted to you pursuant to the paragraph immediately above, and 50% against the account of each member of the Purchase Group, including yourselves, proportionately according to its participation in the original purchase of Bonds from the Company, and your determination of the amount thereof shall be final and conclusive.

Upon the termination of the Selling Groups you shall render an accounting to the several members of the Purchase Group of their final net profits or losses (after deduction of a pro rata share of known expenses and a pro rata share of a reserve to cover possible additional expenses, as provided in the paragraph immediately above), delivering over at the same time (in the proportion that the amount of each member's Bonds offered to members of the Selling Groups bears to the total amount of Bonds offered to the Selling Groups) any of the Bonds delivered to you on the closing date for delivery to the members of the Selling Groups but not taken up by members of the Selling Groups or sold by you for the account of the several members of the Purchase Group or theretofore divided by you among the several members of the Purchase Group, pursuant to the provisions of this agreement; and will deliver over at the same time (in proportion to their respective participations in the original purchase of the Bonds from the Company) any Bonds purchased and held for the respective accounts of members of the Purchase Group at the termination of the Selling Groups. You shall not be under any duty to account for any interest on funds of the members of the Purchase Group at any time in your hands.

5. Each member of the Purchase Group authorizes you in your discretion, during the life of the Selling Groups, to buy and sell bonds in the open market or otherwise for the account of the respective members of the Purchase Group, who shall participate in the profits or losses in proportion to their respective participations in the original purchase of Bonds from the Company; provided, however, that at no time shall the net commitment either for long or short account exceed $2,000,000 principal amount of Bonds. Each member of the Purchase Group agrees to pay to you on demand the full purchase price of any bonds so purchased for its account.

6. Upon application to you, you will inform any member of the Purchase Group as to the states in which you believe the Bonds have been qualified for sale under the respective Securities or Blue Sky Laws of such states, but you do not assume any responsibility or obligation as to the right of any member of the Purchase Group to sell the Bonds in any state.

If any of the members of the Purchase Group shall cancel his agreement with the Company in accordance with the terms of the agreement, Exhibit A, the obligations hereunder of the members so cancelling shall thereupon immediately cease and determine, except to pay his proportionate share of all expenses. No member shall cancel its agreement with the Company except after notice to all the other members and with the consent of members of the Purchase Group agreeing to purchase not less than 50% of the aggregate principal amount of the issue.

Any Bonds sold by a member of the Purchase Group (except Bonds sold to the Selling Groups), which shall be purchased during the life of the Selling Groups by the Managers of the Selling Groups in the open market, at or below the public offering price, shall be repurchased at a price equal to the cost of such purchase in the open market by the member of the Purchase Group to whom the Bonds were originally delivered.

We hereby authorize you to take such action as you may deem advisable in respect of all matters pertaining to the agreement, Exhibit A, it being understood that you shall act only as agent for the several members of the Purchase Group. It is our understanding that you shall be under no liability for or in respect of the value of the Bonds, the validity or the form of or the representations contained in the Bonds, the Mortgage Indenture securing the Bonds or the Registration Statement, Prospectus, or the agreement Exhibit A; or for the delivery of the Bonds or for the performance by the Company or by others of any agreement on its or their part. You shall not be liable to the undersigned for the qualification of the Bonds for sale under the laws of any jurisdiction, nor shall you be liable for any of the provisions of this agreement of, in, or for any matter connected therewith, except for lack of good faith and except for obligations expressly assumed by you in this agreement. Nothing herein contained shall constitute the several members of the Purchase Group partners or render any member liable for the participation of any other member and the participations and liabilities of each of the several members of the Purchase Group are several in accordance with their respective interests and are not joint.

We confirm that we have examined the Registration Statement and amendments thereto filed in respect to the Bonds, and are willing to accept the responsibilities of underwriters thereunder; that we have read the Prospectus, and are willing to proceed with the public offering of the Bonds in the manner contemplated; and that the form of Selling Group letter attached hereto as Exhibit B is satisfactory to us.

Please confirm that the foregoing correctly states the understanding between us by signing and returning to each of the undersigned a counterpart of this letter, all of which taken together will constitute one and the same agreement.

Very truly yours,

Speyer & Co.
(Speyer & Co.)

The First Boston Corporation
By George D. Woods, V.P.

Hallgarten & Co.
(Hallgarten & Co.)

Goldman, Sachs & Co.
(Goldman, Sachs & Co.)

Bancamerica-Blair Corporation
By Hearn W. Streat, V.P.

Lazard Freres & Company, Incorporated
By John D. Harrison, V.P.

Hornblower & Weeks
(Hornblower & Weeks)

Lee Higginson Corporation
By James J. Lee
Asst. Secty.

Kuhn, Loeb & Co.
(Kuhn, Loeb & Co.)

The foregoing is hereby confirmed:

Edward B. Smith & Co.
(Edward B. Smith & Co.)

Field, Glore & Co.
(Field, Glore & Co.)

Chapter XVIII

SELLING GROUPS

The Distributing Problem

In the preceding chapter, the process of originating new security issues was traced, and the steps taken by investment houses in purchasing and carrying new flotations pending their distribution were described. American investment banking houses seldom wish to hold issues which they purchase for any length of time. They are in the business of merchandising securities, and a cardinal precept of modern merchandising in general is a quick turnover. Hence, the most important part of the investment banking process is the actual sale of the new offerings to investors.

Practices connected with the negotiation and purchase of new security issues have been profoundly changed in recent years. The business of origination is largely restricted to a relatively small number of houses with wide connections and resources, who now bear the full burden of underwriting and carrying new issues in process of syndication. Methods of distributing securities have been changed correspondingly, but in general to a lesser extent.

In considering distributing syndicates, it is important to note that three distinct and sometimes conflicting aims are striven after. The first is a reasonable and, if possible, large profit to the participants. Secondly, speed is of the essence in successful syndicate operations, since purchase group members are eager to terminate their liability and free their resources for other transactions. The longer a syndicate remains open, the greater the risk of unforeseen developments which may interfere with the successful consummation of the offering. In the third place, the syndicate aims at wide and permanent distribution of the securities as far as possible, both for the satisfaction of the vendor government or cooperation, assuring permanent relations with it, and to prevent dissatisfaction among clients by later sharp declines in price caused by poor distribution.

The assurance of a profit is closely related to the factor of speed. The purchase of securities from the vendor by the purchase group is usually made on terms dictated by the state of the securities market. If it is felt by the bankers that a bond issue can be sold successfully at 95, they may purchase it at 92. Unless the sale is effected as quickly as possible, however, the market may change and only an average of 93 may be realized, leaving perhaps a net loss after necessary syndicate expenses have been met.

The Selling Group

The selling group is almost universally the type of syndicate utilized today to effect final distribution of a new issue of securities among investors.

Before the Federal Securities Act was enacted, the actual sale of a new offering of securities was effected through either a distribution syndicate or a selling group. The *distribution syndicate* both underwrote the issue, thus virtually releasing the purchase group from responsibility, and actually sold it. The *selling group* assumed no underwriting liability, restricting itself entirely to distribution, any unsold balance reverting to the members of the purchase group.

Even before the Act was enacted, however, the distribution syndicate became less popular, and the selling group came to be widely preferred. Several reasons explained this. First, the existence of numerous retailers with small resources made them less ready to underwrite, and there was more doubt about their ability to make good on their commitment if the issue proved a failure. In fact, during the early depression years dealers turned down freely invitations to join distribution syndicates because of their unwillingness to assume the risks involved. Secondly, as profit margins have tended to become narrower, originators have become less willing to grant members of a selling group the larger share of the gross spread which they want in the event that they share the underwriting liability.

The fact that under the federal Securities Act the underwriters may not sell until the registration statement is effective, at the end of a 20-day waiting period, has assured that the selling group will dominate security distribution.

The nature of the selling group itself has changed in recent years. Formerly, it was customary to keep a new issue intact, except for a portion earmarked for sale abroad or withdrawn for some other special purpose, until the day of public offering through a distribution syndicate or selling group. This is no longer the case. Now, the selling group is concerned with the sale only of that portion of a new offering which is not actually sold by purchase group members. In order to avoid additional transfer taxes on the bonds or stock sold by purchase group members, it is usual for these houses to sell indirectly from their underwriting participation the bonds they can dispose of at retail, only the balance going to the selling group. In fact, for the most part, purchase group members do not now technically join the selling groups on their own issues.

Choosing the List

The first important step in the formation of a selling group is the choice of a list of security houses to constitute its membership. This is a delicate and difficult task, for the best issues of securities may prove failures if backed by a group of firms with inadequate distributing facilities.

The chief criterion in the choice of selling group members is their ability to place bonds with more or less permanent investors. Formerly, it was common to include houses of financial strength in distribution syndicates merely because of their financial responsibility and strong reputation. This is no longer the case, such firms being sought now for the purchase group, which alone assumes an underwriting liability.

Ability to place bonds may be secured by a house in several ways. The most common is through a corps of salesmen who have a clientele reached by direct solicitation. In the second place, a number of security houses have investment trust affiliations with whom substantial amounts of bonds may be placed, thus greatly improving their distributing power. Finally, it is not uncommon for investment trusts to be given places on selling groups because of the large amount of an issue they can take.

The chief consideration in the choice of members of a selling group is, therefore, distribution power. The large originating houses keep a record of the past performance of security houses which they propose to invite to join new syndicates, and thus are in a position constantly to weed out houses which chronically fail successfully to place bonds and stock allotted them, while increasing participations for those which are successful. A separate card or loose-record sheet is generally kept for each syndicate participant, recording his participation and the record of his success or failure in handling it. A sample of such a card is shown in Fig. 15.

Name........................

Address..................... ....
Number of Offices

DATE	ISSUE	PARTICIPATION		SALES	REPURCHASES
		OFFERED	ACCEPTED		

FIG. 15. CARD FORM TO RECORD PERFORMANCE OF SYNDICATE MEMBERS

The multiplication of institutional investors in recent years has made it increasingly difficult for the small dealer to hold his own. When the commercial bank, the savings bank, the investment trust and the insurance companies are all getting bonds below the offering price, at what they regard as a "wholesale price" to which they are entitled by virtue of the large-scale buying they do, the small security dealer finds he cannot sell to these worth-while customers at a profit. The Investment Bankers Association has sought to correct this situation, and at the same time to limit competition in the security business, by publishing lists of authorized dealers who alone are considered entitled to syndicate membership or to dealers' discounts.

The first published list of authorized dealers, compiled by the investment houses which are members of the Association in each part of the country, was distributed in 1929. In describing its purposes, the Investment Bankers Association of America made the following statement:

> It is desirable that all members of the Association conform in so far as possible and in the territories covered, to the list of dealers in the granting of concessions to dealers and in the offering of syndicate or selling group participations.
>
> In compiling the list, no responsibility is assumed by the Investment Bankers Association of America or any of the Groups thereof with regard to the moral and/or financial responsibility of any dealer listed therein or for any errors or omissions in the list. Several of the Groups have furnished their lists to all members of the Association in printed pamphlet form; and at least three Group lists have classified certain dealers as being eligible to receive syndicate participations and dealers' discounts, and certain other dealers as being eligible for dealers' discounts only. In reproducing the lists in the pamphlet, it was determined, for sake of uniformity and simplicity, that the dealers should not be divided into classes. Revisions of lists will be made by the Groups from time to time.
>
> The list is not limited to members of the Association, but includes all dealers entitled to recognition as such in the opinion of the respective Groups, whether members or non-members of the Association.
>
> The list is compiled for the use of members of the Investment Bankers Association of America only and has been copyrighted.

The Investment Bankers Code sought to achieve this same end, providing:

> No investment banker proposing to organize a selling syndicate or a selling group shall invite or permit any person to be a participant in such selling syndicate or a member in such selling group unless such person is an investment banker actually engaged in the investment banking business.

The security dealer generally finds that he must adopt a consistent policy with regard to the acceptance of selling group invitations. If he turns down an offer to join a group formed to sell an issue not altogether desirable, he may very possibly be left out of the list of houses invited to join the next group organized by the same underwriters to put out a highly desirable offering. The leading originating houses universally demand that participants in their syndicates take the good with the bad, as they come along. Only in this way can they build up an efficient security-distributing machine of permanent character.

For the smaller security house without much originating power of its own, a regular place on the selling group lists of large originating houses is often its most valuable asset. Such a place can be won, however, only by consistently accepting invitations to join syndicates and by proving that participations can actually be placed with investors. This curtails to a certain extent, of course, the ability of the house to run its business solely in the interest of clients, as it means that sometimes securities will be taken which the house, if left to its own judgment, would not care to sell to its clients.

One alternative to joining selling groups for the smaller house is to "sell off the list" of a larger house, and many small dealers and banks do so as a regular thing. This is accomplished by securing the printed offering list of an issue house and offering to sell securities from it at the prices therein stated. The house whose offering sheet is used allows a special dealers' discount of, say, ¼ of 1 per cent on such sales.

Also, selling group agreements usually allow a dealer's discount on orders from those who want securities for resale. The majority of dealers do not join selling groups as a rule, selling for a dealer's discount or specializing in obscure local securities or special types of issues such as municipals or investment trusts.

A final consideration in connection with the choice of houses in the formation of a selling syndicate or group is the number to be included in the invitation. This will depend on the general state of the market and, more specifically, on the reception investors are expected to accord the issue. If there is uncertainty as to its reception, it is customary to invite dealers who may want substantially more than the amount of the offering, as many participants may be able to place only part of the bonds they ask for. In the case of a larger issue, several hundred houses will be approached.

In certain cases of very large offerings, more than 500 houses have been included in the selling groups.

Letter of Invitation

When the list of prospective members has been prepared, the next step in the formation of the selling group is the sending out of the invitations to participate.

Since actual sales of a new security issue, even by the purchase group to the selling group, may not take place until the offering has been registered and the 20-day waiting period has elapsed, the formation of the selling group is necessarily delayed until then. Of course, informal "feelers" can be put out earlier, but under the Act no sale can be made without giving the buyer a prospectus. Hence, dealers cannot be formally asked to join the selling group until the registration statement is effective.

Another complication was introduced by a provision of the Code of Fair Practice for Investment Bankers, to which many houses conform, requiring delivery of an adequate description or prospectus of the security to each investment banker who is to be offered a participation in a group at least three days before the date of public offering. This wise provision, designed to end extreme high-pressure methods in the formation of selling groups, thus conflicted with the Securities Act.

This problem has been solved by sending out a preliminary or "red herring" prospectus and selling group letter, which contain no reference to price, commissions, etc., to prospective selling group members three days before the date when the registration statement is scheduled to become effective. The term "red herring" arises from the fact that a notation indicating its tentative and preliminary character is printed across its face in red ink. Then, usually at one minute past midnight on the day when the statement becomes effective, the purchase group manager sends telegrams to all selling group members completing the preliminary prospectus and selling group letters.

The public offering price, the selling group concession and the amount offered to each dealer are thus inserted. Prospective selling group members may be provided with large quantities of prospectuses which are delivered at telegraph offices in advance and released by wire on the public offering date.

Dealers usually have until 11 A.M. or noon of the day when the registration statement becomes effective to accept the offering or reject it, in accordance with the terms of the offering letter.

The selling group letter constitutes the contract that regulates the operation of the group. Since no underwriting is involved, a simple reply, or a countersigning of a copy of this letter, constitutes the selling group agreement.

Types of Selling Groups

Two main types of selling groups are in general use. One offers the participant the right to make a firm subscription, on the morning of the offering date, for a fixed amount of the bonds or stock. If accepted in whole or in part, the selling group member knows how many bonds or shares he is certain to get. Such a participation is not subject to allotment.

The usual wording of a selling group letter provision permitting a firm subscription is as follows:

> One or more of the several Underwriters are reserving for purchase by you, and hereby offers to sell you,
>
> $....................
>
> principal amount of the Bonds when, as and if issued and accepted by the several Underwriters and subject to the approval of their counsel and to the terms and conditions hereof. Your acceptance of this offer, which may be in whole or in part, must be received by us by eleven o'clock A.M. (Standard Time), September 15, 1936, in your city, and should be addressed to........................ Bonds offered, but not accepted, may be reoffered and sold by us in our uncontrolled discretion.

The Investment Bankers Code referred to a selling group operating in this manner as a selling syndicate, but this terminology does not appear to have gained general acceptance.

A second type of selling group letter invites dealers to subscribe for the issue in any amount they wish, but the actual amount is subject to allotment by the syndicate manager. The usual wording of such a general request for subscriptions, subject to allotment, is as follows:

> The several Underwriters are offering to certain investment bankers (herein called the Selling Group), in which they are pleased to include you, the right to subscribe, subject to allotment, to . . . shares, part of the issue of such Stock.
>
> Subscriptions subject to allotment must be received by........

The first form, in which a fixed amount of bonds is offered to the dealers, has generally been the more popular. An attractive issue, readily salable, will almost invariably be offered by the purchase group on a firm basis. A less desirable issue, on the other hand, will be offered for subscriptions in any amount, as a rule. The acceptance may be for a part, as well as for the whole, of the amount proffered in many cases, although partial acceptance is not always acceptable.

The Selling Group Agreement

The operation of the selling group is governed by the agreement embodied in the letter of the manager. This agreement varies considerably in form and content. It is generally a simply worded and concise document, but experience has caused the insertion of a number of provisions to prevent the development of abuses in operation. A sample selling group letter is presented in the appendix to this chapter.

The chief points in the usual selling group agreement are the following:

1. Description of issue
2. Concessions to members
3. Handling repurchased securities
4. Allowances to other dealers
5. Termination of group
6. Expenses

In individual cases, any other provisions are included as found necessary.

1. *Description of Issue.*—Under the Securities Act it is necessary to make the selling group letter refer to "the enclosed

prospectus." The latter gives a full description of the issue and the issuer. Finally, it should be indicated that the securities are being offered "when, as and if issued and accepted by the underwriters," and "subject to the approval of counsel." This will cover those unusual but real contingencies when the transaction is not completed for one reason or another. If the securities were not actually delivered, the selling group member or his customer could sue for damages unless this protective clause is used, thus making the contract conditional.

2. *Concessions.*—Members of a selling group may subscribe to a new issue at the public offering price, less a concession given only to them. This concession is usually a substantial portion of the gross spread between the price received by the issuer and that paid by the public, the balance of the difference being absorbed by the purchase group and the selling group manager.

3. *Handling Repurchased Securities.*—During the life of the selling group, it is almost always provided, no member may offer the issue below the public offering price. This is necessary in order to permit the selling effort to proceed, without scaring away potential buyers because of a drop in market price. The syndicate manager, to assure that the price will be maintained, almost invariably pegs the quotation in the market through placing orders to buy at the public offering price.

A typical provision of this kind runs as follows:

> During the life of the bond selling syndicate you shall not offer the bonds at a price below the initial public offering price. In the event that, during the life of the bond selling syndicate any member of the underwriting group through the managers of the bond selling syndicate contracts for or purchases in the open market at or below the initial public price offering any of the bonds theretofore delivered to you, the managers reserve the right to withhold the above-mentioned concession in respect of such bonds and in addition to charge you with the broker's commission paid thereon.

Formerly, selling group managers had the option of either delivering bonds purchased in the open market in connection with pegging operations back to the member to whom they had been originally delivered, or canceling the selling group commission on these bonds and returning them to the unsold balance in the hands of the group. Currently, it is usual merely to cancel the commission and to add brokerage costs in connection with the repurchase. Repurchased securities are not now forced back upon houses that may not be able to sell them. It is recognized that they will throw them on the market or otherwise dispose of them at the first opportunity, to free their funds for other business, thus unsettling the market after the dissolution of the syndicate. Where an issue is likely to be particularly hard to sell, or where the lack of a market makes resale unlikely, no provision whatever may be made for market support or penalties covering repurchased securities.

In order to fix the liability of the several syndicate members to repurchase bonds which the manager buys in the market, a careful record is kept of the numbers of bonds delivered to different participants. When bonds are repurchased at or below the offering price, the manager is then in position to trace them.

Where a new offering is part of an already outstanding issue, the trading account usually has to buy a substantial block of the security from old holders in pegging the market. The agreement generally provides in such cases that the maximum repurchases shall not exceed a certain percentage, say 10 per cent, of the amount of the new issue.

4. *Allowances to Other Dealers.*—It is usually provided that a selling group member may reallow a portion of his concession, usually ¼ of 1 per cent of the face value, to other dealers. Before 1927, such concessions were also usually given financial institutions and large investors. This type of price concession came to be regarded as an abuse, however, and was specifically termed an unfair trade practice by the Investment Bankers Association of America in 1927, except when allowed *bona fide* security dealers. The Investment Bankers Code also barred all deductions and commissions from the public offering price except for permission to "allow to another investment banker a commission or concession if and to the extent that provision is made therefore in the agreement creating the selling syndicate or the selling group." However, banks that buy bonds for resale to clients, and even large institutional investors, do obtain dealers' allowances in numerous instances. It specifi-

cally added that any dealer obtaining such concession automatically became subject to the requirement that all sales be at the public offering price during the life of the syndicate.

5. *Termination of Group.*—The duration of the selling group is one of the most important matters that must be specifically provided in the agreement. The most common provision is that the group shall have an existence of 30 days, subject to earlier termination by the manager, while it may be extended for a period up to 30 days more by members representing 75 per cent of the issue. In several cases an initial life of 45 days is provided.

Quick termination of syndicates is favored by many investment bankers. They contend that the existence of many open syndicates at one time gives the bond market an artificial character and tends to frighten buyers away from new issues, thus demoralizing the market even at times when fundamental conditions are favorable to the large-scale distribution of securities.

6. *Expenses.*—The selling group incurs certain expenses, apart from those of the purchase group. These may be charged in some cases against the member dealers, but it is far more usual to have the purchase group absorb these outlays.

Selling Group Operation

In the operation of the selling group, the manager has supreme power within the limitations of the agreement. In order to remove any doubt on this score, a paragraph may be inserted in the agreement which provides that the managers "shall have full power and authority to act in all syndicate matters," without any obligation "except for want of good faith." In the event of a default by a participant, the manager reserves the right to substitute another house.

While the important but routine details connected with the formation of the group are being completed, the manager proceeds with the public offering of the issue. The first important task in this connection is the distribution of the prospectus and other offering literature.

The federal Securities Act provides for the form of prospectus that must be used for registered issues, and the tendency has been to follow suit with non-registered issues. Newspaper

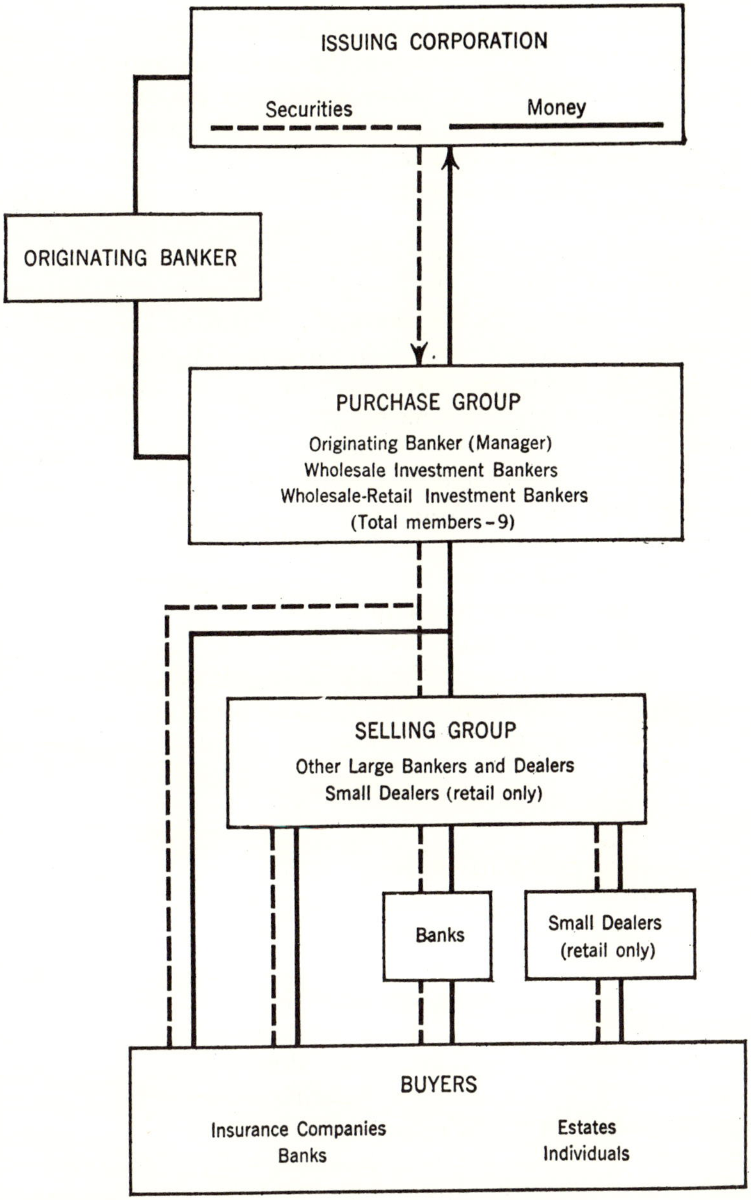

FIG. 16. CHART ILLUSTRATING THE OPERATION OF PRESENT-DAY SYNDICATION METHODS

advertisements and other forms of advertising literature also must conform to regulations of the Securities and Exchange Commission. Even before the Securities Act was enacted, however, investment bankers sought to raise standards in connection with offering circulars.

The general use of disclaimers and the tendency to include only favorable information in offering circulars have been frequently criticized by committees of the Investment Bankers Association of America. In 1929, the Association began the practice of issuing specifications of information regarded as necessary for circulars for each important type of security. Furthermore, provision was made for quick action against members who violated these standards, complaints being received by the chairman of committees of the Association devoted to the different classes of securities and then turned over by them to the Association's Committee on Business Conduct.

The Investment Bankers Code also set up standards of disclosure in the advertising of new issues.

The manager generally disclaims responsibility for seeing that regulations governing the sale of securities in the various states have been complied with. The complex subject of blue-sky laws, as these legal regulations are called, is discussed in Chapter XXII.

The Offering

The selling group having been formed, the actual offering proceeds. In the case of larger issues, extensive preparations may be undertaken. Advance publicity is sought, perhaps by means of "news releases" sent out through the financial agency which is to handle the advertising. The filing of the registration statement and amendments assures much advance attention also, in the press and financial services.

In choosing the actual day of offering, it is good practice to avoid periods of temporary congestion in the security markets, the occurrence of an unfavorable event, or any other circumstance which seems to make delay advisable. The managers retain full discretion on this score, being able to delay actual offering even though the 20-day waiting period elapses; and participants who actually sell securities publicly before the formal offering date are guilty of the practice of "beating the gun."

Offerings in most cases are made in the morning, although in individual instances an issue may be formally offered in the afternoon. Municipal bonds are frequently placed on formal sale as soon as awarded, which may be at any time through the day. In general, however, the manager receives subscriptions for the issue at the opening of business on the offering date chosen. In the quaint language of finance, which originated in the days when subscriptions to new issues of securities were received in the public rooms of taverns or coffee houses and inscribed in big recording books, the process of making the formal public offering is called "opening the books." When the books are opened, the manager accepts subscriptions to the issue from both selling group participants and outsiders. The privilege is retained "to reject these subscriptions in whole or in part," except where firm subscriptions may be made by selling group members. Outside subscribers may not have much prospect of getting allotments if the demand for it is heavy.

The manager reserves the right to close the books at his discretion. If the demand for the issue is very great, the books may be closed immediately on opening, and announcement is made that the issue has been over-subscribed. Where the results are not good, the books may remain open for weeks and months. In fact, they may never be formally closed, the unsold bonds being distributed to members of the purchase group on its expiration date. It is understood, of course, that announcement of over-subscription does not by any means indicate that the entire issue has been placed with investors. Members of the purchase and selling groups and other dealers place the orders. They may be padded purposely, and, because of the need for haste, many of these subscriptions are blindly made before there has been an opportunity to check up on the actual demand for securities among the clients of the subscribing house. Hence, over-subscription usually means over-subscription by dealers, who then still face the task of making a distribution to the investing public. It is for this reason that the Investment Bankers Association of America has objected to the use of a statement in the offering advertisement to the effect that the entire issue has been sold, when, as a matter of fact, subscriptions have come in the main from investment houses who still have before them the task of selling these securities to investors. A form of statement which meets this criticism is that "orders have been received from dealers and others for an amount of these securities in excess of the offering."

The problem of allotting securities against subscriptions where there has been an over-subscription is faced not only by the manager, but also by each member as among its own clients. The practice frequently followed is to have a conference of the salesmen, at which old customers and large buyers of securities are given special consideration; the effort may also be made to satisfy as fully as possible orders for small lots because they are considered to represent a *bona fide* investment demand.

Payment by Investors

Subscriptions are accepted and confirmed in the usual case without any cash payment being made. Orders for new issues are taken at the time of offering and confirmed shortly thereafter, and payment against the delivery of temporary securities representing the issue is not required usually for a period averaging almost two weeks. The period was formerly much longer.

This custom arises from the speed with which such operations are carried out. Even despite the 20-day waiting period provided by the Securities Act, there is often insufficient time for the advance preparation and distribution of temporary securities, and so delivery cannot be made. Also, if payment were required immediately, the underwriters would have to put up the cash pending the receipt of funds from buyers Furthermore, it is felt that investors should be given a little leeway before being asked to turn over the full cash purchase price of the purchase. Nevertheless, this custom of delaying the payment encourages speculators to "take a ride" by buying the securities in the hope of selling out at a scalping profit before the date of payment. In some quarters, the remedy has been proposed of requiring a small down payment with the order, but this has not as yet been adopted to any extent.

The Investment Bankers Code provided for a 5 per cent down payment by subscribers to new offerings.

On the date of payment, temporary securities are delivered against cash payment by subscribers. It usually takes six months or more to prepare permanent engraved certificates of bonds or stock, especially of the former, with their coupons. Hence, it is common practice to deliver temporary certificates that can be printed quickly. Such temporary securities are negotiable and represent the final securities in all transactions until the latter are issued.

If for any reason temporary bonds or stocks, as the case may be, cannot be delivered by the issuing corporation, then the underwriters may issue receipts, usually termed *interims,* against payment by investors. The Investment Bankers Association of America, and the Investment Bankers Code, have both provided that the underwriters shall hold actual securities or cash in a separate trustee account, to protect holders of the interims. Where securities are held, the underwriters' receipt, which in appearance resembles a temporary bond or stock, is known as an interim certificate, and if cash is held it is then an interim receipt. Where the securities or cash are held by a trust company which issues a receipt of its own, then the latter is known as a trust certificate or trust receipt. Where a dealer issues his own receipt, it is known as a dealer's receipt.

In view of the 20-day waiting period under the Act, it is now usual to have temporary bonds or stocks from the issuer available before the stated settlement date, making the use of interims and dealers' receipts unnecessary.

Syndicate Abuses

A number of practices have developed in the operation of selling groups which are not strictly in accord with the terms of the agreements or the intentions of the managers. In certain instances, these practices have constituted abuses which are recognized as undesirable. In other cases, these deviations arise from the force of circumstances, and may in time become recognized as necessary and ethically correct practices.

The most important series of abuses is connected with the "shading" of the agreed offering price of an issue by participants in the syndicate. If the securities are not moving at a satisfactory rate, the participant in the syndicate may share his profit with his client by reducing the price. This sometimes takes the form of offering the issue at an institutional or dealers' discount to those not properly entitled to such rebate. Such price-cutting is stimulated by dealers whose large participations in a syndicate are ill-considered because of the speed with which decisions must be reached, or by keen competition among investment houses eager to curry favor with large investors.

A more subtle way in which price-cutting is often carried out is through the practice of "over-trading," or accepting other securities in exchange above their market prices. This has been made common because of the fact that individual salesmen can thus increase their sales and obtain commissions even if the customer has no ready cash for further investment. Although this is frequently specifically forbidden in the syndicate agreement, effective methods to halt this practice have been very difficult to devise.

In order to cure the over-trading evil, the Investment Bankers Code took the extreme stand that a member of a selling group could not effect "switches" for his clients from old issues into the new offering. Instead, he could accept the old security only as a broker, selling it at the usual commission rates and then applying the proceeds to payment for the new security.

Over-trading undoubtedly constitutes a violation of the spirit, at least, of the provision of the purchase and selling group agreements barring sales below the public offering price. However, where an investment house in the capacity of dealer purchases a security from a client and applies the proceeds to payment for a new issue, it is difficult to draw the line where over-trading begins. Particularly with unlisted securities, there may be a considerable spread between the bid and asked prices, so that a favorable price may be paid for the security accepted in exchange without seeming violation of the rule against price shading.

The establishment of a trading account through which securities offered in the market at or below the purchase price are bought in by the manager constitutes a peril to group members who indulge in price-cutting practices. If bonds or stock, as the case may be, are sold below the offering price and are purchased by the manager, the participant loses his selling commission, so that he suffers an actual monetary loss from his sale below the public offering price. In order to avoid the danger of such resales during the life of the syndicate, the buyer at these reduced prices is usually asked to give assurance that he will keep the securities at least during the life of the syndicate. This is termed a purchase "investment guaranteed." As a result, when new offerings do not meet with much success, there grows up an "investment guaranteed" market in which the issue is privately offered below the original offering price, always with the understanding that securities sold in this way will not be thrown back upon the market for a period of 60 days or so. Dealers outside the syndicate may obtain securities in this way at the full selling commission and can sell them profitably below the public offering price, as these outside dealers are not subject to the terms of the syndicate agreement. The invoice covering such bonds usually bears some such notation as "syndicate bonds—protect."

Prevention of the price-cutting abuse is sought in the syndicate agreement by provisions permitting the cancellation of the participation of the offending house by the manager. However, since these abuses are most marked where the public response is poor, such cancellation may be quite desirable from the viewpoint of the offending house. Hence, the more effective cure is publicity for houses which regularly and willfully violate agreements, so that they can be debarred from future group participations. The Investment Bankers Association of America, which has spent much time and labor in an effort to improve syndicate practices, is coming to rely upon the reporting of these violations as a cure for them.

The argument has been advanced in some quarters that the investment guaranteed market is by no means an unmixed evil. It constitutes a check on underwriters and dealers seeking to sell securities at excessive prices. From the point of view of the investor, it permits him to buy a new issue at a price that may be much fairer than the public offering price. In German investment banking practice, in fact, the buyer for investment who agrees to hold an issue for a stated period of time in many cases openly receives a concession, as compared with the buyer who does not choose to tie himself up in this way.

A second group of abuses is connected with the practice of "beating the gun," or endeavoring to sell the issue before the date of public offering. The members of the purchase group, and especially the originator, are in a position to give clients advance information concerning the issue, and thus to secure orders before smaller dealers can find out about it. The result is that clients tend on an increasing scale to do business with the larger houses. The spread of advance information concerning a new issue cannot be prevented as a rule, especially where preliminary publicity is desired. But salesmen of group managers and members sometimes accept subscriptions and even make firm sales, thus putting certain clients on a favored basis and getting an advantage over those houses which wait for the "firing of the gun"—the official offering day.

The Investment Bankers Association made beating the gun an unfair trade practice, and the Investment Bankers Code also outlawed the practice. However, owing to keen competition among investment dealers, and particularly individual salesmen, these efforts had limited practical success.

With the enactment of the federal Securities Act, a new element was introduced. The law bars the offering of a security, except an exempt issue, without registration if use is made "of any means or instruments of transportation or communication in interstate commerce or of the mails." While the law thus hits this practice directly, it also encourages it through the introduction of the 20-day waiting period. Now, far more precise and complete advance information is available on a new offering than ever before.

Winding Up Selling Groups

When the market is asked to absorb too many issues at one time, or when bond prices are declining for other reasons, the maintenance by syndicates of quotations on new issues creates for them an artificial level of values. In such cases, the public tends to lose confidence in all new offerings, and they necessarily fall off in volume. Often this happens at a time when fundamental conditions in the security markets are favorable. In order to avoid such situations, it has been considered good practice to shorten the life of bond syndicates and permit the trend of prices to take its normal course as soon as feasible.

Where a new offering is out of line, the quotation will drop several points as soon as price restrictions are removed, as dealers seek to get out of their commitments and free their funds for other uses. Investors are expected to gain greater confidence in new offerings if there is less artificial control of the market after issuance, and there will be less fear of a sharp drop in price on the expiration of the syndicate because of the "dumping" of bonds by those unable to carry them longer.

Another practice sometimes resorted to by less successful syndicates, especially in municipal issues, is to form a "secondary" selling group, which takes over from the original syndicate the unsold balance of the offering. In this way, extensive "dumping" of such securities is prevented. The new group, including houses not in the first syndicate, puts new organizations to work in selling the issue, and is expected to hasten its distribution. The bonds are usually turned over at cost by the first distributing syndicate.

Another expedient sometimes encountered is to permit selling group members to trade among themselves, so that houses which have taken down more securities than they can sell turn them over to those who have a shortage of supply, at or near the public offering price less the full selling group concession. This is known as *intertrading*. The selling group letter will so provide if intertrading among syndicate members at the full concession is to be specifically authorized. In most cases the selling group manager, to keep control of the situation, prefers to have all deals among group members go through him at the full or partial concession, except that members can, of course, sell to each other at the offering price less the usual dealers' concession.

The market action of a new issue both before and after the closing of the syndicate will have a strong effect on the attitude of the clientele of the group members, and the public in general, toward the participating houses. The question of security price movements, with special reference to the subject of pegging quotations of specific issues, is treated in Chapter XX.

References

Biddle, C. P., and Bates, G. E., *Investment Banking: A Case Book,* New York, 1931, part iii.

Bishop, A. L., *The Financing of Business Enterprises,* New York, 1929, chap. xxi.

Callaway, Trowbridge, *Ethical Problems of Investment Banking* (Investment Bankers Association of America publication), Chicago, 1929.

Dewing, A. S., *Financial Policy of Corporations,* New York, 1934, book v, chaps. ix and x.

Fraser, C. E., *Problems in Finance,* Chicago, 1927, part ii.

Galston, A., *Security Syndicate Operations,* New York, 1928, chaps. iv–xi.

Gerstenberg, C. W., *Financial Organization and Management,* New York, 1932, chap. xxii.

Montgomery, R. H., *Financial Handbook,* second edition, New York, 1933, section 22.

Twentieth Century Fund, *The Security Markets,* New York, 1935, chap. xiii.

University of Illinois Bureau of Business Research, *Investment Banking in Chicago,* Urbana, 1931.

Appendix

A TYPICAL SELLING GROUP LETTER

$25,000,000
The Hamilton Electric Company
First Mortgage Bonds, 3¼% Series Due 1966

Dated August 1, 1936 Due August 1, 196

New York, August 18, 193

Messrs. Zilch & Company
16 Wide Street,
New York, N. Y.

Dear Sirs,

We and certain associates, namely Warwick & Co., Orange Securities Corporation, White Williams & Co., Incorporated, Fell & C and Keller & Co. (we and such associates being hereinafter referred to as the Underwriters), have severally agreed to purchase, when, as and if issued and accepted by the Underwriters and approved by counsel for the Underwriters, at 100% of the principal amount thereof plus accrued interest to the date of payment therefor, an aggregate of $25,000,000 principal amount of The Hamilton Electric Company First Mortgage Bonds, 3¼% Series Due 1966, dated August 1, 1936, due August 1, 1966 (hereinafter sometimes called the Bonds), and more fully described in the enclosed copy of the Offering Prospectus.

The Underwriters are offering a part of the $25,000,000 First Mortgage Bonds, 3¼% Series Due 1966 for sale, subject to the conditions of their purchase from the Company and to the terms and conditions hereof, to certain dealers (hereinafter collectively referred to as the Selling Group), at the public offering price less a concession of ¾%, payable as hereinafter provided. No deduction from this concession will be made for expenses.

The public offering price is to be 102% and accrued interest. Out of the above-stated concession of ¾% dealers may allow a concession not in excess of ⅛% to brokers, dealers, banks or bankers only, provided that in the case of banks or bankers such purchase is made upon the order and for the account of a customer, and provided that in all cases the public offering price to the customer is maintained.

We shall advise you by telegram on the morning of the public offering of the principal amount of Bonds which we, as Manager of the Selling Group, have reserved for purchase by you, subject to the terms and conditions hereof. We shall reserve such Bonds for purchase by you until 5 o'clock P.M. (standard time in your city), Wednesday, August 18, 1936. Please advise us, at our office, 8 High Street, New York City, by the time specified whether or not you agree to purchase, on the above-described terms and conditions, all or any part of such reserved Bonds. Applications for Bonds in excess of the amount so reserved and applications received after 5 o'clock P.M. (standard time in the applicant's city), August 18, 1936, will be received only subject to allotment by us in our uncontrolled discretion.

We have been advised by The Hamilton Electric Company that a Registration Statement in respect of these Bonds under the Securities Act of 1933, as amended, became effective on or before August 18, 1936. Neither you nor any other person is authorized by the Company or by the Underwriters to give any information or make any representations, other than those contained in the Offering Prospectus, in connection with the issue and sale of the Bonds. No member of the Selling Group is authorized to act as agent for the several Underwriters when offering the Bonds to the public or otherwise. The Hamilton Electric Company has agreed with the Underwriters that for a period of one year after the public offering of the Bonds, if any change shall have occurred as a result of which the Offering Prospectus includes an untrue statement of a material fact or omits to state any material fact necessary in order to make the statements in the light of the circumstances under which they were made not misleading, forthwith to prepare and to furnish to the Underwriters, and to the members of the Selling Group and, upon request, to any other dealer making such request, an amendment or amendments to said Prospectus which will correct the Prospectus so that as corrected it will not contain any untrue statement of a material fact or omit to state any material fact necessary in order to make the statements in the light of the circumstances in which they were made not misleading.

The members of the Selling Group are not permitted to buy from or sell to each other any of the Bonds prior to the termination of the Selling Group, at any price lower than the initial public offering price less a concession of not more than the 1/8% provided for in the preceding paragraph. Williams & Co., as representative of the several Underwriters, however, may themselves purchase from and/or sell Bonds to any member of the Selling Group at the public offering price, less the Selling Group concession or any part thereof.

Bonds purchased by you may be re-offered to the public at no less than the initial public offering price immediately upon you receipt of telegraphic advice from us to the effect that the issue i released for offering, but subject to the terms and conditions hereo and to the securities laws of the various states. During the life o the Selling Group you shall not offer the Bonds at a price belov the initial public offering price. In the event that, during the lif of the Selling Group, any Underwriter through the Managers o the Selling Group contracts for or purchases in the open marke at or below the initial public offering price any of the Bonds there tofore delivered to you, the Managers reserve the right to withhol the above-mentioned concession in respect of such Bonds and i addition to charge you with any Broker's commission paid thereor

Upon application to the Managers you will be informed as t the states in which it is believed the Bonds have been qualified fo sale under the respective securities laws of such states, but the Managers assume no obligation or responsibility as to the right of any member of the Selling Group to sell the Bonds in such states.

In connection with the Securities Exchange Act of 1934, your attention is called to the fact that in the agreement between the Underwriters and the Company, the Company agrees, upon request of the representative of the Underwriters, to make application to have the Bonds listed on the New York Stock Exchange, or on such other Exchange as Williams & Co., as representative of the Underwriters, may designate, which is registered as a National Securities Exchange under said Act, and to have the Bonds registered thereon.

The Selling Group will terminate thirty (30) days from this date or at such earlier date as we may determine or may be extended for a period or periods not exceeding in the aggregate sixty (60) days, provided that no such extension shall become effective except upon the consent of dealers purchasing Bonds hereunder and Underwriters retaining Bonds for direct sale who in the aggregate have so purchased or so retained 75% of this issue. As promptly as possible after the termination of the Selling Group the Managers will settle all accounts with the members thereof.

Public advertisement of these Bonds will be made on August 18, 1936. After such advertisement has appeared, subject to the applicability of local laws, you are free to advertise at your own expense, but your advertisement must conform in all respects to the requirements of the Securities Act of 1933, as amended, particularly in respect of Section 2 (10) and Section 10 of such Act, and to the rules and regulations thereunder.

The Bonds purchased by the Underwriters which are not being ffered to dealers in the Selling Group are being offered for sale by ertain of the Underwriters, all of whom have agreed with respect o the sale of such Bonds to comply with the terms and conditions f this Agreement. All of such Underwriters have agreed that they vill not sell, offer or solicit offers to buy Bonds prior to the public ffering.

Payment for Bonds purchased by you is to be made by certified heck at the office of Williams & Co., 8 High Street, New York ity, at the public offering price of 102% and accrued interest to he date of payment therefor, on August 31, 1936, in New York nds to the order of Williams & Co. against delivery of temporary onds, exchangeable for definitive Bonds when prepared. The ncession to which you shall be entitled will be paid to you upon the termination of this Agreement. Notwithstanding the distribution of any such amount to you, you shall be liable for your proportionate share of any claim, demand or liability asserted against you and the other members of the Selling Group or any of them or the Managers of the Selling Group based on the claim that the members of the Selling Group constitute an association, unincorporated business or other separate entity.

The Underwriters reserve the right to make purchases or sales in the open market or otherwise of any of the securities of the Company, before or after the public offering of the Bonds either directly or through the Managers, and Williams & Co. is authorized and empowered to buy or sell Bonds in their discretion in the open market in a limited amount for the account of the several Underwriters and such fact is disclosed in the Prospectus.

The Managers of the Bond Selling Syndicate shall have full authority to take such action as it may deem advisable in respect of all matters pertaining to the Bond Selling Syndicate, but the Managers shall act only as agent for the several members thereof. The Managers shall be under no liability for or in respect of the value of the Bonds, or the validity of, or the form of the representations contained in, the Bonds, or the Registration Statement or Prospectus or any agreement or other instruments executed by the Company or by others; or for the delivery of the Bonds or for the performance by the Company or by others of any agreement on its or their part; nor shall the Managers be liable for the qualification of the Bonds for sale under the laws of any jurisdiction; nor shall they be liable under any of the provisions of this agreement, or in or for any matter connected therewith, except want of good faith; and no obligation not expressly assumed by the Managers in this agreement shall be implied therefrom.

The Managers of the Bond Selling Syndicate agree to cause to be filed a further state notice representing the aforesaid securities to be offered to the public in New York, in the form required by and pursuant to the provisions of Article 23-A of the General Business Law of the State of New York.

Additional copies of the Prospectus will be supplied in reasonable quantities upon request to the office of Williams & Co., 8 High Street, New York, N. Y., or to the offices of any of the other Underwriters.

All communications to the Managers should be addressed to Williams & Co., 8 High Street, New York, N. Y.

Any notice from the Managers to any member of the Bond Selling Syndicate shall be deemed to have been duly given if mailed or telegraphed to such member at the address to which this agreement is mailed.

Please confirm your agreement to purchase the Bonds held firm for acceptance by you by telegraph or telephone and later by signing and returning at once the duplicate copy of this letter enclosed herewith.

Very truly yours,
By

Williams & Co, Managers

Williams & Co.,
8 High Street,
New York City.
Dear Sirs:

The undersigned hereby confirms acceptance of the firm offering of Bonds in accordance with all of the terms and conditions stated in the attached letter. The undersigned hereby acknowledges receipt of the Prospectus relating to the above new issue of Bonds and the undersigned further states that in agreeing to purchase such Bonds the undersigned has relied solely on said Prospectus and on no other statement whatsoever, written or oral.

Dated ______________________

By ______________________

Official Capacity

Address ______________________

Chapter XIX

SECURITY SELLING

Analysis of the Market

The success of the investment banker in distributing depends, of course, upon his establishing an adequate buying clientele upon which he can regularly depend.

Basic differences in the practices pursued to attain this end exist in different countries. They may perhaps be best illustrated by the case of the United States and Great Britain. In the latter country the customer is attracted largely by general confidence in the issue or selling house. In the United States, on the other hand, although it has been believed necessary to develop a much more highly specialized and personal mechanism for disposing of securities, while confidence in the sponsoring is an important factor, a much more aggressive procedure for placing the issue in the hands of the investor is deemed desirable. This distinction in point of view illustrates a fundamental aspect of investment banking—the type of solicitation or selling method which has been developed as most acceptable to, and most likely to succeed with, the investing public in any given case.

The selling method used depends a great deal on the character and habits of the group in the community to which the selling appeal must be made. Thus a nation which is largely given to the placing of its surplus capital in savings banks, and which is not accustomed to the judging and holding of securities directly, is not likely to offer a particularly satisfactory field for the selling of bonds to individual investors. In similar fashion, a group of bond buyers who have been habituated, like the rank and file of French investors, to the purchase of securities largely on the basis of low yields with a high degree of safety, are not likely to be strongly appealed to by offerings of more speculative issues whose chief attraction is not intrinsic security, but high yields or participation in prospective profits.

Classes of Security Buyers

The character of the public to be approached will largely determine the methods to be used in reaching them. The first step toward an analysis of his market by the investor as a distributor of securities is a classification of available purchasers. These fall into the following major groups:

1. Institutional or professional buyers—those who are themselves reasonably familiar with the character of the issues they are purchasing and are fairly well able to judge it. In this class may be included:

(a) Banks, investment trusts and other investing institutions which purchase for their own account and risk.

(b) Trust companies, investment counsel, and other fiduciaries which purchase on behalf of the owners of funds that have been intrusted to their care.

(c) Institutional investors, such as insurance companies, which have very clearly defined needs and buy securities with a view to meeting peculiar technical requirements of their own.

2. Trade buyers who purchase with a view to retailing the securities. Among these may be recognized:

(a) Investment houses which sell to small investors, earning a profit from the selling group concession or dealers' discount.

(b) Houses that take a position in an issue with a view to sale after its anticipated appreciation.

3. General investment buyers, including:

(a) Individuals who have a surplus income over expenditure, or who are in possession of accumulated funds which they wish to use as a basis for future income.

(b) Business establishments which find themselves from time to time with surplus funds in hand, and, not wishing to leave these funds idle, or earning only a nominal income as bank time deposits, prefer to purchase securities with them.

In the years following 1933 institutional buyers were by far the most important in most issues, accounting for the great bulk of the sales of new bond issues.

Modes of Approach

It is evident that a special method of approach will be needed in these different cases if the purchaser is to be induced to apply his funds in the direction desired by the investment banker. Broadly speaking, the investment banker may decide to operate on a wholesale[1] or retail basis, that is, to endeavor to dispose of his issues in large blocks or to take upon himself the task of reaching the general rank and file of the public. Should he determine to sell in large blocks, he will be inclined to address himself to institutional investors of the various classes already outlined and to interest them as far as practicable. In so doing he will necessarily rely to a great extent upon his general reputation and standing. Profit margins are smaller, and hence sales effort per unit sold must be limited.

In retail distribution, far greater reliance rests on direct personal representation and solicitation. While it may be that the individual bond buyer is more or less directly reached and influenced by advertising of the right kind, it is also true in a great majority of cases that the advertising alone is not sufficient to induce him to buy. If he be inexperienced, he may refer the question of purchase of securities to his own banker for advice; or, in other cases, without any reference to experience, he may decide to buy what are called "seasoned bonds," that is, those that are already listed and proved on the exchanges of the country. In either case, his funds are not likely to go to the investment banker who is just bringing out a new issue, without special effort on the latter's part.

It is evident that the choice of a method of security selling in any given case must be largely influenced by the number of prospects and the size of average purses which may be expected. Prior to the World War, a prevalent rough estimate placed the total number of habitual bond buyers in the United States at

[1] Not to be confused with security wholesaling in the technical sense, which means to sell or originate new issues as outlined in Chapter XVII.

probably about 300,000. The number of stockholders was considerably greater, but consisted to a large extent of owners of closed corporations, who were not therefore investors in the proper sense. It also undoubtedly included a great number of persons who held shares only temporarily, having purchased their holdings on a speculative basis.

The number of *bona fide* security investors in this country before the war, therefore, was about 600,000. Several factors may be noted which have broadened the field of demand. It will be remembered that during the World War extraordinary efforts were made to distribute Liberty Bonds among as large a proportion of the population as possible, not only because of the government's need for the funds, but also because of the general system of war finance which had been determined on by the western countries, which dictated the value of as widely extended a distribution of public bonds as circumstances would permit. It is estimated that in the United States the total number of security holders thus developed eventually amounted to 15,000,000, including, of course, a great number of duplications and speculators.[2] Although many of these buyers were temporary and sporadic, a great many others retained the habit of putting their funds into securities; and, although they may have disposed of their Liberty Bonds soon after the close of the war, they shifted over into other fields of investment and became buyers of other types of securities, instead of as in former years relying almost exclusively upon savings banks, farm and city mortgage investments, and purely local securities of various kinds as outlets for their savings. The American capital market was thus made truly national in scope.

After the war was over, a new era of expansion and of recapitalization set in in most countries, particularly in the United States, and large amounts of new capital were called for, both on home and on foreign account; this new capital had to be provided by appealing widely to the community for its savings. The business of issuing, dealing in, and distributing securities became immensely broadened and enlarged, and large groups in the community which had formerly been un-

[2] Based on 1924 tax returns. Joseph S. McCoy, Government Actuary, estimated there were only three million separate individuals owning corporate securities in that year. Tax returns, however, are believed by many statisticians unreliable as a source of data on such subjects.

familiar with bonds and investments began to take an interest in them. The depression and deflation of the early 'thirties caused widespread losses to individual investors and reduced the number of regular buyers of securities. For a time at least, it made direct investment less popular, and indirect investment through financial institutions, more so. The period of credit inflation that began in 1933 tended to check this new trend.

It has been estimated that at present the total number of habitual security buyers in the United States is not less than seven millions. A majority of them now probably own stock, although a decade ago, bonds rather than stock made up the greater part of their holdings. Stock ownership has been popularized by customer campaigns by public utilities, periods of sharply rising quotations, and the greater relative stability of many industrial enterprises. In 1927, the Investment Research Committee of the Financial Advertisers Association estimated there were approximately 3,000,000 bond buyers in this country.

The Rôle of the Salesman

Widespread solicitation by bond salesmen who visit the customer and suggest to him the desirability of putting his funds into specified issues, long in vogue in this country, has been the outgrowth of the desire of investment bankers to reach a large clientele of individual investors. It implies the organization of a considerable staff and the preparation of lists of prospective customers, assignment of names to each member of the staff, and direct visits to the customer to induce him to part with his money in exchange for the bonds. Bond salesmen of this variety have usually been given some training, at least by the establishment which has employed them, and are expected to be able to furnish desired information with respect to general investment conditions, interest trends and the like, and to supply to the prospective buyer detailed data concerning the particular issue in which he may be interested.

Of late years, bond salesmen have usually taken upon themselves the additional task of giving general investment advice, keeping track of the holdings of bonds owned by each of their customers, suggesting appropriate times at which to dispose of old issues and buy new ones, and aiding in the preservation of a fair amount of diversification by the security buyer. Under such conditions, the bond salesman becomes a kind of investment counselor to the customer or bond buyer. He takes the place which the broker assumes under the British method of bond distribution. His motive to sell, however, is stronger than that of his British contemporary, and his advice is very often unsolicited, whereas that of the British broker is usually furnished only on request.

The sales force of the investment house is recruited to a large extent from the graduating classes of colleges. The young recruits are put through a short training course in the elements of bond investment and the general principles of selling. Taken as a whole, bond salesmen do not adopt a strictly professional attitude toward their work by making an intensive study of security values and the needs of individual customers. They often stress such factors as possible rapid price appreciation and others which are not strictly of an investment character, in order to hasten sales. Intensive competition may compel the salesman in the future, in self-protection, to make himself far more expert than he is now in the intricacies of the securities business and the problem of security valuation, and in this task the technically trained man is certain to win eventually.

Men tend to concentrate in any business and profession in which the gains are large, regardless of their own personal fitness for the work. So the security business, which was of limited scope before the war, attracted many thousands of men and some women from other walks of life to join in establishing large selling organizations which were created almost over night by the sudden growth of an investment class in this country. Between 1921 and 1928, the bond market enjoyed a remarkably sustained bull movement, in which the yields of representative bonds fell approximately 50 per cent. Under such conditions, of course, it was unusually easy to sell new security issues. On many occasions no selling effort at all was required, as investors, tempted by the possibility that the new bonds would rise in price even before they would have to pay for them, eagerly scrambled for the privilege of having their orders accepted. The later stabilization of bond prices brought on a period of more drastic competition, but the switch of investors' interest to more speculative stock issues again brought forward the appreciation factor. During the high money period which followed, salesmen turned to stock selling to get enough business to keep going, and the pure bond salesman faced a difficult state of affairs.

The investment bankers' code laid down certain standards for bond salesmen, designed to raise the competence and professional standing of persons engaged in this activity. The depression worked havoc with employment in this field. In later years there has been less emphasis upon personal selling, while the fact that distribution has been more largely to financial institutions also has reduced the number of salesmen required.

Salesmen's Compensation

The security salesman relies for his compensation chiefly upon a commission for each bond sold, or for each share of stock if sold by the house as part of its regular offerings. In certain cases, the commission system is modified by the payment of a fixed salary, generally of small amount. A study of practices in compensating salesmen in use among investment houses was completed by the Investment Bankers Association of America in 1928.[3] It revealed a wide variation among forty typical houses studied. They were fairly evenly divided on the basis of paying fixed salaries or merely permitting drawing accounts against future commissions. Houses which paid fixed salaries actually paid commissions in most cases only when earned commissions were in excess of the salary; but in several instances, it was found that small commissions were paid on all sales, in addition to the salary. Thus, one house paid its salesmen $1,500 to $5,000 a year, plus a credit of $1 per $100 face value of sales, paid monthly. This total payment was deducted from the aggregate commissions earned, determined on a basis of percentage of gross profit earned on each sale, and any balance was paid the salesman. After 1930, the straight commission

[3] Interim Report of the Sub-Committee on Salesmen's Compensation, *Investment Bankers Association of America Bulletin*, 1928, vol. xvi, pp. 122-127.

basis of compensation became more nearly universal as profit margins narrowed.

In computing commissions, investment houses generally give either a flat rate per bond or a percentage of the gross profit earned on the issue. Typical flat rate payments are $2 to $6 per thousand for general bonds, and $1.25 per thousand for municipal issues. Typical percentage commissions are from 20 to 40 per cent of the dealer's gross "spread." Some houses have a sliding scale of commissions, increasing the rate with the total volume of sales effected. Special credit may be given for bringing in new customers. In one instance $10 was paid for each new customer on the third sale.

Salesmen selling to institutions often get a lower rate of commission per unit, because of their larger sales volume, and also because of the fact that in many cases the buyers are so well informed that they are little better than mere order-takers. Special bonuses based on competition among the salesmen or on length of service are also common.

Finally, the question of establishing a uniform rate of commission has been agitated. Such a practice would doubtless tend to make the salesman more impartial as an adviser to his client, for he would not be interested then in pushing one or a few issues on which specially high rates were being paid. On the other hand, the present system of paying a percentage of gross profit with extra allowances when business is poor, as followed by many houses, doubtless imparts considerable elasticity to investment banking organization, permitting the speeding up of sales effort when necessary by offering larger rewards.

Advertising

Direct selling effort is supplemented in many security houses by a fairly complete advertising organization. Often a special department which acts as an auxiliary to the sales department is maintained for this purpose. Advertising is now used on a large scale, and in several different ways. First, new issues are given publicity through offering advertisements which appear in numerous newspapers. Some houses use different varieties of smaller "follow-up ads," which appear after the original offering date and are aimed at further complete distribution of an issue on bonds with investors. Some bond houses also distribute and advertise monthly offering lists. A fourth type of advertising copy in common use is of a general institutional nature, where the investment house merely seeks to stress the advantages of investment in general and of its own services in particular, prominently displaying the name of the house at the same time. Institutional advertising also may take the form of "cards," or single-column advertisements about six inches in length which briefly state the name of the house and the character of the business it transacts.

This advertising is not restricted to the newspapers. Conservative magazines frequently have separate financial advertising departments, and car poster and billboard advertising has also been not uncommon in the larger cities. Mail-order selling methods also have been developed, further reflecting the popularization of the investment market. Lists of prospects, gathered in various ways, are sent carefully designed letters and circulars in order to broaden the list of clients of the house. A good description of advertising and mail-order methods from the practical standpoint is contained in the volume entitled *Advertising Investment Securities*, which was prepared by the Financial Advertisers Association. The organization of an advertising department in relation to the rest of the bond house is suggested in Fig. 17 on the following page.

The growth of investment advertising is most marked during periods of widespread popular interest in direct investment as in the late 'twenties. Then, when mass distribution method are feasible, advertising represents a real source of economy Paving the way for both direct sales and mail-order sales b newspaper, periodical and poster advertising increases the vol ume of sales and so reduces the burden of total selling expens per bond sold. More extensive advertising permits a reductio of the bond salesman's work and his rate of commission, but a the same time it gives him the opportunity to dispose of a muc larger volume of securities.

Advertising efforts are supplemented to a large extent b newspaper publicity, which plays a very important part in hel ing the sale of new security issues. The newspapers today d pend for their financial news largely upon announcemen issued by large corporations and financial houses through advertising agencies. The latter receive their compensation primarily from the newspapers with which they place the advertising of their clients, while in addition they have a news department, made up usually of experienced journalists, which prepares "hand-outs" for the press. Under this system, the financial press of America has to a degree abdicated in favor of the advertising agency in furnishing news about new security offer-

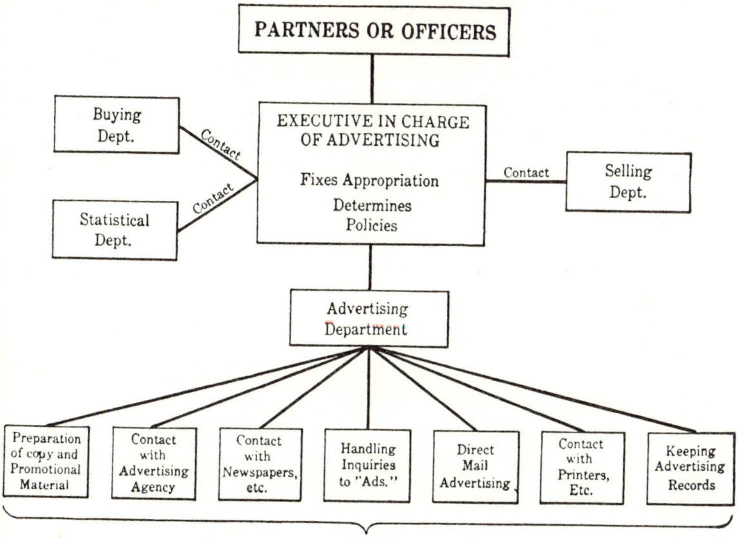

FUNCTIONS

FIG. 17. ORGANIZATION OF A TYPICAL ADVERTISING DEPARTMENT IN AN INVESTMENT HOUSE

ngs to the public, and many houses have learned to make effec- ive use of this situation.

Selling to Institutions

With the development of large corporate organizations and he broadening of the capital market to take in many new industries, the individual investor has found the task of choosing ecurities for investment increasingly complex. So long as the ecurities offered to a buyer related to enterprises in his own mmediate neighborhood, the prospective investor was able to pursue the dictates of common sense in selecting his securities, and to guide himself more or less by what has been called those "slight but unmistakable evidences of veracity" which can be ascertained through personal contact, though usually not otherwise. The purchase of securities representing the credit of corporations or nations at a distance involves resort to a scientific analysis of underlying values, for which the individual is often not qualified. Hence, he has had to resort to some source of professional advice, or to that form of cooperative buying which we have termed "institutional." Since the depression, as we have seen, this tendency has been intensified.

The danger involved in such cases is, of course, that those who are furnishing advice for the guidance of the individual will be selfish or, in extreme cases, venal. Investment trust promoters, for example, have on occasion sought to take for themselves the benefits of good judgment shown in making purchases, and allowed to the investor only a very moderate or "normal" rate of return, while requesting him to carry the risk of losses from depreciation of securities whenever their investment judgment turned out to have been bad. It is fair to suppose that a large proportion of investment will continue to assume the cooperative or institutional form, especially as such institutions develop higher standards of ethics. Institutional investment, in fact, bids fair to be the ultimate general type of individual access to the market.

In making a study of the demand for securities, therefore, the creator or distributor of such securities naturally gives a substantial part of his attention to the wants of institutional buyers; and in analyzing their wants, he first of all directs attention to the statutory requirements which limit them in their operation. We have seen at an earlier point (Chapters V and VI) what these are. Obviously institutions which are limited to a specified list of securities are customers only for those classes of issues. There is thus established at once for the investment houses which specialize in institutional business a buying nucleus of a fairly measurable volume of demand, that volume from year to year being indicated by the annual growth in the total amount of resources placed in the hands of such institutions, plus "switches" and replacements of issues paid off. The annual increase, for example, in holdings of trust funds committed to the hands of trust companies affords one measure of the trust companies' demand for so-called "legals." The total will be largely swelled, of course, in years when refunding becomes common because of a fall in the level of money rates. Similarly, premium income of insurance written annually by life insurance companies may be taken as another measure of the market for new securities of the kinds already indicated as being legal for the investment of their funds.

Broadening of Legal Requirements

Recent experiences have tended to show more and more clearly the existence of a trend away from the narrow limitation of institutional buyers to rigidly prescribed classes of securities, and toward a plan which would base the choice of such buyers upon the quality and character of such securities rather than upon any purely artificial or descriptive test. Originally, savings bank investment statutes limited purchases to mortgage bonds of specified railroads. Later, provisions of law were broadened to include any mortgage railroad bonds which present a definite income record on behalf of their issuers and meet certain other criteria. Today, the trend is toward removing limitations as regards particular industries, setting up more general criteria of investment soundness instead. Several such broad classifications are being made. Thus the Standard Statistics Corporation has devised a method of rating bonds which is described by it as follows:

In the process of rating any issue of bonds, all factors of influence are carefully considered. There are, however, three fundamental factors that to a very great extent determine the real investment worth of any bond. These factors in the order of their importance are earning power, asset value and marketability.

Standard bond ratings are offered primarily as guide posts in furtherance of the investigation of bond values and are therefore not intended to be accepted as final.

The Moody Investors' Service has worked out the following symbols in their bond rating system:

Aaa: Meet the highest tests in asset value, earning power and stability.

Aa: Rank well into the high-grade field.

A: Entirely sound obligations of representative companies, but lacking the higher degree of protection obtainable in bonds of Aaa and Aa grades.

Baa: Generally make a good showing in the tests, but warrant more discrimination.

Ba: Always have some characteristics of uncertainty.

B: Always characterized by speculative features.

Caa: Usually have a decidedly poor statistical standing and fall short of all tests such as asset value, earning power and stability.

Ca: Show marked weakness of one kind or another.

C: Not to be classed as investments at all.

As we have seen earlier, official recognition has been given such investment ratings by the Comptroller of the Currency, in laying down regulations to govern investments of national banks (see Chapter V). Such security ratings possess material value, however, only in connection with bonds. In the field of stock issues, where present and prospective earnings per share constitute the important factor in value determination, they are virtually meaningless.

Investors, in making their choice of bonds, must of course use these symbols of classification as indicative simply of the judgment which has been formed concerning these securities by a statistical and analytical agency that can usually consider and appraise only a few of the numerous factors that go to determine security values. Allowing that no ulterior influences or considerations have acted upon the minds of those who do the rating, they are, of course, subject to the same limitations that apply to any judgments. Their opinions must accordingly be accepted with due reserve, and without any effort to take the decisions so announced as more than merely advisory or suggestive. A careful investor, both institutional and individual, must undertake to check carefully upon the ratings of the statistical services by himself examining the statistics upon which they are based, and other pertinent data.

Adaptation to Needs of Investors

Much can be done in issuing new securities to adapt them to the needs of buyers. In order to accomplish this, attention must be given to the extent and character of the restrictions or qualifications that are imposed by existing law upon investors, particularly institutional buyers. If, for example, a given kind of underlying security is required by law or by custom as widely observed and followed, the result is to limit buyers of this class of investment security to those issues which correspond to their needs. A new issue may often be made to conform to the needs of such buyers by clearing out of the way underlying issues of securities which conflict with these requirements. Also, it is sometimes possible to arrange that specified requirements as to earnings be met by controlling capitalizations accordingly. Thus, railroads may hold down the amount of their bond financing to meet a requirement that they earn interest 1½ or 2 times over a given period of years. In these ways a new issue which would not otherwise be available for some classes of customers can be made to accord with their actual or imaginary needs, thereby causing them to buy it.

The broadening of legal requirements, to which reference has been made in a preceding paragraph, is tending to modify difficult conditions of this kind, and to get rid of restrictions that no longer have a real meaning because of the change in circumstances since the original restrictions were established.

Education of the Investor

As important as broadening of actual legal requirements is the education of the investor to look at investment problems from a broader point of view. Many investors a few years ago had been in the habit of purchasing bonds only, in the belief that they afforded a safer or better-protected kind of investment than they could otherwise get. This has been modified as the risks inherent in buying only fixed-income securities, arising from changing general levels of money rates and currency policies, have become better understood.

The individual's habit of restricting his buying along specified lines may be largely the result of prejudice or ignorance. An explanation to him of all the pertinent factors involved in investment, and a recognition on his part of the underlying fact that it is not the legal forms of securities so much as their essential characteristics that fit them for a place in an investment list, will often result in broadening his demand or changing its direction from narrowly specialized channels into much larger fields.

An example of what may be done in this direction is afforded by the rapid growth within recent years of the practice of buying common stocks instead of preferred issues or bonds. Recognition that the security, in any case, depends primarily upon the earning power of a given enterprise, and that the possession of a legal lien upon corporate property is not usually of itself an especially valuable protection to an investor, naturally leads to a shifting of his interest from one type of securities to the other. The average investor seldom operates on the basis of any definite and consistent theory of investment, and when he does, it is likely to be erroneous in whole or in part.

The ideas of investors and their attitude toward the whole investment problem, in fact, change slowly from period to period. Such changes, however, when they do occur, often come unexpectedly, and baffle both bankers and investors for a time. They may arise from changes in the business situation, which result in holding out hopes of large profits to be made through participation in the actual ownership of the business, thus rendering stocks more attractive than the bonds whose ownership places the individual in the position of creditor. Changes in currency and credit policy, taxation, business law and ethics of business management may also exercise an influence in bringing about such results.

Preferences also vary according to the changing position of the individual himself. The "business man's investment" is one which presumably is suitable for those able to follow changing conditions, for it should be closely watched by observers who have access to a reasonably constant and reliable supply of data in order to protect themselves adequately. The investment to be made by the same person upon his retirement from business and withdrawal from active life will probably be quite different in its character. As the individual changes his relationship to property ownership and to other members of the community, the criteria which determine his selection of securities for investment likewise change.

The problem of selling securities involves the education of the investor in order that he may properly understand the point of view underlying securities issue and the real character of the protection that is offered to him by various types of obligations. Conversely, the attitude of the investor as a customer changes according to the investor's general knowledge of business and his varying appreciation of the elements of value underlying it. Changes in the popular point of view on this whole subject account for broad transfers of demand from one group of securities to another—changes often attributed to alterations of rates or competitive conditions, when in reality they are the result of modification of the investor's attitude and scope of information, in part through the education influence of the activities of the investment house, and especially of its salesmen.

The new federal security legislation enacted in 1933 and 1934 largely expanded the volume of information available to investors, and has facilitated the educational process materially. Registration statements and prospectuses furnish a mass of pertinent factual material, while the provisions of this legislation should also tend to raise the standards of accuracy and reliability of published information.

References

Financial Advertisers Association, *Advertising Investment Securities,* New York, 1928.

Long, John D., and Farwell, John E., *Fundamentals of Financial Advertising,* New York, 1927.

McCord, F. A., *The Art of Selling Bonds,* Philadelphia, 1924.

Morgan, Leslie, *Security Salesmanship* (printed privately by the Investment Bankers Association of America, 1930).

Starch, Daniel, *Principles of Advertising,* Chicago, 1926, chap. xxxvii.

Townsend, W. W., *Bond Salesmanship,* New York, 1924.

Chapter XX

MAINTAINING THE MARKET

Price Stability

Particularly during the process of initial distribution, but also to some extent thereafter, the investment banker faces the problem of maintaining the market quotation of his new issues. Assuming that the investment houses sponsoring the issue have substantial investment clients, so that investment buyers will absorb the bulk of it at the initial offering, price stability should largely depend during the early stages of the new security's history upon the degree of skill and judgment that have been shown in adapting its issue price to the general level prevailing in the market at that time. But this is far from being a full statement of the case.

As a matter of fact, a security will maintain its quotation in the open market only if there are buyers on hand ready to take all offerings at the current price. If that does not prove to be the case, then offerings will be made at concessions by those who feel impelled to liquidate, until buying is attracted from one quarter or another. Furthermore, buyers must be on hand just when the offers are made. If they arrive on the scene too late, price concessions may already have been established.

Now when a new issue of securities is sold, it is likely that salesmen may have had to exert special effort to make each of the original sales. When certain of these buyers subsequently offer the securities they have purchased in the market, however, this specific sales effort is absent; and hence it is natural that the price tends to decline forthwith unless supporting orders are placed in the market by those specially interested in preventing a drop in the quotation—the investment banking houses sponsoring the issue.

Investment bankers ordinarily, therefore, undertake to maintain the market at the public offering price during the period in which the issue is being sold to investors. The process of distributing a new issue of securities generally takes considerable time. It is not possible to forecast what disturbances will occur in the market during that period, and it is very desirable that while salesmen are selling to attract orders from investors the confidence of the latter shall not be undermined by a decline in the quoted price of the security.

Of course, there are exceptions to this practice of price maintenance. If an unusual demand for the issue arises because of certain desirable features or favorable general market conditions, it may immediately sell at a premium, and no market maintenance problem arises. At other times, however, it may prove that the new issue of securities, after getting into the hands of investors, suddenly encounters some severe stock market disturbance. There is no reason why it should not "sell off" or "go to pieces" to the same extent that others of like strength do, and the offering syndicate may quickly withdraw its bids in the open market to avoid getting back the entire issue. Indeed, it is likely that since the new issue has not become firmly placed in the investment portfolios of institutions and individuals, it will suffer even more severely than other issues which may not be as good. Fluctuation in price immediately after issue under such circumstances does not necessarily indicate that the buyer has been imposed upon or that there has been an error of judgment on the part of the issuer.

Duty of the Investment Banker

In his effort to adapt the price of new issues to valuations existing in the market, the investment banker naturally is guided by his judgment of existing conditions and of the attitude investors will display toward his offerings. However, in order to help the new issues surmount the difficulties of the period of initial distribution, actual market support is usually thought necessary for a certain period.

The question as to how far an investment banker is confronted by an actual duty to support market prices has evoked wide difference of opinion, especially after the primary distribution process has been completed and the offering syndicate dissolved. A house, for example, which is in the habit of entering into syndicate or other agreements looking to the maintenance of a given price for an issue of bonds during a period of say, two months, may not be willing to release itself from responsibility at the end of that period if it fears that customers will resent its action. If successive issues of securities decline substantially in price, it may not be able to retain a clientele. The investment house thus tends to remain continuously in the market as a stabilizing factor operating in those securities which it has itself put out.

Formerly, it was quite common for investment bankers and brokerage houses to concern themselves with the maintenance of the quotation of a security not only during the period immediately after its original offering to the public, but also over a more extended period of time. Often, such plans for controlling the market were worked out in conjunction with the issuing corporation.

Activities of this kind have been greatly curtailed in recent years for several reasons. In the first place, the serious losses incurred by investment bankers, issuers and brokerage houses in connection with market support operations in the period 1928-1932 have taught that they can be very costly to those who sponsor them. They may give the market a fictitious stability while the support operation is carried on. During a subsequent deflation period, heavy liquidation by those who have been conducting support operations may cause the quotation to decline far more severely than would have been the case otherwise.

In the second place, the capital resources of investment or brokerage houses at present are usually far smaller in relation to the volume of business done than was the case before 1930. As a result, there is a tendency to avoid operations involving a large measure of risk, among which market support transactions are particularly prominent.

Thirdly, operations of this kind are subject to the legal restrictions contained in the Securities Exchange Act of 1934. Section 9 of this Act is devoted to prohibitions and limitations on manipulation operations. While stabilization activities as such are not barred, transactions such as wash sales and matched orders are made criminal offences. Several types of market control formerly encountered are no longer practicable for legal reasons.

Not only have market support operations subsequent to the offering period been largely eliminated, but also the period immediately after the public offering date in which prices are regularly pegged has been considerably shortened. This is part of the trend to segregate as much of the risk element as possible from the business of originating and selling securities, and thus constitutes a move toward making security distribution a more specialized function than was the case in the past.

Methods of Market Control

Methods of pegging security prices, either during the period of initial distribution or thereafter, have been fairly well standardized. They fall into five main categories.

The first and most common method, still generally pursued at the present time, is to have the selling group manager place a support order for an unlimited amount of securities at the public offering price in the open market. As long as the price rises above this support level, then the house which places the support order will not purchase any securities and the peg becomes unnecessary. However, should the security decline to the support price, it may be that the only buyer will be the selling group manager, and he may have to make large purchases to prevent the price from declining below the offering level.

In connection with such pegging operations, it was formerly not uncommon for the selling group manager to allot more of a security to initial subscribers than the amount of the issue. Thus, if a flotation of $5,000,000 of bonds was being made, the manager would allot $5,500,000 of the issue, thus assuming a technical short position of $500,000. He would count upon his market support operations, as well as the probable cancellation of some of the other subscriptions, to provide the additional bonds with which to cover the short position. Of course, if the demand for the security proved larger than expected, then the selling group manager would have to enter the market and bid against other buyers for his own security in order to cover the short position, with the result that he might be responsible for driving it up to a substantial premium.

More recently, in view of the increased importance of large institutional buyers who are certain to want all of the bonds allotted to them, and in view of the fact that the purchase group will itself sell a large part of the issue, it has become far less usual for the selling group manager to assume a short position in his issue.

A second type of market control sometimes undertaken in connection with the distribution of a security by continuous or "tap" selling is a gradual advance at the price over a period of time. One of the most successful operations of this kind was carried out by the United Founders Corporation during 1929; and the Cities Service Corporation, through affiliations, consummated a similar support operation at about the same time.

This method of market control consists of advancing the pegged price by, say, one-eighth or one-quarter point during each trading season. Prospective buyers of the securities, seeing the stock rise steadily and the opportunity for profits missed, often succumb and purchase without much regard to the other investment factors involved. Needless to say, operations of this kind can prove very costly when they are continued in the face of general liquidation in the security markets. Their legality now is questionable in the light of the provisions of Section 9 of the Securities Exchange Act of 1934.

A third market control method involves the placing of orders on a "scale down" or a "scale up." Thus, if a bond is offered at a price of 98, after the syndicate support order is removed the banker may place orders in the market for 10 bonds at 97½, 20 bonds at 97, 30 bonds at 96½, and 50 bonds at 96. Conversely, he may place selling orders similarly on a scale up. These orders place a considerable backlog of support behind the security on a decline, while bonds thus acquired are sold when the market rises and thus prevent an undue advance. This has been done in the past to stabilize stocks like that of the Pennsylvania Railroad. Stabilization of price today comes within the practices which are authorized, subject to regulations of the Securities and Exchange Commission, by the Securities Exchange Act of 1934.

Another method of control involves the setting aside of a special fund for this purpose. Thus, some corporations have used part of their liquid cash for this purpose, or have created a subsidiary to accomplish this end. In other cases, a group of persons, including perhaps the issuing corporation, its directors or investment banking houses, have formed a special syndicate for this purpose often known as a "pool." Here again, we are confronted with operations of the kind no longer permitted by law. The pool may begin operations with cash, a block of the security in question, or options to buy such securities at fixed prices.

A fifth method for maintaining the market, commonly used in the case of bonds and to a lesser extent preferred stock issues, is the sinking fund device. This throws the burden of market maintenance from the shoulders of the investment banker to those of the original issuer of the security—government or corporation. The sinking fund creates a periodical demand for the issue in the open market, either through purchase or through redemption at stated prices. In either case, the visible supply is cut down and the technical position of the market strengthened.

Sinking funds are usually treated as if they were of chief interest to the investor, but the banker also has an interest in them. The establishment of a satisfactory sinking fund provision naturally has the effect of creating a demand for the issue, which has a corresponding effect in maintaining its value. If the sinking fund is carried on by direct reinvestment in the bonds to which it relates, the effect is the same as that of maintaining or pegging the market, within a limited range. For example, if the sinking fund calls for the purchase annually of 5 per cent of the total original issue of a series of bonds at a price not to exceed par, it evidently has the effect of creating a fixed annual demand for them up to a certain specified price, and, as the issue grows older, this annual demand becomes a larger and larger percentage of the total amount outstanding. In some cases, therefore, it may have a powerful stabilizing effect upon values, if its terms are lived up to rigidly. The investment banker, therefore, is wise to require the insertion of such a provision as a part of the purchase agreement.

The market price of a security may be controlled indirectly by making it convertible into some other issue, or by attaching privileges which entitle the holder to buy some other issue at a fixed price. Thus, if a bond is made convertible into common stock, the quotation of the bond will not decline below its conversion parity, so that the price of the stock will tend to have a supporting effect on the quotation of the bond. A similar effect would be obtained by attaching to the bond the privilege of buying, let us say, ten shares of common stock at $20 a share. Then, if the price of the common stock should rise materially above $20 a share, the bond would tend to be strong also. The existence of the warrant, as long as it is not detached from the bond, is thus a supporting factor for the price of the latter.

In a few cases, this same objective has been sought by giving the bond a more direct participation in profits, by entitling it to additional interest payments when earnings of the corporation rise above a certain level. Such securities are known as participating bonds.

The Problem of Listing

One fundamental problem connected with market control is the question of listing. The investment banker may hope to place his issues of securities in the hands of people who will "put them away and forget about them," but in practice he knows that this cannot be done. They are certain to form the subject of trading as owners find that they must sell them. Even though he may for a short period arrange matters in such a way as to prevent excessive speculative dealings in the issue, the investment banker cannot very long compel the buyers of the securities to adhere to any such plan. He must therefore decide, quite early in the discussion of a given issue, whether it is to be listed upon an organized exchange, such as the New York Stock Exchange, provided, of course, that the consent of that organization can be obtained, or whether it will be sufficient to leave the issue to be dealt in on the over-the-counter market; and if the latter, whether any special arrangements shall be made to assure an active demand there by interesting dealers in the issue.

As a result of the registration provisions of the Securities Exchange Act of 1934, listing requirements have become almost uniform on all registered security exchanges. Hence, unless purely local distribution alone is desired, the tendency will be to list on the New York Stock Exchange or the New York Curb, if it is desired to list the security on any exchange. Corporations which desire to avoid full disclosure of their affairs will prefer to register their issues on the over-the-counter market. However, it should be kept in mind that it is the avowed objective of the Securities and Exchange Commission to bring about the publication of as much information on securities dealt in over-the-counter as in the case of issues that are listed. In some instances, investment bankers prefer to have the issues which they float unlisted, because of the added possibility of earning a profit by maintaining a market with a reasonably wide spread between bid and asked prices after the security has been sold.

The Security and Exchange Commission has not generally shown itself partial to the maintenance of unlisted markets in securities. At the same time, however, it has also in some of its reports recognized the value of the more informal and flexible public markets provided by over-the-counter dealers, especially for smaller issues. It has avoided measures that might tend to disrupt that market. Furthermore, the question of listing has received special attention from state authorities, and in general they favor it as an added protection to the individual investor. This is reflected by the fact that many states exempt from their blue-sky laws issues listed on recognized exchanges. The Attorney-General of New York State, in July, 1928, made the following statement on the subject:

> This office desires to again state its published opinion that an open public market where buyers and sellers of securities can be represented is so far preferable to a private market in its abilities to reflect values, to secure honesty of execution, and to abolish as far as possible unfair practices, as to be incomparable in its results. This office feels that any market which affords facilities for openly bringing buyer and seller together benefits the public, permitting as it does an open reflection of values.

Listing New Issues

When an investment banker decided to list a new offering, he formerly found it possible to list the issue on a "when, as, and if" basis immediately after public offering. Even more common was the practice of beginning trading on this basis on the unlisted department of the New York Curb, and after certain formalities were consummated the security could then be shifted to the New York Stock Exchange. The Securities Exchange Act of 1934 prevents "when, as, and if issued" trading. Hence, a market in a new issue can now be immediately established only over the counter. Trading in an issue on the Exchange can be begun only after registration has been completed and the actual security is available for delivery. Exceptions are made only in the case of securities issued in exchange for already listed issues.

Technical Conditions of the Market

If an issue is subject to special manipulation it generally fluctuates more easily when the floating supply in the hands of short-term traders is small, for it is a widely observed fact that it is usually difficult to induce investors to part with long-pull holdings of securities. On the other hand, margin traders are easily induced to take profits after a rise. Therefore, most manipulative activities are based upon buying up the floating supply, then moving the price up without much resistance to a higher level, and then disposing of the issue to the public again. Experience has shown that the small traders and even the small investors are attracted to issues which are rising rapidly, and this facilitates the distribution process.

Where an issue has been largely distributed and the floating supply is small, the investment banking house can usually discourage much manipulation and keep quotations fairly stable by placing scale buying and selling orders, as was seen above. This device for stabilizing well-seasoned and well-regarded issues breaks down as a rule only at times of severe liquidation or in periods of wild speculative buying. Where the floating supply is larger, however, it becomes more difficult to prevent wide price movements in this way.

Pool Operations

The most common type of manipulation, and the most effective, has been the pool operation.

A speculative stock pool was a syndicate formed by a group of men who join for the purpose of acting together in raising or lowering the price of a security. Most pools aimed at higher prices—some belonged to the class of "bear pools" which profited by a decline.

In the typical "bull pool" operation, there were three important stages. They were:

1. *Accumulation.*—Here the pool, having been organized, sought to acquire a block of the stock without disturbing the price. When skillfully conducted, this was accomplished without any public indication being given of what was going on. The particular stock was bought whenever it declined, especially when the general market was weak and liquidation occurred. When the stock tended to rise, the pool would leave the market alone, or, if necessary, it threw a block of the already purchased stock on the market to lower the price.

2. *Advancing the Price (Marking Up)*.—Having accumulated the stock, the pool was ready for the advance in price, as a result of which it would be established at a higher level and thus give it a paper profit. Under the best conditions, the pool would not have to buy much stock to put it up, relying on a few days of unusual activity to attract a public following. Such outside buying then automatically raised the price because the pool had already cleaned up the floating supply and thus made the quotation highly sensitive, as long as it did not itself interfere to prevent a premature rise by throwing a block of the stock on the market. In other cases, however, the pool would have to take large blocks of the stock sold by the public or others before the price could be advanced as desired.

3. *Distribution.*—In this third stage, the pool was ready to take its profit. If the public following was very large, it could usually dispose of the stock at the end of the rise, selling it in large blocks as the public buying became particularly intense. At other times, the pool would sell on the down-grade. This was done on the theory that the public would buy after a moderate decline, expecting the stock to return to its previous high price.

The above exposition of the typical pool action does not allow for particular developments which the pool often foresaw and which would greatly facilitate its activities. While many a pool engaged merely in manipulation, the majority doubtless planned to discount some particular development which would tend to increase the value of the stock. Large earnings, a higher dividend, a stock dividend, a merger—these were a few of the contingencies which pools sought to take advantage of through the process of accumulation, marking up and distribution. They were thus an incident to the speculative market, making price movements more rapid and decisive.

The fact is that the so-called "public" is, from the speculative point of view, inert for the most part. It follows the "leader," "tips," and seeks suggestions from every source. The "insiders" and professional speculators, including banking houses and brokers, with their organization, superior means and better knowledge of the affairs of the individual company and of the technique of the securities market in general, show the way. In the long run, nothing attracts public buying so much as a steady rise in price of a security, accompanied by active trading.

It must not be supposed that such manipulation was always successful, even under what appeared the most favorable auspices. When the expected development did not occur, or, more frequently, when general conditions suddenly turned adverse and liquidation became general throughout the market, the pool might be forced to "unload." The pool was almost invariably a margin trader, borrowing on the stock which it bought. Frequently, it pyramided on thin margins, buying more after it had raised the price of the stock already bought the consequent higher market quotation permitting it to borrow on the first block the funds with which to pay for the second. Let an avalanche of selling hit the market, and the weak and badly conceived pools would see their stocks thrown on the market by brokers and bankers who found the margin impaired. The annals of the Exchange are replete with stories of pools that failed in this way.

Manipulative activities of the kind described were not necessarily carried on by groups as indicated. A single brokerage or banking house could accomplish a similar purpose. Again many variations may be found in the method of procedure. Frequently, owners of a large block of stock in which no active market existed would give a brokerage house or professional speculator an option to buy stock at a fixed or rising scale of prices. By raising the price of the stock above these figures, the brokerage house could sell out the optioned stock at a profit, thus earning a return for the creation of the market. Options are still in rather common use, although their legal status is yet to be clarified.

The formation of pools was carried out in many different ways. In the case of large pools in well-known issues, an invitation would sometimes be broadcast, on a confidential basis of course, among Wall Street brokerage and investment houses. The latter would then aid in the distribution process by issuing circulars and other analytical data to the public, including their own clients.

One actual letter of invitation of this sort, with the names deleted, was as follows:

The undersigned agree and covenant to become parties to a trading account in shares of the ———————— issue.

It is understood that each party signing hereto assumes a 25% liability in the account and, as a condition of his becoming a member of this group, deposits immediately with ———————— $—— as initial margin.

It is understood by all parties concerned that this account is to be conducted strictly in accordance with the Stock Exchange usage and margins may be called from time to time in accordance with the Wall Street custom.

It is further understood that the maximum number of shares which this account can be long at any time is ———— and it is further understood that purchases and sales may be made from time to time in the discretion of the manager or such person as he may designate to act for him in his absence from the city.

Mr. ———— is hereby designated as manager with full powers to act for the signers of this agreement and also to appoint any person, either interested or not interested in this account, to act as manager for this account during his temporary absence.

This account shall run for six months and may be extended for a further period not in excess of six months at the discretion of the manager.

Each party on signing this agreement becomes a participant to the extent of one-quarter of the entire account and shall be liable only for his proportion.

Date ———.

Legal Restrictions

Section 9 of the Securities Exchange Act of 1934 divides market control operations into two main groups. The first, consisting of manipulative operations, are absolutely prohibited. The second, which come within the category of stabilization operations, are made subject to regulations of the Securities and Exchange Commission.

The manipulative operations which are prohibited fall within five main groups. These are:

1. "Wash sales," or transactions in which the buyer and seller are identical so that no actual change in ownership occurs. Obviously, transactions of this kind are designed merely to give a fictitious appearance of activity and to raise published prices, thus preventing the market from carrying on its actual function as a trading place in which securities are transferred and prices fixed by supply and demand forces.

2. "Matched orders," wherein two or more parties acting collusively transact both buying and selling orders among themselves, so that after they are completed no change in ownership takes place. These are similar in effect to wash sales, and are just as misleading to the outside public.

3. A series of transactions designed to influence the price of a security, such as the pool operations just considered, and shorter-term operations sometimes referred to as "jiggles."

4. The dissemination of untrue or misleading facts, for consideration, for the purpose of influencing the price of security.

5. The dissemination of information concerning manipulation of security prices by others.

The Act provides, in the second place, that the Securities

and Exchange Commission shall regulate market stabilization or pegging operations, the use of options, and short selling. At this writing, the Commission has not yet promulgated such regulations. Until it does, these transactions may be carried on freely, provided they do not contravene other prohibitions specified in the law, or involve fraud.

References

BOND, F. D., *Stock Movements and Speculation,* New York, 1929, chap. xvi.

FLYNN, JOHN T., *Security Speculation,* New York, 1934.

LINCOLN, E. E., *Applied Business Finance,* Chicago, 1925, chap. xi.

MEEKER, J. E., "Distribution of Securities through the Stock Market," pamphlet, New York, 1929.

MEEKER, J. E., *The Work of the Stock Exchange,* New York, 1922, chap. viii.

MEYERS, C. H., *The Securities Exchange Act of 1934 Explained,* New York, 1934.

SIMMONS, E. H. H., *Modern Capitalism,* New York, 1927, pp. 107–132.

TWENTIETH CENTURY FUND, *The Security Markets,* New York, 1934.

Chapter XXI

INVESTMENT MANAGEMENT

Function of Management

In an earlier chapter[1] the organization of investing institutions was outlined, and the savings bank, trust company, investment trust and others were assigned their places in the general structure of American investment banking as developed within recent years. Only general reference was there made to the work of these institutions in their regular operation. It is now time to consider in some detail the practical application of that phase of investment banking which may be described as investment management—the care and supervision of the funds and investments of individuals or corporations by institutions that make it their sole or at least primary business to invest for others.

Such institutions may, from this point of view, be divided into two broad groups. The first group receives funds from depositors or purchasers of their securities, and manages them in a common pool. Their earnings may be regarded as including two elements—a return on the capital employed, and a profit which represents the additional income earned through the special efforts of the management of the institution. Where such management is specifically designed to gain a maximum return, as in the case of the investment trust, this additional profit element may assume large proportions. The second group of investing institutions, typified by the trust company, specifically segregates the funds of individual investors, who thus receive the profits and sustain the losses on the capital they assign to the investing institution. The latter is remunerated by a fixed payment that normally has no relation to the results achieved in the investing process.

[1] Chap. v, on Investing Institutions.

Management Institutions

While there are many institutions which might by some stretch of language be described as investment management institutions inasmuch as the funds intrusted to them are applied for the benefit of others to whom they really belong, we shall here consider only those which make the function of investment their primary task. This excludes the institutional investors, such as life insurance companies and large corporations, considered in Chapter VI. These latter usually apply the same general investment policies, but adapted to their own particular needs. Among the investing institutions, the savings banks are too closely restricted by law to evolve comprehensive management policies. We shall therefore restrict our discussion in the main to three types of such institutions, the investment trust, investment counsel and trust company.

In all three of these types of investing institutions, the fiduciary relationship to the investor is conspicuous. The client turns over his wealth to the institution for the express purpose of having it managed by those who are more closely in touch with conditions than the client believes himself to be. The investment counsel may not actually take possession of the property in its own name, but may limit itself simply to giving advice; but in other cases, the counsel actually takes possession of the wealth on behalf of its clients. In either case, however, there is a relationship of trust. The investment trust takes the funds of its security holders, pools them and invests them. The trust company maintains a complete separation of each deposit of wealth placed in its hands for investment, and carries on the process as an individual matter.

Enough has already been said in the foregoing chapters of the technique of organization of the trust company and of the investment trust; the investment counsel represents a new type of institution whose organization is still unstandardized. We now turn to a survey of the actual methods by which such institutions deal with the sums of wealth intrusted to them by their clients. Such a discussion naturally includes two general fields or branches: their management policy (1) when the institution is left to deal with the funds intrusted to it practically without restriction, as its own best judgment may dictate, and (2) when it is guided by certain general requirements, whether of law or of individual establishment, which restrict its judgment in placing funds in the market.

Theory of Investment Management

Where any institution is intrusted by a client with a fund which is to be managed or invested for him, even where such management is left entirely to the discretion of the institution, the first question to be raised is, of course, one of theory or principle: by what standards or principles of conduct shall such an institution be controlled in its placement of the funds? Experience has dictated certain general principles or canons of policy which are generally recognized. The actual methods pursued by investment managers in dealing with the funds under their control may be taken as an illustration of the theory of investment, showing the extent to which they have been guided by such principles in their actions.

A survey of current management institutions which are able to direct their funds as they choose shows that there is no single or standard type of portfolio management policy, but that managers still follow theories of investment which differ from one another. Even where there is substantial agreement on basic theories, in practice they adopt points of view that are widely at variance with one another, because of the fact that investment methods necessarily differ widely according as the needs and requirements of individual beneficiaries differ among themselves. Nevertheless, there are a few general canons of investment management which are substantially similar in most of these institutions. These are the quality of securities, diversification, and sales policy. The discussion of these principles will be carried on with special reference to the general management investment trust, as the least regulated type of investing institution.

Quality of Securities

Subject to such general limitations as a given investment institution may have set for itself, it desires, first of all, to have its purchases, whatever they are, "safe." This means in practice that depreciation in price will be unlikely, and that a large income or appreciation of principal is to be reasonably expected. Every purchase therefore must be tested from the standpoint of soundness, and this involves statistical analysis of such factors as assets, earnings, character of control, management, and the economic condition of the country in which the security is issued. These factors, and others of the same general description, have been touched on in the chapter on security analysis, and may be found fully discussed in any standard work on investment analysis.

Investment management first of all concerns itself with this kind of study, in order to make sure that within the general groups or types of securities which are to be bought, those which are actually selected for purchase shall come up fully to the standard of the group, and shall conform to such canons of desirability as the purchaser has laid down, however broadly or vaguely. In general, the desire of investment managers is to buy securities that have been "seasoned," although where a management believes itself to be in close touch with a group of originators or promoters in whom it has confidence, it may allow itself to take a position in issues which have not been seasoned but which have great possibilities of profit. This policy is of course more frequently to be noted in the case of investment trusts which are specifically organized for the purpose of carrying on investment in fields in which great profits are expected through appreciation of values, but in which any given security may, on account of the fact that it is new or the management untested, have an unfortunate experience. Illustrations of this practice of buying securities that are not seasoned, but represent distinctly new fields of investment, are furnished by chain store investment trusts, aviation trusts, and others of like kind. The existence of such exceptions does not prevent recognition of the general rule that investment management concerns, even where free to exercise their own judgment, are inclined to adhere to seasoned securities.

Some sample tests that are applied in judging of seasoned securities may be enumerated. A favorite one is that of requiring the existence of a continuous dividend or interest record over a period of years. Another is an earnings test, insisting upon the exclusion from purchase of securities which do not show regular earnings bearing a certain relationship to dividends or interest. Thus, for example, a general rule may be followed that no bonds are to be purchased unless the issuing concern has earned twice the interest for a given period of years.

Marketability is another test widely applied. It is not unusual to require that only those securities shall be bought that are definitely listed upon specified exchanges, the object in view being that of insuring at least a reasonable degree of salability in case the managers should find it desirable to liquidate the commitment. Limitation of securities bought to an amount small enough to insure that the actual control of the concern shall rest elsewhere is intended to prevent the management institution from getting into the position of operating or being responsible for an undertaking in which investment is made.

Diversification

A second canon of conduct on the part of investment managers is that of diversification. By diversification is meant the distribution of investments in such a way as to avoid too great a concentration of risk. This diversification may take four different forms: that of division between types of securities, individual enterprises, types of industry and country. The chief illustration of diversification of the first type is found in the effort to apportion holdings between stocks and bonds. American investment trusts show a general tendency to favor stocks. In Great Britain, good practice seems to call for the holding of about 40 per cent of all investments in bonds, 20 per cent in preferred, and 40 per cent in common stock. One plan of recent development here has been that of carrying bonds and preferred stock sufficient to provide income for meeting the interest and preferred dividend charges of the trust, the balance then being put into stocks.

More elaborate still are the restrictions that are in effect under the second head, the diversification of securities held, so as to avoid undue concentration in any one enterprise. A common requirement is that of prohibiting holdings in the securities of any one concern to an amount of more than 5 to 10 per cent of the sum handled by the investment trust. It is customary also to provide that not more than, say, 5 or 10 per cent of the aggregate amount of a security outstanding shall be purchased by the investment manager. Similar rules may govern the proportion of the investment fund which may be placed in any one industry.

Geographical diversification is afforded by prohibiting the investment of more than, say, one-third of the total fund in securities issued in any one foreign country. In most instances, also, there is a limit on the percentage of resources that may be placed outside domestic securities, for all foreign holdings may be adversely affected by wars and other special developments.

Policy as to Sales

No account of investment management would be adequate if confined entirely to the buying side of the portfolio. The question when to sell and when to "take profits" is, of course, the correlative of the question when to buy; and the two together constitute the problem of what is called "turnover policy." Every investment trust of the general management type expects to improve its position at least to some extent through this process of turnover. In other words, it regards the income of the enterprise as consisting essentially of two factors, the return derived from dividend and interest, and that derived from profits on selling.

One of the principal American investment trusts asserted in 1919 that it expected to make nearly one-half of its annual income out of turnover profits of this kind, which it estimated at anywhere from 14 to 16 per cent on the average capital employed by it. Obviously, no such profit can be made without some substantial skill in selling. In a general way, the investment manager desires to purchase securities that are moving downward or are at a low level, and he desires to sell when they are moving upward or are at peak point. He wishes, in other words, to foreshadow in some degree the cyclical movement of prices. By adapting their theory of business cycles to conditions in the various groups of shares, many investment managers believe it possible to get out of fluctuating securities, such as stocks, at favorable moments and shift their funds into securities that fluctuate little, such as bonds, and again to shift them back again when the more volatile securities have reached low point. In other cases, the cyclical theories are ignored, and instead securities are bought on the basis of advance knowledge of favorable developments in individual companies or industries. Other investment managers have claimed the ability to maintain a constant process of appreciation in investments through the shifting of funds from one market or country to another which is at a different stage of the business cycle or general economic development. There has as yet been no demonstration of ability to do any such thing over extended periods of time and through various types of markets. More particularly, developments during the panic period of 1929 and the subsequent depression have given little evidence that would encourage belief in, or reliance upon, a policy of this kind as a continuing source of profits. It is quite true, however, that through the maintenance of careful statistical and trading departments, and through constant comparison of values between different groups of securities, it is possible for an investment manager to shift by prompt action from one security or group of securities into others in which the possibilities of profit are greater.

Difference Between Discretionary and Dictated Funds

Up to this point we have been speaking of the management of funds which have been placed in the hands of an investment trust or investment counsel to use practically as it sees fit, making it possible to apply an unrestricted technique of investment. We turn next to cases where this discretion is rigidly restricted, as, for example, in trusts growing out of the fact that deceased persons have left funds for management by others, or that living persons who are not capable or are not disposed to manage their own affairs desire to turn over the function of management. In such cases, the transfer of the management function may be accompanied by an agreement to leave the entire conduct of affairs to the manager, in which case the situation approximates that of the investment trust; or the transfer may take place subject to the laws of the community dealing with estates and fiduciary transactions. At other times, the specific provisions of a will or other document, in which definite conditions are laid down for the management of the funds, govern the process. Work of this kind is more and more generally, especially in the United States, placed in the hands of trust companies, and is sometimes referred to as fiduciary banking. It is accompanied by the performance of many other functions which have only an indirect relationship to investments, such as corporate trusts.

In the exercise of its function as investment manager, the trust company, under all circumstances, keeps the general canons of investment before it as a guide. In addition, it must conform to two other series of regulations. These are:

1. The trust deed or instrument that accompanies the placement of funds with a trust company, and which is designed to indicate to the concern the desire of the person creating the trust.

2. The fiduciary law of the jurisdiction in which the trust is established, and which, in the absence of any specific instructions on the part of the original owner of the property, dictates the manner in which it shall be administered in the interest of its ultimate possessors. Such law may control or direct the use and disposition of the property in exceptional instances in a manner contrary to the expressions conveyed in the trust instrument itself.

A survey was made in 1925 of the investment policy of more than 200 trust companies and trust departments of national banks. This study revealed that trust companies, taken together, followed about the same policies in investing "legal" trust funds as those which were subject to their discretion, except for a moderately larger percentage of the latter invested in corporate securities. The distribution for discretionary funds was approximately as follows:[2]

[2] Smith, James R., *Trust Companies in the United States*, pp. 427ff.

Investment	Percentage of Funds Invested
Real estate, mortgages and mortgage bonds	56.7
U. S. bonds	12.8
Municipals	9.1
Railroad bonds	4.6
Railroad stock	.7
Public utility securities	5.4
Industrial bonds	4.5
Industrial stock	2.6
Bank and insurance stocks	1.4
Foreign bonds	.5
Miscellaneous	1.7
Total	100.0

Lately there has been a marked tendency to invest a substantial portion of discretionary estates in seasoned stocks, largely in response to the desire of clients of the trust companies who reflect the growing public favor seasoned equities now meet.

The trust company, in its work as individual trustee, acts usually as executor, administrator, guardian and trustee. In all individual trusts, the first and essential step on the part of the trustee is to obtain at the outset a copy of the trust instrument and to familiarize himself with its terms, thereafter guiding his conduct entirely by the orders therein given in so far as they are not in conflict with existing law or legal and judicial practice. If the trust instrument has afforded definite instructions which leave no element of judgment open to the trustee as, for example, if the fund placed in the hands of the trustee is in cash and is accompanied by instructions to purchase a specified kind of securities, keep the fund invested in these same securities and pay the income to designated persons, the matter is relatively simple. But in most cases an element of judgment emerges; and even where the instructions appear to be perfectly plain and unmistakable, it not infrequently happens that changing conditions, the withdrawal or retirement of given securities, the failure of others, and so forth, throw into the hands of the trustee a degree of discretion not expected at the outset. This makes it important to know in general terms what the position of the courts on the subject has been and exactly where the investment responsibility of the trustee begins and ends. This is outlined in full in the appendix to the chapter.

Organization for Management

The conduct of management institutions has increasingly taken on a standardized character. Research and statistical work are carried on in separate departments where broad economic conditions and the status of particular industries are studied, and the analysis of particular companies and securities is effected.

Supervisors then seek to translate this work into specific buying and selling recommendations for each account, in the light of the circumstances that affect the investment problems of the client. In addition, in the case of investment counsel and related types of institutions, "account executives" carry out the dual functions of acting as salesmen and giving routine personal service to clients.

Increasingly, it is coming to be felt that mere buying and selling recommendations are not enough. In addition, the client as far as possible must be made to see the reasons for the steps taken, and the background of the steps suggested. Thus, he will see that a rational course of procedure is being followed, rather than a program that is little more than guesswork.

Flexibility

One great handicap of investment management work is the tendency for those responsible to lose flexibility. The need for obtaining a ready market in which large amounts of securities can be bought and sold without disturbance to price is very important, particularly in the case of larger investing institutions. It is pointed out that large trust companies and investment counsel organizations are no longer in a position to buy and sell readily because the market cannot absorb major holdings, particularly in depression periods.

This inability to buy and sell substantial blocks of securities readily will probably lead to further modification of portfolio policies by these institutions, so as to place more stress than ever upon long-term holdings.

References

Chamberlain, L., and Edwards, G. W., *Principles of Bond Investment,* New York, 1927, chap. iv.

Dice, C. A., *The Stock Market,* Chicago, 1927, chap. xxvii.

Kirshman, I. E., *Principles of Investment,* Chicago, 1924, part v.

Lyon, Hastings, *Investment,* New York, 1926, chap. xxvii.

Riddle, N. G., *The Investment Policy of Trust Institutions,* Chicago, 1934.

Rose, Dwight C., *The Practical Application of Investment Management,* New York, 1933.

Smith, J. G., *The Development of Trust Companies in the United States,* New York, 1928, chap. xvii.

Vance, Ray, *Investment Policies That Pay,* New York, 1929, *passim.*

Appendix

The following survey of the question of trustee responsibility has been prepared by a counsellor of one of the principal trust companies of New York City, who has sketched therein the outlines of the present legal and judicial situation as applicable to it:

Legal Responsibility of Trustee for Investment of Trust Funds

SUMMARY

1. *General Factors in Choice of Investments:*
   - a. The trust investment:
     - Wording necessary to vest discretion
     - Effect of consent of adult beneficiary—not a minor or an incompetent
   - b. Statutes and court decisions
   - c. Situation and needs of the beneficiaries
   - d. Economic conditions

2. *General Duties of Trustee Regarding Investments:*
   - a. To invest within a reasonable time
   - b. To invest within court's jurisdiction
   - c. To make no individual profit from trust funds
     - Sale of securities to trusts
     - Mortgage participations

d. To keep trust funds separate
Temporary deposits in banking department
Deposit designated as Trust Fund

3. *Legal Principles Governing Nature of Investment:*
a. "Prudent man" theory
b. Speculation excluded, but investment permitted
c. Relative importance of safety of principal versus amount of income
d. Reasonable diversification required
e. Trustee not surcharged for losses on perfectly proper securities

4. *Continuation of Investments:*
a. Those made by creator of trust
b. Those received from predecessor trustee
c. Business of decedent

5. *Concrete Restrictions on New Investments:*
a. Margin stock speculation barred
b. Active conduct of business barred
c. Company must
NOT BE NEW
HAVE DIVIDEND RECORD
HAVE AMPLE PROPERTY
d. Security must be SEASONED and BE WELL REGARDED AS AN INVESTMENT
e. Trustee must consider condition of the industry
f. Industrial common stocks admitted

DETAILED ANALYSES

1. *General Factors in Choice of Investments:*
Each trust's investments present a separate problem. The choice of its investments depends upon four factors:

a. The Trust Instrument
b. Statutes and Court decisions
c. Situation and need of beneficiaries
d. Economic conditions

The definite instructions, if any, contained in the trust instrument and the intention of the trustor as indicated in a reading of the entire document are the most important.

a. *The Trust Instrument:*

The Trust Instrument may appoint the Company sole trustee or co-trustee. It may place varying degrees of responsibility upon the Company by making the investments

1. controlled by the donor or others, so that the Company acts merely as agent
2. subject to the approval of the donor
3. controlled solely by the Company

From another point of view, trusts fall into two classes:

1. Those in which existing investments are turned over to the Company as trustee and the question of their retention or change merely arises
2. Those in which a sum of money is turned over to the Company as Trustee, which it is to invest

Regardless of the party upon whom responsibility for investments is placed, the trust instrument may either:

1. Permit new investment only in legal securities
2. Permit wide discretion in investing funds

If the instrument is silent as to character of investments permitted, the Company, as trustee in New York State, may follow only the dictates of the State Law.

If it invests outside the "legal list," it does so at its own risk and must bear loss resulting therefrom. It makes no difference whether or not the Company invested with ordinary care and prudence, but it is liable just as if it had disregarded the instructions contained in the instrument and invested in securities other than those specified therein. Many trusts, however, vest discretion in the Company as Trustee to invest as it sees fit in "non-legals" outside the authorized list, but its discretion is not arbitrary or uncontrolled.

The instructions vesting general discretion in the Company as Trustee must be clear and specific. The wording is now well understood.

In a legal trust, however, where all the beneficiaries are of full age and under no legal disabilities, their consent sanctions the investment and waives their right to hold the Company as Trustee, responsible for loss. It must appear that the beneficiary knew all the facts, was apprised of his legal rights and under no disability to assert them. He must have acted freely, deliberately and advisedly, with the intention of confirming a transaction which he knew, or with reasonable diligence ought to have known, to be impeachable. The Company, as trustee, sustains the burden of proof.

b. *Statutes and Court decisions:*

Regardless of the discretion conferred, the conduct of the Company, as trustee, is subject to review by the Court. Reckless and willful abuse is not permitted, but good faith is required, even though the discretion granted be absolute. Most of the investment principles represent older ideas rather than current views, and most of the instruments creating trusts were drawn years ago. The Trustee is held to strict accountability and emphasis is placed upon conservatism.

Trust Companies as trustees are subject to the same rules of law as are individual trustees, but it is possible that they may be the more subject to a standard of reasonable conduct by the courts in considering the facts in a particular case.

c. *Situation and need of beneficiaries:*

The Company as trustee must consider the interests of both life beneficiary and remainderman. It must carry out the purpose of the trust to provide for both and adapt its investments to their requirements.

d. *Economic conditions:*

Finally, the Company must consider the general economic situation when investing trust funds. The economic outlook for an industry determines the desirability of investing in its securities. The general economic situation makes investment in bonds preferable at certain times to investment in stocks, or investment in long-term obligations preferable to investment in short-term.

2. *General Duties of Trustee Regarding Investments:*

The general duties with respect to investments of the Company as trustee, are four in number:

a. To invest within a reasonable time
b. To invest within the court's jurisdiction
c. To make no individual profit from the trust funds
d. To keep the trust funds separate from its own

a. *To invest within a reasonable time:*

In order to make the trust estate produce an income the Company as trustee is required to invest the trust funds within a reasonable time. This rule applies also to any interest or increase which comes to the estate and which is not distributed. A "reasonable" time has been variously defined by the courts; but, in New York State, negligently permitting the funds to remain idle renders the Company as trustee liable for interest on the funds at the legal rate.

b. *To invest within the court's jurisdiction:*

The Company, as trustee, must not make investments that will remove trust property beyond the jurisdiction of the court supervising the trust. This requirement dates back and applies to the time when real estate was a leading form of property bequeathed, and is not applicable to stocks, bonds and similar securities.

c. *To make no individual profit from the trust funds:*

The Company, as trustee, is not permitted to purchase from itself or at its own sale, except at a mortgage foreclosure sale, to protect the beneficiaries. The law does not stop to inquire into the fairness of the sale or the adequacy of the price, but stamps its disapproval upon the transaction which creates a conflict between the self-interest and the integrity of the trustee. The trustee is not permitted to obtain any profit, direct or indirect, from its dealings with the trust property, other than its lawful compensation. If it does, it is liable not only for the entire fund and interest thereon, but also for such profit as it may have made, the beneficiary having the option to elect whether to take the fund with interest or with the profit.

This matter is of importance to institutions which have a bond department. Two questions arise in such cases: first, should the bond department sell securities to the trust department; and if so, second, upon what basis? California institutions, e.g., answer the question in two ways. Some execute all orders for the purchase of securities through an outside dealer and buy securities only from outside sources in the open market—never from the institution itself. Others, however, feel that they have special facilities and desire to give their trusts the benefit of their expert opportunities, knowledge and judgment. Hence when they are syndicate members, they sell securities to their trusts at the wholesale price, feeling that the good will resulting will indirectly prove ample compensation.

In New York State no direct legal decisions exist on the matter. An exception is made of participating mortgages in which the Company is specifically authorized to invest trust funds. The Company holds the mortgage and issues participating certificates to the various beneficiaries. The small estate benefits by becoming productive at once. The practice was recognized as proper by the Court of Appeals in 1916, confirmed in 1918 by an amendment to Sec. III of the Decedent's Estate Law and Sec. 21 of the Personal Property Law, and further approved by an opinion of the Attorney-General of the State of New York in 1924.

d. *To keep the trust funds separate:*

Since the trust company must have no personal interest in its dealings with the trust property, it must keep the trust funds entirely separate and not mingle them either with its own funds or with those of other trusts. Sec. 231 of the Surrogates Court Act specifically required this in the case of testamentary trusts, although the statutes are silent as to voluntary trusts.

The trust company, however, may temporarily deposit in its banking department trust funds awaiting investment by the trust department. Sec. 188 Sub. 11 of the New York Banking Law permits such deposit in its name as trustee. On sums of not less than $100 the Company shall allow interest at not less than 2% per annum until expended or distributed. If unexpended or undistributed for one year, it is added to the principal of the trust fund, and is itself subject to interest.

3. *Legal Principles Governing Nature of Investment:*

The Courts in certain leading cases have laid down a few fundamental principles to be observed in investing trust funds, in the absence of words in the will conferring greater discretion. Massachusetts does not limit trustees by statutory enactment to certain classes of securities, and in 1830 the Court in Harvard College *vs.* Amory laid down the following guide for the trustee:

"to observe how men of prudence, discretion and diligence

manage their own affairs, not in regard to speculation, but in regard to the permanent disposition of the funds, considering the probable income as well as the probable safety of the capital to be invested."

The New York Courts have adopted the same tests, in particular for those trusts which vest discretion in the trustee, the leading case being Matter of Hall, handed down in 1900.

The decision contains several significant features:

a. It lays down a "prudent man" theory.
b. It distinguishes between speculation and investment.
c. It emphasizes amount of income as well as safety of principal.

Good faith is of course, fundamental.

a. *"Prudent man" theory:*

The general rule was early stated (1869) in the following words: "The trustee is bound to employ such diligence and such prudence in the care and management, as in general, prudent men of discretion and intelligence in such matters employ in their own like affairs."

The degree of care to which the trustee is held is not his opinion of the security nor that of some interested party, but what a normal or prudent man would think of it as applied to his own personal transactions.

b. *Speculation excluded, but investment permitted:*

In view of the "prudent man" theory, the courts exclude speculation as distinct from investment.

The tests of a speculative transaction have been laid down in various cases. They are included in the following pronouncements:

1. Investment for an uncertain and doubtful rise in the market.
2. Its purpose is to increase the estate or realize a profit from the transaction, while the purpose of an investment is to secure an income.
3. It will generally be conceded that a mere business chance or prospect, however promising, is not a proper place for trust funds. While, of course, all investments, however carefully made, are more or less liable to depreciate and become worthless, experience has shown that certain classes of investments are peculiarly

> liable to such depreciation and loss. These, of course, should be avoided by every prudent man who is investing his own money with a view to permanency and security rather than chance of profit. A trustee should, therefore, avoid them, even though he sincerely believes a particular investment of that class to be safe as well as profitable.

The exclusion of speculation raises the question—may the trustee purchase common stocks with trust funds? (Sec. 5f.)

c. *Relative importance of safety of principal versus amount of income:*

In view of these tests of speculation, it is not surprising to find that Courts of Law generally hold that it is the primary duty of a trustee to maintain the principal of the trust intact.

Hence a decrease in the income of the trust can be more easily explained than a decrease in the principal, but a decrease in income would incur the ill will of the beneficiary.

d. *Reasonable diversification required:*

In addition to these requirements, the courts oppose overheavy investment in one security, regardless of the merit of the security. The mere fact that a substantial investment is made originally does not absolve the trustee from liability for a substantial further investment in the same security.

e. *Trustee not surcharged for losses on perfectly proper securities:*

In a legal trust the trustee is surcharged for losses if it selects investments from outside the legal list. In a discretionary trust, it is surcharged only in case it fails to heed the requirements laid down in 3 a–d just given. Where a trustee buys only perfectly proper securities, hence exercises sound discretion, he is not surcharged in the event that some depreciate. In a case where some common stocks were included among the securities purchased, the court stated that "he should receive the benefit of the care and prudence with which he has administered the estate and not be mulcted in damages when the whole estate has been administered so as to yield a profit, because certain of the investments may not have turned out as had been anticipated." No case has yet been decided in which an aggregate loss ensued in place of an aggregate gain.

4. *Continuation of Investments:*

Some trusts, as already stated, involve the question whether or not investments received from others should be continued. It is necessary to distinguish three cases, according to the origin and nature of the investment:

a. Those made by the creator of the trust
b. Those received from a predecessor trustee
c. Those involving continuation of the decedent's business.

Two questions arise:

1. How far may the trustee go in disposing of the securities he holds?
2. What are the circumstances under which he comes under a duty to dispose of the securities, as a preliminary to reinvestment?

a. *Those made by creator of trust:*

The first duty of the trustee is to call in the estate preparatory to investment. The trust instrument, however, may specifically authorize a continuance of the investments made by the creator of the trust. Otherwise, in New York State it has been decided that the investments the creator made afford no criterion for the trustee and that it is the latter's duty to call in the estate and invest it in authorized securities. As a general rule, this must be done within one year, but a trustee is permitted to use his discretion and may not be liable if he retains the investments for a longer period, awaiting a favorable market. In the discretionary as distinct from the legal trust, the trustee may continue investments made by the creator, which the trustee in the exercise of good faith and ordinary care considers safe. The fact that the creator made the investments may be considered a recommendation or suggestion that they are worthy of retention. One decision states:

"There is a great difference between an investment made by the trustees of moneys forming a part of the estate and the retention of securities purchased by the testator and held by him at the time of his decease. In one case the investment, whether wise or unwise, is the independent

> uncontrollable act of the owner, and in the other it is the act of the trustees whose discretion is limited and whose duties are prescribed and each is to be subjected, therefore, to wholly different rules of law, if indeed, the act of the owner is subject to any rules whatever."

If the trust instrument makes a specific gift of certain stocks or securities, the trustee is not liable in retaining them.

b. *Those received from predecessor trustee:*

A trustee may have unauthorized investments turned over to him by a predecessor trustee. He should ascertain which have been purchased by the predecessor, as distinct from the creator of the trust, and dispose of them. He is allowed a reasonable time in which to investigate the investments he takes over and make such changes as may be necessary. But where a court forces a trustee to take over from his predecessor securities of speculative value and possibly unsalable, he is required merely to act in good faith in dealing with them and is not liable for loss if he uses his best judgment.

c. *Business of decedent:*

The general rule is that in the absence of express authority either in the document creating the trust or by order of the court, an executor, administrator or trustee may not continue a trade or business carried on by the decedent at the time of his death. The reason is that trades and businesses are hazardous and conduct of them is not within the scope of administrative functions. Even when the power to continue a business is conferred by the trust instrument, it is strictly construed.

In certain cases, an executor, administrator or trustee will be permitted to carry out contracts made by the decedent, or to carry on a business or to complete the manufacture of unfinished articles, or to incur liabilities when such a course is for the best interests of the estate, but even in the exceptional case the trustee should protect himself by an order of the court.

The trustee should not continue the business as a sole proprietorship or partnership, but as a corporation, so as to limit its own liability. The instrument should specially relieve the trustee from the consequences of poor business judgment. It is asked in such cases to do more than the ordinary trustee and to undertake more work.

5. *Concrete Restrictions in New Investments:*

The general principles stated in Sec. 3 have been applied in a number of specific instances. As a result, the following concrete restrictions on new investments have been laid down:

a. Margin stock speculation is barred.
b. Active conduct of business is barred.
c. The company whose securities are purchased must
    a. Not be new.
    b. Have a dividend record.
    c. Have ample property.
d. The security must be seasoned and be well regarded as an investment.
e. The trustee must consider conditions in the industry.
f. Industrial common stocks may be purchased for a discretionary trust.
g. Express or implied power to invest is necessary.

These restrictions are especially important for those securities not on the legal list. They relate primarily to the individual security, and do not penalize a trustee who buys at the top price in the market, provided that he buys a standard security.

a. *Margin stock speculation barred:*

The courts have opposed margin stock speculation, even where begun by the testator and merely continued by the trustee.

b. *Active conduct of business barred:*

The courts frown upon active participation in the affairs of corporations, even where the trustee claims that he is carrying out the developmental plans of the testator by engaging in such new ventures. Only business undertaken by the decedent can be carried on under the conditions mentioned in 4 c.

c. *Company must:*

not be new;
have dividend record;
have ample property.

These requirements obviously hark back to the idea of a

prudent man investing his funds with care, for they represent commonly accepted tests for an investment security. In case of a consolidation, the company must not represent such expansion as to be substantially a new company.

d. *The security must be seasoned and be well regarded as an investment:*

These requirements are allied to those contained in c. A company which is not new, so that it has been conducted successfully over a long period of time, has a dividend record and has built an ample property, soon enters the class of seasoned investments. Thus established, its securities become well regarded as investment issues and acquire the confidence of investors.

e. *The trustee must consider conditions in the industry:*

Investment involves consideration of the company, the issue and the underlying conditions in the industry in question. Most decisions refer to the condition of the company, but a few consider the immediate and prospective situation in the industry at the time of investment. This requirement adds greatly to the trustee's responsibility.

In 1924 a trustee inexperienced in investment matters, who sought the advice of a well-known financial institution, was surcharged with the amount of bonds of a steamship company which defaulted soon after organization, on the ground among others, that he should have realized that in 1919 the steamship business was grossly inflated.

6. *Industrial Common Stocks May Be Purchased for a Discretionary Trust:*

Much controversy exists on the merits of common stocks as investments for trust funds. A trustee is permitted, under various decisions, to purchase common stocks which meet the tests laid down in the preceding sections.

Chapter XXII

REGULATION OF SECURITY SELLING

History of Regulation

While banking regulation has been known in this country from the time of the establishment of the first commercial banks, the security business escaped specific regulation until recent years. Investment banking was fully developed long after commercial banking, and it affected directly, until recently, a much smaller segment of the population. The banks, especially in their note issue function, came into contact with virtually all elements in the community. Hence, the demand for government control was not as great.

Although laws to regulate the issuance of securities were known in Germany and France before 1900, and in England such legislation was passed at the opening of the present century, no such general laws appeared on the statute books of an American state until 1911. Only in the case of railroad and public utility securities did the states pass laws giving jurisdiction over their issuance to duly constituted commissions with varying degrees of power. A number of legal enactments were made in several states governing security trading, as distinct from new issues. Some of these, such as the laws of 1812 forbidding short selling in New York State, fell into disuse or were repealed, while others remained on the statute books.[1]

The first state law regulating the sale of investment securities was passed in Kansas in 1911. It bore the name of blue-sky law, a term which has since been applied generally to this type of legislation. The name was first applied to "high-pressure" promoters who at that time infested the state and sold fraudulent securities to farmers in huge volume. These promoters had come to be called "blue-sky merchants" because

[1] A discussion of older exchange and brokerage law may be found in Goldman, S. P., *Stock Exchange Law*.

some of them were said to be bold enough to offer to the farmers, unversed in investment matters, title in fee simple to the blue sky itself.

The Kansas law, passed without regard to European experience and the nature of the investment banking business, was too extreme in its original form. It made the state the guardian of the people's investments. A Charter Board was created which was to allow the sale within the state only of securities which held out promise of dividend payments, and which were issued by businesses which were "honestly, fairly and justly managed." The law expected too much of the Charter Board, and as a matter of fact that body soon reduced its investigations to a perfunctory basis. Nevertheless, the blue-sky merchants were frightened and their depredations were sharply reduced. Later, Kansas modified her law to involve less jurisdiction over the speculative quality of securities by the Charter Board, in response to an adverse decision of the Supreme Court.

The Kansas statute was almost immediately copied by the province of Manitoba, Canada. Other states successively passed laws along similar lines. For several years, the fate of the blue-sky laws hung in the balance because of litigation over their validity and scope. They were attacked chiefly on grounds of unconstitutionality, and their opponents won a number of victories in the state and lower federal courts. However, the Supreme Court came to the rescue, and in 1917 a series of cases declared the blue-sky laws of Ohio, Michigan and South Dakota constitutional as an exercise of the police power of the state.[2] On the other hand, the states were prevented by the highest court from exercising jurisdiction over sales of securities within their borders from without the state, through the use of the mails or other forms of communication. The case of Hall *vs.* Geiger Jones Company (242 U. S. 539) declared such sales made from outside the borders of a state to be interstate commerce, and hence subject to the jurisdiction of the federal government. The court held in this decision that the states have the power to license and regulate all persons who dispose of securities within the state, even when they originate

[2] Merrick *vs.* Halsey, 242 U. S. 568, was a leading case bringing out this doctrine.

from the outside, as "a police regulation strictly." Where there is no person so doing reachable, however, the state is powerless. Before the enactment of the federal Securities Act of 1933, it was generally declared that the bulk of security frauds took place through the use of the mails, the state blue-sky laws having sharply reduced intrastate fraudulent selling of this kind.

A total of 43 states now have blue-sky laws properly so called. The jurisdiction over security issues in these states is put into the hands of security commissioners, who, in the interest of effective cooperation to prevent security frauds, have formed a National Association of Securities Commissioners. New York, New Jersey, Maryland and Delaware have not adopted such legislation, strictly speaking, but have what is known as an anti-fraud type of law. Only Nevada, among the states, has no security legislation at all. In their efforts to reach the fraudulent security vendor, these regulations affect the business of the legitimate investment banker, and he must make sure that he meets such legal requirements, as well as those of the federal government, before selling new issues in the various states.

Blue-sky Laws

The basic theory behind the blue-sky laws is that a corporation, being a creature of the state, has an implied approval by the state in the issue of its securities. If these securities are fraudulent, the state which has created the corporation or authorized it to do business within its borders has authorized their issue. Hence, because of this implied approval, supervision of these security issues becomes desirable.[3]

Blue-sky laws regulate security issues chiefly through two important channels. In the first place, dealers and brokers offering these securities may be required to get a license from the securities commissioner or cognate officer, or at least to register with him. In this way, unreliable or fraudulent individuals and firms can be kept out of the securities business in the state. Secondly, specific issues of securities are under certain circum-

[3] This theory is not the one which the Supreme Court adopted in upholding the legality of blue-sky laws, however. It adopted chiefly the police power theory, as has already been seen.

stances required to be qualified or "blue-skyed" by the securities commissioner.

Both the qualification of the security issue and the licensing or registration of the dealer offering it are required in many states; but there are several, such as Texas, which rely upon the qualification of securities or the issuing corporations themselves, rather than licensing the dealers putting them out. In states like Illinois and others where the dealer or agent offering the security is merely registered with the Secretary of State under a relatively small bond, the major reliance of the law is upon the requirements concerning the security issue itself, which must be fulfilled before it may be offered for sale within the state. Registration mainly serves the purpose of facilitating the service of legal process on dealers who violate the law. The Illinois law, in fact, specifically states that "the Secretary of State shall not issue any certificate or written evidence to any person registered as an owner, dealer, broker, solicitor or agent." In this way, the state avoids giving an implied assurance of the reliability of dealers, such as is given in states where formal licensing is required.

Regulation of Dealers

In their regulations licensing dealers, the blue-sky laws have wo distinct aims. In the first place, many of the laws seek to licit enough information before granting a license to assure hat the dealer is solvent and financially responsible. Secondly, y the mere act of registration, the state authorities are enabled o keep watch on the activities of dealers, and to trace those who re engaging in doubtful or fradulent practices.

As an example of the requirements governing the licensing f dealers in those states which stress this aspect of blue-sky aw practice, the Indiana law may be cited. This is of special nterest as showing what legitimate investment houses must do n order to do business in that state.

> Every dealer before engaging in business in this state shall file in e office of the commission an application for registration in writg in such form as the commission may prescribe, duly verified by th, which shall state the principal office of the applicant, wherever tuated, and the location of the principal office and all branch of-

fices in this state, if any, the name or style of doing business, the names, residence and business addresses of all persons interested in the business as principals, co-partners, officers and directors, specifying as to each his capacity and title, the general plan and character of business and the length of time the dealer has been engaged in business. The commission may also require such additional information as to applicant's previous history, record and association, as it may deem necessary to establish the good repute in business of the applicant.

Every dealer shall file with his application an irrevocable written consent to the service of process upon the commission in actions against such dealer in manner and form as hereinabove provided in section 9.

Every applicant for a dealer's license shall also file with his application a bond in the sum of five thousand dollars ($5,000) running to the State of Indiana in such form, if any, as the commission may designate, such bond to be conditioned upon the faithful compliance with the provisions of this act by said dealer and by all agents registered by him. Such bond shall be executed as surety by a surety company having a net worth of not less than one million dollars ($1,000,000) and authorized to do business in this state.

If the commission shall find that the applicant is of good repute and has complied with the provisions of this section, including the payment of the fee hereinafter provided, it shall register such applicant as a dealer.

Upon the written application of a registered dealer and general satisfactory showing as to good character, and upon the payment of the proper fee, the commission shall register as agents of such dealer, such natural persons as the dealer may request.

The names and addresses of all persons approved for registration as dealers or agents and all orders with respect thereto shall be recorded in a register of dealers and agents kept in the office of the commission which shall be open to public inspection. Every registration under this section shall expire on the 31st day of December in each year, but new registrations for the succeeding year shall be issued upon written application and upon payment of the fee as hereinafter provided, without the filing of further statements or furnishing any further information unless specifically required by the commission. Applications for renewals must be made not less than thirty nor more than sixty days before the first day of the ensuing year, otherwise they shall be treated as original applications. The fee for such registration and for each renewal shall be twenty-five dollars ($25) in the case of dealers, and five dollars ($5) in the case of agents.

In their regulations licensing dealers, most blue-sky laws distinguish between dealers who offer securities in their own names and brokers who merely transact business as agents for others. There is no desire to control the operations of brokers except in so far as they are used to float new securities within the state. "Investment companies," within the meaning of the blue-sky laws, may include all dealers in securities and corporations making direct offerings of their own securities. The term is not to be confused with the group of companies more commonly termed investment trusts.

In several states, there has been a tendency in the law to favor dealers resident within the state at the expense of those operating from without who send salesmen and other representatives into the state. Thus, the Virginia law, as amended in 1928, provided that securities shall be exempted from the provisions of the law when offered by a licensed dealer, who "must be a regular dealer in securities and must have been in business in this state for a period of one year prior to the date of his application for license as a licensed dealer under this act." Discussing this type of provision, which makes it difficult for outside houses to do business in Virginia, the Legislation Committee of the Investment Bankers Association of America has stated:

> Forty-six states have some form of law which was enacted to protect the public against misrepresentation, deceit and fraud in the sale of securities. The clearly indicated purpose of such law is to protect the citizens of the state. It is contrary to the recognized purpose of such legislation that such law should become the medium, whether intentional or otherwise, by which unfair competition is accomplished by one class of dealers against another class of dealers. Classifications made by such law should be on reasons that have a legitimate, fair, just and reasonable relation to the purpose of such legislation.
>
> Such discriminations are also objectionable for the reason that they act as a barrier to the proper distribution of sound securities, whereas it is essential to the growth, development and prosperity of the nation that investment funds of the public shall be free to flow

in any natural channel when there is no fraud or deception, and that legitimate business wherever located shall have the opportunity of free access to the available capital of the general public in all parts of the country with the least possible burden.

In states where such favoritism is shown to local security dealers, the practice is common for outside houses to sell securities only to such local dealers, rather than to the general public, for these dealers are exempt from the operation of the blue-sky law. Thus, in Pennsylvania, security dealers, selling to investors there, must be licensed in the state. Unlicensed dealers, in advertising new issues in Pennsylvania, state in their advertisements that "the above offering is confined to banks, savings institutions and trust companies created under the laws of Pennsylvania and to persons and companies registered under the securities act approved June 14, 1923." Thus such regulations increase the business of dealers within the state, but may not conduce to the best interests of investors.

Regulation of Specific Issues

In qualifying a new issue, the first important task facing the investment banker is to determine whether or not any given offering is subject to the provisions of the blue-sky laws in the various states.[4] It is to the advantage of the originating house to make new issues exempt, if possible, as in this way delay and expense may be avoided. By keeping these regulations in mind when negotiating an issue and making proper provision in advance, this may be accomplished without difficulty.

The first important class of exemptions is government securities, which are generally exempt in most states. This exemption applies not only to obligations of the United States government, the states and municipalities, but also to foreign governments and often to government-guaranteed obligations as well.

A second important class of exemptions relates to securities listed on specified exchanges. Often this exemption is widened by a provision that securities senior to these listed securities

[4] For this purpose, an up-to-date compilation of blue-sky laws is necessary. Such a service is given by the Commerce Clearing House Securities Law Service, which gives in loose-leaf form texts and annotations of both state and federal legislation.

are exempt also. In both cases, the theory is that these issues have been adequately investigated by the exchange before listing. Thirteen states in 1929 had such exemptions for issues listed on the New York Stock Exchange, and nine for those listed on the New York Curb. Public utility securities, including railroad issues, since they are issued by companies subject to regulation by governmental bodies, also are generally exempted. There are such exemptions in twenty-eight states as of a recent date.

The exemption list is frequently, for the large investment banking house, the most important part of the blue-sky law. While qualification under several of the state security laws involves so many delays and uncertainties as to discourage selling effort by investment houses in those states, simple conformance to the exemption requirements eliminates this difficulty. Hence, there is a special advantage in coming under these exemptions where possible. Thus, a number of investment trust issues were originally listed on the Boston Stock Exchange because this gives exemption under the blue-sky laws in several states. By listing in Boston rather than New York, two advantages were gained. There was less difficulty in maintaining the market on the smaller exchange, and less stringent regulations governed listing there before 1934. Listing is but one example of how exemption may be gained for a security under blue-sky law provisions.

The tests applied by state commissions in passing on applications for permits for the sale of securities differ, both in accordance with law and according to the known predilections of the state securities commissioner or similar officer given jurisdiction in the application of the blue-sky laws. In Massachusetts, the chief legal test is the character of the principals. Michigan stresses chiefly asset values. Thus, this state forbade at one time the sale of preferred stock of Dodge Brothers, Inc., within the state, after about $1,500,000 of the stock had been sold there, because the book value of the shares based on the balance sheet as published was only $1 per share. Earning power is stressed in Illinois and Wisconsin. Still another test applied is whether or not the issue is speculative, securities of an uncertain character being discriminated against. Finally, there are a number of states having no known policy in granting permits. These rely upon a combination of earning power, asset value and character of management in judging an issue, approval of which is applied for.

In a number of states, actual qualification of a new issue of securities is not required. Instead, it is merely necessary to file certain data concerning it with the state security commissioner. This process is sometimes referred to as *notification*, as distinct from *qualification*, and is similar to registration under the federal Securities Act. Until a stop-order is issued in such cases by the security commissioner, selling may go forward after the requisite data have been placed on file with the latter.

Blue-sky law proceedings must be expedited by bankers, especially in those states which require preliminary approval of an issue before it is actually offered to the public. This is done in Massachusetts, Rhode Island, Michigan, Illinois, Wisconsin, Georgia and Missouri. In the first two states named, and in Georgia, approval is given as soon as a "notice of intention" to make the issue is received from a licensed dealer. In Michigan, such approval may or may not be forthcoming. Illinois and Wisconsin grant preliminary approval only to securities belonging to the non-speculative class, as measured by the criteria set up in the blue-sky laws.

Final qualification is secured for an issue after the issuing company makes out full papers on forms furnished by the security commissioners. Bankers generally see that these forms are filled in by the company, and that no delay occurs in filing them. A provision that this be done as soon as practicable is often included in the purchase agreement.

When securities are sold in violation of blue-sky laws, the latter frequently provide that sales are void or voidable at the option of the purchaser. In addition, "teeth" are put into the law by providing fines and prison terms for parties selling securities contrary to certain of its provisions.

The lack of uniformity in blue-sky legislation makes it difficult for the legitimate security dealer, whose prime requisite is speed of operation, to do business in several of the states where the regulations are most severe. In practice, this often means either avoiding those states, or doing business through dealers who are close to the situation there and will be able to get securities through the commission with the least friction and delay. Law firms specializing in blue-sky practice also are often in a position to hasten such procedure. In fact, the personal element enters largely in many instances in licensing securities, the commissioners having confidence and respect for leading dealers in their own state, and being more severe with others. Efforts to bring about greater uniformity in blue-sky legislation are constantly being made by the National Association of Security Commissioners which meets annually. Its members keep in constant touch with one another in endeavoring to improve the enforcement of the several blue-sky laws. The Investment Bankers Association of America also has worked for the enactment of a uniform blue-sky law.

Investment Trust Regulation

Progress toward more uniform methods of administration of blue-sky laws is illustrated by regulations adopted by the National Association of Security Commissioners covering such flotations. Individual trusts have been required to fill out a uniform blank which calls for full information as to their organization and personnel. Provision has been made for such further information as the case requires, but the following general requirements were laid down:

1. The securities offered should be in marketable form and negotiable by endorsement.

2. The personnel of the office and management should show a clear record of good business repute, and should be men of integrity and investment experience.

3. The officers, promoters or managers should make an investment of their own funds sufficient to assure a personal interest in the proper conduct thereof.

4. Certain essential fundamentals should be present in the charter or agreement which should be of such character as to amount to a covenant with the investors. Some of these are as follows:

(a) Adequate provision in the charter or trust agreement or like indenture definitely and accurately stating the plan and policy of operation.

(b) Provision for periodic statements of the financial condition of the company, including balance sheet in detail, income and disbursement statement, and, in the case of a fixed trust, an itemized list of investments held in the portfolio, or, in the case of a management trust, a classification of investments held; this information to be furnished the share or unit holders at periodic intervals.

(c) Provision that the capital assets cannot be distributed during the life of the trust through dividends.

(d) Provision for the establishment of reserves and of surplus out of the current net cash earnings from whatever source.

(e) Definite statement as to the cost of management and the expense incurred in the raising of capital.

(f) A clear statement of any privilege accorded the incorporators, officers or managers.

The report of the Association's committee on investment trusts stated further:

We believe that all States equipped with blue-sky laws can, through a careful analysis of the applications, fairly judge the merits of the various companies that may appear before them to the end that the honest and ably managed companies will not be precluded from carrying on legitimate and profitable enterprises.

We believe that in time the practice of furnishing to investors and prospective investors clear and adequate information which will enable them to judge the management and to know in what way their funds are being handled will tend to weed out the undesirable and loosely managed trusts and leave those institutions which are inevitably to become a more important and ever-increasing factor in the financial growth of the country.

Utility Security Regulation

In the regulation of public utilities, considerable difference exists in the practices of different states. In the first place, not every state regulates all types of utilities, many leaving this task to the municipalities in which the utilities operate. Thus, Florida regulates only street railways and telephone and telegraph companies. Nearly all the states do regulate through their state commissions electric light and power and gas companies. In connection with this regulation, however, only a limited number of states retain jurisdiction over the capitalization of these companies, requiring approval of issues of securities. Those which do, according to a survey made by the Investment Bankers Association, are Alabama, Arizona, California, Georgia, Illinois, Indiana, Maine, Maryland, Massachusetts, Michigan, Missouri, Nebraska, New Hampshire, New Jersey, New York, North Dakota, Ohio, Tennessee, Texas, Vermont and Wisconsin. In a few other cases, jurisdiction is given over one or two types of utilities only in respect to financing.

The Public Utility Act of 1935 established a comprehensive system of security issue regulation for holding-company systems to its provisions, as well as subsidiaries of the latter.

Anti-fraud Laws

The security laws of New York, New Jersey and Maryland are of the anti-fraud type,[5] in that no attempt is made to set up a securities commission to pass on new issues as made. Instead, a mechanism has been set up to aid the state Attorney General in investigating and prosecuting those who sell fraudulent securities. This is accomplished in New York under the Martin Law by requiring that dealers file a statement, recently made rather intensive, giving information about themselves and the securities they offer. Some of this information is published in the bulletin, which thus contains the information on the basis of which the Attorney General of the state may proceed against offenders. A brief statement is also required of each new offering. Government, public utility, bank and other specified classes of securities are exempt from this publication requirement. This information has in certain cases been of great aid in securing convictions of fraudulent security sellers and reducing the scope of their activities in the state.

The Martin Act authorizes the Attorney General of the state

[5] The Connecticut law of 1929 largely transformed the former strict blue-sky law of the state into the anti-fraud type of law.

to bring an action as soon as he has satisfactory reason, based on complaint or otherwise, to believe that fraudulent practices in the sale of securities are to be undertaken. The court then may grant a preliminary injunction and call for witnesses stated by the Attorney General to be necessary in the case, and a referee may be appointed to gather additional evidence. Either with or without such examination, "an order or a judgment may be entered awarding such preliminary or final injunction as may be proper."

Efforts have been made from time to time to have the ordinary type of blue-sky law passed in New York State. However, investment bankers have opposed it because of the delays that would result, since the great bulk of new issues are originally offered in New York. Enactment of the Federal Securities Act of 1933 has made this consideration less potent, since a waiting period before actual offering is there provided.

The chief difference between the blue-sky and the anti-fraud types of securities laws is that the first is largely preventive in character, while the latter is punitive. Blue-sky laws in many instances—although this is on the whole decreasingly true—seek to prevent frauds before their commission by seeking preliminary scrutiny of security offerings and dealers before the actual sale to the public. The anti-fraud law creates a machinery for facilitating the prosecution and making more severe the punishment of those convicted of already having committed such frauds. Obviously, the investment banker finds the latter law is much less hampering to his regular operations.

E. H. H. Simmons, former president of the New York Stock Exchange, gave the reasons why investment bankers favor the punitive or anti-fraud type of law, as follows:

> Despite the enormous number of elaborate state laws enacted during recent years on security frauds, the security swindler has shown undoubted cleverness in continuing his activities. It is my opinion that essentially preventive legislation against security frauds has in general considerably hampered the legitimate security business without providing any actual or genuine solution to the security fraud problem. Very often just those states which have the most elaborate preventive legislative codes in connection with the

issuance and sale of securities there, are the ones which complain the most bitterly concerning the continued ravages committed on the savings of their people by security sharpsters and tricksters.

It is therefore natural that, as far as legislation against fraud is concerned, the tendency has set in almost throughout the country to depend on punitive rather than preventive fraud legislation, and to punish the swindler speedily and severely rather than attempt to construct elaborate legal traps which are as likely as not to cause the most trouble to honest security dealers who are not particularly on the lookout for them. The swindler in securities belongs to the more intelligent class of criminals. He does not engage in swindling operations without a very careful balancing of the risks which he must take as compared with the gains which he may obtain. As a rule, he can successfully elude the legal traps which preventive legislation has attempted to set for him. But the one thing which will invariably halt him is the prospect of undergoing a speedy and severe jail sentence. There is nothing new or attractive about this program. It is a remedy as old as the Pyramids. Nevertheless, many states today, after vain experiments with preventive legislation, are turning to punitive laws, and where these are wisely formulated and sternly enforced they have invariably proved effectual.

But whatever the specific form which anti-fraud legislation may take, no such law can hope to succeed without the earnest and hearty cooperation of legitimate security salesmen and dealers themselves. It is all very well to create additional anti-fraud powers to be exercised by state officials, or to appoint a commission with regulatory powers and a few rooms and a few clerks in the state capitol. This is only a part of the real answer to the security fraud problem. The state officials who administer security fraud laws rarely have sufficient appropriations to prosecute their work on the scale required. They are compelled to consider only those cases of fraud which are brought to their attention by the victim of fraud or some party acting in his behalf. The considerable reticence of investors who have been swindled to make a public exhibit of their past credulity in this way, as well as their inexperience in dealing with the legal machinery established to protect them, largely isolates state investigating officers from the swindling activities that they are attempting to abate.

The federal Securities Act, in addition to its registration provisions, contains a general anti-fraud section.

Earlier Federal Regulation

Legislation of an anti-fraud character to govern interstate security selling was on the federal statute books long before the enactment of the Securities Act of 1933.

Section 215 of the U. S. Criminal Code makes it a crime and provides a penalty for using the mails in furtherance of "any scheme or artifice to defraud." (Also U. S. Code, Title 18, Section 338.) In addition, the fraud order section of the law authorizes the Postmaster General to issue "stop orders" forbidding delivery of mail and payment of money orders to anyone found conducting any "scheme or device for obtaining money or property of any kind through the mail by means of false or fraudulent pretenses, representations or promises." The fraud order sections of the law (U. S. Revised Statutes, 3929, 4041; U. S. Code, Title 39, Sections 259, 732) were first introduced in 1872, and since 1895 have applied to all classes of mail. Unlike the criminal section of the law, the fraud order sections aim at prevention.

The Postmaster General acts as a fact-finding officer in connection with fraud orders, and his judgment is held to be final, except that it may be reviewed by the courts where it is alleged to be arbitrary or palpably wrong. However, in order to carry out this work effectively, a large staff of inspectors is needed, and this has not been provided. The need for this has largely passed with the enactment of the federal Securities Act of 1933.

The federal government exercises special supervision over security issues of railroad, utility holding, and interstate communication companies through the Interstate Commerce Commission. No railroad corporation may issue any securities, except notes running less than two years amounting in the aggregate to less than 5 per cent of the total capitalization of the company, without its approval. The Interstate Commerce Commission has assumed jurisdiction over every aspect of the sale of railroad securities, and has on different occasions changed the price of offering, the method of sale, the amount, the interest rate and the form of proposals for new issues by railroad companies.

Cooperative Regulation

While state and federal governments have thus established agencies for the regulation of the sale of securities, investment banking interests have organized cooperative agencies of their own to detect security frauds and raise the general standards of practice in the security-selling business. Among other reasons for this cooperative effort has been the desire to discourage stricter state legislation through corrective efforts of their own.

The nation-wide system of Better Business Bureaus is one important factor in this situation. Originally developed by the Associated Advertising Clubs of the World, the National Better Business Bureau was organized in 1927 as a separate organization. In time 26 local Better Business Bureaus were set up to work with it. The organization is maintained by contributions from leading firms and financial institutions. It keeps extensive files concerning new promotions and doubtful security dealers, and sends out a corps of investigators to check up on these matters. Developing in this way the most complete existing collection of data on security frauds, the Better Business Bureaus make this evidence available to both prospective investors and the legal authorities. Estimates of annual sales of fraudulent securities have run as high as $500,000,000 annually, and the elimination of these frauds would naturally make available an equal amount of money for legitimate investment or speculation.

The Investment Bankers Association of America constitutes a second important agency seeking to reduce the number of security frauds. The legislation committee of this Association, while opposed to legislation of a type which burdens the legitimate dealer, has worked out a uniform blue-sky law and has cooperated with the Better Business Bureaus. The stock exchanges also have sought to fight security frauds.

Regulation *vs.* Education

While efforts have been made continuously to improve and simplify the operation of blue-sky laws, it has been generally recognized that the best protection against security frauds lies in the education of investors. The growth in the investment banking business, with the consequent increasing difficulty of adequately controlling the quality of new issues, has made education of investors more necessary than ever before. The need for education of the many millions of investors who have little knowledge or experience in this field was described as follows by an official of the National Association of Securities Commissioners:[6]

> The surplus-creating ability of this country has scarcely been scratched, and this fast-growing surplus should be protected and encouraged. It is not always realized how markedly the agricultural Middle West and Southwest and South have developed in an investment way in the last twenty years. As an indication, it is common experience of Middle West investment dealers to sell in dozens of small villages of a thousand to fifteen hundred inhabitants which invest monthly $10,000 to $25,000 with a single house.
>
> Blue-sky legislation became necessary because of the new situation; but there can be no question that the gradual improvement in this type of law and the building up of trained forces to administer the laws have achieved a great deal in narrowing the twilight zone of the securities faker. At the same time, while the securities commissioners feel that there should be a constant improvement and a uniform betterment of these laws, we also feel that the law cannot do everything. It is not a substitute for common sense.
>
> For this reason we are making an effort in our Association to broaden the economic education of our grade and high schools so that the generation coming on will not only know how to make a dollar but will have a better knowledge of taking care of that dollar after it has been earned and has gone into surplus. I've recently appointed a member of our Association to head a committee to establish this educational effort. We hope in time it will be extended to every state in the Union. Some conception of the magnitude of this undertaking can be realized if you will recall that there are about 800,000 school teachers in this country. With several hundred thousand of these giving a small part of their time to the task, the financial illiteracy, now so outstanding a handicap in the economic situation, will largely disappear and the opportunities for the faker be pushed toward the vanishing point.

[6] Statement by Jesse V. Craig, president of the National Association of Securities Commissioners, to newspaper men at the convention of the Investment Bankers Association of America, October 15, 1928.

References

Commerce Clearing House, *Securities Law Service.*
Lagerquist, W. E., *Investment Analysis,* New York, 1927, chap. xii.
Montgomery, R. H., *Financial Handbook,* New York, 1933, section 22.
Simmons, E. H. H., *Modern Capitalism,* New York, 1927, pp. 209–231, 233–251.

Chapter XXIII

INVESTMENT BANKING HERE AND ABROAD

Value of Comparisons

As has been seen in Chapter VIII on the history of investment banking, our investment banking mechanism has grown up rapidly in response to pressing needs, and the growth has at times been haphazard and unduly influenced by accident and extraneous conditions. Accordingly, there is no reason to think that the present American mechanism of methods of investment banking are either inevitable or stabilized. Rather, continuous evolution and change are perhaps its chief characteristics, and no one seems more imbued with the appreciation of the need for constant adaptation to new conditions than investment bankers themselves, as shown in the work of the Investment Bankers Association of America.

In order to arrive at a proper appraisal of American practice in comparison with that of other countries, it is desirable to review the organization and operation of investment banking in other countries. The number of countries in which a well-developed investment banking mechanism exists is decidedly limited, however. In fact, only in England, France and Germany do the volume of transactions at times attain an amount large enough to create first-class capital markets where the volume of transactions raises problems similar to our own. In smaller countries like Belgium, Holland, Switzerland and Austria, there are fairly important international financial centers, but methods there largely reflect those used in the larger centers. Hence, this review of foreign investment banking organization and operation will be restricted to the three largest. During the depression, furthermore, investment banking methods were profoundly affected, but it is difficult to judge how permanently.

Great Britain

Security Issuance

Investment banking was developed on a large scale in Great Britain before it became a broad activity in any other country. This was largely because of the early date at which the Industrial Revolution took place there. While famous banking houses were built up in Germany and Italy during and after the Middle Ages, it was in Great Britain that investing in securities first became a popular activity, and thus led to the development of a complete investment mechanism.

In England, even more than in this country, commercial and investment banking have been segregated and different institutions provided for handling each. The great British joint-stock banks are commercial banking institutions possessing numerous branches extending throughout the country and abroad. They have generally refrained from entering the securities business.[1] It is true that, because of their close contact with the individual investor in their various branches, they have of late been willing to exercise orders to buy securities.

They also frequently handle the mechanical details in connection with a new flotation, receiving applications and payments from subscribers.

The investment banking houses of Great Britain are divided into two fairly distinct groups: merchant bankers like Baring Brothers & Company, Morgan, Grenfell & Company, Lazard Brothers & Company, and J. Henry Schroeder & Company, and distributing brokers. This division, which separates the wholesale from the retail fields in the security business, permits the broker who sells directly to the public to be relatively independent in his advice to customers, as he is not tied down in his dealings to a limited number of issues through syndicate participation, as is the case in this country. On the other hand, it does result in less direct contact between investment bankers and industry than is the case where issue houses also sell securi-

[1] The reason for this which is usually advanced is that the joint-stock banks have too little capital and cash reserves against liabilities to enter investment banking on a large scale. The chief joint-stock banks are the Midland, Barclay's, Lloyd's and National Provincial.

ties on a large scale; and to that extent investment banking has been less helpful in developing domestic British industry than some have thought desirable. This point is stressed in the report of the Macmillan Committee covering British economic and financial policies.

The issuance of securities in Great Britain, when not done directly by the borrowing government or vendor corporation through an "offer by prospectus," is generally carried out either by underwriters who buy entire issues and distribute them by "offers for sale," or by "Stock Exchange introduction," where the underwriter places the issue privately with a small group that distributes it on the Stock Exchange. As a rule, smaller flotations are handled by the last-mentioned method.

The houses of issue frequently handle a small or medium-sized issue alone, without forming a syndicate of other houses to aid them. Where a syndicate is formed, the participants "sub-underwrite" a portion of the issue by agreeing to purchase it at the public offering price, less a commission, as is the case with selling groups here. The sub-underwriters generally pay down 5 or 10 per cent on the amount sub-underwritten. When the offering is made, orders are received from various sources through the regular distribution channels presently to be described, and the underwriters then announce what proportion of the issue has not been taken by the public, and therefore is automatically subscribed for by the underwriters. If an announcement is made that a substantial proportion of the issue has "remained with the underwriters," the security issued will doubtless immediately sell at a discount. On the other hand, an over-subscribed issue often starts off at a substantial premium. No effort is made to peg the price, and syndicate members are not expected to maintain the offering price in their sales, once an allotment has been made at the close of the public offering date, as is the case here. The desire is for a free and open market from the start, as British investors do not buy securities for short turns as a rule, and will often ignore a price decline of two or three points shortly after the offering date.

The underwriter obtains an over-riding commission of a fraction of 1 per cent, while sub-underwriters obtain an underwriting commission that often exceeds 2 per cent. These sub-underwriters usually take a small participation in each case, usually a block of several thousand pounds. It should be understood, furthermore, that in the case of an offer by prospectus, the most popular type, the underwriting agreement covers only that portion of the flotation not absorbed by the corporation's stockholders, or public investors. If the latter should fail to take up their subscriptions, furthermore, the issuer can retain only the payment of 15 to 30 per cent that usually accompanies the subscription. Thus, outside of cases where the securities have actually been sold to underwriters for an offer for sale or Stock Exchange introduction, underwriting is not complete.

The actual selling of securities is largely done by brokers, who receive a commission that averages 1/4 point. Brokers may act as sub-underwriters, but this is not always the case.

They are located all over the country, and build up lists of clients who have confidence in them. These clients often learn to look upon the broker as a professional man whose integrity and reliability they are assured of. Business is transacted usually by calling on or writing to the broker; the bond salesman is unknown.[2] The British broker combines in his work the functions of the American stock brokerage house and the retail security dealer. On the whole, however, it might be said that he does less independent analysis of his own and pays more attention to the quality of banking sponsorship, in advising clients.

The Stock Exchange

Brokers are known as "inside" or "outside," the former belonging to the London Stock Exchange. The London Stock Exchange is different in numerous fundamental respects from the kind of securities market known in this country and typified in the New York Stock Exchange. It has several times as many issues listed, but there is less trading. Transactions do not get the full publicity known here, as no stock quotation tickers are maintained, and brokers may or may not publish their transactions or "mark their bargains," as they wish. The financial papers give a full list of quotations of such transac-

[2] The British Companies Act of 1929 prohibits actually house-to-house solicitation of orders for securities in that country.

tions as are reported, but do not indicate sales as opening, high, low, close, because they are not reported in that way.

Members of the stock exchange are divided sharply into two groups: jobbers and brokers. The jobber resembles in a way the specialist of the American exchange, except that he has no dealings with the public, spending his time on the floor and specializing in one group of securities in which he stands ready to make bid and asked quotations when requested by the brokers who deal with the outside public. The jobber makes his profit out of the spread between the bid and asked prices he quotes, like our own over-the-counter dealers, while the broker charges the client a fixed rate of commission.

One feature of the London Stock Exchange is the greater use often made of it in the distribution of new security flotations. Many new issues, as we have seen, are not publicly offered and sold before listing, as is the case here, but are listed first and then gradually disposed of after a market has been established by stock exchange introduction.

The daily settlement of stock exchange transactions that prevails in the United States is uncommon to London. London, like most foreign stock exchanges, has adopted the term settlement system, whereby purchases and sales are settled twice a month. This permits a great deal of speculation to go on through buying and selling during the period between settlement dates, thus greatly reducing the need for collateral loans. A mechanism has been devised for avoiding the necessity for payment in cash for purchases, or delivery of securities against sales, on the settlement date, or "contango," so that commitments may be "carried over" into the next period. Margins to protect the broker against loss must be deposited with him, however, as is the case here. This margin is relatively small, moreover, as it is retained by him merely as an assurance against loss and represents no real outlay of funds as long as actual payment for the securities is delayed. If high margins remain in effect in this country, brokers may reverse their traditional hostility to the term settlement system here in order to revive speculative activity.

There are a number of special investment banking institutions in Great Britain which often play a direct rôle in the issuance of securities. Investment trusts, finance companies, insurance companies and large investors frequently become sub-underwriters for the purpose of getting their investment securities cheaper, pocketing the underwriting profit instead if the public actually takes the issue. The investment trust and finance company have generally flourished in Great Britain. The true British investment trust makes turnover profits secondary, regarding as earnings only regular interest and dividend receipts on its security holdings and using realized profits to write down the book cost of the portfolio. The finance company is more like a number of American trusts, having a more speculative character and often controlling or promoting all kinds of financial and industrial enterprises.

France

Types of Institutions

The French banking system has undergone considerable change since the pre-war period, and the process of evolution is far from completed. One characteristic of French banking hitherto has been the hesitation about advancing capital freely for the development of domestic industry. Instead, the banks have in the past concentrated on the security business, and on the whole have preferred foreign issues which gave them a wide margin of profit. The purely commercial banking business was left in substantial measure to the Bank of France, which, unlike other central banks, deals directly with the public through a nation-wide network of branches.

There are three important classes of investment banking institutions in France. First, there are the great credit banks, including three old-established and powerful institutions with nation-wide chains of branches—the Crédit Lyonnais, the Comptoir National d'Escompte, and the Société Générale. These banks, especially before the war, were heavily interested in the business of distributing securities. France has probably a greater number of individual security holders than any other country except the United States. They are served mainly by the credit banks through their several thousand branches. The French security-buying public has been relatively docile, generally leaning heavily on the advice of the credit banks. Each credit bank branch, therefore, is a retailer of securities, and more attention may be paid to this branch of the business than to the deposit and discount activities. Compensation of branch bank managers before the war was in part based on the amount of securities sold through the branch, and this practice is still followed to a large extent.

As security distributors, the credit banks occupy a foremost position in France. They are not equally important in the originating business, preferring to take part in syndicates or consortiums headed by wholesaling or originating houses.

The second type of banking institution is the *banque d'affaires,* which specializes in the origination of securities and the long-term financing of industries. This form of investment house participates in the management of industry to a substantial extent, frequently taking permanent stock participations in companies which it organizes or finances. In this respect, it tends to become more than a mere merchandizer of securities, and acts as an investment banker in a fuller sense, making loans and carrying them itself over extended periods of time until the success of the enterprise or market conditions make feasible the sale of the securities to the public at a desirable price. The largest of the *banques d'affaires* is the Banque de Paris et des Pays Bas, others being the Banque de l'Union Parisienne, the Crédit Mobilier and the Crédit Français.

The third type of bank is the private banking house owned by an individual or family partnership, and engaged in security origination, foreign trade financing, management of estates and a variety of other operations carried on in this country mostly by investment houses and trust companies. At the head of the private banking houses stands a small group of leading firms called collectively the *haute banque.* The leader among these is the house of Rothschild, which no longer holds its old position of preeminence, but remains a wealthy and influential banking firm. Others are Hottinguer et Cie., Lazard Frères, Heine et Cie., Mallet Frères et Cie., etc.

The brokerage business in France is organized along continental lines, but with many special features. The seventy brokers on the floor or *parquet* of the Paris Bourse have few dealings with the outside public, transacting practically all of their business on commission for other banking institutions. These brokers are jointly and severally liable in their dealings. In addition, in the peristyle of the Bourse building, a distinct market of nearly equal importance exists. It is comparable to the Curb here, and is called the *coulisse,* or side wing. It is subject to far less stringent regulations than the *parquet.* The term settlement system is in vogue in both parts of the stock exchange on a large number of securities, thus avoiding the tying up of large amounts of credit in stock exchange loans, as is done in the United States.

Investment Banking Policy

Because of both the conservatism of the French investor and his implicit confidence in the judgment of the credit banks, obviating the general need for security salesmen,[3] the cost of distribution of securities in France could well be perhaps the lowest in the world, despite the relatively small average size of each investor's holdings. Criticism has been leveled at the manner in which the credit banks partly abused this opportunity before the war, neglecting the development of home industry and putting out in rapid succession numerous second- and third-rate foreign loans, including billions of francs of Russian securities. The desire of the government to use the export of capital as a medium for gaining political influence furthered this policy, and resulted in a severe shock to the French investment market during and after the war, with wholesale defaults in Russia and the Balkan States, in which the bulk of French foreign investments had been placed. Investors also sustained enormous losses through the devaluation of the franc in the 'twenties. The credit banks generally frowned on stock investments for their clientele, which would have offset part of the loss resulting from the decline of the franc, but larger investors developed a keen interest in stock purchases in the United States after 1934.

One tendency in recent years has been the development of

[3] French banks do have agents corresponding to the "new business" men of our banks, who seek investment as well as bank accounts. They are called *commissaires.* When an account is secured, however, their function ends.

a more aggressive commercial banking policy, especially on the part of the *banques d'affaires*, which had to enter this field after the war because of the practical cessation of the foreign loan business. At the same time, there has been more interest in domestic investment banking, including the formation of holding companies to advance the cause of industrial and public utility consolidation in France, a country in which the combination movement had been backward. The small investor, whose dependence on the credit bank has continued, has turned to French government securities as the chief commitment for his surplus funds.

Germany

The Great "D" Banks

The German banking system, in contrast to the British, has long been dominated by a single type of institution which performs virtually all banking functions. This so-called continental type of banking is similar to what is known as "department store banking" in the United States, where the leading metropolitan commercial banks in the post-war decade developed along general lines long familiar in Germany.

The "D" banks, including before 1931 the Deutsche Bank, Disconto Gesellschaft, Darmstadter Bank and Dresdner Bank, combined the functions of commercial banking along branch banking lines, investment banking in all its aspects, trust work, security brokerage, etc. We are interested here primarily in their investment banking functions.

The German banks, plentifully supplied with capital and managed by ambitious and energetic boards of directors, assumed the rôle of industrial promoters in large part. While the British joint-stock banks sought to restrict their operations to short-term working capital requirements of industry, and the French credit banks favored foreign government loans for their customers, the great German banks took the leadership in the promotion and amalgamation of public utility and industrial enterprises, and were in a measure responsible for the rapidity of the industrialization of Germany after 1870. Whereas in the United States banking may be said to have been the handmaid of industry, in Germany the banks were for a time the masters of industry. However, after 1900, this was true to a decreasing extent. They also encouraged public stock ownership, especially of industrial shares.

Taking so important a part in the management of industrial enterprises, the "D" banks, and a number of smaller but similar banking institutions, also assumed the dominating rôle in the origination of new security issues. In this function, the banks competed with private banking houses, many of them of long standing, such as the firm of M. M. Warburg & Company of Hamburg and Mendelsohn & Company before the war, and Gebrueder Arnhold and Simon Hirschland after the conflict. As with the *banques d'affaires* in France, the "D" banks and the private banking houses in Germany often retained purchased securities in their portfolios for considerable periods of time before attempting their sale, and in general regarded their function as being much more than the mere buying and selling of securities for a merchandising profit.

In the selling of securities, the "D" banks and the other large commercial banks exercised a leading part, operating through a number of branches scattered throughout the country. As elsewhere in Europe, the security salesman is unknown, the bank officers dealing directly with the local clientele at the branch office. Much of the selling is done through the medium of order blanks prepared in connection with the security offering list of the bank. These blanks are obtained by the customer at the branch office and, when filled out, become orders which are executed generally through the main office. The large private banks do a great deal of direct selling to larger clients.

An interesting feature of German security selling is the recognized existence of an "investment guaranteed" market. In this country, as has been seen in Chapter XVIII on syndicate selling operations, the sale of a new issue below the offering price on an investment guaranteed basis is considered an abuse. In Germany, it is regarded as a valuable device whereby the banks can favor permanent investors who will assure more or less final distribution of the issue as against speculators and short-term holders. In their offering lists, banks may quote two prices for each issue, one the regular price, and the other, reduced by from ½ to 5 points, on an investment guaranteed basis, the buyer promising not to dispose of the issue within six months or so.

The banking collapse of 1931 in Germany, and the establishment of a Fascist régime in 1933, brought drastic changes in banking in that country. The combination of commercial with investment banking was discredited, not only in Germany but elsewhere in Europe, when banks called upon to repay their depositors found that they were not able to do so. In Germany, the "D" banks were combined with others, and a large measure of government aid was given them. After 1933, with the establishment of a system of rigid government control of industry, the capital market was largely contracted, and various indirect means were utilized to finance the government's very heavy armaments and public works programs.

Stock Exchange

Germany has a number of stock exchanges, but they are organized and operated for the most part along similar lines, and that of Berlin has a dominant position. The discussion here is restricted to the latter.

The Berlin boerse has no limit on its membership, anyone acceptable to the authorities being able to join upon payment of the annual fees. The boerse is regarded as a government institution, and is under close public supervision.

There are three kinds of brokers operating on the boerse. The makler or "sworn broker" corresponds to our specialist to a degree, but he does not trade for his own account. He receives orders from the other members of the exchange. and fixes the quotation at a price at which the maximum number of orders can be executed. This price applies to all transactions of the day.

The second type of boerse member, the "free broker," acts for others in the main, having little contact with the public. He executes orders chiefly for the banks. "Free brokers" often eke out their activities with some independent floor trading. Finally, the banks and private banking houses take an active interest in the boerse, the larger ones having several representatives of their own on its floor. It is these banking members who receive orders from the public, and carry margin accounts for traders.

There are three types of trading on the Berlin boerse. Most of the securities listed thereon, although in the main the in-active ones, are dealt in on a "cash" basis. The brokers and bank members present their orders to the sworn broker, who then indicates on a blackboard with plus or minus signs the trend of these orders. Based on these indications, floor traders and others place additional orders, and finally the sworn broker fixes the official quotation of the day at which orders are filled, prices being fixed to include the largest number of bids and offers. In the second place, there is "variable trading" in many stocks, where the opening and closing prices are officially fixed as above, but where buying and selling go on much as on the New York Stock Exchange the rest of the session. Thirdly, there is trading for future delivery in a limited number of stocks, these generally being the most active and accounting for the bulk of daily transactions. Settlement for these transactions is arranged monthly, with arrangements for a carry-over.

Other banking institutions carrying on investment functions in Germany are municipal and cooperative savings banks, which have gathered vast sums and purchased gilt-edged securities; and state, provincial and private mortgage banks for real estate financing. Mortgage bank bonds have long been a staple form of individual investment in Germany, and have generally had an excellent record.

Comparisons with American Conditions

Differences Between American and Foreign Practice

There have grown up a number of outstanding differences between investment banking in this country and in the leading foreign capital centers. Perhaps the most important difference, as far as the individual investor is concerned, is the large rôle played here by the bond salesman. The bond salesman has established personal contact between the investment banker and the purchaser of securities, and thus has been very important in pushing the development of popular investment. His function in the past has been a vital one, and to the profession of bond salesmanship is unquestionably due, in considerable measure, credit for the rapidity with which the American investment market has grown.

In France and Germany, the well-articulated branch banking system which prevails has permitted personal contact to exist between the client and the bank without the mediation of salesmen. The American small-unit banking system, which has tended to keep local commercial banks out of the security business, is thus in part responsible for the presence of and need for security salesmen in investment banking here.

On the other hand, the bond salesman in this country has been and to a lesser extent is today often motivated by factors which in the long run are not altogether sound. His eventual objective is to sell securities, and in order to increase his sales volume there is strong temptation to switch investors frequently from one issue to another equally or even less desirable. Again, the salesman is interested usually in selling new securities, and therefore he will normally prefer to sell a new and perhaps unseasoned and less desirable issue rather than an outstanding one on which he will make no commission. Doubtless, many individual salesmen do not permit these interested motives to dominate their activities. Also, the same motives operate to some extent under any system of security selling.

But the prevalence of the use of bond salesmen is not alone responsible for a lack of disinterested advice. Since security retailers participate in the syndication of new security issues, they usually have a limited number of favored issues for sale. To push these issues is not always consistent with giving wholly disinterested advice to the security buyer, however. The fact that most members of selling groups no longer underwrite has ameliorated this condition in some measure.

Compared with foreign practice, we find the British capital market organized to give the individual investors more disinterested advice. The broker often makes about as much on an old as on a new issue. In France, conditions are nearer those in America in character, the branch bank manager often acting much as does a bond salesman here in seeking to push issues sponsored by his house. In Germany, the big banks had such wide interests that they often could, without damage to their own interests, give clients fairly independent advice on securities.

A second important characteristic of American investment banking which differentiates it from foreign practice is the artificial character of markets for new issues of securities. Pegging of quotations exists to some extent all over the world. Only in this country, however, is it so inevitable and regular a feature of new offerings. The broad geographical expanse of the United States and the fact that investors are sensitive to price changes largely account for this. It takes longer to distribute an issue here than abroad, and during the process of primary distribution pegging is generally regarded as necessary. On the other hand, perhaps nowhere else do so many people like to subscribe when a promising issue is being publicly offered, in order to make a "scalping profit" of a few points, as in England. These "joy riders," known as "stags" in the London market, are not discouraged by the fact that a fractional down payment is required with subscriptions. The scramble for promising new offerings partly reflects the fact that speculators there cannot trade on margin as easily as here, and consequently prefer to buy new issues on which only a small initial payment at the time of offering is required.

In England, pegging of the market on new issues is not usual. In France, it has been done on many occasions, although there the market in new issues does not generally show much activity.

Stock Exchange Organization

A third characteristic of the American market is the peculiar organization of the stock exchange, with its daily clearings. This involves a vastly greater amount of clerical work than the European term settlement system, and also tends to tie up a much larger amount of bank credit in the shape of brokers' loans. On the other hand, there is a possible advantage in a system which gives the broker an income from speculative accounts through the payment of an excess interest charge on debit balances. This gives the broker a rather smaller motive for inducing customers to turn over their speculative holdings rapidly.[4]

Another vital feature of the security market in this country is the greater volume of popular speculative activity which is carried on. There is a larger number of individual speculators in the American market than in any other country, and the range of stock price movements is generally wider. There is good reason to believe that pool operations and other manipulative phenomena were more highly developed here than elsewhere, but this has lately been restricted by legislation. Among the factors which have fostered speculative activity have been the success of numerous American corporations, the well-developed stock exchange machinery, the case of opening margin accounts and the efficient collateral call loan market.

Another important characteristic of the security markets here has been the large amount of direct public investing in common stocks, especially since the war. The European investor generally has preferred government securities and corporate bonds, although Germany, Belgium, and Holland have been partial exceptions. Investments in common stocks in England, consisting in the main of foreign shares, have occurred to a large extent through the medium of the investment trust, while in France and Germany the banks have acted in part as large investing organizations in equities. In this country, the rank and file of investors have long shown interest in common stocks, although after the war this tendency became far more pronounced. The severe deflation of the early 'thirties checked this tendency, but it was resumed under the stimulus of the bank credit inflation of the middle 'thirties.

Tendencies in American Investment Banking

During the past few years, a number of clear-cut tendencies have developed in American investment banking which promise new and vital changes for the future.

The first vital change is the entry of the American commer-

[4] This gain is largely offset in many cases, however, through the customers' man's desire to show a larger amount of business done by him, and results from interposing between the brokerage house and the customer an individual who has assumed an advisory capacity, in addition to executing the routine task of receiving and recording orders.

cial bank, the most important factor in our financial institutional organization, into the investment banking field. This was accomplished first through the establishment of bond departments and security affiliates. It has been intensified since 1932 by the vast expansion of the bond investments of commercial banks. This tendency has been manifest also in Great Britain.

A second important change is the multiplication of investing organizations in this country. The investment trust and investment counsel movements have been a direct expression of the public need for supervision and organization of its investment activities, especially in view of the pronounced tendency to favor stocks as against bonds as a medium for investment, which has in turn profoundly affected the position of investment banking institutions.

The tendencies in recent years toward a more equal distribution of wealth, making the small investor relatively more important and the large one less so, also increase the need for suitable investing institutions.

Finally, American investment banking has become a highly regulated activity, and many changes are likely to result from this fact. This refers not only to the security legislation, but also to the centralization of control over the whole banking system of the nation.

These trends are in large measure typical of investment banking in other countries also.

References

DAVIES, A. E., *Investments Abroad,* Chicago, 1927, chaps. vii and viii.

DOWLING, S. W., *The Exchange of London,* London, 1929, chap. iii.

GREENWOOD, W. J., *American and Foreign Stock Exchange Methods,* New York, 1921.

MADDEN, J. T., and NADLER, M., *International Money Markets,* New York, 1935.

MYERS, M. G., *Paris as a Financial Centre,* New York, 1936.

NASH, BRADLEY D., *Investment Banking in England,* Chicago, 1924.

WILLIS, H. P., and BECKHART, B. H., *Foreign Banking Systems,* New York, 1929, chaps. vii, viii and xvii.

Appendix I

SECURITIES ACT OF 1933

[PUBLIC—NO. 22—73D CONGRESS]

[H.R. 5480]

AN ACT

To provide full and fair disclosure of the character of securities sold in interstate and foreign commerce and through the mails, and to prevent frauds in the sale thereof, and for other purposes.

Be it enacted by the Senate and House of Representatives of the United States of America in Congress assembled,

TITLE I

SHORT TITLE

SECTION 1. This title may be cited as the "Securities Act of 1933."

DEFINITIONS

SEC. 2. When used in this title, unless the context otherwise requires—

(1) The term "security" means any note, stock, treasury stock, bond, debenture, evidence of indebtedness, certificate of interest or participation in any profit-sharing agreement, collateral-trust certificate, preorganization certificate or subscription, transferable share, investment contract, voting-trust certificate, certificate of deposit for a security, fractional undivided interest in oil, gas, or other mineral rights, or, in general, any interest or instrument commonly known as a "security," or any certificate of interest or participation in, temporary or interim certificate for, receipt for, guarantee of, or warrant or right to subscribe to or purchase, any of the foregoing.[1]

---

[1] The matter appearing in bold-face type with footnote references represents subsections and subparagraphs *as amended*. This and subsequent footnotes contain the text prior to amendment. Bold-faced type without footnote references indicates *provisions added* by amendment. The amendments, effective July 1, 1934, are contained in Title II of Securities Exchange Act of 1934, approved June 6, 1934.

(1) The term "security" means "any note, stock, treasury stock, bond, debenture, evidence of indebtedness, certificate of interest or participation in any

(2) The term "person" means an individual, a corporation, a partnership, an association, a joint-stock company, a trust, any unincorporated organization, or a government or political subdivision thereof. As used in this paragraph the term "trust" shall include only a trust where the interest or interests of the beneficiary or beneficiaries are evidenced by a security.

(3) The term "sale," "sell," "offer to sell," or "offer for sale" shall include every contract of sale or disposition of, attempt or offer to dispose of, or solicitation of an offer to buy, a security or interest in a security, for value; except that such terms shall not include preliminary negotiations or agreements between an issuer and any underwriter. Any security given or delivered with, or as a bonus on account of, any purchase of securities or any other thing, shall be conclusively presumed to constitute a part of the subject of such purchase and to have been sold for value. The issue or transfer of a right or privilege, when originally issued or transferred with a security, giving the holder of such security the right to convert such security into another security of the same issuer or of another person, or giving a right to subscribe to another security of the same issuer or of another person, which right cannot be exercised until some future date, shall not be deemed to be a sale of such other security; but the issue or transfer of such other security upon the exercise of such right of conversion or subscription shall be deemed a sale of such other security.

(4) The term "issuer" means every person who issues or proposes to issue any security; except that with respect to certificates of deposit, voting-trust certificates, or collateral-trust certificates, or with respect to certificates of interest or shares in an unincorporated investment trust not having a board of directors (or persons performing similar functions) or of the fixed, restricted management, or unit type, the term "issuer" means the person or persons performing the acts and assuming the duties of depositor or manager pursuant to the provisions of the trust or other agreement or instrument under which such securities are issued; except that in the case of an unincorporated association which provides by its articles for limited liability of any or all of its members, or in the case of a trust, committee, or other legal entity, the trustees or members thereof shall not be individually liable as issuers of any security issued by the association, trust, committee, or other legal entity; except that with respect to equipment-trust certificates or like securities, the term "issuer" means the person by whom the equipment or property is or is to be used; and except that with respect to fractional undivided interests in oil, gas, or other mineral rights, the term "issuer" means the owner of any such right or of any interest in such right (whether whole or fractional) who creates fractional interests therein for the purpose of public offering.[2]

---

profit-sharing agreement, collateral-trust certificate, preorganization certificate or subscription, transferable share, investment contract, voting-trust certificate, certificate of interest in property, tangible or intangible, or, in general, any instrument commonly known as a security, or any certificate of interest or participation in, temporary or interim certificate for, receipt for, or warrant or right to subscribe to or purchase, any of the foregoing."

[2] "(4) The term 'issuer' means every person who issues or proposes to issue any security or who guarantees a security either as to principal or income; except that with respect to certificates of deposit, voting-trust certificates, or collateral-trust certificates, or with respect to certificates of interest or shares in an

(5) The term "Commission" means the Federal Trade Commission.*

(6) The term "Territory" means Alaska, Hawaii, Puerto Rico, the Philippine Islands, Canal Zone, the Virgin Islands, and the insular possessions of the United States.

(7) The term "interstate commerce" means trade or commerce in securities or any transportation or communication relating thereto among the several States or between the District of Columbia or any Territory of the United States and any State or other Territory, or between any foreign country and any State, Territory, or the District of Columbia, or within the District of Columbia.

(8) The term "registration statement" means the statement provided for in section 6, and includes any amendment thereto and any report, document, or memorandum accompanying such statement or incorporated therein by reference.

(9) The term "write" or "written" shall include printed, lithographed, or any means of graphic communication.

(10) The term "prospectus" means any prospectus, notice, circular, advertisement, letter, or communication, written or by radio, which offers any security for sale; except that (a) a communication shall not be deemed a prospectus if it is proved that prior to or at the same time with such communication a written prospectus meeting the requirements of Section 10 was sent or given to the person to whom the communication was made, by the person making such communication or his principal, and (b) a notice, circular, advertisement, letter, or communication in respect of a security shall not be deemed to be a prospectus if it states from whom a written prospectus meeting the requirements of Section 10 may be obtained and, in addition, does no more than identify the security, state the price thereof, and state by whom orders will be executed.[3]

(11) The term "underwriter" means any person who has purchased from an issuer with a view to, or sells for an issuer in connection with, the distribution

---

unincorporated investment trust not having a board of directors (or persons performing similar functions) or of the fixed, restricted management, or unit type, the term 'issuer' means the person or persons performing the acts and assuming the duties of depositor or manager pursuant to the provisions of the trust or other agreement or instrument under which such securities are issued; and except that with respect to equipment-trust certificates or like securities, the term 'issuer' means the person by whom the equipment or property is or is to be used."

* See Secs. 27 and 28, infra, being Sections 210 and 211, Title II of Securities Exchange Act of 1934, providing for transfer to "Securities and Exchange Commission" of all powers, duties, and functions of the Federal Trade Commission.

[3] "(10) The term 'prospectus' means any prospectus, notice, circular, advertisement, letter, or communication, written or by radio, which offers any security for sale; except that (a) a communication shall not be deemed a prospectus if it is proved that prior to such communication a written prospectus meeting the requirements of section 10 was received, by the person to whom the communication was made, from the person making such communication or his principal, and (b) a notice, circular, advertisement, letter, or communication in respect of a security shall not be deemed to be a prospectus if it states from whom a written prospectus meeting the requirements of section 10 may be obtained and, in addition, does no more than identify the security, state the price thereof, and state by whom orders will be executed."

of any security, or participates or has a direct or indirect participation in any such undertaking, or participates or has a participation in the direct or indirect underwriting of any such undertaking; but such term shall not include a person whose interest is limited to a commission from an underwriter or dealer not in excess of the usual and customary distributors' or sellers' commission. As used in this paragraph the term "issuer" shall include, in addition to an issuer, any person directly or indirectly controlling or controlled by the issuer, or any person under direct or indirect common control with the issuer.

(12) The term "dealer" means any person who engages either for all or part of his time, directly or indirectly, as agent, broker, or principal, in the business of offering, buying, selling, or otherwise dealing or trading in securities issued by another person.

EXEMPTED SECURITIES

SEC. 3. (a) Except as hereinafter expressly provided, the provisions of this title shall not apply to any of the following classes of securities:

(1) Any security which, prior to or within sixty days after the enactment of this title, has been sold or disposed of by the issuer or bona fide offered to the public, but this exemption shall not apply to any new offering of any such security by an issuer or underwriter subsequent to such sixty days;

(2) Any security issued or guaranteed by the United States or any Territory thereof, or by the District of Columbia, or by any State of the United States, or by any political subdivision of a State or Territory, or by any public instrumentality of one or more States or Territories, or by any person controlled or supervised by and acting as an instrumentality of the Government of the United States pursuant to authority granted by the Congress of the United States, or any certificate of deposit for any of the foregoing, or any security issued or guaranteed by any national bank, or by any banking institution organized under the laws of any State or Territory or the District of Columbia, the business of which is substantially confined to banking and is supervised by the State or Territorial banking commission or similar official; or any security issued by or representing an interest in or a direct obligation of a Federal Reserve Bank;[4]

(3) Any note, draft, bill of exchange, or bankers' acceptance which arises out of a current transaction or the proceeds of which have been or are to be used for current transactions, and which has a maturity at the time of issuance of not

[4] "(2) Any security issued or guaranteed by the United States or any Territory thereof, or by the District of Columbia, or by any State of the United States, or by any political subdivision of a State or Territory, or by any public instrumentality of one or more States or Territories exercising an essential governmental function, or by any corporation created and controlled or supervised by and acting as an instrumentality of the Government of the United States pursuant to authority granted by the Congress of the United States, or by any national bank, or by any banking institution organized under the laws of any State or Territory, the business of which is substantially confined to banking and is supervised by the State or territorial banking commission or similar official; or any security issued by or representing an interest in or a direct obligation of a Federal reserve bank."

exceeding nine months, exclusive of days of grace, or any renewal thereof the maturity of which is likewise limited;

(4) Any security issued by a person[5] organized and operated exclusively for religious, educational, benevolent, fraternal, charitable, or reformatory purposes and not for pecuniary profit, and no part of the net earnings of which inures to the benefit of any person, private stockholder, or individual;

(5) Any security issued by a building and loan association, homestead association, savings and loan association, or similar institution, substantially all the business of which is confined to the making of loans to members (but the foregoing exemption shall not apply with respect to any such security where the issuer takes from the total amount paid or deposited by the purchaser, by way of any fee, cash value or other device whatsoever, either upon termination of the investment at maturity or before maturity, an aggregate amount in excess of 3 per centum of the face value of such security), or any security issued by a farmers' cooperative association as defined in paragraphs (12), (13), and (14) of section 103 of the Revenue Act of 1932;

(6) Any security issued by a common carrier which is subject to the provisions of section 20a of the Interstate Commerce Act, as amended;

Amendment to Section 3 (a) (6) of the Securities Act of 1933, as amended

The "Motor Carrier Act of 1935" (approved August 9, 1935), Section 214, amended section 3 (a) (6) of the Securities Act of 1933 to read as follows:

"(6) Any security issued by a common *or contract* carrier, *the issuance of which* is subject to the provisions of section 20a of the Interstate Commerce Act, as amended";

The new law added is in italics.

(7) Certificates issued by a receiver or by a trustee in bankruptcy, with the approval of the court;

(8) Any insurance or endowment policy or annuity contract or optional annuity contract, issued by a corporation subject to the supervision of the insurance commissioner, bank commissioner, or any agency or officer performing like functions, of any State or Territory of the United States or the District of Columbia;

(9) Any security exchanged by the issuer with its existing security holders exclusively where no commission or other remuneration is paid or given directly or indirectly for soliciting such exchange;

(10) Any security which is issued in exchange for one or more bona fide outstanding securities, claims or property interests, or partly in such exchange and partly for cash, where the terms and conditions of such issuance and exchange are approved, after a hearing upon the fairness of such terms and conditions at which all persons to whom it is proposed to issue securities in such exchange shall have the right to appear, by any court, or by any official or agency of the United States, or by any State or Territorial banking or insurance commission or other governmental authority expressly authorized by law to grant such approval;[6]

(11) Any security which is a part of an issue sold only to persons

---

[5] "Corporation."

[6] The first clause of the following former Sec. 4 (3) has been replaced by Sec 3 (a) (9) and the second clause by Sec. 3 (a) (10): "(3) The issuance of a security of a person exchanged by it with its existing security holders exclusively, where no commission or other remuneration is paid or given directly or

resident within a single State or Territory, where the issuer of such security is a person resident and doing business within, or, if a corporation, incorporated by and doing business within, such State or Territory.[7]

(b) The Commission may from time to time by its rules and regulations, and subject to such terms and conditions as may be prescribed therein, add any class of securities to the securities exempted as provided in this section, if it finds that the enforcement of this title with respect to such securities is not necessary in the public interest and for the protection of investors by reason of the small amount involved or the limited character of the public offering; but no issue of securities shall be exempted under this subsection where the aggregate amount at which such issue is offered to the public exceeds $100,000.

EXEMPTED TRANSACTIONS

SEC. 4. The provisions of section 5 shall not apply to any of the following transactions:

(1) Transactions by any person other than an issuer, underwriter, or dealer; transactions by an issuer not involving any public offering; or transactions by a dealer (including an underwriter no longer acting as an underwriter in respect of the security involved in such transaction), except transactions within one year after the first date upon which the security was bona fide offered to the public by the issuer or by or through an underwriter (excluding in the computation of such year any time during which a stop order issued under section 8 is in effect as to the security), and except transactions as to securities constituting the whole or a part of an unsold allotment to or subscription by such dealer as a participant in the distribution of such securities by the issuer or by or through an underwriter.[8]

---

indirectly in connection with such exchange; or the issuance of securities to the existing security holders or other existing creditors of a corporation in the process of a bona fide reorganization of such corporation under the supervision of any court, either in exchange for the securities of such security holders or claims of such creditors or partly for cash and partly in exchange for the securities or claims of such security holders or creditors."

[7] The following former Sec. 5 (c) has been supplanted by Sec. 3 (a) (11): "(c) The provisions of this section relating to the use of the mails shall not apply to the sale of any security where the issue of which it is a part is sold only to persons resident within a single State or Territory, where the issuer of such securities is a person resident and doing business within, or, if a corporation, incorporated by and doing business within, such State or Territory."

[8] "(1) Transactions by any person other than an issuer, underwriter, or dealer; transactions by an issuer not with or through an underwriter and not involving any public offering; or transactions by a dealer (including an underwriter no longer acting as an underwriter in respect of the security involved in such transaction), except transactions within one year after the last date upon which the security was bona fide offered to the public by the issuer or by or through an underwriter (excluding in the computation of such year any time during which a stop order issued under section 8 is in effect as to the security), and except transactions as to securities constituting the whole or a part of an unsold allotment to or subscription by such dealer as a participant in the distribution of such securities by the issuer or by or through an underwriter."

(2) Brokers' transactions, executed upon customers' orders on any exchange or in the open or counter market, but not the solicitation of such orders.

PROHIBITIONS RELATING TO INTERSTATE COMMERCE AND THE MAILS

SEC. 5. (a) Unless a registration statement is in effect as to a security, it shall be unlawful for any person, directly or indirectly—

(1) to make use of any means or instruments of transportation or communication in interstate commerce or of the mails to sell or offer to buy such security through the use or medium of any prospectus or otherwise; or

(2) to carry or cause to be carried through the mails or in interstate commerce, by any means or instruments of transportation, any such security for the purpose of sale or for delivery after sale.

(b) It shall be unlawful for any person, directly or indirectly—

(1) to make use of any means or instruments of transportation or communication in interstate commerce or of the mails to carry or transmit any prospectus relating to any security registered under this title, unless such prospectus meets the requirements of section 10; or

(2) to carry or to cause to be carried through the mails or in interstate commerce any such security for the purpose of sale or for delivery after sale, unless accompanied or preceded by a prospectus that meets the requirements of section 10.

REGISTRATION OF SECURITIES AND SIGNING OF REGISTRATION STATEMENT

SEC. 6. (a) Any security may be registered with the Commission under the terms and conditions hereinafter provided, by filing a registration statement in triplicate, at least one of which shall be signed by each issuer, its principal executive officer or officers, its principal financial officer, its comptroller or principal accounting officer, and the majority of its board of directors or persons performing similar functions (or, if there is no board of directors or persons performing similar functions, by the majority of the persons or board having the power of management of the issuer), and in case the issuer is a foreign or Territorial person by its duly authorized representative in the United States; except that when such registration statement relates to a security issued by a foreign government, or political subdivision thereof, it need be signed only by the underwriter of such security. Signatures of all such persons when written on the said registration statements shall be presumed to have been so written by authority of the person whose signature is so affixed and the burden of proof in the event such authority shall be denied, shall be upon the party denying the same. The affixing of any signature without the authority of the purported signer shall constitute a violation of this title. A registration statement shall be deemed effective only as to the securities specified therein as proposed to be offered.

(b) At the time of filing a registration statement the applicant shall pay to the Commission a fee of one one-hundredth of 1 per centum of the maximum aggregate price at which such securities are proposed to be offered, but in no case shall fee be less than $25.

(c) The filing with the Commission of a registration statement, or of an amendment to a registration statement, shall be deemed to have taken place upon the receipt thereof, but the filing of a registration statement shall not be deemed to have taken place unless it is accompanied by a United States postal money order or a certified bank check or cash for the amount of the fee required under subsection (b).

(d) The information contained in or filed with any registration statement shall be made available to the public under such regulations as the Commission may prescribe, and copies thereof, photostatic or otherwise, shall be furnished to every applicant at such reasonable charge as the Commission may prescribe.

(e) No registration statement may be filed within the first forty days following the enactment of this Act.

INFORMATION REQUIRED IN REGISTRATION STATEMENT

SEC. 7. The registration statement, when relating to a security other than a security issued by a foreign government, or political subdivision thereof, shall contain the information, and be accompanied by the documents, specified in Schedule A, and when relating to a security issued by a foreign government, or political subdivision thereof, shall contain the information, and be accompanied by the documents, specified in Schedule B; except that the Commission may by rules or regulations provide that any such information or document need not be included in respect of any class of issuers or securities if it finds that the requirement of such information or document is inapplicable to such class and that disclosure fully adequate for the protection of investors is otherwise required to be included within the registration statement. If any accountant, engineer, or appraiser, or any person whose profession gives authority to a statement made by him, is named as having prepared or certified any part of the registration statement, or is named as having prepared or certified a report or valuation for use in connection with the registration statement, the written consent of such person shall be filed with the registration statement. If any such person is named as having prepared or certified a report or valuation (other than a public official document or statement) which is used in connection with the registration statement, but is not named as having prepared or certified such report or valuation for use in connection with the registration statement, the written consent of such person shall be filed with the registration statement unless the Commission dispenses with such filing as impracticable or as involving undue hardship on the person filing the registration statement. Any such registration statement shall contain such other information, and be accompanied by such other documents, as the Commission may by rules or regulations require as being necessary or appropriate in the public interest or for the protection of investors.

TAKING EFFECT OF REGISTRATION STATEMENTS AND AMENDMENTS THERETO

SEC. 8 (a) The effective date of a registration statement shall be the twentieth day after the filing thereof, except as hereinafter provided, and except that in case of securities of any foreign public authority, which has continued the full service of its obligations in the United States, the proceeds of which are to be devoted to the refunding of obligations payable in the United States, the registration statement shall become effective seven days after the filing thereof. If any amendment to any such statement is filed prior to the effective date of such statement, the registration statement shall be deemed to have been filed when such amendment was filed; except that an amendment filed with the consent of the Commission, prior to the effective date of the registration statement, or filed pursuant to an order of the Commission, shall be treated as a part of the registration statement.

(b) If it appears to the Commission that a registration statement is on its face incomplete or inaccurate in any material respect, the Commission may, after notice by personal service or the sending of confirmed telegraphic notice not later than ten days after the filing of the registration statement, and opportunity for hearing (at a time fixed by the Commission) within ten days after such notice by personal service or the sending of such telegraphic notice, issue an order prior to the effective date of registration refusing to permit such statement to become effective until it has been amended in accordance with such order. When such statement has been amended in accordance with such order the Commission shall so declare and the registration shall become effective at the time provided in subsection (a) or upon the date of such declaration, whichever date is the later.

(c) An amendment filed after the effective date of the registration statement, if such amendment, upon its face, appears to the Commission not to be incomplete or inaccurate in any material respect, shall become effective on such date as the Commission may determine, having due regard to the public interest and the protection of investors.

(d) If it appears to the Commission at any time that the registration statement includes any untrue statement of a material fact or omits to state any material fact required to be stated therein or necessary to make the statements therein not misleading, the Commission may, after notice by personal service or the sending of confirmed telegraphic notice, and after opportunity for hearing (at a time fixed by the Commission) within fifteen days after such notice by personal service or the sending of such telegraphic notice, issue a stop order suspending the effectiveness of the registration statement. When such statement has been amended in accordance with such stop order the Commission shall so declare and thereupon the stop order shall cease to be effective.

(e) The Commission is hereby empowered to make an examination in any case in order to determine whether a stop order should issue under subsection (d). In making such examination the Commission or any officer or officers designated by it shall have access to and may demand the production of any books and papers of, and may administer oaths and affirmations to and examine, the issuer, underwriter, or any other person, in respect of any matter relevant to the examination, and may, in its discretion, require the production of a balance sheet exhibiting the assets and liabilities of the issuer, or its income statement, or both, to be certified to by a public or certified accountant approved by the Commission. If the issuer or underwriter shall fail to cooperate, or shall obstruct or refuse to permit the making of an examination such conduct shall be proper ground for the issuance of a stop order.

(f) Any notice required under this section shall be sent to or served on the issuer, or, in case of a foreign government or political subdivision thereof, to or on the underwriter, or, in the case of a foreign or Territorial person, to or on its duly authorized representative in the United States named in the registration statement, properly directed in each case of telegraphic notice to the address given in such statement.

COURT REVIEW OF ORDERS

SEC. 9. (a) Any person aggrieved by an order of the Commission may obtain a review of such order in the Circuit Court of Appeals of the United States, within any circuit wherein such person resides or has his principal place of business, or in the Court of Appeals of the District of Columbia, by filing in such court, within sixty days after the entry of such order, a written petition praying that the order of the Commission be modified or be set aside in whole or in part. A copy of such petition shall be forthwith served upon the Commission, and thereupon the Commission shall certify and file in the court a transcript of the record upon which the order complained of was entered. No objection to the order of the Commission shall be considered by the court unless such objection shall have been urged before the Commission. The finding of the Commission as to the facts, if supported by evidence, shall be conclusive. If either party shall apply to the court for leave to adduce additional evidence, and shall show to the satisfaction of the court that such additional evidence is material and that there were reasonable grounds for failure to adduce such evidence in the hearings before the Commission, the court may order such additional evidence to be taken before the Commission and to be adduced upon the hearing in such manner and upon such terms and conditions as to the court may seem proper. The Commission may modify its findings as to the facts, by reason of the additional evidence so taken, and it shall file such modified or new findings, which, if supported by evidence, shall be conclusive, and its recommendation, if any, for the modification or setting aside of the original order. The jurisdiction of the court shall be exclusive and its judgment and decree, affirming, modifying, or setting aside, in whole or in part, any order of the Commission, shall be final, subject to review by the Supreme Court of the United States upon certiorari or certification as provided in sections 239 and 240 of the Judicial Code, as amended (U.S.C., title 28, secs. 346 and 347).

(b) The commencement of proceedings under subsection (a) shall not, unless specifically ordered by the court, operate as a stay of the Commission's order.

INFORMATION REQUIRED IN PROSPECTUS

SEC. 10. (a) A prospectus—

(1) when relating to a security other than a security issued by a foreign government or political subdivision thereof, shall contain the same statements made in the registration statement, but it need not include the documents referred to in paragraphs (28) to (32), inclusive, of Schedule A;

(2) when relating to a security issued by a foreign government or political subdivision thereof shall contain the same statements made in the registration statement, but it need not include the documents referred to in paragraphs (13) and (14) of Schedule B.

(b) Notwithstanding the provisions of subsection (a) —

(1) When a prospectus is used more than thirteen months after the effective date of the registration statement, the information in the statements contained therein shall be as of a date not more than twelve months prior to such use, so far as such information is known

to the user of such prospectus or can be furnished by such user without unreasonable effort or expense.[9]

(2) there may be omitted from any prospectus any of the statements required under such subsection (a) which the Commission may by rules or regulations designate as not being necessary or appropriate in the public interest or for the protection of investors.

(3) any prospectus shall contain such other information as the Commission may by rules or regulations require as being necessary or appropriate in the public interest or for the protection of investors.

(4) in the exercise of its powers under paragraphs (2) and (3) of this subsection, the Commission shall have authority to classify prospectuses according to the nature and circumstances of their use, and, by rules and regulations and subject to such terms and conditions as it shall specify therein, to prescribe as to each class the form and contents which it may find appropriate to such use and consistent with the public interest and the protection of investors.

(c) The statements or information required to be included in a prospectus by or under authority of subsection (a) or (b), when written, shall be placed in a conspicuous part of the prospectus in type as large as that used generally in the body of the prospectus.

(d) In any case where a prospectus consists of a radio broadcast, copies thereof shall be filed with the Commission under such rules and regulations as it shall prescribe. The Commission may by rules and regulations require the filing with it of forms and prospectuses used in connection with the sale of securities registered under this title.

CIVIL LIABILITIES ON ACCOUNT OF FALSE REGISTRATION STATEMENT

SEC. 11. (a) In case any part of the registration statement, when such part became effective, contained an untrue statement of a material fact or omitted to state a material fact required to be stated therein or necessary to make the statements therein not misleading, any person acquiring such security (unless it is proved that at the time of such acquisition he knew of such untruth or omission) may, either at law or in equity, in any court of competent jurisdiction, sue—

(1) every person who signed the registration statement;

(2) every person who was a director of (or person performing similar functions) or partner in, the issuer at the time of the filing of the part of the registration statement with respect to which his liability is asserted;

(3) every person who, with his consent, is named in the registration statement as being or about to become a director, person performing similar functions, or partner;

(4) every accountant, engineer, or appraiser, or any person whose profession gives authority to a statement made by him, who has with his consent been named as having prepared or certified any part of the registration statement, or as having prepared or certified any report or valuation which is used in connection with the registration statement, with respect to the statement in

---

[9] "(1) when a prospectus is used more than thirteen months after the effective date of the registration statement, the information in the statements contained therein shall be as of a date not more than twelve months prior to such use."

such registration statement, report, or valuation, which purports to have been prepared or certified by him;

(5) every underwriter with respect to such security.

If such person acquired the security after the issuer has made generally available to its security holders an earning statement covering a period of at least twelve months beginning after the effective date of the registration statement, then the right of recovery under this subsection shall be conditioned on proof that such person acquired the security relying upon such untrue statement in the registration statement or relying upon the registration statement and not knowing of such omission, but such reliance may be established without proof of the reading of the registration statement by such person.

(b) Notwithstanding the provisions of subsection (a) no person, other than the issuer, shall be liable as provided therein who shall sustain the burden of proof—

(1) that before the effective date of the part of the registration statement with respect to which his liability is asserted (A) he had resigned from or had taken such steps as are permitted by law to resign from, or cease or refused to act in, every office, capacity, or relationship in which he was described in the registration statement as acting or agreeing to act, and (B) he had advised the Commission and the issuer in writing that he had taken such action and that he would not be responsible for such part of the registration statement; or

(2) that if such part of the registration statement became effective without his knowledge, upon becoming aware of such fact he forthwith acted and advised the Commission, in accordance with paragraph (1), and, in addition, gave reasonable public notice that such part of the registration statement had become effective without his knowledge; or

(3) that (A) as regards any part of the registration statement not purporting to be made on the authority of an expert, and not purporting to be a copy of or extract from a report or valuation of an expert, and not purporting to be made on the authority of a public official document or statement, he had, after reasonable investigation, reasonable ground to believe and did believe, at the time such part of the registration statement became effective, that the statements therein were true and that there was no omission to state a material fact required to be stated therein or necessary to make the statements therein not misleading; and (B) as regards any part of the registration statement purporting to be made upon his authority as an expert or purporting to be a copy of or extract from a report or valuation of himself as an expert, (i) he had, after reasonable investigation, reasonable ground to believe and did believe, at the time such part of the registration statement became effective, that the statements therein were true and that there was no omission to state a material fact required to be stated therein or necessary to make the statements therein not misleading, or (ii) such part of the registration statement did not fairly represent his statement as an expert or was not a fair copy of or extract from his report or valuation as an expert; and **(C) as regards any part of the registration statement purporting to be made on the authority of an expert (other than himself) or purporting to be a copy of or extract from a report or valuation of an expert (other than himself), he had no reasonable ground to believe and did not believe, at the time such part of the registration statement became effective, that the statements therein were untrue**

or that there was an omission to state a material fact required to be stated therein or necessary to make the statements therein not misleading, or that such part of the registration statement did not fairly represent the statement of the expert or was not a fair copy of or extract from the report or valuation of the expert; and (D) as regards any part of the registration statement purporting to be a statement made by an official person or purporting to be a copy of or extract from a public official document, he had no reasonable ground to believe and did not believe, at the time such part of the registration statement became effective, that the statements therein were untrue, or that there was an omission to state a material fact required to be stated therein or necessary to make the statements therein not misleading, or that such part of the registration statement did not fairly represent the statement made by the official person or was not a fair copy of or extract from the public official document.[10]

(c) In determining, for the purpose of paragraph (3) of subsection (b) of this section, what constitutes reasonable investigation and reasonable ground for belief, the standard of reasonableness shall be that required of a prudent man in the management of his own property.[11]

(d) If any person becomes an underwriter with respect to the security after the part of the registration statement with respect to which his liability is asserted has become effective, then for the purposes of paragraph (3) of subsection (b) of this section such part of the registration statement shall be considered as having become effective with respect to such person as of the time when he became an underwriter.

(e) The suit authorized under subsection (a) may be to recover such damages as shall represent the difference between the amount paid for the security (not exceeding the price at which the security was offered

[10] "(C) as regards any part of the registration statement purporting to be made on the authority of an expert (other than himself) or purporting to be a copy of or extract from a report or valuation of an expert (other than himself), he had reasonable ground to believe and did believe, at the time such part of the registration statement became effective, that the statements therein were true and that there was no omission to state a material fact required to be stated therein or necessary to make the statements therein not misleading, and that such part of the registration statement fairly represented the statement of the expert or was a fair copy of or extract from the report or valuation of the expert; and (D) as regards any part of the registration statement purporting to be a statement made by an official person or purporting to be a copy of or extract from a public official document, he had reasonable ground to believe and did believe, at the time such part of the registration statement became effective, that the statements therein were true, and that there was no omission to state a material fact required to be stated therein or necessary to make the statements therein not misleading, and that such part of the registration statement fairly represented the statement made by the official person or was a fair copy of or extract from the public official document."

[11] "(c) In determining for the purpose of paragraph (3) of subsection (b) of this section, what constitutes reasonable investigation and reasonable ground for belief, the standard of reasonableness shall be that required of a person occupying a fiduciary relationship."

to the public) and (1) the value thereof as of the time such suit was brought, or (2) the price at which such security shall have been disposed of in the market before suit, or (3) the price at which such security shall have been disposed of after suit but before judgment if such damages shall be less than the damages representing the difference between the amount paid for the security (not exceeding the price at which the security was offered to the public) and the value thereof as of the time such suit was brought: Provided, that if the defendant proves that any portion or all of such damages represents other than the depreciation in value of such security resulting from such part of the registration statement, with respect to which his liability is asserted, not being true or omitting to state a material fact required to be stated therein or necessary to make the statements therein not misleading, such portion of or all such damages shall not be recoverable. In no event shall any underwriter (unless such underwriter shall have knowingly received from the issuer for acting as an underwriter some benefit, directly or indirectly, in which all other underwriters similarly situated did not share in proportion to their respective interests in the underwriting) be liable in any suit or as a consequence of suits authorized under subsection (a) for damages in excess of the total price at which the securities underwritten by him and distributed to the public were offered to the public. In any suit under this or any other section of this title the court may, in its discretion, require an undertaking for the payment of the costs of such suit, including reasonable attorney's fees, and if judgment shall be rendered against a party litigant, upon the motion of the other party litigant, such costs may be assessed in favor of such party litigant (whether or not such undertaking has been required) if the court believes the suit or the defense to have been without merit, in an amount sufficient to reimburse him for the reasonable expenses incurred by him, in connection with such suit, such costs to be taxed in the manner usually provided for taxing of costs in the court in which the suit was heard.[12]

(f) All or any one or more of the persons specified in subsection (a) shall be jointly and severally liable, and every person who becomes liable to make any payment under this section may recover contribution as in cases of contract from any person who, if sued separately, would have been liable to make the same payment, unless the person who has become liable was, and the other was not, guilty of fraudulent misrepresentation.

(g) In no case shall the amount recoverable under this section exceed the price at which the security was offered to the public.

CIVIL LIABILITIES ARISING IN CONNECTION WITH PROSPECTUSES AND COMMUNICATIONS

SEC. 12. Any person who—

(1) sells a security in violation of section 5, or

(2) sells a security (whether or not exempted by the provisions of section

[12] "(e) The suit authorized under subsection (a) may be either (1) to recover the consideration paid for such security with interest thereon, less the amount of any income received thereon, upon the tender of such security, or (2) for damages if the person suing no longer owns the security."

3, other than paragraph (2) of subsection (a) thereof), by the use of any means or instruments of transportation or communication in interstate commerce or of the mails, by means of a prospectus or oral communication, which includes an untrue statement of a material fact or omits to state a material fact necessary in order to make the statements in the light of the circumstances under which they were made, not misleading (the purchaser not knowing of such untruth or omission), and who shall not sustain the burden of proof that he did not know, and in the exercise of reasonable care could not have known, of such untruth or omission,

shall be liable to the person purchasing such security from him, who may sue either at law or in equity in any court of competent jurisdiction, to recover the consideration paid for such security with interest thereon, less the amount of any income received thereon, upon the tender of such security, or for damages if he no longer owns the security.

LIMITATION OF ACTIONS

Sec. 13. No action shall be maintained to enforce any liability created under section 11 or section 12 (2) unless brought within one year after the discovery of the untrue statement or the omission, or after such discovery should have been made by the exercise of reasonable diligence, or, if the action is to enforce a liability created under section 12 (1), unless brought within one year after the violation upon which it is based. In no event shall any such action be brought to enforce a liability created under section 11 or section 12 (1) more than three years after the security was bona fide offered to the public, or under section 12 (2) more than three years after the sale.[13]

CONTRARY STIPULATIONS VOID

SEC. 14. Any condition, stipulation, or provision binding any person acquiring any security to waive compliance with any provision of this title or of the rules and regulations of the Commission shall be void.

LIABILITY OF CONTROLLING PERSONS

SEC. 15. Every person who, by or through stock ownership, agency, or otherwise, or who, pursuant to or in connection with an agreement or understanding with one or more other persons by or through stock ownership, agency, or otherwise, controls any person liable under section 11 or 12, shall also be liable jointly and severally with and to the same extent as such controlled person to any person to whom such controlled person is liable, **unless the controlling person had no knowledge of or reasonable grounds to believe in the existence**

[13] "SEC. 13. No action shall be maintained to enforce any liability created under section 11 or section 12 (2) unless brought within two years after the discovery of the untrue statement or the omission, or after such discovery should have been made by the exercise of reasonable diligence, or, if the action is to enforce a liability created under section 12 (1), unless brought within two years after the violation upon which it is based. In no event shall any such action be brought to enforce a liability created under section 11 or section 12 (1) more than ten years after the security was bona fide offered to the public."

of the facts by reason of which the liability of the controlled person is alleged to exist.

ADDITIONAL REMEDIES

Sec. 16. The rights and remedies provided by this title shall be in addition to any and all other rights and remedies that may exist at law or in equity.

FRAUDULENT INTERSTATE TRANSACTIONS

Sec. 17. (a) It shall be unlawful for any person in the sale of any securities by the use of any means or instruments of transportation or communication in interstate commerce or by the use of the mails, directly or indirectly—

(1) to employ any device, scheme, or artifice to defraud, or

(2) to obtain money or property by means of any untrue statement of a material fact or any omission to state a material fact necessary in order to make the statements made, in the light of the circumstances under which they were made, not misleading, or

(3) to engage in any transaction, practice, or course of business which operates or would operate as a fraud or deceit upon the purchaser.

(b) It shall be unlawful for any person, by the use of any means or instruments of transportation or communication in interstate commerce or by the use of the mails, to publish, give publicity to, or circulate any notice, circular, advertisement, newspaper, article, letter, investment service, or communication which, though not purporting to offer a security for sale, describes such security for a consideration received or to be received, directly or indirectly, from an issuer, underwriter, or dealer, without fully disclosing the receipt, whether past or prospective, of such consideration and the amount thereof.

(c) The exemptions provided in section 3 shall not apply to the provisions of this section.

STATE CONTROL OF SECURITIES

Sec. 18. Nothing in this title shall affect the jurisdiction of the securities commission (or any agency or office performing like functions) of any State or Territory of the United States, or the District of Columbia, over any security or any person.

SPECIAL POWERS OF COMMISSION

Sec. 19. (a) The Commission shall have authority from time to time to make, amend, and rescind such rules and regulations as may be necessary to carry out the provisions of this title, including rules and regulations governing registration statements and prospectuses for various classes of securities and issuers, and defining accounting, **technical**, and trade terms used in this title. Among other things, the Commission shall have authority, for the purposes of this title, to prescribe the form or forms in which required information shall be set forth, the items or details to be shown in the balance sheet and earning statement, and the methods to be followed in the preparation of accounts, in the appraisal or valuation of assets and liabilities, in the determination of depreciation and depletion, in the differentiation of recurring and nonrecurring income, in the differentiation of investment and operating income, and in the preparation, where the Commission deems it necessary or desirable, of consolidated balance sheets or income accounts of any person directly or indirectly controlling or controlled by the issuer, or any person under direct or indirect common control with the issuer; but insofar as they relate to any common carrier subject to the provisions of section 20 of the Interstate Commerce Act, as amended, the rules and regulations of the Commission with respect to accounts shall not be inconsistent with the requirements imposed by the Interstate Commerce Commission under authority of such section 20. The rules and regulations of the Commission shall be effective upon publication in the manner which the Commission shall prescribe. **No provision of this title imposing any liability shall apply to any act done or omitted in good faith in conformity with any rule or regulation of the Commission, notwithstanding that such rule or regulation may, after such act or omission, be amended or rescinded or be determined by judicial or other authority to be invalid for any reason.**

(b) For the purpose of all investigations which, in the opinion of the Commission, are necessary and proper for the enforcement of this title, any member of the Commission or any officer or officers designated by it are empowered to administer oaths and affirmations, subpena witnesses, take evidence, and require the production of any books, papers, or other documents which the Commission deems relevant or material to the inquiry. Such attendance of witnesses and the production of such documentary evidence may be required from any place in the United States or any Territory at any designated place of hearing.

INJUNCTIONS AND PROSECUTION OF OFFENSES

SEC. 20. (a) Whenever it shall appear to the Commission, either upon complaint or otherwise, that the provisions of this title, or of any rule or regulation prescribed under authority thereof, have been or are about to be violated, it may, in its discretion, either require or permit such person to file with it a statement in writing, under oath, or otherwise, as to all the facts and circumstances concerning the subject matter which it believes to be in the public interest to investigate, and may investigate such facts.

(b) Whenever it shall appear to the Commission that any person is engaged or about to engage in any acts or practices which constitute or will constitute a violation of the provisions of this title, or of any rule or regulation prescribed under authority thereof, it may in its discretion, bring an action in any district court of the United States, United States court of any Territory, or the Supreme Court of the District of Columbia to enjoin such acts or practices, and upon a proper showing a permanent or temporary injunction or restraining order shall be granted without bond. The Commission may transmit such evidence as may be available concerning such acts or practices to the Attorney General who may, in his discretion, institute the necessary criminal proceedings under this title. Any such criminal proceeding may be brought either in the district wherein the transmittal of the prospectus or security complained of begins, or in the district wherein such prospectus or security is received.

(c) Upon application of the Commission the district courts of the United States, the United States courts of any Territory, and the Supreme Court of the District of Columbia, shall also have jurisdiction to issue writs of mandamus commanding any person to comply with the provisions of this title or any order of the Commission made in pursuance thereof.

HEARINGS BY COMMISSION

SEC. 21. All hearings shall be public and may be held before the Commission or an officer or officers of the Commission designated by it, and appropriate records thereof shall be kept.

JURISDICTION OF OFFENSES AND SUITS

SEC. 22. (a) The district courts of the United States, the United States courts of any Territory, and the Supreme Court of the District of Columbia shall have jurisdiction of offenses and violations under this title and under the rules and regulations promulgated by the Commission in respect thereto, and, concurrent with State and Territorial courts, of all suits in equity and actions at law brought to enforce any liability or duty created by this title. Any such suit or action may be brought in the district wherein the defendant is found or is an inhabitant or transacts business, or in the district where the sale took place, if the defendant participated therein, and process in such cases may be served in any other district of which the defendant is an inhabitant or wherever the defendant may be found. Judgments and decrees so rendered shall be subject to review as provided in sections 128 and 240 of the Judicial Code, as amended (U.S.C., title 28, secs. 225 and 347). No case arising under this title and brought in any State court of competent jurisdiction shall be removed to any court of the United States. No costs shall be assessed for or against the Commission in any proceeding under this title brought by or against it in the Supreme Court or such other courts.

(b) In case of contumacy or refusal to obey a subpena issued to any person, any of the said United States courts, within the jurisdiction of which said person guilty of contumacy or refusal to obey is found or resides, upon application by the Commission may issue to such person an order requiring such person to appear before the Commission, or one of its examiners designated by it, there to produce documentary evidence if so ordered, or there to give evidence touching the matter in question; and any failure to obey such order of the court may be punished by said court as a contempt thereof.

(c) No person shall be excused from attending and testifying or from producing books, papers, contracts, agreements, and other documents before the Commission, or in obedience to the subpena of the Commission or any member thereof or any officer designated by it, or in any cause, or proceeding instituted by the Commission, on the ground that the testimony or evidence, documentary or otherwise, required of him, may tend to incriminate him or subject him to a penalty or forfeiture; but no individual shall be prosecuted or subjected to any penalty or forfeiture for or on account of any transaction, matter, or thing concerning which he is compelled, after having claimed his privilege against self-incrimination, to testify or produce evidence, documentary or otherwise, except that such individual so testifying shall not be exempt from prosecution and punishment for perjury committed in so testifying.

UNLAWFUL REPRESENTATIONS

SEC. 23. Neither the fact that the registration statement for a security has been filed or is in effect nor the fact that a stop order is not in effect with respect thereto shall be deemed a finding by the Commission that the registration statement is true and accurate on its face or that it does not contain an untrue statement of fact or omit to state a material fact, or be held to mean that the Commission has in any way passed upon the merits of, or given approval to, such security. It shall be unlawful to make, or cause to be made, to any prospective purchaser any representation contrary to the foregoing provisions of this section.

PENALTIES

SEC. 24. Any person who willfully violates any of the provisions of this title, or the rules and regulations promulgated by the Commission under authority thereof, or any person who willfully, in a registration statement filed under this title, makes any untrue statement of a material fact or omits to state any material fact required to be stated therein or necessary to make the statements therein not misleading, shall upon conviction be fined not more than $5,000 or imprisoned no more than five years, or both.

JURISDICTION OF OTHER GOVERNMENT AGENCIES OVER SECURITIES

SEC. 25. Nothing in this title shall relieve any person from submitting to the respective supervisory units of the Government of the United States information, reports, or other documents that are now or may hereafter be required by any provision of law.

SEPARABILITY OF PROVISIONS

SEC. 26. If any provision of this Act, or the application of such provision to any person or circumstance, shall be held invalid, the remainder of this Act, or the application of such provision to persons or circumstances other than those as to which it is held invalid, shall not be affected thereby.

Sec. 27. Upon the expiration of sixty days after the date upon which a majority of the members of the securities and exchange commission appointed under Section 4 of Title I of this act have qualified and taken office, all powers, duties and functions of the Federal Trade Commission under the Securities Act of 1933 shall be transferred to such commission, together with all property, books, records and unexpended balances of appropriations used by or available to the Federal Trade Commission for carrying out its functions under the Securities Act of 1933. All proceedings, hearings or investigations commenced or pending before the Federal Trade Commission arising under the Securities Act of 1933 shall be continued by the Securities and Exchange Commission. All orders, rules and regulations which have been issued by the Federal Trade Commission under the Securities Act of 1933 and which are in effect shall continue in effect until modified, superseded, revoked, or repealed. All rights and interests accruing or to accrue under the Securities Act of 1933, or any provision of any regulation relating to, or out of action taken by, the Federal Trade Commission under such act, shall be followed in all respects and may be exercised and enforced.

Sec. 28. The commission is authorized and directed to make a study and investigation of the work, activities, personnel and functions of protective and reorganization committees in connection with the reor-

ganization, readjustment, rehabilitation, liquidation, or consolidation of persons and properties and to report the result of its studies and investigations and its recommendations to the Congress on or before January 3, 1936.[14]

SCHEDULE A

(1) The name under which the issuer is doing or intends to do business;

(2) the name of the State or other sovereign power under which the issuer is organized;

(3) the location of the issuer's principal business office, and if the issuer is a foreign or territorial person, the name and address of its agent in the United States authorized to receive notice;

(4) the names and addresses of the directors or persons performing similar functions, and the chief executive, financial and accounting officers, chosen or to be chosen if the issuer be a corporation, association, trust, or other entity; of all partners, if the issuer be a partnership; and of the issuer, if the issuer be an individual; and of the promoters in the case of a business to be formed, or formed within two years prior to the filing of the registration statement;

(5) the names and addresses of the underwriters;

(6) the names and addresses of all persons, if any, owning of record or beneficially, if known, more than 10 per centum of any class of stock of the issuer, or more than 10 per centum in the aggregate of the outstanding stock of the issuer as of a date within twenty days prior to the filing of the registration statement;

(7) the amount of securities of the issuer held by any person specified in paragraphs (4), (5), and (6) of this schedule, as of a date within twenty days prior to the filing of the registration statement, and, if possible, as of one year prior thereto, and the amount of the securities, for which the registration statement is filed, to which such persons have indicated their intention to subscribe;

(8) the general character of the business actually transacted or to be transacted by the issuer;

(9) a statement of the capitalization of the issuer, including the authorized and outstanding amounts of its capital stock and the proportion thereof paid up, the number and classes of shares in which such capital stock is divided, par value thereof, or if it has no par value, the stated or assigned value thereof, a description of the respective voting rights, preferences, conversion and exchange rights, rights to dividends, profits, or capital of each class, with respect to each other class, including the retirement and liquidation rights or values thereof;

(10) a statement of the securities, if any, covered by options outstanding or to be created in connection with the security to be offered, together with the names and addresses of all persons, if any, to be allotted more than 10 per centum in the aggregate of such options;

(11) the amount of capital stock of each class issued or included in the shares of stock to be offered;

(12) the amount of the funded debt outstanding and to be created by the security to be offered, with a brief description of the date, maturity, and character of such debt, rate of interest, character of amortization provisions, and the security, if any, therefor. If substitution of any security is permissible, a

[14] Secs. 27 and 28 are Secs. 210 and 211, Title II, of Securities Exchange Act of 1934, approved June 6, 1934, effective July 1, 1934.

summarized statement of the conditions under which such substitution is permitted. If substitution is permissible without notice, a specific statement to that effect;

(13) the specific purposes in detail and the approximate amounts to be devoted to such purposes, so far as determinable, for which the security to be offered is to supply funds, and if the funds are to be raised in part from other sources, the amounts thereof and the sources thereof, shall be stated;

(14) the remuneration, paid or estimated to be paid, by the issuer or its predecessor, directly or indirectly, during the past year and ensuing year to (a) the directors or persons performing similar functions, and (b) its officers and other persons, naming them wherever such remuneration exceeded $25,000 during any such year;

(15) the estimated net proceeds to be derived from the security to be offered;

(16) the price at which it is proposed that the security shall be offered to the public or the method by which such price is computed and any variation therefrom at which any portion of such security is proposed to be offered to any persons or classes of persons, other than the underwriters, naming them or specifying the class. A variation in price may be proposed prior to the date of the public offering of the security, but the Commission shall immediately be notified of such variation;

(17) all commissions or discounts paid or to be paid, directly or indirectly, by the issuer to the underwriters in respect of the sale of the security to be offered. Commissions shall include all cash, securities, contracts, or anything else of value, paid, to be set aside, disposed of, or understandings with or for the benefit of any other persons in which any underwriter is interested, made, in connection with the sale of such security. A commission paid or to be paid in connection with the sale of such security by a person in which the issuer has an interest or which is controlled or directed by, or under common control with, the issuer shall be deemed to have been paid by the issuer. Where any such commission is paid the amount of such commission paid to each underwriter shall be stated;

(18) the amount or estimated amounts, itemized in reasonable detail, of expenses, other than commissions specified in paragraph (17) of this schedule, incurred or borne by or for the account of the issuer in connection with the sale of the security to be offered or properly chargeable thereto, including legal, engineering, certification, authentication, and other charges;

(19) the net proceeds derived from any security sold by the issuer during the two years preceding the filing of the registration statement, the price at which such security was offered to the public, and the names of the principal underwriters of such security;

(20) any amount paid within two years preceding the filing of the registration statement or intended to be paid to any promoter and the names of the principal underwriters of such security;

(21) the names and addresses of the vendors and the purchase price of any property, or good will, acquired or to be acquired, not in the ordinary course of business, which is to be defrayed in whole or in part from the proceeds of the security to be offered, the amount of any commission payable to any person in connection with such acquisition, and the name or names of such person or persons, together with any expense incurred or to be incurred in connection with such acquisition, including the cost of borrowing money to finance such acquisition;

(22) full particulars of the nature and extent of the interest, if any, of every

director, principal executive officer, and of every stockholder holding more than 10 per centum of any class of stock or more than 10 per centum in the aggregate of the stock of the issuer, in any property acquired, not in the ordinary course of business of the issuer, within two years preceding the filing of the registration statement or proposed to be acquired at such date;

(23) the names and addresses of counsel who have passed on the legality of the issue;

(24) dates of and parties to, and the general effect concisely stated of every material contract made, not in the ordinary course of business, which contract is to be executed in whole or in part at or after the filing of the registration statement or which contract has been made not more than two years before such filing. Any management contract or contract providing for special bonuses or profit-sharing arrangements, and every material patent or contract for a material patent right, and every contract by or with a public utility company or an affiliate thereof, providing for the giving or receiving of technical or financial advice or service (if such contract may involve a charge to any party thereto at a rate in excess of $2,500 per year in cash or securities or anything else of value), shall be deemed a material contract;

(25) a balance sheet as of a date not more than ninety days prior to the date of the filing of the registration statement showing all of the assets of the issuer, the nature and cost thereof, whenever determinable, in such detail and in such form as the Commission shall prescribe (with intangible items segregated), including any loan in excess of $20,000 to any officer, director, stockholder or person directly or indirectly controlling or controlled by the issuer, or person under direct or indirect common control with the issuer. All the liabilities of the issuer in such detail and such form as the Commission shall prescribe, including surplus of the issuer showing how and from what sources such surplus was created, all as of a date not more than ninety days prior to the filing of the registration statement. If such statement be not certified by an independent public or certified accountant, in addition to the balance sheet required to be submitted under this schedule, a similar detailed balance sheet of the assets and liabilities of the issuer, certified by an independent public or certified accountant, of a date not more than one year prior to the filing of the registration statement, shall be submitted;

(26) a profit and loss statement of the issuer showing earnings and income, the nature and source thereof, and the expenses and fixed charges in such detail and such form as the Commission shall prescribe for the latest fiscal year for which such statement is available and for the two preceding fiscal years, year by year, or, if such issuer has been in actual business for less than three years, then for such time as the issuer has been in actual busines, year by year. If the date of the filing of the registration statement is more than six months after the close of the last fiscal year, a statement from such closing date to the latest practicable date. Such statement shall show what the practice of the issuer has been during the three years or lesser period as to the character of the charges, dividends or other distributions made against its various surplus accounts, and as to depreciation, depletion, and maintenance charges, in such detail and form as the Commission shall prescribe, and if stock dividends or avails from the sale of rights have been credited to income, they shall be shown separately with a statement of the basis upon which the credit is computed. Such statement shall also differentiate between any recurring and nonrecurring income and between any investment and operating income. Such statement shall be certified by an independent public or certified accountant;

(27) if the proceeds, or any part of the proceeds, of the security to be issued is to be applied directly or indirectly to the purchase of any business, a profit and loss statement of such business certified by an independent public or certified accountant, meeting the requirements of paragraph (26) of this schedule, for the three preceding fiscal years, together with a balance sheet, similarly certified, of such business, meeting the requirements of paragraph (25) of this schedule of a date not more than ninety days prior to the filing of the registration statement or at the date such business was acquired by the issuer if the business was acquired by the issuer more than ninety days prior to the filing of the registration statement;

(28) a copy of any agreement or agreements (or if identic agreements are used the forms thereof) made with any underwriter, including all contracts and agreements referred to in paragraph (17) of this schedule;

(29) a copy of the opinion or opinions of counsel in respect to the legality of the issue, with a translation of such opinion, when necessary, into the English language;

(30) a copy of all material contracts referred to in paragraph (24) of this schedule, but no disclosure shall be required of any portion of any such contract if the Commission determines that disclosure of such portion would impair the value of the contract and would not be necessary for the protection of the investors;

(31) unless previously filed and registered under the provisions of this title, and brought up to date, (a) a copy of its articles of incorporation, with all amendments thereof and of its existing bylaws or instruments corresponding thereto, whatever the name, if the issuer be a corporation; (b) copy of all instruments by which the trust is created or declared, if the issuer is a trust; (c) a copy of its articles of partnership or association and all other papers pertaining to its organization, if the issuer is a partnership, unincorporated association, joint-stock company, or any other form of organization; and

(32) a copy of the underlying agreements or indentures affecting any stock, bonds, or debentures offered or to be offered.

In case of certificates of deposit, voting trust certificates, collateral trust certificates, certificates of interest or shares in unincorporated investment trusts, equipment trust certificates, interim or other receipts for certificates, and like securities, the Commission shall establish rules and regulations requiring the submission of information of a like character applicable to such cases, together with such other information as it may deem appropriate and necessary regarding the character, financial or otherwise, of the actual issuer of the securities and/or the person performing the acts and assuming the duties of depositor or manager.

SCHEDULE B

(1) Name of borrowing government or subdivision thereof;

(2) specific purposes in detail and the approximate amounts to be devoted to such purposes, so far as determinable, for which the security to be offered is to supply funds, and if the funds are to be raised in part from other sources, the amounts thereof and the sources thereof, shall be stated;

(3) the amount of the funded debt and the estimated amount of the floating debt outstanding and to be created by the security to be offered, excluding intergovernmental debt, and a brief description of the date, maturity, character of such debt, rate of interest, character of amortization provisions, and the security, if any, therefor. If substitution of any security is permissible, a statement of the

conditions under which such substitution is permitted. If substitution is permissible without notice, a specific statement to that effect;

(4) whether or not the issuer or its predecessor has, within a period of twenty years prior to the filing of the registration statement, defaulted on the principal or interest of any external security, excluding intergovernmental debt, and, if so, the date, amount, and circumstances of such default, and the terms of the succeeding arrangement, if any;

(5) the receipts, classified by source, and the expenditures, classified by purpose, in such detail and form as the Commission shall prescribe for the latest fiscal year for which such information is available and the two preceding fiscal years, year by year;

(6) the names and addresses of the underwriters;

(7) the name and address of its authorized agent, if any, in the United States;

(8) the estimated net proceeds to be derived from the sale in the United States of the security to be offered;

(9) the price at which it is proposed that the security shall be offered in the United States to the public or the method by which such price is computed. A variation in price may be proposed prior to the date of the public offering of the security, but the Commission shall immediately be notified of such variation;

(10) all commissions paid or to be paid, directly or indirectly, by the issuer to the underwriters in respect of the sale of the security to be offered. Commissions shall include all cash, securities, contracts, or anything else of value, paid, to be set aside, disposed of, or understandings with or for the benefit of any other persons in which the underwriter is interested, made, in connection with the sale of such security. Where any such commission is paid, the amount of such commission paid to each underwriter shall be stated;

(11) the amount or estimated amounts, itemized in reasonable detail, of expenses, other than the commissions specified in paragraph (10) of this schedule, incurred or borne by or for the account of the issuer in connection with the sale of the security to be offered or properly chargeable thereto, including legal, engineering, certification, and other charges;

(12) the names and addresses of counsel who have passed upon the legality of the issue;

(13) a copy of any agreement or agreements made with any underwriter governing the sale of the security within the United States; and

(14) an agreement of the issuer to furnish a copy of the opinion or opinions of counsel in respect to the legality of the issue, with a translation, where necessary, into the English language. Such opinion shall set out in full all laws, decrees, ordinances, or other acts of Government under which the issue of such security has been authorized.

TITLE II

SECTION 201. For the purpose of protecting, conserving, and advancing the interests of the holders of foreign securities in default, there is hereby created a body corporate with the name "Corporation of Foreign Security Holders" (herein called the "Corporation"). The principal office of the Corporation shall be located in the District of Columbia, but there may be established agencies or branch offices in any city or cities of the United States under rules and regulations prescribed by the board of directors.

SEC. 202. The control and management of the Corporation shall be vested in a board of six directors, who shall be appointed and hold office in the following manner: As soon as practicable after the date this Act takes effect the Federal Trade Commission (hereinafter in this title called "Commission") shall appoint six directors, and shall designate a chairman and a vice chairman from among their number. After the directors designated as chairman and vice chairman cease to be directors, their successors as chairman and vice chairman shall be elected by the board of directors itself. Of the directors first appointed, two shall continue in office for a term of two years, two for a term of four years, and two for a term of six years, from the date this Act takes effect, the term of each to be designated by the Commission at the time of appointment. Their successors shall be appointed by the Commission, each for a term of six years from the date of the expiration of the term for which his predecessor was appointed, except that any person appointed to fill a vacancy occurring prior to the expiration of the term for which his predecessor was appointed shall be appointed only for the unexpired term of such predecessor. No person shall be eligible to serve as a director who within the five years preceding has had any interest, direct or indirect, in any corporation, company, partnership, bank or association which has sold, or offered for sale any foreign securities. The office of a director shall be vacated if the board of directors shall at a meeting specially convened for that purpose by resolution passed by a majority of at least two-thirds of the board of directors, remove such member from office, provided that the member whom it is proposed to remove shall have seven days' notice sent to him of such meeting and that he may be heard.

SEC. 203. The Corporation shall have power to adopt, alter, and use a corporate seal; to make contracts; to lease such real estate as may be necessary for the transaction of its business; to sue and be sued, to complain and to defend, in any court of competent jurisdiction, State or Federal; to require from trustees, financial agents, or dealers in foreign securities information relative to the original or present holders of foreign securities and such other information as may be required and to issue subpenas therefor; to take over the functions of any fiscal and paying agents of any foreign securities in default; to borrow money for the purposes of this title, and to pledge as collateral for such loans any securities deposited with the Corporation pursuant to this title; by and with the consent and approval of the Commission to select, employ, and fix the compensation of officers, directors, members of committees, employees, attorneys, and agents of the Corporation, without regard to the provisions of other laws applicable to the employment and compensation of officers or employees of the United States; to define their authority and duties, require bonds of them and fix the penalties thereof, and to dismiss at pleasure such officers, employees, attorneys, and agents; and to prescribe, amend, and repeal, by its board of directors, bylaws, rules, and regulations governing the manner in which its general business may be conducted and the powers granted to it by law may be exercised and enjoyed, together with provisions for such committees and the functions thereof as the board of directors may deem necessary for facilitating its business under this title. The board of directors of the Corporation shall determine and prescribe the manner in which its obligations shall be incurred and its expenses allowed and paid.

SEC. 204. The board of directors may—

(1) Convene meeting of holders of foreign securities.

(2) Invite the deposit and undertake the custody of foreign securities which have defaulted in the payment either of principal or interest, and issue receipts or certificates in the place of securities so deposited.

(3) Appoint committees from the directors of the Corporation and/or all other persons to represent holders of any class or classes of foreign securities which have defaulted in the payment either of principal or interest and determine and regulate the functions of such committees. The chairman and vice chairman of the board of directors shall be ex officio chairman and vice chairman of each committee.

(4) Negotiate and carry out, or assist in negotiating and carrying out, arrangements for the resumption of payments due or in arrears in respect of any foreign securities in default or for rearranging the terms on which such securities may in future be held or for converting and exchanging the same for new securities or for any other object in relation thereto; and under this paragraph any plan or agreement made with respect to such securities shall be binding upon depositors, providing that the consent of holders resident in the United States of 60 per centum of the securities deposited with the Corporation shall be obtained.

(5) Undertake, superintend, or take part in the collection and application of funds derived from foreign securities which come into the possession of or under the control or management of the Corporation.

(6) Collect, preserve, publish, circulate, and render available in readily accessible form, when deemed essential or necessary, documents, statistics, reports, and information of all kinds in respect of foreign securities, including particularly records of foreign external securities in default and records of the progress made toward the payment of past-due obligations.

(7) Take such steps as it may deem expedient with the view of securing the adoption of clear and simple forms of foreign securities and just and sound principles in the conditions and terms thereof.

(8) Generally, act in the name and on behalf of the holders of foreign securities the care of representation of whose interests may be entrusted to the Corporation; conserve and protect the rights and interests of holders of foreign securities issued, sold, or owned in the United States; adopt measures for the protection, vindication, and preservation or reservation of the rights and interests of holders of foreign securities either on any default in or on breach or contemplated breach of the conditions on which such foreign securities may have been issued, or otherwise; obtain for such holders such legal and other assistance and advice as the board of directors may deem expedient; and to do all such other things as are incident or conducive to the attainment of the above objects.

Sec. 205. The board of directors shall cause accounts to be kept of all matters relating to or connected with the transactions and business of the Corporation, and cause a general account and balance sheet of the Corporation to be made out in each year, and cause all accounts to be audited by one or more auditors who shall examine the same and report thereon to the board of directors.

Sec. 206. The Corporation shall make, print, and make public an annual report of its operations during each year, send a copy thereof, together with a copy of the account and balance sheet and auditor's report, to the Commission and to both Houses of Congress, and provide one copy of such report but not more than one on the application of any person and on receipt of a sum not exceeding $1: *Provided,* That the board of directors in its discretion may distribute copies gratuitously.

Sec. 207. The Corporation may in its discretion levy charges, assessed on a pro rata basis, on the holders of foreign securities deposited with it: *Provided,* That any charge levied at the time of depositing securities with the Corporation shall not exceed one fifth of 1 per centum of the face value of such securities:

Provided further, That any additional charges shall bear a close relationship to the cost of operations and negotiations including those enumerated in sections 203 and 204 and shall not exceed 1 per centum of the face value of such securities.

SEC. 208. The Corporation may receive subscriptions from any person, foundation with a public purpose, or agency of the United States Government, and such subscriptions may, in the discretion of the board of directors, be treated as loans repayable when and as the board of directors shall determine.

SEC. 209. The Reconstruction Finance Corporation is hereby authorized to loan out of its funds not to exceed $75,000 for the use of the Corporation.

SEC. 210. Notwithstanding the foregoing provisions of this title, it shall be unlawful for, and nothing in this title shall be taken or construed as permitting or authorizing, the Corporation in this title created, or any committee of said Corporation, or any person or persons acting for or representing or purporting to represent it—

(a) to claim or assert or pretend to be acting for or to represent the Department of State or the United States Government;

(b) to make any statements or representations of any kind to any foreign government or its officials or the officials of any political subdivision of any foreign government that said Corporation or any committee thereof or any individual or individuals connected therewith were speaking or acting for the said Department of State or the United States Government; or

(c) to do any act directly or indirectly which would interfere with or obstruct or hinder or which might be calculated to obstruct, hinder or interfere with the policy or policies of the said Department of State or the Government of the United States or any pending or contemplated diplomatic negotiations, arrangements, business or exchanges between the Government of the United States or said Department of State and any foreign government or any political subdivision thereof.

SEC. 211. This title shall not take effect until the President finds that its taking effect is in the public interest and by proclamation so declares.

SEC. 212. This title may be cited as the "Corporation of Foreign Bondholders Act, 1933."

Approved May 27th 1933.

Appendix II

SECURITIES EXCHANGE ACT OF 1934[1]

AND AMENDMENTS

[PUBLIC—NO. 291—73D CONGRESS]

[H. R. 9323]

AN ACT

To provide for the regulation of securities exchanges and of over-the-counter markets operating in interstate and foreign commerce and through the mails, to prevent inequitable and unfair practices on such exchanges and markets, and for other purposes.

Be it enacted by the Senate and House of Representatives of the United States of America in Congress assembled,

TITLE I—REGULATION OF SECURITIES EXCHANGES

SHORT TITLE

SECTION 1. This act may be cited as the "Securities Exchange Act of 1934."

NECESSITY FOR REGULATION AS PROVIDED IN THIS TITLE

SEC. 2. For the reasons hereinafter enumerated, transactions in securities as commonly conducted upon securities exchanges and over-the-counter markets are affected with a national public interest which makes it necessary to provide for regulation and control of such transactions and of practices and matters related thereto, including transactions by officers, directors, and principal security holders, to require appropriate reports, and to impose requirements necessary to make such regulation and control reasonably complete and effective, in order to protect interstate commerce, the national credit, the Federal taxing power,

---

[1] The matter appearing in bold-face type with footnote references represents sections, subsections, and subparagraphs *as amended.* Footnotes contain the text prior to amendment. Bold-face type without footnote references indicates *provisions added* by amendment. The amendments, with varying effective dates, as indicated, are contained in Public, No. 621, 74th Cong., approved May 27, 1936.

to protect and make more effective the national banking system and Federal Reserve System, and to insure the maintenance of fair and honest markets in such transactions:

(1) Such transactions (a) are carried on in large volume by the public generally and in large part originate outside the States in which the exchanges and over-the-counter markets are located and/or are effected by means of the mails and instrumentalities of interstate commerce; (b) constitute an important part of the current of interstate commerce; (c) involve in large part the securities of issuers engaged in interstate commerce; (d) involve the use of credit, directly affect the financing of trade, industry, and transportation in interstate commerce, and directly affect and influence the volume of interstate commerce; and affect the national credit.

(2) The prices established and offered in such transactions are generally disseminated and quoted throughout the United States and foreign countries and constitute a basis for determining and establishing the prices at which securities are bought and sold, the amount of certain taxes owing to the United States and to the several States by owners, buyers, and sellers of securities, and the value of collateral for bank loans.

(3) Frequently the prices of securities on such exchanges and markets are susceptible to manipulation and control, and the dissemination of such prices gives rise to excessive speculation, resulting in sudden and unreasonable fluctuations in the prices of securities which (a) cause alternately unreasonable expansion and unreasonable contraction of the volume of credit available for trade, transportation, and industry in interstate commerce, (b) hinder the proper appraisal of the value of securities and thus prevent a fair calculation of taxes owing to the United States and to the several States by owners, buyers, and sellers of securities, and (c) prevent the fair valuation of collateral for bank loans and/or obstruct the effective operation of the national banking system and Federal Reserve System.

(4) National emergencies, which produce widespread unemployment and the dislocation of trade, transportation, and industry, and which burden interstate commerce and adversely affect the general welfare, are precipitated, intensified, and prolonged by manipulation and sudden and unreasonable fluctuations of security prices and by excessive speculation on such exchanges and markets, and to meet such emergencies the Federal Government is put to such great expense as to burden the national credit.

DEFINITIONS AND APPLICATION OF TITLE

SEC. 3. (a) When used in this title, unless the context otherwise requires—

(1) The term "exchange" means any organization, association, or group of persons, whether incorporated or unincorporated, which constitutes, maintains, or provides a market place or facilities for bringing together purchasers and sellers of securities or for otherwise performing with respect to securities the functions commonly performed by a stock exchange as that term is generally understood, and includes the market place and the market facilities maintained by such exchange.

(2) The term "facility" when used with respect to an exchange includes its premises, tangible or intangible property whether on the premises or not, any right to the use of such premises or property or any service thereof for the purpose of effecting or reporting a transaction on an exchange (including, among other things, any system of communication to or from the exchange, by

ticker or otherwise, maintained by or with the consent of the exchange), and any right of the exchange to the use of any property or service.

(3) The term "member" when used with respect to an exchange means any person who is permitted either to effect transactions on the exchange without the services of another person acting as broker, or to make use of the facilities of an exchange for transactions thereon without payment of a commission or fee or with the payment of a commission or fee which is less than that charged the general public, and includes any firm transacting a business as broker or dealer of which a member is a partner, and any partner of any such firm.

(4) The term "broker" means any person engaged in the business of effecting transactions in securities for the account of others, but does not include a bank.

(5) The term "dealer" means any person engaged in the business of buying and selling securities for his own account, through a broker or otherwise, but does not include a bank, or any person insofar as he buys or sells securities for his own account, either individually or in some fiduciary capacity, but not as a part of a regular business.

(6) The term "bank" means (A) a banking institution organized under the laws of the United States, (B) a member bank of the Federal Reserve System, (C) any other banking institution, whether incorporated or not, doing business under the laws of any State or of the United States, a substantial portion of the business of which consists of receiving deposits or exercising fiduciary powers similar to those permitted to national banks under section 11 (k) of the Federal Reserve Act, as amended, and which is supervised and examined by State or Federal authority having supervision over banks, and which is not operated for the purpose of evading the provisions of this title, and (D) a receiver, conservator, or other liquidating agent of any institution or firm included in clauses (A), (B), or (C) of this paragraph.

(7) The term "director" means any director of a corporation or any person performing similar functions with respect to any organization, whether incorporated or unincorporated.

(8) The term "issuer" means any person who issues or proposes to issue any security; except that with respect to certificates of deposit for securities, voting-trust certificates, or collateral-trust certificates, or with respect to certificates of interest or shares in an unincorporated investment trust not having a board of directors or of the fixed, restricted management, or unit type, the term "issuer" means the person or persons performing the acts and assuming the duties of depositor or manager pursuant to the provisions of the trust or other agreement or instrument under which such securities are issued; and except that with respect to equipment-trust certificates or like securities, the term "issuer" means the person by whom the equipment or property is, or is to be, used.

(9) The term "person" means an individual, a corporation, a partnership, an association, a joint-stock company, a business trust, or an unincorporated organization.

(10) The term "security" means any note, stock, treasury stock, bond, debenture, certificate of interest or participation in any profit-sharing agreement or in any oil, gas, or other mineral royalty or lease, any collateral-trust certificate, preorganization certificate or subscription, transferable share, investment contract, voting-trust certificate, certificate of deposit, for a security, or in general, any instrument commonly known as a "security"; or any certificate of interest or participation in, temporary or interim certificate for, receipt for, or warrant or right to subscribe to or purchase, any of the foregoing; but shall not include currency or any note, draft, bill of exchange, or banker's acceptance which has a

maturity at the time of issuance of not exceeding nine months, exclusive of days of grace, or any renewal thereof the maturity of which is likewise limited.

(11) The term "equity security" means any stock or similar security; or any security convertible, with or without consideration, into such a security, or carrying any warrant or right to subscribe to or purchase such a security; or any such warrant or right; or any other security which the Commission shall deem to be of similar nature and consider necessary or appropriate, by such rules and regulations as it may prescribe in the public interest or for the protection of investors, to treat as an equity security.

(12) The term "exempted security" or "exempted securities" shall include securities which are direct obligations of or obligations guaranteed as to principal or interest by the United States; such securities issued or guaranteed by corporations in which the United States has a direct or indirect interest as shall be designated for exemption by the Secretary of the Treasury as necessary or appropriate in the public interest or for the protection of investors; securities which are direct obligations of or obligations guaranteed as to principal or interest by a State or any political subdivision thereof or any agency or instrumentality of a State or any political subdivision thereof or any municipal corporate instrumentality of one or more States; and such other securities (which may include, among others, unregistered securities, the market in which is predominantly intrastate) as the Commission may, by such rules and regulations as it deems necessary or appropriate in the public interest or for the protection of investors, either unconditionally or upon specified terms and conditions or for stated periods, exempt from the operation of any one or more provisions of this title which by their terms do not apply to an "exempted security" or to "exempted securities."

(13) The terms "buy" and "purchase" each include any contract to buy, purchase, or otherwise acquire.

(14) The terms "sale" and "sell" each include any contract to sell or otherwise dispose of.

(15) The term "Commission" means the Securities and Exchange Commission established by section 4 of this title.

(16) The term "State" means any State of the United States, the District of Columbia, Alaska, Hawaii, Puerto Rico, the Philippine Islands, the Canal Zone, the Virgin Islands, or any other possession of the United States.

(17) The term "interstate commerce" means trade, commerce, transportation, or communication among the several States, or between any foreign country and any State, or between any State and any place or ship outside thereof.

(b) The Commission and the Federal Reserve Board, as to matters within their respective jurisdictions, shall have power by rules and regulations to define technical, trade, and accounting terms used in this title insofar as such definitions are not inconsistent with the provisions of this title.

(c) No provision of this title shall apply to, or be deemed to include, any executive department or independent establishment of the United States, or any lending agency which is wholly owned, directly or indirectly, by the United States, or any officer, agent, or employee of any such department, establishment, or agency, acting in the course of his official duty as such, unless such provision makes specific reference to such department, establishment, or agency.

SECURITIES AND EXCHANGE COMMISSION

SEC. 4. (a) There is hereby established a Securities and Exchange Commission (hereinafter referred to as the "Commission") to be composed of five commissioners to be appointed by the President by and with the advice and consent of the Senate. Not more than three of such commissioners shall be members of the same political party, and in making appointments members of different political parties shall be appointed alternately as nearly as may be practicable. No commissioner shall engage in any other business, vocation, or employment than that of serving as commissioner, nor shall any commissioner participate, directly or indirectly, in any stock-market operations or transactions of a character subject to regulation by the Commission pursuant to this title. Each commissioner shall receive a salary at the rate of $10,000 a year and shall hold office for a term of five years, except that (1) any commissioner appointed to fill a vacancy occurring prior to the expiration of the term for which his predecessor was appointed, shall be appointed for the remainder of such term, and (2) the terms of office of the commissioners first taking office after the date of enactment of this title shall expire, as designated by the President at the time of nomination, one at the end of one year, one at the end of two years, one at the end of three years, one at the end of four years, and one at the end of five years, after the date of enactment of this title.

(b) The Commission is authorized to appoint and fix the compensation of such officers, attorneys, examiners, and other experts as may be necessary for carrying out its functions under this Act, without regard to the provisions of other laws applicable to the employment and compensation of officers and employees of the United States, and the Commission may, subject to the civil-service laws, appoint such other officers and employees as are necessary in the execution of its functions and fix their salaries in accordance with the Classification Act of 1923, as amended.

TRANSACTIONS ON UNREGISTERED EXCHANGES

SEC. 5. It shall be unlawful for any broker, dealer, or exchange, directly or indirectly, to make use of the mails or any means or instrumentality of interstate commerce for the purpose of using any facility of an exchange within or subject to the jurisdiction of the United States to effect any transaction in a security, or to report any such transaction, unless such exchange (1) is registered as a national securities exchange under section 6 of this title, or (2) is exempted from such registration upon application by the exchange because, in the opinion of the Commission, by reason of the limited volume of transactions effected on such exchange, it is not practicable and not necessary or appropriate in the public interest or for the protection of investors to require such registration.

REGISTRATION OF NATIONAL SECURITIES EXCHANGES

SEC. 6. (a) Any exchange may be registered with the Commission as a national securities exchange under the terms and conditions hereinafter provided in this section, by filing a registration statement in such form as the Commission may prescribe, containing the agreements, setting forth the information, and accompanied by the documents, below specified:

(1) An agreement (which shall not be construed as a waiver of any constitutional right or any right to contest the validity of any rule or regulation) to comply, and to enforce so far as is within its powers compliance by its members, with the provisions of this title, and any amendment thereto and any rule or regulation made or to be made thereunder;

(2) Such data as to its organization, rules of procedure, and membership, and such other information as the Commission may by rules and regulations

require as being necessary or appropriate in the public interest or for the protection of investors;

(3) Copies of its constitution, articles of incorporation with all amendments thereto, and of its existing bylaws or rules or instruments corresponding thereto, whatever the name, which are hereinafter collectively referred to as the "rules of the exchange"; and

(4) An agreement to furnish to the Commission copies of any amendments to the rules of the exchange forthwith upon their adoption.

(b) No registration shall be granted or remain in force unless the rules of the exchange include provision for the expulsion, suspension, or disciplining of a member for conduct or proceeding inconsistent with just and equitable principles of trade, and declare that the willful violation of any provisions of this title or any rule or regulation thereunder shall be considered conduct or proceeding inconsistent with just and equitable principles of trade.

(c) Nothing in this title shall be construed to prevent any exchange from adopting and enforcing any rule not inconsistent with this title and the rules and regulations thereunder and the applicable laws of the State in which it is located.

(d) If it appears to the Commission that the exchange applying for registration is so organized as to be able to comply with the provisions of this title and the rules and regulations thereunder and that the rules of the exchange are just and adequate to insure fair dealing and to protect investors, the Commission shall cause such exchange to be registered as a national securities exchange.

(e) Within thirty days after the filing of the application, the Commission shall enter an order either granting or, after appropriate notice and opportunity for hearing, denying registration as a national securities exchange, unless the exchange applying for registration shall withdraw its application or consent to the Commission's deferring action on its application for a stated longer period after the date of filing. The filing with the Commission of an application for registration by an exchange shall be deemed to have taken place upon the receipt thereof. Amendments to an application may be made upon such terms as the Commission may prescribe.

(f) An exchange may, upon appropriate application in accordance with the rules and regulations of the Commission, and upon such terms as the Commission may deem necessary for the protection of investors, withdraw its registration.

MARGIN REQUIREMENTS

SEC. 7. (a) For the purpose of preventing the excessive use of credit for the purchase or carrying of securities, the Federal Reserve Board shall, prior to the effective date of this section and from time to time thereafter, prescribe rules and regulations with respect to the amount of credit that may be initially extended and subsequently maintained on any security (other than an exempted security) registered on a national securities exchange. For the initial extension of credit, such rules and regulations shall be based upon the following standard: An amount not greater than whichever is the higher of—

(1) 55 per centum of the current market price of the security, or

(2) 100 per centum of the lowest market price of the security during the preceding thirty-six calendar months, but not more than 75 per centum of the current market price.

Such rules and regulations may make appropriate provision with respect to the carrying of undermargined accounts for limited periods and under specified conditions; the withdrawal of funds or securities; the substitution or additional purchases of securities; the transfer of accounts from one lender to another; special or different margin requirements for delayed deliveries, short sales, arbitrage transactions, and securities to which paragraph (2) of this subsection does not apply; the bases and the methods to be used in calculating loans, and margins and market prices; and similar administrative adjustments and details. For the purposes of paragraph (2) of this subsection, until July 1, 1936, the lowest price at which a security has sold on or after July 1, 1933, shall be considered as the lowest price at which such security has sold during the preceding thirty-six calendar months.

(b) Notwithstanding the provisions of subsection (a) of this section, the Federal Reserve Board, may, from time to time, with respect to all or specified securities or transactions, or classes of securities, or classes of transactions, by such rules and regulations (1) prescribe such lower margin requirements for the initial extension or maintenance of credit as it deems necessary or appropriate for the accommodation of commerce and industry, having due regard to the general credit situation of the country, and (2) prescribe such higher margin requirements for the initial extension or maintenance of credit as it may deem necessary or appropriate to prevent the excessive use of credit to finance transactions in securities.

(c) It shall be unlawful for any member of a national securities exchange or any broker or dealer who transacts a business in securities through the medium of any such member, directly or indirectly to extend or maintain credit or arrange for the extension or maintenance of credit to or for any customer—

(1) On any security (other than an exempted security) registered on a national securities exchange, in contravention of the rules and regulations which the Federal Reserve Board shall prescribe under subsections (a) and (b) of this section.

(2) Without collateral or on any collateral other than exempted securities and/or securities registered upon a national securities exchange, except in accordance with such rules and regulations as the Federal Reserve Board may prescribe (A) to permit under specified conditions and for a limited period any such member, broker, or dealer to maintain a credit initially extended in conformity with the rules and regulations of the Federal Reserve Board, and (B) to permit the extension or maintenance of credit in cases where the extension or maintenance of credit is not for the purpose of purchasing or carrying securities or of evading or circumventing the provisions of paragraph (1) of this subsection.

(d) It shall be unlawful for any person not subject to subsection (c) to extend or maintain credit or to arrange for the extension or maintenance of credit for the purpose of purchasing or carrying any security registered on a national securities exchange, in contravention of such rules and regulations as the Federal Reserve Board shall prescribe to prevent the excessive use of credit for the purchasing or carrying of or trading in securities in circumvention of the other provisions of this section. Such rules and regulations may impose upon all loans made for the purpose of purchasing or carrying securities registered on national securities exchanges limitations similar to those imposed upon members, brokers, or dealers by subsection (c) of this section and the rules and regulations thereunder. This subsection and the rules and regulations thereunder shall not apply (A) to a loan made by a person not in the ordinary course of his business, (B) to a loan on an exempted security, (C) to a loan to a dealer to aid in the financing of the distribution of securities to customers not through the medium of a national securities exchange, (D) to a loan by a bank on a security other than an equity security, or (E) to such other loans as the Federal Reserve Board shall, by such rules and regulations as it may deem necessary or appropriate in the public interest or for the protection of investors, exempt, either unconditionally or upon specified terms and conditions or for stated periods, from the operation of this subsection and the rules and regulations thereunder.

(e) The provisions of this section or the rules and regulations thereunder shall not apply on or before July 1, 1937, to any loan or extension of credit made prior to the enactment of this title or to the maintenance, renewal, or extension of any such loan or credit, except to the extent that the Federal Reserve Board may by rules and regulations prescribe as necessary to prevent the circumvention of the provisions of this section or the rules and regulations thereunder by means of withdrawals of funds or securities, substitutions of securities, or additional purchases or by any other device.

RESTRICTIONS ON BORROWING BY MEMBERS, BROKERS, AND DEALERS

SEC. 8. It shall be unlawful for any member of a national securities exchange, or any broker or dealer who transacts a business in securities through the medium of any such member, directly or indirectly—

(a) To borrow in the ordinary course of business as a broker or dealer on any security (other than an exempted security) registered on a national securities exchange except (1) from or through a member bank of the Federal Reserve System, (2) from any nonmember bank which shall have filed with the Federal Reserve Board an agreement, which is still in force and which is in the form prescribed by the Board, undertaking to comply with all provisions of this Act, the Federal Reserve Act, as amended, and the Banking Act of 1933, which are applicable to member banks and which relate to the use of credit to finance transactions in securities, and with such rules and regulations as may be prescribed pursuant to such provisions of law or for the purpose of preventing evasions thereof, or (3) in accordance with such rules and regulations as the Federal Reserve Board may prescribe to permit loans between such members and/or brokers and/or dealers, or to permit loans to meet emergency needs. Any such agreement filed with the Federal Reserve Board shall be subject to termination at any time by order of the Board, after appropriate notice and opportunity for hearing, because of any failure by such bank to comply with the provisions thereof or with such provisions of law or rules or regulations; and, for any willful violation of such agreement, such bank shall be subject to the penalties provided for violations of rules and regulations prescribed under this title. The provisions of sections 21 and 25 of this title shall apply in the case of any such proceeding or order of the Federal Reserve Board in the same manner as such provisions apply in the case of proceedings and orders of the Commission.

(b) To permit in the ordinary course of business as a broker his aggregate indebtedness to all other persons, including customers' credit balances (but excluding indebtedness secured by exempted securities), to exceed such percentage of the net capital (exclusive of fixed assets and value of exchange membership) employed in the business, but not exceeding in any case 2,000 per centum, as the Commission may by rules and regulations prescribe as necessary or appropriate in the public interest or for the protection of investors.

(c) In contravention of such rules and regulations as the Commission shall prescribe for the protection of investors to hypothecate or arrange for the hypothecation of any securities carried for the account of any customer under circumstances (1) that will permit the commingling of his securities without his written consent with the securities of any other customer, (2) that will permit such securities to be commingled with the securities of any person other than a bona fide customer, or (3) that will permit such securities to be hypothecated, or subjected to any lien or claim of the pledgee, for a sum in excess of the aggregate indebtedness of such customers in respect of such securities.

(d) To lend or arrange for the lending of any securities carried for the account of any customer without the written consent of such customer.

PROHIBITION AGAINST MANIPULATION OF SECURITY PRICES

SEC. 9. (a) It shall be unlawful for any person, directly or indirectly, by the use of the mails or any means or instrumentality of interstate commerce, or of any facility of any national securities exchange, or for any member of a national securities exchange—

(1) For the purpose of creating a false or misleading appearance of active trading in any security registered on a national securities exchange, or a false or misleading appearance with respect to the market for any such security, (A) to effect any transaction in such security which involves no change in the beneficial ownership thereof, or (B) to enter an order or orders for the purchase of such security with the knowledge that an order or orders of substantially the same size, at substantially the same time, and at substantially the same price, for the sale of any such security, has been or will be entered by or for the same or different parties, or (C) to enter any order or orders for the sale of any such security with the knowledge that an order or orders of substantially the same size, at substantially the same time, and at substantially the same price, for the purchase of such security, has been or will be entered by or for the same or different parties.

(2) To effect, alone or with one or more other persons, a series of transactions in any security registered on a national securities exchange creating actual or apparent active trading in such security or raising or depressing the price of such security, for the purpose of inducing the purchase or sale of such security by others.

(3) If a dealer or broker, or other person selling or offering for sale or purchasing or offering to purchase the security, to induce the purchase or sale of any security registered on a national securities exchange by the circulation or dissemination in the ordinary course of business of information to the effect that the price of any such security will or is likely to rise or fall because of market operations of any one or more persons conducted for the purpose of raising or depressing the prices of such security.

(4) If a dealer or broker, or other person selling or offering for sale or purchasing or offering to purchase the security, to make, regarding any security registered on a national securities exchange, for the purpose of inducing the purchase or sale of such security, any statement which was at the same time and in the light of the circumstances under which it was made, false or misleading with respect to any material fact, and which he knew or had reasonable ground to believe was so false or misleading.

(5) For a consideration, received directly or indirectly from a dealer or

broker, or other person selling or offering for sale or purchasing or offering to purchase the security, to induce the purchase or sale of any security registered on a national securities exchange by the circulation or dissemination of information to the effect that the price of any such security will or is likely to rise or fall because of the market operations of any one or more persons conducted for the purpose of raising or depressing the price of such security.

(6) To effect either alone or with one or more other persons any series of transactions for the purchase and/or sale of any security registered on a national securities exchange for the purpose of pegging, fixing, or stabilizing the price of such security in contravention of such rules and regulations as the Commission may prescribe as necessary or appropriate in the public interest or for the protection of investors.

(b) It shall be unlawful for any person to effect, by use of any facility of a national securities exchange, in contravention of such rules and regulations as the Commission may prescribe as necessary or appropriate in the public interest or for the protection of investors—

(1) any transaction in connection with any security whereby any party to such transaction acquires any put, call, straddle, or other option or privilege of buying the security from or selling the security to another without being bound to do so; or

(2) any transaction in connection with any security with relation to which he has, directly or indirectly, any interest in any such put, call, straddle, option, or privilege; or

(3) any transaction in any security for the account of any person who he has reason to believe has, and who actually has, directly or indirectly, any interest in any such put, call, straddle, option, or privilege with relation to such security.

(c) It shall be unlawful for any member of a national securities exchange directly or indirectly to endorse or guarantee the performance of any put, call, straddle, option, or privilege in relation to any security registered on a national securities exchange, in contravention of such rules and regulations as the Commission may prescribe as necessary or appropriate in the public interest or for the protection of investors.

(d) The terms "put," "call," "straddle," "option," or "privilege" as used in this section shall not include any registered warrant, right, or convertible security.

(e) Any person who willfully participates in any act or transaction in violation of subsection (a), (b), or (c) of this section, shall be liable to any person who shall purchase or sell any security at a price which was affected by such act or transaction, and the person so injured may sue in law or in equity in any court of competent jurisdiction to recover the damages sustained as a result of any such act or transaction. In any such suit the court may, in its discretion, require an undertaking for the payment of the costs of such suit, and assess reasonable costs, including reasonable attorneys' fees, against either party litigant. Every person who becomes liable to make any payment under this subsection may recover contribution as in cases of contract from any person who, if joined in the original suit, would have been liable to make the same payment. No action shall be maintained to enforce any liability created under this section, unless brought within one year after the discovery of the facts constituting the violation and within three years after such violation.

(f) The provisions of this section shall not apply to an exempted security.

REGULATION OF THE USE OF MANIPULATIVE AND DECEPTIVE DEVICES

SEC. 10. It shall be unlawful for any person, directly or indirectly, by the use of any means or instrumentality of interstate commerce or of the mails, or of any facility of any national securities exchange—

(a) To effect a short sale, or to use or employ any stop-loss order in connection with the purchase or sale, of any security registered on a national securities exchange, in contravention of such rules and regulations as the Commission may prescribe as necessary or appropriate in the public interest or for the protection of investors.

(b) To use or employ, in connection with the purchase or sale of any security registered on a national securities exchange or any security not so registered, any manipulative or deceptive device or contrivance in contravention of such rules and regulations as the Commission may prescribe as necessary or appropriate in the public interest or for the protection of investors.

SEGREGATION AND LIMITATION OF FUNCTIONS OF MEMBERS, BROKERS, AND DEALERS

SEC. 11. (a) The Commission shall prescribe such rules and regulations as it deems necessary or appropriate in the public interest or for the protection of investors, (1) to regulate or prevent floor trading by members of national securities exchanges, directly or indirectly for their own account or for discretionary accounts, and (2) to prevent such excessive trading on the exchange but off the floor by members, directly or indirectly for their own account, as the Commission may deem detrimental to the maintenance of a fair and orderly market. It shall be unlawful for a member to effect any transaction in a security in contravention of such rules and regulations, but such rules and regulations may make such exemptions for arbitrage transactions, for transactions in exempted securities, and, within the limitations of subsection (b) of this section, for transactions by odd-lot dealers and specialists, as the Commission may deem necessary or appropriate in the public interest or for the protection of investors.

(b) When not in contravention of such rules and regulations as the Commission may prescribe as necessary or appropriate in the public interest or for the protection of investors, the rules of a national securities exchange may permit (1) a member to be registered as an odd-lot dealer and as such to buy and sell for his own account so far as may be reasonably necessary to carry on such odd-lot transactions, and/or (2) a member to be registered as a specialist If under the rules and regulations of the Commission a specialist is permitted to act as a dealer, or is limited to acting as a dealer, such rules and regulations shall restrict his dealings so far as practicable to those reasonably necessary to permit him to maintain a fair and orderly market, and/or to those necessary to permit him to act as an odd-lot dealer if the rules of the exchange permit him to act as an odd-lot dealer. It shall be unlawful for a specialist or an official of the exchange to disclose information in regard to orders placed with such specialist which is not available to all members of the exchange, to any person other than an official of the exchange, a representative of the Commission, or a specialist who may be acting for such specialist; but the Commission shall have power to require disclosure to all members of the exchange of all orders placed with specialists, under such rules and regulations as the Commission may prescribe as necessary or appropriate in the public interest or for the protection of investors. It shall also be unlawful for a specialist acting as a broker to effect on the exchange any transaction except upon a market or limited price order.

(c) If because of the limited volume of transactions effected on an exchange, it is in the opinion of the Commission impracticable and not necessary or appropriate in the public interest or for the protection of investors to apply any of the foregoing provisions of this section or the rules and regulations thereunder, the Commission shall have power, upon application of the exchange and on a showing that the rules of such exchange are otherwise adequate for the protection of investors, to exempt such exchange and its members from any such provision or rules and regulations.

(d) It shall be unlawful for a member of a national securities exchange who is both a dealer and a broker, or for any person who both as a broker and a dealer transacts a business in securities through the medium of a member or otherwise, to effect through the use of any facility of a national securities exchange or of the mails or of any means or instrumentality of interstate commerce, or otherwise in the case of a member, (1) any transaction in connection with which, directly or indirectly, he extends or maintains or arranges for the extension or maintenance of credit to or for a customer on any security (other than an exempted security) which was a part of a new issue in the distribution of which he participated as a member of a selling syndicate or group within six months prior to such transaction: *Provided,* That credit shall not be deemed extended by reason of a bona fide delayed delivery of any such security against full payment of the entire purchase price thereof upon such delivery within thirty-five days after such purchase, or (2) any transaction with respect to any security (other than an exempted security) unless, if the transaction is with a customer, he discloses to such customer in writing at or before the completion of the transaction whether he is acting as a dealer for his own account, as a broker for such customer, or as a broker for some other person.

(e) The Commission is directed to make a study of the feasibility and advisability of the complete segregation of the functions of dealer and broker, and to report the results of its study and its recommendations to the Congress on or before January 3, 1936.

REGISTRATION REQUIREMENTS FOR SECURITY

SEC. 12. (a) It shall be unlawful for any member, broker, or dealer to effect any transaction in any security (other than an exempted security) on a national securities exchange unless a registration is effective as to such security for such exchange in accordance with the provisions of this title and the rules and regulations thereunder.

(b) A security may be registered on a national securities exchange by the issuer filing an application with the exchange (and filing with the Commission such duplicate originals thereof as the Commission may require), which application shall contain—

(1) Such information, in such detail, as to the issuer and any person directly or indirectly controlling or controlled by, or under direct or indirect common control with, the issuer, and any guarantor of the security as to principal or interest or both, as the Commission may by rules and regulations require, as necessary or appropriate in the public interest or for the protection of investors, in respect of the following:

(A) the organization, financial structure and nature of the business;

(B) the terms, position, rights, and privileges of the different classes of securities outstanding;

(C) the terms on which their securities are to be, and during the preceding three years have been, offered to the public or otherwise;

(D) the directors, officers, and underwriters, and each security holder of record holding more than 10 per centum of any class of any equity security of the issuer (other than an exempted security), their remuneration and their interests in the securities of, and their material contracts with, the issuer and any person directly or indirectly controlling or controlled by, or under direct or indirect common control with, the issuer;

(E) remuneration to others than directors and officers exceeding $20,000 per annum;

(F) bonus and profit-sharing arrangements;

(G) management and service contracts;

(H) options existing or to be created in respect of their securities;

(I) balance sheets for not more than the three preceding fiscal years, certified if required by the rules and regulations of the Commission by independent public accountants;

(J) profit and loss statements for not more than the three preceding fiscal years, certified if required by the rules and regulations of the Commission by independent public accountants; and

(K) any further financial statements which the Commission may deem necessary or appropriate for the protection of investors.

(2) Such copies of articles of incorporation, bylaws, trust indentures, or corresponding documents by whatever name known, underwriting arrangements, and other similar documents of, and voting trust agreements with respect to, the issuer and any person directly or indirectly controlling or controlled by, or under direct or indirect common control with, the issuer as the Commission may require as necessary or appropriate for the proper protection of investors and to insure fair dealing in the security.

(c) If in the judgment of the Commission any information required under subsection (b) is inapplicable to any specified class or classes of issuers, the Commission shall require in lieu thereof the submission of such other information of comparable character as it may deem applicable to such class of issuers.

(d) If the exchange authorities certify to the Commission that the security has been approved by the exchange for listing and registration, the registration shall become effective thirty days after the receipt of such certification by the Commission or within such shorter period of time as the Commission may determine. A security registered with a national securities exchange may be withdrawn or stricken from listing and registration in accordance with the rules of the exchange and, upon such terms as the Commission may deem necessary to impose for the protection of investors, upon application by the issuer or the exchange to the Commission; whereupon the issuer shall be relieved from further compliance with the provisions of this section and section 13 of this title and any rules or regulations under such sections as to the securities so withdrawn or stricken. An unissued security may be registered only in accordance with such rules and regulations as the Commission may prescribe as necessary or appropriate in the public interest or for the protection of investors. Such rules and regulations shall limit the registration of an unissued security to cases where such security is a right or the subject of a right to subscribe or otherwise acquire such security granted to holders of a previously registered security and where the primary purpose of such registration is to distribute such unissued security to such holders.

(e) Notwithstanding the foregoing provisions of this section, the Commission may by such rules and regulations as it deems necessary or appropriate in the public interest or for the protection of investors permit securities listed on any exchange at the time the registration of such exchange as a national securities exchange becomes effective, to be registered for a period ending not later than July 1, 1935, without complying with the provisions of this section.

(f) Notwithstanding the foregoing provisions of this section, any national securities exchange, upon application to and approval of such application by the Commission and subject to the terms and conditions hereinafter set forth, (1) may continue unlisted trading privileges to which a security had been admitted on such exchange prior to March 1, 1934; or (2) may extend unlisted trading privileges to any security duly listed and registered on any other national securities exchange, but such unlisted trading privileges shall continue in effect only so long as such security shall remain listed and registered on any other national securities exchange;[2] or (3) may extend unlisted trading privileges to any security in respect of which there is available from a registration statement and periodic reports or other data filed pursuant to rules or regulations pescribed by the Commission under this title or the Securities Act of 1933, as amended, information substantially equivalent to that available pursuant to rules or regulations of the Commission in respect of a security duly listed and registered on a national securities exchange, but such unlisted trading privileges shall continue in effect only so long as such a registration statement remains effective and such periodic reports or other data continue to be so filed.[3]

No application pursuant to this subsection shall be approved unless the Commission finds that the continuation or extension of unlisted trading privileges pursuant to such application is necessary or appropriate in the public interest or for the protection of investors. No application to extend unlisted trading privileges to any security pursuant to clause (2) or (3) of this subsection shall be approved except after appropriate notice and opportunity for hearing. No application to extend unlisted trading privileges to any security pursuant to clause (2) or (3) of this subsection shall be approved unless the applicant exchange shall establish to the satisfaction of the Commission that there exists in the vicinity of such exchange sufficiently widespread public distribution of such security and sufficient public trading activity therein to render the extension of unlisted trading privileges on such exchange thereto necessary or appropriate in the public interest or for the protection of investors. No application to extend unlisted trading privileges to any security pursuant to clause (3) of this subsection shall be approved except upon such terms and conditions as will subject the issuer thereof, the officers and directors of such issuer, and every beneficial owner of more than 10 per centum of such security to duties substantially equivalent to the duties which would arise pursuant to

---

[2] By sec. 12 of Public, No. 621, 74th Cong., the provisions of this clause do not become effective until 90 days after May 27, 1936.

[3] By sec. 12 of Public, No. 621, 74th Cong., the provisions of this clause do not become effective until 6 months after May 27, 1936.

this title if such security were duly listed and registered on a national securities exchange; except that such terms and conditions need not be imposed in any case or class of cases in which it shall appear to the Commission that the public interest and the protection of investors would nevertheless best be served by such extension of unlisted trading privileges. In the publication or making available for publication by any national securities exchange, or by any person directly or indirectly controlled by such exchange, of quotations or transactions in securities made or effected upon such exchange, such exchange or controlled person shall clearly differentiate between quotations or transactions in listed securities, and quotations or transactions in securities for which unlisted trading privileges on such exchange have been continued or extended pursuant to this subsection. In the publication or making available for publication of such quotations or transactions otherwise than by ticker, such exchange or controlled person shall group under separate headings (A) quotations or transactions in listed securities, and (B) quotations or transactions in securities for which unlisted trading privileges on such exchange have been continued or extended pursuant to this subsection.

The Commission shall by rules and regulations suspend unlisted trading privileges in whole or in part for any or all classes of securities for a period not exceeding twelve months, if it deems such suspension necessary or appropriate in the public interest or for the protection of investors or to prevent evasion of the purposes of this title.

Unlisted trading privileges continued for any security pursuant to clause (1) of this subsection shall be terminated by order, after appropriate notice and opportunity for hearing, if it appears at any time that such security has been withdrawn from listing on any exchange by the issuer thereof, unless it shall be established to the satisfaction of the Commission that such delisting was not designed to evade the purposes of this title or unless it shall appear to the Commission that, notwithstanding any such purpose of evasion, the continuation of such unlisting trading privileges is nevertheless necessary or appropriate in the public interest or for the protection of investors. On the application of the issuer of any security for which unlisted trading privileges on any exchange have been continued or extended pursuant to this subsection, or of any broker or dealer who makes or creates a market for such security, or of any other person having a bona-fide interest in the question of termination or suspension of such unlisted trading privileges, or on its own motion, the Commission shall by order terminate, or suspend for a period not exceeding twelve months, such unlisted trading privileges for such security if the Commission finds, after appropriate notice and opportunity for hearing, that by reason of inadequate public distribution of such security in the vicinity of said exchange, or by reason of inadequate public trading activity or of the character of trading therein on said exchange, such termination or suspension is necessary or appropriate in the public interest or for the protection of investors.

In any proceeding under this subsection in which appropriate notice and opportunity for hearing are required, notice of not less than ten days to the applicant in such proceeding, to the issuer of the security involved, to the exchange which is seeking to continue or extend or

has continued or extended unlisted trading privileges for such security, and to the exchange, if any, on which such security is listed and registered, shall be deemed adequate notice, and any broker or dealer who makes or creates a market for such security, and any other person having a bona-fide interest in such proceeding, shall upon application be entitled to be heard.

Any security for which unlisted trading privileges are continued or extended pursuant to this subsection shall be deemed to be registered on a national securities exchange within the meaning of this title. The powers and duties of the Commission under subsection (b) of section 19 of this title shall be applicable to the rules of an exchange in respect of any such security. The Commission may, by such rules and regulations as it deems necessary or appropriate in the public interest or for the protection of investors, either unconditionally or upon specified terms and conditions, or for stated periods, exempt such securities from the operation of any provision of section 13, 14, or 16 of this title.[4]

PERIODICAL AND OTHER REPORTS

SEC. 13. (a) Every issuer of a security registered on a national securities exchange shall file the information, documents, and reports below specified with the exchange (and shall file with the Commission such duplicate originals thereof as the Commission may require), in accordance with such rules and regulations

---

[4] Attention is directed to sec. 2 of Public, No. 621, 74th Cong., which reads:

SEC. 2. Any application to continue unlisted trading privileges for any security heretofore filed by any exchange and approved by the Commission pursuant to clause (1) of subsection (f) of section 12 of the Securities Exchange Act of 1934 and rules and regulations thereunder shall be deemed to have been filed and approved pursuant to clause (1) of said subsection (f) as amended by section 1 of this act.

Prior to the amendment sec. 12 (f) read as follows:

(f) The Commission is directed to make a study of trading in unlisted securities upon exchanges and to report the results of its study and its recommendations to Congress on or before January 3, 1936. Notwithstanding the foregoing provisions of this section, the Commission may, by such rules and regulations as it deems necessary or appropriate for the protection of investors, prescribe terms and conditions under which, upon the application of any national securities exchange, such exchange (1) may continue until June 1, 1936, unlisted trading privileges to which a security had been admitted on such exchange prior to March 1, 1934, and for such purpose exempt such security and the issuer thereof from the provisions of this section and sections 13 and 16, or (2) may extend until July 1, 1935, unlisted trading privileges to any security registered on any other national securities exchange which security was listed on such other exchange on March 1, 1934. A security for which unlisted trading privileges are so continued shall be considered a "security registered on a national securities exchange" within the meaning of this title. The rules and regulations of the Commission relating to such unlisted trading privileges for securities shall require that quotations of transactions upon any national securities exchange shall clearly indicate the difference between fully listed securities and securities admitted to unlisted trading privileges only.

as the Commission may prescribe as necessary or appropriate for the proper protection of investors and to insure fair dealing in the security—

(1) Such information and documents as the Commission may require to keep reasonably current the information and documents filed pursuant to section 12.

(2) Such annual reports, certified if required by the rules and regulations of the Commission by independent public accountants, and such quarterly reports, as the Commission may prescribe.

(b) The Commission may prescribe, in regard to reports made pursuant to this title, the form or forms in which the required information shall be set forth, the items or details to be shown in the balance sheet and the earning statement, and the methods to be followed in the preparation of reports, in the appraisal or valuation of assets and liabilities, in the determination of depreciation and depletion, in the differentiation of recurring and nonrecurring income, in the differentiation of investment and operating income, and in the preparation, where the Commission deems it necessary or desirable, of separate and/or consolidated balance sheets or income accounts of any person directly or indirectly controlling or controlled by the issuer, or any person under direct or indirect common control with the issuer; but in the case of the reports of any person whose methods of accounting are prescribed under the provisions of any law of the United States, or any rule or regulation thereunder, the rules and regulations of the Commission with respect to reports shall not be inconsistent with the requirements imposed by such law or rule or regulation in respect of the same subject matter, and, in the case of carriers subject to the provisions of section 20 of the Interstate Commerce Act, as amended, or carriers required pursuant to any other Act of Congress to make reports of the same general character as those required under such section 20, shall permit such carriers to file with the Commission and the exchange duplicate copies of the reports and other documents filed with the Interstate Commerce Commission, or with the governmental authority administering such other Act of Congress, in lieu of the reports, information and documents required under this section and section 12 in respect of the same subject matter.

(c) If in the judgment of the Commission any report required under subsection (a) is inapplicable to any specified class or classes of issuers, the Commission shall require in lieu thereof of the submission of such reports of comparable character as it may deem applicable to such class or classes of issuers.

PROXIES

Sec. 14. (a) It shall be unlawful for any person, by the use of the mails or by any means or instrumentality of interstate commerce or of any facility of any national securities exchange or otherwise to solicit or to permit the use of his name to solicit any proxy or consent or authorization in respect of any security (other than an exempted security) registered on any national securities exchange in contravention of such rules and regulations as the Commission may prescribe as necessary or appropriate in the public interest or for the protection of investors.

(b) It shall be unlawful for any member of a national securities exchange or any broker or dealer who transacts a business in securities through the medium of any such member to give a proxy, consent, or authorization in respect of any security registered on a national securities exchange and carried for the account of a customer in contravention of such rules and regulations as the Commission may prescribe as necessary or appropriate in the public interest or for the protection of investors.

OVER-THE-COUNTER MARKETS

Sec. 15. (a) No broker or dealer (other than one whose business is exclusively intrastate) shall make use of the mails or of any means or instrumentality of interstate commerce to effect any transaction in, or to induce the purchase or sale of, any security (other than an exempted security or commercial paper, bankers' acceptances, or commercial bills) otherwise than on a national securities exchange, unless such broker or dealer is registered in accordance with subsection (b) of this section.[5]

(b) A broker or dealer may be registered for the purposes of this section by filing with the Commission an application for registration, which shall contain such information in such detail as to such broker or dealer and any person directly or indirectly controlling or controlled by, or under direct or indirect common control with, such broker or dealer, as the Commission may by rules and regulations require as necessary or appropriate in the public interest or for the protection of investors. Except as hereinafter provided, such registration shall become effective thirty days after the receipt of such application by the Commission or within such shorter period of time as the Commission may determine.

An application for registration of a broker or dealer to be formed or organized may be made by a broker or dealer to which the broker or dealer to be formed or organized is to be the successor. Such application shall contain such information in such detail as to the applicant and as to the successor and any person directly or indirectly controlling or controlled by, or under direct or indirect common control with, the applicant or the successor, as the Commission may by rules and regulations require as necessary or appropriate in the public interest or for the protection of investors. Except as hereinafter provided, such registration shall become effective thirty days after the receipt of such application by the Commission or within such shorter period of time as the Commission may determine. Such registration shall terminate on the forty-fifth day after the effective date thereof, unless prior thereto the successor shall, in accordance with such rules and regulations as the Commission may prescribe, adopt such application as its own.

If any amendment to any application for registration pursuant to this subsection is filed prior to the effective date thereof, such amendment shall be deemed to have been filed simultaneously with and as part of such application; except that the Commission may, if it appears necessary or appropriate in the public interest or for the protection of investors, defer the effective date of any such registration as thus amended until the thirtieth day after the filing of such amendment.

The Commission shall, after appropriate notice and opportunity for hearing, by order deny registration to or revoke the registration of any

[5] By sec. 12 of Public, No. 621, 74th Cong., the provisions of this subsection do not become effective until 90 days after May 27, 1936.

broker or dealer if it finds that such denial or revocation is in the public interest and that (1) such broker or dealer whether prior or subsequent to becoming such, or (2) any partner, officer, director, or branch manager of such broker or dealer (or any person occupying a similar status or performing similar functions), or any person directly or indirectly controlling or controlled by such broker or dealer, whether prior or subsequent to becoming such, (A) has willfully made or caused to be made in any application for registration pursuant to this subsection or in any document supplemental thereto or in any proceeding before the Commission with respect to registration pursuant to this subsection any statement which was at the time and in the light of the circumstances under which it was made false or misleading with respect to any material fact; or (B) has been convicted within ten years preceding the filing of any such application or at any time thereafter of any felony or misdemeanor involving the purchase or sale of any security or arising out of the conduct of the business of a broker or dealer; or (C) is permanently or temporarily enjoined by order, judgment, or decree of any court of competent jurisdiction from engaging in or continuing any conduct or practice in connection with the purchase or sale of any security; or (D) has willfully violated any provision of the Securities Act of 1933, as amended, or of this title, or of any rule or regulation thereunder. Pending final determination whether any such registration shall be denied, the Commission may by order postpone the effective date of such registration for a period not to exceed fifteen days, but if, after appropriate notice and opportunity for hearing, it shall appear to the Commission to be necessary or appropriate in the public interest or for the protection of investors to postpone the effective date of such registration until final determination, the Commission shall so order. Pending final determination whether any such registration shall be revoked, the Commission shall by order suspend such registration if, after appropriate notice and opportunity for hearing, such suspension shall appear to the Commission to be necessary or appropriate in the public interest or for the protection of investors. Any registered broker or dealer may, upon such terms and conditions as the Commission may deem necessary in the public interest or for the protection of investors, withdraw from registration by filing a written notice of withdrawal with the Commission. If the Commission finds that any registered broker or dealer, or any broker or dealer for whom an application for registration is pending, is no longer in existence or has ceased to do business as a broker or dealer, the Commission shall by order cancel the registration or application of such broker or dealer.

(c) No broker or dealer shall make use of the mails or of any means or instrumentality of interstate commerce to effect any transaction in, or to induce the purchase or sale of, any security (other than commercial paper, bankers' acceptances, or commercial bills) otherwise than on a national securities exchange, by means of any manipulative, deceptive, or other fraudulent device or contrivance. The Commission shall, for the purposes of this subsection, by rules and regulations define such devices or contrivances as are manipulative, deceptive, or otherwise fraudulent.

(d) Each registration statement hereafter filed pursuant to the Securities Act of 1933, as amended, shall contain an undertaking by the issuer of the issue of securities to which the registration statement relates to file with the Commission, in accordance with such rules and regulations as the Commission may prescribe as necessary or appropriate in the public interest or for the protection of investors, such supplementary and periodic information, documents, and reports as may be required pursuant to section 13 of this title in respect of a security listed and registered on a national securities exchange; but such undertaking shall become operative only if the aggregate offering price of such issue of securities, plus the aggregate value of all other securities of such issuer of the same class (as hereinafter defined) outstanding, computed upon the basis of such offering price, amounts to $2,000,000 or more. The issuer shall file such supplementary and periodic information, documents, and reports pursuant to such undertaking, except that the duty to file shall be automatically suspended if and so long as (1) such issue of securities is listed and registered on a national securities exchange, or (2) by reason of the listing and registration of any other security of such issuer on a national securities exchange, such issuer is required to file pursuant to section 13 of this title information, documents, and reports substantially equivalent to such as would be required if such issue of securities were listed and registered on a national securities exchange, or (3) the aggregate value of all outstanding securities of the class to which such issue belongs is reduced to less than $1,000,000, computed upon the basis of the offering price of the last issue of securities of said class offered to the public. For the purposes of this subsection, the term "class" shall be construed to include all securities of an issuer which are of substantially similar character and the holders of which enjoy substantially similar rights and privileges. Nothing in this subsection shall apply to securities issued by a foreign government or political subdivision thereof or to any other security which the Commission may by rules and regulations exempt as not comprehended within the purposes of this subsection.[6]

---

[6] By sec. 12 of Public, No. 621, 74th Cong., the provisions of this subsection do not become effective until 90 days after May 27, 1936.

Attention is directed to sections 10 and 11 of Public, No. 621, 74th Cong., which reads:

SEC. 10. All brokers and dealers for whom registration is in effect on the date of enactment of this Act in accordance with rules and regulations of the Commission prescribed pursuant to section 15 of the Securities Exchange Act of 1934 shall be deemed to be registered pursuant to section 15 of such Act as amended by section 3 of this Act.

SEC. 11. Nothing in this Act shall be deemed to extinguish any liability which may have arisen prior to the effective date of this Act by reason of any violation of section 15 of the Securities Exchange Act of 1934 or of any rule or regulation thereunder.

Prior to the amendment sec. 15 read as follows:

SEC. 15. It shall be unlawful, in contravention of such rules and regulations as the Commission may prescribe as necessary or appropriate in the public interest and to insure to investors protection comparable to that provided by and under authority of this title in the case of national securities exchanges,

DIRECTORS, OFFICERS, AND PRINCIPAL STOCKHOLDERS

SEC. 16. (a) Every person who is directly or indirectly the beneficial owner of more than 10 per centum of any class of any equity security (other than an exempted security) which is registered on a national securities exchange, or who is a director or an officer of the issuer of such security, shall file, at the time of the registration of such security or within ten days after he becomes such beneficial owner, director, or officer, a statement with the exchange (and a duplicate original thereof with the Commission) of the amount of all equity securities of such issuer of which he is the beneficial owner, and within ten days after the close of each calendar month thereafter, if there has been any change in such ownership during such month, shall file with the exchange a statement (and a duplicate original thereof with the Commission) indicating his ownership at the close of the calendar month and such changes in his ownership as have occurred during such calendar month.

(b) For the purpose of preventing the unfair use of information which may have been obtained by such beneficial owner, director, or officer by reason of his relationship to the issuer, any profit realized by him from any purchase and sale, or any sale and purchase, of any equity security of such issuer (other than an exempted security) within any period of less than six months, unless such security was acquired in good faith in connection with a debt previously contracted, shall inure to and be recoverable by the issuer, irrespective of any intention on the part of such beneficial owner, director, or officer in entering into such transaction of holding the security purchased or of not repurchasing the security sold for a period exceeding six months. Suit to recover such profit may be instituted at law or in equity in any court of competent jurisdiction by the issuer, or by the owner of any security of the issuer in the name and in behalf of the issuer if the issuer shall fail or refuse to bring such suit within sixty days after request or shall fail diligently to prosecute the same thereafter; but no such suit shall be brought more than two years after the date such profit was realized. This subsection shall not be construed to cover any transaction where such beneficial owner was not such both at the time of the purchase and sale, or the sale and purchase, of the security involved, or any transaction or transactions which the Commission by rules and regulations may exempt as not comprehended within the purpose of this subsection.

---

(1) for any broker or dealer, singly or with any other person or persons, to make use of the mails or any means or instrumentality of interstate commerce for the purpose of making or creating, or enabling another to make or create, a market, otherwise than on a national securities exchange, for both the purchase and sale of any security (other than an exempted security or commercial paper, bankers' acceptances, or commercial bills, or unregistered securities the market in which is predominantly intrastate and which have not previously been registered or listed), or (2) for any broker or dealer to use any facility of any such market. Such rules and regulations may provide for the regulation of all transactions by brokers and dealers on any such market, for the registration with the Commission of dealers and/or brokers making, or creating such a market, and for the registration of the securities for which they make or create a market and may make special provision with respect to securities or specified classes thereof listed, or entitled to unlisted trading privileges, upon any exchange on the date of the enactment of this title, which securities are not registered under the provisions of section 12 of this title.

(c) It shall be unlawful for any such beneficial owner, director, or officer, directly or indirectly, to sell any equity security of such issuer (other than an exempted security), if the person selling the security or his principal (1) does not own the security sold, or (2) if owning the security, does not deliver it against such sale within twenty days thereafter, or does not within five days after such sale deposit it in the mails or other usual channels of transportation; but no person shall be deemed to have violated this subsection if he proves that notwithstanding the exercise of good faith he was unable to make such delivery or deposit within such time, or that to do so would cause undue inconvenience or expense.

(d) The provisions of this section shall not apply to foreign or domestic arbitrage transactions unless made in contravention of such rules and regulations as the Commission may adopt in order to carry out the purposes of this section.

ACCOUNTS AND RECORDS, REPORTS, EXAMINATIONS OF EXCHANGES, MEMBERS, AND OTHERS

SEC. 17. (a) Every national securities exchange, every member thereof, every broker or dealer who transacts a business in securities through the medium of any such member, and **every broker or dealer registered pursuant to section 15 of this title,**[7] shall make, keep, and preserve for such periods, such accounts, correspondence, memoranda, papers, books, and other records, and make such reports, as the Commission by its rules and regulations may prescribe as necessary or appropriate in the public interest or for the protection of investors. Such accounts, correspondence, memoranda, papers, books, and other records shall be subject at any time or from time to time to such reasonable periodic, special, or other examinations by examiners or other representatives of the Commission as the Commission may deem necessary or appropriate in the public interest or for the protection of investors.

(b) Any broker, dealer, or other person extending credit who is subject to the rules and regulations prescribed by the Federal Reserve Board pursuant to this title shall make such reports to the Board as it may require as necessary or appropriate to enable it to perform the functions conferred upon it by this title. If any such broker, dealer, or other person shall fail to make any such report or fail to furnish full information therein, or, if in the judgment of the Board it is otherwise necessary, such broker, dealer, or other person shall permit such inspections to be made by the Board with respect to the business operations of such broker, dealer, or other person as the Board may deem necessary to enable it to obtain the required information.

LIABILITY FOR MISLEADING STATEMENTS

SEC. 18. (a) Any person who shall make or cause to be made any statement in any application, report, or document filed pursuant to this title or any rule or regulation thereunder **or any undertaking contained in a registration**

---

[7] Sec. 4 of Public, No. 621, 74th Cong., substituted the matter appearing in bold-face type for "every broker or dealer making or creating a market for both the purchase and sale of securities through the use of the mails or of any means or instrumentality of interstate commerce," which was deleted by that amendment.

statement as provided in subsection (d) of section 15 of this title, which statement was at the time and in the light of the circumstances under which it was made false or misleading with respect to any material fact, shall be liable to any person (not knowing that such statement was false or misleading) who, in reliance upon such statement, shall have purchased or sold a security at a price which was affected by such statement, for damages caused by such reliance, unless the person sued shall prove that he acted in good faith and had no knowledge that such statement was false or misleading. A person seeking to enforce such liability may sue at law or in equity in any court of competent jurisdiction. In any such suit the court may, in its discretion, require an undertaking for the payment of the costs of such suit, and assess reasonable costs, including reasonable attorneys' fees, against either party litigant.

(b) Every person who becomes liable to make payment under this section may recover contribution as in cases of contract from any person who, if joined in the original suit, would have been liable to make the same payment.

(c) No action shall be maintained to enforce any liability created under this section unless brought within one year after the discovery of the facts constituting the cause of action and within three years after such cause of action accrued.

POWERS WITH RESPECT TO EXCHANGES AND SECURITIES

SEC. 19. (a) The Commission is authorized, if in its opinion such action is necessary or appropriate for the protection of investors—

(1) After appropriate notice and opportunity for hearing, by order to suspend for a period not exceeding twelve months or to withdraw the registration of a national securities exchange if the Commission finds that such exchange has violated any provision of this title or of the rules and regulations thereunder or has failed to enforce, so far as is within its power, compliance therewith by a member or by an issuer of a security registered thereon.

(2) After appropriate notice and opportunity for hearing, by order to deny, to suspend the effective date of, to suspend for a period not exceeding twelve months, or to withdraw, the registration of a security if the Commission finds that the issuer of such security has failed to comply with any provision of this title or the rules and regulations thereunder.

(3) After appropriate notice and opportunity for hearing, by order to suspend for a period not exceeding twelve months or to expel from a national securities exchange any member or officer thereof whom the Commission finds has violated any provision of this title or the rules and regulations thereunder, or has effected any transaction for any other person who, he has reason to believe, is violating in respect of such transaction any provision of this title or the rules and regulations thereunder.

(4) And if in its opinion the public interest so requires, summarily to suspend trading in any registered security on any national securities exchange for a period not exceeding ten days, or with the approval of the President, summarily to suspend all trading on any national securities exchange for a period not exceeding ninety days.

(b) The Commission is further authorized, if after making appropriate request in writing to a national securities exchange that such exchange effect on its own behalf specified changes in its rules and practices, and after appropriate notice and opportunity for hearing, the Commission determines that such exchange has not made the changes so requested, and that such changes are necessary or appropriate for the protection of investors or to insure fair dealing in securities traded in upon such exchange or to insure fair administration of such exchange, by rules or regulations or by order to alter or supplement the rules of such exchange (insofar as necessary or appropriate to effect such changes) in respect of such matters as (1) safeguards in respect of the financial responsibility of members and adequate provision against the evasion of financial responsibility through the use of corporate forms or special partnerships; (2) the limitation or prohibition of the registration or trading in any security within a specified period after the issuance or primary distribution thereof; (3) the listing or striking from listing of any security; (4) hours of trading; (5) the manner, method, and place of soliciting business; (6) fictitious or numbered accounts; (7) the time and method of making settlements, payments, and deliveries and of closing accounts; (8) the reporting of transactions on the exchange and upon tickers maintained by or with the consent of the exchange, including the method of reporting short sales, stopped sales, sales of securities of issuers in default, bankruptcy or receivership, and sales involving other special circumstances; (9) the fixing of reasonable rates of commission, interest, listing, and other charges; (10) minimum units of trading; (11) odd-lot purchases and sales; (12) minimum deposits on margin accounts; and (13) similar matters.

(c) The Commission is authorized and directed to make a study and investigation of the rules of national securities exchanges with respect to the classification of members, the methods of election of officers and committees to insure a fair representation of the membership, and the suspension, expulsion, and disciplining of members of such exchanges. The Commission shall report to the Congress on or before January 3, 1935, the results of its investigation, together with its recommendations.

LIABILITIES OF CONTROLLING PERSONS

SEC. 20. (a) Every person who, directly or indirectly, controls any person liable under any provision of this title or of any rule or regulation thereunder shall also be liable jointly and severally with and to the same extent as such controlled person to any person to whom such controlled person is liable, unless the controlling person acted in good faith and did not directly or indirectly induce the act or acts constituting the violation or cause of action.

(b) It shall be unlawful for any person, directly or indirectly, to do any act or thing which it would be unlawful for such person to do under the provisions of this title or any rule or regulation thereunder through or by means of any other person.

(c) It shall be unlawful for any director or officer of, or any owner of any of the securities issued by, any issuer of any security registered on a national securities exchange, without just cause to hinder, delay, or obstruct the making or filing of any document, report, or information, required to be filed under this title or any rule or regulation thereunder **or any undertaking contained in a registration statement as provided in subsection (d) of section 15 of this title.**

INVESTIGATIONS; INJUNCTIONS AND PROSECUTION OF OFFENSES

SEC. 21. (a) The Commission may, in its discretion, make such investigations as it deems necessary to determine whether any person has violated or is about to violate any provision of this title or any rule or regulation thereunder, and may require or permit any person to file with it a statement in writing, under oath or otherwise as the Commission shall determine, as to all the facts and circumstances concerning the matter to be investigated. The Commission is authorized, in its discretion, to publish information concerning any such violations, and to investigate any facts, conditions, practices, or matters which it may deem necessary or proper to aid in the enforcement of the provisions of this title, in the prescribing of rules and regulations thereunder, or in securing information to serve as a basis for recommending further legislation concerning the matters to which this title relates.

(b) For the purpose of any such investigation, or any other proceeding under this title, any member of the Commission or any officer designated by it is empowered to administer oaths and affirmations, subpena witnesses, compel their attendance, take evidence, and require the production of any books, papers, correspondence, memoranda, or other records which the Commission deems relevant or material to the inquiry. Such attendance of witnesses and the production of any such records may be required from any place in the United States or any State at any designated place of hearing.

(c) In case of contumacy by, or refusal to obey a subpena issued to, any person, the Commission may invoke the aid of any court of the United States within the jurisdiction of which such investigation or proceeding is carried on, or where such person resides or carries on business, in requiring the attendance and testimony of witnesses and the production of books, papers, correspondence, memoranda, and other records. And such court may issue an order requiring such person to appear before the Commission or member or officer designated by the Commission, there to produce records, if so ordered, or to give testimony touching the matter under investigation or in question; and any failure to obey such order of the court may be punished by such court as a contempt thereof. All process in any such case may be served in the judicial district whereof such person is an inhabitant or wherever he may be found. Any person who shall, without just cause, fail or refuse to attend and testify or to answer any lawful inquiry or to produce books, papers, correspondence, memoranda, and other records, if in his power so to do, in obedience to the subpena of the Commission, shall be guilty of a misdemeanor and, upon conviction, shall be subject to a fine of not more than $1,000 or to imprisonment for a term of not more than one year, or both.

(d) No person shall be excused from attending and testifying or from producing books, papers, contracts, agreements, and other records and documents before the Commission, or in obedience to the subpena of the Commission or any member thereof or any officer designated by it, or in any cause or proceeding instituted by the Commission, on the ground that the testimony or evidence, documentary or otherwise, required of him may tend to incriminate him or subject him to a penalty or forfeiture; but no individual shall be prosecuted or subject to any penalty or forfeiture for or on account of any transaction, matter, or thing concerning which he is compelled, after having claimed his privilege against self-incrimination, to testify or produce evidence, documentary or otherwise, except that such individual so testifying shall not be exempt from prosecution and punishment for perjury committed in so testifying.

(e) Whenever it shall appear to the Commission that any person is engaged or about to engage in any acts or practices which constitute or will constitute a violation of the provisions of this title, or of any rule or regulation thereunder, it may in its discretion bring an action in the proper district court of the United

States, the Supreme Court of the District of Columbia, or the United States courts of any Territory or other place subject to the jurisdiction of the United States, to enjoin such acts or practices, and upon a proper showing a permanent or temporary injunction or restraining order shall be granted without bond. The Commission may transmit such evidence as may be available concerning such acts or practices to the Attorney General, who may, in his discretion, institute the necessary criminal proceedings under this title.

(f) Upon application of the Commission the district courts of the United States, the Supreme Court of the District of Columbia, and the United States courts of any Territory or other place subject to the jurisdiction of the United States, shall also have jurisdiction to issue writs of mandamus commanding any person to comply with the provisions of this title or any order of the Commission made in pursuance thereof **or with any undertaking contained in a registration statement as provided in subsection (d) of section 15 of this title.**

HEARINGS BY COMMISSION

SEC. 22. Hearings may be public and may be held before the Commission, any member or members thereof, or any officer or officers of the Commission designated by it, and appropriate records thereof shall be kept.

RULES AND REGULATIONS; ANNUAL REPORTS

Sec. 23. (a) The Commission and the Board of Governors of the Federal Reserve System shall each have power to make such rules and regulations as may be necessary for the execution of the functions vested in them by this title, and may for such purpose classify issuers, securities, exchanges, and other persons or matters within their respective jurisdictions. No provision of this title imposing any liability shall apply to any act done or omitted in good faith in conformity with any rule or regulation of the Commission or the Board of Governors of the Federal Reserve System, notwithstanding that such rule or regulation may, after such act or omission, be amended or rescinded or be determined by judicial or other authority to be invalid for any reason.[8]

(b) The Commission and the Federal Reserve Board, respectively, shall include in their annual reports to Congress such information, data, and recommendation for further legislation as they may deem advisable with regard to matters within their respective jurisdictions under this title.

INFORMATION FILED WITH THE COMMISSION

SEC. 24. (a) Nothing in this title shall be construed to require, or to authorize the Commission to require, the revealing of trade secrets or processes in any application, report, or document filed with the Commission under this title.

(b) Any person filing any such application, report, or document may make

[8] SEC. 23. (a) The Commission and the Federal Reserve Board shall each have power to make such rules and regulations as may be necessary for the execution of the functions vested in them by this title, and may for such purpose classify issuers, securities, exchanges, and other persons or matters within their respective jurisdictions.

written objection to the public disclosure of information contained therein, stating the grounds for such objection, and the Commission is authorized to hear objections in any such case where it deems it advisable. The Commission may, in such cases, make available to the public the information contained in any such application, report, or document only when in its judgment a disclosure of such information is in the public interest; and copies of information so made available may be furnished to any person at such reasonable charge and under such reasonable limitations as the Commission may prescribe.

(c) It shall be unlawful for any member, officer, or employee of the Commission to disclose to any person other than a member, officer, or employee of the Commission, or to use for personal benefit, any information contained in any application, report, or document filed with the Commission which is not made available to the public pursuant to subsection (b) of this section: *Provided,* That the Commission may make available to the Federal Reserve Board any information requested by the Board for the purpose of enabling it to perform its duties under this title.

COURT REVIEW OF ORDERS

SEC. 25. (a) Any person aggrieved by an order issued by the Commission in a proceeding under this title to which such person is a party may obtain a review of such order in the Circuit Court of Appeals of the United States, within any circuit wherein such person resides or has his principal place of business, or in the Court of Appeals of the District of Columbia, by filing in such court, within sixty days after the entry of such order, a written petition praying that the order of the Commission be modified or set aside in whole or in part. A copy of such petition shall be forthwith served upon any member of the Commission, and thereupon the Commission shall certify and file in the court a transcript of the record upon which the order complained of was entered. Upon the filing of such transcript such court shall have exclusive jurisdiction to affirm, modify, and enforce or set aside such order, in whole or in part. No objection to the order of the Commission shall be considered by the court unless such objection shall have been urged before the Commission. The finding of the Commission as to the facts, if supported by substantial evidence, shall be conclusive. If either party shall apply to the court for leave to adduce additional evidence, and shall show to the satisfaction of the court that such additional evidence is material and that there were reasonable grounds for failure to adduce such evidence in the hearing before the Commission, the court may order such additional evidence to be taken before the Commission and to be adduced upon the hearing in such manner and upon such terms and conditions as to the court may seem proper. The Commission may modify its findings as to the facts, by reason of the additional evidence so taken, and it shall file such modified or new findings, which, if supported by substantial evidence, shall be conclusive, and its recommendation, if any, for the modification or setting aside of the original order. The judgment and decree of the court, affirming, modifying, and enforcing or setting aside, in whole or in part, any such order of the Commission, shall be final, subject to review by the Supreme Court of the United States upon certiorari or certification as provided in sections 239 and 240 of the Judicial Code, as amended (U. S. C., title 28, secs. 346 and 347).

(b) The commencement of proceedings under subsection (a) shall not, unless specifically ordered by the court, operate as a stay of the Commission's order.

UNLAWFUL REPRESENTATIONS

SEC. 26. No action or failure to act by the Commission or the Federal Reserve Board, in the administration of this title shall be construed to mean that the particular authority has in any way passed upon the merits of, or given approval to, any security or any transaction or transactions therein, nor shall such action or failure to act with regard to any statement or report filed with or examined by such authority pursuant to this title or rules and regulations thereunder, be deemed a finding by such authority that such statement or report is true and accurate on its face or that it is not false or misleading. It shall be unlawful to make, or cause to be made, to any prospective purchaser or seller of a security any representation that any such action or failure to act by any such authority is to be so construed or has such effect.

JURISDICTION OF OFFENSES AND SUITS

SEC. 27. The district courts of the United States, the Supreme Court of the District of Columbia, and the United States courts of any Territory or other place subject to the jurisdiction of the United States shall have exclusive jurisdiction of violations of this title or the rules and regulations thereunder, and of all suits in equity and actions at law brought to enforce any liability or duty created by this title or the rules and regulations thereunder. Any criminal proceeding may be brought in the district wherein any act or transaction constituting the violation occurred. Any suit or action to enforce any liability or duty created by this title or rules and regulations thereunder, or to enjoin any violation of such title or rules and regulations, may be brought in any such district or in the district wherein the defendant is found or is an inhabitant or transacts business, and process in such cases may be served in any other district of which the defendant is an inhabitant or wherever the defendant may be found. Judgments and decrees so rendered shall be subject to review as provided in sections 128 and 240 of the Judicial Code, as amended (U. S. C., title 28, secs. 225 and 347). No costs shall be assessed for or against the Commission in any proceeding under this title brought by or against it in the Supreme Court or such other courts.

EFFECT ON EXISTING LAW

SEC. 28. (a) The rights and remedies provided by this title shall be in addition to any and all other rights and remedies that may exist at law or in equity; but no person permitted to maintain a suit for damages under the provisions of this title shall recover, through satisfaction of judgment in one or more actions, a total amount in excess of his actual damages on account of the act complained of. Nothing in this title shall affect the jurisdiction of the securities commission (or any agency or officer performing like functions) of any State over any security or any person insofar as it does not conflict with the provisions of this title or the rules and regulations thereunder.

(b) Nothing in this title shall be construed to modify existing law (1) with regard to the binding effect on any member of any exchange of any action taken by the authorities of such exchange to settle disputes between its members, or (2) with regard to the binding effect of such action on any person who has agreed to be bound thereby, or (3) with regard to the binding effect on any such member of any disciplinary action taken by the authorities of the exchange as a result of violation of any rule of the exchange, insofar as the action taken is not inconsistent with the provisions of this title or the rules and regulations thereunder.

VALIDITY OF CONTRACTS

Sec. 29. (a) Any condition, stipulation, or provision binding any person to waive compliance with any provision of this title or of any rule or regulation thereunder, or of any rule of an exchange required thereby shall be void.

(b) Every contract made in violation of any provision of this title or of any rule or regulation thereunder, and every contract (including any contract for listing a security on an exchange) heretofore or hereafter made the performance of which involves the violation of, or the continuance of any relationship or practice in violation of, any provision of this title or any rule or regulation thereunder, shall be void (1) as regards the rights of any person who, in violation of any such provision, rule, or regulation, shall have made or engaged in the performance of any such contract, and (2) as regards the rights of any person who, not being a party to such contract, shall have acquired any right thereunder with actual knowledge of the facts by reason of which the making or performance of such contract was in violation of any such provision, rule or regulation.

(c) Nothing in this title shall be construed (1) to affect the validity of any loan or extension of credit (or any extension or renewal thereof) made or of any lien created prior or subsequent to the enactment of this title, unless at the time of the making of such loan or extension of credit (or extension or renewal thereof) or the creating of such lien, the person making such loan or extension of credit (or extension or renewal thereof) or acquiring such lien shall have actual knowledge of facts by reason of which the making of such loan or extension of credit (or extension or renewal thereof) or the acquisition of such lien is a violation of the provisions of this title or any rule or regulation thereunder, or (2) to afford a defense to the collection of any debt or obligation or the enforcement of any lien by any person who shall have acquired such debt, obligation, or lien in good faith for value and without actual knowledge of the violation of any provision of this title or any rule or regulation thereunder affecting the legality of such debt, obligation, or lien.

FOREIGN SECURITIES EXCHANGES

Sec. 30. (a) It shall be unlawful for any broker or dealer, directly or indirectly, to make use of the mails or of any means or instrumentality of interstate commerce for the purpose of effecting on an exchange not within or subject to the jurisdiction of the United States, any transaction in any security the issuer of which is a resident of, or is organized under the laws of, or has its principal place of business in, a place within or subject to the jurisdiction of the United States, in contravention of such rules and regulations as the Commission may prescribe as necessary or appropriate in the public interest or for the protection of investors or to prevent the evasion of this title.

(b) The provisions of this title or of any rule or regulation thereunder shall not apply to any person insofar as he transacts a business in securities without the jurisdiction of the United States, unless he transacts such business in contravention of such rules and regulations as the Commission may prescribe as necessary or appropriate to prevent the evasion of this title.

REGISTRATION FEES

SEC. 31. Every national securities exchange shall pay to the Commission on or before March 15 of each calendar year a registration fee for the privilege of doing business as a national securities exchange during the preceding calendar year or any part thereof. Such fee shall be in an amount equal to one five-hundredths of 1 per centum of the aggregate dollar amount of the sales of securities transacted on such national securities exchange during the preceding calendar year and subsequent to its registration as a national securities exchange.

PENALTIES

Sec. 32. (a) Any person who willfully violates any provision of this title, or any rule or regulation thereunder the violation of which is made unlawful or the observance of which is required under the terms of this title, or any person who willfully and knowingly makes, or causes to be made, any statement in any application, report, or document required to be filed under this title or any rule or regulation thereunder or any undertaking contained in a registration statement as provided in subsection (d) of section 15 of this title, which statement was false or misleading with respect to any material fact, shall upon conviction be fined not more than $10,000, or imprisoned not more than two years, or both, except that when such person is an exchange, a fine not exceeding $500,000 may be imposed; but no person shall be subject to imprisonment under this section for the violation of any rule or regulation if he proves that he had no knowledge of such rule or regulation.

(b) Any issuer which fails to file information, documents, or reports pursuant to an undertaking contained in a registration statement as provided in subsection (d) of section 15 of this title shall forfeit to the United States the sum of $100 for each and every day such failure to file shall continue. Such forfeiture, which shall be in lieu of any criminal penalty for such failure to file which might be deemed to arise under subsection (a) of this section, shall be payable into the Treasury of the United States and shall be recoverable in a civil suit in the name of the United States.[9]

[9] SEC. 32. Any person who willfully violates any provision of this title, or any rule or regulation thereunder the violation of which is made unlawful or the observance of which is required under the terms of this title, or any person who willfully and knowingly makes, or causes to be made, any statement in any application, report, or document required to be filed under this title or any rule or regulation thereunder, which statement was false or misleading with respect to any material fact, shall upon conviction be fined not more than $10,000, or imprisoned not more than two years, or both, except that when such person is an exchange, a fine not exceeding $500,000 may be imposed; but no person shall be subject to imprisonment under this section for the violation of any rule or regulation if he proves that he had no knowledge of such rule or regulation.

SEPARABILITY OF PROVISIONS

SEC. 33. If any provision of this act, or the application of such provision to any person or circumstances, shall be held invalid, the remainder of the act, and the application of such provision to persons or circumstances other than those as to which it is held invalid, shall not be affected thereby.

EFFECTIVE DATE

SEC. 34. This act shall become effective on July 1, 1934, except that sections 6 and 12 (b), (c), (d), and (e) shall become effective on September 1, 1934; and sections 5, 7, 8, 9 (a) (6), 10, 11, 12 (a), 13, 14, 15, 16, 17, 18, 19, and 30 shall become effective on October 1, 1934.

TITLE II—AMENDMENTS TO SECURITIES ACT OF 1933

SECTION 201. (a) Paragraph (1) of section 2 of the Securities Act of 1933 is amended to read as follows:

"(1) The term 'security' means any note, stock, treasury stock, bond, debenture, evidence of indebtedness, certificate of interest or participation in any profit-sharing agreement, collateral-trust certificate, preorganization certificate or subscription, transferable share, investment contract, voting-trust certificate, certificate of deposit for a security, fractional undivided interest in oil, gas, or other mineral rights, or, in general, any interest or instrument commonly known as a 'security,' or any certificate of interest or participation in, temporary or interim certificate for, receipt for, guarantee of, or warrant or right to subscribe to or purchase, any of the foregoing."

(b) Paragraph (4) of such section 2 is amended to read as follows:

"(4) The term 'issuer' means every person who issues or proposes to issue any security; except that with respect to certificates of deposit, voting-trust certificates, or collateral-trust certificates, or with respect to certificates of interest or shares in an unincorporated investment trust not having a board of directors (or persons performing similar functions) or of the fixed, restricted management, or unit type, the term 'issuer' means the person or persons performing the acts and assuming the duties of depositor or manager pursuant to the provisions of the trust or other agreement or instrument under which such securities are issued; except that in the case of an unincorporated association which provides by its articles for limited liability of any or all of its members, or in the case of a trust, committee, or other legal entity, the trustees or members thereof shall not be individually liable as issuers of any security issued by the association, trust, committee, or other legal entity; except that with respect to equipment-trust certificates or like securities, the term 'issuer' means the person by whom the equipment or property is or is to be used; and except that with respect to fractional undivided interests in oil, gas, or other mineral rights, the term 'issuer' means the owner of any such right or of any interest in such right (whether whole or fractional) who creates fractional interests therein for the purpose of public offering."

(c) Paragraph (10) of such section 2 is amended to read as follows:

"(10) The term 'prospectus' means any prospectus, notice, circular, advertisement, letter, or communication, written or by radio, which offers any security for sale; except that (a) a communication shall not be deemed a prospectus if it is proved that prior to or at the same time with such communication a written prospectus meeting the requirements of section 10 was sent or given to the person to whom the communication was made, by the person making such communication or his principal, and (b) a notice, circular, advertisement, letter, or communication in respect of a security shall not be deemed to be a prospectus if it states from whom a written prospectus meeting the requirements of section 10 may be obtained and, in addition, does no more than identify the security, state the price thereof, and state by whom orders will be executed."

SEC. 202. (a) Paragraph (2) of section 3 (a) of such Act is amended to read as follows:

"(2) Any security issued or guaranteed by the United States or any Territory thereof, or by the District of Columbia, or by any State of the United States, or by any political subdivision of a State or Territory, or by any public instrumentality of one or more States or Territories, or by any person controlled or supervised by and acting as an instrumentality of the Government of the United States pursuant to authority granted by the Congress of the United States, or any certificate of deposit for any of the foregoing, or any security issued or guaranteed by any national bank, or by any banking institution organized under the laws of any State or Territory or the District of Columbia, the business of which is substantially confined to banking and is supervised by the State or Territorial banking commission or similar official; or any security issued by or representing an interest in or a direct obligation of a Federal Reserve bank";

(b) Paragraph (4) of such section 3 (a) is amended by striking out "corporation" and inserting in lieu thereof "person."

(c) Such section 3 (a) is further amended by striking out the period at the end of paragraph (8) and inserting in lieu thereof a semicolon, and by inserting immediately after such paragraph (8) the following new paragraphs:

"(9) Any security exchanged by the issuer with its existing security holders exclusively where no commission or other remuneration is paid or given directly or indirectly for soliciting such exchange;

"(10) Any security which is issued in exchange for one or more bona fide outstanding securities, claims or property interests, or partly in such exchange and partly for cash, where the terms and conditions of such issuance and exchange are approved, after a hearing upon the fairness of such terms and conditions at which all persons to whom it is proposed to issue securities in such exchange shall have the right to appear, by any court, or by any official or agency of the United States, or by any State or Territorial banking or insurance commission or other governmental authority expressly authorized by law to grant such approval;

"(11) Any security which is a part of an issue sold only to persons resident within a single State or Territory, where the issuer of such security is a person resident and doing business within or, if a corporation, incorporated by and doing business within, such State or Territory."

SEC. 203. (a) Paragraph (1) of section 4 of such Act is amended (1) by striking out "not with or through an underwriter and"; and (2) by striking out "last" and inserting in lieu thereof "first."

(b) Paragraph (3) of such section 4 is hereby repealed.

SEC. 204. Subsection (c) of section 5 of such Act is hereby repealed.

SEC. 205. Paragraph (1) of section 10 (b) of such Act is amended to read as follows:

"(1) When a prospectus is used more than thirteen months after the effective date of the registration statement, the information in the statements contained therein shall be as of a date not more than twelve months prior to such use, so far as such information is known to the user of such prospectus or can be furnished by such user without unreasonable effort or expense."

SEC. 206. (a) Section 11 (a) of such Act is amended by adding after the last line thereof the following new sentence: "If such person acquired the security after the issuer has made generally available to its security holders an earning statement covering a period of at least twelve months beginning after the effective date of the registration statement, then the right of recovery under this subsection shall be conditioned on proof that such person acquired the security relying upon such untrue statement in the registration statement or relying upon the registration statement and not knowing of such omission, but such reliance may be established without proof of the reading of the registration statement by such person."

(b) Clauses (C) and (D) of paragraph (3) of section 11 (b) of such Act are amended to read as follows: "(C) as regards any part of the registration statement purporting to be made on the authority of an expert (other than himself) or purporting to be a copy of or extract from a report or valuation of an expert (other than himself), he had no reasonable ground to believe and did not believe, at the time such part of the registration statement became effective, that the statements therein were untrue or that there was an omission to state a material fact required to be stated therein or necessary to make the statements therein not misleading, or that such part of the registration statement did not fairly represent the statement of the expert or was not a fair copy of or extract from the report or valuation of the expert; and (D) as regards any part of the registration statement purporting to be a statement made by an official person or purporting to be a copy of or extract from a public official document, he had no reasonable ground to believe and did not believe, at the time such part of the registration statement became effective, that the statements therein were untrue, or that there was an omission to state a material fact required to be stated therein or necessary to make the statements therein not misleading, or that such part of the registration statement did not fairly represent the statement made by the official person or was not a fair copy of or extract from the public official document."

(c) Subsection (c) of such section 11 is amended to read as follows:

"(c) In determining, for the purpose of paragraph (3) of subsection (b) of this section, what constitutes reasonable investigation and reasonable ground for belief, the standard of reasonableness shall be that required of a prudent man in the management of his own property."

(d) Subsection (e) of such section 11 is amended to read as follows:

"(e) The suit authorized under subsection (a) may be to recover such damages as shall represent the difference between the amount paid for the security (not exceeding the price at which the security was offered to the public) and (1) the value thereof as of the time such suit was brought, or (2) the price at which such security shall have been disposed of in the market before suit, or (3) the price at which such security shall have been disposed of after suit but before judgment if such damages shall be less than the damages representing the difference between the amount paid for the security (not exceeding the price at which the security was offered to the public) and the value thereof as of the time such suit was brought: *Provided,* That if the defendant proves that any portion or all of such damages represents other than the depreciation in value of such security resulting from such part of the registration statement, with respect to which his liability is asserted, not being true or omitting to state a material fact required to be stated therein or necessary to make the statements therein not misleading, such portion of or all such damages shall not be recoverable. In no event shall any underwriter (unless such underwriter shall have knowingly received from the issuer for acting as an underwriter some benefit, directly or indirectly, in which all other underwriters similarly situated did not share in proportion to their respective interests in the underwriting) be liable in any suit or as a consequence of suits authorized under subsection (a) for damages in excess of the total price at which the securities underwritten by him and distributed to the public were offered to the public. In any suit under this or any other section of this title the court may, in its discretion, require an undertaking for the payment of the costs of such suit, including reasonable attorney's fees, and if judgment shall be rendered against a party litigant, upon the motion of the other party litigant (whether or not such undertaking has been required) if the court believes the suit or the defense to have been without merit, in an amount sufficient to reimburse him for the reasonable expenses incurred by him, in connection with such suit, such costs to be taxed in the manner usually provided for taxing of costs in the court in which the suit was heard."

SEC. 207. Section 13 of such act is amended (a) by striking out "two years" wherever it appears therein and inserting in lieu thereof "one year"; (b) by striking out "ten years" and inserting in lieu thereof "three years"; and (c) by inserting immediately before the period at the end thereof a comma and the following: "or under section 12 (2) more than three years after the sale."

SEC. 208. Section 15 of such act is amended by inserting immediately before the period at the end thereof a comma and the following: "unless the controlling person had no knowledge of or reasonable ground to believe in the existence of the facts by reason of which the liability of the controlled person is alleged to exist."

SEC. 209. (a) The first sentence of subsection (a) of section 19 of such Act is amended by inserting after the word "accounting" a comma and the word "technical."

(b) Subsection (a) of such section 19 is further amended by adding at the end thereof the following new sentence: "No provision of this title imposing any liability shall apply to any act done or omitted in good faith in conformity with any rule or regulation of the Commission, notwithstanding that such rule or regulation may, after such act or omission, be amended or rescinded or be determined by judicial or other authority to be invalid for any reason."

SEC. 210. Upon the expiration of sixty days after the date upon which a majority of the members of the Securities and Exchange Commission appointed under section 4 of title I of this Act have qualified and taken office, all powers, duties, and functions of the Federal Trade Commission under the Securities Act of 1933 shall be transferred to such Commission, together with all property, books, records, and unexpended balances of appropriations used by or available to the Federal Trade Commission for carrying out its functions under the Securities Act of 1933. All proceedings, hearings, or investigations commenced or pending before the Federal Trade Commission arising under the Securities Act of 1933 shall be continued by the Securities and Exchange Commission. All orders, rules, and regulations which have been issued by the Federal Trade Commission under the Securities Act of 1933 and which are in effect shall continue in effect until modified, superseded, revoked, or repealed. All rights and interests accruing or to accrue under the Securities Act of 1933, or any provision of any regulation relating to, or out of action taken by, the Federal Trade Commission under such Act, shall be followed in all respects and may be exercised and enforced.

SEC. 211. The Commission is authorized and directed to make a study and investigation of the work, activities, personnel, and functions of protective and reorganization committees in connection with the reorganization, readjustment, rehabilitation, liquidation, or consolidation of persons and properties and to report the result of its studies and investigations and its recommendations to the Congress on or before January 3, 1936.

Approved, June 6, 1934, 12:15 p. m.

Appendix III

Regulation T

of the Board of Governors of the Federal Reserve System

EXTENSION AND MAINTENANCE OF CREDIT BY BROKERS, DEALERS, AND MEMBERS OF NATIONAL SECURITIES EXCHANGES

SECTION 1. SCOPE AND EFFECTIVE DATE OF REGULATION

This regulation is issued pursuant to the requirements of sections 7 and 8 (a) of the Securities Exchange Act of 1934 for the purpose of preventing the excessive use of credit for the purchasing or carrying of securities and applies to the extension and maintenance of credit by members of national securities exchanges and by brokers and dealers transacting a business in securities through the medium of such members.

This regulation shall not be construed as applying to the extension or maintenance of credit on registered securities for any purpose other than the purpose of purchasing or carrying securities or of evading or circumventing the provisions of this regulation.

This regulation shall become effective on October 1, 1934.

Such further regulations as the Board deems necessary or appropriate to carry out the provisions of sections 7 and 8 (a) of the Securities Exchange Act of 1934 will be issued from time to time.

SECTION 2. DEFINITIONS

For the purposes of this regulation—

(*a*) The terms **"person," "member," "broker," "dealer," "buy," "purchase," "sale," "sell," "security," "equity security,"** and **"bank"** shall have the meanings given them in section 3 (a) of the Securities Exchange Act of 1934, which is printed in the appendix to this regulation.

(*b*) The term **"creditor"** means any member of a national securities exchange or any broker or dealer who transacts a business in securities through the medium of any such member.

(*c*) The term **"account"** means any account (whether a "combined account" or a "special account" or any other account) representing any financial relationship between any creditor and any customer or any group of customers acting jointly.

(*d*) The term **"combined account"** means the combination of all accounts (except "special accounts") between any creditor and any customer, or any group of customers acting jointly, to or for whom such creditor is extending or maintaining any credit, directly or indirectly, on registered securities (other than exempted securities) for the purpose of purchasing or carrying securities.

(*e*) The term **"special account"** means any account recorded separately in conformity with sections 3 (*b*), 3 (*c*), 3 (*d*), 5 (*b*), 6, or 7 (*a*) of this regulation; and, when so recorded, such accounts shall be excluded, for the purposes of this regulation, from all calculations involving "combined accounts."

(*f*) The term **"exempted security"** or **"exempted securities"** shall include securities which are direct obligations of or obligations guaranteed as to principal or interest by the United States; such securities issued or guaranteed by corporations in which the United States has a direct or indirect interest as shall be designated for exemption by the Secretary of the Treasury as necessary or appropriate in the public interest or for the protection of investors; securities which are direct obligations of or obligations guaranteed as to principal or interest by a State or any political subdivision thereof or any agency or instrumentality of a State or any political subdivision thereof or any municipal corporate instrumentality of one or more States; and such other securities as the Securities and Exchange Commission may, by such rules and regulations as it deems necessary or appropriate in the public interest or for the protection of investors, either unconditionally or upon specified terms and conditions or for stated periods, exempt from the operation of any one or more provisions of section 7 and/or 8 (a) of the Securities Exchange Act of 1934, which by their terms do not apply to an "exempted security" or to "exempted securities."

(*g*) The term **"registered security"** means any security which is registered on a national securities exchange, or which, in consequence of its having unlisted trading privileges on a national securities exchange, must, under the provisions of section 12 (f) of the Securities Exchange Act of 1934, be considered a "security registered on a national securities exchange."

(*h*) The term **"maximum loan value"** of a security means the maximum amount of credit which, at any given time, may be extended by any creditor on such security, in conformity with section 3. The "maximum loan value" of the securities in an account, at any given time, is the sum of the maximum loan values at such time of the individual securities in such account, including securities bought for the account of the customer but not yet debited to his account, but excluding securities sold for the account of the customer for which payment has not yet been credited to his account and excluding contracts for the purchase or sale of unissued securities.

(*i*) The term **"unrestricted account"** means an account in which at any given time the adjusted debit balance equals or is less than the maximum loan value at such time of the securities in the account; and any account which is an unrestricted account at the beginning of business on any given day may for the purposes of this regulation be considered an unrestricted account throughout such day.

(*j*) The term **"restricted account"** means an account in which, at the beginning of business on any given day, the adjusted debit balance exceeds the maximum loan value at such time of the securities in the account: *Provided, however,* That, if during the course of a day, as a result of the deposit of cash and/or securities or the sale or substitution of securities by or on behalf of the customer the maximum loan value of the securities in the account becomes equal to or greater than the adjusted debit balance, such account may be deemed an unrestricted account throughout such day.

(*k*) The term **"initial extension of credit"** means any new extension of credit in an account or any increase in the amount of credit outstanding in an account.

(*l*) The term **"net withdrawal"** means any payment or delivery from an account of money and/or registered and/or exempted securities having an aggregate current market value exceeding that of any money and/or registered and/or exempted securities paid or delivered into the account on the same day.

(*m*) The term **"customer"** means any person to or for whom, or any group of persons to or for whose joint account, a creditor is extending or maintaining any credit and includes any partner in a firm to whom such firm is extending credit for the purpose of purchasing or carrying securities: *Provided, however,* That a partner shall not be deemed to be a customer of his firm within the meaning of this regulation with reference to his financial relations to the firm as reflected in his capital and ordinary drawing accounts.

(*n*) The term "days" as distinguished from "business days" and "full business days," means calendar days, but if the last day of a specified period of days be a Saturday, a Sunday, or a holiday, such period shall be considered to end on the next full business day.

SECTION 3. MARGIN REQUIREMENTS

(*a*) **General rule.**—No creditor shall make any initial extension of credit to any customer on any registered security (other than an exempted security) for the purpose of purchasing or carrying any security, in an amount which causes the total credit extended on such registered security to exceed the maximum loan value of such registered security. (See supplement below for actual margin requirements established in 1936.)

(*b*) **Extensions of credit to other members, brokers, and dealers.**—In a special account recorded separately, any creditor may extend credit on any registered security to any other member, broker, or dealer in an amount not greater than the maximum loan value of such security, which shall be (except in the case of an exempted security) 80 per cent of the current market value of such security: *Provided,* That (1) such other member, broker, or dealer is subject to the provisions of this regulation or has places of business only in foreign countries, (2) such credit is extended or maintained solely for the purpose of enabling such member, broker, or dealer to carry accounts for his customers other than his partners, and (3) any credit extended or maintained by such creditor to or for such other member, broker, or dealer for the purpose of purchasing or carrying securities for his own account or for the account of his firm or any of his partners shall not be included in such special account and shall be subject to the other provisions of this section.

(*c*) **Extension of credit to distributors, syndicates, etc.**—In a special account recorded separately, any creditor may extend credit on any registered security in an amount not greater than the maximum loan value thereof, which shall be (except in the case of an exempted security) 80 per cent of the current market value of such security:

(1) To any dealer, for the purpose of financing the distribution of an issue of securities at wholesale or retail; or

(2) To any group, joint account or syndicate, for the purpose of underwriting or distributing an issue of securities.

(*d*) **Arbitrage accounts.**—If such transactions are recorded separately in a special account and are not used for the purpose of evading or circumventing the provisions of this regulation, any *bona fide* arbitrage transactions in securities and any credit extended or maintained to or for a customer for the purpose of financing such transactions shall be exempt from the other provisions of this regulation: *Provided,* That the customer shall maintain a margin equal to 2 per cent of any net debit balance in such account, unless the account contains no securities except exempted securities.

(*e*) **Exempted securities.**—In an account which contains both exempted securities and registered nonexempted securities, the maximum loan value of an exempted security shall be regarded as not more than the current market value of such security: *Provided, however,* That nothing in this regulation shall be construed as preventing any exchange or any creditor from requiring margin on, or assigning lower loan values to, exempted securities.

(*f*) **Adjusted debit balance.**—For the purpose of this regulation, the adjusted debit balance of an account shall be calculated by taking the sum of the following items:

(1) The net debit balance, if any, of the account;

(2) Any amount to be paid for securities (other than unissued securities) bought for the account of the customer but not yet debited to his account;

(3) The current market value of any securities sold short in the account (other than unissued securities) *plus* the margin customarily required by the creditor on such short commitments;

(4) The amount of any margin customarily required by the creditor on every future commitment in unissued securities, in commodities, or in foreign exchange, and/or in connection with the creditor's indorsement or guaranty of any put, call or other option, *plus* any unrealized loss on each such commitment and/or *minus* any unrealized gain on each such commitment not exceeding the margin thereon; *and*

(5) In the case of a guarantor's account, the aggregate of the amounts required to make each account guaranteed by such guarantor an unrestricted account: *Provided,* That in the case of no such guaranteed account shall the amount exceed that to which the guaranty is limited;

and deducting therefrom the sum of the following items:

(6) The net credit balance, if any, of the account;

(7) Any amount to be received for securities (other than unissued securities) sold for the account of the customer but for which payment has not yet been credited to his account; *and*

(8) Any amount needed but not yet received by the creditor to provide any margin required by this regulation: *Provided,* That (*a*) a demand for such margin shall have been made in, or confirmed by, a letter or telegram which the creditor shall have sent to the customer at his last known address and (*b*) the time within which the creditor is required by this regulation to obtain such margin has not expired.

For the purposes of this regulation, the adjusted debit balance of every account in which any credit is extended or maintained for the purpose of purchasing or carrying securities shall be computed in accordance with the above rules, regardless of whether it be a combined account or a special account. In case a customer has more than one account (other than special accounts) with a creditor, his adjusted debit balance and the maximum loan value of the securities in his account shall be calculated, for the purposes of this regulation, on the basis of his combined account, taking into consideration all accounts between such customer and such creditor except special accounts. In computing the adjusted debit balance of each special account, there shall be taken into consideration only the items involved in that particular account.

(*g*) **Current market value.**—For the purpose of ascertaining the current market value of a security at the time of and in connection with a purchase or sale of such security, the price at which such security is purchased or sold (whether or not as part of a substitution of securities or other transaction), shall be used in computing the current market value of such security within the meaning of this regulation.

For the purpose of ascertaining the current market value of any security in an account, at any time other than the time of its purchase or sale, the creditor shall have the option of using as the price of such security either the closing sale or the closing bid price for such security on the preceding business day, as shown by any regularly published reporting or quotation service used by such creditor (except that such bid price shall not be deemed to be the current market value of a security sold short). In the absence of any such closing sale price, the creditor shall have the option of using either any such bid price on such preceding business day (except that such bid price shall not be deemed to be the current market price of a security sold short), or the price at which the last sale was recorded, if such sale occurred during the current or preceding calendar month, as shown by any regularly published reporting or quotation service used by such creditor. In the event that none of the prices above described is available, the creditor may use any reasonable estimate of the market price of such security.

SECTION 4. EXTENSION AND MAINTENANCE OF CREDIT

(*a*) **Statutory provision.**—Under the provisions of subsection (c) of section 7 of the Securities Exchange Act of 1934, it is unlawful for any member of a national securities exchange or any broker or dealer who transacts a business in securities through the medium of any such member, directly or indirectly, to extend or maintain credit or arrange for the extension or maintenance of credit to or for any customer on any registered security (other than an exempted security) in contravention of the regulations of the Federal Reserve Board.

(*b*) **General rule.**—A creditor may permit credit to be maintained in any account in accordance with the provisions of this section, regardless of reductions in the customer's equity resulting from changes in market prices and/or from charges to the account of the customer permitted under section 8 (*b*) of this regulation.

(*c*) **Transactions in unrestricted accounts.**—A creditor shall not permit any customer to make in an unrestricted account any transaction or combination of transactions which would cause such account to become a restricted account, unless he demands, in accordance with section 4 (*e*) of this regulation, additional margin in an amount sufficient to make such account an unrestricted account.

(*d*) **Transactions in restricted accounts.**—A creditor shall not permit a customer to make in a restricted account any transaction which, in combination with any other transactions made on the same day and together with demands for additional margin in connection therewith, results in any increase of the excess of the adjusted debit balance of the account over the maximum loan value of the securities in the account, or results in any net withdrawal of cash and/or securities: *Provided, however,* That a creditor may permit a customer to make any transaction or combination of transactions which causes the account to become an unrestricted account: and *Provided,* That any substitution of securities consisting of a sale of securities in the account and the purchase of other securities, if completed within a period of two successive business days, may be considered for the purposes of this section as a single transaction occurring on the day on which the purchase occurs.

(*e*) **Time when margin must be obtained.**—Whenever the creditor is required to demand additional margin in order to comply with this regulation, he shall demand the required amount of margin as promptly as possible and shall obtain such margin as promptly as possible in view of the established usages of the trade and the circumstances of the case and in all events before the expiration of three full business days (exclusive of Saturdays, Sundays and holidays) from the date of the purchase or other transaction on account of which such margin is required, unless, within such time such account is brought into conformity with this regulation by some other method: *Provided,* That, in exceptional cases, any regularly constituted committee of a national securities exchange having jurisdiction over the business conduct of its members, of which exchange the creditor is a member or through which his transactions are effected, may grant a further extension of time, not exceeding ten days, on application of the creditor, if such committee is satisfied that the creditor is acting in good faith and that the circumstances warrant such action: *Provided, however,* That, if the account be a restricted account (1) in the case of a withdrawal of cash, the necessary amount of securities must be deposited on the same day; (2) in the case of a withdrawal of securities, the necessary amount of cash must be deposited on the same day; and (3) in the case of a substitution of securities (not involving a sale of securities in the account and the purchase of other securities), the securities substituted must be deposited on the same day that the securities for which they are substituted are withdrawn.

(*f*) **Time when payment or margin is deemed to be received.**—For the purposes of this regulation, any creditor who shall in good faith accept any check or draft drawn on a bank which in the ordinary course of business is payable on presentation or any order on a savings account with passbook attached, shall be deemed to have received payment of the amount of such check, draft, or order within the meaning of this regulation at the time such check, draft, or order is received; and any creditor who shall in good faith ship securities with sight draft attached shall be deemed to have received payment of the amount of such sight draft at the time of the shipment of the securities to which such sight draft is attached: *Provided,* That, if such check, draft, order, or sight draft is not paid on the day of presentation, the creditor shall, before the expiration of three full business days from the receipt of notice of such nonpayment, obtain actual payment, cancel the sale, resell the securities for the account of the customer, or obtain the deposit of additional securities having a loan value sufficient to provide the margin needed.

Any member, broker, or dealer who shall receive payment of any amount in any foreign currency capable of being converted without restriction into United States currency, shall be deemed, for the purposes of this regulation, to have received payment of an amount equal to the value of the foreign currency so paid, computed at the buying rate for cable transfers of such foreign currency on the preceding business day as determined and certified by the Federal Reserve Bank of New York and published by the Secretary of the Treasury pursuant to the provisions of section 522 of title 4 of the Tariff Act of 1930. Any person who shall deposit with a creditor any such foreign currency may, for the purpose of determining the adjusted debit balance in an account of such person, be credited with the value of such foreign currency computed as hereinabove prescribed.

In the case of any special account which grows out of regular correspondent relationships between a creditor and a customer who is not located in the same city and who is a member, broker, or dealer, securities which are in transit from such customer to the creditor for the purpose of increasing the customer's margin may, for the purposes of this regulation, be deemed to have been received by the creditor at the time he receives and accepts in good faith a telegram or letter from the customer stating that such securities have been shipped to the creditor.

SECTION 5. EXTENSION OR MAINTENANCE OF CREDIT WITHOUT COLLATERAL OR ON COLLATERAL OTHER THAN EXEMPTED OR REGISTERED SECURITIES

(*a*) **General rule.**—Under the provisions of subsection (c) of section 7 of the Securities Exchange Act of 1934, it is unlawful for any member of a national securities exchange or any broker or dealer who transacts a business in securities through the medium of any such member, directly or indirectly to extend or maintain credit or arrange for the extension or maintenance of credit to or for any customer without collateral or on any collateral other than exempted and/or registered securities except as expressly permitted by this regulation.

(*b*) **Credit not for purchasing or carrying securities.**—In a special account recorded separately, a creditor may, notwithstanding any other provision of this regulation, extend credit to any customer, without collateral or on any collateral other than non-exempted registered securities, for any *bona fide* commercial, industrial, or other purpose except the purpose of purchasing or carrying securities or of evading or circumventing the provisions of this regulation.

SECTION 6. CASH TRANSACTIONS

Notwithstanding any other provision of this regulation, a creditor may, in a special cash account recorded separately, subject to the conditions specified in this section, (1) effect *bona fide* cash transactions and transactions incidental thereto and (2) make, for limited periods not exceeding seven days, extensions of credit which are incidental to *bona fide* cash transactions.

A *bona fide* cash transaction is (1) a transaction in which a customer buys a security (whether registered or unregistered), through a creditor acting as broker or from a creditor acting as dealer, pursuant to an agreement made in good faith, and not to evade or circumvent the provisions of this regulation, that the customer will promptly make full cash payment for such security, or (2) a transaction in which a customer sells, through a creditor acting as broker or to a creditor acting as dealer, a security (whether registered or unregistered) which the creditor holds in the special cash account of such customer or which, pursuant to an agreement made in good faith and not to evade or circumvent the provisions of this regulation, is to be deposited in or transferred to such account.

The creditor shall record the full details of every *bona fide* cash transaction and of every transaction incidental thereto which is effected in the special cash account provided for in this section and shall record in the special cash account itself the following details: (1) in the case of every security purchased by the customer, the name of the customer, the date of payment by the creditor, and the date of payment by the customer, and (2) in the case of every security sold by the customer the name of the customer, the date of deposit of the security in or the transfer thereof to the account, the date of payment to the customer, and the date of the crediting of the proceeds of the sale to the account.

No extension of credit which is incidental to any such *bona fide* cash transaction shall constitute a violation of this regulation (1) if, within the time specified above, payment is received by the creditor (who may disregard for the purpose of this clause any sum due not exceeding $50), or (2) if, within two full business days after the time when payment should have been received under this section, the creditor (*a*) in the case of any security purchased by the customer from the creditor acting as dealer, cancels the sale or resells the security, or (*b*) in the case of any security purchased through the creditor acting as broker, sells the security, or (*c*) in the case of any security sold through the creditor acting as broker, resells the security or is repaid by the customer: *Provided, however,* That, in exceptional cases, any regularly constituted committee of a national securities exchange having jurisdiction over the business conduct of its members, of which exchange the creditor is a member or through which his transactions are effected, may, on application of the creditor, grant a further extension of time not exceeding 35 days or, in the case of a registered security, authorize the creditor to extend credit on such security subject to the provisions of this regulation, if such commitee is satisfied that the transaction was a *bona fide* cash transaction, that the creditor is acting in good faith in making the application, and that the circumstances warrant such action.

The special cash account provided for in this section shall not be used in any way for the purpose of evading or circumventing any provision of this regulation. No transactions shall be effected in such account except *bona fide* cash transactions and transactions incidental thereto, and no extension of credit shall be made in such account except extensions incidental to *bona fide* cash transactions.

NOTE.—The Board's rulings numbered 16, 27, 34, and 35 interpreting Regulation T may be disregarded with respect to transactions occurring on and after the effective date of the foregoing amendment. After enactment of Amendment No. 3, Ruling No. 36 interpreting Regulation T will still be controlling as to the facts stated in the ruling but it is contemplated that the ruling will be of less general interest because of the possibility under Amendment No. 3 of transferring unregistered, nonexempted securities from a combined account to a cash account for the purpose of effecting their sale as a *bona fide* cash transaction.

SECTION 8. ADMINISTRATIVE ADJUSTMENTS AND DETAILS

(*a*) **Borrowing and lending securities.**—Neither the *bona fide* deposit of cash, in order to borrow securities for the purpose of making delivery of such securities in the case of short sales, delayed deliveries, and other similar transactions, nor the *bona fide* lending of securities for such purposes shall be considered an extension or maintenance of credit within the meaning of this regulation.

(*b*) **Interest, commissions, etc.**—Interest on credit maintained in an account, commissions on transactions in an account, sale or transfer taxes on transactions in an account, premiums on securities borrowed in connection with short sales or to effect delivery, dividends, interest, rights or other distributions due on borrowed securities, and any service charges which the creditor may impose, may be debited to such account in accordance with the usual practice and shall be taken into consideration in calculating the net balance of such account; but the debiting of any such item to an account shall not be considered a violation of this regulation, whether or not such account is a restricted account and whether or not the debiting of such item causes an unrestricted account to become a restricted account.

Nothing in this regulation shall be construed to prevent a creditor from paying to or for a customer from any account (including any restricted account) interest and/or cash dividends collected by the creditor for the customer's account, if such payment is made within 35 days after the day on which, in accordance with the creditor's usual practice, such interest or dividends are credited to the account, and if the crediting of such interest or dividends has not served in the meantime to permit in the account any purchase of securities or other transaction which could not otherwise have been effected in accordance with this regulation.

(*c*) **Declaration as to purpose of loan.**—Every extension of credit on a registered security (other than an exempted security) shall be deemed for the purposes of this regulation to be for the purpose of purchasing or carrying securities, unless the customer shall file with the creditor a written declaration signed by the customer which shall state the use to be made of such credit and which shall state specifically that such credit is not for the purpose of purchasing or carrying securities or of evading or circumventing the provisions of this regulation. In any case in which a creditor is required to comply with the provisions of this regulation if an extension of credit is for the purpose of purchasing or carrying securities, he may rely upon a written declaration of the customer such as that required above, unless he knows the statement to be false or has information which would put a prudent man upon inquiry and if investigated with reasonable diligence would lead to the discovery of the falsity of the statement.

(*d*) **Guaranteed accounts.**—Notwithstanding the definitions of the terms "unrestricted account" and "restricted account," a creditor may regard as an unrestricted account any account which is guaranteed in writing for an amount sufficient to make such account an unrestricted account by a person who has an account with such creditor containing securities of sufficient loan value to make such guaranteed account an unrestricted account in addition to providing the margin required by this regulation on the guarantor's account.

(*e*) **Transfer of accounts.**—In the event of the transfer of an account from one creditor to another, such account may be treated for the purposes of this regulation as if it had been maintained by the transferee from the date of its origin.

(*f*) **Credit for clearance of securities.**—The extension or maintenance of any credit which is maintained for only a fraction of a day (that is, for only part of the time between the beginning of business and midnight on the same day) shall be disregarded for the purposes of this regulation, if it is incidental to the clearance of transactions in securities directly between members or through an agency organized or employed by the members of a national securities exchange for the purpose of effecting such clearances.

(*g*) **Innocent mistakes.**—If any failure to comply with this regulation results from an innocent mistake made in good faith in executing a transaction, recording, determining, or calculating any loan, balance, market price, loan value, or other administrative adjustment or detail, the creditor shall not be deemed guilty of a violation of this regulation: *Provided,* that (1) the mistake is corrected promptly, (2) any additional margin required is obtained within the time allowed by this regulation from the date of the discovery of the mistake.

(*h*) **Transactions outside United States.**—In view of the provisions of section 30 (b) of the Securities Exchange Act of 1934, nothing in this regulation shall apply to any creditor in so far as he transacts a business in securities without the jurisdiction of the United States, unless he transacts such business in contravention of such rules and regulations as the Securities and Exchange Commission may prescribe as necessary or appropriate to prevent the evasion of the Securities Exchange Act of 1934.

SECTION 9. REPORTS

Every member of a national securities exchange and every broker or dealer who transacts a business in securities through the medium of any such member, shall, in the manner and form to be prescribed by the Federal Reserve Board, make such periodic, special, and/or other reports as the Federal Reserve Board may require from time to time.

SECTION 10. BORROWINGS BY MEMBERS, BROKERS, AND DEALERS

(*a*) **General rule.**—Under the provisions of section 8 of the Securities Exchange Act of 1934 it is unlawful for any member of a national securities exchange, or any broker or dealer who transacts a business in securities through the medium of any such member, directly or indirectly to borrow in the ordinary course of business as a broker or dealer on any registered security (other than an exempted security) except:

(1) From or through a member bank of the Federal Reserve System; or

(2) From any nonmember bank which shall have filed with the Federal Reserve Board an agreement which is still in force and which is in the form prescribed by this regulation; or

(3) To the extent to which, under the provisions of this regulation, the Federal Reserve Board permits loans between such members and/or brokers and/or dealers, or to meet emergency needs.

(*b*) **Borrowing from nonmember banks.**—Each nonmember bank which has filed an agreement in the form prescribed by this regulation will be given a certificate evidencing that fact. Interested persons may obtain from the Federal Reserve agent at any Federal Reserve bank the names of banks which have filed such agreements and information as to whether in each case the agreement is still in force.

(*c*) **Borrowing from other members, brokers, and dealers.**—A creditor may borrow from another creditor in the ordinary course of business as a broker or dealer on any registered security to the extent and subject to the terms upon which the latter may extend credit to him in accordance with the provisions of this regulation and subject to such rules and regulations as the Securities and Exchange Commission may prescribe under the provisions of section 8 (c) of the Securities Exchange Act of 1934.

(*d*) **Emergency loans.**—Notwithstanding any other provision of this regulation, any member of a national securities exchange, or any group of such members, may, with the approval of any regularly constituted committee of a national securities exchange having jurisdiction over the business conduct of such members, make loans to meet the emergency needs of any other such member or of a broker or dealer transacting business through the medium of any such member; and all such loans, whether made prior or subsequent to the effective date of this regulation, may be maintained, renewed, and/or extended until the Federal Reserve Board shall determine that the emergency justifying such loan has ceased to exist: *Provided,* That any such committee approving the making, renewal, or extension of any such loan, made after the effective date of this regulation, shall, within 10 days, make a written report of all facts relative thereto to the Federal Reserve agent of the district in which such exchange is located. Any member of a national securities exchange and any broker or dealer who transacts a business in securities through the medium of any such member may borrow in accordance with the provisions of this section for the purpose of meeting his emergency needs.

SECTION 11. QUALIFICATION OF NONMEMBER BANKS TO LEND TO MEMBERS, BROKERS, AND DEALERS

(*a*) **Form of agreement.**—In order to qualify, pursuant to the provisions of subsection (a) of section 8 of the Securities Exchange Act of 1934, as a bank from which it is lawful for any member of a national securities exchange or any broker or dealer who transacts a business in securities through the medium of any such member, to borrow, in the ordinary course of business as a broker or dealer, on registered securities (other than exempted securities), a bank which is not a member of the Federal Reserve System and which is not included in the classes of banks referred to in subsection (*b*) of this section, shall file, in the manner hereinafter prescribed, an agreement on F.R.B. Form T–1, which form is hereby made a part of this regulation. The execution of such agreement shall be authorized by the adoption by the board of directors or other governing body of the bank of a resolution in the form contained in F.R.B. Form T–1 and the agreement when filed shall be accompanied by a copy of such resolution certified by the secretary or other duly authorized officer of the bank in the manner provided for in F.R.B. Form T–1.

(*b*) **Banks in territories or insular possessions; branches of foreign banks.**—In order to qualify, pursuant to the provisions of subsection (a) of section 8 of the Securities Exchange Act of 1934, a bank which is not a member of the Federal Reserve System and which has its principal place of business in a Territory or insular possession of the United States (including the Philippine Islands and the Canal Zone) or which is not a member of the Federal Reserve System and which has its principal place of business in a foreign country and has a branch or agency in the United States, shall file in lieu of the agreement on F.R.B. Form T–1 an agreement on F.R.B. Form T–2, which form is hereby made a part of this regulation. Such agreement when filed shall be accompanied by proof of the authorization of its execution in the manner provided on F.R.B. Form T–2.

(*c*) **Method and evidence of filing.**—Duplicate originals of F.R.B. Form T–1, when properly executed, shall be delivered to the Federal Reserve agent at the Federal Reserve bank of the district in which is situated the qualifying bank's principal place of business and such delivery shall constitute filing with the Federal Reserve Board. A certificate evidencing such filing will thereupon be delivered to the qualifying bank by the Federal Reserve agent.

Duplicate originals of F.R.B. Form T–2, when properly executed, shall be delivered to the Federal Reserve agent at the Federal Reserve Bank of New York or the Federal Reserve agent at the Federal Reserve Bank of San Francisco and delivery to either such Federal Reserve agent shall constitute filing with the Federal Reserve Board. The Federal Reserve agent to whom such delivery is made shall thereupon send a certificate evidencing such filing to the qualifying bank and to each branch or agency of the qualifying bank which is listed in F.R.B. Form T–2 and shall at the same time send appropriate notice of such filing to the Federal Reserve agent at the Federal Reserve bank in each Federal Reserve district in which is situated one or more of such branches or agencies.

(*d*) **Termination of agreements.**—Any agreement on F.R.B. Form T–1 or F.R.B. Form T–2 filed with the Federal Reserve Board shall be subject to termination at any time by order of the Board, after appropriate notice and opportunity for hearing, because of any failure by the bank filing such agreement to comply with the provisions thereof or with the provisions of the Securities Exchange Act of 1934, the Federal Reserve Act, as amended, or the Banking Act of 1933, which are applicable to member banks and which relate to the use of credit to finance transactions in securities, or with such rules and regulations as may be prescribed pursuant to such provisions of law or for the purpose of preventing evasions thereof. For any willful violation of such agreement, the offending bank will be subject to the penalties prescribed by the Securities Exchange Act of 1934 for violations of rules and regulations prescribed thereunder.

(*e*) **Forms available.**—Copies of F.R.B. Form T–1 and F.R.B. Form T–2 may be obtained from the Federal Reserve agents at the Federal Reserve banks.

SECTION 12. ADDITIONAL REQUIREMENTS BY EXCHANGES AND CREDITORS

Nothing in this regulation shall be construed as preventing an exchange from adopting and enforcing any rule or regulation requiring its members to secure or maintain higher margins or otherwise restricting the amount of credit which may be extended by such members.

Nothing in this regulation shall be construed as modifying the right of any creditor to require additional security for the maintenance of any credit or as restricting the right of any creditor to refuse to extend credit or to sell any securities or property held as collateral for any loan or credit extended by him.

Supplement to Regulation T

(Effective April 1, 1936)

MAXIMUM LOAN VALUES OF REGISTERED SECURITIES (OTHER THAN EXEMPTED SECURITIES) FOR PURPOSES OF REGULATION T

Pursuant to the provisions of section 7 of the Securities Exchange Act of 1934 and section 3 of its Regulation T, as amended, the Board of Governors of the Federal Reserve System hereby prescribes the following maximum loan values of registered securities (other than exempted securities) for the purposes of Regulation T:

(1) **General rule.**—Except as provided in paragraphs (2) and (3) of this supplement, the maximum loan value of a registered security (other than an

exempted security) shall be 45 per cent of the current market value of the security.

(2) **Extension of credit to other members, brokers and dealers.**—The maximum loan value of a registered security (other than an exempted security) in a special account with another member, broker or dealer, which special account complies with subsection (*b*) of section 3 of Regulation T, as amended, shall be 60 per cent of the current market value of the security.

(3) **Extension of credit to distributors, syndicates, etc.**—The maximum loan value of a registered security (other than an exempted security) in a special account with a distributor, syndicate, etc., which special account complies with subsection (*c*) of section 3 of Regulation T, as amended, shall be 80 per cent of the current market value of the security.

Appendix IV

Regulation U

of the Board of Governors of the Federal Reserve System

LOANS BY BANKS FOR THE PURPOSE OF PURCHASING OR CARRYING STOCKS REGISTERED ON A NATIONAL SECURITIES EXCHANGE

EXPLANATORY FOREWORD

(Not a part of the regulation)

This regulation is issued pursuant to the provisions of section 7 of the Securities Exchange Act of 1934 and relates only to loans made on or after May 1, 1936. It is not retroactive.

The regulation does not restrict the right of a bank to extend credit, whether on securities or otherwise, for any commercial, agricultural, or industrial purpose, or for any other purpose except the purchasing or carrying of stocks registered on a national securities exchange.

The regulation does not prevent a bank from taking for any loan collateral in addition to that required by the regulation, nor does it require a bank to reduce any loan, to obtain additional collateral for any outstanding loan, or to call any outstanding loan because of insufficient collateral.

Any inquiry relating to this regulation should be addressed to the Federal Reserve bank of the district in which the inquiry arises.

SECTION 1. GENERAL RULE

On and after May 1, 1936, no bank shall make any loan secured directly or indirectly by any stock *for the purpose of purchasing or carrying any stock registered on a national securities exchange* in an amount exceeding the maximum loan value of the collateral, as prescribed from time to time for stocks in the supplement to this regulation and as determined by the bank in good faith for any collateral other than stocks.

For the purpose of this regulation, the entire indebtedness of any borrower to any bank incurred on or after May 1, 1936, for the purpose of purchasing or carrying stocks registered on a national securities exchange shall be considered a single loan; and all the collateral securing such indebtedness shall be considered in determining whether or not the loan complies with this regulation.

After any such loan has been made, a bank shall not at any time permit withdrawals or substitutions of collateral that would cause the maximum loan value of the collateral at such time to be less than the amount of the loan. In case such maximum loan value has become less than the amount of the loan, a bank shall not permit withdrawals or substitutions that would increase the deficiency; but the amount of the loan may be increased if there is provided additional collateral having maximum loan value at least equal to the amount of the increase.

SECTION 2. EXCEPTIONS TO GENERAL RULE

Notwithstanding the foregoing, a bank may make and thereafter maintain any loan for the purpose specified above, without regard to the limitations prescribed above, if the loan comes within any of the following descriptions:

(*a*) Any loan to a bank or to a foreign banking institution;

(*b*) Any loan to any person whose total indebtedness to the bank at the date of and including such loan does not exceed $1,000;

(*c*) Any loan to a dealer, or to two or more dealers, to aid in the financing of the distribution of securities to customers not through the medium of a national securities exchange;

(*d*) Any loan to a broker or dealer that is made in exceptional circumstances in good faith to meet his emergency needs;

(*e*) Any loan for the purpose of purchasing a stock from or through a person who is not a member of a national securities exchange and is not a broker or dealer who transacts a business in securities through the medium of any such member, or for the purpose of carrying a stock so purchased;

(*f*) Any temporary advance to finance the purchase or sale of securities for prompt delivery which is to be repaid in the ordinary course of business upon completion of the transaction;

(*g*) Any loan against securities in transit, or surrendered for transfer, which is payable in the ordinary course of business upon arrival of the securities or upon completion of the transfer;

(*h*) Any loan which is to be repaid on the calendar day on which it is made;

(*i*) Any loan made outside the 48 States of the United States and the District of Columbia.

SECTION 3. MISCELLANEOUS PROVISIONS

(*a*) In determining whether or not a loan is for the purpose specified in section 1 or for any of the purposes specified in section 2, a bank may rely upon a statement with respect thereto, accepted by the bank in good faith, signed by an officer of the bank or by the borrower.

(*b*) No loan, however it may be secured, need be treated as a loan for the purpose of "carrying" a stock registered on a national securities exchange unless the purpose of the loan is to enable the borrower to reduce or retire indebtedness which was originally incurred to purchase such a stock, or, if he be a broker or dealer, to carry such stocks for customers.

(*c*) In determining whether or not a security is a "stock registered on a national securities exchange," a bank may rely upon any reasonably current record of stocks so registered that is published or specified in a publication of the Board of Governors of the Federal Reserve System.

(*d*) The renewal or extension of maturity of a loan need not be treated as the making of a loan if the amount of the loan is not increased except by the addition of interest or service charges on the loan or of taxes on transactions in connection with the loan.

(*e*) A bank may accept the transfer of a loan from another lender, or permit the transfer of a loan between borrowers, without following the requirements of this regulation as to the making of a loan, provided the loan is not increased and the collateral for the loan is not changed.

(*f*) A loan need not be treated as collateralled by securities which are held by the bank only in the capacity of custodian, depositary or trustee, or under similar circumstances, if the bank in good faith has not relied upon such securities as collateral in the making or maintenance of the particular loan.

(*g*) Nothing in this regulation shall be construed to prevent a bank from permitting withdrawals or substitutions of securities to enable a borrower to participate in a reorganization.

(*h*) No mistake made in good faith in connection with the making or maintenance of a loan shall be deemed to be a violation of this regulation.

(*i*) Nothing in this regulation shall be construed as preventing a bank from taking such action as it shall deem necessary in good faith for its own protection.

(*j*) Every bank shall make such reports as the Board of Governors of the Federal Reserve System may require to enable it to perform the functions conferred upon it by the Securities Exchange Act of 1934.

(*k*) Terms used in this regulation have the meanings assigned to them in such portions of section 3 (a) of the Securities Exchange Act of 1934 as are printed in the appendix to this regulation, except that the term "bank" does not include a bank which is a member of a national securities exchange.

(*l*) The term "stock" includes any security commonly known as a stock, any voting trust certificate or other instrument representing such a security, and any warrant or right to subscribe to or purchase such a security.

Supplement to Regulation U

(Effective May 1, 1936)

For the purpose of section 1 of Regulation U, the maximum loan value of any stock, whether or not registered on a national securities exchange, shall be 45 per cent of its current market value, as determined by any reasonable method.

Loans to brokers and dealers.—Notwithstanding the foregoing, a stock, if registered on a national securities exchange, shall have a special maximum loan value of 60 per cent of its current market value, as determined by any reasonable method, in the case of a loan to a broker or dealer from whom the bank accepts in good faith a signed statement to the effect (1) that he is subject to the provisions of Regulation T (or that he does not extend or maintain credit to or for customers except in accordance therewith as if he were subject thereto), and (2) that the securities hypothecated to secure the loan are securities carried for the account of his customers other than his partners.

INDEX

Wall Street

and the

Security Markets

An Arno Press Collection

Abbott, Charles Cortez. **The New York Bond Market, 1920-1930.** 1937

Adams, Henry C. **Public Debts:** An Essay in the Science of Finance. 1898

Black, Hillel. **The Watchdogs of Wall Street.** 1962

Bond, Frederic Drew. **Stock Movements and Speculation.** 1930

The Boston Stock Exchange. 1975

Burr, Anna Robeson. **The Portrait of a Banker: James Stillman, 1850-1918.** 1927

Carret, Philip L. **The Art of Speculation.** 1930

Chamberlain, Lawrence. **The Work of the Bond House.** 1912

The Chicago Securities Market. 1975

Finance and Industry: The New York Stock Exchange. 1886

Flynn, John T. **Investment Trusts Gone Wrong!** 1930

Forgan, James B. **Recollections of a Busy Life.** 1924

Fowler, John Francis, Jr. **American Investment Trusts.** 1928

Galston, Arthur. **Security Syndicate Operations.** [1928]

Glass, Carter. **An Adventure in Constructive Finance.** 1927

Grayson, Theodore J[ulius]. **Investment Trusts:** Their Origin, Development, and Operation. 1928

Greef, Albert O. **The Commercial Paper House in the United States.** 1938

Haney, Lewis H., Lyman S. Logan and Henry S. Gavens. **Brokers' Loans.** 1932

Hardy, Charles O[scar]. **Odd-Lot Trading on the New York Stock Exchange.** 1939

Hillhouse, A[lbert] M. **Municipal Bonds:** A Century of Experience. 1936

Hodgson, James Goodwin, comp. **Wall Street:** Asset or Liability? 1934

King, Jos[eph] L. **History of the San Francisco Stock and Exchange Board.** 1910

Lamont, Thomas W. **Henry P. Davison:** The Record of a Useful Life. 1933

Lefèvre, Edwin. **The Making of a Stockbroker.** 1925

McElroy, Robert [McNutt]. **Levi Parsons Morton:** Banker, Diplomat and Statesman. 1930

Medina, Harold R. **Corrected Opinion of Harold R. Medina, United States Circuit Judge in United States of America, Plaintiff, V. Henry S. Morgan, Harold Stanley, et al., Doing Business as Morgan Stanley & Co., et al., Defendants.** 1954

Meeker, J[ames] Edward. **Short Selling.** 1932

Meeker, J[ames] Edward. **The Work of the Stock Exchange.** [1930]

Moody, John. **The Long Road Home:** An Autobiography. 1933

Moody, John. **Profitable Investing.** [1925]

Moulton, Harold G. **Financial Organization and the Economic System.** 1938

Moulton, Harold G. **The Financial Organization of Society.** [1930]

Moulton, Harold G. **The Formation of Capital.** 1935

Moulton, Harold G., George W. Edwards, James D. Magee and Cleona Lewis. **Capital Expansion, Employment, and Economic Stability.** 1940

The New York Stock Market. 1975

Nicolson, Harold. **Dwight Morrow.** [1935]

Palyi, Melchior. **The Chicago Credit Market:** Organization and Institutional Structure. [1937]

Peach, W[illiam] Nelson. **The Security Affiliates of National Banks.** 1941

Pratt, Sereno S. **The Work of Wall Street.** 1921

Regulation of the Security Markets. 1975

Reis, Bernard J. **False Security:** The Betrayal of the American Investor. 1937

Rice, Samuel O., ed. **Fundamentals of Investment.** 1925

Sakolski, A[aron] M. **Principles of Investment.** [1925]

Satterlee, Herbert L. **J. Pierpont Morgan:** An Intimate Portrait. 1939

Scott, James Brown. **Robert Bacon:** Life and Letters. 1923

Herbert D. Seibert & Co. **The Business and Financial Record of World War Years.** |1939|

Steiner, William Howard. **Investment Trusts: American Experience.** |1929|

Sturgis, Henry S. **Investment:** A New Profession. 1924

Townsend, William W. **Bond Salesmanship.** 1924

Twentieth Century Fund. **The Security Markets.** 1935

Two Private Banking Partnerships. 1975

U.S. Congressional House Committee on Banking and Currency. **Report of the Committee Appointed Pursuant to House Resolutions 429 and 504 to Investigate the Concentration of Control of Money and Credit.** 1913

U.S. Senate Committee on Banking and Currency. **Stock Exchange Practices.** 1934

Van Antwerp, W|illiam| C|larkson|. **The Stock Exchange From Within.** 1913

Warburg, Paul M. **The Federal Reserve System:** Its Origin and Growth. 2 Volumes. 1930

Weissman, Rudolph L. **The New Wall Street.** 1939

Willis, Henry Parker. **The Federal Reserve System:** Legislation, Organization and Operation. 1923

Willis, H|enry| Parker and Jules I. Bogen. **Investment Banking.** 1936